STRATEGIES FOR

COLLEGE

SUCCESS

THIRD EDITION

MARY C. STARKE
Ramapo College

PRENTICE HALL Upper Saddle River, New Jersey 07458

I dedicate this book to my parents, Eva and
David Celnik, who taught me the value of
striving for success and to my husband, Charles
Starke, and children, Katherine and Robert, who
make striving worthwhile. I thank them for their
support, their love, and their understanding.

STARKE, MARY C.
    Strategies for college success / Mary C. Starke. — 3rd ed.
        p.   cm.
    Includes bibliographical references (p.   ) and index.
    ISBN 0-13-449570-5 (pbk.)
    1. College student orientation—United States.   2. Study skills—
United States.   3. College students—United States—Conduct of
life.   4. College students—Health and hygiene—United States.
5. College students—United States—Time management.   I. Title.
LB2343.32.S74   1996
378.1'98—dc20   96-32392
                                                          CIP

Editor-in-Chief: *Charlyce Jones Owen*
Acquisition Editor: *Maggie Barbieri/Todd Rossell*
Editorial Assistant: *Lee Mamunes*
Director of Production and Manufacturing: *Barbara Kittle*
Managing Editor: *Bonnie Billor*
Project Manager: *Fran Russello*
Project Editor: *Publications Development Company of Texas*
Manufacturing Manager: *Nick Sklitsis*
Prepress and Manufacturing Buyer: *Mary Ann Gloriande*
Cover Design: *Marianne Frasco, Artwork by Michael Linley, "Man Climbing Book Stack"*

This book was set in 10 point Palatino by Publications Development Company of
Texas and was printed and bound by Quebecor Printing Semline.
The cover was printed by Quebecor Printing Semline.

© 1997, 1993, 1990 by Prentice-Hall, Inc.
Simon & Schuster/A Viacom Company
Upper Saddle River, New Jersey 07458

Printed in the United States of America
10 9 8 7 6 5 4 3 2 1

ISBN 0-13-449570-5

Prentice-Hall International (UK) Limited, *London*
Prentice-Hall of Australia Pty. Limited, *Sydney*
Prentice-Hall Canada Inc., *Toronto*
Prentice-Hall Hispanoamericana, S.A., *Mexico*
Prentice-Hall of India Private Limited, *New Delhi*
Prentice-Hall of Japan, Inc., *Tokyo*
Simon & Schuster Asia Pte. Ltd., *Singapore*
Editora Prentice-Hall do Brasil, Ltda., *Rio de Janeiro*

Brief Contents

Detailed Contents

Preface

The college experience! It is an exciting time: a time of dreams, hopes, and fears, of great joys, major adjustments, and some disappointments. It is a time to grow, to develop intellectual and emotional competencies, to learn about oneself and others, and to develop academic and interpersonal skills.

The freshman year is the gateway to this experience. It is the year in which you will acquire the skills and knowledge that will lay the foundation for the balance of your college career.

When I went to college in the sixties, students were expected to learn these types of skills and knowledge on their own. Many did learn them and they became successful college graduates. Others did not, and they did not fare as well, some even dropped out of college.

College students today come from a broader variety of backgrounds. We have more minority students, more students who have interrupted their education to work or to raise families, more students who need help with basic academic skills, more students who have physical or learning disabilities of various sorts, more students who must work to finance their college educations, and more students who are the first members of their families to attend college. Life is also more complex; there are greater pressures, more uncertainties, and more choices to make.

As a result of the broader mixture of student backgrounds and the greater complexities in life choices, many educators feel that college students benefit from a course that teaches the skills needed for success and helps them make the transition from high school or work to the college environment. Students enter institutions of higher education with varying degrees of preparation. This textbook is designed to help students acquire the academic, personal, and interpersonal skills that will ensure their success in college.

Let me say a few words about the goals for this text and the type of course—sometimes known as the college seminar. Some of the goals are academic. The text will help you improve your writing, reasoning, and research skills; you will, therefore, find numerous writing assignments in this text. You will learn through these assignments to think critically and to relate your own experiences to readings from assigned texts and to materials from library research. You may find the questions at the end of each chapter—"Reflections for Your Journal"—particularly helpful in setting your goals, evaluating your skills, exploring your values, reviewing the material in the chapter, and improving your writing.

The text will also help you improve your verbal skills and feel more comfortable when you speak in front of a group. For this reason, this text asks you to complete many oral presentation assignments.

You will find yourself participating in units on study skills, note-taking skills, library skills, computing skills, reading skills, test-taking skills, and time management skills. These chapters contain notes in the margins that highlight important strategies, concepts, guidelines, and key terms. Review those notes after you have read the chapter. This review will help you remember the most important points. These margin notes will also serve as models for the kinds of notes you should be making in your other textbooks to help you study more effectively. This text will help you to become a successful student who gets the most from your college education!

This text also has a number of personal and interpersonal goals. One goal is that you will come to understand and like yourself better and that you will also come to understand others better and be more accepting of their differences, whether these differences are based on race, ethnic group, gender, sexual orientation, age, or disabilities. To this end, you will have readings, activities, and films on values and communication.

If you are to succeed in college, you must take care of your physical and mental "plant." This text will help you to lead a healthier lifestyle; it includes units on stress, relaxation, nutrition, and drug and alcohol abuse. To succeed in college, you must also acquire or reaffirm responsible values regarding interpersonal relationships. For this purpose, you will explore issues in communication, conflict resolution, values, and intimacy.

This text should help to make you feel secure in your college environment. It will do this by familiarizing you with campus support services and policies, by having you participate in campus activities, by letting you know what you may expect from a college education, and also by giving you an idea of what the faculty and staff expect from you as a college student. The text will also help you take advantage of academic advisement so that you make informed choices about courses, majors, and careers.

The activities in the text will help make learning an active, participatory experience for you, as research shows that students feel better about themselves and their college when they are actively involved in campus activities. Students not only feel better, but they also perform better and are less likely to drop out of school. The purpose of the text is to help you graduate with the best possible education. That will happen only if you take advantage of both extracurricular opportunities and academic opportunities offered at your college.

This text will also help you maximize your participation in class. You will experience relatively little lecturing in this course; rather you will find yourself writing about your research, giving oral presentations about your experiences, interacting with guest speakers, participating in exercises and small group discussions, reacting critically to controversial films, keeping journals, and occasionally attending events with your class.

The text has several goals in promoting all of this activity: students learn better when they participate actively in the learning process. In addition, students gain a better understanding of themselves and others when they are involved in these sorts of activities and discussions. Finally, students learn to interact more comfortably and competently with both faculty and their fellow students through this process.

Welcome to the freshman seminar, a course that will help you grow and become a successful college student. I do hope that you will make the most of your valuable college experience!

■ A WORD TO THE INSTRUCTOR

The preface presents the goals and rationale for this text.

The text is organized so that each major section is followed by an activity through which your students can practice the skill that has just been described. For example, in Chapter 5, the text first describes the rationale for marking and underlining textbooks; it then presents guidelines on how to write in textbooks most effectively. It goes on to give students a practice session in underlining and marking a passage and then offers them feedback by showing them the same passage with too much, too little, and more appropriate markings. Each major section of the text is organized in the same way, offering your students the opportunity to **learn by doing as well as reading.** The supplemental videos and audiocassettes reinforce this **kinesthetic** and **right-brain learning** through **visual and auditory channels.**

The idea for such a course is not new; the first known course of this type offered for credit was given at Reed College in 1911.[1] What *is* new today is the increasing number of institutions that offer such a course. Surveys by the American Council on Education and the National Center for the Study of the Freshman Year Experience reveal that almost 78 percent of the American institutions of higher learning offer a course in coping with the college experience and that the percentage of institutions is increasing.[2]

The increasing popularity of such courses is not surprising. National surveys reveal that more than one-third of the freshmen at American colleges and universities drop out during their first year of college.[3] Longitudinal studies at a growing number of institutions show that students who have enrolled in freshman seminar courses persist in college in greater numbers than students who have not taken such a course. The difference in retention rates varies among institutions, but the rates consistently favor students who have taken freshman seminar courses.[4]

It may well be that the various bonds these seminar students establish at their colleges are responsible for their higher persistence rates. For example, surveys at many institutions reveal that first-year students who enroll in these freshman seminar courses attend more events on campus, belong to more extracurricular organizations, are more familiar with campus services, feel more comfortable approaching faculty if they have a problem, and speak with faculty more frequently outside of the class than first-year students who have not taken such a course.[5]

Students appreciate the value of this seminar. In one survey, for example, 78 percent of the first-year students who had taken the seminar recommended that it be given to first-year students in the future.[6] Other data indicate that seminar students see more of an improvement in their study habits and use the library more frequently than students who have not enrolled in the seminar.[7] A number of studies also find evidence of higher grade point averages among seminar enrollees than among students who have not taken the freshman seminar.[8]

So, a freshman seminar course will help your first-year students do better in their studies and increase the likelihood that they will graduate. This text will be your best tool in this course because it offers both readings and activities. Researchers have found that students learn better by doing than by just reading or hearing material. Our format of readings interspersed with exercises is more likely than the traditional format to hold the students' attention.

The text contains many different types of activities. You may not have time to use all of them in class. Tailor the exercises to fit your course. For example, you may wish to assign some activities to be completed by students on their own outside of class. Other assignments may be completed outside of class and submitted as written assignments to the instructor. You may choose to have students write and discuss some exercises in class. For example, the questions at the end of each chapter in the "Reflections for Your Journal" section encourage students to relate and integrate their own experience with the material they have read in the text. These items may be used as the stimulus for a writing assignment that is collected by the instructor on a regular basis, as the basis for small or large group discussions in class, or simply as review questions at the end of the chapter that encourage student self-exploration.

The text is particularly detailed in the sections dealing with multicultural diversity, women's issues, sexually transmitted diseases, substance abuse, and a healthier lifestyle. Many colleges do not offer courses in these areas, yet knowledge about these topics can make the difference between a successful student and one who is forced to withdraw from college. The students' knowledge about abstinence, sexually transmitted diseases, and alcohol/substance abuse may literally mean the difference between life and death. If you do not wish to cover this material in class, you might consider assigning it solely as outside reading. The sections are complete enough so that students can learn this important information on their own.

Faculty across the nation are reporting that the freshman seminar helps them see the college experience from a new perspective. A survey at Ramapo College revealed that 95 percent of the instructors who had taught freshman seminar were interested in teaching it again. I hope that you will become as enthusiastic about this text and learning experience as we have.

The Third Edition

This third edition of *Strategies for College Success* includes new units on learning styles, choosing college majors, sexual harassment and dating abuse, crime on campus, conflict resolution, the Internet, World Wide Web, and e-mail. I have also added **46 new videos** to the list of films reviewed which formed part of the **annotated bibliography of audio-visual resources** in the *Instructor's Manual* of the second edition.

I have thoroughly updated other sections with 160 recent citations in areas such as costs and benefits of a higher education, careers after graduation, computers, substance abuse, STDs, nutrition, and exercise. Changing trends in the area of substance abuse, for example, are reflected by discussions of new drugs such as Rohypnol, increasing abuse of methamphetamines and heroin, an expanded section on tobacco, and a smaller unit on cocaine.

New activities have been added to the third edition such as "Identifying Your Preferred Learning Style," "Implementing Abstinence," "Warning Signs of an Eating Disorder," "Understanding People Who Have AIDS," "Talking about Condoms," "Recognizing Signs of a Learning Disorder," "When Smokers Quit," and "Playing God: A Question of Values."

Supplement Package

The text is complete in itself, but if time permits, the supplementary package, additional videos, and guest speakers can enhance your teaching. I have put together an extensive supplementary package that includes an Instructor's Manual with sample syllabi, a package of videotapes, several audiocassettes, and a Student Planner. All of this material is free upon adoption of this book for your class. Additional books such as a dictionary and reference on careers may be packaged with the text for a nominal charge. Please contact your **local Prentice Hall representative or call the Instructors' Service Line at 1-800-526-0485** to get copies of this material for preview and use.

The *Instructor's Manual* offers chapter-by-chapter guidelines to help you diversify your classes and make them successful. I have found that variety is the key to maintaining the students' interest. The *Instructor's Manual* describes videos and other resources along these lines and offers additional activities, **sample syllabi,** chapter-by-chapter summaries of the text, suggestions for additional topics, transparency masters, test items, and course evaluation forms.

The **package of videotapes and ABC news clips** consists of videos in areas such as substance abuse, multicultural diversity, sexually transmitted diseases, nutrition, health, and exercise. These videos, recent professional productions featuring lively music and MTV-type formats, target a college audience. Several have won Oscars or other awards in the short documentary class. They are lively, moving, and provocative. I have chosen them because they dramatically raise key issues and stimulate class discussion.

The audiocassettes, which are on critical thinking, and deal with stress and exam anxiety, talk right to the needs of college students. They teach skills which helps students focus on a task so they can perform at their best. Both of these supplements are particularly helpful in reinforcing the material in the text, diversifying the class experience, and strengthening the skills that help students succeed in college. They can also be used as backup for instructors who may not be comfortable or familiar with teaching these topics to students. These videotapes and audiocassettes are available free to instructors who adopt this text.

The *Student Planner* is designed to help students organize and manage their time more effectively. It includes a daily planner, monthly planner, calendars for 1997 through 2001, an address book, course and class planners, and other organizing tools. Every copy of the text will be accompanied by the Student Planner. I discuss its use in detail in Chapter 3, Time Management.

FREE TEACHER SUPPLEMENTS PACKAGE

- 300-Page Instructor's Manual with sample syllabus
- Objective and Essay Tests for each chapter, printed on separate pages, ready to copy and distribute to students
- Answer Keys for Objective and Essay Tests
- Annotated Bibliography of Additional Video and Referral Resources
- Transparency Masters
- Student Planner
- Video Package: Dramatic, lively, and thought-provoking films and ABC clips on substance abuse, prejudice, STDs, date rape, and a healthy lifestyle. For further information about ordering the videos, visit our web page at http://www.netsurftech.com/collegesuccess
- Prentice Hall Critical Thinking Audio Study Cassette
- Stress Management and Essay Exam Anxiety Audiocassette

■ ACKNOWLEDGMENTS

I am grateful to Charles Starke for his support and encouragement, his editorial assistance, and the battles he has won for me with the computer.

I am pleased to acknowledge the following faculty and staff who suggested materials to be included in this book and helped me with the research: Amy Pollock, Director of Student Development and a tireless source of videos and other resources; Jean Balutanski, Director of Specialized Services; Al Frech, Director, Center for Personal Development; Judith Jeney, Reference Librarian; Ellen Ross, Professor of History and Women's Studies at Ramapo College; M. Carol May, Associate Director of Domestic Conferences and University 101 Instructor; Gail McGrail, Instructor University 101, at the University of South Carolina; Christine Paustian, reviewer for Jump City and *What's on the Web*; and Rick Poverny, Health Education Services at Rutgers University.

I thank the staff at Prentice Hall, especially my editors, Maggie Barbieri and Todd Rossell, whose encouragement and support have helped this book become a reality and their assistants, Joan Polk and Jennifer Collins, who were always ready to search out the answers to my questions and soothe my nerves; the project manager, Fran Russello, and the production editors, Nancy Marcus Land and Jennifer Gage, who successfully juggled a difficult layout job.

I also wish to acknowledge the feedback from reviewers who read earlier drafts of this manuscript.

Notes

1. V. N. Gordon and T. J. Grites, 1984. The Freshman Seminar Course: Helping Students Succeed. *Journal of College Student Personnel*, pp. 315–320.

2. J. Gardner, 1991. Paper presented at Fifth National Conference on Student Retention, New York, NY. E. El-Kawas, Ed., 1985. *Campus Trends, 1984: A Survey of the American Council on Education, Higher Education Report, 65.* Washington, DC: American Council on Education, p. 9.

3. "National Dropout Rates." The American College Testing Program. Compiled from ACT Institutional Data File. Iowa City, IA: Noel-Levitz Center for Student Retention, 1996.

4. M. C. Starke. "Retention, Bonding, and Academic Achievement: Effectiveness of the Freshman Seminar in Promoting Success in College." Paper presented at the Ninth National Conference on Student Retention, New York, NY, July 1995. P. P. Fidler "Evidence of the Effectiveness of the Freshman Seminar," in J. N. Gardner and M. L. Upcraft, Eds. *Enhancing the Success of the First Year Students: The Freshman Experience.* San Francisco: Jossey-Bass, 1989, Chap. 15. L. Dunphy et al., in M. M. Stodt and W. M. Klepper, Eds., 1987. *Increasing Retention: Academic and Affairs Administrators in Partnership: New Directions for Higher Education.* San Francisco: Jossey-Bass.

5. M. C. Starke. "A Longitudinal Study of the Freshman Seminar Program" Paper presented at Eleventh National Conference on the Freshman Year Experience, Columbia, SC: February 1994; P. P. Fidler "Evidence of the Effectiveness of the Freshman Seminar," in J. N. Gardner and M. L. Upcraft, Eds., 1989. *Enhancing the Success of the First Year Students: The Freshman Experience.* San Francisco: Jossey-Bass, Chap. 15.

6. M. Harth, personal communication, 1987.

7. M. C. Starke. "Retention and Bonding: The Success of the Freshman Seminar Program at Ramapo College." Paper presented at Fourth National Conference on Student Retention, Washington, DC, July 1990.

8. P. P. Fidler. "Evidence of the Effectiveness of the Freshman Seminar," in J. N. Gardner and M. L. Upcraft, Eds., 1989. *Enhancing the Success of the First Year Students: The Freshman Experience,* San Francisco: Jossey-Bass, Chap. 15.

CHAPTER

BENEFITS AND GOALS OF A COLLEGE EDUCATION

According to the National Center for Education Statistics, over 14.5 million students are enrolled in college programs in the United States. More than two million of them are first-year students; so take heart, you have lots of company.[1]

In the 1980s and early 1990s, the cost of a college education rose by twice the rate of inflation.[2] According to the College Board, the average tuition at private four-year colleges totaled $18,000 in 1995, and at public institutions, prices rose by as much as 12 percent. Although schools are reining in costs, the College Board reports that undergraduates will pay 6 percent more for tuition and fees in 1996–1997 than they did a year before. For example, Princeton University, in announcing a record low in increases, reported that the cost of tuition, room, and board would come to $28,325 in 1996–1997.[3] At the University of Vermont, the highest priced state system, total costs for state residents come to more than $11,000; the national average for state universities, including room and board is approximately $7,500.[4] Experts predict that by the year 2000, an Ivy League undergraduate education could cost $155,000, while an in-state public college education is expected to cost $52,404.[5]

Costs are not the only aspect of a college education that are rising. According to "College Debt and the American Family," a recent analysis by The Education Resources Institute and the Institute for Higher Education Policy shows that college students borrowed as much money for college in the first five years of the 1990s as students in the 1960s, 1970s, and 1980s *combined*. The rate of borrowing has increased almost three times as fast as college costs and four times as fast as personal incomes. The percentage of students receiving loans broke previous records in the two most recent years of the study and increased fastest for students at public colleges and universities.[6]

As more and more students find that they must borrow and work in order to pay for a college education, the number of years that students typically spend on campus is also increasing. Due to competing pressures from jobs, family responsibilities, or the need to raise basic skills in reading, writing, or math to the college level, many colleges are finding that the majority of their students no longer complete a bachelor's degree in the traditional four years. An increasing number of students are requiring five, six, or even more years to graduate.

■ REASONS FOR ATTENDING COLLEGE

Why are so many people willing to spend considerable amounts of time, effort, and money to attain a college education? For many students, the goals of a college education are career related; for others, the benefits of college involve personal satisfactions such as developing one's mind, undertaking an exciting

1

ACTIVITY

Reflecting on Your Reasons for Attending College

The list that follows presents many of the reasons students commonly give for attending college. Look over the list; then put a 1 next to the item that represents your main reason for enrolling in college, a 2 next to the item that comes next in importance for you, and a 3 next to the item that describes your third most important reason for attending college. Then go back and put a 21, a 22, and a 23 next to the three items that were least important in influencing your decision to enroll in college.

I enrolled in college to

———— prepare for a job or profession

———— find a spouse or mate

———— gain knowledge

———— get a degree

———— learn problem-solving skills

———— learn how to learn

———— have something to do

———— please my parents

———— make friends

———— raise my economic prospects

———— gain security

———— gain prestige or status

———— become more mature

———— have fun

———— become a more productive member of society

———— open new avenues

———— learn to think and question

———— gain self-confidence and self-esteem

———— find a focus for my life

———— advance in my career

———— understand myself better

———— other ————————————————

———— other ————————————————

challenge, learning new skills or acquiring knowledge, and meeting new people. The advantages of a college degree run the gamut from higher salaries to better health, from happier marriages to greater satisfaction with careers, from higher self-esteem to better parenting skills. The more you know about what college can offer you and the clearer you are about your goals for your own college experience, the more likely it is that you will get the most from that experience.

We know that many jobs are open only to individuals who have earned college degrees, and young adults today find it harder to advance without a degree than earlier generations did. Our increasingly technical economy has lost many of the low-skill jobs that allowed people to learn on the job, and this pattern will continue. According to "Workforce 2000," a study commissioned by the U.S. Department of Labor, 52 percent of all new jobs created in the 1990s will require a college education.[7] The pathways that connected many entry-level jobs with promotional opportunities higher up on the ladder have been broken. Low-level jobs today tend to be dead-end jobs that do not give workers the opportunity to advance in their careers. They also tend to provide less job security and fewer benefits.

We also know that a college degree means a higher starting salary and a greater probability of promotion in many companies. For example, a thirty-year study of managers at AT&T revealed that just earning a college degree has a strong influence on whether employees move up the management ladder.[8]

According to Richard Freeman, a Harvard economist, "College graduates are the only males who've gotten any real pay increase in the last ten years. Less educated people have taken a tremendous beating."[9] Fifteen years ago, college-educated workers earned about 40 percent more than high school graduates. Now a college degree is worth almost 60 percent more.[10] The average income for a male college graduate, 25 to 34 years of age, is more than $59,000 compared to only $30,000 for the same man who has only a school diploma.[11] This represents one million dollars more in earned income over the course of a career.

Other benefits associated with a college degree may be even more important than the financial ones. College graduates tend to get jobs that are more stimulating and challenging, that offer them greater safety from physical hazards, and that give them greater responsibility and freedom to prove their talents. College-educated individuals tend to be more flexible and adapt better to changes in their personal lives and careers, they enjoy better health, they seem to have happier marriages, their children tend to perform better in school and achieve more than the children of parents who have not attended college. They also tend to be more satisfied with their lives in general. Among women who are college graduates, for example, 95 percent said that things were going at least fairly well, compared with only 3 percent of the women who had not completed high school.[12]

■ DECIDING ON A MAJOR AND CHOOSING A CAREER DIRECTION

Once you have decided to earn a college degree, your next question is, "What type of education should I pursue?" Many students these days are choosing majors in technical fields such as engineering, business, and computer science, where demand and starting salaries are high. The latest survey of first-year American college students conducted by the Higher Education Research Institute reports that 19 percent intend to pursue professional studies, 16 percent plan to major in business, 10 percent plan to focus on education, and 8 percent propose to specialize in engineering.[13]

Students feel more secure about these majors, as they seem to directly prepare them for a particular job after college. Yet studies show that very few people stay in the same line of work over the course of their working lives. "Experts used to predict that the average person would have four jobs in a lifetime. Now, because of social, economic, and technological changes, the average person is likely to have four careers."[14] "Throughout the economy . . . , job security for both sexes will become a relic of the past: automation, swifter product obsolescence, cutthroat competition from abroad, and the need . . . for even the largest, most stable corporations to become leaner will mean many of today's jobs will disappear."[15] According to Martin John Yate, author of *Knock 'Em Dead with Great Answers to Tough Interview Questions,* eight out of ten people will be fired at some point in their careers.[16]

No one can predict accurately which particular job skills will be in demand in ten years, much less in twenty or thirty years. As you change jobs, the best preparation for career success will be the knowledge of how to learn new skills and the willingness to undertake that learning. An education that emphasizes critical thinking skills will provide the key to success. A course of study is necessary that teaches you the ability to understand and interpret complex relationships and to analyze and question basic assumptions about how things are done. You must also learn how to work effectively with different types of people and how to communicate, orally and in writing. These abilities are not necessarily fostered by a course of education that teaches technical skills designed to fit you for a particular job. These are abilities traditionally fostered by a liberal arts education—courses in history, literature, psychology, economics, philosophy, and political science, to name a few. This is the reason that 93 percent of all two- and four-year colleges have general education requirements for all students regardless of their major;[17] even the most technical majors require a year or two of liberal arts courses before you begin to specialize in business, engineering, or computer courses.

Perhaps this is also the reason that a survey of two thousand graduates from the University of Virginia revealed that 91 percent of them recommend a liberal arts major.[18] Graduates holding varied positions, such as bank vice president, assistant district attorney, physician, editorial producer, and systems analyst, all felt that liberal arts prepared them for the most successful careers. Although these students often ended up in jobs that seem far removed from their undergraduate majors, they felt that a liberal arts background gave them the thinking, research, and communications skills to ensure flexibility and, therefore, success in a broad range of career shifts dictated by changes in their interests or in the economy's needs.

Interviews conducted by Katy Koontz revealed, for example, that Joe Paterno, the legendary head football coach at Pennsylvania State University, majored in English because he had planned to go to law school, "I've always told my own kids not to be so concerned about exactly what they want to do. . . . The world moves so quickly these days that it's unrealistic to zero in on a career when you're 20 years old." Paterno's only regret is that he did not take his English major further and earn a graduate degree in English literature while his coaching career was still getting off the ground.[19]

Jane Metzroth, senior vice president of human resources for The Gap, Inc., has no regrets about her biochemistry major. She had planned to go on to medical school before she got married but discovered that she could not afford medical school tuition; "I have absolutely no regrets," she reports. "Not majoring in business hasn't hampered my career one bit." Metzroth believes that she learned how to manage a heavy work load and set priorities as a result of majoring in biochemistry. She also learned how to work in groups: "In labs, I learned how to work for the good of the team without being overpowering or underwhelming. I now have a department of 80 people, and the principles I use in working with others are the same."[20]

In contrast, Edward Tabor, M.D., associate director for biological carcinogenesis at the National Cancer Institute, majored in English and ended up in medicine. He was interested in law and writing and planned *not* to go into medicine. According to Tabor, "Not only is majoring in science unnecessary, . . . but the better med schools actively look for at least some students who have majored in other areas. . . . In science and medicine, if you know how to write, you're way ahead of everyone else."[21]

Magician and psychic investigator Andre Kole landed in his unusual career after majoring in psychology. His research has taken him to Africa to study the work of witch doctors and to the Philippines to investigate psychic surgeons for *Time* magazine. He also consults with people who have been deceived by what he calls psychic charlatans and fraudulent faith healers. "We magicians use a lot of psychology in our performances," he says, "and even though most of it isn't the type they teach in universities, I'm still glad I got my degree."[22]

An informal survey by Lynne Cheney revealed that the communications world is dominated by liberal arts majors.[23] For example, Thomas H. Wyman, chairman of CBS, and Cathleen Black, publisher of *USA Today*, both majored in English. William Raspberry, columnist for the *Washington Post*, studied history, and NBC news anchorman Tom Brokaw specialized in political science.

Business executives such as Donald Regan, who headed Merrill Lynch, and Malcolm Baldrige, who steered Scoville Manufacturing before entering government service, are not unusual in their liberal arts backgrounds. A report in *Fortune* magazine revealed that 38 percent of the current chief executive officers majored in the liberal arts.[24] *The New York Times*[25] reported that nine of the top thirteen executives at IBM were liberal arts majors, and the AT&T study mentioned earlier found that humanities and social science majors were more successful in the managerial ranks of that company than engineering and business majors. A study by Northwestern University reported that many large companies planned to increase their hiring of liberal arts majors. They are looking for students with strengths in broader areas. They will then give these successful graduates the technical training they need for specific jobs.[26]

These surveys are not mentioned here to dissuade you from pursuing a major in business, engineering, or computer science. The starting salaries in these fields are higher than those in liberal arts, and there are many job openings available in these areas. The more technical fields may be particularly appropriate for nontraditional students whose previous background in college or in the workplace gives them very focused career objectives. By all means, enroll in these courses if you enjoy them. I mention these surveys in the hopes of dissuading you from pursuing a major that does not interest you just because it seems to offer initial job security. I have, unfortunately, seen many students try to cram themselves into a mold that doesn't suit them. It is not a strategy that is likely to breed success or happiness.

It might be a better investment of your college time to major in a field that interests you rather than to force yourself through courses that are boring just for the sake of improving your prospects for that first job. If you are interested in your courses, you will be motivated to study and get the best education you can in college. This will give you a better edge in the job market than you would receive from specific training in a field that you do not enjoy and that may not be in demand by the time you graduate. If you are interested in your job, you are less likely to "burn out" quickly and more likely to put in the long hours and effort that will ensure success and satisfaction.

It is a good idea, however, to keep abreast of specific skills you can learn in college that might enhance your employability after graduation. If the option is open to you, I advise you to take a second major or a minor that will open additional opportunities for you after college graduation. I also recommend taking courses in computer literacy, accounting, management, and a foreign language if these might be helpful along the career path you are considering. A survey by the Modern Language Association of America found that more college students are enrolled in foreign language courses than ever before, with Japanese, Russian, and Spanish showing the greatest growth in enrollment.[27] Many experts predict that a knowledge of one of the Chinese languages will be increasingly useful as the world's most populous country enters the mainstream economy of the twenty-first century. The 18 percent increase found in enrollment of foreign language courses undoubtedly reflects the expansion of the global economy and the increasing heterogeneity of our domestic multicultural markets and workforce. The ability to communicate in several languages is an asset for virtually all careers in the business, service, and management sectors.

Use your college years to expand your horizons, to broaden and strengthen your mind, to follow your intellectual curiosity, and to enjoy the stimulation of your instructors and peers. Even if this does not lead directly to the field with the highest starting salary immediately after graduation, it may well be the course that leads to ultimate career success in both financial and personal terms.

■ EXTRACURRICULAR ACTIVITIES

In addition to your major and the actual courses you take, you will find that college offers you exposure to a wealth of experiences outside the classroom. Many of these experiences are organized in the extracurricular programs of the college. If you enjoy writing, there is the college newspaper or literary magazine. If you are interested in government or politics, there is the student government structure, where you can work actively to influence the quality of campus life; there are also local political campaigns where you can volunteer your services and learn about the electoral process. If you enjoy music, you may wish to join the college choir or learn to play an instrument.

There are opportunities to work on and off campus in cooperative education, internships, and research positions related to your studies. These activities offer you the chance to develop leadership skills; to collaborate as part of a team; to work with people from different backgrounds; to initiate, organize, and implement programs; and to learn skills that cannot be taught in a classroom. Both a University of Virginia study and an AT&T study found that extracurricular activities and other kinds of experiential learning (internships, summer jobs, and cooperative education), along with personal initiative, were highly correlated with success in a chosen career.[28] So even if you are a commuter or a returning student who is juggling the conflicting responsibilities of a job, a family, and an education, take advantage of these opportunities to develop your abilities and your career prospects.

Research shows that students who make connections with their peers at college are much less likely to drop out than students who dash in and out of class, attending only to their academic responsibilities. Even if you are a commuter or a nontraditional student whose main social networks are located off campus, take the time to become acquainted and exchange phone numbers with at least one student in each of your classes. Becoming involved in the social fabric of the school will increase your commitment to completing your college education and may also be helpful if you need to catch up on the notes you missed in class the day your car broke down or your child got sick.

A C T I V I T Y

Getting Acquainted

This activity will help you meet the other members of your class. You will have ten minutes to circulate around the room to find out the answers to the following questions:

1. Write the names of two people in this class who have the same major as you do:

   a. _____

   b. _____

2. Write the names and majors of two people in this class who do not have the same major as you do:

   a. _____

   b. _____

3. Write the names of three people in this class whose major is "undecided."

   a. _____

   b. _____

   c. _____

4. Write the names and hometowns of three people who are not from your hometown.

   a. _____

   b. _____

   c. _____

5. Write the names of two people in this class who do *not* have part-time jobs.

   a. _____

   b. _____

6. Write the names of two people in this class who hold full-time jobs.

   a. _____

   b. _____

7. Write the names of two people in this class who recently saw the same movie you did.

   a. _____

   b. _____

8. Write the names of two people in this class who live on campus.

   a. _____

   b. _____

9. Write the names of two people in this class who commute to college.

   a. _____

   b. _____

A C T I V I T Y

Determining Your College Goals

This activity is meant to help you clarify your goals for a college education, get to know the other members of your class, and practice some public speaking skills.

1. Sit next to someone you do not know and discuss the following questions. Record each other's answers, because you will be introducing this person to the rest of the class when you have finished talking with each other.

Name: _____

Hometown: _____

Favorite activities, hobbies, interests: _____

_____

_____

_____

If you could be anyone else in the world, who would you choose to be? _____

_____

Reasons for attending college: _____

_____

_____

_____

Reasons for attending this particular college: _____

_____

_____

_____

Two most memorable experiences (good or bad) that you have experienced at college so far: _____

_____

_____

_____

Probable major(s) or career: (Don't be afraid to say "undecided.") _____

_____

2. When you have completed your individual conversations, your instructor will ask each of you to introduce your partner to the class.

✍ REFLECTIONS FOR YOUR JOURNAL

Keeping a journal of your college experiences will help you practice writing, emphasize and realize your goals in college, and integrate your college experiences with who you are as a person. This will enhance the changes you can expect during your college career and help you develop your full potential. The questions that follow each chapter are suggested as guidelines for your journal entries.

1. What are the goals you hope to realize during your years at college? List at least three and explore how you expect your college experience to help you reach these goals.
2. List your major (or several possible majors if you have not yet decided on one); explain why you are attracted to this field of study.
3. If your college is one of the many institutions of higher education that requires general education courses in English, mathematics, history, science, the social sciences, or other areas, explain why all students are required to complete these courses before they graduate from college.
4. Which extra-curricular activities offered at your college do you find attractive? How will participation in these activities enhance your college experience and your prospects after graduation?

Notes

1. U.S. Department of Commerce, Bureau of the Census, *Statistical Abstracts of the United States, 1995* (Washington, DC: Government Printing Office, 1995), Table 228, p. 151; Table 281, p. 181.
2. "Back to School," *The Serious Investor* (New York: Shearson-Lehman Brothers, August 1991), p. 1.
3. P. Appelbome, "After Rising Faster Than Inflation for Years, Tuition Begins to Drop at Many Colleges," *New York Times,* 24 January 1996, p. B7.
4. W. H. Honan, "State Universities Reshaped in the Era of Budget Cutting," *New York Times,* 22 February 1995, pp. A1, B7.
5. "Back to School," p. 1.
6. "Families Reel from Borrowing Explosion," *On Campus,* March 1996, *Vol. 15, no. 6,* p. 3, Washington, DC: American Federation of Teachers.
7. Bureau of Labor Statistics, Hudson Institute in "Jobs for Women in the Nineties," *Ms. Magazine,* July 1988, p. 74.
8. G. Dessler, "Just Earning College Degree Is Important," *Bergen County (NJ) Record,* 8 September 1986.
9. F. Rose, "Pragmatic Approach," *New York Times,* 4 August 1991, section 4A, p. 20.
10. M. M. Weinstein, "Why They Deserve It," *New York Times Magazine,* 19 November 1995, p. 103.
11. U.S. Department of Commerce, op. cit., Table 742, p. 479.
12. T. Lewin, "Women Are Becoming Equal Partners," *New York Times,* 5 November 1995, p. A27.
13. U.S. Department of Commerce, op. cit., Table 294, p. 187.
14. Martin, John Yate in C. McIntosh, "Giving Good Answers to Tough Interview Questions," *McCall's,* May 1991, p. 38.
15. "Jobs for Women in the Nineties," op. cit., p. 74.
16. Martin John Yate, op. cit., p. 40.
17. U.S. Department of Commerce, op. cit., Table 271, p. 162.
18. S. T. Hitchcock and R. Benner in "Life After Liberal Arts," by W. Raspberry, *Bergen County (NJ) Record,* 19 June 1986.
19. K. Koontz, "Major Matters, or Does It?" *Connections,* Winter Preview, 1989, American Express Card, pp. 3–4, 16.
20. Ibid. p. 4.
21. Ibid. p. 16.
22. Ibid. p. 4.

23. L. Cheney, "Students of Success," *Newsweek,* 1 September 1986, p. 7.

24. Ibid.

25. "What Value Education? Counting the Whys," *New York Times,* 3 October 1987, p. 29.

26. Ibid.

27. "Students in Language Are Found At New High," *New York Times,* 25 September 1991, p. B6.

28. "Life After Liberal Arts," op. cit.

CHAPTER

COLLEGE RESOURCES

Your college or university is a large organization, and like any other organization it has a structure and a set of rules by which it functions. In order to succeed in your college, you must learn its rules and you must know where to go to find help. It is a sad fact that one-third of the freshmen enrolled in American colleges and universities drop out during their first year.[1] This chapter will familiarize you with college resources that can help you succeed: the professors, the student support services, the publications that give you important information about your school's structure and policies, the academic advisors, the college catalog, and the extracurricular activities.

■ COLLEGE PROFESSORS

One of the best resources for help at your institution is the faculty. After all, professors are responsible for what happens in the college classroom. I have always found it strange that students will invest more time asking questions about a blind date with whom they plan to spend 3 or 4 hours one evening than checking out an instructor in whose class they will be sitting for 45 hours over the course of an entire semester. The professor you choose can make or break your course: An enthusiastic instructor who knows how to engage students and make his or her subject come alive can turn even the most boring subject into a thrilling adventure; a teacher who has been reading the same lecture notes for the past 20 years can render the most fascinating course a torturous, dreary disaster.

Before you enroll in a course with an instructor, ask for feedback from other students who have taken courses with him. Organize discussion sessions in your dorm to trade information about instructors a week or two before registration. Approach upperclass students in your major. Direct conversations with your peers before class begins along these lines. When you are hanging out in the cafeteria or taking a study break in the library, ask your peers about the professors they have had. Take the time to sit in on a class taught by your prospective instructor the semester before you enroll with him. Wait outside the door of an instructor's classroom and ask one of the students who is leaving for feedback about her teaching style.

Schedule an appointment with the professor (or, if you must cut corners, correspond with her via e-mail) and ask about the course requirements, the reading materials, and other aspects of the course. Read the section in Chapter 5 that deals with learning styles, and try to match your preferred style with the teaching style of your prospective instructor. Purchase a copy of the course review catalog that is published in many schools which rates professors and their courses. Ask your advisor which instructor is the best teacher for a course you plan to take. If your first choice is not available that semester, you may do better to wait until the preferred teacher is teaching the course and you can get into his section. This could make the difference between an enjoyable, intellectually stimulating semester and four months of drudgery, receiving an inferior grade in an important course, and failing to learn material that is key to future courses in your major and your vocational plans.

You will get a better education and you are more likely to succeed if you understand your instructors and the expectations they hold for college students. You will find that their expectations differ in important ways from those of your high school teachers. For example, college faculty expect you to take greater responsibility for your education and to manage your assignments and your time more independently. You may find that some of them do not take attendance regularly and they may not check your assignments on a daily basis. This does not mean that they do not care about you or your education; it means that they trust you to manage more of your work on your own.

Your college professors want you to become an educated, well-rounded person who is interested in a broad range of subjects that affect your life, your

ACTIVITY

Interviewing a Faculty Member

This activity is meant to acquaint you with at least one of your instructors, give you practice in arranging an appointment with a faculty member, familiarize you with faculty expectations, and give you practice in public speaking or in writing.

Choose one of the instructors at your college and make an appointment for a ten- to fifteen-minute interview at his or her office. (You may wish to choose an instructor who teaches courses in a major that interests you.) Bring your questions with you, and write down the answers so that you may share them with the other members of your class or with your freshman seminar instructor if this is to be a written assignment. The following exercise gives you some suggested interview questions. You may wish to add others.

General Questions

Professor's name: _____

Department in which the professor teaches: _____

Discipline: _____

Reasons the professor chose to teach in his or her particular discipline: _____

_____

_____

_____

_____

_____

_____

_____

Type(s) of work the professor has performed other than college teaching: ⎯⎯

⎯⎯⎯⎯⎯⎯⎯⎯⎯⎯⎯⎯⎯⎯⎯⎯⎯⎯⎯⎯⎯⎯⎯⎯⎯⎯⎯⎯⎯⎯⎯⎯⎯⎯

⎯⎯⎯⎯⎯⎯⎯⎯⎯⎯⎯⎯⎯⎯⎯⎯⎯⎯⎯⎯⎯⎯⎯⎯⎯⎯⎯⎯⎯⎯⎯⎯⎯⎯

⎯⎯⎯⎯⎯⎯⎯⎯⎯⎯⎯⎯⎯⎯⎯⎯⎯⎯⎯⎯⎯⎯⎯⎯⎯⎯⎯⎯⎯⎯⎯⎯⎯⎯

Reasons the professor chose to teach at the college level: ⎯⎯⎯⎯⎯⎯⎯

Reasons the professor chose to teach at your particular college: ⎯⎯⎯⎯

Expectations the professor has for the ideal student: ⎯⎯⎯⎯⎯⎯⎯⎯

Characteristics of a poor student (what bothers the professor most about students today): ⎯⎯⎯⎯⎯⎯⎯⎯⎯⎯⎯⎯⎯⎯⎯⎯⎯⎯⎯⎯⎯

Optional Questions

What the professor likes most and least about his or her job: ⎯⎯⎯⎯⎯

Institutions where the professor received undergraduate and graduate degrees; the degrees obtained: ⎯⎯⎯⎯⎯⎯⎯⎯⎯⎯⎯⎯⎯⎯⎯⎯⎯⎯⎯⎯

The professor's area of research or specialization: ⎯⎯⎯⎯⎯⎯⎯⎯⎯

The professor's interests or hobbies: ⎯⎯⎯⎯⎯⎯⎯⎯⎯⎯⎯⎯⎯⎯

country, and your world. They do not see a college education as only a means to a better-paying job. They hope it will lay the foundation for a lifetime of learning, thinking, and analyzing the world around you. They want to stimulate your mind and help you to grow intellectually.

You will find that college professors do not want you to spout back the information you have heard in class or read in the texts. They expect you to analyze and criticize the ideas of others, to develop your own ideas, and to support those ideas with research. You will find that they sometimes disagree with the authors of your textbooks. This is to teach you that there is more than one way to look at a problem. They will often raise more questions than they answer. They do this so that you will learn to question what you read. They want to help you grow and develop into a critical thinker.

Most instructors teach at the college level because they are enthusiastic about their disciplines and wish to pass on their enthusiasm and knowledge to others. They have spent years studying, researching, and writing about their discipline, and they want to share this knowledge with their students. They welcome your interest and participation in the course. This is one of the reasons that professors are often particularly enthusiastic about nontraditional or returning students who have had more experience outside the classroom and can bring that experience to bear on the course material. Many professors specifically apportion a part of the student's grade for quality of class participation, so do not be afraid to interact with your instructors!

You should be aware that your instructors are expected to perform many tasks in addition to teaching. Significant portions of their time must be spent on research to discover new knowledge, on reading to keep up with the latest developments in their fields, on writing to communicate new knowledge to other researchers or to students (through journal articles, books for professionals, and textbooks), on presenting papers to other researchers at conferences, on updating their class presentations, on administrative work, and on advisement.

In order to fulfill all of their obligations, instructors must manage their time efficiently. This is the reason that instructors schedule office hours. If you have questions about a course or wish to talk about other matters, tell your instructor that you would like to come by during his or her office hours or make an appointment for another mutually convenient time. It is part of your professor's job to schedule office hours so that he or she can advise students about the course. When you make an appointment, write it down so that you remember it. If you cannot keep the appointment, let your teacher know that you will not be stopping by. If you need to contact your instructor at some other time, leave a message and your phone number with the department secretary or contact your instructor through e-mail, and he or she will get back to you. Most instructors look forward to talking with students about their work so do not hesitate to see them outside of class. The activity on pages 12–13 will help you become acquainted with an instructor.

■ STUDENT SUPPORT SERVICES

Most schools offer services that are helpful to students throughout their college careers. You should become familiar with the nonacademic support services that are available so that you know where to turn for help when you need it. One of the best sources for this information is the student handbook. If your college does not publish a handbook, consult the dean of students or the student services office for a listing of the services available on your campus. The goal of the activity on page 15 is to familiarize you with the many support services your college offers.

ACTIVITY

Using Student Support Services

Pair up with another member of your seminar. (Choose someone in the class you do not know; one goal of this exercise is to help you learn to work with new people.) Choose one of the following listed support services that your college offers. Call the person in charge of that service and request a brief interview so that you and your partner may learn what services are offered by that office. You should take notes on the types of services available, the days and hours when the office is open, the special restrictions regarding eligibility for services, and the location and phone number of the office. Request a sample of the office's literature so that you may pass it around in class (e.g., a schedule of games from the athletics department, a brochure from the child care center, a pamphlet about birth control from the health services department). Prepare a presentation for the class with your partner. Report on the service you have researched so that your classmates may learn what is available at that office. Fill in the location and phone extension of each service on the list that follows as it is presented in class.

LIST OF SUPPORT SERVICES

	Room Number	Telephone Number	Person in Charge
Dean of Students	_____	_____	_____
Residence Life	_____	_____	_____
Specialized Services	_____	_____	_____
Health Services	_____	_____	_____
Athletics	_____	_____	_____
Counseling Center	_____	_____	_____
Office of Orientation	_____	_____	_____
Student Activities	_____	_____	_____
Child Care Center	_____	_____	_____
Career Planning	_____	_____	_____
Cooperative Education	_____	_____	_____
International Students	_____	_____	_____
Registrar	_____	_____	_____
Campus Security	_____	_____	_____
Student Newspaper	_____	_____	_____
Women's Center	_____	_____	_____
Academic Affairs	_____	_____	_____
Educational Opportunity Program	_____	_____	_____
Financial Aid	_____	_____	_____
Academic Advisement Center	_____	_____	_____
Academic Skills Center	_____	_____	_____
Student Government	_____	_____	_____
Student Radio Station	_____	_____	_____
Other	_____	_____	_____

■ ACADEMIC ADVISEMENT

Academic advisement is an important part of your college experience. If you do not make good use of your advisor, you are not likely to get the best education possible, and you may even be forced to postpone graduation because you have not fulfilled the necessary requirements. When you meet with your advisor, he or she will check to see that you are fulfilling college requirements for graduation. Your advisor may help you decide on a major, choose among several electives or courses in your major, make recommendations about the best sequence in which to take certain courses, or suggest changes in your overall course load or scheduling that will increase your chances for success.

Academic advisors may also give you helpful information about the course of study that best fits your needs. For example, if your career objective is to help disturbed children, your advisor will tell you that you can reach this goal by obtaining a PhD in clinical or developmental psychology, an MSW in social work, an EdD in education, an MA in counseling, a PsyD in psychology, an MD with specialization in child psychiatry, or an MA in special education. You may then choose which route will best fulfill your goals. You will find that you must complete different courses in college in order to pursue certain options in graduate school. Which programs should you choose and which courses must you take? Your advisor is a valuable resource in gathering the information that will help you make these decisions.

Your advisor can also serve as a resource person if you experience any problems at college from failure in a course to hassles with your roommate or problems raising money for tuition. He or she knows your school and can direct you to the office that will help you succeed.

During your first two years at college, you may have a general advisor who will mainly work with you on courses required of all students at the college, regardless of major. Later in your college career, you will find it helpful to have an advisor who specializes in your major as you may have questions about graduate programs or career opportunities in your field.

Schedule an appointment with your advisor if you

■ Are doing poorly in one of your classes.
■ Are thinking about dropping a course.
■ Know it is time to plan your schedule for the following semester.
■ Are not sure about requirements for graduation or your major.
■ Are doing poorly in most or all of your classes.
■ Are thinking of stopping out or dropping out of school.
■ Are considering summer courses at another college.
■ Would like information about the honors program or any other special program.
■ Are undecided about a major.
■ Would like to discuss career options available through your major.
■ Would like to change your major.
■ Would like information about graduate school or professional programs.
■ Would like to discuss career choices.

Advisement Documents

Keep a copy of your initial college catalog.

The faculty at the college consider you an adult. Therefore, they expect you to take on adult responsibilities for keeping advisement appointments, planning your program, and holding onto copies of your academic records. It is helpful to keep a copy of the college catalog that was issued the year you enrolled. College requirements change, but the college will usually allow you to graduate according to the requirements in place when you first enrolled. If an advisor or an administrator tells you that you are exempt from a certain course requirement, have that person put the exemption in writing and keep a copy of this document in your file of academic papers. It could make the difference between graduating and spending an extra semester at the college!

Have all course exemptions put in writing.

If you keep a cumulative record of the courses you have completed that fulfill various requirements, you will find that advisement and registration go more smoothly. Many schools have several categories of requirements for graduation. For example, you may have to take certain courses to fulfill general education requirements, other courses to fulfill requirements in your major, and still other courses to fulfill requirements for your department or school. Within each of these categories, you may be able to choose among several courses that fulfill a particular requirement.

The best way to keep track of which requirements you have fulfilled and which courses you still have to take is to make a master sheet that lists all the required categories. When you meet with your academic advisor each semester, write down each course in which you are enrolling next to the category of requirement it fulfills. Keep a separate list at the end of the required categories for elective courses. In this way, when you reach your senior year and you are trying to figure out whether you fulfilled the "Sophomore Level General Education" requirement in "Culture and Civilization," you will know that that requirement was the reason you enrolled in "History 215, Affluence and Anxiety in the Twentieth Century."

Keep a list of courses you have completed and the requirements they fulfill.

In summary, keep a copy of the college catalog, or other document that describes your major program, along with a list of any other courses that you are required to take over the course of your college career; keep these papers with the master list of courses you have taken. You will then be ready to face each semester's registration period with confidence about the courses you need to take in order to progress toward graduation.

■ CHOOSING A MAJOR

Many students agonize over choosing a major. They believe that this decision will lock them into a particular career path and determine their future success. In fact, choosing a particular college major may have relatively little impact on the direction your career will take or on your success after you graduate from college. A number of surveys indicate that only a tiny percentage of students end up working in fields related to their college major. More than half eventually work in jobs that did not even exist when they were attending college.

Many students select their major with an eye toward the job market; they look toward the fields where jobs are opening up. But recent trends in the workplace indicate that the job market is a very volatile place: Fields that hire at a furious pace in one year, are often "oversubscribed" five years later. If you select your major primarily because you think it will offer you the greatest number of job opportunities after graduation, you may be in for a very unpleasant surprise.

A better strategy would involve learning the basic skills that all employers value: oral and written communication, problem solving, analytical and critical thinking, organization and management, the ability to work effectively with different types of people. These are skills that you will acquire in your general education courses and in the courses required for almost any major.

Next, choose a major by finding an area that interests you and a subject where you have some ability. This will not necessarily be the major toward

ACTIVITY

Matching Successful People with Their Majors

This activity will emphasize the gap that often exists between the choice of a college major and one's final career direction. Match each of the individuals described in column A with a major from column B by writing the letter of the corresponding major next to the person's name. When you have completed the activity, check your answers with the list on page 29 which displays the individuals' true choice of major.

Column A

_____ 1. Jim Manzi, president and chief executive officer, Lotus Development, the second-largest software company in the world

_____ 2. Joe Paterno, legendary football coach, Pennsylvania State University

_____ 3. Roger Corman, the "Louis B. Mayer" of B movies

_____ 4. Jonathan Winters, comedian

_____ 5. Jane Metzroth, senior vice president for The Gap

_____ 6. Edward Tabor, physician and associate director for biological carcinogenesis, American Cancer Institute

_____ 7. Patrick Ewing, center for the Knicks

_____ 8. Andre Cole, magician and psychic investigator

_____ 9. Greta Martin, Hat Box Girl in the Broadway musical, "Guys and Dolls"

_____ 10. Bill Bradley, senator from New Jersey

_____ 11. Julian Sahni, chef and author, "Classic Indian Cooking"

_____ 12. Sam Perkins, forward, Seattle SuperSonics

_____ 13. Bob Garfield, commentator, National Public Radio

_____ 14. Blanche Roberts, national pug breeder

_____ 15. Ellen Gould, actress

_____ 16. Lori Cole, designer of computer games such as the "Quest for Glory" fantasy series

_____ 17. Harry Blackstone Jr., magician

_____ 18. Mary C. Starke, clinical psychologist, psychology professor, author of *Strategies For College Success*

Column B

a. engineering
b. mathematics
c. classics
d. American history
e. English
f. biochemistry
g. art
h. theatre arts, communications
i. English
j. art
k. sociology
l. English
m. communications
n. elementary education
o. drama
p. architecture, urban planning
q. psychology
r. Spanish

The information in this exercise is based on articles by M. Kaufman, "College Majors Often Proven Minor"[2] and K. Koontz, "Major Matters, or Does It?"[3]

which your parents are pushing you, nor the major that most of your friends are choosing, nor the major that is "hot" or currently has the greatest number of job openings. This should be the major which interests you enough so that you will be happy to put in the long hours of work and study that are required for success in any career. Be realistic about you abilities. If you have trouble with math, computer engineering may not be the best career choice for you. If you are getting D's in your accounting courses, try marketing or business management instead. If you hate science, a pre-med major may not be the best choice for you.

Don't worry if you have not reached a decision about your major during your first or second year. The largest percentage of first-year students belongs to the "undecided" major. Use your freshman and sophomore years to explore various options by completing the general education courses that are required for a college degree in any major. Ask your advisor about additional elective courses that may help you make a decision about your major. Talk with juniors and seniors about their majors. Make appointments with academic advisors who specialize in counseling students who are undecided. Complete some of the first steps described in the "Four-Year Career Guide Activity" in Chapter 15 of this text. Look through the majors listed in your college catalog and find a field you love.

■ THE COLLEGE CATALOG

The most complete source for information about your college's structures, policies, and requirements is the college catalog. It includes a wealth of information, such as course descriptions, tuition fees, beginning and ending session dates, withdrawal dates, minimum grade point average, faculty and administrative titles and departments, grading policies, and requirements for majors. As you look through the college catalog, you may find some interesting fields of learning you did not know existed. The following activity will help familiarize you with your college's catalog and rules.

ACTIVITY

Using Your College Catalog

Read the general information section of your college catalog and the program descriptions for two majors that might interest you in order to find the answers to the questions.

The Academic Calendar

1. During what dates will the college be closed for holidays this semester?

   _____

2. What is the last date on which you may add or drop courses? _____

3. What is the last date on which you may withdraw from a course and still receive a partial refund on your tuition? _____

4. On what dates will registration for next semester take place?

   _____

5. If your school offers you the option of taking a grade of "incomplete," what is the last date to request this grade?

_____

6. What is the last date on which you can withdraw from a course?

_____

7. When is final exam week scheduled? _____

8. What is the last day of classes? _____

9. What is the first day of classes next semester? _____

General Background Information

1. When was your college founded? _____

2. Does your college have any particular mission, focus, or area of specialization? If so, what is it?

_____

_____

_____

3. Is your college accredited by any national organization(s)? Which one(s)?

_____

4. How many students are enrolled in the college? _____

Your College's Organizational Structure

1. How is your institution organized (colleges, schools, divisions, departments)?

_____

_____

2. List three examples of departments or majors within your institution.

_____

3. Does your institution offer graduate or professional programs? List three programs.

_____

_____

_____

Financial Information

1. What is the annual tuition that applies to you at your college? (At most public institutions, state or county residents pay lower tuition than out-of-state residents.)

_____

2. What types of financial aid programs are available (scholarships, work/study programs, loans)?

_____

_____

3. Where would you go to find more information about financial aid?

   _____

Academic Policies and Grades

1. Does your college offer credit for advanced courses taken in high school? _____

2. Does your college accept transfer credits from other institutions? _____

3. Does your college give credit for certain types of life experience outside the classroom? _____

4. What is the grading system? (List the grades that may be given by instructors.)

   _____

   _____

   _____

5. Explain the following grade options if your college offers them:

   Incomplete

   _____

   _____

   Pass/Fail

   _____

   _____

   Repeat (If a course is taken a second time)

   _____

   _____

   Audit

   _____

   _____

   Withdrawal

   _____

   _____

6. List any other special grade options offered by your college.

   _____

   _____

7. What is the minimum grade point average that a student may earn and still remain in satisfactory academic standing?

   _____

   _____

8. What happens if your grade point average falls below the minimum required for satisfactory academic standing?

   _____

   _____

9. How does your institution deal with the following violations of academic integrity?

Cheating

_____

_____

Plagiarism

_____

_____

Other academic misconduct

_____

_____

Special Programs

1. If your college offers an honors program or programs, what are the eligibility criteria?

_____

_____

2. Does your college offer any other forms of recognition for academic excellence while you are working toward your degree (e.g., dean's list, scholarships, assistantships)? List several.

_____

_____

3. If your college offers a program to study abroad, what are the prerequisites for participation?

_____

4. If your college offers cooperative education or internship programs, what are the prerequisites for participation? (Cooperative education programs allow students to work off campus for pay while earning credits toward their degrees.)

_____

_____

5. Describe any other special programs your college offers that might interest you.

_____

_____

_____

Graduation Requirements

1. What are the requirements for graduation other than completing a major?

_____

_____

_____

2. What is the minimum grade point average required for graduation? _____

3. What is the minimum grade point average in your major required for graduation?

   _____

4. Is it possible to graduate with more than one major? _____

5. Does your college offer minors or concentrations? _____

6. What honors or awards does your college extend to graduating seniors who have shown evidence of academic excellence?

   _____

   _____

Academic Programs

1. Skim the list of majors offered by your college. How many are there? _____

2. Skim the list of minors offered by your college. How many are there? _____

3. What major interests you? _____

   How many credits are required to complete this major? _____

   What particular courses are required for this major?

   _____

   _____

   _____

   Must courses be taken in a certain sequence for this major? Are some courses prerequisites for others? Are some courses restricted to the junior or senior years? If so, give examples.

   _____

   _____

   _____

4. What other major interests you? _____

   How many credits are required to complete this major? _____

   What particular courses are required for this major?

   _____

   _____

   _____

   Must courses be taken in a certain sequence for this major? Are some courses prerequisites for others? Are some courses restricted to the junior or senior years? If so, give examples.

   _____

   _____

   _____

5. Can you combine two majors or create your own major at your college? _____

6. What minor interests you? _____

How many credits are required to complete this minor? _____

What particular courses are required for this minor?

_____

_____

_____

Must courses be taken in a certain sequence? Are some of the courses prerequisites for others? Are some of the courses restricted to the junior or senior year? If so, give examples.

_____

_____

_____

■ SURVIVING IN THE SYSTEM

Your college is a large organization. As happens in many large organizations, there may come a time when you run afoul of the organization's rules or structures. This may happen if you receive a lower grade on a paper than you expected, if the computer loses the record of your tuition payment, or if the registrar's office misplaces your application for graduation. By the time most students become seniors, they have learned how to thread their way through the college's structural maze quite effectively.

The system is a little more confusing for freshmen; a few hints may help you find your way through the system. These suggestions will also stand you in good stead during other life experiences when you have to tackle large organizations such as the credit bureau that gives you an unfair credit evaluation, the bank that loses the record of your mortgage payment, or the car company that refuses to honor the warranty on the "lemon" you bought.

Creating a File for College Documents

Keep all important college documents in a file.

Early in your college career, begin a file in which to save important documents. Place in it a copy of the catalog that was issued the year you matriculated or began taking courses at your college. Most schools will allow you to graduate under the policies that were in effect when you entered, even if regulations change after you have enrolled. If you have a copy of that catalog, you can readily produce it in your senior year to prove that you need only one laboratory course rather than the two that may be currently required for graduation. The same advice holds true for any prerequisites or requirements that may be waived for you on an individual basis. Ask the dean or advisor who is waiving the requirement to put the special exception in writing, and keep a copy in your file. When you are ready to graduate, that person may no longer be working at the college, and there may be no other way to confirm the dispensation that he or she made for you.

Keep a record of all financial dealings with your college.

You should also keep records and receipts of all your financial dealings with the college (tuition receipts, bookstore receipts, library fine receipts, etc.). In these days of high-tech computer billing, errors are all too frequent. Many colleges will hold up your grade report or refuse to mail out a transcript for an

application to graduate school until all bills have been paid. Errors in this area are easily resolved if you can produce a receipt or canceled check proving that you have paid the charges.

Seeking a Grade Adjustment

Keep a copy of all papers you submit for course work until you have received your grade report for that semester. Although most professors are conscientious, it is possible that a paper might be lost or that a grade might be incorrectly entered in an instructor's grade book. For this reason, you should also keep copies of exams that are returned to you until you receive the grade report at the end of the semester. You cannot depend on your professor to remember that your paper was one of the 125 handed in or that you received a 92 percent on an exam if the records show otherwise. If, on the other hand, you can produce a copy of the document in question, the problem is easily resolved.

Keep a copy of all papers and exams you have written until you receive your final grade report for the semester.

If you feel that you have been graded unfairly on a paper or in a course, you should make an appointment to speak to your instructor about it first. Professors enjoy the right of academic freedom, which means that any administrator will be reluctant to interfere with an instructor's way of teaching or with his or her grading policies. You will not gain anything by going to the chair of the department and complaining about the situation before speaking with your instructor. The first question you will be asked is whether you have discussed the problem with your professor. If you indicate that you are reluctant to complain to the instructor for fear that future grades might be jeopardized, the department chair will reply that there is little he or she can do to help you. Usually, a complaint that identifies the involved parties and describes the situation must be put in writing before a department chair or any other administrator can act on it.

In most cases, a professor will not become prejudiced against you if you question his or her grading policies or teaching methods. College instructors generally are fair people who enjoy the give and take of discussions even when their points of view are being questioned. Do not attack your instructor in front of a whole roomful of students—he or she will naturally feel defensive under those conditions. Make an office appointment to see your instructor, and present your case as diplomatically and persuasively as you can. If the situation affects other students as well, you might wish to bring with you to the meeting a few tactful students who share your view.

If you cannot resolve the problem with your instructor and still feel that you have been treated unfairly, you must take the next step up the ladder. The procedures for pursuing a grievance vary from one college to another. In most institutions, the next step is to make an appointment with the department chair. The chair will ask you to describe the problem. If he or she feels you have some basis for complaint, you will probably have to submit a written account of the situation. Putting the problem in writing allows all parties involved to be sure that they are responding to the same facts. It also gives the professor a chance to defend his or her position. The department chair will then follow up with the instructor and try to mediate between the two of you.

If you do not receive satisfaction from the department chair, you will have to repeat the process with the dean or the vice president. Most professors try to treat their students fairly. Cases do exist, however, in which disagreements must be mediated between students and faculty, and students are within their rights to complain about grading practices, teaching methods, or sexual harassment. If you control your temper, state your case clearly, and follow the appropriate steps, you can succeed in achieving a fair resolution of your problem.

Read about the procedure for a grade dispute that exists on your campus. List the steps you would take if you disagreed with an instructor about the grade for a course. In each case, list the title of the administrator to whom you would make your appeal.

Step   Title of Administrator

_____

_____

_____

_____

■ GRADE POINT AVERAGES (GPAs)

A survey of grading systems used in colleges across the United States revealed a considerable variety of practices.[4] Most colleges, however, use some variation of the alphabetic system (i.e., *A, B, C, D, F*), and there is a growing tendency to include plus and minus modifiers along with the letter grades (e.g., *B*+ or *C* −).

The calculation of grade point average (GPA) described here is based on the most common alphabetic grading system and a numerical scale ranging from 0.0 to 4.0 grade quality points. If your college uses a different system, familiarize yourself with it by checking the college catalog or asking your academic advisor about it.

Each letter is associated with a certain number of grade points. The particular numbers and letters will vary from college to college, but the following system is the most common:

A = 4.0
B = 3.0
C = 2.0
D = 1.0
F = 0.0

Intermediate grades such as A − or B+ have intermediate values depending on the college's system, so that an A − might equal 3.5 or 3.67 grade points.

Figure 2.1 shows a sample grade report for a student enrolled in 16 credits of coursework. The activity on page 27 demonstrates how to calculate a GPA for the semester.

This student's GPA for the semester is 2.0, which is equivalent to a *C*. You will notice that courses worth more credits affect your GPA more than courses worth fewer credits. If your only consideration were your GPA, it would pay to put more work into a 5-credit course so that the higher grade will be multiplied by 5 (for a 4-credit course, the grade will be multiplied only by 4, etc.). Rarely, however, is the GPA the only consideration. Some courses may be more important to you because they are in your major or because of your vocational goals. At other times, you may wish to do better in a course because the material interests you or is more meaningful to you. *Grades should not be the primary considerations that guide your college studies.*

You will also notice that a grade of F brings your whole average down. Although an F results in 0.0 grade points earned, the grade still counts against you when your average is calculated because the number of course credits in the denominator is not balanced out by the 0.0 in the numerator. In some cases, you may wish to withdraw from a course if you believe that you will not be

Figure 2.1   *Calculation of a GPA*

Course Title	Number of Credits	Grade Earned		Grade Points Earned
Introduction to Accounting	3	C	2.0 × 3 credits =	6
Freshman English	3	B	3.0 × 3 credits =	9
Biology	5	D	1.0 × 5 credits =	5
Introduction to Psychology	3	A	4.0 × 3 credits =	12
Music Appreciation	2	F	0.0 × 2 credits =	0
Total number of credits attempted	= 16		*Total of grade points earned =*	32

Total grade points earned divided by total number of credits attempted = 32/16 = 2.0 GPA

ACTIVITY

Computing Your GPA

Read the section of your college catalog that describes the grading system used in your institution. Using Figure 2.1 as a guide, complete the following activity.

First, write down the courses you are taking this semester and make a hypothetical list of grades that you might receive at the end of the semester. Do not give yourself all *A*s; use a broad range of possible grades. Then compute your hypothetical GPA.

Course Title	Number of Credits	Grade Earned	Grade Points Earned
_____	_____	_____	_____
_____	_____	_____	_____
_____	_____	_____	_____
_____	_____	_____	_____
_____	_____	_____	_____
_____	_____	_____	_____
_____	_____	_____	_____
_____	_____	_____	_____

Total number of credits attempted   =   _____   *Total grade points earned*   =   _____

GPA earned for the semester _____

able to pass it. You may then enroll in the course at a future date when your chances of learning the material are better.

■ SUPPLEMENTING YOUR EDUCATION THROUGH EXTRACURRICULAR ACTIVITIES

Many campuses offer a wide variety of extracurricular activities. Clubs may focus on hobbies, such as photography or cycling; majors, such as psychology or history; on vocations, such as accounting or law; or on a particular religion. Other extracurricular activities are more directly involved with services to the campus such as the student government, the newspaper, or the campus radio station. Many athletic departments sponsor a variety of teams that offer a good physical workout and a focus for campus spirit. Sororities and fraternities serve social functions and may also provide community services such as a food cooperative, a recycling project, or support for a political campaign.

Participation in these activities can offer relief from academic pressure, entertainment, and educational experiences. Research shows that students who are involved in extracurricular activities are much less likely to drop out of college than students who do not participate in the extracurriculum. Extracurricular activities can help you to develop social and leadership skills. They can also introduce you to students with interests similar to yours, help you explore closer and less formal relationships with faculty, and give you valuable information about careers and majors.

Many employers look closely at the extracurricular activities of job applicants because these employers value the initiative, leadership, and social skills that the activities foster. Students who have been active in extracurricular activities are more likely to be well-rounded people who will make good members of a company team. These students may have had direct organizational experience that will be helpful in the vocational setting; they probably know

ACTIVITY

Getting Involved in Extracurricular Activities

1. This activity will encourage you to get involved in extracurricular activities on campus. Choose at least five organizations or campus events that you will attend over the course of the semester. Listings of organizations and events are usually available in the student handbook, the student activities office, a campus bulletin, or the student newspaper. Make one of your choices a club meeting; a second, a student government meeting; a third, an athletic event; a fourth, a community service organization meeting; and a fifth, some type of cultural campus event.

2. Attend the meeting or event, and write a brief summary. Include the date, the location, the name of the organization or event, the principal people involved (e.g., the names of the performing group or speaker, the club's president and faculty advisor, the teams involved), a brief summary of the main events, and your reaction to the event.

Your instructor may choose to collect this as a homework assignment or may ask you to share one or two events with the class so that you can benefit from each others' experiences.

how to cooperate with others on a group project; and they are more likely to follow up on interests and translate them into concrete products.

Graduate and professional program administrators are likely to have similar views about students who participate in extracurricular activities related to their majors. Like employers, these program administrators value initiative, organizational experience, and commitment to a specific area of interest. Even if you are a commuter or a nontraditional student juggling family and job responsibilities, do not view extracurricular activities as a luxury that must take a back seat to academic assignments and job-related pressures. Consider these activities as a valuable part of the college learning experience and as a way to enjoy yourself.

Answers to Activity "Matching Successful People with Their Majors"

1. c	6. e	11. p	16. n
2. i	7. g	12. m	17. h
3. a	8. q	13. l	18. r
4. j	9. b	14. o	
5. f	10. d	15. k	

REFLECTIONS FOR YOUR JOURNAL

1. One of the best predictors of a student's success in college is the quality of his or her relationships with faculty. Finding a faculty member to serve as your guide or mentor can make all the difference in your college career. Think of the teachers you had in elementary and high school. Was there anyone who made a difference in your life? What qualities did this teacher possess? Keep an eye out for college professors who possess similar qualities.

2. Have you ever made friends with a teacher? How did this relationship affect you?

3. A grade is an assessment of how well you have mastered the material in a course. It is not always an accurate appraisal of your learning, and it is certainly not a good predictor of how well you will do later in your life. Motivation, persistence, planning, and luck are all more important. Think about a time when you were disappointed by a grade. How did you handle it? How might you have handled it better?

4. Think of a problem that might arise during your college career, for example, an attendance problem with a course, a serious dispute with a spouse, boyfriend or girlfriend, difficulty in getting together enough money to stay in college. Where would you go for help with such a problem?

5. After considering the extracurricular activities available at your college, choose one that interests you most. What might you gain from participating or assuming a leadership role in this activity?

Notes

1. "National Dropout Rates." The American College Testing Program. Compiled from ACT Institutional Data File. Iowa City, IA: Noel-Levitz Center for Student Retention, 1996.

2. M. Kaufman, "College Majors Often Proven Minor," *New York Times*, 4 April 1993, Section 4A, Education Life, p. 21.

3. K. Koontz, "Major Matters, or Does It?" *Connections*, Winter Preview, 1989, American Express Card, pp. 3–4, 16.

4. M. C. Starke and G. Bear, "Grading in Higher Education: A Survey of American Systems and Practices," *Journal of Research and Development in Education*, 21 no. 4 (1988), pp. 62–68.

CHAPTER

3

TIME MANAGEMENT

Think of it as a formula:

Planning + Prioritizing = Productivity

Those three Ps in turn produce another P bonus: Pleasure

Marilyn Gardner[1]

The efficient management of time is vital for success in any career. Learn to manage your time effectively now, and you will not only survive your first year at college, but you will also acquire a skill that becomes increasingly important as your life grows more complex and as you take on a larger number of roles. *Now* is the time to learn better ways to use your time. When you find that you must juggle commitments to your career, spouse, children, other family members, friends, community, or charitable organizations, and still want to find time for a weekly softball, bridge, or poker game, you will really appreciate the time management skills you learned in college!

Many students entering college do not have strong time management skills. This is one of the reasons that so many first-year students do not succeed. Perhaps you were able to succeed in high school without practicing effective time management because the work load was lighter, there was less competition from your peers, or your time was managed for you. In college, the work load will be heavier, and the competition from your peers will be tougher because only the more able students who graduate from high school go on to college. You will also find that time is not structured for you the way it was in high school. Courses will not meet every day as they do in many high schools. Often instructors will not take attendance in class, and the school will certainly not send a note home to your parents when you are absent. Study halls will not be scheduled for you. Instructors will not collect daily homework assignments to make sure that you have read or studied a particular chapter. Parents will not ask you whether you finished your homework before you run out the door to a movie.

College instructors expect you to behave in an adult manner with regard to time management. If your responsibilities are met, then you will succeed; if they are not, then it is your own problem. Many first-year students fail or drop out of college because they have not developed an effective time management system. If you do not keep up with college assignments on a regular basis, these assignments accumulate until you are overwhelmed by due dates for exams, papers, and projects.

Yet most good students find time to join a club, play some sports, hang out with their friends, complete their responsibilities to their jobs and their families, and still get a good college education. If you learn to use your time efficiently, you will be rewarded. You will have leisure time to use as you please; you will enjoy yourself without feeling guilty because you are not studying; you will have better health because you are getting enough sleep; you will experience less stress because you do not have to cram for an exam or write a paper the night before it is due; and you will learn more while getting better

30

grades! Time management skills can be learned. This chapter will help you learn how to work smarter, not harder.

■ SETTING GOALS

Choosing and using goals can set a tone and pattern for your life. Use your time at college to reflect upon your life goals and values. The values you adopt will shape your life pattern over a span of years. Shorter term goals, such as passing a course or learning a new skill, can give you a sense of purpose over a time span of months and can also allow you to set a reward for your own behavior while you work toward longer range goals such as completing your college education or launching a rewarding career. Most people find that they work better toward long-range goals when they use both short-term goals and a reward for a job well done.

Even short-term goals, with a time frame of days or weeks, allow you to plan and give structure to your time. When you accomplish a task that you have set for yourself, you can reward yourself with anything from a pat on the back, or an excursion to the movies, to a trip to Bermuda. Setting and accomplishing short-term objectives will make you feel as though you are master or mistress of your own fate; you will not feel as though you are at the mercy of events beyond your control. Having both short- and long-term goals is the way to impose structure and value on your life and the world.

Modern life can be quite harried and seemingly without structure. You can give it structure by having good, regular daily habits (e.g., getting enough sleep, eating three well-balanced meals a day, making time for physical exercise) and by having regular, appointed tasks and objectives. Learn to set these objectives at a level so that you can accomplish them but also experience some degree of challenge. The goals must be high enough to keep you interested, but not so high that you will become frustrated. The rewards must be frequent enough so that you remain motivated. It is important to set realistic goals so that you can accomplish them and feel like an effective, valued, and purposeful person.

■ SETTING TASK PRIORITIES

The effective management of time requires decision making and planning. You must decide on your priorities: What is most important to you? What must you accomplish today? Tomorrow? Next week? Do not put equal time and energy into every task. List all the things you have to do and decide which ones are really important and which ones will not make that much difference. For example, you may know that you should read that chapter in your economics textbook and write a detailed outline. But this is the week that the big project is due that will determine half of your grade in your history course. Can you read that economics chapter carefully, but save time by not writing a detailed outline? Can you save additional time this week by buying a cake for your daughter's birthday party instead of baking one from scratch?

There is never enough time to do everything you must do in addition to everything that you want to do. Should you stay up late and party with your friends or get a good night's sleep before that important physics exam tomorrow? Should you go to work or finish the English paper that is due the next day? Should you go home and visit with your family this weekend or catch up on the reading for your anthropology course? Establish your priorities on a general basis so that you do not have to agonize over daily decisions that cause conflict and waste precious time. The following activities will help you determine how much time you need for course work and for other obligations so you can make decisions about the best way to use your time.

A C T I V I T Y

Keeping a Time Journal

Using the Time Journal

The time journal shown on pages 33–34 is designed to help you determine exactly how you spend your time. Many of us think we know where our time goes. When we actually write down what we do minute by minute, however, we are surprised by all the little interruptions and time wasters we encounter and by the amount of time we actually spend on various activities.

Time seems to fly by when you are having fun, and it seems to crawl along at a snail's pace when you are involved with a task that does not interest you.

Did you really spend an hour studying for that chemistry exam or was most of that hour spent talking "briefly" with the friend who stopped by your house for a moment? Keeping a time journal will show you exactly how your time is spent. You will then be in a better position to determine whether you need to make changes in the way you manage your time and what those changes should be.

Keep a time journal for at least two weekdays. During the evening, before you begin recording in the journal, make a list of things you have to do the next day. Assign each item a priority number based on the total number of items on your list. For instance, your rating scale might extend from most important (1) to least important (8) if there are eight items on your list. Your list might look like the following example.

Prioritize Daily Activities

4   Attend biology class
3   Attend computer class
5   Attend basketball practice
1   Study for economics exam (scheduled tomorrow)
2   Drive sister to work
6   Review biology notes
7   Prepare draft of English paper (due in three weeks)
8   Get oil changed in car

Carry the time journal with you. As the day goes on, record each activity, the time it began, and the amount of time used for the activity. If you wait to record your activities until the end of the day, you will forget many of the fifteen-minute interruptions (phone calls, brief chats, daydreaming lapses) that may actually eat up so much of your time.

At the end of the day, evaluate how you have used your time. Did you accomplish everything that had to get done? Did you waste time that could have been put to better use? Did you finish high-priority items before taking time for activities that were not essential? Make comments in the last column of your time journal, with an eye to improving your time management (e.g., study at desk instead of in bed, move an item to the end of the day, use break between classes for study in library, avoid scheduling social activities the night before an important exam, eliminate specific time wasters, avoid watching television during the day). On page 36, write down ways you can improve your time management system.

The Science Teacher General has determined that procrastinating may be hazardous to your sense of wellbeing and state of mind (and your science grade).

Melissa Robin, The Hackley School

The Time Journal Form

Name _____ Day/Date _____

Priority Rating: 1 = Most Important . . . . 7 = Least Important

Goals for Today:

1. _____ 5. _____

2. _____ 6. _____

3. _____ 7. _____

4. _____ 8. _____

Time	Activity	Amount Time Used	Priority Rating	Comments

The Time Journal Form

Name _____ Day/Date _____

Priority Rating: 1 = Most Important . . . . 7 = Least Important

Goals for Today:

1. _____ 5. _____

2. _____ 6. _____

3. _____ 7. _____

4. _____ 8. _____

Time	Activity	Amount Time Used	Priority Rating	Comments

ACTIVITY

Keeping a Weekly Schedule

Now that you have made some improvements in the day-to-day use of your time, do a little arithmetic to set your priorities and improve your weekly planning. Make a photocopy of the weekly schedule form on page 46 to write out a typical schedule for your week. Write in the hours that you should be in class, that you spend at your job, that you commit to any regularly scheduled family or house-hold obligations, and that you spend commuting. Then calculate and record, on the weekly expenditure of time form on page 36, the number of hours you spend on activities. In recording time for meals, don't automatically put down an hour for each meal; calculate the time you need based on the actual amount of time you spent eating when you were keeping the time journals.

Add up the total number of hours you spend in classes, at work, on fam-ily responsibilities, for commuting, and on personal needs. Subtract that num-ber from 168, the total number of hours in a week. This gives you the number of hours you have available for study and leisure.

On the form for weekly expenditure of time in study at the bottom of page 36, list your courses and estimate the number of study hours you are willing to devote to each course in order to achieve the grade you want. Remember that the traditional rule of thumb suggests that you spend two or three hours of study and preparation time outside of class for every hour you spend in class. This rule will vary, of course, depending on how good a student you are, how difficult a particular course is for you, and how heavy the work load (reading assignments, papers, exams) is for that particular course over the span of the semester. You will have a better idea of how much time each course requires once the first two weeks of the semester have passed. Up to a certain point, the greater the number of hours you are willing to devote to a course, the more you should learn in it, and the higher your grade in that course should be.

Add weekly study time to the total number of hours you have calculated for classes, work, and personal needs, and subtract that number from 168. The answer is the number of hours you have available per week for leisure. You should schedule at least some time for exercise, relaxation, or leisure activities each day.

Practice prioritizing your activities. In the following box, list the activi-ties that you should accomplish tomorrow and give each one a priority number beginning with 1, your most important goal.

Prioritize Your Activities for Tomorrow

Priority
Rating   Activity

_____   _____

_____   _____

_____   _____

_____   _____

_____   _____

_____   _____

Weekly Expenditure of Time for Personal Needs, Classes, Job, Family Responsibilities, and Commuting

Number of hours per week you need to sleep _____

Number of hours per week used for meals _____

Number of hours per week used for personal grooming _____

Number of hours per week spent on fixed family and household duties (laundry, child care, meal preparation, cleaning) _____

Number of hours per week spent in class _____

Number of hours per week spent at work, if you are employed _____

Number of hours per week spent commuting (between school, home, and work, or among classes) _____

a. Total number of hours: _____

168 − total number of hours from a = Number of hours available for study and leisure: _____

Weekly Expenditure of Time in Study (Reading, Exams, Papers, etc.)

Course 1

_____ _____

Course 2

_____ _____

Course 3

_____ _____

Course 4

_____ _____

Course 5

_____ _____

b. Total number of study hours per week: _____

168 − total number of hours from a − total number of hours from b = Number of hours available for leisure: _____

Based on what you have learned from keeping the time journal, what changes can you make to improve your time management system?

Improvements I can make in managing my time:

1.

2.

3.

4.

5.

■ MAKING TIME FOR LEISURE ACTIVITIES

If you work more than twenty hours per week, carry significant family obligations, enroll in difficult courses, or read slowly, you may find that you have little leisure time. You may have to reevaluate your priorities in order to make time for leisure activities. Decrease the number of hours you spend on meals, personal needs, family and household obligations, or work. If this is not possible, you may have to drop a course or adjust the goals you have set for grades in your courses. It is generally better to drop a course than to plan on scraping by just to receive a passing grade. Pick up the course again during a summer session or a less harried semester when work or family commitments decrease. No iron-clad rule says you must graduate in four years. As a matter of fact, more than half of all college students take longer to complete their bachelor's degree.

■ STRATEGIES FOR EFFECTIVE TIME MANAGEMENT

After you have given some thought to your priorities and weekly schedule, incorporate the following suggestions to help you use your time more effectively and avoid procrastination.

Identify your peak efficiency times during the day—when you are most alert and energetic and when you do your best work. For most people, these are the morning hours. Use these peak times to schedule classes, study periods, and other high-priority items that must be completed. Be realistic about scheduling study times. Sunday morning is not a good time to schedule study time if you stay out late Saturday night or enjoy sleeping in on weekends. *Schedule high priority activities for peak energy times.*

Tackle your most difficult assignments during your peak energy times, and leave other more mechanical tasks for times when you are tired. For example, composing a paper, reading a difficult assignment, or studying for an exam should be done during your peak efficiency hours. Copying a lab report, typing a paper, alphabetizing the sources for your bibliography, going through your mail, straightening up your room, or doing laundry can be left for other time periods when you are not working at peak efficiency. Make a habit of starting your study period with the most difficult task for the day. The beginning of a study period is when your mind is most alert and rested. Leave short, trivial, or routine tasks for the end of your study period. *Schedule most difficult activities for peak times and do them first.*

Make up a schedule for each week. Sunday evening is a good time to do this. Include classes, meals, time at your job, meetings and appointments (social, medical, school related, etc.), exercise, and *study time*. Add items to your schedule as they come up during the week, and check your schedule each morning so that you leave home with all the materials you need for that day. It does not pay to get to the library, planning to read a chapter in your psychology text, only to find that you have left the textbook in your room. *Make weekly schedule.*

Check schedule daily.

Try to schedule study time for each particular course in a time period soon before or after that class meets. This will allow you to relate reading assignments to class lectures more easily, help you to participate in class discussions more readily, and prime you to review class notes while they are still fresh in your mind. It will also keep you from having to carry an extra book as you will already have the notebook or text with you for a course when you attend class. *Schedule study time close to class time.*

Use your time in class effectively so that you do not have to study as much outside of class. Sit in the front row. Sitting in front encourages you to pay attention and helps convince the professor that you are an interested, motivated student. Complete your reading assignments *before* class so that you have an overall framework into which you can place your class notes and you are familiar with the topics and terms your professor will be using. Listen and take notes, but do not try to write down everything the professor says. Write down *Use your time in class efficiently.*

Read assignments before class.

Record important information only.

Fill in gaps after class.

Ask questions.

Learn from your mistakes.

Schedule specific study assignments.

Establish a regular study schedule.

Change study subjects every 45 to 55 minutes.

Take breaks.

Use odd hours for study.

Study with a partner.

key words and phrases and fill in the gaps after class. This will give you time to analyze what is being said, as well as the opportunity to ask intelligent questions. (Professors appreciate students who ask intelligent questions.)

When a professor returns your exam or paper, read over the comments she or he has written and talk with the professor about them. This will communicate to the professor that you are a student who is serious about the work, it will help you to learn better, and it will keep you from making the same mistakes the next time.

When you schedule study time, write down specifically what you are going to study. For example, instead of writing just "study biology," write "read Chapter 6 for biology," "proofread history paper," or "review psychology class notes." The more specific you make your commitment on your schedule, the more likely it is that you will be "psyched" to start your study period on time. Do not waste valuable study time hunting through your syllabus for the next assignment or rummaging through your desk to find the draft of the history paper. When you see a specific item listed on your schedule for the day, use the previous night to prepare whatever materials you need; or, you can prepare in the morning before you leave your room.

Once you schedule study time, be sure to use that time to study. Do not wait until you feel like studying. It is too easy to put it off or to hang out with a friend if you wait until you are in the right mood. If you regularly schedule certain times and places for study, you can condition yourself to study under those circumstances. Your mind will automatically prepare itself, and it will become easier for you to get to work and concentrate once you have established a regular routine. If you consistently associate certain stimuli with studying, you can even condition yourself so that those stimuli trigger a frame of mind conducive to studying. You might even wish to prompt yourself with a certain piece of music, specific lighting, certain clothes, or a particular place that you use only for study. In addition, studying in a place that you use only for study means that you will not have to lose time cleaning off your study area or gathering up your study materials.

You should be studying approximately 2 to 3 hours for every hour that you spend in class. Spread out your study time for any particular course into several sessions over the week rather than in one long marathon session. Your mind will remain more alert if you change subjects every 45 to 55 minutes. This advice does not apply if you are really into the groove of writing a paper or if you have to catch up for an exam that is scheduled for the next day. Plan to take a short break (approximately 10 minutes) after studying for 45 to 55 minutes, regardless of whether you are changing subjects. If your schedule is really tight, that "break" might have to consist of paying bills, moving your laundry from the washer to the dryer, or reviewing your daily schedule for the next day. The break will work better if you can take the time to prepare a snack, read the newspaper, or look through your junk mail. A break from studying will refresh your mind, maintain your concentration, improve retention of the material, and reward you for sticking with the study schedule.

Take advantage of odd hours to catch up on study time. You might be able to review course notes during the time you spend waiting for an appointment with a doctor or a professor. If lines in your supermarket are long, bring your English book and complete part of your reading assignment. While you are walking to your math class, practice reciting formulas that must be memorized. If you drive to class, play a tape of irregular Spanish verbs and practice conjugating them. You will get your work done sooner and have more time for leisure.

Schedule study time with a friend if this helps motivate you, but choose your study partner wisely. This strategy can backfire if you spend the time socializing instead of studying. Choose your study area carefully so that you are not tempted by distractions and do not waste valuable time traveling to the study area. It is not easy to study in the cafeteria if all your friends are hanging out there. Use an empty classroom to review notes between classes if the library is located all the way across campus. Do not return to your room after classes if you know that you will be tempted to take a nap or turn on the television. Instead, schedule this study session in the library or in a quiet lounge.

Choose your study area carefully to avoid distractions.

If your are tempted by the television set when you return to your room, move it into the closet, unplug it, or tape a sheet over it in the morning when you leave for classes; hide the remote control in the closet, tape over the power button, or make plans to study in a different room. If you use your computer for study, copy your games onto a disk and store them in the closet. If you listen to background music when you study, put your "study" CD or cassette in the stereo before you leave your room in the morning. Store your other tapes and CDs in the closet.

Minimize distractions before you leave your room.

If your concentration is easily interrupted, buy ear plugs and use them to minimize distracting noise. Instrumental music can be used to drown out other distractors. If you use the same music consistently, you will "condition" yourself to study when that music comes on. Using a headset will block out distractions and discourage others from interrupting your work.

Use ear plugs or music to drown out distractions.

Use some operant conditioning on yourself, and reward yourself *after* you have studied. Do not allow yourself to go through your mail, call your friend, read the newspaper, or watch a television program until you have completed a scheduled study activity. Take that candy or soda break *after* you have written the laboratory report. Allow yourself ten or fifteen minutes to socialize in the lounge *after* you have finished the marketing assignment. Schedule leisure and social activities when possible, so that they occur after work periods. Many of these leisure activities should be scheduled in the more relaxing evening hours unless this is your peak efficiency time. Write the leisure activities down on your schedule so that you can motivate yourself to study and earn them. Reward yourself for sticking to your study schedule by going to a party or a movie. You will find it easier to settle down to study if you apply this rule consistently. Do not allow yourself to attend the event if you have "goofed off."

Condition yourself and reward yourself after study.

Schedule your leisure time so that you can look forward to activities you really enjoy; do not fritter away time just because you have nothing better to do. Seeing enjoyable items on your schedule will help you avoid the temptation to socialize or daydream during times that you have scheduled for study. You may have to learn to be more assertive (see Chapter 9, "Relationships") so that you can say "No" to friends who ask you to socialize, to a parent who invites you to go shopping, or to a child who requests help with a long homework assignment during a time slot that you have scheduled for study. If you stick to your schedule, you will be able to enjoy your leisure time without guilt or anxiety, knowing that your work will get done during the scheduled work time. Be sure that you do schedule some physical exercise or recreation every day.

Write leisure activities on a schedule.

Practice assertiveness skills to guard your study time.

Avoid heavy partying on week nights. You need that time to study or to get enough sleep so that you can function efficiently the next day. Schedule extra study time during peak work times, such as midterms and finals weeks, so that you can avoid late-night cramming. Try not to meet your study needs by cutting back on your need for sleep. You will pay for it in the long run through lowered efficiency the next day or by getting sick because your resistance to infection is decreased.

Avoid partying during the week.

If you get enough sleep, you will have more energy and your concentration will be better. You will learn the material in less time and remember it better. People who try to study when they are sleepy or distracted are fooling themselves. They *think* they are studying; in reality, they are just flipping pages, while most of the information does not even enter their brains. It's not

Get enough sleep.

how many hours you study that counts, it's how well you retain the information. Don't study more; study more efficiently.

List and prioritize your daily goals.

Keep and check your long-range schedule.

Establish the habit of listing, in the evening, the things you have to do the following day; prioritize those activities so that the most important ones are completed first. Be sure to check your list in the morning before you leave your room. Carry your weekly schedule with you so that you can refer to it during the day to keep yourself on target and add appointments or assignments as they come up. You should also keep a yearly schedule so that you can make note of long-range due dates over the course of the semester. You should check this schedule every Sunday when you are writing out your weekly schedule, so that you can plan ahead for the extra study sessions before an exam or a project deadline. Use the monthly and long-range forms in the planner that comes with this textbook.

■ SPECIAL TIME MANAGEMENT STRATEGIES FOR COMMUTERS

Many colleges do not have residential facilities so that all students are commuters. At other colleges, the student body is made up of both commuters and students who live on campus. Students over 25 years of age make up 43 percent

ACTIVITY

Calculating Number of Hours Required for Family and Household Duties per Week for Commuters

Family and Household Duties

Child care and/or care of elderly or disabled relatives   _____

Chauffeuring children and/or elderly or disabled relatives   _____

Shopping (children's clothing and school supplies, sports equipment)   _____

Car maintenance   _____

Household maintenance (lawn and grounds; repairs; maintenance for appliances, heating/air conditioning systems)   _____

Financial responsibilities (paying bills, preparing taxes, monitoring investments)   _____

House cleaning   _____

Laundry   _____

Meal preparation   _____

Marketing   _____

Entertaining   _____

Volunteer work (PTA, community organizations, block association, local government)   _____ of the nation's college students.[2] The majority of these students are commuters who work full time.[3] Together with younger commuters, they make up a group of students who face particular challenges in managing their time.

If you are one of these students, you may find that there are many demands on your time that compete with course work. When you use the "Weekly Expenditure of Time for Classes, Personal Needs, Job, Family Responsibilities, and Commuting" form on page 36 to calculate the number of hours you have available for study and leisure, be sure that you include the items in the activity on page 40 in your calculations for the number of hours per week spent on family and household duties.

Calculate the number of hours you have for leisure.

Consider the number of hours you have available for leisure activities once you have subtracted the number of hours you need for classes and study time (two to three hours outside of class for every hour you spend in class) plus the number of hours you devote to commuting, your job, your personal needs, and your family and household responsibilities from 168, the total number of hours in a week. Do you feel that you have enough time for leisure activities? (You will not have as much time for leisure and socializing as students who live on campus, but remember that you do need some time for exercise and relaxation as well as some leisure time with your family.)

Enlist your family's support with household duties.

If you do not feel that you have enough time left for leisure activities, sit down with your family and hold a planning session. Enlist your family's support in helping you cope with your numerous responsibilities. You might start by considering the advantages the family will gain from your college education: a happier, more fulfilled parent/spouse who has greater self-confidence and self-esteem, increased family income, and the benefits that that can buy.

Find ways to cut back on time spent on household duties.

Consider with your family how you can cut back on the time you must devote to family and household responsibilities that would cause the least discomfort to other family members. Figure 3.1 lists some of the possibilities.

Is your course load too heavy?

If it is not possible to enlist your family's help in meeting more of the household responsibilities or to hire help in meeting these responsibilities, consider whether your course load is realistic. You may have to cut back on the number of courses you carry and plan on taking courses during the summer session or graduating at a later date. Nowhere is it written in stone that students must graduate in four years. As a matter of fact, the majority of students today take longer than four years to graduate, and many attend college for six or seven years before receiving their degrees. It is better to get a good education and postpone graduation than to scrape by, doing the minimum for passing grades or to stress yourself and your family beyond the breaking point.

Figure 3.1 *Strategies to Decrease Time Spent on Household Responsibilities*

- Eat out more often
- Use more convenience foods
- Have family members help with cleaning, laundry, food preparation, or other household tasks
- Lower your standards on how neat and clean the house must be
- Pay someone else to help with household duties or child care
- Subscribe to more hours at the child care center
- Buy clothes that require less care in the laundry

Coordinate household and campus calendars.

Once you have determined that your work load is realistic, coordinate your household and campus calendars. Schedule family activities (children's parties, social events, family entertaining, Christmas or Chanukah celebrations) to minimize conflict with the time you need to study for exams and end-of-semester crunch time (term papers, final exams). It may be necessary to reschedule family activities or celebrations for other times, to modify the nature of the celebration so that preparation for it is less time-consuming, or to cut back on the amount of time that you must devote to it.

Review stress management skills in Chapter 11.

Practice relaxation skills.

Regardless of how cooperative your family is and how good your time management skills are, you will still experience stress from the strain of managing too many conflicting roles with too little time. This will be particularly true at pressure points during the semester or when emergencies arise, such as a car that breaks down, a child who becomes sick, a parent or spouse who is hospitalized, or a roof that begins to leak. Read Chapter 11 on stress management and coping techniques. Practice the relaxation exercises described in the chapter and on the audiocassette described on page 384 so that you are ready for these times. Try to maintain a balanced perspective and your sense of humor.

Review assertiveness training Chapter 9.

If you find that family members or others are disrupting your study times, review the section on assertiveness training in Chapter 9. It may be necessary for you to improve your ability to say "No" to your spouse, your children, your in-laws, your parents, or your friends who do not take your school commitment seriously. You must learn to protect your study time from people who make unreasonable demands on you.

Define a study area and distinguish study times.

Arrange alternate activities for family members.

Study with family members.

Select a study area and study times at home carefully. Mark them off physically (by using a "Do Not Disturb" sign or wearing your "Study Hat" or head phones, for example) so that family members know when you should not be disturbed. Studying at the kitchen table invites family members to interrupt you by asking for a snack or help with the taxes. If you select a particular study area or specific study hours and stick to them, family members will learn to respect your need to work without interruption. If there are young children living in your household and you cannot isolate your study area, you may need to arrange activities that keep them occupied while you are studying or study while they attend a daycare program. If your children are old enough, you may wish to schedule study time together so that you work side-by-side. Working side-by-side can also establish camaraderie with your spouse if she or he brings work home from the job.

Schedule breaks between classes.

Study between classes.

Schedule study time on campus.

Try to schedule time between classes so that you can review notes or prepare reading assignments. Commuters are often tempted to schedule their classes in blocks to minimize commuting time and time spent on campus. This scheduling strategy actually works against you. Scheduling all your courses in a row will make it more difficult for you to pay attention and absorb material as the day goes on. It is better to take breaks from the intense concentration required to sit in class, take notes, absorb large amounts of information, and participate actively and intelligently in class discussions. Find a quiet room or lounge so that you can use the breaks between classes to review your notes and prepare reading assignments for the next class. You will also find that studying on campus reduces disruptions from your family members or staff members at work. It is difficult for them to interrupt you at the college library or in an empty classroom where you are studying. For this reason, you may wish to add extra study time on campus by arriving before classes or staying after your classes are over.

Review study strategies for exams.

Learn to decrease exam anxiety.

Learn to study for exams efficiently. Review the strategies described in Chapter 6. If you experience high levels of anxiety when you are faced with examinations, review the techniques described on pages 99–100, 222–228, and on the Stress Management audiocassette described on page 384. Practice these techniques or seek help at the counseling center on campus.

If you have children, build up child care credit during school vacations by doing more than your share of carpooling and taking your friends' children on outings. When your schedule is tight around exams or at the end of the semester, you will be relieved as your friends reciprocate with child care or carpools.

Build up carpool and child care "credit" during vacations.

Be prepared for emergencies. If your children are old enough, have them wear the house key around their necks. You can also exchange keys with a neighbor so that someone can let your children into the house if you are delayed by car trouble or a snowstorm. Carry a book with emergency telephone numbers with you. (Space for these numbers is provided in the planner that comes with this textbook.) This book should contain the telephone numbers of your pediatrician or physician, dentist, orthodontist, two or three neighbors, children's schools or day care center, children's friends, children who are on the same bus route as your children, your carpool partners, local taxi services, your friends or study partners in each course, your professors and their office hours, and a local courier service or the fax number at the college. (The day will undoubtedly come when you will have that paper done but will not be able to get it to campus on time.)

Prepare for emergencies.

Carry important phone numbers in your daily planner.

■ A SAMPLE WEEKLY SCHEDULE

You are now ready to plan your schedule for the week. Make a copy for future use of the blank weekly schedule form that appears on page 46. Use the sample weekly schedule in Figure 3.2 as a guide and fill in the blank weekly schedule form with your own schedule. Remember to use the suggestions for effective time management when you design your schedule.

Figure 3.2 *Sample Weekly Schedule*

		Monday	Tuesday	Wednesday	Thursday	Friday	Saturday	Sunday
A.M.	6	Sleep	Sleep	Rev. Bio Notes for Quiz	Sleep	Rev. Procedure for Bio. Lab.	Sleep and Relax	Sleep and Relax
	7	Breakfast AND Grooming	Breakfast and Grooming	Breakfast and Grooming	Breakfast and Grooming	Breakfast and Grooming		
	8	Biology Class	Listen to Music Assignment and Write Analysis	Bio. Class	Read Bio. Chp. 3	Bio. Class		
	9	Review Bio Notes Study for Bio. Quiz.	Read Ch 3 Marketing Text	Rev. Bio. Notes Finish Hist ch. 5	Read Marketing Ch. 4 Rev. Notes	Rev Bio. Notes Read Ch. 4		Work out in Gym
	10	History Class	Marketing Class	Hist Class	Marketing Class	History Class		
	11	Read History Text ch. 4 Library Write Lab Report Bio. Review Hist. notes.	Lunch Rev. Marketing Notes	Rev. Hist. Paper	Begin Research for Marketing Class in Library	Rev. Hist. Notes Lunch	Brunch	Rewrite Marketing Paper
	12			Write Hist. Paper Read Soc. Ch 7		Prepare Oral Presentation for Soc	Work and Commuting time	
P.M.	1	Lunch Rev. Soc. Notes	Music Class	Lunch Rev. Soc. Notes	Music Class	Soc. Class Cont. Rev. Hist. Notes		Listen to Music Assignment and Write Analysis
	2	Soc. Class	Basketball Practice	Soc. Class	Basketball Practice	Library Read Soc. Ch. 8 Research for Marketing Paper Bio ch 2 & 3	Work and Commuting time	Work and Commuting Time
	3	Ski Club Meeting		Prepare Oral Presentation for Soc. Rewrite Hist. Paper				
	4	Prepare Outline & Draft for Hist. paper Library	Work and Commuting Time		Rev. Bio. Ch. 3		Draft Marketing Paper	
	5				Dinner	Dinner		
	6	Dinner		Dinner	Type History Paper	Movie with Jane	Laundry and Chores	Dinner
	7	Work and Commuting Time	Dinner	Work and Commuting Time	Type History Paper		Dinner	Read ch. 5 Bio
	8		Study for Bio. Quiz		Proof-read History Paper	Snack Socializing	party at Jim's	T.V. Relax Socialize
	9		Read Hist. Ch. 5		Arrange Bibliography for Hist. Paper Type + Proofread			
	10	Hang Out in Lounge	T.V.	Work-out in Gym	T.V.			Makeup Schedule for Next Week
	11			Hang Out in Lounge				
	12	Sleep	Sleep	Sleep	Sleep	Sleep	Sleep	
	1			Sleep	Sleep	Sleep		

Figure 3.3   Sample Monthly Schedule

October

SUNDAY	MONDAY	TUESDAY	WEDNESDAY	THURSDAY	FRIDAY	SATURDAY
3 4pm Dinner at Parents	**4**	**5**	**6** PTA	**7**	**1**	**2** 9am Laura's Soccer
10	**11** Columbus Day-day off	**12** Econ Test	**13** English Paper due	**14**	**8**	**9** 9am Laura's Soccer
17	**18**	**19**	**20**	**21**	**15** 7pm Nancy's b-day party	**16** 9am Laura's Soccer
24	**25** Drive Carpool for Daycare	**26**	**27**	**28**	**22**	**23** 9am Laura's Soccer
31 Halloween			Biology Test →		**29**	**30** 9am Laura's Soccer

THE WEEKLY SCHEDULE FORM

	Monday	Tuesday	Wednesday	Thursday	Friday	Saturday	Sunday
A.M. 6							
7							
8							
9							
10							
11							
12							
1							
2							
3							
4							
5							
6							
P.M. 7							
8							
9							
10							
11							
12							
1							

THE MONTHLY SCHEDULE FORM

Fill in the month at the top. Determine which day the month begins on and begin numbering each box sequentially from that day.

Sunday	Monday	Tuesday	Wednesday	Thursday	Friday	Saturday

REFLECTIONS FOR YOUR JOURNAL

1. If you find that you must manage your time more effectively now that you are attending college, reflect upon why this is so.
2. After keeping your time journal for two days, you may find that you waste time in certain predictable ways. Identify these time-wasting activities and patterns; think about why they are attractive to you. (What needs do they serve?) Identify other ways to fulfill these needs that would allow you to use your time more effectively.
3. Are there any activities you have had to give up since you began attending college because you no longer have time for them? If these activities are important to you, can you make changes in your schedule that will allow you to find time for these activities?
4. Even the best time managers find areas in which they can make improvements. Which of the strategies discussed in this chapter would allow you to lead a more satisfying or productive life?

Notes

1. M. Gardner, "19 Tips Guaranteed To Give You What You Want," *Working Mother,* February 1996, p. 19.
2. L. Smith and T. Walter, *The Adult Learner's Guide to College Success.* Belmont, CA: Wadsworth, 1995.
3. C. Sims, "Late Bloomers Come to Campus," *New York Times,* 4 August 1991, Section 4A, pp. 16–17.

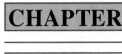

CHAPTER 4

COLLEGE LECTURES
Listening and Taking Notes

■ CRITICAL THINKING IMPROVES YOUR LISTENING SKILLS

Many college professors lecture. Therefore, if you wish to learn the information they are teaching, you must know how to listen. The bad news is that listening for the purpose of learning is not a natural, passive process; it is not the same as hearing or even paying attention. It is an active process in which you convert the material you hear so that it becomes meaningful to your mind. You organize it, you relate it to your experiences, and you make it part of yourself. The good news is that you *can* learn to listen effectively.

One aspect of effective listening involves figuring out the professor's purpose in lecturing. Is it to help you solve a particular problem, to discuss and raise questions, to demonstrate certain trends, or to show you how the course material relates to your own life? The professor often states his or her purpose at the beginning of the lecture. (This is one good reason to arrive on time for classes.) If this is not done, go over your notes after class and see if you can determine the purpose.

Identify purpose of lecture.

Identify your professor's main point or points. Is he or she explaining how individual citizens' private debts lead to inflation? Is the professor stating that the American Revolution was primarily caused by economic considerations and not by patriotic factors? Is he or she contending that corporal punishment and tougher discipline will increase learning in the schools? There should be no more than four or five main points in a one-hour lecture.

Identify main point or points.

Once you have decided what your teacher's main point is, examine how the main idea is supported. Do the presented statistics demonstrate a correlation between balances on individuals' MasterCard accounts and inflation? Does a relationship exist over the years between increasing interest payments and spiraling prices? Are the theories of famous economists used to support the main point?

Examine supporting evidence.

Identifying the main points and supporting details of the lecture will help you to understand and learn the material more easily. Deciphering your professor's organizational plan will also help you to remember and to study more effectively. Is the professor using a chronological organization, telling you about events that happened early in the course of the American Revolution and then tracing the sequence of later events? Is the lecture organized by comparison and contrast, explaining how the American Revolution was similar to the French and Latin American revolutions, but then going on to note the differences among them?

Note the organizational plan.

Is the presentation based on cause and effect, showing you what led up to the Boston Tea Party or the Boston Massacre and then explaining the

49

ACTIVITY

Listening to a Sample Lecture

This activity is part of a lecture on the history of mental illness. Your instructor may choose to read the lecture to you in class so that you can practice listening for the purpose, main points, and organizational structure. If your instructor assigns this exercise as homework, ask a friend to read the lecture to you. Before you have your friend read you the lecture, look over the questions that follow it so that you know what information to listen for. Think critically about the lecture. How does it relate to your experience or readings? Is the lecturer biased? Is sound support offered for the main thesis?

A SAMPLE LECTURE

Today we will take a historical look at the concept of mental illness. We will examine how, during various time periods, people have explained the causes of mental illness. We will also examine how these views have affected the treatment of emotionally disturbed individuals. By the end of the lecture, you will appreciate the very different approaches society has taken in dealing with the mentally ill and how these approaches are linked to the greater values and belief systems espoused by a society.

It seems that ancient people believed that many illnesses, including mental illnesses, were caused by spirits or demons. We have evidence of this belief in the art, writings, and skulls that remain from this period. For example, paleontologists have collected numerous skulls from Stone Age people that show evidence of trephination, a primitive surgical procedure during which a hole was made in the patient's skull so that the evil spirits would be free to depart. Subsequent healing tells us that many of these early patients survived the surgery. Patients may even have benefited from the procedure in cases where fluid was putting pressure on the brain and resulting in disordered behavior.

Another treatment method associated with the demon possession theory was used by ancient Greeks, Hebrews, and Chinese: exorcism. Praying, noise-making, and in some cultures, starvation and beating were used to drive the evil spirits out of the afflicted individual. Societies and subcultures still exist in America today where root doctors and shamans engage in a variety of rituals to drive demons from the bodies of unfortunate victims.

A change in the views of mental illness occurred around 2,500 years ago when a number of Greek physicians and philosophers espoused naturalistic, rather than supernatural, explanations of mental illness. They believed that emotionally disturbed behavior was caused by disease of the brain or by imbalances in the body's vital fluids. Hippocrates, for example, recommended a peaceful environment, moderate exercise, abstinence from sexual activity, and a balanced diet in treating melancholia, a condition associated with symptoms of depression. Although many of the specific explanations and treatments recommended by the Greeks are no longer followed today, the general view of natural, rather than supernatural, causation of mental illness is currently widely held.

As society entered the Dark and Middle Ages (approximately A.D. 400–1500), the naturalistic beliefs of the Greeks and Romans gave way to the ancient superstitious views of mental illness. People believed that illness was God's punishment for wrongdoing. Bands of flagellants traveled from town to town, whipping themselves to achieve forgiveness and a state of ecstasy. Fear often afflicted large groups of people so that they danced and writhed madly in the streets, raving and, finally, collapsing in convulsions. This form of mass hysteria was called *tarantism,* and it spread from Italy to the rest of Europe.

As the feudal structure collapsed and war, famine, and bubonic plague killed large numbers of people, panic spread throughout Europe. People looked to the church for guidance, and the church reinforced the spreading belief that demons and witches were responsible for these catastrophes. Torture was sanctioned as an acceptable means of obtaining confessions from suspected witches. People who were seen as peculiar or different, such as many of the emotionally disturbed, were particularly vulnerable to accusations of witchcraft. Sometimes their own delusions or feelings of guilt caused them to confess to associations with the devil. At other times, torture was used to extract the desired confession. Society believed that associations with the devil or other demons explained these individuals' strange behavior. The usual "treatment" was torture and death.

As the Middle Ages came to an end, there was a resurgence in the naturalistic beliefs espoused by the ancient Greeks. However, the mentally ill continued to be badly treated through the early nineteenth century. They were viewed as animals or criminals and incarcerated in dungeons, prisons, poorhouses, or asylums. They were beaten and chained, naked and starving, to be exhibited in cages to the public for a fee. It was not until Phillipe Pinel's daring experiment with moral therapy that the concept of humane treatment for the mentally ill became widely accepted.

By the twentieth century, medical explanations for mental illness became prevalent, and mental patients were treated by doctors in large mental hospitals located in rural areas. Patients continued to suffer abuse, however, in these large, isolated mental institutions where they were often warehoused for life under inhumane physical conditions with no hope for treatment.

By the 1960s, many professionals believed that emotional disorders were caused by problems in living and not by medical problems. The community mental health movement was inaugurated to keep the emotionally disturbed in their own communities where they would receive compassionate treatment and return to their families and jobs. Unfortunately, local facilities were not adequately staffed or funded. They were not able to cope with the large numbers of patients discharged from the mental hospitals. As our society continues to shun the emotionally disturbed, we are faced with a growing population of homeless people, many of whom suffer from the dual afflictions of emotional disturbance and poverty.

Questions about the Lecture

Answer the following questions about the lecture you have just heard:

1. What is the purpose of the lecture?

_____

_____

_____

_____

_____

2. What are the speaker's main points?

_____

_____

_____

_____

_____

3. What types of supportive evidence does the speaker use to back up the main points?

_____

_____

_____

_____

_____

4. What is the organizational structure of the lecture?

_____

_____

_____

_____

_____

5. Evaluate the lecture. Is the speaker biased? Are the conclusions sound? How does the content of the lecture relate to your experience or knowledge of the subject?

_____

_____

_____

_____

_____

_____

consequences these events had for later developments on the road to the revolution? Is the professor presenting one main idea and then going on to give you many examples that support that idea? For example, he or she may contend that the revolution was based on economics and then discuss the stamp tax, the trade restrictions, and the billeting of soldiers as examples of English actions that hurt the colonists' pocketbooks. If you can follow the lecture's organization, you will find yourself understanding and remembering the material better.

Listen critically and evaluate what you hear.

As you listen to the lectures in your classes, you should also try to evaluate what you are hearing. Do not just accept ideas at face value. Question, criticize, and compare them to your own experiences and to material you have read or heard from other sources. Is it a fact that tougher discipline will help children in schools to develop better learning skills, or is it an opinion? What types of data support the statement? Does your professor offer results from surveys of educators or parents? Does he or she compare test scores from schools that allow corporal punishment with those that do not allow it? Is your professor biased in regard to this question based on his or her own experiences or values? If you question and listen critically, you will become actively involved with the material. You will find yourself learning better and more easily!

■ IMPROVING YOUR NOTE-TAKING SKILLS

Record it or lose it.

Note taking is a major survival skill in college. Taking notes forces you to pay closer attention in the first place and to remember the material better at a future date. Studies have shown that you will remember up to 78 percent of the information you record. If you do not write it down, you will remember only 5 to 34 percent. Although you may understand the contents of a lecture while your professor is speaking, within two weeks you will probably forget 80 percent of what you hear. After four weeks, 95 percent of what you hear will be gone! Ideas that were clear and simple in class often seem hazy and complicated a few weeks later, and they may make no sense at all a month later when you are studying for an exam.

Some students make the mistake of thinking that someone else's notes are an adequate substitute for attending class. It's true that any notes are better

than no notes at all, but someone else's notes are likely to be even less intelligible than your own notes, and you will miss the professor's emphasis on certain topics. You will also miss the opportunity to hear material that could trigger the recall of an item that will answer a test question, but did not make it into your (or your classmate's) notes.

Strategies for Note Taking

Professors go over the most important material in class. Many of them base tests solely or primarily on the information they present in class. This is true for information presented in the lecture as well as points raised by students during discussions. If you are going to succeed in college, you must learn that information, and the only way to guard against the insidious process of forgetting is to take notes immediately so that you can review the information later.

Take notes during each class.

If you take more complete notes, you will do better on exams. Take notes during every class! Date each set of notes so that you can ask the instructor or a friend for help if your notes are not clear to you later when you are studying for the exam. If you miss a class, borrow a set of notes as soon as possible from a classmate who takes good notes. Put your name, address, and phone number in your notebook.

Date each set of notes.

Record your name and phone number in your notebook.

Keep all your notes for a particular course together in one place so that you can review them more easily. A looseleaf notebook is convenient because you can insert the syllabus and any handouts right into the book along with your class notes for the course. Leave the back of each page of notes blank so that you can integrate summaries from your reading assignments next to the appropriate lecture notes. Use full size paper that is at least 8-½ by 11 inches so that you can readily see the organization of the lecture. When notes are chopped up and spread over a large number of small pages, it is hard to see the relationships among different points.

Keep course notes together.

Leave blank pages.

Use full-size paper.

You will find it easier to take notes and you will take better notes if you come to class prepared. Read the assignment before class so that you are familiar with key words, concepts, and relationships. This preview will also help you ask intelligent questions so that you do not have to spend time later making an appointment with your professor to clear up uncertainties. If you do not have time to complete the reading assignment before coming to class, at least scan the chapters so you have a general idea of the material's organization and the topics that will be discussed. This overview will help you to organize your class notes and to zero in on major points.

Read ahead.

Your class notes should provide a summary of the main points of the lecture and enough details and examples to trigger your memory several weeks later. You are not training to become a stenographer; copying down everything your instructor says will not help you earn a better grade. In fact, you may perform more poorly because you will miss the forest for the trees. (You may miss the main points and connections because you are too busy trying to copy down every word.) Along with margin notes to summarize main ideas, you can use an outline format to show the relationships between ideas and to emphasize which points are most important. You should be able to accomplish these goals most effectively if your notes follow these general guidelines:

Summarize main points.

- Main ideas should be summarized in the margins of the page.
- Major subgroups in your outline should be indented.
- More subordinate examples or details in your outline should be indented even further.

Use outline format.

Note organization and relationships.

Such an outline will allow you to see the organization and the relationships in the material without having to copy down the entire lecture. It is not practical to write down everything your professor says. Lecturers usually speak at 125 words per minute. Even the best shorthand system will not allow you to record everything. Furthermore, if you are constantly scrambling to get every word down, you will not have time to understand or think about what is being said, to see the relationships between ideas, or to realize which points are most important. Tape recording lectures is not a good idea because it is too time-consuming to play the tapes back. You can use that same study time more efficiently by reviewing the main points of the presentation.

Summarize major ideas and examples.

Summarize each major idea in a phrase or two, and try to write down a phrase for each detail that illustrates or explains the major point. If your instructor gives four or five examples, record two or three in your outline so that you will be able to understand the point and illustrate it several weeks later. Write "ex." in the margin next to the example so that you recognize the relationship between the concept and the example indented under it.

Record definitions and enumerated items.

Record chalkboard items.

Several types of information must be recorded. If your professor gives a definition, write it down. If he or she enumerates items, record them. For example, "There are five classes of occupation . . . ," can be written, "classes of occupation," with the five classes written in outline form under it. Instructors will often indicate that a particular item is important by repeating the item, slowing down their rate of speech as they present it, changing their tone of voice, or emphasizing the item. If your professor writes an item on the chalkboard, tells you that it is important, or relates it to previous material, write it down! You should also make a note to yourself in the margin next to that item (by writing an asterisk [*] or the word *important*), indicating that this material was emphasized by your instructor.

Use abbreviations.

Develop a system of abbreviations so that you may write down as much information as necessary in the shortest period of time. A number of common abbreviations are listed in Figure 4.1, but you can make up your own shorthand as long as you make a note of a particular abbreviation (e.g., *comp = comparison*). If you do not write down these abbreviations, you may have an unintelligible set of notes as you try to decide several weeks later whether *comp* means *comparison, computation,* or *completion.*

Keep a key of abbreviations.

If certain words come up repeatedly during a course or lecture, create your own abbreviations, but keep a key of these abbreviations at the front of your notebook. For example, it will save you considerable time to write *OD* instead of *organizational development, rft* for *reinforcement,* and *MBO* in place of *management by objective.*

Leave blanks.

Sit in front.

Participate.

Stay alert.

If you miss information during the lecture, leave blank spaces and compare notes after class with a classmate or with your instructor. If your attention wanders during class, keep bringing it back. One way to help yourself concentrate is to sit in front of the class. You are less likely to nod off or to daydream if you are looking directly at your instructor and know that he or she is looking at you. Ask questions or think of relevant examples to keep yourself alert. Sitting in the front row also conveys a positive attitude of interest and motivation to your professor. Do not allow fatigue toward the end of class to slow down your note taking. Teachers sometimes mistime their lectures and have to cram important information into the last few minutes of class. This is particularly true for the last class before an exam. The instructor will probably have made up the test and will be trying to fit in some of the material that appears on the exam during this last class. This is not the time to nod off!

Review notes.

Form questions.

Review your notes as soon after class as possible, while the lecture is still fresh in your mind. Fill in blank spaces with information that you remember. Clarify phrases that will not make sense in a week or two. Add any new abbreviations to the abbreviation key in the front of your notebook. Jot down notes

Figure 4.1 *List of Common Abbreviations*

Common Word	Abbreviations
with, without	w/, w/o
and	&
definition	def
introduction	intro
example	ex
important	imp't
continued	cont'd
therefore	$\therefore$
leads to	$\rightarrow$
organization	org
information	info
does not equal	$\neq$
frequency	f
organism, individual, individuals	$\bigcirc$, $\odot$, $\circledS$
compare	cf
department	dept
liberal	lib
capitalism	cap
subject, subjects	subj or S, subjs or Ss,
totalitarianism	tot
individual	ind
association, associate	assoc
biological	biol
background	bkgrnd
problem	prblm
government	gvt, gov't
amount	am't
checking	chkg
against	vs

Leave out the words *a* and *the.*
Leave out auxiliary or unimportant verbs.
Write out a term or phrase the first time; the next time, use initials: *The American Psychological Association* becomes *APA.*

Coordinate notes with readings.

in the margin that will help you study for an exam (e.g., "key concept," "important definition"). Based on your notes, make up questions that might appear on your exam; write these questions in the margin. Each of the main themes and subtopics can be turned into a good exam question. Review these questions, and try to answer them at least once a week. Coordinate notes from your textbook readings by adding them to the backs of your class notes where appropriate. Note the relationships between the material covered in class and the material covered in assigned readings.

Get feedback on your notes.

If you find that you did not perform well on an exam despite adequate study time, you may wish to compare your class notes with a student who did well on the exam. Sometimes, students think they are taking good notes when, in fact, they are not. A note-taking system that served you well in high school may not be adequate in the more competitive atmosphere of college. If you do

Taking Notes from a Sample Lecture

Your instructor may assign this activity as homework or choose to have you do it in class. If you complete the activity in class, your instructor will read the lecture on cocaine to you so that you can practice taking notes. If the activity is assigned for homework, have a friend read the practice lecture while you take notes on it. Then compare your notes with the sample notes that follow.

A SAMPLE LECTURE

Cocaine

Today we will consider the crisis caused by cocaine in the United States. First we will take a brief look backward at the history of cocaine. Then we will examine the effects this drug is having on individuals and on our society as a whole.

Dr. Mark Gold, researcher and founder of 800-COCAINE, the national cocaine hotline, reports that 25 million Americans have used cocaine at least once. One million Americans report that they are so dependent on the drug that they cannot stop using it even though it is destroying their lives and those of their loved ones. Three thousand teenagers and adults try the drug for the first time every day.

Statistics like these, along with the increasing daily reports of murders, robberies, and assaults associated with the drug's use, have forced Americans to realize that we have a crisis on our hands. The long-term threat to our society is emphasized by events in South America where widespread corruption and terror caused by the drug's traffickers have reached the highest levels of the government and the law enforcement system. A look at cocaine's history and effects may place the seriousness of this problem in better perspective.

Experts believe that the coca plant, *erythroxylum coca,* has existed on this planet longer than people. It grows wild in South America, but careful cultivation has resulted in successful crops in Europe, Asia, and the United States. South America is by far the largest producer, with yields increasing dramatically over the past ten years. Bolivia, for example, produces three times as much cocaine now as it did a decade ago.

Native peoples in South America have chewed coca leaves for several thousand years. They believe that this practice gives them a number of benefits: increased energy, decreased appetite, greater tolerance for the effects of altitude, better digestion, and elevated mood. The plant played a role in religious ceremonies and in political control of the Inca. Indeed, coca leaves may have aided native survival in these inhospitable regions. One hundred grams of coca leaves satisfies the U.S. government's daily recommended allowance for vitamin A, vitamin B2, vitamin E, calcium, phosphorous, and iron. The same 100 grams of coca leaves also supply 305 calories, 19 grams of protein, and 40 grams of carbohydrates.

Of the fourteen alkaloids present in coca leaves, only cocaine aroused the major interest of Europeans in the nineteenth century, and this interest was not based on its nutritional value. Europeans in the mid-nineteenth century touted cocaine for its medicinal and recreational properties. It was included as an ingredient in a number of popular elixirs, and Coca Cola became known as a health drink in the United States. Since the amount of cocaine contained in these drinks was small, overdoses and other medical complications did not constitute a major problem.

Sigmund Freud was one of the early advocates of cocaine, recommending it as a cure for asthma, morphine addiction, and digestive disorders and also as a local anaesthetic. He described its pleasurable stimulatory properties based on his own personal experimentation. Cocaine became widely used as a local anaesthetic; it was touted by medical communities on both sides of the Atlantic as a cure for everything from seasickness to masturbation to head colds. We know now that cocaine is not an effective treatment for any of these disorders, and other drugs have replaced it as an anaesthetic. By the beginning of the twentieth century, the medical community's love affair with the drug had ended, based on disastrous case reports and on its highly addictive properties.

It is these negative properties of cocaine that concern us today. The most dramatic attention has been given to sudden, unexplained deaths in healthy individuals who have experimented with cocaine. These deaths have occurred in chronic users, but they have also been reported in individuals with little or no previous experience with cocaine.

These deaths might occur because cocaine has dramatic stimulatory effects on electrical and chemical activity in the brain and on heart rate, blood pressure, and breathing. It is difficult to predict the precise effects cocaine may have on any given individual because these effects depend on the dose and purity of the drug, the mode of administration, and the individual's personal physical make-up. Some individuals cannot metabolize the drug, and this can lead to an overdose from small quantities. The "Casey Jones" reaction immortalized in a song by the Grateful Dead can result in failure of the body's major systems leading to convulsions and death within a few minutes.

Cocaine can result in mild to life-threatening symptoms in the respiratory system. Any of the following four symptoms are grounds for an immediate trip to the hospital emergency room: gasping for breath, irregular breathing, accumulation of fluid in the lungs, and failure to breathe. Freebasing also leads to symptoms usually associated with smoking cigarettes: bronchitis, hoarseness, and coughing. Symptoms frequently experienced by individuals who snort cocaine are asthma, chronic respiratory infections, rhinitis (clogged, inflamed, swollen, runny, and bleeding nose), and damage to the vessels or septum of the nose.

Cocaine's effects on the cardiovascular system also run the gamut from uncomfortable to deadly. Any of the following four symptoms require emergency medical attention: irregular heart rate; sudden, rapid decrease in blood pressure; weak or irregular pulse; blue or gray skin color resulting from lack of oxygen.

Malnutrition and severe vitamin deficiency are common in chronic cocaine users. These disorders lower the individual's resistance and open him or her to infection and disease by any of the organisms commonly found in the environment. Sleep disorders, digestive disorders, hallucinations, and seizures are all disturbing symptoms frequently reported by cocaine users.

The question remains as to why the drug has become so popular despite the dangers and discomforts previously described. The answer seems to be the cocaine high. Users report that they feel confident, competent, energetic, alert, powerful, and in total control. Many users feel that cocaine helps them to perform better socially and on the job. Unfortunately, the feelings of euphoria are short-lived, and then the crash occurs. The feelings of enhanced competence are mostly illusory, particularly at higher levels of cocaine.

And cocaine users do go on to higher levels. Very few individuals can control a cocaine habit for long. The brief high is followed by a severe slump, and addicted users feel that the only way out of the depression is through another dose. Larger and larger doses are required to reach the high, and the time between doses becomes shorter and shorter. These reports are in keeping with definitions of addiction where users become habituated so that larger doses become necessary to achieve the drug's effect. Additional evidence of dependency involves the fact that users' lives become centered around the drug, and they cannot function without it. It is horrifying to read reports, from successful individuals in every age group, that describe how cocaine has taken over their lives.

Successful doctors, students, engineers, athletes, business executives, songwriters, and lawyers have all reported the same result: cocaine destroyed their lives. It is a powerfully addictive drug, and many are not able to give it up. They lose their families, careers, fortunes, and self-respect, and they also lose the values that formed the foundations of their lives. Devoted sons steal from their mothers, successful models prostitute themselves, devoted fathers leave their children hungry and penniless, ethical lawyers steal from their clients; they do these things to finance a habit that grows more and more expensive until it consumes their lives and the lives of their loved ones.

Cocaine is a drug that poses a serious threat to our society. It attacks the health of individuals, breaks down the relationships that bind people together, threatens our moral fiber and values, and costs us dearly in terms of increased crime and law enforcement, medical treatment, and loss of job productivity. It is a problem for which we must find a solution if we are to survive as a nation.

Now compare the notes you took with the sample notes that begin on page 58.

Now compare the notes you took with the sample notes that begin on page 58.

Much of the material in this sample lecture is summarized from Mark S. Gold, *800-Cocaine*, 6th printing, New York: Bantam Books.

Sample Notes on Cocaine Lecture

Cocaine

I. Amer. Crisis
    A. 25 mil. Amers. used cocaine at least once
    B. 1 mil. Amers. dependt on drug
       1. can't stop using it
    C. 3000 new users try it every day
    D. corruptn + terror in S. Amer. gov'ts + legal sys.

II. Hist.
    A. native S. Amer plant — grows wild
       1. predates man

origin + prodctn: S. Amer.

       2. natives chew leaves — many benefits
          a. incrsd energy
          b. decrsd appetite
          c. betr tolerance of altitude
       3. impt to Inca
          a. relig rites
          +. politicl contrl
    B. 19th cent. Europe + Amer.
       1. medicl + recreatl properts
          a. populr elixirs
          b. Coca Cola = health drink
          c. Freud

pop in 19th centry — medical uses

             1. cure for asthma, morphine addictn + oth. disords.
          d. useful anaesthetic

popularity declined in 20th cent.

          f. no medicl uses now
       2. by 1900, doctors against cocaine
          a. bad cases
          b. addictive

III. Negative Properts
    A. Sudden Unexplained Deaths

affect brain, heart + breathg

       1. in healthy people
       2. in users + first timers
       3. Casey Jones reactn
          a. sudden death from convulsns.

→ sud. death respiratory

       4. affects brain, heart, + breathg
    B. Respirtly Damage
       1. warning signs →

damage + disords.

          Emergncy Rm.
          a. failure to breathe
          b. irreg. breathg/gaspg

Sample Notes on Cocaine Lecture

Abbreviations

HR= heart rate

B-P = blood
            pressure

O_2 = oxygen

c. fluid in lungs

ex.   2. bronchitis
ex.   3. asthma
ex.   4. rhinitis = inflamed, runny, bleedg nose

C. Cardiovasclr Damage
    1. warng signs → Emergcy Rm.
      a. irreg H-R
      b. suddn fall in B-P
      c. weak/irreg pulse
      d. blue/gray skin — not enuf O_2

heart +
circulatn
damage +
disords.

D. Malnutrition
    1. → infection or illness

E. Oth. Disords.

susceptbl.
to infectn
+ illnss

ex.   1. sleep
ex.   2. halucinats.
ex.   3. seizures

F. Warnings

**important:
written on
blackboard

    1. to peop. susceptbl. to heart or circulatory probs.
    2. " " " " " diabetes
    3. " " " " " epilepsy or seizures
    4. " " " " " asthma

IV. Why is it Popular?

    A. "High" = Euphoria

ex.   1. alert
ex.   2. powerful
ex.   3. energetic

high → low

    B. "High" → "Low"
      1. nd. anothr dose to get out of depressn.
      2. nd. bigger + bigger doses mo. often
      3. life centered ar. drug

def. of
addctn

main pt.

V. Dangers to Socty

indiv.
tragedies

crime

    A. Ruin lives — even most successfl peop.
      1. lose families, jobs, $, self-respect, + health
    B. Incr. Crime
    C. Expensive
      1. law enforcemt

costs to
society

      2. medicl costs
      3. prodctvty + jobs

not wish to compare notes with a classmate, you might consider showing your notes to a tutor or to the professor of the course. He or she may be able to tell you whether you are taking down relevant information or give you suggestions that will help you take better notes. If you are going to do this, it is best to do it early in the semester, immediately after the first test, if possible.

✍ REFLECTIONS FOR YOUR JOURNAL

1. What should you do differently when listening to a professor's lecture than when you are listening to a friend's conversation?
2. Which of the strategies described in the section on *critical thinking* is more likely to help you pay attention and learn the material in your classes better? Why do you think that strategy is most likely to help you?
3. Evaluate your note taking skills. How can you improve them? Choose three of the strategies discussed in the section on taking notes that you will put into practice immediately.

CHAPTER 5

STUDY TECHNIQUES, LEARNING STYLES, READING AND MARKING TEXTBOOKS

Just as listening to a college lecture is not the same as listening to a friend's account of a football game, reading a textbook is not the same as reading for pleasure. When you read a textbook, you are reading to acquire information. It is not enough just to read the material; you must study and learn it so that you can apply the information to future tasks in class, on exams, or at work.

■ TAKING ADVANTAGE OF YOUR PREFERRED LEARNING STYLE

There are a number of different processing or learning styles. A learning style refers to the way you usually process or take in and make sense of information: your dominant way of looking at the world. Not everyone learns the same way. When you were young, you probably discovered a way to collect and store information that was most convenient and made the most sense for you. As you grew older, you probably continued to use this particular learning style so that it was reinforced and became stronger. Eventually it became your habitual or preferred way of dealing with incoming information. This preferred learning style is probably the reason that you like certain subjects better than others and find that certain material is easier for you to learn.

Identifying your preferred or dominant mental processing habits can help you take advantage of your strengths and compensate for your weaknesses. Knowing your learning style can make it easier to grasp new material, choose instructors whom you will enjoy, use your strengths to do well in classes, help you to understand why you may be having difficulty with certain courses or instructors, and pinpoint what you might have to change to make improvements. Awareness of your instructors' teaching styles may help you study more effectively and perform better on exams. Learning to use several different processing styles and tailoring them to different courses can help you to learn even more effectively. The activity, "Identifying Your Preferred Learning Style," presents an informal approach to exploring your individual learning styles. More formal measures of learning style, available through your college counseling center, are discussed later in the chapter.

A majority of people tend to be visual processors. They learn best by seeing. They find figures, charts, diagrams, and pictures to be the most useful learning aids. They often think quickly, in terms of the overall picture. They often use visual imagery when they communicate with others: "Do you see the point?" "I get the picture." "Is this clear to you?" These people often communicate clearly and precisely. When they are trying to remember information, they may visualize where on the page they read or saw it. Copying and recopying their notes may help them to learn material better. They often are most

A C T I V I T Y

Identifying Your Preferred Learning Style

The goal of this activity is to help you become more aware of your preferred learning or processing style. Becoming aware of your preferred style and learning to adapt to several different styles will enhance your education and grades.

Remember that no one processing style is better than another; most of us use more than one style, but we tend to adopt a dominant style to process the bulk of our information.

For each group of statements, circle the letter of the item that best describes your preference.

1. a. I learn best in courses with hands-on activities.
   b. I learn best in courses that primarily involve lectures.
   c. I learn best from texts and books.

2. a. I prefer essay exams.
   b. I prefer multiple choice or other objective-item exams.
   c. I prefer a project where I have the opportunity to apply what I have learned.

3. a. If I need to find a place, I want a map that clearly shows orientation for north, south, east, and west.
   b. If I need to find a place, I want precise, written instructions with street names, right and left turns.
   c. If I need to find a place, I want to follow someone the first time.
   d. If I need to find a place, I want someone to describe to me how to get there.

4. a. I tend to do best on tests that involve reading comprehension.
   b. I tend to do best on tests that involve calculations or problem solving.

5. a. I tend to do well on crossword puzzles.
   b. I tend to do well on jig saw puzzles.

6. a. I prefer exams that cover small units of material or facts.
   b. I prefer cumulative exams that take a broad overview of the course.

7. a. I study best by taking notes and playing or reading my notes to myself.
   b. I study best by copying and recopying my notes.
   c. I study best by pacing back and forth while reviewing key concepts.

8. a. When taking a stand on a controversial issue I usually make up my mind by consulting my "gut feeling" or intuition.
   b. When taking a stand on a controversial issue I usually try to sort out the facts rationally and then come to a conclusion.

9. a. I am descriptive when I talk or write. I use metaphors, similes, figures of speech, descriptive terms.
   b. I use language carefully and precisely when I communicate. I choose my words carefully and am aware of grammar and punctuation.

10. a. I use outlines to learn concepts and their relationships to each other.

b. I use diagrams to learn concepts and their relationships to each other.

11. a. When faced with a problem, I like to look at the various parts and follow a logical and systematic order of steps.

b. When faced with a problem, I like to get an overview first, find a pattern, if possible, and fit the pieces into the whole.

12. a. I use images to help remember material.

b. I make up rhymes or use key words to help remember material.

c. I use gestures or act out concepts to remember material.

13. a. When I am trying to persuade someone to do something, I use my own experiences, I try to enlist his or her emotions, I express my feelings vividly.

b. When I am trying to persuade someone to do something, I use facts and figures, logic and analysis to move him or her in the best direction.

14. a. I would prefer to diagram or sketch a solution to a problem.

b. I would prefer to write out a verbal description of a solution to a problem.

c. I would prefer to role play or act out a solution to a problem.

15. a. I prefer to know in advance what I am expected to do.

b. I like to be free to do things at the last minute.

16. a. I prefer to deal with concrete or applied problems.

b. I prefer to deal with abstract or theoretical problems.

When you have finished the first part of this activity, transfer each of your answers to the scoring key which follows by circling the appropriate item. Then mark one point for each of your circled items in the total points column at the far right of each learning style. This will give you a clearer picture of the pattern that most closely matches your style or styles.

Total
Points

Visual Learning Style

1c   3b 4a 5a   7b   12a   14a

Auditory Learning Style

1b   3d   7a   12b

Kinesthetic Learning Style

1a 2c 3c   5b   7c   12c   14c

Right Brain Learning Style

2a 3a 4b 5b 6b   8a 9a 10b 11b   13a 14a 15b 16a

Left Brain Learning Style

2b 3b 4a 5a 6a   8b 9b 10a 11a   13b 14b 15a 16b

Many items in this activity are adapted from material in N. L. Matte and S. H. G. Henderson. *Success, Your Style: Right- and Left-Brain Techniques For Learning*, NY: Wadsworth, 1995.[1]

comfortable with instructors who use the blackboard to illustrate important concepts or who distribute outlines of their lectures.

Kinesthetic processors make up a smaller, but significant portion of the population. These people are particularly aware of feelings and the sense of touch. They are sensitive to other people's emotions, and indeed, they tend to focus on feelings rather than reasoning or logic. They are good at applied, hands-on tasks. They usually find *doing* to be the best way of learning. They prefer to walk through a demonstration or project, write down information, and apply it to real-life circumstances. Kinesthetic learners often find it helpful to gesture, to act out information, to get up and pace around while they are studying. They often have "gut-level feelings" about the best way to approach a problem. They look for "intuitive" solutions that "feel" right.

Auditory processors use a third approach to learning. They often feel most comfortable understanding, learning, and remembering concepts through lectures or discussions. They are good listeners and often repeat words or phrases out loud to themselves when they are trying to fix information in their minds. They are sensitive to sounds and may lose their concentration when confronted with auditory distractions. They frequently remember the *sounds* of words. They will often say that something "sounds right." They can often hear words they read or remember the tone that someone used to describe a concept.

All human brains are divided into left and right hemispheres that communicate with each other through a bridge called the corpus callosum. The two halves of our brains tend to specialize in different types of information and processing. Increasing research shows that some people rely more on one hemisphere or type of learning than the other.

People who are best at using their left brain or hemisphere tend to be logical, analytical individuals who approach facts in a linear, sequential, step-by-step manner. They use analytical thinking, breaking down the parts of the whole, coming to conclusions after gathering the facts. They use outlines and charts. They are orderly. They use lists and keep track of time and sequence. They are very good with words, language, and writing. They listen, talk, and recite, preferring verbal forms of communication.

Figure 5.1 presents an example of the type of diagram that might be used by people who tend to rely on visual or right brain learning styles. It is based on ecology and biology research that highlights the complex, interrelated cycle of events involved in Lyme disease epidemics and outbreaks of gypsy moths. Note that this cycle implicates many variables: the size of the acorn crop, the white-footed mouse, the gypsy moth larva, the scapularis tick (adult and nymph stages), the spirochete that causes Lyme disease, the white-tailed deer, hunters, and oak trees.[2]

Every few years, oak trees produce bumper crops of acorns which are rich in proteins and fats. This gives them an advantage over other tree seeds, but also makes them a favorite food of mice and deer. If the oaks produced large acorn crops every year, they would sustain a large population of mice and deer who would eat the acorns every year. To evade this problem, the trees have adopted a feast-and famine strategy: occasional bumper crops separated by years in which many deer and mice starve because there are not enough acorns for all of them. Then when a large crop of acorns comes along, there are not enough deer and mice to eat all of them, so many survive to become acorn seedlings.

During the years of acorn bumper crops, the white-tailed deer move into the oak-dominated parts of the forest bringing with them adult ticks which drop off and lay eggs in the leaves beneath the oak trees. The tick larvae hatch the following summer just as the forest is overrun by large numbers of their

Figure 5.1 *Diagram of an Ecological Cycle*

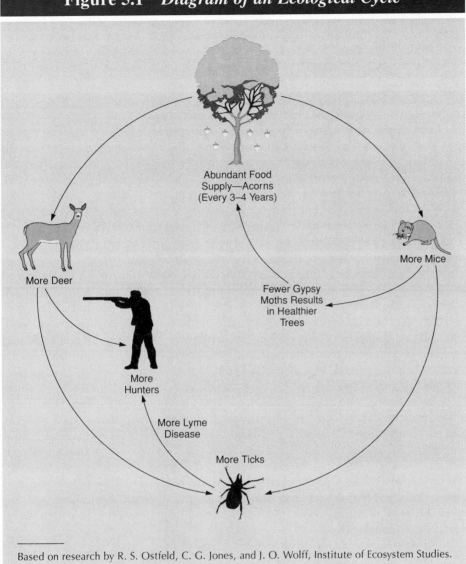

Abundant Food
Supply—Acorns
(Every 3–4 Years)

More Deer

More Mice

Fewer Gypsy
Moths Results
in Healthier
Trees

More
Hunters

More Lyme
Disease

More Ticks

Based on research by R. S. Ostfeld, C. G. Jones, and J. O. Wolff, Institute of Ecosystem Studies.

favorite host, the white-footed mouse whose population has also expanded due to the bumper crop of acorns. The larvae pick up the spirochete that causes Lyme disease when they feed on their mouse hosts and then molt to become nymphs. The following spring, these nymphs, infected with Lyme disease, attach themselves to various mammals, including humans, to whom they transmit the disease. The nymphs molt to become adults in the late summer; the adults wait for a deer to come by and the cycle begins again. Without mice, the deer ticks would be a nuisance, but they would not cause illness because when they hatch from eggs, they are free from the disease; they pick up the Lyme spirochete only after a blood meal from a mouse.

Besides a fondness for acorns, the mice have another habit that influences the forest: they enjoy the taste of gypsy moth pupae. As long as the mice are abundant, they control the gypsy moth population. When mouse numbers drop due to small acorn crops, many gypsy moth pupae survive to become moths. The population of moths then builds up over several years until there are too many moths for the mice to control. The moths damage or kill thousands of trees by eating their leaves. This may delay or eliminate acorn bumper crops, and it may change the composition of the forest by encouraging the growth of other trees' saplings. Gypsy moth populations also rise and fall in cycles because after they kill off many trees, the next generation of caterpillars finds that food is in short supply. Deer populations go through similar cycles, and they are also influenced by the greater number of hunters who are attracted to the forest when deer populations are large.

You might find it easier to learn the multifaceted, tangled cycle of events that governs this ecosystem by diagramming it rather than by memorizing all the individual components of the interaction. Even if you do not usually make use of a right-brain learning approach, this might be the most efficient way to learn and remember this particular information.

You will also find that instructors use different learning styles and that this may influence your study strategies in various courses. An instructor who uses terms such as *list, define, outline, label,* or *summarize* in handouts for assignments, in his or her syllabus, in stating goals for the course, or in sample test questions will expect you to be very specific in papers. He or she will tend to ask for factual information on examinations. This type of instructor might ask you to list three advantages of a particular classification system, briefly summarize four consequences of the Battle of Lexington, or label the parts of a cell. She or he might be more likely to use objective test items that ask you to reason or draw conclusions from facts. If you know what to expect and adapt your study techniques to the instructor's expectations, you will learn more and perform better in the course.

Individuals who prefer to use their right brain or hemisphere tend to be more intuitive. They look for patterns and relationships. They take the pieces and put them together to make a whole. They are very conscious of space and visual-spatial patterns. They tend to have a good sense of direction and excellent map skills. They respond to feelings, body language, and emotions. They often use intuitions, hunches, and feelings to solve problems. They respond particularly well to musical patterns, to patterns of color, to pictures and images. They tend to be more physical than analytical. They use diagrams, sketches, and metaphors.

An instructor partial to this approach might use words such as *ideas, concepts, theories, interpretation,* or *analysis* in his or her lecture, handouts, and syllabus. The exams for this course might ask you to *compare, criticize, evaluate, discuss, explain, describe, analyze, justify,* or *relate* various theories or events. This type of instructor would probably prefer essay to multiple choice exams.

Remember that no one processing style is better than another. They are just different tools which we have become accustomed to using when we organize our world. Most of us use more than one style, but we tend to rely on a habitual or dominant way for making sense of much of the information that bombards us. There are several standardized tests or inventories that can give you information about your preferred processing style and what kind of learning environment works best for you.

The Myers-Briggs Type Inventory and David Kolb's Learning Style Inventory are probably the most popular instruments that can give you feedback about what type of environment makes it easiest for you to study, how you like to learn, and what form of information you assimilate best. These are often available through your college's counseling office. A counselor should help you interpret the results. Becoming aware of your preferred processing style, choosing your instructors according to the teaching styles that mesh best with your learning style, and learning to adapt to several different styles will enhance your education and grades.

■ MAKING THE MOST OF YOUR TEXTBOOKS

We have said that looking at information is usually not enough; if we want to remember it, we must study it. A few quick examples will reinforce the point that active processing is necessary to really learn information. We have all used telephones thousands of times, yet we do not usually study them. Can you remember which letters of the alphabet are missing from the telephone keypad? Most of us handle coins every day. Which words appear on most American coins besides "In God We Trust"? (There tend to be about nine additional words.) Do you remember whose picture appears on a dime? Is he wearing a tie?[3] Despite the fact that we handle these items very frequently, most of us cannot answer all of these questions correctly. Looking at information is usually not enough; if we want to remember it, we must process it in some way. Research has shown that one of the best ways to process or study material is the SQ3R system.

■ THE SQ3R SYSTEM: SURVEY, QUESTION, READ, RECITE, REVIEW

The SQ3R system is a reading and study system based on information-processing theory developed by Francis P. Robinson in 1941. It is still the most widely used and the most effective way to study. The system works for several reasons:

1. It gives you an overview of your reading assignment.
2. It helps you learn the organization of the chapter so that you have a framework into which you can connect the many loose pieces of new information.
3. It helps you focus on the reading; you form questions and search for particular answers rather than plod aimlessly through the paragraphs.
4. It provides you with the repetition and rehearsal that are necessary to ensure learning.

The Basic Steps in SQ3R

The first step in using the SQ3R system is to survey, preread, or skim, the assignment in your textbook. Read the title and the introduction of your assignment. If the introduction is very long, read only the first paragraph of the introduction. Now you know the general content and purpose of your assignment. Next read each of the section headings (they are usually printed in boldfaced type) and the first sentence after each heading. These will tell you more about the content and organization of your chapter. Examine any graphs, tables, and pictures. Finally, read the chapter summary or last paragraph and review the study questions at the beginning or end of the chapter.

> *Survey, or preread, assignment title, introduction, section headings, figures, summary, questions.*

Prereading takes only a few minutes. You will make up for that time by being able to read faster because you are familiar with the material and the organization of the chapter. Your survey will motivate you to go on to the reading, and it will help you to relate your assignment to information you already know about the topic. Prereading also provides an extra review of the most-important points in the assignment, and review is vital to learning and remembering the material. Students who survey their assignments understand and remember the material better than students who do not use this technique.

The second step of the SQ3R system is to form questions as you read. Turn each section heading into a question. For a section with the title "Memory Storage," you might ask, "How are memories stored?" If a heading is titled

> *Form questions as you read.*

"The Process Approach," you might ask, "Why should you use the process approach?" If you see a heading titled "Advantages of Capitalism," you can ask a question such as, "What are the advantages of capitalism?" Jot down your questions in the margin of the text. You will find these questions helpful when you review the material. If the text you are reading does not have section headings, turn the first sentence of each paragraph into a question.

Ask How? Why? What? You will find that questions beginning with the words *how, why,* or *what* are most useful. A heading such as "World War II" can be transformed into questions such as, "What caused World War II?" or "Why did World War II happen?" or "How did World War II come about?" These questions require more thought and deeper reading than questions such as, "When did World War II begin?" or "Where did World War II begin?" or "Who started World War II?" When you ask questions that require more thought and deeper processing, you will discover that you are learning more.

Read and find answers. As you transform section headings into questions, you will find yourself setting goals for your reading, which is the third step of the SQ3R system. You will read to find answers to your questions. Have you ever had the experience of sitting down to read an assignment, and then, about 15 or 20 minutes into your study period suddenly realized that you have absolutely no idea what you have been reading? (Or worse, have you read an assignment for class, and then realized, when your instructor asked you a question about the reading or gave a pop quiz during class, that you had no idea what the assignment contained?) If this has happened to you, it is not because you have "forgotten" the material; it never got into your brain in the first place. You were not paying attention!

Many students, especially when they are bored, tired or distracted, tend to fool themselves by thinking they are studying long hours. (After all, they are running their eyes over the print and turning the pages, right?) Instructors do not give grades based on the number of hours you "studied." Grades are based on how well you learn the material. If you are not concentrating or attending to the material, you will not be able to learn or remember it. Forming questions and reading to find the answers to those questions will help you focus your attention.

Get actively involved. It will be useful for you to underline or take notes on key ideas, definitions, and names as you read and answer your questions; the next section will give you some helpful hints about underlining and notetaking. It is also useful for you to get actively involved while you are reading. Evaluate the material. Is it true or false? Is the author biased? How does the material relate to what you know? How does this information make a difference in your life? When you are actively involved in your reading, you will find yourself learning better.

Recite. Now that you have surveyed the reading, asked questions for each section, and read each section, it is time for you to go to the fourth step of SQ3R: recitation. Before you leave a section to go to the next part of an assignment, be sure that you can answer the question you posed for that section. Look away from the text for a few moments, and say the important points in your own words. This is a form of rehearsal or practice. As you may remember from grade school, "practice makes perfect." This step is important in helping you *Recite out loud.* remember the material better. It is also more effective if you "recite" out loud. When you talk to yourself silently, it is easier to get away with incomplete thoughts or the assurance that you know that concept. Reciting out loud helps you to catch gaps in your learning that will interfere with your ability to retrieve the information later on.

Review each section. The final stage of the SQ3R system involves reviewing. When you have completed the entire assignment, go back to each section heading and answer *Answer each question.* each question you posed. If you cannot answer the question, review the section again until you find the answer. Practice giving definitions and examples (out loud) for all the important concepts and terms. The recitation and reviewing

ACTIVITY

Using SQ3R with a Sample Text

SQ3R SYSTEM TECHNIQUES

Use the SQ3R system techniques in the following list to study the "Managers and Management" sample reading selection in this activity.

1. Use a highlighter to mark the sections that you would read during your survey.
2. Turn each section heading and boldfaced term into a question; write the question in the margin.
3. Read each section.
4. Answer the question(s) you have posed for each section as you finish reading it.
5. Review the entire selection by going back to the beginning and answering all the questions you have posed. Write your answer in the margin underneath your question. If you are unable to answer a question for a particular section, read that part again until you find your answer.

A SAMPLE TEXTBOOK SELECTION

Learning Objectives

After reading this chapter, you should be able to:

1. Define an organization.
2. Define management.
3. Describe what managers do.

Chapter 1   Managers and Management

This book is about managers and management. In this chapter we want to introduce you to managers and management by answering, or at least beginning to answer, these questions: *Who* are managers? *What* is management and *what* do managers do? And *why* should you spend your time studying management?

Who Are Managers?

Managers work in a place we call an organization. Therefore, before we can identify who managers are, it is important to clarify what we mean by the term *organization.*

An *organization* is a systematic arrangement of people to accomplish some specific purpose. Your college or university is an organization. So are fraternities, government agencies, churches, the Xerox Corporation, your neighborhood gas station . . . and the United Way. These are all organizations because they all have three common characteristics. First, each has a distinct purpose. This is typically expressed in terms of a goal or set of goals. Second, each is composed of people. Third, all organizations develop a systematic structure that defines and limits the behavior of its members.

Managers work in organizations, but not everyone in an organization is a manager. For simplicity's sake, we can divide organizational members into two categories: operatives or managers. *Operatives* are those who work directly on a job or task and have *no* responsibility for overseeing the work of others. In contrast, *managers* direct the activities of other people.

What Is Management and What Do Managers Do?

Just as organizations have common characteristics, so do managers. In this section, we define management; present the classical functions of management;

review recent research on managerial roles; and consider the universal applicability of managerial concepts.

Defining Management   The term *management* refers to the process of getting activities completed efficiently with and through people. The process represents the functions or primary activities engaged in by managers. These functions are typically labeled planning, organizing, leading, and controlling. We elaborate on these functions in the next section.

Management Functions   In the early part of this century, a French industrialist by the name of Henri Fayol wrote that all managers perform five management functions: they plan, organize, command, coordinate, and control. The most popular textbooks (and this one is no exception) still continue to be organized around *management functions,* though these have generally been condensed down to the basic four: planning, organizing, leading, and controlling. Let's briefly define what each of these functions encompasses.

If you don't know where you're going, any road will get you there. Since organizations exist to achieve some purpose, someone has to define that purpose and the means for its achievement. Management is that someone. The *planning* function encompasses defining an organization's goals, establishing an overall strategy for achieving these goals, and developing a comprehensive hierarchy of plans to integrate and coordinate activities.

Managers are also responsible for designing an organization's structure. We call this function *organizing.* It includes the determination of what tasks are to be done, who is to do them, how the tasks are to be grouped, who reports to whom, and where decisions are to be made.

Summary

An organization is a systematic arrangement of people to accomplish some specific purpose. It has a distinct purpose, includes people or members, and contains some type of systematic structure. Management is defined as the process of getting activities completed efficiently with and through other people. Managers work in an organization and direct the activities of other people. They should perform four functions: planning, organizing, leading, and controlling.

How does your work compare with the markings on the selection that follows? The highlighted sections are the ones that you should have read during your surveying, or prereading. Go back over your exercise; mark any items that you missed for the survey and any questions or answers you missed during the question, recitation, or review phases of your studying.

TEXTBOOK SELECTION MARKED FOR SQ3R

Learning Objectives

After reading this chapter, you should be able to:

1. Define an organization.
2. Define management.
3. Describe what managers do.

Chapter 1   Managers and Management

This book is about managers and management. In this chapter, we want to introduce you to managers and management by answering, or at least beginning to answer, these questions: *Who* are managers? *What* is management and *what* do managers do? And *why* should you spend your time studying management?

Who Are Managers?

Managers work in a place we call an organization. Therefore, before we can identify who managers are, it is important to clarify what we mean by the term *organization.*

An *organization* is a systematic arrangement of people to accomplish some specific purpose. Your college or university is an organization. So are fraternities,

What is an organizatn?

government agencies, churches, the Xerox Corporation, your neighborhood gas station . . . and the United Way. These are all organizations because they all have three common characteristics. First, each has a distinct purpose. This is typically expressed in terms of a goal or set of goals. Second, each is composed of people. Third, all organizations develop a systematic structure that defines and limits the behavior of its members.

Managers work in organizations, but not everyone in an organization is a manager. For simplicity's sake, we can divide organizational members into two categories: operatives or managers. *Operatives* are those who work directly on a job or task and have *no* responsibility for overseeing the work of others. In contrast, *managers* direct the activities of other people.

What Is Management and What Do Managers Do?

Just as organizations have common characteristics, so do managers. In this section, we define management; present the classical functions of management; review recent research on managerial roles; and consider the universal applicability of managerial concepts.

Defining Management   The term *management* refers to the process of getting activities completed efficiently with and through people. The process represents the functions or primary activities engaged in by managers. These functions are typically labeled planning, organizing, leading, and controlling. We elaborate on these functions in the next section.

Management Functions   In the early part of this century, a French industrialist by the name of Henri Fayol wrote that all managers perform five management functions: they plan, organize, command, coordinate, and control. The most popular textbooks (and this one is no exception) still continue to be organized around *management functions,* though these have generally been condensed down to the basic four: planning, organizing, leading, and controlling. Let's briefly define what each of these functions encompasses.

If you don't know where you're going, any road will get you there. Since organizations exist to achieve some purpose, someone has to define that purpose and the means for its achievement. Management is that someone. The *planning* function encompasses defining an organization's goals, establishing an overall strategy for achieving these goals, and developing a comprehensive hierarchy of plans to integrate and coordinate activities.

Managers are also responsible for designing an organization's structure. We call this function *organizing*. It includes the determination of what tasks are to be done, who is to do them, how the tasks are to be grouped, who reports to whom, and where decisions are to be made.

Summary

An organization is a systematic arrangement of people to accomplish some specific purpose. It has a distinct purpose, includes people or members, and contains some type of systematic structure. Management is defined as the process of getting activities completed efficiently with and through other people. Managers work in an organization and direct the activities of other people. They should perform four functions: planning, organizing, leading, and controlling.

Stephen Robbins, *Management*, 2/e, © 1988, pp. 3–8. Reprinted by permission of Prentice-Hall, Inc., Englewood Cliffs, NJ.

steps encourage you to evaluate the material and to identify the most important points. Narrow down the amount of material that you have to remember, and then review the major points. Rehearsal or review is the most effective technique for remembering information. You may find it helpful to write down the answers to your questions. You will then have an excellent set of study notes for class discussions or exams.

When you complete an assignment using the SQ3R system, you will have an overview of the subject, you will understand the relationships among the topics, you will have read the material carefully, and you will have reviewed the main points at least four times. You will learn better, you will remember better, you will save time studying for tests, and you will not have to cram for exams!

■ MARKING YOUR TEXTBOOK

Underline judiciously.

Underlining a textbook is the most popular study technique used in college. When you highlight an item so that it stands out against its background, you will find it easier to remember that item. Underlining is effective, however, only if it is practiced judiciously. The most common mistake students make is to underline too much. Many students read along mindlessly, underlining almost everything. This is almost no better than just reading passively. It does not force you to identify the major points in the text. It also means that you will have to reread practically the whole text when you study for an exam. Indiscriminate underlining is useless!

First read then underline key phrases.

It is best to read a paragraph first, then go back and underline the important points. This allows you to identify the main points, and it also gives you an extra review of the key material. Use the section headings and the questions you pose in the SQ3R system to help you identify the main points in each paragraph. Underline the parts of the paragraph that answer your questions. Do not underline complete sentences, but do underline complete thoughts so that the material will make sense when you reread just the underlined sections.

The sample paragraph in Figure 5.2 is an example from a student who has underlined too little. The student will miss important information and will have to go back and reread the entire text because the underlinings are just unrelated words that don't make sense.

The paragraph in Figure 5.3 is an example from a student who has underlined too much. This student has not distinguished key points from background material and will have to reread practically the entire text when reviewing the underlinings.

The final paragraph in Figure 5.4 is an example of an appropriate approach to underlining. Key points are emphasized, and the underlined phrases make sense on their own.

Underline about one-third of a paragraph.

In general, you will find that underlining about one-third of each paragraph will allow you to highlight the important points. If you underline too

---

Figure 5.2 *Sample Paragraph with Too Little Underlining*

<u>Resources</u> are <u>scarce</u>. Scarcity is a relationship between how much there is of something and how much it is wanted. Resources are scarce compared to all of the uses we have for them. If we want to <u>use more</u> than there is of an item, it is <u>scarce</u>. Note that this definition is different from the usual definition of scarce, which means "<u>rarely found in nature</u>." How are they different? Consider this example. Is water scarce? How could anyone argue that water is scarce in the usual sense? Water covers nearly two-thirds of the earth's surface. Yet an economist would say that water is scarce. Why? The reason is that there are so many competing uses for water that more water is needed than is available. If you find this hard to believe, ask farmers and ranchers in the West, where water rights are among the most jealously guarded properties. As soon as someone is willing to pay for a good, or a resource, it is scarce by the economist's definition.

Figure 5.3 *Sample Paragraph with Too Much Underlining*

<u>Resources are scarce</u>. <u>Scarcity is a relationship between how much there is of something and how much it is wanted</u>. Resources are scarce compared to all of the uses we have for them. <u>If we want to use more than there is of an item, it is scarce</u>. Note that <u>this definition is different from the usual definition of scarce, which means "rarely found in nature." How are they different? Consider this example. Is water scarce?</u> How could anyone argue that water is scarce in the usual sense? <u>Water covers nearly two-thirds of the earth's surface. Yet an economist would say that water is scarce. Why? The reason is that there are so many competing uses for water that more water is needed than is available.</u> If you find this hard to believe, ask farmers and ranchers in the West, where <u>water rights are among the most jealously guarded properties. As soon as someone is willing to pay for a good, or a resource, it is scarce by the economist's definition.</u>

much, you will not distinguish key points from background material, and you will find yourself rereading practically the entire text when you review your underlinings. If you underline too little, you will miss important information or have to reread the entire text because your underlinings are just unrelated words that don't make sense.

Margin Notes

It is helpful to distinguish main points from supporting details while you are underlining. You may wish to use two different colors of highlighter to make this distinction, or you may prefer to develop a system of notations in the margin that helps you to make this differentiation (e.g., an asterisk [*] for main points and a plus sign [+] for support material). Sometimes a sentence in your

Distinguish main points from support material.

Figure 5.4 *Sample Paragraph with Appropriate Underlining*

<u>Resources are scarce</u>. Scarcity is a relationship between how much there is of something and how much it is wanted. Resources are scarce compared to all of the uses we have for them. <u>If we want to use more than there is of an item, it is scarce</u>. Note that <u>this definition</u> is <u>different from</u> the <u>usual</u> definition of scarce, which means "rarely found in nature." How are they different? <u>Consider</u> this <u>example. Is water scarce?</u> How could anyone argue that water is scarce in the usual sense? Water covers nearly two-thirds of the earth's surface. Yet an <u>economist would say that water is scarce. Why?</u> The reason is that there are so many competing uses for water that <u>more water is needed than is available</u>. If you find this hard to believe, ask farmers and ranchers in the West, where water rights are among the most jealously guarded properties. <u>As soon as someone is willing to pay for a good</u>, or a resource, <u>it is scarce</u> by the economist's definition.

Paragraphs in Figures 5.2, 5.3, and 5.4 are excerpted from A. J. Hoag and J. H. Hoag, © 1986, *Introductory Economics*, pp. 4–5. Reprinted by permission of Prentice-Hall, Inc., Englewood Cliffs, NJ.

ACTIVITY

Underlining and Marking Your Textbooks

Read the paragraph that follows and then underline the important points. Be sure that the phrases you underline make sense when read on their own. Make margin notes that distinguish the main idea from the support material. Add other margin notes to summarize ideas and highlight important points.

A SAMPLE SELECTION FROM A TEXTBOOK

Chapter 1   The Meaning of Economics

The chapter starts with a definition of economics. In each of the remaining sections, one concept in the definition will be discussed. We must take the definition apart before it can be put together in a meaningful way.

Economics is a social science that studies how society chooses to allocate scarce resources, which have alternative uses, to provide goods and services for present and future consumption.

The definition starts "Economics is," and that is what is being defined. So the remaining words need to be understood to make sense of economics. Let us start with "goods and services."

Goods and Services

What exactly are goods and services? A *good* is anything that satisfies a want. That is the purpose of production—to provide goods that satisfy wants. Therefore goods are produced, and the consumption of those goods satisfies wants. Goods can be tangible or intangible. Tangible goods are physical items such as bulldozers or pizzas. Intangible goods such as medical care or education are called services. Both goods and services satisfy wants and therefore can be called goods.

Resources

The satisfaction of wants can only be accomplished by using up resources, the so-called factors of production or means of production. These resources can be classified as land, labor, and entrepreneurship.

Now compare your underlinings and margin notes with those in the following selection. Did you underline too much or too little? Are there markings in the margin that you might have added to help you focus and review?

SELECTION WITH UNDERLINING AND NOTES IN THE MARGINS

Chapter 1   The Meaning of Economics

The chapter starts with a <u>definition of economics</u>. In each of the remaining sections, one concept in the definition will be discussed. We must <u>take the definition apart</u> before it can be put together in a meaningful way.

<u>Economics</u> <u>is a social science that studies how society chooses to allocate scarce resources, which have alternative uses, to provide goods and services for present and future consumption.</u>

a def. of ec.

The definition starts "Economics is," and that is what is being defined. So the remaining words need to be understood to make sense of economics. Let us start with "goods and services."

1. def. of goods
a. purp. of pdtn =
prov. gds tht satif.
wants

Goods and Services

What exactly are goods and services? <u>A *good*</u> <u>is anything that satisfies a want</u>. That is the <u>purpose of production</u>—to <u>provide goods that satisfy wants</u>. Therefore goods are produced, and the consumption of those goods satisfies wants. Goods can be tangible or intangible. <u>Tangible goods are physical items such as bulldozers</u> or pizzas. <u>Intangible goods such as medical care</u> or education <u>are called services</u>. <u>Both goods and services</u> satisfy wants and therefore <u>can be called goods</u>.

b. tangbl gds =
  phys. items
c. intangbl gds =
  svcs
d. use up resources →
  satisfact of wants
e. categs. of resources
  1. land
  2. labor
  3. entrepshp

Resources

The <u>satisfaction of wants</u> can only be <u>accomplished by using up resources</u>, the so-called factors of production or means of production. These <u>resources can be classified as land, labor, and entrepreneurship</u>.

Excerpted with permission from A. J. Hoag and J. H. Hoag, © 1986, *Introduction to Economics*, pp. 4–5. Reprinted by permission of Prentice Hall, Inc., Englewood Cliffs, NJ.

---

text will be too long or complicated to underline effectively. Summarize or paraphrase these difficult or lengthy points in brief phrases in the margin.

Margin notes are also helpful for marking definitions ("defs") and classifications or enumerations (e.g., "causes of trade deficits '#1,' '#2,' '#3,'" etc.). You may draw arrows in the margins as a shorthand way to indicate causal relationships between the ideas you have highlighted. Circle words you do not understand so that you can look them up in the dictionary or glossary after you have finished reading. Use margin notes such as "good test item," "reread," and "?" to flag items that need review or consultation with the instructor.

Highlight definitions, enumerations, and items for review with margin notes.

Making these types of notes in the margin is an active process that forces you to evaluate the information. Both underlining and marking help you to concentrate by keeping you physically involved. They help focus your attention on the key points. They force you to see the organization of the material and the relationships between ideas. They encourage you to evaluate these ideas. They highlight the main points and make it easier for you to remember them.

Get involved with the text.

At the end of each week, take notes in outline form on the sections you have underlined. If you are using a looseleaf notebook, insert these notes next to the class lecture notes you have taken on the same subject. If you are using a spiral notebook, write the notes on the backs of the pages where you have written your lecture notes. Review your lecture notes at this time, and note the relationships between texts and lectures.

Outline underlined sections and add to class notes.

■ ADDITIONAL STUDY TECHNIQUES FOR PARTICULAR SUBJECTS

The SQ3R study system and the strategies for marking textbooks will help you succeed in most of the courses you are taking. But for some of your classes, you will need additional study techniques to reach your full potential.

■ STUDY SKILLS FOR MATH COURSES

The majority of colleges and universities require that their students complete a math course such as calculus, college algebra, or statistics before they can graduate, regardless of the major the student has chosen. But many students, especially older, nontraditional students, experience anxiety about these math requirements. Use the following study techniques to help you succeed in math courses. You will also find these techniques helpful in advanced physics and chemistry courses which rely on mathematical reasoning. This success can be an important factor in reducing anxiety about math and science performance.

Address math anxiety directly.

You might also wish to review the relaxation exercises described in Chapter 11 and the techniques for coping with exam anxiety described in Chapter 6 if

Use relaxation and visualization techniques.

you are uncomfortable approaching math courses. The Stress Management audiocassette described on page 384 will lead you through more extensive exercises aimed at reducing anxiety about particular subjects. If you still find anxiety interfering with your performance in math after improving your math skills and practicing these exercises, consult the college's counseling center. An advisor can help you deal with math anxiety rather quickly and easily, and you will be on your way to completing an important college course successfully.

Devote more time to math study.

Despite the fact that so many educators believe that mathematical reasoning is important for success in our society, more than half the students enrolled in math courses are taking remedial math because their skills are not up to college-level work. If math is a relatively difficult subject for you, you may find that you have to make a greater time commitment to studying math than your other subjects.

Choose your instructor carefully.

Some professors are better than others when it comes to helping students overcome math "blocks" and learn the basic concepts and processes. Read over the suggestions in Chapter 2 for choosing the best instructor. If math is a difficult subject for you, take particular time and care in choosing a teacher who will ease you through this course.

Add a practice step.

Since math courses require that you learn particular skills in addition to information, you will have to add a practice step to your study techniques in order to succeed.

Review the previous assignment.

It is often helpful to review the previous assignment before you begin using the SQ3R method on the assignment for the next class because math is a sequential subject that builds on skills you have previously mastered. Review the last assignment, then study the next one using the SQ3R method, learn any new terms or formulas, and study the sample problems carefully.

Work the practice problem without looking at the book.

Be sure that you can do the sample problems for the section you have studied without looking at the book before you go on to the next section in the chapter. Complete the practice problems at the end of the chapter and on your study sheets. If you have difficulty with any of the problems assigned for homework, go back and review the section and work through the sample problems again. If you find yourself becoming frustrated or anxious, take a break by working on an assignment for another course. You are likely to come back to the math feeling refreshed and successful from completing the other assignment.

Never fall behind.

If you are still having difficulty, get help as soon as possible from your professor, a math laboratory assistant, a classmate, or a tutor. Do not let yourself fall behind. Math is a subject that builds on skills you have previously learned. If you miss one skill, you will not be able to learn the ones that are based on it.

Complete practice problems at end of chapter.

It is often helpful to do all of the practice problems at the end of an assigned chapter, even if your professor has not specifically asked you to complete them. This type of practice results in overlearning, which gives you confidence and allows you to complete that type of problem quickly, correctly, and without anxiety when you see it on an exam. You might also try to practice under time pressure. Time yourself while you solve a set of problems. Then try to do another set of similar problems in less time.

Use timed drills.

Use index cards to practice formulas, definitions, and calculations.

Use index cards to learn formulas, symbols, or rules. Figure 5.5 shows a sample index card you might construct to practice the formula, definition, and calculation for the mathematical term *variance*. Write *variance* on the front of the card. On the back, write the definition, the formula, and a sample problem that shows how to calculate the variance. Practice and test yourself often on blank cards or sheets of paper until you can write out the definition and formula for variance and work a sample problem without looking at your index card. Check your work by consulting the flashcard you have created.

Simplify word problems.

Index cards are also good for practicing word problems. Word problems often have lots of information that is not necessary in order to solve the problem.

Figure 5.5   *Back of Index Card Used to Learn Concept of Variance*

Definition: Variance is the sum of the squared deviations from the mean divided by *N*.

Formula: $S^2 = \dfrac{(X - \overline{X})^2}{N}$

Example: for 5 scores ($N = 5$)

1. Calculate the mean by adding the 5 scores and dividing by the number of scores:	**2.** Subtract the mean from each score:	**3.** Square each number and add them up:	**4.** Divide by *N*:
			$\dfrac{16}{5} = 3.2$
	$(X - \overline{X})$	$(X - \overline{X})^2$	$S^2 = 3.2$
3	$3 - 4 = -1$	1	
7	$7 - 4 = 3$	9	
5	$5 - 4 = 1$	1	
2	$2 - 4 = -2$	4	
$\underline{3}$	$3 - 4 = -1$	$\underline{1}$	
20		16	

Mean = 20/5 = 4

Cross out or ignore irrelevant information. Highlight what it is that the problem wants you to find. (This information is usually at the end of the problem, often in the last sentence.) Go back and decide what formulas or processes you will need to solve the problem. Highlight the key numbers and terms that you will need to complete the problem. If you are having difficulty with a problem, try a diagram. Making a picture or visual representation can often clear your way.

Highlight key terms and numbers.

Diagram the problem.

Figures 5.6 and 5.7 present a problem to help you practice using an index card in the solution of word problems. Write a sample problem on the front of a card. Write the problem and the steps you will use to solve it along with your calculations on the back of the card.

Note that most students are attracted to choice *d*, since that is the average of 35 and 40; it just *seems* like the right answer. (Of course, it isn't.) On multiple choice questions like this one, avoid the quick and easy solution that seems like the right answer unless you know it is right. Many students are also attracted to numbers that are repeated from the question (alternatives *a* and *e*). These are not usually the correct answer either. Once you have eliminated three of the options, *a, d,* and *e,* you are left with two possible alternatives: *b* and *c*. At this point, if you really do not know how to do this type of problem, you have a fifty percent chance of getting it right by guessing.

Do not forget to check your answer with common sense, with an estimate, or with the opposite mathematical process whenever possible. For example, if you spend $12 on six books, and the question asks you to calculate the cost of each individual book, common sense tells you that each book must cost less than the $12 you spent for all of them. You can also check your answer by reversing the mathematical process you used. Take the answer you calculated ($2) and complete the reverse mathematical operation of multiplying (6 × 2),

Check answers with common sense, estimation, or reverse mathematical processes.

ACTIVITY

Creating a Flashcard to Learn a Math Concept

If you are enrolled in a math course this semester, choose one of the concepts from your text and create a flashcard that will help you learn the definition and the formula for that concept and give you a practice example in calculating it. You may diagram that concept in the box provided below. If you are not taking math this semester, choose a math term such as *arithmetic mean* or the formula for calculating the hypotenuse of a triangle when you know the area and the length of the other sides. Show how you would set up the back of your flashcard.

Sample Flashcard

Definition:

Formula:

Example:

and you will arrive at the number you started with ($12). You can check differentiation problems by integrating, square root problems by squaring, addition problems by subtracting, and so on. When possible, try to estimate the answer to a problem before you work it. You will then know if the answer you calculate is in the right ballpark.

Figure 5.6 *Front of Index Card Used to Practice Word Problem*[4]

A woman driving on a sunny day experienced delays due to road construction and could only average 30 miles per hour on her way to work. On the return trip home, it was raining. The road crews had packed up, and so she was able to travel home at an average speed of 40 miles per hour. If her total traveling time was one hour, what was the total number of miles in the round trip?

a. 30   b. $30^{1/7}$ c. $34^{2/7}$ d. 35   e. 40

Figure 5.7 *Back of Index Card Used to Practice Word Problem*

A woman driving ~~on a sunny day experienced delays due to road construction and could only~~ average 30 miles per hour on her drive to work. On the return trip home, ~~it was raining. The road crews had packed up, and so she was able to~~ travel home at an average speed of 40 miles per hour. If her total traveling time was one hour, what was the total number of miles in the round trip?

a. 30   b. 30$\frac{1}{7}$ c. 34$\frac{2}{7}$ d. 35   e. 40

Solving the problem:

Step 1: Cross out irrelevant information.

Step 2: Highlight what it is that the problem wants you to find. (This information is usually at the end of the problem, often in the last sentence.)

Roundtrip distance = ?

Step 3: Go back and decide what formulas or processes you will need to solve the problem.

distance = rate $\times$ time

time = distance $\div$ rate

Step 4: Highlight the key numbers and terms that you will need to complete the problem.

y = distance one way; 2 $\times$ y = roundtrip
rate^1 = 30 mph
rate^2 = 40 mph
total time = 1 hour

Step 5: Write out the processes you will use.

The formula for the average distance travelled at each speed.

$$1 \text{ hour} = \frac{y}{40 \text{ mph}} + \frac{y}{30 \text{ mph}}$$

Convert fractions to a common denominator.

$$1 \text{ hour} = \frac{30y}{1200} + \frac{40y}{1200}$$

Addition $1 \text{ hour} = \dfrac{70y}{1200}$

Division   1 hour $\times$ 1200 = 70y

Multiplication & division   y = 1200 $\div$ 70

y = 17.143 = distance one way

Multiplication 2 $\times$ y = 34.29 = roundtrip distance

The answer is c: 34$\frac{2}{7}$

STUDY SKILLS FOR SCIENCE COURSES

Draw diagrams.   Many of the techniques discussed in the previous section, Study Skills for Math Courses, also apply to advanced physics and chemistry courses which rely on mathematical reasoning. In other science courses you will often find chains of reactions or complex processes such as reproduction that you must learn. Draw diagrams of the different steps of cell division involved in reproduction, and look at the diagrams as you recite the steps or processes you must learn. These diagrams may be easier to remember than long chains of unfamiliar words, and the acts of drawing and labeling offer you an extra recitation session. Drawing and labeling may also be useful tools for learning the parts of a cell as shown in Figure 5.8 or the interaction of variables in a complex ecosystem as shown in Figure 5.1.

A C T I V I T Y

Creating a Study Card That Summarizes an Experiment

You may find it easier to organize and study this information if you put it on a flashcard. Choose an experiment described in one of your science or social science textbooks and create a study card. The front of the card might say "Smith & Jones's 1993 experiment on superconductors." On the back of the card, state the hypothesis, describe the experiment, explain how the data collected support the hypothesis, and describe the consequences for other research in this area. You may fill in that information on the card shown below.

Study Card with Summary of Experiment

Name of researcher(s):

Year in which the research was published:

Hypothesis (or purpose):

Description of experiment:

How do the data support (or fail to support) the hypothesis?

What consequences does this research have for the field?

Figure 5.8 *Study Diagram for Parts of a Plant Cell*

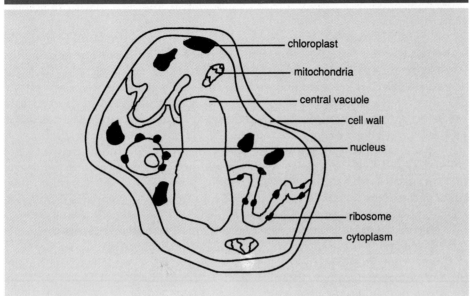

Scientists conduct a great deal of research, and you will be asked to learn certain facts that result from this research. But your professor is likely to put more emphasis on learning to think like a scientist than on just memorizing facts. For an important experiment, you may be asked to learn the hypothesis or theory that led the scientist to do the work, you will need to know how the research was carried out (what was the experiment like?), you will be asked how the evidence collected supports (or fails to support) the hypothesis, you will need to explain how this research affects the rest of the field, and you may be asked to remember the names of the scientists who conducted the experiment.

State the hypothesis.

Describe the experiment.

Explain the results.

Describe the implications.

■ STUDY SKILLS FOR SOCIAL SCIENCE COURSES

In social science courses such as psychology, sociology, anthropology, economics, or political science, you will be learning a whole new vocabulary. Use flashcards to help you learn these new words by writing the important term on the front of the card and the definition on the back. You may find it easier to learn this vocabulary if you translate the definition into your own words.

Use flashcards to learn vocabulary.

You will also find a great deal of emphasis on different theories. You will need to know who proposed a theory, what evidence supports it, what advantages and disadvantages it has over other theories, and what implications it has for the rest of the field. You will often be asked to compare theories, so it might be helpful to plan ahead by making charts or outlines that compare, for example, Freud's stages of human development with Erikson's stages.

Outline information about theories.

Diagram and compare theories.

Whenever you encounter important research or experiments, study them as you would the science experiments previously described. Learn the hypothesis, describe the experiment, explain the results, and determine the implications of the research for other theories or knowledge in the field.

■ STUDY SKILLS FOR HISTORY, FOREIGN LANGUAGE, AND LITERATURE

You may find that many of the techniques described can be adapted to help you study more effectively for some of your other courses as well. For example, in history courses you may be expected to learn sequences of events or to

Use diagrams, time lines, and outlines.

analyze major events such as revolutions in terms of their causes and effects. Diagrams, outlines, time lines, and flashcards can be very helpful in linking separate events so that they form a whole picture that is easier to remember than the separate pieces.

Practice during odd moments.

To study effectively for courses in foreign languages, you will have to add a great deal of repetition and practice. Repeat new words or phrases during the day as you are walking to classes, waiting in lines, doing household chores, or commuting to your job. Listening to a tape on which you have recorded new vocabulary or the conjugation of an irregular verb can be helpful. Carry flashcards for conversational phrases, with English on one side and the translation on the other so that you can practice during odd moments of your day.

Use cassette tapes.

In literature courses you will find it helpful to highlight the names of characters and key events. Events that relate to major themes of the book and plot summaries can be diagrammed for easier review before a test. Stylistic features of different authors can be outlined for purposes of comparison and contrast in preparing for an essay exam.

Figure 5.9 presents a diagram of the themes, characters, atmospheric elements, and symbols portrayed in "The Masque of the Red Death," a short story by Edgar Allen Poe. Constructing such a diagram helps you to focus on the important points of the story, and the visual cues may make it easier for you to review and remember key elements.

REFLECTIONS FOR YOUR JOURNAL

1. What is your preferred learning style (visual, kinesthetic, auditory; right-brain or left-brain)? Describe a strategy to strengthen your abilities in a learning style that does not come easily to you.
2. Analyze the weaknesses in your study habits. Do you survey an assignment before reading it? Do you read actively, asking and answering questions, jotting down comments and criticisms, noting major points and supporting

Figure 5.9 *Diagram of "The Masque of the Red Death" by Edgar Allen Poe*

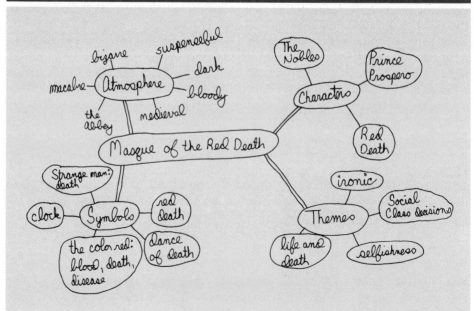

material in the margins as you go along? Do you review the major points after reading the assignment?

3. Study and review differ from each other. Study refers to learning material for the first time. Review involves going over material that you have already learned. Review ensures that you will remember the new material. It is more effective soon after study because most forgetting takes place immediately after learning. How do you incorporate study and review in your learning?

4. Evaluate your system for marking textbooks: highlighting, underlining, making notes in the margins, integrating notes from your textbook with your class notes. How can you improve your system?

5. Which of the special study techniques described for mathematics, science, social science, history, foreign language, or literature courses is likely to be most useful to you?

Notes

1. N. L. Matte and S. H. G. Henderson. *Success, Your Style: Right- and Left-Brain Techniques For Learning.* NY: Wadsworth, 1995.

2. R. S. Ostfeld, C. G. Jones, and J. O. Wolff, *Bioscience,* May 1996, in L. Line, "Ticks and Moths, Not Just Oaks, Linked to Acorns," *New York Times,* 16 April 1996, pp. C1, C8.

3. These examples are taken from K. Higbee, *Your Memory: How It Works and How to Improve It.* Englewood Cliffs, NJ: Prentice Hall, 1993.

4. A. Robinson and J. Katzman. *Cracking the SAT 1996: The Princeton Review.* NY: Random House, 1995, p. 144.

CHAPTER 6

EXAMINATIONS
Studying, Improving Your Memory, and Reducing Anxiety

■ THE PURPOSE OF EXAMS

Exams have been with us since the first colleges and universities. Contrary to the opinion of many students, exams were not invented by sadistic instructors to torture hapless students. It may also interest you to know that most professors dislike making up and grading exams almost as much as you dislike taking them.

Exams actually serve a number of useful purposes. Test scores let professors know how well their teaching techniques are working and whether they need modification. They also give instructors feedback on how well students have mastered important skills and information. They can be helpful to administrators, admissions officers, and employers in making decisions about which students have mastered the material best. Tests give students and their parents feedback on how well the students are doing. They are also useful in motivating students to learn; there is nothing like an upcoming exam to encourage students to hit the books. Finally, perhaps the best justification for examinations is that they serve as a learning experience; in reviewing and studying for a test, you are forced to learn the material better.

■ EFFECTIVE EXAM PREPARATIONS

Exams are unlikely to go away. If you want to succeed in college, it is worthwhile learning how to study for exams effectively. Studying for exams involves organizing, reviewing, and learning the key material from your class lectures and reading assignments. If you practice the skills you have learned in the sections on listening, note taking, identifying the most effective learning styles, and reading and marking textbooks, this will be a piece of cake! If you use these techniques to keep up with your assignments and the weekly reviews of your class notes, you will never have to cram the night before an exam, and you will find that you already know most of the material.

Avoid cramming.

Last-minute cramming is never a good idea. Cramming the day before an exam is likely to tire you out and raise your anxiety level so that on the day of the exam you will not think as clearly as you usually do. You also will not remember the material as well as you would if you had learned it in smaller portions over a period of several weeks. Many studies have shown that breaking up your study time results in more efficient learning. Three two-hour study sessions are better than one six-hour study session. Even better are 40- to 50-minute sessions separated by breaks. Your brain automatically reviews what you have been studying while you wash dishes, call your mother, or have a snack. The break gets your blood circulating, refreshes your mind, and keeps you from nodding off.

Distribute study sessions.

Take breaks.

Organize your study area so that you get the most out of your study time. Reduce interference. Do not study near a tempting television or in a tempting bed. People who try to study when they are sleepy or distracted are fooling themselves. They think that they are studying, but in fact, they are not concentrating. They may even fall asleep! If music or roommates distract you, go to the library. Clear your desk. Do not leave that letter to your friend (the one you meant to answer last week) in plain sight when you have to study for an exam. Have your study area organized so that pens, paper, books, and other materials you need are at hand.

Organize study area.

Spread your study time for a major exam over a one- to two-week period before the test date. Review your textbook underlinings and class notes. Summarize the notes and underlinings; organize them according to the topics outlined in your syllabus so that lecture topics and textbook topics are integrated. Condense and streamline these notes until you have three to five pages of key terms, ideas, and relationships. Include supporting details, examples, definitions, graphs, and diagrams. You will want to review these notes several times before the exam. You should certainly review them the night before and the morning of the exam. If an auditory learning style works best for you, you may wish to record your notes on an audiocassette and play these back to yourself.

Spread out your study time.

Summarize and condense notes.

Make practice tests with the questions you have posed in the margins of your text and lecture notes. Include questions that occur to you as you review your underlinings and notes. Add questions from the end-of-chapter exercises and from a student study guide if your text comes with these study aids. Brainstorm with a study group, and make up a collective list of test questions. Answer these questions and compare your answers with those of your study partners. Ask your instructor if he or she can provide you with copies of tests from previous years or with sample items like those that will be on the exam. Although past exams will not be identical to the one you will take, you will gain a better understanding of what information your professor thinks is important and how he or she tests for it.

Make practice tests.

Obtain sample tests.

Answering practice test questions is an effective study technique, and it also helps to reduce some of the anxiety you will experience when you take the exam. Ask your instructor about the format of the test so that you can study most effectively. Different study strategies are effective for essay as opposed to objective tests. Essay and fill-in questions rely on recall memory. You must be able to supply terms, definitions, and supporting details, and you must be able to organize the material. If your instructor is going to ask for it, you must be prepared to write out a word such as *phenylketonuria* (which is a metabolic disorder that may result in mental retardation). For multiple choice and matching

Ask about test format.

Calvin & Hobbes © 1988. B. Watterson. Distributed by Universal Press Syndicate. Reprinted with permission. All rights reserved.

items, you need not reproduce the word itself, but you must be able to recognize the disorder, to distinguish it from other disorders, and to know about its causes, consequences, and treatment.

Practice solving similar problems.

Examinations in science, math, and many technical areas require that you know how to solve various types of problems. In order to do this, you may have to memorize certain formulas, tables, or values. You must understand and know how to apply certain problem-solving strategies. The best way to prepare for these exams is to practice solving similar problems. Review the study techniques described on pages 75–82 of Chapter 5. If time pressure is a problem for you, practice solving sets of problems with a kitchen timer or alarm clock.

Prepare answers.

Essay questions require well-organized replies. Prepare outlines for sample questions that synthesize your class notes with your reading notes. Plan out answers to possible questions ahead of time so that you can readily explain the major theories, compare and contrast several approaches, give advantages and disadvantages of different strategies, provide examples of various principles, and explain the causes and consequences of major events. Study those outlines before you come to the exam.

Memorize certain material.

"Overlearn" material.

Although most college professors stress understanding of a subject rather than memorization of facts, you will find that there are certain situations in which memorization is helpful. If you are asked to write an essay comparing Erikson's stages of human development with Freud's developmental stages, you will not be able to do so effectively unless you remember the stages that each writer describes. Similarly, instructors may require that you memorize certain formulas so that you can solve problems on the test. Memorize enough material so that the answers to questions come quickly to mind. Take your practice test several times before the test day, and check your answers for accuracy and completeness. Remember that "overlearning" the material will be beneficial in helping you to remember items when you are experiencing the tension of the exam situation.

■ STRATEGIES FOR ANSWERING MULTIPLE-CHOICE AND TRUE/FALSE ITEMS

Some students test well; they perform better on exams than others even when they do not know the material as well. This ability is not related to luck or heredity. Many of these students have learned techniques for studying that, like the ones described in the preceding paragraphs, give them an edge. You can learn these, too.

The following section focuses on strategies that are helpful once you are taking the exam. These strategies apply to multiple-choice, true/false, and matching examinations, and you can use them when you are not sure which answer is correct. *These strategies are not a substitute for studying thoroughly or for reading the exam questions carefully, but they can be helpful when you are stuck and need to guess.*

Choose longest answers.

Choose middle answers.

Few generalizations about the world we live in can be stated in simple or black-and-white terms. For this reason, the longest or most complicated option in a multiple-choice question is more often the correct answer. On true/false tests, longer items that give you more information are more likely to be true than false. It also happens to be true that instructors are less likely to place the correct answer as the first or last option. (This is not true for computer-generated exams. The computer randomly allocates correct responses to all possible positions.) If you have to guess, your choice of one of the middle options is more likely to be correct when your professor has made up the test. This is particularly true if the middle item is longer.

Choose qualified answers.

Most truths are relative rather than absolute so that multiple-choice answers qualified by terms such as *often, most,* and *generally* are more likely to be

ACTIVITY

Applying Strategies to Objective Tests

Here is some practice in applying a number of strategies for taking objective tests. Read the test strategies shown in Figure 6.1. Then answer the practice questions that follow. Choose the best answer, and then indicate why you chose that particular option. The correct answers are on page 100.

Sample Test Items

1. *True or false.* Many decision makers select information more for its accessibility than for its quality.

   Answer: _____

   Strategy number: _____

2. *True or false.* Organizational structures never influence solutions to problems.

   Answer: _____

   Strategy number: _____

3. *Choose the best answer.* The French Revolution was caused by

   a. economic forces

   b. ideological forces

   c. a combination of economic and ideological forces

   d. particular leaders

   e. the American Revolution

   Answer: _____

   Strategy number: _____

4. *Choose the best answer.* Antifederalists opposed ratification of the Constitution because they feared

   a. decentralization

   b. centralization

   c. the British

   d. the army

   Answer: _____

   Strategy number: _____

5. *Choose the best answer.* Parents who abused their children

   a. wants children but can't afford them

   b. hate children

   c. were themselves abused as children

   d. believe in discipline

   Answer: _____

   Strategy number: _____

Reject absolute answers.

the correct choice. There are exceptions to almost every rule, especially in the social sciences and humanities, so options that include absolute words such as *always, everyone,* and *never* are more often wrong. Advice to avoid absolute statements should be followed only after you have carefully read the question, because some questions do not follow this general rule. A true/false item such as "Every monopoly has complete control" is true even though it includes the absolute terms *every* and *complete.*

Use process of elimination.

If two multiple-choice items are opposite in meaning, it is likely that one of them is the correct answer. You may then be able to eliminate the other choices and focus on which of these two opposite options is correct.

Read all answers.

Read the instructions for each question. If your instructor asks for the *best* answer, you must read all choices carefully; several answers may be correct, but only one will be the best. This advice is particularly true for multiple-choice exams. Read all the options before choosing one; it does not pay to choose the first correct answer if the last option reads "all of the above," and indeed all of the answers are correct. Before you choose "none of the above" as your answer, be sure that *none* of the three or four options you have read is correct.

Try questions with answers.

If you have read all of the choices and cannot single out the correct one, try reading the question again and following it with the first option. Next read the question and try answering it with the second option. Continue doing this until you have tried all of the choices. It is often confusing to read four or five complicated choices one after the other; "hearing" the question next to each option may make your choice clearer.

Narrow down choices.

If you are dealing with matching items, read all the choices in both columns before you begin to answer the questions. An item in Column B may fit several items in Column A, but it may represent the *best* match for only one. Complete the easiest items first, to narrow the number of options you must deal with for the remaining questions. Check the directions, or ask your instructor whether you can use items for more than one match. If you may use an item only once, cross off each option as you use it. You may be able to get an item correct by using the process of elimination.

Simplify the question.

If your exam includes complicated true/false items, try to simplify the grammar. Remember, for example, that two negatives make a positive: "You *won't* be *un*prepared for tests if you make up practice questions for study," is equivalent to "You will be prepared for tests if you make up practice study questions." The second version of the statement is less likely to trip you up, so convert the original item by eliminating the negatives. As with multiple-choice items, statements that include absolute terms such as *every* or *never* are less likely to be accurate; mark them "false." Items based on terms such as *some* or *occasionally* are more likely to be true. Figure 6.1 gives some general hints for using test strategies.

■ STRATEGIES FOR ANSWERING SHORT-ANSWER QUESTIONS

Many exams contain questions that ask for a short answer: a word, a sentence, several sentences, or a paragraph. Examples of such open-ended short-answer questions are:

Give a definition of a fugue.
Describe one disadvantage of a market economy.
What is a novel?
List two medications used to treat schizophrenic symptoms.
How many chromosomes are there in a gamete?

Figure 6.1 *Hints for Using Test Strategies*

1. Answers that have qualifying terms such as *some, usually, probably,* and *many* are more likely to be correct.
2. Answers that have absolute terms such as *none, never, always,* and *everyone* are less likely to be correct.
3. Long answers, particularly those that are qualified, are more likely to be correct or "true" than short, unqualified answers.
4. If your instructor made up the exam, options located in the middle position are more often correct than options in the first or last position.
5. If two multiple-choice options are opposite in meaning, one of them is likely to be the correct answer.
6. If you have difficulty choosing an option, read the question followed by each option in turn. Often grammatical agreement between question and answer can hint at the correct answer.
7. In order for a true/false item to be "true," all parts of it must be true. Mark an item false if you know that any part of it is false.
8. True/false tests frequently have more true answers than false ones. If you must guess, marking an item "true" is more likely to get you extra points.

It is sometimes difficult to know how much detail your professor expects. The answer to the question "What is a novel?" could be stated in one sentence or in one paragraph or it could take up an entire book! The number of points allotted to the question, the length of the test, the amount of time you have to answer the question, your professor's expectations, and the amount of information you know about the topic will all be important in determining the length and detail of your answer. *Determine how much detail is necessary.*

The best way to make sure that your answers are satisfactory is to answer one or two items and ask your professor whether your responses are complete enough to merit full credit for the questions. His or her reply will give you an idea of the amount of information you have to supply to get the best grade possible. Unless you are very sure of the information and have lots of extra time, it is best not to volunteer more information than is necessary; professors often take off points for incorrect information, and the errors make a poor impression that could affect your grade. *Check the professor's expectations.*

■ STRATEGIES FOR ANSWERING ESSAY QUESTIONS

Essay questions require that you use your own words to write about a subject at some length. Many students find that this kind of question creates the greatest amount of anxiety on a test. But if you understand how essays are graded and follow some effective strategies, you may find that essays become your favorite kind of question.

When professors grade essay exams, they do not simply count the number of facts that you write down. They are more interested in your ability to reason: do you state your points clearly and support them with accurate information? Research shows that professors award the greatest number of points when students

How to earn the greatest number of points.

- ■ Stick to the question (points and facts that are relevant).
- ■ Think and reason effectively.
- ■ Give accurate information.
- ■ Organize the answer well.
- ■ Express thoughts clearly.
- ■ Answer the question completely.

Knowing facts is not enough.

Obviously you must know your facts well or else you will not be able to use them to reason. But knowing the facts is not enough; you must present them in such a way that you show your ability to think, to organize, to relate concepts to each other, to make your points clearly, and to answer the question.

Read instructions carefully.

One of the most important steps on an essay exam is to read the instructions carefully. If the instructions tell you to answer three questions, and you answer only two, you will automatically lose one-third of the points on the exam even if everything you do write is perfect! On the other hand, if you answer three questions when the instructions tell you to respond only to two, chances are that you will not have enough time to spend on all those essays to achieve full credit on any of them.

Read all questions first.

Read all the questions on the exam before you begin writing. This will permit you to select the questions you can answer most effectively if the instructor has given you a choice of essays. It will help you to budget your time on the test more effectively. It will also allow you to tackle the questions you can answer most easily at the beginning of the test so that you do not get bogged down on a difficult essay and run out of time.

Pay close attention to key words.

Pay very close attention to the key words that tell you how to answer the question. A list of the most common guiding words and their definitions appears in Figure 6.2. Circle, underline, or highlight the key words so that you answer the question completely. If you discuss only the differences between two theories when the instructor asks you to compare them, you will receive only half credit on that essay no matter how good your answer is because you have not answered the other half of the question, "What are the similarities?" Similarly, if you include only two examples when the question asks for three examples, you will lose one-third of the points for that part of the question.

Budget your time.

Budget your time carefully. Questions that are worth more points should receive more time. Otherwise divide the amount of time you have evenly among all of the questions. Check the time you have left periodically so that you can keep to your schedule.

Answer the easiest questions first.

Answer the easiest questions first. You will be more likely to earn full credit for the questions you know best—you will not be pressured or forced to stop working on them because of the time deadline. This strategy will keep you from wasting time and becoming panicky because you are stuck on a difficult question. You will also feel better once you have completed a question successfully, and your positive feelings will help you to perform better on the more difficult items. Finally, you will be able to blame some of your incomplete or poor performance on the more difficult questions on the fact that you were pressured by the time deadline.

Outline your answer before writing.

Outline your answer before you begin writing. Jotting down an outline should take only a few moments, but it will vastly improve the organization and clarity of your answer. You will be less likely to forget important points or examples; this is particularly true if you run into time pressure. If you do run out of time, you will be able to hand in your outline and receive partial credit for your answer even though you did not finish writing it out.

Begin with a statement of purpose.

Do not take the time to present a fancy or lengthy introduction to your essay, but write a sentence or two at the beginning that states what you will do and the order you will follow. This will organize your essay and make it easier

Figure 6.2 *Key Words Used in Essay Examinations*

Key Word	Meaning	Key Word	Meaning
Compare	Examine the qualities of two things in order to reveal their similarities and differences.	Interpret	Explain the meaning of a term or concept.
Contrast	Examine two items in order to highlight their differences.	Justify	Prove or make a case for something using logic or facts.
Criticize	Evaluate the good and bad points of an idea.	List	Present a series of terms or names; enumerate.
Define	Explain the meaning of an item.	Outline	Describe the main points or ideas in a brief form (not necessarily in outline form).
Demonstrate	Show or prove that a statement is true through logic or evidence.	Prove	Demonstrate that something is true; give evidence or logic supporting it.
Describe	Paint a detailed picture in words.		
Differentiate	Contrast or show the differences between two ideas or items.	Relate	Show the connections between two ideas or events.
Discuss	Examine in detail, considering pros, cons, or facts.	State	Explain briefly and specifically.
Enumerate	List or state points one by one.	Summarize	Cover the main points of a topic.
Evaluate	Judge; give an opinion stating strengths and weaknesses.		
Explain	Give the reasons for or causes of; make something understandable.	Support	Back up an argument with proof.
Identify	List items that belong to a certain category.	Trace	Describe the development of a process; outline its major stages or events.
Illustrate	Give examples.		

to read and write. You might want to use part of the instructor's question in your first sentence to state how you will answer the item (Figure 6.3).

You may also wish to include a brief summary sentence or conclusion at the end of your essay that states your main point. In between the introductory and summary sentences, you should present your main points along with sup- *Use transitional words.* porting examples or facts. Try to include transitional words and sentences so that your reader understands when you are going from one point to another. Words such as *however, in addition, for example, for this reason,* and *finally* make

Figure 6.3 *Sample Introduction for an Essay Question*

Sample Question:	Support or argue against the view that the decision to commit suicide cannot be made rationally.
Sample Answer:	Suicide has long been a controversial issue in the area of mental health. I will justify the view that suicide cannot be a rational action.

your essay easier to follow. They also make your writing appear clearer and more logical.

Be brief.

Stick to the subject.

Be concise and keep to the subject. Answer the question completely, but do not try to stretch your essay out. Longer answers are not necessarily better answers. When professors have to read a large number of essays, they become angry and bored with long, rambling, and poorly organized essays. Bored or angry professors are more likely to miss the important points you do make, and they are more likely to give you a lower grade.

Write neatly.

Write neatly and legibly, use a pen, leave a margin (in case you need to add a point you forgot), and write on only one side of the paper. These techniques will make your essays easier to read. If professors have to struggle to read your answers, they may be distracted from the points you are making or form a poor opinion of you.

State your best points early.

Use your best points and ideas early in the essay if possible. This creates a good impression on your instructors, and they are likely to be less critical readers as they go through the rest of your exam.

Support your opinions.

Do not state opinions unless you can support them with facts or with logic. This is an important part of the way you demonstrate your ability to reason.

Avoid factual errors.

Avoid errors in writing.

Try to avoid making mistakes in the facts you present, in your spelling, and in your grammar. Even if your instructors say that they are not grading you on the basis of your writing skills, poor writing and sloppiness create a bad impression. Remember that essays are graded more subjectively than multiple-choice items. Professors may unconsciously give you a lower grade when they think you are a poor student. If you have time after finishing the exam, read over your answers to check for errors or items you have left out.

■ SUCCESS ON EXAM DAY

Be prepared.

One of the best ways to reduce exam anxiety is to be prepared: read and study the assignments, take good notes in class, and review both assignments and class notes. Test yourself on the key terms and definitions; go over the enumerations and review how they are related; review the items that you and your professor had flagged as important. It is normal to feel somewhat nervous when you take an exam; if you have prepared as well as you can, however, you are much less likely to panic and forget what you have studied.

Review notes and go directly to bed.

Get enough sleep.

Make a final review of your notes the night before the exam, then go directly to bed. Your brain will automatically continue to review the material as you drop off to sleep. If you get involved in television programs or heated debates with your roommates, it is possible that the content of these activities will interfere with the material you studied. This interference results from a phenomenon psychologists call *retroactive inhibition,* where new information coming into the brain interferes with the memory of other information that was previously learned. Get a solid night's sleep so that you will be functioning at your best when you take the exam.

Review notes.

Bring the necessary materials.

Arrive early.

Wake up a half hour earlier than necessary on the day of the exam, and review your notes again. If there are items that you had to memorize, such as formulas, dates, or examples, review those several times. If you are tense, take a shower, do some exercises, take a walk, breathe deeply. Make sure that you bring all the materials you need with you (e.g., pens or pencils, calculator, watch, and text or notes, if these are allowed). Plan to arrive a little early for the exam. Being late raises your anxiety level and adds unnecessary time pressure while you are working on the test; it may also cause you to miss important last-minute instructions or hints that the instructor delivers. Take the opportunity to review your notes again while you are waiting for the exam to begin. Stay calm. Breathe deeply. If your head is bursting with formulas or dates that

you may forget, write those down on the back of your exam paper as soon as you receive it.

Listen to your professor's instructions and read over the instructions on the exam before you rush into it. Put your name on the answer sheet. Make sure you have all the pages and that they are in the correct order. (This is particularly important on objective portions of the exam. Collators do sometimes make mistakes!) Take a moment to scan the exam; note the number and extent of the questions so you can budget your time appropriately. If your instructor has included point allotments next to the questions, use these as guides to the length of your answers. You should spend roughly twice as much time on the question worth 30 points as you do on the question worth only 15 points. If you have time, read over the essay questions before you answer the multiple choice items. You may come across material in the objective questions that can help you with your essays.

Read instructions.

Scan exam.

Budget time.

Go through the exam and first answer the questions that come easily to you. Put an asterisk (*) or some sort of notation next to the items you skip so that you remember to come back to them. This instills confidence as you realize that you do in fact know a lot of the material. It also ensures that you will have time to complete the questions you know while leaving yourself the maximum amount of time to go back and work on the difficult items. Part of your mind will continue to work on the difficult questions, and you may find yourself remembering the answers when you return to these items later. This strategy is also useful because you may find that later test items give you hints or information that you can use to answer earlier ones that you missed.

Answer easy questions first.

Read the instructions for each question carefully. Underline key words in the questions such as the verb (e.g., *compare, contrast, define, give an example of*). Circle the number of items that you have to complete (e.g., "Choose *two* of the following four essays."). If your professor wants you to answer *A* or *B*, it does not pay to waste valuable time in answering both parts. If the question asks for two examples, you will receive only half the credit if you give just one example.

Read instructions carefully.

Answer all the questions unless you are penalized for wrong answers. If you leave a question blank, you automatically get a zero for it. If you guess, particularly when you can eliminate one or two of the options, you have a chance of getting it right. Even if you cannot answer an essay question, put down whatever you can think of that relates to the item. Your instructor may be able to give you partial credit for the information you put down.

Answer all questions.

Always outline your response to an essay question. This is especially true if it is to be a lengthy essay. An outline ensures that your response will be organized and that you will not forget to include information that you know because of the pressures of the exam situation. It is also more likely that you will remember to answer the question completely. (If the instructor asks you to compare and contrast, you will get only half the credit if you forget to contrast.) The outline may also be the only information you are able to get down if you run out of time. In that case, you will at least get partial credit for the item. After you have written your answer, reread the question to be sure that you have answered it correctly and completely.

Outline essay response.

If you have difficulty understanding a question or if two answers seem correct, ask your professor to clarify the item or explain your difficulty to him or her. Your professor will not give you the answer but may be able to rephrase the question or give you some other type of helpful hint. If your instructor is not present during the exam or will not entertain questions, write a comment on the exam explaining the nature of the ambiguity. You may be able to get full credit even if you choose the wrong answer.

Ask the professor for clarification.

Comment on ambiguity.

After you have completed the exam, check it over to make sure that you have answered all items and the correct number of parts for essay questions.

Check exam.

Again, unless there is a penalty for guessing, answer every question even if you are unsure of the answer. Read over your answers to check that they are complete. If you have time, review the objective items to be sure that you have answered them correctly. Often information that you receive from later items may cause you to reevaluate an earlier answer correctly. Note your track record on one or two tests so that you can determine whether you are one of the people who changes wrong answers to the right ones or whether you belong to the group that tends to change right answers to wrong ones when you are checking over your work. If you belong to the second group, resist the temptation to change your answers.

Analyze your test performance.

Do not miss the first few classes after an exam. You want to be present when the instructor goes over the exam. This is your opportunity to find out how you can improve your performance on the next exam. I usually take half a period or more to review my expectations for particular exam questions, to have students read some of the best responses, and to answer questions about the multiple choice items. This is your opportunity to find out how your instructor thinks and what she expects. This is also your opportunity to trouble shoot your exam-taking skills. Analyze why you missed the questions you got wrong. Look for patterns and then make the appropriate changes for the next test.

Did you misread the question? (Was this due to carelessness or anxiety? Use a highlighter to focus on key words. Practice relaxation exercises.)

Did you "forget" to study certain information because it didn't seem important to you? (Re-evaluate your perceptions of what is important. Check your ideas against those of your study partners or ask your instructor.)

Did you misunderstand the question? (How can you insure that this does not happen on the next exam?)

Did you miss words like *not, except,* or *false?* (Use a highlighter to mark those words or underline them whenever you see them on future exams.)

Did you study the material, but have difficulty recalling it on the exam? (Was this due to inadequate study or to anxiety? Plan to study longer or practice relaxation techniques.)

Did you mark the first option that seemed correct instead of reading the entire question? (Many instructors ask questions where "all of the above" is the correct answer.)

Was the question unclear? (Should you have asked for clarification from the instructor during the exam or written a note on the exam indicating the ambiguity?)[1]

◼ IMPROVING YOUR MEMORY

If your studying is going to pay off on exam day, you will have to remember a great deal of what you read. For this reason, it is worth knowing a little about the human memory so that you can make the best use of your memory when you study. Psychologists believe that there are three kinds of memory: sensory memory, short-term memory, and long-term memory.

Sensory memory registers everything that makes an impression on one of your five senses at any moment. These memories are very short-lived unless you single them out as important in some way.

If the information is important, you then transfer it to your short-term memory system. You can keep limited amounts of information alive here for only a few moments unless you rehearse it. A good example is a new phone number that you can remember only long enough to dial unless you repeat it over and over or process it in some other way that ties it into information you already know. If you want the information to last more than a few minutes, you will have to do some more processing so that it can be transferred to long-term memory.

Once you transfer material to long-term memory, it is permanently stored, but retrieving it for use may be tricky unless you have processed it well. Information must be organized or hooked in with other information in your memory for you to be able to get at it. The more connections you make between the new material and the information you already know, the easier it is for you to remember or retrieve these new facts when you need them.

It is always easier to remember information that is organized in some meaningful way than to memorize random facts. As an example, how easy do you think it would be for you to memorize the number 149,162,536,496,481 and retrieve it for an exam two months later? If you organized that number in a different way, however, and fit it in with information you already know, you would have no difficulty remembering it ten years from now. Remembering the numbers 1 4 9 16 25 36 49 64 81 (the squares of 1, 2, 3 . . . 9) as a specific series is much easier than remembering 149, 162, 536, 496, 481. This is the reason that you should try to follow the organization of a lecture or a chapter: you will find it easier to learn the information. This is also the reason that you should relate the new material to information that is already familiar. You will be able to remember it more easily.

Organize material in a meaningful way.

Connect material with other information.

It is also much easier to retrieve information if it has been "overlearned." Many studies have demonstrated that continuing to rehearse material past the point where you have gotten it perfect the first time will result in better scores when you are tested. Continued drill or practice is the most effective technique for learning information so that you can retrieve it later. This is the reason that you should use the SQ3R system; it involves at least four opportunities to review the most important aspects of an assignment.

"Overlearn" material.

Strategies for Improving Your Memory

1. Study over a period of time—do not cram.
2. Organize the material and relate it to what you already know.
3. Review and rehearse until you have overlearned the material.
4. Use the mnemonic devices described in the following section.

Mnemonic Devices

There will be times when you have to memorize information. Mnemonic devices can be very helpful at these times because they build on material that is already familiar to you. I learned a sentence in fourth grade that helped me to remember the order of the planets of our solar system according to their distance from the sun. Although I never used this information after fourth grade, I remembered it twenty-eight years later when I had to help my seven-year-old son with his science project!

Use mnemonics.

Mnemonic for Planets in the Solar System

Man   Very   Early   Made   Jars   Serve   Useful   Needs   (Period)
Mercury, Venus, Earth, Mars, Jupiter, Saturn, Uranus, Neptune, Pluto

The name "ROY G. BIV" has helped thousands of students through their physics courses when they had to memorize the order of colors in the light spectrum. (You can also use this mnemonic to show off your knowledge about rainbows.)

Mnemonic for Colors in the Light Spectrum

R   O   Y   G.   B   I   V
Red, Orange, Yellow, Green, Blue, Indigo, Violet

Do you need to memorize the reciprocal of pi for a math course?

Mnemonic for the Reciprocal of Pi

Can I remember the reciprocal?

> **Count the number of letters in each word of the preceding sentence and you will have your answer any time you need it.**

> **The reciprocal of pi = .3 1 8 3 10.**

Is your zoology professor going to ask you whether a Bactrian camel has two humps or one? How about a dromedary?

Mnemonic for Bactrian Camel versus Dromedary

> **Place the *B*, for the Bactrian camel, on its back like this: ʙ**
> **How many "humps" do you see?**

> **Place the *D*, for dromedary, on its back in the same way: ◠**
> **Count the "humps."**

Do you always forget how to spell the word *geography?* Try the following mnemonic:

Mnemonic for Spelling Geography

> **George Elliot's Old Grandfather Rode A Pig Home Yesterday.**
> **G   E   O   G   R   A   P   H   Y**

Mnemonic for First Four Hydrocarbons of the Alkane Class

> **My   Eggs   Peel   Better.**
> **Methane Ethane Propane Butane**

We all realize how useful rhymes can be in helping us retrieve information such as the number of days in each month:

Mnemonic for Number of Days in the Months

> **Thirty days hath September, April, June, and November.**

> **All the rest have 31 except February which has 28 till leap year gives it 29.**

Do you have difficulty remembering the musical notes on the treble clef for your music exam? Here is a sentence that will help:

Mnemonic for Notes on Treble Clef

> **Every Good Boy Does Fine**
> **E   G   B   D   F**

A C T I V I T Y

Making Up Mnemonics

Here is a practice problem. Make up a sentence that will help you remember the following classifications in the order they are used in biology. The first word in your sentence should begin with a *k*, the second with a *p*, the third with a *c*, and so on. If you make the sentence vivid and unusual, you are more likely to remember it.

Kingdom	Phylum	Class	Order	Family	Genus	Species

Mnemonic devices cannot guarantee *A*s on all your exams, as they can assist you only in recalling information. They cannot help you to understand it or to apply it. When an exam calls for memorizing certain facts, however, try a mnemonic to get you through.

Imagery and the Method of Loci

Psychologists have found that imagery can be a powerful tool in boosting the efficiency of your memory. If you visualize information, you can expand the capacity of your memory. This is particularly true if you use startling or unusual images.

Greek and Roman orators who had to remember long speeches used the method of "loci" to trigger their memories. This was also one of the methods used by an amazing subject who was studied by the noted psychologist, Alexander Luria.[2] He was able to memorize books in foreign languages that he did not know and recite whole chapters of these books twenty years later!

A C T I V I T Y

Using the Method of Loci

1. In using the method of loci, visualize a room or route that is familiar to you. Then place each of the items you wish to remember in a location along that route and "pick it up" as you take a mental walk around that room. For example, if you wish to memorize the presidents of the United States in order, you might deposit a dramatic image of each president in strategic locations around your house.

Use the method of loci.

Start in the front yard of your house, and visualize George Washington chopping down your favorite tree. Then, as you open your front door, you are greeted by John Adams whose Adam's apple is wildly bobbing up and down

Create dramatic imagery.

while he pumps your hand in greeting. You walk through the front hall into the living room to see a short "Mutt" and a tall "Jeff" sitting next to each other on the couch. Jeff's son (Jefferson) is sitting on his father's lap and shrieking at the top of his lungs because he wants some candy from the dish located on the lamp table next to the couch. You then see James *Mad*ison, hopping *mad,* jumping up and down next to the lamp table because Jeff's son has broken the lamp while trying to get at the candy dish.

Continue through the house "picking up" a president at each stop along your route. The more vivid and unusual you make the images, the easier it will be to remember your items. This method need not be used with only the rooms in your house; any familiar route, such as a street with particular shops, will work as well.

2. Here is a list of the first ten presidents of the United States. Next to each name write an image that is associated with a room in your house or a stop along a route you know well. Read the list over twice after you have completed it, imagining the scenes as clearly as possible. Then test yourself by writing down the names of the ten presidents in order. Check your answers against this list.

George Washington   chopping down a cherry tree in the front yard
_____

John Adams   _____
_____

Thomas Jefferson   _____
_____

James Madison   _____
_____

James Monroe   _____
_____

John Quincy Adams   _____
_____

Andrew Jackson   _____
_____

Martin Van Buren   _____
_____

William Henry Harrison   _____
_____

John Tyler   _____
_____

■ REDUCING EXAM ANXIETY

It is normal to feel somewhat nervous as you sit down to take an exam. Not only is this anxiety normal, it is also helpful! If you feel totally calm and collected during a test, you may not perform as well as you could. A small amount of anxiety is helpful in arousing all your systems so that you are motivated to do your best.

On the other hand, too much anxiety is disruptive; it interferes with your concentration. If you are worrying about your pumping heart, churning stomach, or sweaty palms, you will not be focusing on the test.

Quick Tension Relievers

If you become tense before exams, try the exercises described in Figure 6.4 the next time you are studying for an exam or when you are actually taking one.

Relaxation Training

The exercises you have just completed can be quite useful in dissipating average levels of tension or anxiety, especially if you have been sitting for a long

Figure 6.4 *Quick Tension Relievers*

- SHOULDER SHRUGS. Let your arms hang limply at your sides (or rest your hands in your lap, keeping your arms relaxed) and hunch your shoulders up as high as you can toward your ears. Then roll your shoulders back trying to touch your shoulder blades together. Finally, allow your shoulders to drop down and forward to a comfortable resting place. Repeat the exercise, but this time, after you hunch your shoulders, roll them forward before you drop them into a comfortable resting position. Repeat the exercise three times.
- CHIN TUCKS AND HEAD TILTS. Let your head drop forward to your chest. Hold 10 seconds, then rest. Bring your right ear as close to your right shoulder as you can while keeping your shoulder down. Hold 10 seconds and relax. Bring your left ear to your left shoulder. Hold for 10 seconds, then relax. Repeat all three exercises again.
- EYE CLOSURE. Close your eyes. Make your hands into fists and press them against your eyes, squinting your eyes tightly at the same time. Give yourself a few seconds to shut out your tension and all other distractions. Drop your hands and open your eyes.
- TENSE AND RELAX. Tense all the muscles in your body at once: Curl your toes towards your head, lift your legs, suck in your stomach, push the small of your back against your chair or the wall, take a deep breath and hold it, hunch up your shoulders, ball your hands into fists and press your forearms against your biceps, push your neck against your chair or the wall, clench your jaws, wrinkle up your nose, squeeze your eyes shut, and bring your eyebrows together in a frown. Then release all the tension at once as you let out your breath and continue breathing normally.
- DEEP BREATHING. Breathe deeply and regularly.

time taking an exam or studying for one. If your anxiety level is higher than average, you may need to use one of the more comprehensive techniques developed by psychologists for reducing anxiety. Two of the most successful techniques that reduce anxiety are relaxation training and systematic desensitization. Relaxation training is discussed in the section on stress of Chapter 11. Practice the exercises in that chapter or, if your anxiety level is higher, try the more comprehensive exercises in the audiocassette described on page 384.

Remember that the best way to reduce exam anxiety is to feel that you are prepared for the exam. If you have not studied adequately, relaxation exercises will not be very helpful. Practice the study strategies discussed in this chapter, and your confidence will soar!

Systematic Desensitization to Exam Anxiety

If your anxiety level is not too high, relaxation exercises can help you to feel more comfortable during exams or other problematic situations. If, on the other hand, anxiety really interferes with your performance, you may wish to consider systematic desensitization in addition to the relaxation exercises.

When you use systematic desensitization, you actually condition yourself to replace anxiety with relaxation during the situations that are troublesome for you. Exam anxiety can offer a good example of how to set up a program of desensitization, but you can tailor a program to fit almost any irrational fear. You first analyze your fear and break it down into the specific situations that make you anxious. You then place those situations in order from least- to most-anxiety-producing, and finally you systematically condition yourself to relax in those situations by coupling them with deep muscle relaxation exercises.

Psychologists have demonstrated the effectiveness of systematic desensitization in thousands of studies. This method has proven successful with a wide range of fears from public speaking to exams to snakes. The audiocassette described on page 384 teaches you how to set up a systematic desensitization program for exam anxiety or you may seek out a professional at the counseling center who can help you with such a program.

Answers to Activity "Applying Strategies to Objective Tests"

1. *true.*   Strategy 1: the term *many* is a qualifier.
2. *false.* Strategy 2: the term *never* is an absolute.
3. *c.*   Strategies 3 and 4: *c* is longer, more complicated, and in the middle position.
4. *b.*   Strategy 5: the answer is one of two opposite choices.
5. *c.*   Strategies 6 and 4: for *c*, there is agreement between the noun in the question (*parents* = plural) and the verb in the correct answer (*were* = plural); for *c*, there is agreement between tense of the verb in the question (*abused* = past tense) and tense of the verb in the answer (*were* = past tense); and *c* is in a middle position.

✍ REFLECTIONS FOR YOUR JOURNAL

1. Compare your method of preparing for exams with the strategies described in this chapter. Are you satisfied with the way you usually study for exams? Which of the techniques suggested in the text would help you prepare more successfully?

2. Do you usually perform best on essay, short answer, multiple choice, or true/false exams? Which of the strategies described in this chapter will help you improve your performance?

3. Preparing for exams should involve reviewing material rather than learning it for the first time. Reviewing is critical because it ensures that you will remember the material you have learned. If you have been studying consistently during the semester, the time needed to prepare for exams is not as great as many students expect. How much study time should you schedule for a quiz? a midterm? a final exam?

4. If anxiety interferes with your ability to perform well on exams, review the suggestions described in the text. Which one(s) will you use to decrease your anxiety?

Notes

1. Adapted from N. L. Matte and S. H. G. Henderson. *Success, your style!* NY: Wadsworth, 1995, pp. 149–152.
2. A. R. Luria, *Mind of a Mnemonist,* trans. L. Solotaroff. New York: Basic Books, 1968.

LIBRARY RESEARCH

■ RESEARCH SKILLS

One of the most important skills you can learn at college is how to find information. You will need research skills when you prepare term papers and oral reports. You will also find these skills useful once you graduate from college if you need to look up statistics for a business presentation, write an article for a newsletter, or decide which automobile to purchase. There has been a tremendous increase in the number of works published in the past decade. It is estimated that more than forty thousand books are published each year in the United States alone, and thousands of newspapers, magazines, and journals come out on a daily, weekly, or monthly basis to add to this information explosion.

Become familiar with the library.

It is well worth your time to become familiar with the services and locations of your college library. Take a tour of the library if your school offers one. Many colleges offer library orientation workshops or courses, pamphlets on library services, or videotapes to acquaint you with what is available and where to find it. The small amount of time you invest in becoming familiar with your library, at the beginning of your college career, will save you much time later when you are working under the pressure of the due date for that important research paper.

Ask the reference librarian for help.

The reference librarian is your best ally in the time-consuming but ultimately rewarding search for information. Learn as much as you can about the library, but always check with a reference librarian if you are stuck about how or where to find the information you need. Even if you have done a thorough research job, the reference librarian may be able to help you locate additional or superior sources. The reference librarian's job is to help people use the library. Do not be afraid to ask for help, no matter how simple your question seems!

Bring assignment guidelines with you.

In order to help you, however, the reference librarian needs certain information from you. Bring your syllabus and the guidelines for your assignment to the library with you in case the librarian has a question about the type of information you need for your assignment. Spend some time choosing a topic and narrowing it down before you approach the librarian. Know what types of sources your instructor expects you to use. For example, an encyclopedia may be fine for certain assignments, but totally inadequate for others; magazine articles may be appropriate for some courses, but only the more scholarly journal articles may be acceptable for others. Do not be afraid to ask for help. As your research skills improve, you will experience less frustration and greater rewards when you use the library.

If you have not used a research library before, you may feel overwhelmed by the size and complexity of your college library. A research library includes many types of services that are not found in your high school or neighborhood library. Although your local library may be simpler, it does not contain many of the resources that you will need for college-level work.

■ LIBRARY SECTIONS AND SERVICES

Familiarize yourself with the main section of the college library in your freshman year. You may in later years also need to become familiar with smaller or more specialized collections that are located in other campus buildings. The central library on a college campus usually includes a main desk where books are checked out, a reference section that contains specialized materials used in research, a card and/or electronic catalog where you may look up the location of books, the stacks where books are shelved, and a periodicals section where journals are housed.

Familiarize yourself with the entire library.

In addition to these areas, there may be audio- and videotape collections, a section for reserve books set aside by instructors for certain courses, shelves where current newspapers and magazines are displayed, a vertical file containing clippings and pamphlets on topics of current interest, and a government documents collection. Many research libraries also include photocopy machines for duplicating materials, microfilm and microfiche machines for reading and duplicating materials printed on film rather than paper, terminals for electronic databases, typing or word-processing areas, and study areas.

Be able to find the tape collection, reserve section, vertical file, and government documents.

■ THE REFERENCE SECTION

The reference section contains sources as diverse as handbooks, thesauri, dictionaries, encyclopedias, indexes, atlases, yearbooks, bibliographies, and directories to guide you with your research. These are usually expensive volumes, and they do not circulate. That means that you may use them in the library, but you may not take them home with you.

You are familiar with dictionaries, but in addition to the general dictionaries that help you with routine spelling and definitions, the reference section contains specialized dictionaries to answer technical questions in a particular field (e.g., *A Dictionary of Biological Sciences, Dictionary of Music and Musicians, Mathematical Dictionary,* and *Dictionary of Quotations*).

Become familiar with the special dictionaries.

The same is true of encyclopedias. In addition to the more general *Encyclopedia Britannica,* you may find more specialized encyclopedias such as the *Encyclopedia of Sports,* the *Encyclopedia of Banking and Finance,* and the *Encyclopedia of Bioethics.* You may not be able to use these as one of your major sources for a research paper, but they are often a good place to begin research. You may find them useful in giving you an overview of a particular topic, helping you to recognize the major subdivisions of an area, or guiding you when you have to narrow down a topic that is too broad.

Find the special encyclopedias.

The reference section also houses the many indexes that will help you locate information published in newspapers, magazines, and journals. *Biological Index,* for example, lists by subject and by author all the articles published in biology for a given year. *Education Index* does the same for the field of education, as does *Sociological Abstracts* for sociology articles and *Historical Abstracts* for historical material. *Bibliographic Index* is an annual publication that lists published bibliographies by subject. Many libraries have replaced printed indexes with electronic bibliographic databases. The information you receive from these databases is much the same as that contained in printed indexes, but you gain access to this information through a computer terminal. As you take more advanced courses in your major, you will find these indexes to be invaluable guides to the information available in your field.

Use indexes to journals or electronic bibliographical databases.

Ask the reference librarian.

The most valuable resource in the reference section, however, is the reference librarian. Whether you need to know the batting average of a particular player, the birth date of a specific author, the address of a certain university, the approved subject heading for a particular topic, or the location of a government document, your reference librarian is your best guide to finding information.

■ THE CARD OR ELECTRONIC CATALOG

The card catalog is your guide to what books your library owns and where to find them. The catalog may be arranged on individual cards, which are housed in wooden files familiar from your high school days. Or, as in more and more libraries, the card catalog may be a computerized listing.

Check the author file.

Check the title file.

The card catalog is divided into three sections. Each book is listed in the author section, under the last name of the person who wrote it. It is also listed in the title section, by the first word in the book's title. (Leave out words such as *The* or *A* if these are the first words in the book's title, and look up the book alphabetically by the second word.) In writing a research paper, however, you may find that the listing in the subject section is most useful to you.

Check the subject file.

Find the Library of Congress subject headings.

Books in the subject section are listed by the topic that they cover. Be aware, however, that the topic or subject that you choose may not be listed under the most obvious subject heading. If you do not find books under a particular heading, ask the reference librarian to show you the *Library of Congress Subject Headings,* a guide to official subject headings. You will find, for example, that books about fraternities are listed under "Greek letter societies," those that deal with teenagers are listed under "youth," and publications on the greenhouse effect are cataloged under "greenhouse atmospheric." Until recently, books about toilets were to be found under "water closets," and works dealing with nuclear power were filed under "atomic power." These last two subject headings were recently updated, so it pays to check the latest edition of *Library of Congress Subject Headings* if you are having difficulty finding your sources. The guide may also suggest additional headings that you might check to find information about your topic.

Note the publisher, date, and place of publication.

The sample cards in Figures 7.1, 7.2, and 7.3 show the listings in the library card catalog for a book entitled *The Jazz Age;* the listings are, respectively, in the subject, author, and title sections of the card catalog. Notice that the cards tell you the name of the publisher, the date, and the place of publication. If you ever misplace some of the bibliographical information you need for your list of references, you will not have to go back to the book itself to trace this information. It can be found in the card catalog. The card also gives you helpful information about how many pages the book has and whether it includes illustrations, bibliography, and index. The subject headings under which the book is listed are printed at the bottom of the card. These subject headings offer good suggestions for additional categories that could yield more books on your topic. The most important information on the card is the call number, which tells you where to find the book. This number appears in the upper left hand corner of the card and on the spine of the book. Write it down carefully, as your library is a big place. If you copy even one of the letters or numbers incorrectly, you are not likely to find the book.

Check the subject headings.

Copy call number carefully.

Electronic catalogs.

The same information that appears in a printed card catalog may be found through a computer terminal if your college is one of the many institutions that has converted to an electronic catalog system. It is estimated that by the year 2000 all medium-size and large academic institutions will have computerized catalogs.

At this time, some libraries list all of their collections in printed card catalogs, some show all of their collections on electronic catalogs, and still others use a combination of printed and electronic catalogs. For example,

Figure 7.1 *Card Catalog Listing by Subject*

Subject Heading

JAZZ MUSIC—UNITED STATES.

Author

Call Number {

ML
3477
.S475
1987

Year of Publication

Shaw, Arnold.

Book Title —— The jazz age: popular music in the
1920's/Arnold Shaw.—New York:—— *Place of Publication*

Publisher —— Oxford University Press, 1987.

Number of Pages — x, 350 p.; 22 cm.

Bibliography — Bibliography: p. 303-309.

"Discography" —p. 311-318. *References in Record Form*

Includes index.
ISBN 0-19-503891-6

Other Library of Congress Subject Headings {

1. Music, Popular (Songs, etc.)—
United States—History and criticism.
2. Jazz music—United States.
3. Musical revue, comedy, etc.—United
States.   4. United States—History—
1919–1933.

NjMahR   RNJAsc   86-33234r88

Figure 7.2 *Card Catalog Listing by Author*

ML
3477
.S475
1987

Shaw, Arnold.
The jazz age: popular music in the
1920's/Arnold Shaw.—New York:
Oxford University Press, 1987.
x, 350 p.; 22 cm.
Bibliography: p. 303-309.
"Discography" —p. 311-318.
Includes index.
ISBN 0-19-503891-6

1. Music, Popular (Songs, etc.)—
United States—History and criticism.
2. Jazz music—United States.
3. Musical revue, comedy, etc.—United
States.   4. United States—History—
1919–1933.   I. Title

NjMahR 15 JUN 88   15081972   RNJAac   86-33234r88

Figure 7.3 *Card Catalog Listing by Book Title*

The jazz age

ML
3477   Shaw, Arnold.
.S475   The jazz age: popular music in the
1987   1920's/Arnold Shaw.—New York:
           Oxford University Press, 1987.
               x, 350 p.; 22 cm.
               Bibliography: p. 303-309.
               "Discography" —p. 311-318.
               Includes index.
               ISBN 0-19-503891-6

NjMahR   RNJAtc   86-33234r88

many libraries list only materials acquired after a certain date in the electronic catalog while older materials are listed in a printed catalog.

Electronic catalogs store the information about the library collection in a computer system, and students may bring that information up on individual screens. These electronic catalogs have menus that list what is available on the program and provide basic instruction on how to use it. In addition, they often have "help" screens that offer explanations beyond the menu's instructions. These are useful if you are not familiar with the particular program at the library you are using.

CD-ROM catalogs. The two most common types of electronic catalogs are CD-ROM (Computer Disk-Read Only Memory) and on-line catalog systems. The CD-ROM is a plastic disk on which data has been encoded by using a laser that burns pits in its surface. It has a storage capacity of about 600,000 catalog records. The disadvantage of CD-ROM is that it cannot be edited; information cannot be added or deleted from it. If you wish to update the information in the file, you must produce a new disk. Most academic libraries update their CD-ROMs once a month or once every two months; materials that are acquired by the library in the time before the CD-ROM is updated must be listed in some other system.

On-line catalogs. On-line catalogs can be updated at any time so they will give you the most current information about your library's holdings. They often include additional information to that contained in a printed catalog. For example, the computer may tell you whether the item in which you are interested is signed out, missing, or sitting on the shelf. In some libraries, only materials acquired after a certain year are listed on-line; you may have to look elsewhere for earlier holdings. On-line systems vary in the ways that information appears on the screen, the amount of information given, and the instructions used for accessing the information. Because instructions vary from one on-line system to another, read the instructions on the terminal for the system you are using before beginning your search. Most instructions are easy to follow, but they must be followed exactly and in the order given for the program to work.

Key words. One advantage of on-line catalogs is that they allow you to search by key word in addition to author, title, call number, or Library of Congress subject heading. The key word allows you to use whatever word or words seem to describe your subject best. It may also allow you to find a poem or short story that appears in a book of collected works and would not be listed on its own in a printed card catalog.

ACTIVITY

Using the Readers' Guide to Periodical Literature

As a practice activity, fill in the bibliographical information for the following article that appears as the fourth listing under "marriage" on page 1350 of the 1994 edition of the *Readers' Guide to Periodical Literature.* You will need to include *all of this information* in the bibliography of your research papers. You will also need this information in order to find the article in the library's periodicals section. If you copy it down carefully, and hold onto it, you will save yourself a great deal of time and frustration!

The allure of old boyfriends [effect of remaining friends on a marriage]. L. Dormen. il. *Redbook* v183 p52–4 Jl '94

Author's name: _____

Date of publication (month and year): _____

Title of article: _____

_____

Title of magazine: _____

_____

Volume number: _____

Page numbers: _____

chronological order: the most recently published sources will appear first on your screen.

The most general index is the *Readers' Guide to Periodical Literature.* This index will give you references that are appropriate for introductory-level courses. If you are doing research for a sophomore-level course, you may need to use a more specialized index or database such as *General Science Index, Humanities Index,* or *Social Science Index.* For junior or senior-level courses, you may need to consult an even more specialized index that will give you citations for more advanced articles such as *Biological Abstracts, Art Index,* or *Psychological Abstracts.*

Consult the Readers' Guide to Periodical Literature *or more specialized indexes.*

The *Readers' Guide to Periodical Literature* lists articles by author and subject that appear in more than 100 popular magazines such as *Reader's Digest, Time,* and *Newsweek.* You will find that the index lists the magazines it covers on a page near the front of the volume. If your instructor wants you to use magazines in your research, this is a good index to consult. Check the *Library of Congress Subject Headings* or a list of subject headings for the database to find the appropriate ones. You may find that articles about your topic are listed under several headings. If you are using a database, you may combine several headings so that the computer will automatically list all articles relevant to your research. If you are using a printed index, make a list of appropriate headings and check each of them in turn to compile a comprehensive list of sources.

List and check subject headings.

If you are doing a paper on marriage, for example, you will find that pages 1350–1352 of volume 54 in the 1994 edition of the *Readers' Guide to Periodical*

Literature list more than 160 articles on this topic. The listing includes articles on marriage counseling, marriage law, marriage customs and rites, and marriage contracts. If, however, you are researching a paper on movie stars, you will find those articles listed under "motion picture actors and actresses" on page 1457. The third article on this topic is listed in a sample citation in Figure 7.4.

The information about the article always appears in the same order, as would other citations from the *Readers' Guide to Periodical Literature:*

Copy bibliographic information carefully or have the computer print citations from the bibliographic database.

1. The subject heading for the article.
2. The title of the article.
3. The author's name (first initial followed by last name). If there is more than one author, you will need the names and initials of all of them for your bibliography. In many cases, there is no author listed for the article.
4. Information about a bibliography or illustrations. Abbreviations for these (e.g., il., bibli.) are indicated if the article includes them.
5. The title of the magazine. You will have to check the list of magazines in the front of the index to interpret the abbreviations used. Please do not guess, as it will make it hard for you to find the magazine. "Psych" could stand for "psychological," "psychiatric," or "psychology." Many journals have similar titles, and you could lose a great deal of time if you make a mistake about the periodical's title.
6. The volume number of the magazine.
7. The page numbers where the article appears.
8. The date of the magazine in which the article was published. Check the list of abbreviations in the front of the index for the key. *Je,* for example, refers to June, and *Ja* stands for January.

Check abbreviations in front of index.

Copy volume number and page number of index.

All abbreviations are listed in the front of the index, and you may have to keep checking these until you become accustomed to the systems used by the various indexes. If you are doing a large research project, you may find it helpful to write down the issue and page number of the *Readers' Guide to Periodical Literature* where you found the citation. In case you miscopy some of the bibliographical information, forget to write some information down, or need to order a magazine through the interlibrary loan network, writing down the issue and page number will save you considerable time in searching through back issues of the *Readers' Guide to Periodical Literature.* If you are using a bibliographic database, the computer will allow you to indicate which citations you want to print as you scan through the list. When you have finished reviewing the

---

Figure 7.4 *Sample Citation from* Readers' Guide to Periodical Literature

Directors make stars from scratch [accidental actors]. J. Giles. il pors. *Newsweek* V123 p67 Ja. 24 '94.

(This citation tells you that the title of the article is "Directors Make Stars from Scratch." The author is J. Giles. The article is illustrated with portraits, and it appeared in *Newsweek* magazine, volume 123, on page 67, of the January 24, 1994 edition.)

items, print those that interest you. This print option will save you much time, and it will ensure accuracy of the bibliographic information.

Once you have copied all the bibliographical information for the articles that interest you, you will have to see whether your library carries those magazines. It is likely that your library does subscribe to most of the magazines listed in the *Readers' Guide to Periodical Literature*. If the periodicals are shelved in open stacks, you must then look up the call number for the magazine you want and locate it in the same way you would locate a book. If the stacks are not open, you will need to fill out a call slip with the bibliographical information so that the librarian can retrieve the magazine for you. Please be careful to write down the bibliographical information correctly so that you do not have to go back to the *Readers' Guide* and check it again!

Look up call number or fill out call slip.

You will find that other indexes work much like the *Readers' Guide to Periodical Literature* so that once you have mastered one, you can easily use others such as the *Education Index*, *Art Index*, or *Engineering Index Monthly*. The example that follows in Figure 7.5 was printed from a technology database, *Computer Data Bases*, for a student who was researching a paper on whether computer display terminals affect pregnant users. The key words supplied for the search were "video display terminal," "VDT," and "pregnant women."[2]

Use specialized indexes or databases.

The *Social Science Index*, on the other hand, covers a broader territory by listing articles published in the more scholarly journals of the social sciences. The difference between a magazine and a journal is that a journal is written for a more specialized, professional audience. It tends to be more scholarly. If you are writing a paper on disciplinary problems of schoolchildren for a psychology course, your professor may not allow you to use magazine articles from *McCalls*, *Reader's Digest*, or even *Psychology Today*. If he or she specifies that you are to use journal articles, then your research job will be easier if you consult The *Social Science Index* or *Psychological Abstracts*. These indexes contain more scholarly articles than the magazine articles featured in the *Readers' Guide to Periodical Literature*.

Use journals instead of magazines for more scholarly papers.

Indexes such as *Sociological Abstracts*, *Historical Abstracts*, or *Biological Abstracts* have an added benefit. In addition to giving you the bibliographical information for an article, they also present abstracts or summaries of the articles. Each index of these volumes is numbered. The number assigned to the

Use abstracts and summaries.

Figure 7.5 *Sample Citation from Computer Database*

0834200 DATABASE: CD FILE 275

The VDT challenge. (results differ for various groups responding to the health hazards associated with video display terminal use)
Schacter, Esther Roditti; Fontaine, Anne Elizabeth
Computer Systems News ISSUE: n463 PAGINATION: p21(1)
PUBLICATION DATE: April 16, 1990
SOURCE FILE: CD File 275

(This citation tells you that the authors of the article are Esther R. Schacter and Anne E. Fontaine; the title of the article is "The VDT Challenge. [results differ for various groups responding to the health hazards associated with video display terminal use]"; the article appeared in issue number 463 of the *Computer Systems News* on April 16, 1990; and it is a one-page article on page 21 of that issue.)

citation in the index volume under author or subject heading corresponds to numbers printed on the spine of the abstracts volume. If you look up that abstract number, you will find a paragraph that summarizes the article. This summary gives you a better idea than the article's title as to whether that article would really be useful for the paper you are writing.

Check the periodical holdings list.

Ask about interlibrary loan.

Once you are using the more specialized indexes, you will undoubtedly find that your library does not subscribe to all the journals listed in the index. You will need to check the list of periodical holdings located at the reference desk or in the periodicals area to see which periodicals your library does own. If the library does not subscribe to a particular journal that you need, ask whether it will order the article for you through an interlibrary loan system. This service is usually free, but you will probably have to wait two to three weeks before you receive the article.

Use newspaper indexes and databases.

Many newspapers have indexes that catalog their articles. The *New York Times Index* and the *Wall Street Journal Index,* for example, list bibliographical information for articles that appear daily in those newspapers. *Data Times* and *Lexus/Nexus* are bibliographic databases that index hundreds of newspapers including some that are printed in other countries. Figure 7.6 is an example of a citation that was printed for a search from *Lexus/Nexus* database for a student who was doing a paper on smoking among college students. The key words used for this search were "cigarettes" and "college students."

Research skills, like writing skills, improve with practice. The more you work in the library, the easier you will find it to locate information. As the quality of your information improves, so does the quality of your papers and your education. Give yourself the time and practice to develop solid research skills.

Figure 7.6   *Sample Citation from* Lexus/Nexus

Level 1–33 of 788 stories
Copyright 1996 The *San Diego Union Tribune*
The *San Diego Union Tribune*
April 28, 1996, Sunday
SELECTION: OPINION; Ed. 1, 2; pg 6-3.
LENGTH: 1026 words
HEADLINE: The battle against underage drinking
BYLINE: JAY T. DURING and ROBERT HANS

(This citation tells you that the title of the article is "The Battle Against Underage Driving"; the authors are J. During and R. Hans; and it appeared in the April 28, 1996 edition of the *San Diego Union Tribune.*) The search brought up 788 articles in response to the key words "cigarettes" and "college students." The articles are listed chronologically, the most recent ones appearing first.

The text of the article is presented by *Lexus/Nexus,* and the key words are highlighted in the text whenever they appear. This article consists of 1026 words, and it was article number 33 offered by the database in response to this search.

The full text of the article is printed and indicates that people who begin using alcohol during the critical 13–16-year-old period are more likely to be current users of alcohol, cigarettes, or marijuana than those who begin drinking when they are older.

A C T I V I T Y

Using the Card or Electronic Catalog

Go to your library and fill in the following requested information:

1. Look in the title section of the card catalog or check the electronic catalog and locate a book entitled *The Myth of Mental Illness*.

    Author (last name, first name, and middle initial): _____

    _____

    Year and city of publication: _____

    Name of publisher: _____

    Number of pages: _____

    Does the book have a bibliography or illustrations? _____

    Under what subject headings is this book listed? _____

    _____

2. In the author's section of the card catalog, look up two books by Ernest Hemingway. Write down the bibliographical information required for a book.

Book 1	Book 2
Author:	Author:
Year of publication:	Year of publication:
Title of book:	Title of book:
City of publication:	City of publication:
Name of publisher:	Name of publisher:

A C T I V I T Y

Researching a Topic with the Card or Electronic Catalog

Choose a topic. If you have a paper due this semester, use the topic for that paper. Otherwise, choose one of the following topics: the Olympics, women's fashions, alcohol, disarmament, or the social security system.

1. Check the *Library of Congress Subject Headings* (or the list of subject headings for your electronic catalog) for three approved headings that will give you information about your subject. Write them down.

Library of Congress Headings

_____

_____

_____

2. Look at the subject section of the card or electronic catalog, and write down the following bibliographical information for two books about your subject:

Author: (last name, first initial, and middle initial)

Book 1   Book 2

_____   _____

Year of publication

Book 1   Book 2

_____   _____

Title of book

Book 1   Book 2

_____   _____

City of publication

Book 1   Book 2

_____   _____

Name of publisher

Book 1   Book 2

_____   _____

Call number

Book 1   Book 2

_____   _____

On what floor of the library would you find these books?

Book 1   Book 2

_____   _____

ACTIVITY

Researching a Topic with the Readers' Guide to Periodical Literature

Use the *Readers' Guide to Periodical Literature* to find an article on your topic. Write down the following information:

Subject heading: _____

Author if it is listed (last name, first name, and middle initial): _____

_____

Date of magazine (month, day, year, if listed): _____

Title of article: _____

_____

_____

Name of magazine: _____

_____

Volume number of magazine: _____

Page numbers of the article: _____

Does your library own the magazine? (Check the periodical holdings listing at the reference desk or periodical section.)

Yes _____   No _____

If your library has open stacks, write down the call number of the journal and find the journal. If your library does not have open stacks, fill out a call slip and get the journal.

Call number: _____

Is the journal bound together with other issues of the journal, or is it available as a single copy? Is it printed on paper or microfilm?

Bound   Yes _____   No _____

Single copy   Yes _____   No _____

Microfilm   Yes _____   No _____

Find the article and copy down the first sentence.

_____

_____

_____

_____

_____

_____

_____

ACTIVITY

Researching a Topic with Another Index or a Bibliographic Database

Use a periodical index other than the *Readers' Guide to Periodical Literature* (e.g., *Business Periodicals Index, Psychological Abstracts, Art Index, Historical Abstracts*) to find an article on your topic; write down the following information.

Title of index or database you used: _____

Author (last name, first initial, and middle initial): _____

_____

Year of publication: _____

Title of article: _____

_____

_____

Name of journal: _____

_____

Volume number (and issue number if listed): _____

Page numbers of article: _____

Does your library own the journal? (Check the periodical holdings list at the reference desk or in the periodicals section.) If your library does not own the journal, fill out an interlibrary loan request and staple it to this page.

Yes _____   No _____

If your library has open stacks, write down the call number and get the journal. If your library does not have open stacks, fill out a call slip and get the journal.

Call number: _____

Is the journal bound together with other issues of the journal, or is it available as a single copy? Is it printed on paper or microfilm?

Bound	Yes _____	No _____
Single copy	Yes _____	No _____
Microfilm	Yes _____	No _____

Find the article, and copy down the first sentence.

_____

_____

_____

_____

ACTIVITY

Researching a Topic with an Index or Database to Newspapers

Use The *New York Times Index,* The *Wall Street Journal Index,* or another newspaper index to find an article on your topic. Write down the following information:

Name and year of index used: _____

_____

Subject heading used: _____

Author (if listed): _____

Date of article: _____

Name of newspaper: _____

Title of article (if listed): _____

_____

_____

Section, page, and column of article: _____

Where would you find the article? Is it on paper or microfilm? _____

Location: _____

Paper	Yes _____	No _____
Microfilm	Yes _____	No _____

✍ REFLECTIONS FOR YOUR JOURNAL

1. Describe a topic or paper you enjoyed researching.
2. Write down the types of sources (e.g., dictionaries, books, indexes, journals, and so on) you would use in researching a term paper. Begin with sources for the most general material and progress to sources for more specialized information.
3. Write down any questions you have about your library. Where would you find the answers to these questions?
4. Do you study at the library? What would make your library a more attractive place to study?

Notes

1. P. Hinsenkamp, *How to Use Undergraduate Libraries for Academic Success.* Ridgefield, NJ: Xerographic Reproduction Center, 1991, p. 205.
2. Ibid., p. 214.

CHAPTER

8

PAPERS
Thinking and Writing Logically

■ CRITICAL THINKING AND THE PURPOSE OF WRITING ASSIGNMENTS

Do you have difficulty translating your thoughts into words? Do you try to avoid courses that require term papers? Do you encounter a "mental block" when you sit down to write a paper? Many students dread writing papers more than they dread taking exams. This is understandable. The writing process often results in feelings of frustration, and writing does require a lot of time and planning. Even professional writers often find it hard to get started, and once they are writing, they spend hours revising their work before it's ready for public view.

This chapter presents hints and techniques that will make the writing process less painful, but first a few words about the purpose of writing assignments that may help you to approach these tasks more enthusiastically. Papers, like exams, give your professor a means for evaluating how much you have learned. The primary purpose of writing assignments, however, is to help you learn about a topic and to teach you how to think, organize, and communicate your thoughts.

When you put ideas into your own words, when you analyze, criticize, summarize, and compare them, you become a critical thinker. Becoming actively involved with the ideas in this way helps you to remember and use them long after the course is over. That is the real reason that instructors assign papers. They want you to make the assigned material a part of yourself. They want you to evaluate critically the ideas that you encounter. They want you to develop your own ideas. They want you to learn how to research a topic and communicate about it.

Research and Communication

The ability to carry out research is one of the most useful skills you will learn in college. You will find that it helps you later in life, for instance, when you are aiming for a competitive job and need to find out more about the company that is about to interview you. You will use it as you advance in your career to keep up with the latest developments in your field. You will need it when you have to decide what type of car to buy, how to go about buying a house, or where to send your child to college.

The ability to communicate clearly is also one of the most important skills you can learn in college. You will find that you are called upon to communicate more often and at more advanced levels as you progress from your freshman year to your senior year at college. You will also find that virtually any career you might choose will require this skill. Written communication becomes particularly important if you want to rise into the managerial or executive ranks in business, but it is just as important if you wish to become a lawyer, a teacher, a psychologist, a writer, a researcher, or any type of administrator.

Once you have learned some basic rules about writing, the key to improving your writing skills is practice. Take the time to review your instructor's comments and suggestions when he or she returns your papers. Try to apply the instructor's suggestions to the next paper you write. Writing is a cumulative skill; each paper you write should help you to improve your skill for the next round.

Success in writing depends on practice.

Review instructor's feedback.

Computers and the Writing Process

A few words about the relationship between writing and computers are in order because so many students now use word processors as a major tool in writing. If you feel comfortable with computers, you may wish to do many of the activities in this chapter such as brainstorming, free-writing, creating an assignment page, and outlining directly on the computer. Or, if you prefer, you may complete those activities in the space provided in the chapter.

Many writing instructors are now holding their classes in computer laboratories rather than in conventional classrooms, and many colleges insist that students own or have access to a computer. If you are not familiar with word processors, it will be worthwhile to read Chapter 16 and complete the exercises on word processing. Then go to the library or to the computer laboratory and practice your skills on a computer. In addition to helping you succeed in college, computer skills have become a major asset in every nook and cranny of the work world.

If you hate writing, you may find, as other students have, that computers make writing enjoyable and exciting.[1] Because corrections and changes are so easy to make, you will feel free to try out new ideas. There is no longer such a thing as a mistake; you can keep making changes until your texts are perfect. You can add sentences, delete words, move paragraphs around, and check spelling, executing each action with a single command. You may rely on the computer's memory so that you are free to move back and forth in your work, focusing on ideas, organization, spelling, or revisions of different sections at various times. Because computers save so much time, you are more likely to experiment with new techniques. You can try free-writing, brainstorming, or heuristic aids to composition.[2] You can compare several drafts to see which organizational structure works best. Writing skills improve because you are more willing to "play" with your work and develop it.

■ SELECTING A TOPIC

The first step in writing a paper usually involves choosing a topic. Before you even tackle the topic, be sure that you understand the assignment. A lab report has different goals than a literary critique. A case study in social work uses a different format than a case study in political science. Professors in history expect different elements in a research paper than do professors in communications.

Identify the type of writing required.

If your instructor has given you written guidelines, read them carefully. If the instructions for the assignment are verbal, take down your professor's words carefully. Ask questions about anything that is not clear, and then review those notes before you choose your topic. If you are absent when an assignment is

Review the assignment.

given, make an appointment with your professor to find out firsthand about the assignment.

Choose an interesting topic.

When you choose a topic, choose one that interests you and one that you know something about. It is easier to motivate yourself to write if you are interested in your subject. You will also have a head start if you have some idea of where or how to approach your topic.

Topic Definition

Narrow topic down.

Once you have chosen a topic, you have to define it. This usually means narrowing it down. Most students make the mistake of choosing topics that are too broad, resulting in a paper that is superficial. You never get a chance to thoroughly discuss or evaluate the topic because you are covering too many bases. You do not have the opportunity to deal with your topic in depth because you are too busy describing all its parameters at a very general level.

Let us say, for example, that you have chosen to do a two-page paper on cars. The subject of cars is much too broad a topic for a two-page paper. Will you discuss types of cars? Production techniques for cars? Advertising for car sales? Environmental impact of cars? To produce an effective paper, you will have to narrow your topic down to one of these, but even they are likely to be too broad. Let us say you are interested in the environmental impact of cars. You will need to narrow your topic down even further. Will you examine fuel economy? Air pollution? Road construction? Encroachment on wilderness preserves? The outline in Figure 8.1 will give you examples of how you might narrow down your subject until you have a topic you can handle competently within the scope of your assignment.

Figure 8.1 *Sample Outline for Narrowing Down a Topic*

I. Cars
   A. Types
      1. Family
      2. Sports
      3. Four-wheel drive
      4. Van
   B. Effect on Lifestyle
      1. Method of commuting to work
      2. Types of vacations taken
      3. Number of cars owned
      4. Level of debt sustained
   C. Production Techniques
      1. Assembly-line production
      2. Multinational company structure
      3. Union participation
      4. Management restructuring
   D. Environmental Impact
      1. Improved fuel economy
      2. Reduced air pollution
      3. Necessity for road construction
      4. Destruction of wilderness preserves

Once you have defined your topic, check it with your professor. He or she will be able to tell you whether the topic is too broad or too narrow. If it is too narrow, you will not be able to find enough information to write a paper of the required length. If it is too broad, you will end up with a superficial paper in which you cannot demonstrate your analytical or critical skills and for which you will receive a poor grade. Your professor will also be able to tell you whether the topic you have chosen is too advanced for you to handle and whether you will be able to find information on it at your level of expertise. It is wise to have more than one idea about possible topics when you go to see your instructor. He or she may guide you as to which one will be easier to research or will result in a better paper. Choose one of the courses in which you are enrolled this semester that requires a paper. List three possible topics on which you might write that paper. Consult with your instructor about which of these topics would result in the best paper.

A C T I V I T Y

Narrowing Down a Topic

Choose one of the following topics and list five major subtopics that narrow it down. Then choose one of the subtopics you have identified and narrow it down again into four narrower topics that might be used for a shorter paper. If you have difficulty thinking of subcategories, try the brainstorming technique. Give yourself five minutes to list all words or phrases that come into your mind when you think about that topic. Do not evaluate the phrases, and do not worry about spelling or handwriting. Just write as much and as quickly as you can in the five minutes. When the time limit is up, go back and review your list. Cross off the words that are not appropriate. Recopy the ones that might be appropriate subtopics for a short paper.

1. Choose one of the following listed topics, cross out the other two, and list five major subtopics under your choice.

Sports   *Occupational Choices*   *Changing Sex Roles*

_____

_____

_____

_____

_____

2. Choose one of the five subtopics you identified, and narrow it down into four smaller subtopics suitable for a short paper. Use the brainstorming technique.

_____

_____

_____

_____

■ COLLECTING INFORMATION

Determine the purpose of your paper.

Once you have defined your topic, check with your instructor about the purpose of the paper. Usually he or she will tell you whether to describe something, explain it, prove something, convince your audience of a certain point of view, or inform your reader about a topic. Each of these assignments has a different purpose and will require different research and writing strategies.

Determine the type of information required.

Take notes on index cards.

The type of assignment will determine what type of information you will need. You may be using your own thoughts and experiences, others' experiences or opinions, assigned readings, or reference materials from the library. If you are doing a paper that requires sources other than your own experience, you will have to take notes from those sources and organize your material. Use three-by-five-inch index cards to take notes. Put one idea on each card. Number the cards so that related or supporting material for ideas follows the original ideas. You will later be able to shuffle these cards and rearrange them to help you organize your material. Look over your cards while you are doing the research so that you can think about the best ways to organize the information.

Use index cards for sources.

Record author name, year of publication, title, journal, volume number, page numbers, city and state of publication, publisher, and edition.

Keep a separate set of three-by-five-inch cards to use as source cards. If you are interviewing people to get information for your paper, write down each person's name, title, agency or business name, and the date. You will have to prepare a bibliography or a list of references for any research paper you write. Keeping track of the bibliographical information as you go along will save you a great deal of time in having to go back and track down a missing date of publication or the page numbers of an article. For each journal article, write down last name and first initial of the author, year of publication, title of the article, title of the journal, volume number of the journal, and page numbers. If you are using a book, you will need author's name, year of publication, title, city and state of publication, name of publisher, edition (if it has been reprinted more than once), and pages used. When it is time to type up your list of references, you will be able to arrange your bibliography cards in alphabetical order and type directly without having to recopy all that information or run to the library to track down missing information.

Give each source card a number.

As you write your paper, you will probably wish to quote or give credit to the authors whose works you are using. In order to cite these sources appropriately, you will need to know the source of the information on your note cards. Give each of your bibliography cards a code number. When you take notes from a book or article, on three-by-five-inch cards, you can put that code number on top of the corresponding information cards. Then as you write your paper from your note cards, you will automatically have the source of each idea, quotation, or statistic available without having to write down the bibliographical information on each note card.

Find a research library.

Where should you look for information about your topic? In order to research most of your college papers, you will need a research library. These may be found in colleges, universities, medical schools, or specialized libraries in large cities. Very few local libraries will have the reference materials or sources necessary for college-level research papers.

Check subject headings of card catalog.

Find the guide to subject headings.

The best advice is to go from the more general sources to the more specialized ones. Start out with an encyclopedia and get an overview of your topic. This will give you an idea of subtopics that you might look for in more specialized works. Check the card catalog under your subject heading for books on your topic. The appropriate subject headings are not necessarily obvious, and you may have to check several headings before you find books that zero in on your topic. Ask a reference librarian to help you locate the appropriate headings in the Library of Congress guide to subject headings. This is a

thesaurus to the subject section of the card catalog. When you find a book that looks promising, write down the author's name, the title, and the call number. The card catalogs of many research libraries are computerized so that you may actually be carrying out this part of your research on a computer screen rather than with a small wooden box.

Magazine, journal, and newspaper articles give you more specific and often more up-to-date information on a topic. If you will be including these sources for your paper, check indexes such as the *Readers' Guide to Periodical Literature,* the *Humanities Index,* and the *New York Times Index.* More specialized indexes also exist for fields such as psychology, biology, and so on. Ask a reference librarian to show you how to find, through these indexes, articles that relate to your topic. Your reference librarian may also be able to make a computer literature search for your paper. This service is available in some schools for advanced undergraduate papers. You must define your topic carefully, and the computer will then check a variety of appropriate indexes to locate books, articles, and dissertations about your topic.

Check journal indexes.

Try to use sources that are current. Books or articles more than fifteen years old may no longer be accurate. This is particularly true in fast-changing fields such as science or medicine; statements made about acquired immunodeficiency disease syndrome (AIDS) six months ago may no longer be accurate. It is also true in areas such as history and literature where new theories or discoveries change current views. There may be older classic material that you will wish to consult, for instance, Freud's original case description of Little Hans. Secondary evaluative literature, however, should be of a more contemporary nature.

Use current sources.

Begin your research as early as you can. This will give you the opportunity to order materials that your library doesn't own. Many college libraries are able to get you any published book or article free of charge through an interlibrary loan system, but the process can take up to three weeks. Give yourself time to gather the best possible materials. Beginning your research early will also allow you to use the materials your library has on hand before they have been checked out by everyone else in the class. If you have to change your topic or gather additional research to complete the paper, you will have time for it. The final advantage of an early start is that it allows you to think about your paper before you have to write it; this will result in a better paper. Your instructor might even be willing to look over the first version of the paper and return it with suggestions so that you can rewrite it for a better grade.

Begin research early.

■ ORGANIZING YOUR PAPER WITH AN ASSIGNMENT PAGE

Sitting down and planning a paper is often the most difficult part of writing. Some instructors recommend that you begin by generating a one-page assignment sheet that will guide your writing.[3] Figure 8.2 provides a sample assignment page.

As you begin to write your paper, refer back to the assignment page in Figure 8.2. Use it as a guide for your paper's organizational structure. You should also use it as a checklist to be certain that you have covered all aspects of the assignment. Many students receive poor grades on papers because they used only two bibliographical sources when an instructor asked for five or used books when the professor specified that the references should be journals. If the assignment calls for you to compare and contrast two stories, you may lose credit for half of the paper if you do only the comparison. If the assignment says that the paper must be typed, the instructor may not accept a handwritten copy, and you may be penalized for handing it in late if it has to be typed.

Use the assignment page to structure your paper.

Check the assignment page to be sure you have completed all aspects of the assignment.

Figure 8.2 *Example of an Assignment Page*

Mary Jane Doe
Freshman Seminar
Professor Starke

Assignment 1
Due: September 30
Suggested Length: Five pages

Description of Assignment

The scandals surrounding college athletes have tarnished the image of team sports. I will discuss the factors responsible for these problems and suggest solutions that might help the institutions and teams regain their integrity and original focus. I will use my own experiences along with newspaper or magazine articles to write a five-page paper that describes the problem, analyzes the causes and effects, and makes recommendations for change.

Audience

The audience will be college freshmen who are familiar with the problem through their readings and experiences as athletes or as spectators at sports events. I hope to show that competition should be reduced and that limits should be placed on the amount of money distributed to college teams.

Organization Strategies

I will begin with a description of the issues, by giving examples of abuse and by describing the magnitude of the problem. I will describe the effects of the abuses on athletes and on colleges. I will compare high school sports with college sports to show how levels of competition increase as fund-raising pressures become more important. I will then recommend guidelines for academic standards and fund-raising that should bring college athletics back as a respected part of the undergraduate experience.

Thesis Statement

I will try to convince my readers that current economic and psychological climates encourage colleges and universities to exploit athletes and to subvert academic standards in an attempt to produce winning teams. As long as college sports remain a key factor in fund-raising and publicity, team managers will knuckle under to strong pressures to win at any cost.

Sources of Information

My own knowledge and experience. Newspaper and magazine articles (with bibliographical references).

A C T I V I T Y

Creating an Assignment Page

This activity instructs you to put an assignment into your own words and to seek feedback from your instructor. You will then find out whether you have interpreted the assignment correctly. Create an assignment page for a paper that has been assigned in one of your courses. Show the page to your instructor and ask whether it fulfills the requirements for the assignment. Many students receive poor grades because they have misinterpreted an assignment. This activity is also a good way to practice your word-processing skills on the computer, but if you prefer, you may complete it on the typewriter.

- Key in a heading that gives your name, the course title, the instructor's name, the due date, and the suggested length for the paper. Then key in a description of the assignment.
- Consider your audience. Are you writing for the general public or for a specific group with special knowledge, background, and attitudes? What is your goal in addressing this audience? Will you inform them of a certain position? Will you try to influence their beliefs or attitudes? Will you try to change their behavior?
- What type of organizational strategy will you use? Will you compare and contrast? Will you use cause and effect? Will you present advantages and disadvantages?
- You might next consider the content of the assignment and the sources of information you will use. You may have to collect information through library research or personal interviews. You may be able to rely on your own experiences or on the information in your text.
- Finally, formulate a thesis statement that describes your goals and tells your reader the direction you will follow.

The example of an assignment page in Figure 8.2 incorporates these elements.

■ PREPARING TO WRITE

Give some thought to the time and place in which you will write. You should set aside time for writing when you are most alert and your concentration is at its best. Like your study area, your writing area should be organized with all the materials you need; it should be free of distractions; and it should allow you to work comfortably (e.g., good lighting, proper support for your back).

Schedule prime time.

Choose good writing area.

Stimulate Ideas Through Brainstorming or Free-Writing

If you are writing a paper from your own experience and need ideas to flesh out your topic, use the brainstorming or free-writing technique. Creative writing instructors often recommend brainstorming as a way to cope with the sudden blanks or the panic that many writers feel when they are confronted by an empty page and the pressure to write. During brainstorming, you sit down and write, as quickly as possible, everything and anything that comes to mind. Do not censor or evaluate this material, just write.

Brainstorm for ideas.

ACTIVITY

Generating Ideas Through Brainstorming or Free-Writing

1. This is another activity that works well on the computer, but it can also be done with paper and pen. Take an assigned topic for a one- or two-page paper or choose one of the topics that follow. Set aside ten minutes and use the brainstorming or free-writing technique to generate as many ideas as possible for your paper.

National health insurance
The high salaries of celebrities
Euthanasia (mercy killing)

_____

_____

_____

_____

_____

_____

_____

_____

2. When the ten minutes are up, go back over your writing and see what you can use in your paper. Eliminate some ideas and add others that occur to you while you are reviewing your notes. Organize these ideas into an outline so that related ideas follow each other. Use patterns such as cause and effect, classification, chronological order, and compare and contrast to help you organize your thoughts in a logical manner. If you are doing a lengthy research paper, go through your note cards and look for patterns. Arrange cards into piles that reflect the major categories of your paper. Then go through and arrange each pile into smaller subcategories. Place the categories and subcategories in order so that they follow a logical train of thought.

Take the ideas you generated in the preceding section of this activity and organize them into an outline in which related ideas follow each other logically.

_____

_____

_____

_____

_____

_____

_____

ACTIVITY

Generating Ideas with the Question Technique

An alternative technique to brainstorming that generates ideas to get you started writing is the question technique. Set aside five minutes and write as many questions as you can think of that relate to your topic. Again, do not criticize or censor the questions. Write all questions as they occur to you. After five minutes, review the questions you have written and make additions or deletions as appropriate.

Use the question technique with a topic assigned in one of your courses or choose one of the following subjects:

Abortion
The high salaries of corporate executives
The death penalty

_____

_____

_____

_____

_____

_____

_____

_____

_____

Did the brainstorming or the question technique work best for you in stimulating the flow of ideas? Explain why.

_____

_____

More ideas and activities for stimulating and organizing ideas are described in Chapter 16. You may find the activities "Using the Journalist's Shell" and "Using the Classical Shell" particularly helpful.

Free-writing is very similar to brainstorming, except that you choose a topic and write about it for ten minutes without stopping. The goal is also to stimulate the flow of thoughts into words. Write whatever comes into your mind about the topic. Do not stop to correct, criticize, or edit anything. If you draw a blank, just repeat the last word until a new idea comes along. Before you begin, if you are using a computer, turn down the brightness knob on your monitor. When you cannot see the words on the screen, you are less likely to be distracted from your train of thought. Here is an example of a free-writing exercise complete with all the typographical errors.

An Example of Free-Writing

The beginning of a paper is always the hardest point for me. I don't know what I want to say or where to start.I It is so tempting to just put off the whole thing, but I know that I have a deadline, and so I have to get this wtritten. I would like to write about vacation time when the stressis off and I don't have to be on a rigid timeschedule all of the time. I can read for pleasure or just lie on a beacch and soak yp the sun. I can stay up all night and not have to worry that I will be exhausted the next morning because I won't have to get up the next morning if I don't feel like it! I only have to make "difficult" decisions like whether to go sailing or windsurfing or snorkeling or just putter around the house enjoyuing the quiet and the freedom to b unproductive. This might be a good place to start pa paper on the benefits of escaping from stress. It certainly does wonders for the mind. I wonder what it does for the body? I am certainly in a better mood for a few weeks after I return from vacation. Daily irritations just seem to roll of my back. My body gets a break and I return ready to face work with new reserves of energy.

A list of ideas elicited by this free-writing episode might include the following:

I. Work Pressures
    A. Difficulties of writing
        1. Finding a starting point
        2. Procrastination
        3. Stress and pressure
            a. Deadlines

II. Vacations: Relief from Pressure
    A. No rigid time schedule
    B. No stress
    C. Preferred activities
        1. Basking on the beach
        2. Reading for pleasure
        3. Sailing
        4. Wind surfing
        5. Snorkeling
    D. Effects on—
        1. Body
        2. Mind
        3. Mood

■ FORMULATING A THESIS STATEMENT

Write thesis statement.

You are now ready to formulate a thesis statement. Look over the outline you generated in part 2 of the brainstorming exercise and check for patterns, trends, or relationships. Summarize your ideas into one clear, detailed sentence that defines the purpose of your paper. This is the sentence that will organize and control your paper. The rest of your paper will be dedicated to explaining, supporting, and defending this thesis statement. The following examples of thesis statements might be used for a short paper called The Changing Trends in Exercise Today:

- ■ An appropriate program of exercise can lead to a more satisfying lifestyle and to a healthy old age.
- ■ Exercise can lead to health problems if it is pursued to extremes.
- ■ The growing popularity of exercise reflects our culture's obsession with the "thin is beautiful" doctrine.

ACTIVITY

Writing a Thesis Statement

Look over the outline you generated in the preceding exercise, and write a thesis statement that might be appropriate for a two-page paper.

_____

_____

_____

_____

_____

_____

_____

_____

_____

_____

A thesis statement is not always easy to write. If one does not come forth after a review of your outline, try the brainstorming technique. Write all possible thesis statements that occur to you in a five-minute period. Then examine each statement to see how much of your outline it would include or exclude. Try to combine several of the thesis statements if you do not wish to eliminate any of your material. If you are still not sure about a statement, let it sit over night. Your brain will continue to work on the problem, and you may have some new insights on the next day.

Once you have chosen a thesis statement, you may have to revise your outline to support it. You may wish to discard some of your research or complete additional research to answer new questions. The complexity and specificity of your thesis statement will depend on the length of your paper and the type of paper you have been assigned. You may wish to check with your instructor as to whether your thesis statement is appropriate to the assignment.

Revise outline.

■ THE FIRST DRAFT

Now that you have your thesis statement and outline, you are ready to write your first draft. Check your professor's instructions for the assignment once again. Make sure that you have followed these instructions, and then begin with an introduction. Your introduction should include your thesis statement. Do not worry about being witty at this point. Do not worry about grammar, spelling, punctuation, or choice of words. Just get your ideas down on paper. Write as though you were telling a story to a friend. Follow your outline and put the ideas down in order. Explain each idea thoroughly, supporting it with examples, reasoning, quotations, or any other supportive material you may have. If new ideas occur to you as you are writing, jot them in the margin and

Read assignment again.

Do not edit, just write.

return to them later. Take breaks while you are writing. Never try to finish a major paper in one day.

■ THE SECOND DRAFT

Revise draft next day.

Supply transitions.

Be brief.

Let your draft sit overnight or for several days. Your mind will continue to work on it even if you are not consciously aware of it. You will return to the paper the next time with new perspectives and better judgment. A paper involves communicating information in a logical, effective manner. You may see patterns in the material; comment on them. Make comparisons and discriminations. You may see holes in your presentation that you did not notice the day before. Fill them in with additional information or transition sentences. You may notice repetitions or inappropriate phrases. Rewrite your material. Be as brief and concise as possible. Do not try to impress your instructor with the length of the paper by adding filler material. Your instructor will just write "redundant" or "repetitious" in the margin. Most professors do not judge quality by the pound. They will get bored, and they will downgrade a repetitious, lengthy paper for poor organization.

Check vocabulary.

Do not use fancy words unless you know what they mean and know how to use them. Misusing complicated words is much worse than using simple words correctly. Misused words obscure your meaning and make you seem pompous. Check your words in the dictionary if you have any doubts about their meaning.

Check grammar.

Check your grammar. Certain errors like run-on sentences, dangling participles, agreement between verbs and nouns, and misspellings should not occur in college-level work. Use the spellcheck feature of your word processor, but note that spellcheck will not flag words that are misused if they are correctly spelled. For example, if you are talking about the heroine in a novel and refer to her as the "heroin," spellcheck will not alert you to the error because "heroin," which refers to the illegal, addictive substance, is a properly spelled word. The statements in the activity, "Correcting Common Writing Errors," take a humorous look at grammatical errors that are frequently seen in students' papers. Find and correct the error in each of the sentences.

ACTIVITY

Correcting Common Writing Errors

The goal of this activity is to reinforce your ability to recognize common writing errors, label them, and make the appropriate corrections. After reading each statement, write a correct version of the sentence on the blank line that follows it.

1. Don't use no double negatives.

   _____

2. Make each pronoun agree with their antecedent.

   _____

3. Join clauses good, like a conjunction should.

   _____

4. About those sentence fragments.
_____

5. When dangling, watch participles.
_____

6. Verbs has to agree with their subject.
_____

7. Between you and I, case is important.
_____

8. Don't write run-on sentences they're hard to read.
_____

9. Don't use commas, that aren't needed.
_____

10. Try not to ever split infinitives.
_____

11. Be sure to use apostrophe's right.
_____

12. Proofread your writing to see if you any words out.
_____

13. Correct spelling iz esential.
_____

14. A preposition is a poor word to end a sentence with.
_____

15. If theirs too or moor weighs of spelling a word, bee sure ewe yews the rite won.
_____

16. begin each sentence with a capital and close with punctuation
_____

From *The Dial*, April/May, 1992, Volume 66, no. 7, p. 9. Tarrytown, NY: The Hackley School, Benedict Avenue, Tarrytown, NY 10591.[4]

■ FURTHER REVISIONS AND FINISHING TOUCHES

The best papers have gone through several drafts. Write, rewrite, and rewrite again. Give yourself two to three revisions and three to five days before completing the final copy of a major paper. Now is the time to check your content, organization, and style. Be aware that your writing style should be different from your speaking style. Slang expressions and contractions do not belong in formal written work. Be sure that you have an introduction and a conclusion or summary. Be sure that your ideas are clearly expressed. Explain, justify, and support your ideas even if you are not writing a research paper. Your instructor is interested in teaching you how to think. He or she does not want just your opinions, so include the foundation on which those opinions are based.

    Check to see whether your ideas are presented in the order you announced in your introduction. Be sure that you have included transition sentences that lead the reader from one idea and paragraph to the next. Be careful in citing the ideas or work of others. Be sure that you include the complete

Write, rewrite, and rewrite again.

Check style, organization, content, clarity, and support.

Check order and transition statements.

source in the proper format for each quotation or citation. Check to see that the ideas you have presented support your entire thesis statement. Arrange a mutual support system with a friend so that you read each other's papers and give each other feedback on items such as clarity and organization of ideas.

Quotations

Provide citations.

Take care with the citation of material from your research. If you quote an author's work word for word, use quotation marks before and after the excerpted material, and then give the author credit, either in parentheses following the quote, in a footnote at the bottom of the page, or in an endnote at the end of the paper. It is generally better to paraphrase an author's ideas rather than to string together long quotations with your brief transition sentences. Use quotations only when you feel that you cannot present the material in words that are different from the author's or when the exact words are important to the point you are making. If you are paraphrasing an author's ideas in your own words, you need not use quotation marks, but you should still give that author the proper credit for his or her ideas. If you present statistics, these should also be footnoted or cited appropriately.

Proofreading

Proofread with care.

Now it is time to proofread. Check your punctuation, your grammar, and your spelling. These will influence your grade even if your instructor is trying to ignore them. Most instructors, however, do not ignore them. They assign part of the grade for the mechanics of writing. After all, a college graduate is supposed to write like a college graduate. Your supervisors at work will expect this as well.

Proofread with a friend.

Proofread out loud.

The best way to proofread is to arrange with a friend to proofread each other's papers. Our eyes tend to skim over the mistakes we have made when we are rereading a paper. Choose a friend who spells and writes reasonably well. If you cannot find someone to read your paper for you, read it to yourself out loud. You are more likely to hear missing words and awkward grammatical constructions. Keep a dictionary by your side and check your spelling. The list shown in Figure 8.3 includes errors that are constantly found even in seniors' papers. These errors should not occur in college-level writing.

Calvin and Hobbes © 1988. B. Watterson. Distributed by Universal Press Syndicate. Reprinted with permission. All rights reserved.

Figure 8.3   *Common Errors in Grammar*

It's means "it is." ("*It's* going to rain.")
Its is the possessive pronoun for an object. ("The dog lost *its* leash.")
Its' does not exist in the English language.

There refers to a location. ("Meet me over *there*.")
Their is the plural form of the possessive pronoun. ("The players won *their* second match.")
They're means "they are." ("*They're* going to a movie tonight.")

Your is a possessive pronoun. ("Don't forget *your* hat.")
You're is a contraction for "you are." ("*You're* a real pain.")

To is used in two ways.
    It directs you to a location. ("I am going *to* school.")
    It precedes a verb. ("I want *to* play.")
Too is used in two ways.
    It means "also." ("I am coming, *too*.")
    It is an adverb. ("I have *too* much money.")
Two is the number that comes after one. ("*One* o'clock, *two* o'clock, *three* o'clock, rock!")

Effect (as a verb) means to bring about. ("His greed *effected* the murder.")
Affect (as a verb) means to have an influence on something. ("The murder *affected* his future tremendously.")

Effect (as a noun) means that something has been influenced. ("The murder had a tremendous *effect* on him.")
Affect (as a noun) is used by psychologists to mean an emotion. ("He showed no *affect* even at his mother's funeral.")

Everyone, anyone, and *no one* are indefinite pronouns that call for a singular verb. ("*Everyone* has HIS or HER own opinion." However, "Everyone has *their* own opinion" is *incorrect*.)

Receive is spelled with the *e* first: *i* before *e* except after *c* and in *neighbor, weird,* and *weigh.*

Develop has no *e* on the end.

Environment and *government* each have an *n* in the middle.

Certain words form the plural by dropping *on* and adding *a.*
Criterion and *phenomenon* become *criteria* and *phenomena* when they are plural.

Type your paper.

Almost all college instructors require that papers be typed. You will find that the same standard applies in the business world, and you may not have your own secretary when you are first starting out. Even if your professor does not require a typed manuscript, you are likely to find that your grade is better when your paper presents a neat, professional appearance. It is a good idea to number your pages and type your last name at the top of each page in case your pages should become separated.

Include a title page.

Keep a copy.

Give your paper a title page that includes your name, the course title, your instructor's name, the date, and the title of your paper. Put your paper in a cover, or at least staple the pages together so that your instructor has all the pages in the proper order when he or she is ready to read your paper. Make a copy of your paper, and keep it in case your instructor loses it.

■ ACADEMIC INTEGRITY, CITATIONS, AND REFERENCES

Do not hand in a paper that someone else has written.

A few words about honesty and plagiarism are in order at this point. It is dishonest to hand in a paper that you have not written. If you are caught, and it is likely that you will be caught, you may fail the course in question, and a letter describing this instance of cheating may be placed in your permanent file at the college. In certain institutions, you may also be expelled from the school. Review your college's policies regarding academic misconduct.

Do not use the same paper or research for two courses.

Most professors also consider it unethical to use a paper you have written for one course over again in another course. If you did this, you would be receiving credit twice for work you did only once, and you would not be learning anything new the second time. Ask permission from your instructor before you use substantial portions of research or writing you have done for another course. Your professor may allow you to do this if you will be expanding or elaborating on your former work enough to earn credit for your work in the current course.

Do not plagiarize.

It is illegal to use another author's ideas, opinions, words, or statistics without giving credit to that author. This practice is called plagiarism, and it can result in sanctions as serious as a failing grade in the course, dismissal from the college, loss of one's job, and imposition of substantial fines by a court of law. A review of your school's policies on plagiarism will convince you that this is a serious offense.

Choose a citation format.

Ask your professor about his or her preferred style for citations. There are several accepted formats for doing this. If your professor has no preference, use the simplest format, as shown in Figure 8.4. This format, endorsed by the *Publication Manual of the American Psychological Association*, includes the author's last name, the year of publication, and the page number of the citation. This information is presented in parentheses in the text of your paper immediately following the citation. You need not include any footnotes nor endnotes, but be sure that the complete bibliographical information appears in your list of references at the end of your paper.

Choose a bibliography format.

If you have used sources other than your own inspiration in researching or writing your paper, these must be listed on a separate page of references at the end of your paper. As there are several acceptable formats for bibliographical listing, ask your instructor which format he or she prefers. In the event that your professor has no preference, use the format presented in Figure 8.4. This format is endorsed by the *Publication Manual of the American Psychological Association*. The fourth edition of this volume was published in 1994, in Washington, DC, by the American Psychological Association. Another popular format is presented in the *MLA Handbook for Writers of Research Papers, Theses, and Dissertations*, 4th ed., published in 1995 in New York by the Modern Language Association. Finally, K. L. Turabian's *A Manual for Writers*, 5th ed., published by

Figure 8.4   *Examples of Citations and References*

1. A direct quote requires quotations marks. After typing the quotation, give credit to the authors in parentheses by listing their names, the year of publication of the work, and the page number of the quote.

   "College students today are more optimistic about career opportunities after graduation" (Smith & Jones, 1997, p. 15).

2. A paraphrase does not require quotation marks, but you must still cite the author and the source.

   Research shows that today's college students believe they will easily find jobs after they graduate from college (Smith & Jones, 1997, p. 15).

3. The following is a bibliographical reference for a journal article. If the quotation or paraphrase you used comes from an article by Smith and Jones, this complete reference should appear in your bibliography at the end of your paper.

   Smith, R. M., & Jones, A. M. (1997). Attitudinal trends in the college class of 1956. *Journal of Higher Education, 14,* 177–81.

4. The following example is a bibliographical reference for a book. If the quotation or paraphrase you used in your paper comes from a book by Smith and Jones, then this complete reference should appear in your bibliography.

   Smith, R. M., & Jones, A. M. (1997). *Current trends in higher education* (pp. 177–181). Upper Saddle River, NJ: Prentice-Hall.

the University of Chicago Press in 1987 is an old classic in the field of writing manuals. Figure 8.4 gives several examples of references and citations.

✍ REFLECTIONS FOR YOUR JOURNAL

1. Evaluate your writing skills. What are your strengths and weaknesses?
2. If you have difficulty writing, which of the strategies suggested in this chapter might be most helpful to you?
3. What type of writing do you enjoy most (e.g., fiction, correspondence, personal experience, lab report, research assignment, and so on)?
4. How important do you think your writing ability will be to your success in the future?
5. Write about an experience that has affected you deeply. Describe how writing helps you to understand what you are thinking or feeling.

Notes

1. T. Hughes, "Word Processing: Changes in the Classroom, Changes in the Writer," *CSSEDC Quarterly* 10 (1988), 3:2–3.
2. W. W. Wresch, "Computers and Composition Instruction: An Update," *College English* 45 (1988), 8:794–799.
3. H. M. Smith and M. L. Kennedy, *Word Processing for College Writers.* Englewood Cliffs, NJ: Prentice-Hall, 1989.
4. *The Dial,* April/May, 1992, Volume 66, no. 7, p. 9. Tarrytown, NY: The Hackley School.

CHAPTER 9

RELATIONSHIPS

■ PERSONAL CHANGE

As you enter college, you will find that your relationships with others change. You may not see as much of your old friends as they go off to different schools or begin careers instead of continuing with their educations. You now may be living in a dormitory or in an apartment with roommates rather than with your family. If you continue to live at home, you may find that your relationships with family members change as you mature and take on new responsibilities. If you are returning to college after some years in the workforce or as a homemaker, you may find that your new perspectives and the demands of course work lead to changes in your relationships with family and friends.

■ COMMUNICATION AND CONFLICT RESOLUTION

These changes in relationships are important and exciting, but all changes require some adjustment. Now that you are taking on new roles and responsibilities, you will have to cope with more varied interpersonal situations on your own. If you are going to get what you need from your college years, you will have to learn to communicate effectively with professors, administrators, classmates, roommates, and friends. Increasing pressure from the added workload of college may also mean that you may have to develop better communication skills to resolve stresses with your spouse, children, parents, or other family members. You will need to polish your conflict resolution skills because differences of opinion are a natural product of many interpersonal situations.

Listening

One of the basic components of communication and conflict resolution involves listening. In order to communicate effectively, you must first understand what the other person is saying. To keep emotions on an even keel, you must also reassure the other person that you have heard what he or she is trying to say. Many people fail to really hear what others say because they are too concerned with making or defending their own points. If you are silently rehearsing what you will say while another person is talking, you will miss large portions of the communication. The other person is also likely to feel that you are not really listening to him and do not care about his point of view.

If you are guilty of "selective listening," you will hear only those parts of the message that confirm your own views. If you are afraid to change, you will block out those aspects of the communication that do not agree with

136

ACTIVITY

Listening and Paraphrasing

Break into pairs and choose one of the following topics. Decide which of you will be the listener first. The speaker will express his or her thoughts on the subject in four or five sentences. The listener will restate the speaker's ideas and feelings and will then ask the speaker if he or she is satisfied with the paraphrasing. Is it accurate and complete? If it is not, the speaker will correct the restatement. Then switch roles so that the speaker becomes the listener, choose another topic, and repeat the exercise.

Some suggested topics are:

Abortion

Death penalty

Minimum age for alcohol consumption

Military draft

Euthanasia

your position. If your main goal is defending yourself, you will not be able to consider the other person's points. If your major objective in listening is to evaluate others, you will make judgments before you have time to really understand their point of view. Perhaps the most difficult part of this is that you may be unconscious of your reactions.

One way to be sure that you are hearing accurately and to show your partner that you are really listening is to restate what the other person has said and to confirm your interpretation with him or her. It is often helpful to do this when you are bogged down in an argument with another person. If you each restate the other's view before responding, you will be more likely to promote accurate communication. This is also an excellent way to reassure each other that you are genuinely trying to understand both points of view. The "Listening and Paraphrasing" activity will allow you to practice effective listening skills. When you are communicating, try to follow the guidelines shown in Figure 9.1.

Figure 9.1   *Strategies for Effective Listening and Conflict Resolution*

- ■ Face each other.
- ■ Make eye contact.
- ■ Listen while the other person is speaking.
- ■ Do not prepare your response while the other person is speaking.
- ■ Take a moment to consider what was said and your reaction to it before you respond.
- ■ Restate the speaker's ideas and feelings in your own words.
- ■ Ask the speaker whether your restatement is complete and accurate.

■ EXPRESSING YOUR IDEAS WITHOUT ALIENATING OTHERS

Listening constitutes one-half of the communication process. Expressing your ideas and feelings makes up the other half. If you are going to get what you need from your college experience, you will have to learn to communicate your thoughts. Assertion involves the appropriate sharing of thoughts and feelings with others. If you communicate your needs and emotions to other people without putting those people down, then you will feel good and your relationships will flourish.

If you nonassertively keep your needs and feelings to yourself, then you may become hurt or angry, and others may lose respect for you. On the other hand, if you become aggressive and abuse others or force your ideas on them, you may find yourself facing interpersonal problems. People will become angry and avoid you. The goal is to communicate your needs and feelings appropriately without abusing others or depriving them of their rights.

Aggressive, Nonassertive, and Assertive Behavior

As an example of the different ways you can react to any set of circumstances, consider the following situation. A customer in a restaurant orders a steak and requests that it be prepared rare. When the steak arrives well done, the customer may make one of the following responses:

1. *Aggressive:* The customer rants and raves at the waiter, accuses him of negligence, refuses to leave a tip, and threatens to never patronize the restaurant again.
   Result: The customer's needs are met, but the waiter feels abused, and the other members of the customer's party may feel embarrassed.

2. *Nonassertive:* The customer eats the steak and says nothing about the poor service. She then feels angry about paying for a meal that she did not enjoy. She becomes angry at herself for being a "wimp," and other members of her party may also lose respect for her.
   Result: The customer feels frustrated and loses respect.

3. *Appropriately assertive:* The customer politely explains to the waiter that the steak was not prepared according to her instructions, and she requests a substitution. She then enjoys her meal and leaves the waiter an appropriate tip for good service.
   Result: The customer's rights and the waiter's dignity and tip are preserved.

In general, nonassertive behavior (example 2) is emotionally dishonest. The person denies her true needs and feelings. She does not stand up for her rights and allows people to take advantage of her. Other people may feel sorry for her, they may get angry at her, and they may even become disgusted with her spineless behavior. Her resentment may result in emotional outbursts if she has been pushed over the brink by a relatively minor incident. This outburst does not make sense to the other people involved because the issue that triggers it might seem so trivial. This resentment and these temper outbursts may eventually jeopardize relationships with others.

Aggressive behavior (example 1) is inappropriately honest and direct. The aggressive customer may be rude and hurt others by blatantly criticizing and intimidating them. She gets her way by trampling over others' rights and feelings. In other areas of life, the aggressive person may often engage in verbally or physically abusive behavior by yelling at others, belittling them through the

ACTIVITY

Differentiating among Assertive, Aggressive, and Nonassertive Behaviors

This activity will help you to differentiate among appropriately assertive, aggressive, and nonassertive behaviors. Read each situation and classify the response as *assertive* (+), *aggressive* (−), or *nonassertive* (*N*). Compare your responses with the answers printed on page 160.

Situation	Response	+, −, or *N*
1. A friend has asked you for the second time in a week to babysit for her child while she runs errands. You have no children of your own and respond,	You're taking advantage of me and I won't stand for it! It's your responsibility to look after your own child.	_____
2. An attendant at a gas station you frequently stop at for gas neglected to replace your gas cap. You notice this and return to inquire about it and you say,	One of you guys forgot to put my gas cap back on! I want it found now or you'll buy me a new one.	_____
3. You'd like a raise and say,	Do you think that, ah, you could see your way clear to giving me a raise?	_____
4. Someone asks for a ride home and it is inconvenient because you're late, and have a few errands, and the drive will take you out of your way. You say,	I am pressed for time today and can take you to a convenient bus stop, but I won't be able to take you home.	_____
5. A student enjoyed the teacher's class and says,	You make the material interesting. I like the way you teach the class.	_____
6. A committee meeting is being established. The time is convenient for other people but not for you. The time is set when it will be next to impossible for you to attend regularly. When asked about the time, you say,	Well, I guess it's OK. I'm not going to be able to attend very much but it fits everyone else's schedule.	_____
7. In a conversation, a man suddenly says, "What do you women libbers want anyway?" The woman responds,	Fairness and equality.	_____
8. You've been talking for a while with a friend on the telephone. You would like to end the conversation and you say,	I'm terribly sorry but my supper's burning, and I have to get off the phone. I hope you don't mind.	_____
9. At a meeting one person often interrupts you when you're speaking. You say,	Excuse me. I would like to finish my statement.	_____
10. You are in a hard-sell camera store, and you have been pressured to purchase an item. You say,	Well, OK, I guess that's pretty much what I was looking for. Yes, I suppose I'll get it.	_____
11. A good friend calls and tells you she desperately needs you to canvass the street for a charity. You don't want to do it and say,	Oh gee, Fran, I just know that Jerry will be mad at me if I say "yes." He says I'm always getting involved in too many things. You know how Jerry is about things like this.	_____
12. You are at a meeting of seven men and one woman. At the beginning of the meeting, the chairman asks you to be the secretary. You respond,	No, I'm sick and tired of being the secretary just because I'm the only woman in the group.	_____

Situation	**Response**	**+, −, or N**
13. A man asks you for a date. You've dated him once before and you're not interested in dating him again. You respond,	Oh, I'm really so busy this week that I don't think I will have time to see you this Saturday night.	_____
14. The local library calls and asks you to return a book which you never checked out. You respond,	What are you talking about? You people better get your records straight—I never had that book and don't you try to make me pay for it.	_____
15. You are in a line at the store. Someone behind you has one item and asks to get in front of you. You say,	I realize that you don't want to wait in line, but I was here first and I really would like to get out of here.	_____
16. A parent is talking with a married child on the telephone and would like the child to come for a visit. When the child politely refuses, the parent says,	You're never available when I need you. All you ever think about is yourself.	_____
17. Plans to vacation together are abruptly changed by a friend and reported to you on the phone. You respond,	Wow, this has really taken me by surprise. I'd like to call you back after I've had some time to digest what's happened.	_____
18. Your roommate habitually leaves the room a mess. You say,	You're a mess and our room is a mess.	_____
19. Your husband wants to watch a football game on TV. There is something else that you'd like to watch. You say,	Well, ah honey, go ahead and watch the game. I guess I could do some ironing.	_____
20. It is your turn to clean the apartment, which you have neglected to do several times in the last month. In a very calm tone of voice your roommate asks you to clean up the apartment. You say,	Would you get off my back!	_____
21. An acquaintance has asked to borrow your car for the evening. You say,	Are you crazy! I don't lend my car to anyone.	_____
22. A loud stereo upstairs is disturbing you. You telephone and say,	Hello, I live downstairs. Your stereo is loud and is bothering me. Would you please turn it down.	_____
23. A friend often borrows small amounts of money and does not return it unless asked. She again asks for a small loan which you'd rather not give her. You say,	I only have enough money to pay for my own lunch today.	_____
24. A neighbor has been constantly borrowing your vacuum cleaner. The last time, she broke it. When she asked for it again, you reply,	I'm sorry, but I don't want to loan my sweeper anymore. The last time I loaned it to you it was returned broken.	_____
25. Your mate wants to go out for a late night snack. You're too tired to go out and say,	I really don't feel like going out tonight. I'm too tired. But I'll go with you and watch you eat.	_____

use of sarcasm, or even using physical force against them. The aggressive person may often feel superior or righteous while in the midst of a temper outburst, but she then feels guilty or regretful about her behavior afterwards. She may jeopardize relationships with others by hurting and humiliating them. People will often be angry at her; they will avoid her or seek revenge for their humiliation.

Assertive behavior (example 3) is emotionally honest. The assertive person expresses her true feelings. She respects herself and demonstrates that respect by standing up for her rights. She also respects others and does not put them down in order to make herself look better. The assertive person gets what she wants more often than the nonassertive person, yet she is not as likely to anger people as the aggressive person. Other people involved in relationships with her usually value her and respect her opinions.

Assertive behavior does involve risks, and you may not wish to be assertive in all situations. For example, it may not be in your interest to tell your boss that he is running the company the wrong way, especially if he is someone who does not take kindly to criticism. If you criticize him, you may risk losing your job. On the other hand, if the situation at work really bothers you and you bottle up your emotions, you will end up feeling angry and resentful. You may eventually blow up at your boss unintentionally and really give him a piece of your mind. In that case you will definitely lose your job. If you can afford the possibility of a job change, it may be worthwhile to make some tactful suggestions for change before events reach the boiling point. If you make constructive suggestions while you are in control of your emotions, you might find yourself with improved working conditions and a raise in pay!

The same situation holds true in personal relationships. You may not wish to refuse your roommate when she asks to borrow your new sweater. On the other hand, if she continually borrows your clothes and returns them in poor condition or fails to return them at all, you will eventually resent her behavior. You will become angry at yourself and at her, and your relationship will suffer even though you give in to her requests. If you assertively tell her how much it disturbs you when your things are not returned and mention that you will only allow her to borrow them if they are returned in good condition, she may change her behavior. In that case, your friendship can continue on a basis of mutual respect.

■ EFFECTIVE COMMUNICATION AND CONFLICT RESOLUTION

Issues involving assertiveness come up frequently. These issues may arise when friends pressure you to have another drink or to take a drug when you do not wish to. They may arise when you are urged to party but feel you should be studying for an important exam the next day. They may come up when your spouse or partner wants to have sex, but you do not wish to. These issues may arise when your mother insists that you eat another piece of the cake that she baked even though she knows you have been dieting strenuously for the past three weeks. They may come up when your spouse buys a new set of golf clubs with the money you have been saving for the children's orthodontist. They may arise when your roommates continuously "borrow" all the food that you buy or when your children blast the stereo while you are trying to study.

"I" Statements versus "You" Statements

The preceding statements describe situations in which emotions run high and in which it is easy for people to lose their tempers. One strategy for keeping

ACTIVITY

Using Effective Communication to Solve Disputes

This activity will give you practice in finding solutions to problems and in expressing yourself assertively. Take an index card and write down at least three situations that raise issues of assertiveness for you. Pass those cards to your instructor. (Do not put your name on the card. This part of the activity is *anonymous*.) Three volunteers will list all of these areas on the board for the class.

Break down into small discussion groups of four students. Your instructor will then assign two problem areas from the list to each of the small groups. Discuss the situations and brainstorm possible solutions to the problem. Then have two of the group members role-play the situation; each of you will take a part and act out the situation and the solution. Each skit should last no more than one or two minutes. Coach each other about the script, the body language, the tone of voice, the eye contact, and so on, so that your skit is as effective as possible. When you have finished with the first problem situation, act out the second one, giving the other two members of the group a chance to star in this skit. Then regroup as a class, and each of the pairs will present its skit. After each skit, have your fellow class members offer suggested improvements or alternate solutions to the problem. Here is a sample script from a sexual situation in which the woman wishes to use a condom and the man does not. She is responding assertively in a sexual situation.

He: I know I don't have any diseases; I haven't had sex with anyone in six months.

She: Thanks for telling me. As far as I know, I am disease-free, too. But I would still like to use a condom since either of us could have an infection and not know it.

He: I don't have any condoms and I don't want to go out and get any.

She: Well, I just happen to have some condoms with me. What color do you like best?

He: It will interrupt sex.

She: Let me put it on for you. You'll love it.[1]

things under control while working toward a constructive solution is to use "I" language rather than "you" language. If you say to someone, "You are inconsiderate," that person is likely to respond, "No, I'm not. You're the inconsiderate one!" The two of you may then get into an argument in which voices keep rising, tempers are lost, and nothing useful is accomplished. If, on the other hand, you say, "I am hurt," and you explain exactly what it is that the other person does that hurts you, that person is more likely to listen to you without becoming defensive.

"You" statements make the other person feel defensive because they criticize, judge, and label. They force the person to come back with a rebuttal to your accusation, and they usually lead to an argument. "I" statements, on the other hand, tell the other person how his or her behavior makes you feel. "I" statements express your feelings, opinions, observations, and goals or desires without putting the other person down. Observe how the following "you" statements can be turned into "I" statements. Imagine someone saying first one and then the other to you. Do you feel less defensive and angry in response to the "I" statement?

"You" statement	"I" statement
You are crazy.	I don't understand.
You make me furious.	I feel angry.
You don't listen to me.	I feel so frustrated.
You don't help me.	I feel overwhelmed.

When you use "I" statements, the other person is more likely to listen to you and to understand your position. The other person is also more likely to sympathize with you, because he or she is not using so much energy in self-defense. Try to use "I" language wherever possible in the activity, "Using Effective Communication to Solve Disputes," and in any confrontations that you face.

■ UNDERSTANDING AND AVOIDING RAPE

You may wonder why a section on rape is included in a chapter on relating to others. Relations between the sexes have become a very sensitive personal and legal issue. They received explosive attention from the media when Professor Anita Hill brought charges of sexual harassment against Supreme Court Justice nominee Clarence Thomas, when William Kennedy Smith defended himself against rape charges in a highly publicized trial, when heavyweight boxing champion Mike Tyson was convicted of raping a beauty queen contestant, and when O.J. Simpson was tried for the murder of his wife. These events, along with an increasing number of lawsuits and charges filed against less famous individuals, have highlighted potential problems in relations between the sexes and emphasized society's willingness to prosecute and imprison men who force sexual attentions on women.

There has been a disturbing increase in a phenomenon called *acquaintance rape*. The U.S. Department of Justice estimates that 8 percent of women (11 percent of black women) will be raped in their lifetimes. Counselors in rape crisis centers estimate even higher figures, and lesser forms of sexual aggression such as attempted rape or forced sexual liberties occur even more often.[2] This section is presented so that you will recognize the tragic consequences that rape can have. It will also suggest ways that you can avoid becoming a rape victim or perpetrator.

Rape is defined as forced sexual intercourse no matter what the circumstances and regardless of whether the assault is committed by a stranger or by an acquaintance. Physical force, threats, and fear are used to overpower and control the victim.[3] Although the stereotype of a knife-wielding stranger jumping from the shadows to attack a woman still persists, the truth is that as many as 80 percent of rape victims know their assailant. Women are raped by neighbors, coworkers, relatives, store clerks or servicemen, and their dates.[4] (Although the FBI estimates that 10 percent of sexual assault victims are male, I will use the pronoun "she" in this section because most rape victims are female.)

In the years I have practiced as a therapist and a college professor, I have seen and heard of unfortunate cases in which women have been forced to drop out of college because they could not deal with the emotional trauma caused by a rape. There have also been an increasing number of cases in which young men have been suspended from college and have faced criminal proceedings because of sexual assaults. A 23-year-old Florida State University junior, for example, was sentenced to one year minus one day in prison in a date rape case that also involved two of his fraternity brothers. His date, a freshman, was unable to remain at school after the incident; she checked into a psychiatric hospital where she tried to kill herself.[5] Women are becoming more willing to file

Think of the six women closest to you.

Now guess which one will be raped this year.

One out of six college women will be sexually assaulted this year. But you can change the odds of it happening. Simply by trying to avoid situations that leave you or your friends vulnerable.

For starters, follow security measures. Don't prop residence hall doors open. Walk with a friend after dark. And be aware that date rape is a major problem on college campuses. With many of these rapes involving drinking.

Then share these facts with six of your friends. And maybe none of them will become another statistic.

© 1990 Rape Treatment Center, Santa Monica Hospital.

Printed courtesy of Rape Treatment Center, Santa Monica Medical Center.

charges in rape cases, and juries are becoming increasingly willing to convict offenders of criminal charges, even when the rapist is a college student or an athlete. As a result, rape can have unfortunate effects on the college careers of both the man and the woman involved.

Even in those cases in which the students involved were not forced to withdraw from college or go to jail, both victim and perpetrator still spent so much time and energy agonizing over the incident that they neglected their studies and found themselves failing courses.

Rape is an emotionally devastating crime that can have severe negative effects on students' social relationships whether or not there are physical injuries, and whether or not the attacker is a stranger. Some young women have come to fear all men and could not enter into a close relationship with any

ACTIVITY

Sex: A Decision for Two Scenario

The goal of this activity is to help you understand how a man and a woman can misunderstand and misinterpret each other's intentions and signals. It will also give you practice in analyzing a sexual situation so that you can give signals that clearly reflect your feelings and can correctly interpret the signals that your partner is sending. Break into small groups of four to six students. Try to balance the groups so that they include roughly similar numbers of men and women in each group. Read the scenario that follows and then use your group discussion to answer each point in the analysis that follows.

THE SCENARIO

8:00 P.M.

"Hurry up," urged Yvonne. "I thought you said Willie would meet us downstairs at 8:00 P.M." Jill, Yvonne's roommate replied, "Yeah, I know. Listen, I forgot to mention—but that guy you know from English is gonna come with us. You remember, he's a good friend of Willie's." Yvonne felt nervous suddenly. "You mean John? You know I think he's really cute. What do I say?" Jill answered, "Just act natural." Yvonne nodded, thinking the party was going to be really good with John there.

8:15

At the party, John was very attentive to Yvonne. She was thrilled. They started to dance. Yvonne knew she was a terrific dancer and she loved to dance, especially with such a cute guy as John. They spent about an hour together, alternating between talking and dancing. Yvonne had a few beers. She could feel her body get looser from the alcohol making her dancing, she felt, even better.

10:30

A slow song came on and John immediately pulled Yvonne close. Yvonne did not feel entirely comfortable dancing in this way but did not say anything. Instead, she put her hands on his chest in an attempt to keep their bodies from pressing too close. John was really enjoying himself. He had noticed Yvonne in English and thought she was attractive. He couldn't believe his luck. He felt he was acting so smooth and charming. He could sense she was responding to it. He decided to kiss Yvonne.

Yvonne was surprised at John's kiss. She was attracted to him, yet felt uncomfortable that he was kissing her in public. She didn't want him to think that she didn't like him so she just tilted her head down to end the kiss. John thought to himself, she really likes me. She is snuggling in after that kiss.

11:30

The dance floor became packed again as the music got fast. Yvonne felt slightly dizzy from the beer and wanted to get some air. John was distressed at the mood change. He felt very turned on and wanted to be alone with Yvonne. He said to her, "Want to go outside for some air? It's pretty stuffy in here." Yvonne looked around for Jill but didn't see her. She said to John, "OK, but just for a little while." She felt very nervous about being with him alone, but she felt silly feeling that way.

11:40

Once outside, John immediately put his arm around Yvonne and began kissing her, thinking how much she wanted to be kissed since she had been dancing so sexy all evening. Yvonne, still unsure about what she wanted, pulled away and began talking about how good her freshman year had been so far. John thought she was quite drunk and was very talkative when drunk. So he continued to kiss her. Yvonne again pulled away and stood up saying, "I think I should get going. Let's find Jill."

12:00

John followed Yvonne inside to the party. They had found that Jill had just left with Willie. John offered to walk Yvonne to her dorm thinking he could spend some more time with her alone. Not wanting to walk alone, Yvonne agreed.

12:30

Arriving at Yvonne's dark suite, John asked, "Aren't your roommates home?" Yvonne told him they were away. John thought to himself, Yvonne wants to be alone with me too. That's why she brought me back here. John said to Yvonne, "Let's go inside then. We don't have to say goodnight out here." Yvonne hesitated. She told John that she was very tired and wanted to go to sleep. John said, "I won't stay long," and took her key from her hand and opened the door. When Yvonne stood in the hall and said goodnight, John laughed. John walked past her into the living room saying, "Come sit for awhile." He motioned to the space next to him on the couch.

Yvonne sat down, still buzzed from the beer, and began to explain once again that she was tired and John should stay only for a few minutes. John, thinking how sexy Yvonne was, moved over and began to kiss her. He pushed her down onto the couch and began to unbutton her shirt. Yvonne did not respond to his kisses and pushed him away muttering, "No, stop." John ignored her, continuing to undress both of them thinking she really wanted it.

Yvonne stopped saying no and began to cry when John began to have intercourse with her.

THE ANALYSIS

Use your small group discussion to answer the following questions.

1. Identify three times during the scenario when John misinterpreted or ignored Yvonne's signals.

   a. _____

   b. _____

   c. _____

2. Identify three times during the scenario when Yvonne made herself more vulnerable.

   a. _____

   b. _____

   c. _____

3. List three things John could have done or said to make sure he was understanding Yvonne's signals.

   a. _____

   b. _____

   c. _____

4. List three things Yvonne could have done or said to make her real feelings clear to John.

   a. _____

   b. _____

   c. _____

5. Date rape often proceeds through three stages; identify behaviors in the scenario at each stage:

    a. Someone (usually the male) enters another's "personal space" in a public place (kissing, hand on breast or thigh, etc.).

    _____

    b. The partner does not assertively stop this intrusion and the aggressor assumes it is OK.

    _____

    c. The aggressor gets the couple to a secluded place where the rape takes place.

    _____

This exercise is reprinted from P. Brick et al., *Teaching Safe Sex*, 1989, Hackensack, NJ: Planned Parenthood of Greater Northern New Jersey. Reprinted, courtesy of Planned Parenthood of Greater Northern New Jersey.

male for many years after a rape experience. Other women have lost the ability to participate in any sexual relationship because of the painful memories this type of relationship elicits. Some young women have lost all sense of security and could not remain in their rooms alone without experiencing tremendous anxiety and panic attacks. They have lost confidence in their ability to judge people, and they cannot tell who is safe and who is dangerous. Many rape victims are unable to return to school, their jobs, or other activities because they are afraid of confronting their attacker.

A recent issue of *Annals of Internal Medicine* linked a host of gastrointestinal disorders to sexual or physical abuse. Doctors are often puzzled by their inability to find the cause of long-standing, chronic disorders in these cases. Researchers are uncovering more and more cases of Post-Traumatic Stress Disorder that occur years after a sexual assault.[6] Women who have been sexually assaulted often feel isolated because they are unable to tell anyone about the rape. They frequently feel that they will not be believed. (This is particularly true in cases of acquaintance rape.) They often experience shame and guilt even though they were not to blame for the attack. Some men have suffered from tremendous feelings of guilt after performing an act that they thought was all right at the time. The consequences of a rape can be tragic for both people who are involved.

If you believe that you need not be concerned about this subject because it could not happen to you, you are wrong! The Coalition Against Sexual Assault estimates that 15 to 25 percent of college-age women have been raped. Acquaintance rape occurs more frequently among college students, and it is more common among freshmen than any other group. Several studies have shown that the average age of both rapists and rape victims is 18. Women are most likely to be raped during the first 10 weeks of school.[7] Students who are new to college often mistakenly think that the campus is a safe place, that nothing bad can happen here; they think that other students share their ideology and tend to give them the benefit of the doubt. They may not be accustomed to the increased freedom that can lead to staying out later, consuming more alcohol, or inviting a date back to a dorm room late at night.

A survey of college women conducted by Carol Pritchard revealed that one-fourth of the women had been raped or were victims of an attempted rape; almost one-half of the women in the survey personally knew someone who had

Varsity Club, Drama Club,
Dean's List, Student Council,
Rapist

One out of 15 male college students reports committing rape or attempting
it. Most of the time, the victim is another student. And the rapist someone
you would least suspect.

The fact is, whenever a man forces a woman to have sex, it is rape. No
matter who he is, it is a criminal offense. And it should be reported.
Because a collection of varsity letters or club offices won't hold off a jail
sentence.

After all, rape isn't a privilege. It's a felony. Even for the biggest man on
campus.

Against her will is against the law.

©1990 Rape Treatment Center, Santa Monica Hospital.

Printed courtesy of Rape Treatment Center, Santa Monica Hospital Medical Center. The tagline "Against her will is against the law" is used with permission of Pi Kappa Phi fraternity.

been raped. One-fourth of the men surveyed admitted that they had used aggression in sexual situations with women. In this college survey, 84 percent of the rapists were dating partners or acquaintances![8] Another national survey found "that 54 percent of 6000 male and female students enrolled at 32 institutions in the country had been victims of rape or attempted rape, and that 57 percent of the incidents occurred on dates.[9] The number of incidents is probably even greater than figures suggest because many women feel too embarrassed to report rape, especially rape by someone they know. Studies have reported that four out of five sexual assaults at colleges and universities are committed by students. One in 12 college men responding to a college survey admitted committing acts that meet the legal definition of rape or attempted rape.[10]

ACTIVITY

Saying "No!" to Sex

The goal of this activity is to create and practice statements you would feel comfortable using when you do not wish to have sex. Break into groups of four and read over the statements. Place a check mark next to the three statements you would be most likely to use when turning down an invitation to sex. Do members of your small group agree on their top three choices? Write in additional statements on the blank lines that follow.

_____ No, I don't feel good about this.

_____ I'm not ready.

_____ No, I don't want it now.

_____ I have my period.

_____ I have herpes (or some other STD).

_____ I really don't want to. Please leave me alone.

_____ Leave me alone. Forget it.

_____ Look, I'm sorry. I'm just not ready yet.

_____ Sorry, but it's that time of month.

_____ Listen, I'm telling you right now to stop.

_____ Say "No!" and leave.

_____

_____

_____

People often have very different views or interpretations of the same situation. The subtle communications of tone and body language involved in an intimate encounter can easily be misread, and the result may be tragic for both parties. Life is much simpler if we are honest about our feelings and desires and if we state those feelings assertively and clearly. In the sexual arena, clear communication is particularly important because it is so easy to misread another's signals. Do not expect your partner to read your mind unless you tell him or her what it is you want. Do not assume that your partner wants one thing when your partner is telling you that he or she wants another.

People have the right to make their own decisions about what to do with their bodies. Respect your partner's right to make those decisions; assume that what your partner says is what he or she means. Figure 9.2 presents some guidelines that may help you avoid an unpleasant or even traumatic situation, the activity "Sex: A Decision for Two Scenario" highlights how easy it is for people to misunderstand each other's signals, and the activity "Saying 'No!' To Sex" will give you practice with statements that turn down an invitation to sex.

Figure 9.2 *Guidelines for Assertive Communication in Sexual Situations*

■ Know your sexual intentions. Be aware of what you want to do and what you do not want to do.

■ Decide, before you go out on a date, how far you want to go with your partner. Stop things (tactfully, but assertively) when you have reached those limits. Do not allow yourself to be coerced or bullied into going beyond your limits.

■ Communicate your intentions clearly. If you wish to say "No," say it firmly and clearly so that your partner knows you really mean it.

■ Respect your partner's right to say "No." If your request for sex is turned down, it does not mean that you are not a "real man" or a "real woman." It does not mean that you are not a worthwhile human being. It does not even mean that your partner does not like you.

■ You may *want* to have sex, but *you do not have to have sex.* You can control your actions.

■ You do not have the right to demand sex from another person if he or she does not wish to have sex, even if you have spent money on that person.

■ You are not obligated to have sex because someone has "wasted" time or money on you. A date is a situation in which two people go out to enjoy each other's company and get to know each other better. Sex is not part of the contract.

■ Be aware that flirting, dressing in a sexy way, or going to a man's room may be interpreted by some men as an agreement to intercourse. It is not necessarily wrong to do these things, but try to communicate your true intentions clearly so that you can avoid unpleasant misunderstandings.

■ Using drugs or alcohol may cloud your ability to read another person's messages accurately or it may hamper your ability to communicate your own intentions clearly. Fifty percent of the women who become rape victims and 75 percent of their attackers have been drinking before the rape occurs.[11] Know your limits and act responsibly. Getting drunk or high is no excuse for seriously hurting another person.

■ If you are raped, seek help at the college counseling center. The counselor will not blame you, embarrass you, or force you to report the incident if you do not wish to do so. He or she will help you come to terms with your own feelings so that the experience does not continue to haunt you.

■ When a woman is drunk or high on drugs, that does not mean she is willing to have sex. Having sexual intercourse with a woman after deliberately getting her drunk or high by forcing or tricking her into taking alcohol or drugs is considered rape. The laws in most states consider that sex with someone who is unconscious or too drunk to give permission *is also rape even if force is not used.* Being drunk oneself does not eliminate any of the responsibility for committing rape.[12]

■ SEXUAL HARASSMENT

Sexual harassment is another area in relations between the sexes that has been the subject of considerable media and legal exposure. Sexual harassment is defined as any form of unwanted sexual attention. An estimated 30 to 50 percent of female undergraduates will experience some from of sexual harassment in school, and 40 to 90 percent of women will experience it during their working lives.[13] The most common form of sexual harassment involves sexually suggestive comments, gestures, or looks (sexual innuendo, jokes about sex, derogatory comments, leering, whistling, insulting sounds), but it may also include unwelcome touching, kissing, or other sexual contact. This is a form of sexual discrimination, and it is illegal on the basis of federal and many state criminal and civil statutes.

According to the president of Cornell University, sexual harassment is "uncivil behavior . . . It expresses disrespect . . . It exploits and undermines relationships based on trust. It interferes with learning and productive work. In short, it is a breach of community."[14] Researchers have pointed out that sexual harassment is unpleasant and frightening, it decreases self esteem and self confidence, and it can result in feelings of depression and anxiety, difficulty in concentrating and physical problems caused by stress.[15] The activity "Checking Stereotypical Views of Male and Female Behavior" will help you recognize some of the stereotyping that can lead to sexual harassment or date rape.

The courts have certainly considered the effects of sexual harassment seriously as evidenced by a number of multimillion-dollar settlements awarded to individuals who were victims of harassment in corporate settings.[16, 17] Politicians have become sensitive to these issues after the nationally-televised senate hearings involving Professor Anita Hill's accusations against Supreme Court nominee Justice Clarence Thomas.

The armed forces have experienced considerable public scrutiny since the Tailhook scandal in which a number of women were sexually groped at a naval aviators' convention. That case resulted in the forced resignation of several high-ranking officers including Navy Secretary H. Lawrence Garrett, III. Another incident of sexual harassment resulted in the court martial of Captain Evertt Greene, "the highest-ranking Navy officer to be court-martialed since World War II," and a third case led to the demotion and forced early retirement of Rear Admiral Ralph Tindale, deputy commander of NATO forces in Spain and Portugal.[18, 19]

The academic community has also experienced the stigma of sexual harassment scandals. It is estimated that between 18 and 25 percent of students and staff have been victims of sexual harassment in the academic setting.[20] In a highly publicized case, an ethics committee at Cornell University criticized a prominent psychology professor known for his research on sleep and dozens of educational films and television specials. They recommended sanctions against him involving pay raises, honors, and assignments after allegations of sexual harassment were brought by four former students.[21]

In the light of all these legal problems and negative publicity, major corporations, institutions of higher education, and the armed services have rushed to adopt policies and sanctions regarding sexual harassment. Many organizations have instituted mandatory training programs in an attempt to sensitize staff members to the issues involved and prevent abuses. Whereas most victims of sexual harassment have been women, one case of male-on-male harassment was successfully brought against a supervisor by a male employee in Alabama, and another case resulted in a settlement against the Domino's Pizza chain as the result of sexual harassment of a male employee by a female supervisor.[22, 23]

ACTIVITY

Checking Stereotypical Views of Male and Female Behavior

1. Many tragic incidents of acquaintance rape and sexual harassment are the result of misunderstanding or misreading the other person's behavior. Our culture offers certain stereotypes, or false models, of male and female behavior that result in misleading beliefs about both sexes. The following questions are meant to help you explore your views about male and female behavior and to help you share those views with your classmates. Write *A* for "agree" next to the following statements with which you agree, and write *D* for "disagree" next to the statements with which you disagree.

_____ 1. The man should be the aggressor in a sexual situation. He should take control and initiate sexual activity.

_____ 2. The woman should be passive. She should wait for the man to make the moves.

_____ 3. If a man does not make a pass, the woman will feel hurt or rejected.

_____ 4. If a man does not make a pass, the woman will think that he is not a man.

_____ 5. If a woman protests against sex, she is just acting because she does not want the man to think that she is too easy. She really wants sex, even if she says "No."

_____ 6. If a woman says "No," she does not want to have sex with the man at that time.

_____ 7. If a woman does not flirt or dress in a sexy way, she will not be able to attract any men.

_____ 8. If a woman flirts or dresses in a sexy way, it is because she wants to have sex.

_____ 9. If a woman stops a man before the kissing gets too hot and heavy, he will think she is a prude and will lose interest in her.

_____ 10. If a woman allows the kissing to get serious, it is because she wants to have sex.

_____ 11. If a woman shows warmth and caring, it is because she wants to go to bed with the man.

_____ 12. If a woman shows warmth and caring, it is because she likes a man and wants to get to know him better.

_____ 13. If a woman goes to a man's room with him, it is because she wants to go to bed with him.

_____ 14. If a woman goes to a man's room with him, it is because she wants to be with him somewhere private where they can talk and get to know each other better. She does not necessarily want to sleep with him.

_____ 15. If a woman gives a man "mixed messages" (she says "No," but giggles, turns her eyes away, or otherwise indicates that she does not really mean "No"), it means that she wants to have sex but does not want the man to think that she is "easy" or sleeps around.

_____ 16. If a woman gives a man "mixed messages," it means that she does not want to hurt his feelings by rejecting him or does not want to risk ending their relationship by turning him off.

2. When you are finished with part 1 of this activity, write the numbers 1 through 16 on a slip of paper and copy your answers from part 1 next to the appropriate numbers. Do not write your name on the paper, but do write "male" or "female" to indicate whether you are a man or a woman. Hand the papers in to your instructor. Have your instructor tally, on the chalkboard, the number of agree and disagree answers for each question, in the male and female response categories.

IMPROVING COMMUNICATION BETWEEN MEN AND WOMEN

3. When you have completed part 2 of this activity, consider the following questions in a class discussion. Use the discussion as a learning experience to show you how to improve communication between men and women.

- Is there much disagreement among class members about the answers? Why?
- Do the males in the class tend to see the situations differently from the females? Why?
- How do your answers compare with your classmates'? Is there a majority view? Why do you agree or disagree with it?
- Do the men think it is fair that they are pressured into the aggressor role? How might you change this?
- Do the women think it is fair that they are expected to be passive and play hard to get? How might you change this?
- How can a man or a woman say "No," so that the other person knows it is a real "No"? Is there more involved in saying "No" than just the actual words used?
- How do you think men and women might work toward a more equal and honest relationship between the sexes so that embarrassing or even tragic errors in communication can be avoided?
- How can you help a friend (male or female) avoid a date rape or sexual harassment situation?

Dealing with Sexual Harassment

Many experts feel that sexual harassment has less to do with sex than with power. It is a way to keep women in their place, to devalue women's role in the work place or school by calling attention to their sexuality. It does not necessarily involve actual sexual overtures, but the creation of a climate where the woman fears that sexual advances will be made. According to Dr. John Gottman, a psychologist at the University of Washington, "Harassment is a way for a man to make a woman feel vulnerable."[24]

Others disagree and believe that sexual harassment stems from the misguided stereotyping of men and women. They feel that harassment occurs when men are ignorant of women's feelings or do not understand how to communicate with them. Some men misunderstand the difference between a compliment and a crude remark.[25] Many women, for example, would appreciate being told that they have pretty eyes, but would feel uncomfortable about a remark that they have nice breasts. Sexual harassment can take a variety of subtle and not-very-subtle forms. Many women are actually physically abused. This form of harassment, which affects approximately 10 percent of undergraduate women, may be more accurately labelled "sexual assault." The perpetrator is often a boyfriend, lover or spouse of the victim. Sexual assault usually occurs under the influence of alcohol or other drugs and may represent a way for the man to "prove" his masculinity, assert his dominance, or vent his anger

Rape 101.

If you think rape can't happen to you, you're in for a real education.

Because statistics show that rape happens more to women in your age group than any other. In fact, this year, one out of six college women will be the victim of rape or attempted rape. Very often by someone she knows. A fellow student. Even a date.

And that's a crime. Because any time a woman is forced to have sex against her will it's a felony.

Rape. It's a subject no one should take lightly.

Printed courtesy of Rape Treatment Center, Santa Monica Medical Center.

at the world in general.[26] After the incident, the man promises that such abuse will never happen again. But, of course, it does, and the woman becomes trapped in a vicious cycle that erodes her self-esteem, isolates her from friends and family who might help her escape from the relationship, and induces her to believe that she somehow deserves the physical or mental abuse. The activity "Recognizing Sexual Harassment" may help you to appreciate the more subtle forms of harassment and clarify communication between the sexes.

If you receive unwelcome sexual advances, say "NO!" to the harasser in a way that leaves no misunderstanding about whether the behavior is welcome. Cornell University's publication on sexual harassment suggests that you might say, "I'd like to keep our relationship strictly professional." If you know of others who have had similar experiences with this person, approach the offender together.[27]

ACTIVITY

Recognizing Examples of Sexual Harassment

The goal of this activity is to sensitize you to behaviors that are typically defined as sexual harassment. Break into small groups of five and check off behaviors that you have witnessed or in which you have engaged. Which of the three categories, verbal, nonverbal, or physical seems to occur most frequently? Which of the examples do the women in your group find most offensive?

Verbal

- Referring to an adult as a girl, hunk, doll, babe, or honey
- Whistling at someone, cat calls
- Making sexual comments or innuendos
- Turning work discussions to sexual topics
- Telling sexual jokes or stories
- Asking about sexual fantasies, preferences, or history
- Asking personal questions about a person's clothing, anatomy, or looks
- Repeatedly asking out a person who is not interested
- Making kissing sounds, howling, and smacking lips
- Telling lies or spreading rumors about a person's personal sex life

Nonverbal

- Looking a person up and down (elevator eyes)
- Staring at someone, leering at one's body; standing too close
- Blocking a person's path
- Following the person
- Giving personal gifts
- Displaying sexually suggestive visuals: pornographic pictures, posters, cartoons, or other materials
- Making facial expressions such as winking, throwing kisses, or licking lips
- Making sexual gestures with hands or through body movements

Physical

- Giving a massage around the neck or shoulders
- Touching the person's clothing, hair, or body
- Kissing
- Hugging
- Patting
- Provocative touching
- Fondling
- Pinching

The list was collected by Elaine Risch, audio-visual librarian, Ramapo College, at a conference and brought back for in-service training at the college.

ACTIVITY

Sharing Experiences of Sexual Harassment and Communicating about It

The goal of this activity is for you to recognize the various forms that sexual harassment may take, to appreciate the effects that it may have on its victims, and to clarify communication between the sexes.

Your instructor will pass out index cards. Do not put your name on your card. This is to be an anonymous response. Write an "M" on top of the card if you are a man. Put a "W" on top of the card if you are a woman. Write a brief description on the card of a sexual harassment situation in which you were the victim or the perpetrator. If you were the victim, describe how the situation made you feel and any consequences that followed. If you were the aggressor in the situation, describe your feelings and the reasons you acted in the way you did. If you have not personally experienced a situation involving sexual harassment, write about an incident that you witnessed or heard about.

Your instructor will collect the cards, shuffle them, and distribute one to each student. If the class is large, you may wish to break up into small groups of five or six students. If the class is not too large, you may all sit in a circle and process this activity as one group. Each of you will read the card you have been given to the other members of your group (or to the class). Discuss your reactions as the cards are read or after all the cards have been read. Consider the questions that follow.

Do men's reactions differ from women's? If so, how do they differ?
What was the cause or purpose of the sexual harassment?
How do you feel about the incidents that were described?
How might you respond if you were in these situations now?
What steps might you take to prevent the occurrence of sexually harassing incidents or to limit their consequences?

If you are working in small groups, choose a spokesperson who will summarize your group's discussion so that the groups may share their views with the class as a whole.

Write a letter to the harasser that describes the offensive behavior and why you object to it or how it makes you feel. Tell him that you want the harassment to stop. Keep a copy of the letter.

Keep a record of what happened including the date, time, place, names of the people involved and witnesses, and who said what to whom for each of the incidents.[28]

If you do not wish to confront the harasser directly, you may seek advice or counseling from the Office of Equal Opportunity on your campus. You may also go to the Dean of Students, a peer counselor or Resident Assistant, the harasser's supervisor, the department chair, or the Student Counseling Center. Even if you are not sure that what you are experiencing is sexual harassment, consulting with a representative from one of these offices will ensure that the problem is handled effectively. Many complaints can be resolved by informal intervention through one of these channels. You may also file a formal complaint with the Office of Equal Opportunity or the department chair. Figure 9.3 summarizes the steps to take when confronted by sexual harassment.

Figure 9.3   *Steps to Take When Confronted by Sexual Harassment*

- Say "NO!" to the harassment
- Put your complaint in writing
- Keep a record of what happened
- Consult the Office of Equal Opportunity, the harasser's supervisor, the Dean of Students, or the college dean

The organizations below can offer support and information in cases involving harassment, sexual assault, and rape.

Centers for Disease Control and
    Prevention
National Center for Injury Prevention
    and Control
Division of Violence Prevention
Mail Stop K-60
4770 Buford Highway, NE
Atlanta, GA 30341-3724
(770) 488-4362

Family Violence Prevention Fund
383 Rhode Island Street, Suite 304
San Francisco, CA 94103-5133
(415) 252-8900

National Clothesline Project
P.O. Box 727
Brewster, MA 02631
(508) 385-7004

National Coalition Against Domestic
    Violence
P.O. Box 18749
Denver, CO 80218
(303) 839-1852

National Resource Center on Domestic
    Violence
1717 Lamont Street, NW, Apt. D
Washington, DC 20010
(202) 387-6729

9to5, National Association of Working
    Women
614 Superior Avenue, NW, Room 852
Cleveland, OH 44113
(800) 522-0925

Rape Crisis Hotline
P.O. Box 34125
Washington, DC 20043
(800) 656-4673

US Public Health Service's Office on
    Women's Health
200 Independence Avenue, SW, Room
    730B
Washington, DC 20201
(202) 690-7650

If you are the victim of harassment, abuse, or rape, contact someone. You might tell a friend, a counselor, a teacher, a minister, or you might call one of the organizations listed above. Above all, get help; do not allow the consequences of the abuse to fester and grow.

■ CRIME AND VIOLENCE ON CAMPUS

Crimes committed on college campuses probably receive major attention from the media because institutions of higher education have traditionally been seen as safe and tranquil enclaves of study. It is difficult to tell whether there actually is more violence on campuses than in the past or whether the increase in reports of college violence is due to greater awareness and openness about the subject.

Since passage of the Student Right-to-Know and Campus Security Act, new students and their parents are greeted at many college orientation

programs with a count of the previous year's crimes and warnings about how to prevent future problems. Examples of violence include the rape and murder of a coed in her dorm room by a drunken fellow student at Lehigh University, the shooting and death of a Yale University sophomore who was held up just a few yards from the university president's house, the shooting murder of five University of Iowa professors and staff members by a former physics graduate student, the killing of a professor and fellow student at Simon's Rock College by an 18-year old student who also wounded four other people, and the murder of a student at Norfolk University and the critical wounding of his roommate by a first-year student.[29, 30]

In the first annual statements required by the federal reporting law, colleges reported more than 7500 incidents of violent crime.[31] That number included 30 murders, nearly 1000 rapes, and more than 1800 robberies. The number of violent crimes was small, however, compared to property crimes such as burglary (32,127) and motor vehicle theft (8,891). National surveys by Towson State University's Campus Violence Prevention Center indicate that the number of crimes is rising somewhat, but what is particularly disturbing is that the intensity of violence has radically increased.

An American college or university averages three reported violent assaults a year, eight incidents of hate crime or hazing violence, 430 property crimes, and numerous alcohol violations. Many additional incidents are not even reported. Over the course of a year, one in three students will be the victim of some kind of campus crime, and in 80 percent of those cases, it will be another student who is responsible for the crime.[32, 33]

Many administrators feel that the increase in campus crime and violence is a reflection of what is happening in society in general. More students have experienced violence in their homes and communities, the incidence of hate and bias crimes against minority group members is receiving more attention, and small differences of opinion may escalate when alcohol or other drugs are being used. National surveys report that over 90 percent of campus crime is alcohol-related.[34] This applies to both victims and perpetrators. Students are more likely to become victims of campus crime when they use drugs or alcohol because their judgment and awareness become compromised; they are also more likely to become the aggressors in violent incidents when they use these substances because their inhibitions are lowered, and their judgment becomes clouded.

Schools are spending increasing sums of money to provide escort services, tamper-proof windows, state-of-the-art exterior lighting, and upgraded alarm and locking systems. Several large institutions such as the University of California at Berkeley, the University of Illinois at Urbana-Champaign, and Ohio State University have formed their own campus SWAT teams, complete with automatic weapons, black fatigues, and special training for particularly dangerous situations.[35] But the quest for increased security is frequently hampered by students themselves. Young adults often subscribe to the "it can't happen to me" view, they believe in their own immortality, they find it hard to imagine that a member of their own college community might pose a threat to them. Check off the steps that you can take to enhance your security:

- ◼ Do not walk alone at night. Use a campus van, call the escort service, or ask a friend to accompany you. Use well-lighted pathways.
- ◼ Memorize the telephone number of campus security and use it if you feel threatened.
- ◼ Do not prop open security doors in residence halls.
- ◼ Abstain from alcohol (and other drugs) or use it in moderation. You are less likely to become a victim or a perpetrator.

Figure 9.4 *Preventing Crime: Protecting Yourself and Your Family*

Security Areas

Always lock security doors to common areas and garages; ask other tenants or students to cooperate so that everyone will be secure.

Never let a stranger into a security entrance for reasons such as: "to leave a package" or "visit a friend."

In a garage or lobby, make sure that the security door locks behind you.

Do not leave the garage door opener in your car.

Locks, Keys, and Doors

Do not hide house keys in mailboxes, planters, or under door mats. Give a duplicate key to a neighbor you trust.

Do not carry personal identification on key rings.

Keep your house keys and car keys on detachable key rings and leave *only* the car key with the car when it is serviced or valet-parked.

If you lose the keys to your home, change the cylinders in your locks immediately.

Use good locks on all exterior doors and windows.

Install a peephole. A short chain can be broken too easily.

Preventing or Dealing with Intruders

Trim overgrown shrubbery and keep the outside of your house well lit.

Have your key ready when entering house or car.

Do not enter your house if it is in disarray.

If you are at home and someone tries to break in, leave right then (through a window or back door) if possible. Call the police.

If confronted by an intruder, choose the safest strategy (e.g., negotiating, running, or complying).

Don't open your door to a stranger requesting help. Make the call yourself.

Don't open the door to anyone you do not know. Verify the person's identity. Ask police, repair, or delivery persons, salespersons, or charity volunteers for identification.

List only your first initials and last name in the telephone book. Do not list your address.

Precautions While Walking or Exercising Outdoors

Never hitchhike

Look confident and purposeful when you walk. Stay alert; observe people and activities around you.

Choose busy, well-lighted streets, and avoid vacant lots, alleys, or construction sites.

If you are being followed by a car, run or walk quickly in the opposite direction.

If you are being followed by a pedestrian, cross the street and walk in the opposite direction.If you choose to run, run as fast as you can and scream. (Shouting "fire" sometimes gets the best response.)

If you jog or bike, choose a safe and well-populated route. Vary your route and schedule to avoid predictable behavior.

Precautions While Driving

Keep your car in good working order.

Never pick up hitchhikers.

If you see a motorist in trouble, do not stop. Signal that you will get help. Telephone the police for assistance.

Park in well-lighted areas. Look around before you get out of your car.

Always remove the key and lock your car doors, no matter how soon you plan to return.

Look inside your car before you unlock it.

If you have car trouble, wait inside your car with the doors locked and the windows closed until police or an authorized serviceperson arrives. If someone offers to help, open your window slightly and ask the person to call the police or tow service.

If you are being followed, drive to the nearest police or fire station and honk your horn, or drive to the nearest open gas station or business to phone for help.

If no "safe areas" are near, honk your horn in short, rapid blasts and turn on your emergency flashers.

Precautions at Work

If you see a suspicious-looking person in an elevator, do not get in. If another person in an elevator makes you uncomfortable, get off at the next floor.

If you are working late or odd hours, alert the building's security personnel that you are there. Ask someone to check in with you at specified intervals. Ask a security guard, coworker, or escort service to accompany you to your car or public transportation.

Confrontation

If you find yourself in an assault situation, consider which strategy is your best response: negotiating, stalling, not resisting, distracting, verbal assertiveness, screaming, or fighting off the attacker.

Sexual Assault

If you are sexually assaulted, go to a counseling center or hospital emergency department for medical care. Don't bathe, shower, douche, change your clothes, eat, drink, smoke, or urinate, if possible. Even if you do not think you have any physical injuries, you should still be examined.

Seek counseling at a rape treatment center. The people there can help you deal with the consequences of the assault.

___

Excerpted with permission from "Being Safe," Santa Monica, CA: Rape Treatment Center, Santa Monica Hospital Medical Center, 1990.

■ Find out whether your campus has alcohol-free residence halls and consider living in one. Your college experience will include fewer hassles and better study conditions.

■ Develop a clear sense of your sexuality and values and practice assertive communication skills.

■ Consider enrolling in a self-defense course.

Figure 9.4 on page 159 presents a list of additional precautions that you can take to safeguard your security.

Answer Key to Activity "Differentiating among Assertive, Aggressive, and Nonassertive Behaviors"

1. −	8. N	15. +	22. +
2. −	9. +	16. −	23. N
3. N	10. N	17. +	24. +
4. +	11. N	18. −	25. N
5. +	12. −	19. N	
6. N	13. N	20. −	
7. +	14. −	21. −	

REFLECTIONS FOR YOUR JOURNAL

1. Are you satisfied with your ability to communicate with your peers, professors, boss, parents, and boyfriend, girlfriend, or spouse? Describe any situation(s) in which you wish to become more (or less) assertive.

2. What changes have occurred in important relationships (e.g., with your parents, children, spouse, boss, friends, and so on) since you entered college? How do you feel about these changes?

3. Describe an experience you have had or heard about in which a person was forced to engage in sexual behavior against his or her will. How do you feel about the experience?

4. Susan Estrich, author of *Real Rape,* has said, "In many cases, the man thought it was sex, and the woman thought it was rape, and they were both telling the truth." Think about communication between the sexes. How does this quotation apply to the increasing number of incidents reported which involve sexual harassment, rape, and spouse abuse?

Notes

1. R. A. Hatcher, et al., *Contraceptive Technology 1988–1989,* 14th ed. Atlanta: Printed Matter, Inc.: New York: Irvington Publishers, 1988.

2. R. A. Hatcher, F. Stewart, J. Trussell, D. Kowal, F. Guest, G. K. Stewart, and W. Cates, *Contraceptive Technology 1990–1992,* 15th ed. New York: Irvington Publishers, 1990, p. 5.

3. Discussion Guide for the film "Campus Rape." Santa Monica, CA: Rape Treatment Center, Santa Monica Hospital Medical Center, 1990.

4. R. Hershenson, "Pain Is Common Thread in Exhibition on Rape," *New York Times,* 25 November 1995, Sectn 13, p. 1.

5. V. Bane, M. Grant, B. Alexander, K. Kelly, S. A. Brown, B. Wegher, and L. Feldon-Mitchell, "Silent No More," *People,* 17 December 1990, pp. 94–104.

6. Hershenson, op. cit.

7. K. S. Lombardi, "New Policy Is Aimed at Preventing Date Rape on Campuses," *New York Times,* 25 October 1992, Section 13, pp. 1, 4, 5.

8. C. Pritchard, *Avoiding Rape On and Off Campus.* Wenonah, NJ: State College Publishing Co., 1985.

9. Hershenson, op. cit.

10. Bane et al., op. cit.

11. Ibid.

12. M. Roden, "What Men Need to Know About Date Rape." Santa Monica, CA: Rape Treatment Center, Santa Monica Hospital Medical Center, 1990.

13. *Get Real: Straight Talk About Women's Health.* Washington, DC: U.S. Public Health Services Office on Women's Health and Society for Advancement of Women's Research, 1995.

14. H. R. Rawlings III, "Sexual Harassment." Ithaca, NY: Cornell University Office of Public Services, 1995.

15. N. Stein, N. L. Marshall, L. R. Trapp, *Secrets in Public: Sexual Harassment,* Center for Research on Women at Wellesley College and NOW Legal Defense Education Fund.

16. T. Lewin, "Chevron Settles Sexual Harassment Charges," *New York Times,* 22 February 1995.

17. C. Goldberg, "Company To Pay Record Amount in L.I. Sexual Harassment Case," *New York Times,* 3 August 1995, A1 & D8.

18. E. Schmitt, "Ex-Head of Navy's Sex Bias Fight Goes on Trial in Harassment Case," *New York Times,* 12 October 1995, A1 & B6.

19. E. Schmitt, "New Navy Scandal: An Admiral Guilty of Sexual Harassment," *New York Times,* 9 December 1995, A1 & A11.

20. M. L. Roark, "Helping High School Students Assess Campus Safety," *The School Counselor, 39* March 1992, pp. 251–256.

21. T. Lewin, "Sexual Harassment Charged at Cornell," *New York Times,* 27 January 1995, p. B5.

22. "Man Wins Harassment Suit Against Man," *New York Times,* 13 August 1995.

23. "Chain Must Pay Male Sex-Harassment Victim," *New York Times,* 24 November 1995.

24. D. Goleman, "Sexual Harassment: It's About Power, Not Sex," *New York Times,* 22 October 1991.

25. J. Gross, "Schools Are Newest Arena For Sex-Harassment Cases," *New York Times,* 11 March 1992.

26. Get Real, op.cit.

27. Rawlings, op. cit.

28. Rawlings, op. cit.

29. A. Mathews, "The Campus Crime Wave," *The New York Times Magazine,* 7 March 1993, pp. 38–47.

30. D. W. Hayes, "Violence: Another Burden For Some Historically Black Colleges and Universities," *Black Issues in Higher Education,* 24 February 1994, pp. 22–25.

31. D. Lederman, "Colleges Report 7500 Violent Crimes . . . ," *The Chronicle of Higher Education,* 20 January 1993, pp. A32–A41.

32. Mathews, op. cit.

33. D. S. Siegel, "What Is Behind the Growth of Violence on Campuses?," *USA Today,* May 1994, pp. 32–34.

34. Mathews, op. cit.

35. "Sunday: Campus SWAT Team," *New York Times Magazine,* 9 October 1994, p. 18.

10 RESPONSIBLE INTIMACY

■ VALUES AND DECISIONS

An article by Richard Keeling in the *Chronicle of Higher Education* described the most important problems challenging young people in colleges and universities as "the epidemics of HIV and other sexually transmitted diseases, substance abuse, sexual assault, and unwanted pregnancy—all problems related to behavior and relationships." Dr. Keeling went on to say that it is not so much a lack of knowledge in these areas that is causing problems for college students as the absence of a clear strong sense of identity and personal values, as well as the absence of practical skills—for example, how to make decisions about sexual activity, how to negotiate with a potential sexual partner, and how to limit the effects of alcohol on judgment.[1] This chapter will review the basic facts that you should know, but more important, it will give you the opportunity to clarify your values and practice important decision-making, problem-solving, and communication skills that will help you avoid the many pitfalls in these areas.

You will find that the area of interpersonal relations requires a number of important value decisions. This process of learning about yourself, becoming close to others, and making decisions about values is often a difficult one. It may become even more difficult during college, when you may be experimenting with greater freedom from your parents and you may be experiencing considerable pressure from your friends about adopting their value systems.

Remember that only you can judge which values work for you. People who respect and value you as a friend will ultimately accept the standards that you set for yourself. Try to resist the pressure to do what everyone else is doing if it does not feel right for you. Often, the "everyone else is doing it" view is misleading. For example, it may seem that everyone in college is sexually experienced, but one report indicated that 44 percent of women and 27 percent of men have not engaged in sexual intercourse before age 18.[2] Apparently *not* everyone is doing it! It is possible to have a close and meaningful relationship that does not involve sex.

■ INTIMATE RELATIONSHIPS

Intimate relationships involve give and take and sharing. Partners must be willing to disclose themselves to each other. This does not necessarily involve sharing every secret, but it does mean sharing what is important to the relationship and allowing your partner to know about your joys, expectations, frustrations, dreams, fears, excitement, and other important feelings. Each person must have a desire to give to the other, help the other, and support the other, so that both partners are fulfilled. Each makes a commitment to stay

with the other through times of crisis and conflict, to give support, and to work things out. The partners agree to accept each other and to tolerate and respect the differences between them.[3]

The higher level of commitment that couples naturally make when they decide to marry may explain why married individuals enjoy a surprising number of advantages. An increasing number of studies indicates that people who marry enjoy better health, more money, and more satisfying sex than single people, divorced individuals, or even couples who live together without marrying. (According to a National Health and Social Life Survey, married men reported having sex twice as frequently as most of the single men and indicated higher levels of satisfaction with their sex lives than either single or cohabiting men.[4])

People who live together without marriage are not necessarily committed to a relationship for the long term. They may focus too much on their individual careers rather than caring for each other, they may not work as hard to keep the relationship going, they may assume that each partner is more responsible for himself or herself rather than giving as much support to their partners. It may surprise you to know that people who live together before marriage have higher divorce rates, are more likely to be incompatible and sexually disloyal, and are generally less happy than married couples.[5]

Apparently, the commitment involved in marriage means that couples are more likely to pool finances and invest in the future. This better financial status is likely to trickle down into better medical care, safer surroundings, better food, a higher standard of living, and less stress. According to Dr. Linda Waite, Professor of Sociology at the University of Chicago, marriage may give people a sense of meaning in their lives and a feeling of obligation to others. This may explain the higher incidence of alcohol abuse, the higher rates of other risk-taking behaviors, and the poorer health experienced by divorced individuals.[6]

Sexual Relationships

An intimate relationship *may* involve a sexual relationship although many intimate friendships do not include sex. Nor must a sexual relationship necessarily involve sexual intercourse. There are ways to share warm, affectionate, physical feelings without engaging in intercourse.

All human beings need touching—for affection, for comfort, for communication. Most people enjoy erotic touching as well. For many, this involves sexual intercourse: sexual contact with the penis in the vagina. But most people get pleasure from a wide range of sexual expressions as well—holding hands, kissing, massaging, mutual masturbation, dancing, oral-genital sex, fantasy, and sharing erotic movies. Taste, smell, vision, hearing, and imagination matter just as much as touch in erotic situations.[7] Sexual expression and affection can be communicated without intercourse. Only you can judge what you should be doing and under what conditions you might be willing to experiment with various types of sexual behavior.

Precautions

If you make a commitment to abstinence, family planners recommend that when you are with a partner, you stay sober, stay out of an empty house, and stay out of the back seat. Otherwise, abstinence may be just too difficult to maintain.[8] On the other hand, if you decide to have a sexually intimate relationship, there is certain information about birth control and sexually transmitted diseases with which you should become very familiar. Figure 10.1 presents some of the shocking facts about unintended pregnancies and births

Figure 10.1   *Facts about Unintended Pregnancy and Childbearing*

■ Eighty-two percent of pregnancies in the United States among women 15- to 19-years old are unintended; among 20- to 24-year olds, the rate of unintended pregnancies is 61 percent (The US Public Health Service, Office on Women's Health, 1995[9]).

■ The United States has the highest rate of unintended teenage childbirth of any major industrialized country in the world. For example, Japan, France, Sweden, Canada, and the United Kingdom all rank lower than the USA in the number of unintended births to teenage mothers (*USA Today,* 1994[10]).

■ The United States ranks higher in the rate of unintended teenage births than less developed countries such as Saudi Arabia, Jordan, Algeria, and Iraq.(Usdansky, *USA Today,* 1994[11]).

■ Two-thirds of the children born to teenage mothers in the United States are born out of wedlock (*New York Times,* 1991[12]).

Reprinted with permission of the Children's Defense Fund.

in this country. This subject is often considered unromantic, awkward, embarrassing, or even disgusting, but such hang-ups in communicating openly about sexual matters seem to be particularly American. As a result *the rate of unwanted pregnancies in the United States is higher than in any other industrialized nation.* Couples in other countries do not seem to have the same unrealistic ideas about what is romantic. That is probably because we get our notions of romance from the media, and the media do not portray relationships between people who live in the real world.

Sharing and caring enough to help each other avoid disease, death, and the emotional trauma of unwanted pregnancy are warm, loving things to do with a partner. There is nothing romantic about getting AIDS or going through an abortion.

There is also nothing romantic about the number of students who are forced to drop out of college each year because they or their partners become pregnant. Nor is there anything romantic about the students who spend so much time worrying whether they have contracted a disease that they neglect their studies and flunk out of college. Do not allow these types of mistakes to ruin your college career.

Even if you think you know everything there is to know on these subjects, please read the following information carefully. The shocking fact remains that the United States has the highest rate of unintended teenage pregnancy of any major industrialized country in the world. Eighty-two percent of pregnancies among women 15 to 19 are unintended; even among women in the age range of 20 to 24 years, 61 percent of pregnancies are unintended.[13] The rate of teen-age pregnancy here is 10 times that in Japan or the Netherlands. For every 1,000 teenagers in the United States, 62 give birth each year. Figure 10.2 shows

Figure 10.2   *Teenage Childbearing: When It Comes to Teenagers Giving Birth, the United States Resembles Developing Countries More Than Industrialized Ones*

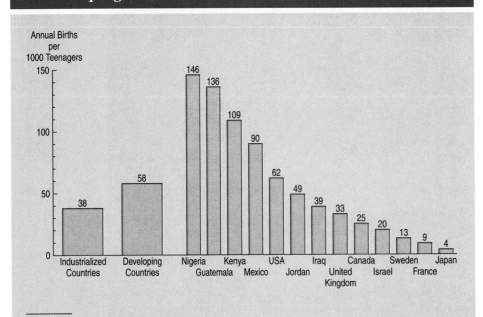

Adapted from M. L. Usdansky, "Teen Births: Formula for Disaster," *USA Today,* 22 February 1994, p. 2A.

the number of teenagers who give birth each year in other countries. In this respect, the United States resembles a developing nation more than an industrialized one. Even less developed countries like Jordan, Algeria, and Iraq all rank lower than the United States in teenage births.[14] Remember that a college degree is necessary for a woman who hopes to find a reasonable job in the United States these days. Almost invariably, teenage mothers in this country doom themselves and their children to lives of poverty, poor education, and unemployment.

Over *one-third of all females* between the ages of fifteen and twenty in the United States *have at least one unwanted pregnancy.*[15] Almost one-third of all children in the United States are born to women who are not married. Among teenagers, where the rate of unplanned pregnancies is highest, more than two-thirds of children are born out of wedlock.[16] Apparently, many young men and women do not know as much about birth control as they should.

What is even more disturbing than the number of unwanted pregnancies are the consequences of those pregnancies. The pregnancies in this young age group result in an astoundingly high percentage of abnormal, physically damaged babies due to birth complications and inadequate prenatal medical care. They also result in a very high number of medical problems for the mothers. Both the mothers and the babies usually experience severe psychological prob-

Reprinted with permission of the Children's Defense Fund.

lems and lives of poverty due to interrupted educations, stressful parental responsibilities, and restricted social opportunities.

Researchers are constantly developing new information and techniques in the area of birth control, and surveys show that many adults are misinformed on these vital subjects. Familiarity with this information could lead to the difference between a satisfying sexual experience and a nightmare involving abortion, unwanted pregnancy, serious illness, or even death. It is not in your interest to become one of these unfortunate, but all too common, statistics.

If you decide that you are ready to enter into a sexually intimate relationship with a partner but you are not planning to start a family, you should be mature and caring enough about your welfare and the welfare of your partner to take responsible action about birth control. The following information will help you to decide what type of birth control to use if you make the decision to become sexually active. The Planned Parenthood Federation of America, with branches listed in the telephone directories of most cities and towns, offers excellent literature and individual counseling should you have additional questions about contraception.

■ ABSTINENCE

The only method of birth control that is 100 percent effective is abstinence. Without sexual intercourse, there cannot be a pregnancy. An additional advantage of sexual expression without intercourse (e.g., kissing, holding hands, caressing) is that it may offer protection from AIDS and other sexually

Abstinence is the only method of birth control that is 100 percent effective.

A C T I V I T Y

Implementing Abstinence

We designed this activity is to encourage you to consider abstinence, even if you have been sexually active in the past. Remember that abstinence is the only method of birth control that is 100 percent effective. In addition, sexual activity without intercourse (e.g., kissing, caressing) may offer protection from AIDS and other sexually transmitted diseases. If you have already made a commitment to abstinence, this activity will help you practice assertive strategies and communication skills that should reinforce your resolve.

The goal of this activity is to practice communicating about abstinence. First read the strategies and statements that are printed in the box that follows.

---

1. Say "No," and say it as if you mean it. Here are a few techniques for saying "No."

Technique	Example
Simple "No"	"No, thanks." or "No."
Emphatic "No"	"No! I don't want to do that!"
Repetitive "No"	"No." "No." "No."
Turn the tables	"You say that if I loved you, I would. But if you loved me, you would listen to me and wouldn't pressure me like this; you wouldn't insist."

Technique	Example
Give a reason	"Look, I'm sorry; I'm just not ready yet."
	"We can't be too careful in this age of AIDS."
	"I have decided to abstain for a while."
	"I'm afraid of getting pregnant."
	"No, this doesn't feel right."
	"I really don't want to. Please leave me alone."
	"Sorry, but it's that time of month.
	Say "No" and leave the scene.

Walk out of there.

2. Steer clear. If you suspect you will be pressured, do not go out with that person.

3. Call in the cavalry. Threaten to tell someone with authority or power (counselor, relative, police, minister, and so on).

4. Safety in numbers. Double date; keep trusted friends nearby and look out for each other.

5. Decide what you want to do about sex at a time when you feel clear-headed, sober, and good about yourself. If you have a partner, decide together at a time when you feel close to each other but not sexual. For example, try talking while you take a walk and hold hands. How could you raise the subject with your partner or how could you respond to your partner's pressure for sex?

6. Decide in advance what sexual activities you will say "Yes" to and discuss these with your partner. Which activities might be included in your "yes" list?

7. Know your personal rights in social relationships: review the section in Chapter 9 on assertive communication (pages 138–141) and Figure 9.2, "Guidelines for Assertive Communication in Sexual Situations" (page 150). You do not owe sexual favors to anyone because he or she has "wasted" time or money on you.

8. Tell your partner very clearly and in advance—not at the last minute in a sexual situation—what activities you will *not* engage in. Which activities might be included on your list?

9. Avoid high-pressure sexual situations: stay sober, stay out of an empty house, stay out of the back seat.

10. Learn more about your body and how to keep it healthy. Appreciate the marvel of your body.

11. Learn about birth control and safer sex, so you will be ready if you change your mind. Always keep condoms around. Always.

12. Learn about emergency birth control options in case you have intercourse when you didn't expect it. (Treatment initiated within 72 hours of unprotected intercourse reduces the risk of pregnancy by 75 percent.)

Much of the material in this activity is adapted by permission, from R. A. Hatcher, J. Trussell, F. Stewart, G. K. Stewart, D. Kowal, F. Guest, W. Cates, & M. Policar, *Contraceptive Technology*, 16th rev. ed. New York: Irvington Publishers, 1994, pp. 141–142 and from student responses made in Professor Starke's College Seminar classes.[17]

When you have finished reading the strategies to implement abstinence, break into groups of four whose membership is as evenly balanced as possible between men and women. (Depending on class size, some groups may have three or five members.) Your instructor will count the number of men in the class and divide that number so that a count off results in approximately two men in each group. The instructor will then do the same with the women. For example, in a class of 10 men and 14 women, the men will count off by fives, and the women will count off by sevens. The male "ones" and "twos" will join the female "ones" and "twos" to form gender-balanced groups of four students, while the men assigned "threes" and "fours" join with the women who were assigned "threes," "fours," and "sevens" to form groups of two men and three women; the male "fives" will join the female "fives" and "sixes" to form groups of one man and two women.

Each group will make up a brief scenario or skit in which one member of a couple wants sex, while the second member has made a commitment to abstinence. Write out the dialog of three or four interchanges between the couple. Incorporate into your skit material from points 3 through 8 in the box above. Integrate additional material that you make up. Two members of the group will take the part of the couple and act out the scene, while the other group members coach and critique: Did the abstainer behave in an assertive (as opposed to an aggressive or unassertive) manner? Was the response effective? How could the respondent have replied more effectively? Were body language, eye contact, verbal tone and volume appropriate?

Do not worry too much about the sex of the actors and actresses. Since some of the students in your group may be gay, it is just as appropriate to practice these responses with same-sex actors.

Next, switch roles so that the "actors" take the role of coaches, while the former coaches take the parts of the couple. The coaches will offer suggestions for improvement.

If time permits, switch roles so that each member of the group has the opportunity to play the part of the abstainer. The coaches will critique this enactment of the scenario, helping each actor or actress to play his or her role most effectively.

Your instructor will circulate around the room while you are practicing your scenarios and may ask one or two of the groups to perform their skits for the whole class. Group discussion may then address issues such as the advantages and disadvantages of abstinence or additional suggestions for making abstinence work more effectively.

---

transmitted diseases. If you make a commitment to abstinence, the strategies presented in the activity "Implementing Abstinence" will help to make it work for you.

■ OTHER METHODS OF BIRTH CONTROL*

If you wish to have intercourse, there are a number of methods that can greatly reduce the chance of pregnancy. In general, two methods are better than one—for example, use the pill and a condom at the same time. About half of all unintended pregnancies in the United States occur when women are not using contraception; the other 50 percent happen to women who used some form of contraception during the month they became pregnant.[18] The most popular contraceptive method today is sterilization, relied upon by 42 percent of contraceptive users. Of the 8.5 million women aged 15 through 19 who use a contraceptive, more than half take oral contraceptives, 44 percent

---

*Much of the information in these sections on the various methods of birth control is summarized from R. A. Hatcher et al., *Contraceptive Technology*, 16th rev. ed. New York: Irvington Publishers, 1994.

ACTIVITY

Assessing Your Contraceptive Method: Comfort and Confidence Scale

This activity will help you evaluate the contraceptive method you are using now or a method that you may consider trying in the future. If you are not comfortable with a contraceptive technique, it is not likely to work for you because you will be tempted not to use it when you think it is "safe." These lapses in contraception will open you up to the risk of pregnancy.

Method of birth control you are considering using: _____

Length of time you used this method in the past: _____

Answer YES or NO to the following questions: YES   NO

1. Have I had problems using this method before?
2. Have I ever become pregnant using this method?
3. Am I afraid of using this method?
4. Would I really rather not use this method?
5. Will I have trouble remembering to use this method?
6. Will I have trouble using this method correctly?
7. Do I still have unanswered questions about this method?
8. Does this method make menstrual periods longer or more painful?
9. Does this method cost more than I can afford?
10. Could this method cause me to have serious complications?
11. Am I opposed to this method because of any religious or moral beliefs?
12. Is my partner opposed to this method?
13. Am I using this method without my partner's knowledge?
14. Will using this method embarrass my partner?
15. Will using this method embarrass me?
16. Will I enjoy intercourse less because of this method?
17. If this method interrupts lovemaking, will I avoid using it?
18. Has a nurse or doctor ever told me NOT to use this method?
19. Is there anything about my personality that could lead me to use this method incorrectly?
20. Am I at any risk of being exposed to HIV (the AIDS virus) or other sexually transmitted infections if I use this method?

Total number of YES answers: _____

    Most individuals will have a few "yes" answers. "Yes" answers mean that potential problems may arise. If you have more than a few "yes" responses, you may want to talk to your physician, counselor, partner, or friend to help you to decide whether to use this method or how to use it so that it will really be effective for you. In general, the more "yes" answers you have, the less likely you are to use this method consistently and correctly at every act of intercourse.

"Contraceptive Comfort and Confidence Scale" is reprinted, by permission, from R. A. Hatcher et al., *Contraceptive Technology,* 16th rev. ed. New York: Irvington Publishers, 1994.[23]

use condoms, and 4 percent rely on other methods. Condoms are used primarily by the partners of teenagers and unmarried women. The diaphragm is used most often by women over 30, and the IUD is used most frequently by women over 35.[19] Figure 10.3 compares the typical failure rates for different contraceptive methods in the United States.

The different methods vary in effectiveness and ease of use, but they only work if they are used according to directions every single time you engage in intercourse. If you have sex just one time (even if it is your very first time) without birth control protection, you risk the chance of pregnancy. If you find a particular contraceptive method uncomfortable or inconvenient, try another one that suits you and your partner. An uncomfortable method will not work because you will be tempted to "skip it just this once." That one time will open you to the risk of pregnancy. Figure 10.4 describes the five contraceptive mistakes that result in the largest number of unwanted pregnancies.

The Pill (Combined Oral Contraceptives)

There are four effective birth control methods that require a medical prescription: the pill, progestin-only contraceptives (Norplant, Depo-Provera), the IUD, and the diaphragm. All four methods are used by the woman. The pill is one of the most common contraceptives used by women, probably because of its convenience and effectiveness. It contains hormonelike substances, and is taken orally. When a woman wishes to become pregnant, she will stop taking the pill. Her regular menstrual cycles should return within one to three months.

Taking the pill must be coordinated with your menstrual cycle, and you must follow your doctor's directions carefully if you expect the pill to work.

Figure 10.3   *Contraceptive Failure Rates (Estimated Percentage of Women Experiencing an Unintended Pregnancy in the First Year of Use)*[20]

Contraceptive Method	Failure Rate (Average Use)
Chance (No contraceptive used)	85
Spermicides	30
Sponge	24
Withdrawal	24
Periodic abstinence (Calendar method)	19
Cervical Cap	18
Diaphragm	18
Condom	16
Pill (Combined Oral Contraceptives)	6
IUD (Copper)	4
Tubal Sterilization	0.5
Depo-Provera	0.4
Vasectomy	0.2
NORPLANT	0.05

Contraceptive Use: Facts In Brief, New York: The Alan Guttmacher Institute, 1996.

Figure 10.4 *Five Biggest Contraceptive Mistakes*[21]

- Neglecting to take the pill every day as directed. Under these circumstances, you may continue to ovulate.
- Using a diaphragm without spermicidal jelly or removing it too soon after sex. (It should remain in place for six to eight hours after intercourse.)
- Waiting to put on a condom until just before intercourse. The small amount of sperm released during foreplay can cause pregnancy even if the penis does not enter the vagina.
- Using spermicidal foams, suppositories, or creams incorrectly. Be sure to use the recommended dosage. Reapply before repeated intercourse.
- Not using birth control during menstruation. This is not necessarily a "safe" time. Sperm can live up to five days inside the reproductive tract; if ovulation occurs soon after menstruation ends, pregnancy can result.

Some pills must be taken every day; others are taken during just twenty-one days of your cycle. The pill can be dangerous for women who have had blood clots, strokes, heart disease, liver disease, unexplained bleeding from the vagina, or cancer. It is also more dangerous to women who smoke because of increased risk of blood clots and phlebitis. A medical examination is necessary in order to prescribe the right pill for you and to be certain that the pill is safe for you.

Some women find that the pill results in problems such as nausea or weight gain. It may also increase the likelihood of more serious disorders such as stroke, heart attack, blood clots, or liver cancer.

Pills can be purchased in a drugstore or in family planning clinics if you have a doctor's prescription. The medical examination, in which the physician determines whether the pill is safe for you and which pill you should take, can be given in a physician's office. Both the examination and the pills may cost less in a family planning clinic that operates on a sliding scale fee than through prescription by a private doctor's office.

Implants and Injections (Norplant and Depo-Provera)

Implants and injections are available that offer contraceptive protection from three months to five years. Norplant, the most popular implant in this country, was approved by the Food and Drug Administration in December 1990 and has been used by approximately 100,000 American women. Public health officials report that the device works well, and there is little concern about its safety because both the drug and the capsule material used in Norplant have been on the market for years.

Norplant may well become the most popular contraceptive in the next few years because of its low failure rate and easy-to-use method. Six matchstick-size capsules are placed under the skin of the woman's upper arm in a ten-minute procedure performed by a doctor or nurse. These capsules provide contraceptive protection for as long as five years, and the procedure can be easily reversed.

Depo-Provera (DMPA) is the most commonly employed injectable progestin. The injection is given every three months and inhibits ovulation. DMPA has been used by more than 15 million women worldwide. It is approved for use in more than 90 countries, including the United States.

Women using these contraceptive methods have reported few side effects, but irregular bleeding, weight gain, and breast tenderness have occurred in some women. In the case of DMPA, the side effects may continue until the medication is cleared from the woman's body (about six to eight months after her last injection). There is a delay in return of fertility averaging six months to one year. Many women who use Norplant have reported that it has eased their menstrual cramps and reduced the amount of bleeding during their periods.

The Intrauterine Device (IUD)

The IUD is a device made of plastic or copper that is inserted into a woman's uterus by a gynecologist or obstetrician. The IUD prevents pregnancy by changing the lining of the uterus so that it is more difficult for pregnancy to take place. Menstruation will continue while the IUD is in place. When a woman wishes to become pregnant, she asks her doctor to remove the IUD.

The IUD is not suitable for women who have heavy menstrual bleeding, anemia, or certain abnormalities of the uterus, ovaries, or cervix. It may also be dangerous for women who have had recent infections in their tubes or ovaries or a history of tubal pregnancy. The IUD may also cause some discomfort (cramps, bleeding, backaches) during the first few months after it is inserted. When an IUD has been inserted, you should return for a checkup soon after your first period, to be sure that the device is still in place. Most pregnancies that occur in IUD users happen because the device falls out and the woman is not aware of it. If you have had an IUD inserted and you think you may be pregnant, notify your physician immediately. A pregnancy that proceeds while an IUD is in place can be very dangerous. There is a greater risk for pelvic infection in IUD users, and some of these can be quite serious if they are not promptly treated by a physician.

Vaginal Barrier Methods: The Diaphragm, Cervical Cap, Contraceptive Sponge, and Female Condom

The diaphragm is a small rubber disk that the woman coats with a spermicidal cream such as nonoxynol-9 and inserts into her vagina each time she has intercourse. It prevents pregnancy by blocking the passage through which sperm swim to unite with the egg. The cream serves as a backup contraceptive by stopping the sperm if the diaphragm becomes dislodged during sex or if it was not properly inserted in the first place. A medical examination is necessary so that the woman can be fitted with the correct size and model of diaphragm. If the diaphragm does not fit correctly or if it is not inserted properly, the sperm will be able to swim through and pregnancy may result. For this reason, the fit should be checked by a physician every two years or sooner if your weight has changed markedly (up or down) or if you have experienced pregnancy.

Diaphragms are not as effective as the pill or the IUD, and they must be inserted each time you have sex. The diaphragm should be left in place for six to eight hours after intercourse. On the other hand, diaphragms do not result in any medical complications of the type mentioned in connection with the pill or the IUD. They can be used safely by most women, especially those who are not eligible for one of the other methods because of their medical histories or other problems. The medical exam and fitting for a diaphragm are done by a gynecologist in his or her office. They can also be performed in a family planning clinic. Diaphragms are sold in both drugstores and clinics.

Compared with the diaphragm, the cap has been less widely used and known in the United States. It looks something like a miniature diaphragm and fits over the cervix to prevent the sperm from uniting with the egg. Like the diaphragm, it should be used in conjunction with a spermicidal cream such as nonoxynol-9. It provides contraceptive protection for 48 hours, but should not be left in place for longer because of the risk of toxic shock. The cervical cap should not be used if you have a history of toxic shock syndrome or an allergy to rubber (latex) or spermicide. It is also contraindicated for women who are prone to urinary tract infections.

The sponge is a small, soft device that is saturated with a spermicidal solution such as nonoxynol-9. The woman inserts it into her vagina where it blocks the passage to the uterus. In addition to blocking the sperms' path, the spermicide reduces the sperms' movement so they cannot swim to join with an egg.

There is no special fitting required for the sponge as it comes in only one size. It should not be removed from the vagina for six hours after the last act of intercourse so that the sperm are effectively neutralized by the spermicide. The sponge may be left in the vagina for twenty-four hours. Do not use it when you are menstruating because it may expose you to the risk of toxic shock syndrome. The sponge is disposable and should never be used a second time.

The sponge requires no prescription. It can be used by any woman who can insert a tampon, and it is available in drugstores and clinics. You can make the sponge even more effective if you back it up with an additional device such as the condom.

If you have difficulty locating or removing a sponge, call your doctor. You should not forget about it or leave one in place longer than 24 hours, as you may develop toxic shock syndrome, which can be fatal.

Some research indicates that the sponge and the cap are not as effective in preventing pregnancy as the diaphragm and the female condom. In addition, re-analysis of data from two studies indicates that a substantial number of pregnancies occur even when the sponge, diaphragm, and cap are used consistently and correctly.[22]

The first female condom, Reality®, was approved for over-the-counter sale in the United States in 1993. It consists of a thin, polyurethane sheath that lines the entire vagina. One of its soft rings, near the closed end, anchors the sheath inside, and the other forms the open edge of the device that remains outside the vagina. The condom is prelubricated, but does not contain spermicide. It is intended for one-time use only and should not be used in conjunction with a male latex condom.

The Condom

The condom (also known as the prophylactic, rubber, or safe) is a contraceptive device that is used by the male during intercourse; it requires no prescription. It is placed over the erect penis before the penis enters the vagina so that the condom catches the sperm and prevents them from the vagina and joining with an egg. The condom offers protection from sexually transmitted diseases in addition to protection against pregnancy. Many young adults who are sexually active or find themselves in a situation where they wish to engage in sexual intercourse, need practice in communicating assertively about condoms. The activity, "Talking About Condoms" will help you become more comfortable discussing this topic.

If you have decided to abstain from sexual intercourse at this time, you may wish to review the assertive responses in the activity, "Implementing Abstinence" on pages 167–169. Sometimes, due to peer pressure, overindulgence in alcohol, or other special circumstances, students who have decided to abstain

ACTIVITY

Talking about Condoms

The goal of this activity is to practice communicating about condoms. First read the statements and responses that are printed below.

Statement	Response
Birth control is not natural, a total turn-off.	Getting an infection or getting pregnant is also a real turn-off.
I don't have a condom with me.	I do or . . . then let's do something else that we like.
Let's do this just this one time without a condom.	Once is all it takes, and I don't want to get pregnant or . . . I don't want to take the chance that one of us might have a disease.
I know I'm clean; I haven't had sex in a long time.	As far as I know, I'm clean, too. Still, I want to use a condom since either of us could have an infection we don't know about.
Condoms are messy, and they smell funny.	They don't have to be. They now make condoms in all kinds of styles and colors. Let's see which we like best.
When I stop to put it on, I'll lose my erection.	Don't worry; I'll make sure that doesn't happen.
It will spoil the feeling.	I could put it on to make it more exciting, and I bet you wouldn't even realize you were wearing one.
You're carrying a condom; all you wanted all along from me was sex.	I wasn't planning to, but it happened. I wanted to be prepared. I care about both of us, so I carry one with me.
None of my other friends uses a condom. A real man isn't afraid.	Look, I'm smarter than your other friends. A real man cares about his lover and thinks about his future.
Everyone else is doing it.	Fine! Then you shouldn't have any trouble finding someone else to do it.
What's the matter? Don't you want me?	Yes, and I want what's right for both of us, too.
I'm hurt that you think I might have AIDS.	Everyone needs to be concerned. Anyone can get AIDS if they're not careful.
You don't trust me.	I didn't say that. I care for you, and a condom will protect both of us.
Only sluts who sleep around need to have their partners use condoms.	That's not true. Once is all it takes to get pregnant or an infection. Anyone who uses a condom is being smart, not a slut.
I'm on the pill so you don't need to use a condom.	The pill only protects you from pregnancy; you can still get an infection.

Statement	Response
But condoms don't work.	Nothing is 100 percent safe (except not doing it). But if you use condoms right, they make sex much safer.
But I hardly ever have sex!	I don't want to risk getting pregnant or an infection. Isn't it better to be safe than sorry?
I could stop to take it out.	Even if you take it out, I could still get pregnant or an infection because even the smallest dribble has a lot of sperm.
I love you. I wouldn't hurt you.	If you loved me, you would listen to me and wouldn't pressure me like this. Besides, I don't want to get pregnant.

You will then break into groups of four whose membership is as evenly balanced as possible between men and women. (Depending on class size, some groups may have three or five members.) Your instructor will count the number of men in the class and divide that number so that a count off results in approximately two men in each group. The instructor will then do the same with the women. For example, in a class of 12 men and 10 women, the men will count off by sixes, and the women will count off by fives. The male "ones" and "twos" will join the female "ones" and "twos" to form gender-balanced groups of four students, while the men assigned "threes" and "fours" join the women who were assigned "threes" and "fours" to form groups of two men and two women; the male "fives" and "sixes" will join the female "fives" to form groups of two men and one woman.

Your instructor will distribute a card containing one of the statements to each member of each group. Each student will have the opportunity to take the role of reader, respondent, and critic. Decide who will be the first reader. That student will read the statement to one of the other members of his or her group, and the second student will make an assertive response indicating that she or he will engage in sex only if the couple uses a condom.

Do not worry about the sex of the reader or the responder. Since some of the students in your group may be gay, it is just as appropriate to practice these responses with same-sex group members. You may use responses from those that you read at the beginning of this exercise or be creative and make up your own responses. You may, if you wish, continue the role play beyond one round of statements and responses.

After completing the second part of this activity, the member(s) of the group who did not read or respond to a statement will critique the "actor's" response. Was it assertive (as opposed to aggressive or unassertive)? Was it effective? How could the respondent have replied more effectively? Were body language, eye contact, verbal tone and volume appropriate?

When one couple has completed the role play, the next reader in the group (who just completed the role of critic in the first skit) will choose a respondent and practice communicating with that person. This process will continue until all members of the group have had the opportunity to play the role of respondent, reader, and critic.

This activity is adapted from "Condoms Are for Everyone . . . Ways to Talk to Your Partner," Mahwah, NJ: Ramapo College Self Treatment and Wellness Center. Originally adapted from a publication of the NCBH Health Program. Portions of this activity are quoted with permission from R. A. Hatcher et al., *Contraceptive Technology*, 16th rev. ed. NY: Irvington Publishers, 1994, p. 170.

from sexual intercourse find themselves in a situation where they decide to try sex "just this once." If this happens to you, you should be prepared to protect yourself against pregnancy and sexually transmitted diseases. It takes only one sexual experience, even if it is your first one, to find yourself in dangerous or even fatal circumstances.

Like the diaphragm, condoms result in no medical complications. They are disposable and inexpensive, and they can be purchased in drugstores, clinics, and through many mail-order catalogs. Plain rubber condoms are the least expensive, and just as effective as animal tissue, lubricated, textured, or colored condoms. In addition, rubber condoms are more effective than those made of animal tissue in preventing the spread of AIDS. They can be purchased by men or women, and there is no restriction on the sale of condoms based on age.

Condoms are effective if they are conscientiously used during each act of intercourse. Condoms can be even more effective if they are used with an additional backup contraceptive such as a spermicidal cream or foam. Should the condom break during intercourse, the cream or foam would stop the sperm from joining the egg.

Condoms rarely break during vaginal intercourse, and lubricated condoms are less likely to tear. They do tend to weaken with exposure to light or heat. Do not try to reuse a condom. Do not store condoms in your wallet next to your body or in other warm places such as your glove compartment for long periods of time. They weaken with age and should be disposed of within two years of purchase or before the expiration date stamped on the package.

Vaginal Spermicides: Foams, Jellies, Creams, Films, Suppositories, and Tablets

All of these contraceptives are inserted into the vagina where they may offer some protection against pregnancy. They should be used in conjunction with a spermicidal cream such as nonoxynol-9 if this spermicide is not one of the ingredients in the product. They do not require medical examinations or prescriptions and cause few medical problems. Instructions on how to use each product come with the package. You should read these instructions carefully, and perhaps even practice with the product once or twice before you use it in a sexual situation.

These products are very useful for boosting the effectiveness of other contraceptives when used in combination with condoms or diaphragms.

Fertility Awareness Methods

Fertility awareness (natural birth control) methods of contraception attempt to prevent pregnancy by avoiding intercourse during the periods of the month when the woman is most fertile. You may recognize these methods by other names such as natural family planning, the rhythm method, the mucus charting method, the basal body temperature charting method, or the ovulation method. Couples use fertility awareness methods to figure out when the woman has released an egg from her ovaries. She is most likely to become pregnant just before, during, and after the time the egg is released. The couple then abstains from sex during those times.

Fertility awareness methods offer no medical complications, and they are acceptable to couples who have religious reservations about the use of other forms of birth control. Thermometers and charts for keeping records of basal body temperature may be purchased in drugstores or at family planning clinics.

Fertility awareness methods are not easy to use. They take time to learn, and after they are learned, the couple must keep very careful daily records in order to ensure accuracy. If a woman does not have regular menstrual cycles, these methods will not work no matter how conscientious the record keeping. Both partners must also be willing to show considerable self-control, because there will be certain days when having sex will expose them to the risk of pregnancy. Some of the spontaneity of lovemaking is lost because of the scheduling and planning that are crucial to the success of these methods.

The two most accurate records to keep are mucus consistency and basal body temperature. Birth control will be much more effective if both of these signs are checked. In using these methods, the couple must refrain from having sex from the end of menstruation until three days after the woman has ovulated. The woman must take her temperature every morning, even before getting out of bed, smoking, or having anything to eat or drink. She must keep a record of her basal body temperature that is accurate to within several tenths of a degree.

The record keeping for fertility awareness methods is complicated. A couple should take a course or consult a counselor at a family planning clinic to learn which signs and times indicate fertile periods. Trying to guess when ovulation has occurred by counting forward from the last menstruation (calendar method) is very risky. This is not an accurate method, and it should not be used unless you are also recording body temperature or checking the vaginal mucus.

Withdrawal

Withdrawal is a method of contraception in which the male attempts to pull his penis out of the woman's vagina before he ejaculates, or "comes." If he is successful in doing this, the sperm will not enter the woman's vagina and fertilize an egg.

This is not a reliable method of birth control for two reasons. First, a man often releases some sperm in the lubricating fluid that he secretes during sexual stimulation before he reaches his climax. The method also requires a great deal of self-control and timing because there is a reflexive reaction to thrust deeper into the woman during intercourse rather than to pull out. This method should only be used as a last resort if no other methods of contraception are available, since it poses the greatest risk of pregnancy.

The Douche

Douching is a technique in which the woman sprays fluid up into her vagina after having intercourse. The douche is supposed to wash the sperm out of the woman's body before the sperm can unite with an egg. It is the most unreliable of all the techniques discussed so far. The sperm begin swimming up to meet an egg before the woman can insert the douching fluid, so many of the sperm are out of the fluid's reach by the time the woman douches. There is even the chance that the pressure of the fluid may give the slower sperm a boost up through the vagina to meet an egg!

Voluntary Sterilization

Sterilization (vasectomy or tubal ligation) is a surgical procedure that prevents the egg from joining with the sperm in the uterus. If the egg and the sperm

ACTIVITY

Making Decisions about Birth Control

The major goal of this activity is that you practice talking with others about this important subject so that you will be comfortable communicating about birth control in the event that you decide to enter into a sexually intimate relationship. Break into groups of four and discuss each situation; decide on the general advice you would give to each couple, the method of contraception you would recommend, and the reasons for your recommendations. Record your answers so that you may share them with the class as a whole.

DIRECTIONS:

In each of the following cases, a couple is making decisions about intercourse and birth control. Discuss the situation with your group and together decide: (1) What general advice would you give the couple? and (2) What birth control method do you recommend for them? Why?

Choices may include:

abstinence—no sex
outercourse—sex without intercourse

condom	foam	diaphragm
condom and foam	sponge	pill

1. Jane and Jim have been going together for over a year. When they began to have intercourse, Jane got the pill—she took it for about six months. Then a month ago they had a fight and decided not to see each other for awhile. Jane stopped taking the pill. Last night they got together, talked things over, and decided to continue with their relationship. Tonight, they're alone at Jim's and really want to resume their sexual relationship.

Advice: _____

_____

Birth Control: _____

Why: _____

_____

2. Jeff and Susan are crazy about each other. For the last three months they've done a lot of heavy petting, but never had intercourse. Tonight is very special because tomorrow Susan leaves the city for a summer job at the shore. They know they won't see each other for at least a month and both want to show their love for each other by having intercourse. They've been to a late movie, parked the car, but they don't have any birth control.

Advice: _____

_____

Birth Control: _____

Why: _____

_____

3. Dave and Janet have been having intercourse once or twice a week for six months. They've been using "withdrawal" and it seemed to work OK—until two weeks ago when Janet's period was late. For ten days they worried that she was pregnant and they both vowed that they'd never have unprotected intercourse again. Finally, Janet's period came, but now she's embarrassed to go to a family planning center. Dave doesn't want to use a condom.

Advice: _____

_____

Birth Control: _____

Why: _____

_____

4. Ken's family has strong religious values including the belief that intercourse should be saved for marriage. Ken respects both his parents and his religion. Ken is dating Cindy, and he cares for her a great deal. Cindy has already had intercourse in a previous relationship (she took the pill then, but stopped it when the relationship broke up three months ago). Cindy thinks it's natural and right that she and Ken should express their love for each other by having intercourse.

Advice: _____

_____

Birth Control: _____

Why: _____

_____

5. Steve and Cathy are married and have one child. The couple has been using condoms for contraception. Steve would like to have a second child, but Cathy prefers to return to her career full-time now that their son is entering school.

Advice: _____

_____

Birth Control: _____

Why: _____

_____

"Choice and Consequences: Making Decisions About Birth Control" is reprinted, by permission, from Peggy Brick and Carolyn Cooperman, *Positive Images: A New Approach to Contraceptive Education* (2d ed.). Planned Parenthood of Bergen County, 1987, pp. 45–46.

ACTIVITY

"Putting Birth Control into Romance"

Break into groups of two (male and female in each pair, if possible) and work with someone of the opposite sex who was not in your group for the previous activity. Complete this activity, and record your answers so that you may share them with the whole class. Once again, the goal of the activity is to reinforce your knowledge about birth control and to help you become more comfortable in discussing birth control with another person.

Directions:

You are to describe a romantic scene in which the couple is discussing the possibility of using birth control. Your description should include:

The Setting:

Describe the place where the couple is having the conversation. Try to make it as vivid as possible so the reader can "see" the spot.

_____

_____

Characters:

Describe, briefly, each of the partners. Include their names, ages, personal characteristics, and interests.

Female: _____

_____

Male: _____

_____

The Relationship:

Tell how the couple met, how long they have known each other, and the present status of their relationship.

_____

_____

_____

_____

The Feelings:

Tell how each partner feels about the possibility of getting and using birth control.

Female: _____

_____

Male: _____

_____

The Dialogue:

Write the verbal exchange between the partners in which they are discussing the possible use of birth control. There should be at least three quotations from each partner.

Here are some examples:

First Partner: I won't feel as much if I have a condom on.

Second Partner: Well, you won't feel anything if you don't have a condom on.

First Partner: It will interrupt sex.

Second Partner: Let me put it on for you. You'll love it.

First Partner: Condoms are a total turnoff.

Second Partner: There's nothing great about getting pregnant either. Please give the condom a try or let's look for alternatives.

First Partner: What alternatives do you suggest?

Second Partner: Just petting and kissing. We could postpone sex, even though we both want it.[23]

Now make up your dialogue for the partners who are discussing the use of birth control.

First Partner: _____

_____

_____

Second Partner: _____

_____

_____

First Partner: _____

_____

_____

Second Partner: _____

_____

_____

First Partner: _____

_____

_____

Second Partner: _____

_____

_____

"Putting Birth Control into Romance" is reprinted, by permission, from Peggy Brick and Carolyn Cooperman, *Positive Images: A New Approach to Contraceptive Education* (2d ed.) Planned Parenthood of Bergen County, 1987, pp. 30–31.

cannot join together, there is no risk of pregnancy. Women who have been surgically sterilized through a tubal ligation (cutting and tying of fallopian tubes) continue to menstruate, but their eggs do not enter the uterus. Men who have undergone a vasectomy (cutting and tying of the vas deferens) continue to ejaculate during sex, but their ejaculate does not contain sperm.

Neither operation should have any effect on a person's sexual behavior. There is no tampering with the hormones so there should also be no change in the person's feelings of femininity or masculinity. Contraceptive sterilization has become one of the most widely used methods of family planning in the world. Female sterilization has become more popular in this country and, together with male sterilization, has outstripped even the pill as the contraceptive method chosen by the highest percentage of women in their childbearing years. Failure rates are lower for sterilization than for the temporary methods of contraception. Failure rates of less than 1 percent are generally reported.

Sterilization is generally permanent and not reversible. For this reason, a couple must be certain, when they make this decision, that they do not wish to have any more children.

The woman's sterilization method, tubal ligation, is more complicated than the man's, and it is performed in a hospital. It involves more risk for medical complications than does the vasectomy, which is usually performed in a doctor's office or a clinic and does not require hospitalization.

As you can see, there are many birth control methods available, and researchers continue to develop new contraceptives; studies are currently underway on a pill taken by men. Therefore, it pays to update your knowledge about birth control from time to time, through your physician or your family planning clinic. Choose an effective method that is most comfortable for you and your partner. If the method you choose does not work out for any reason, discuss it and try another method. The Planned Parenthood Federation of America, a neighborhood family planning clinic, or your college's health services division can be very helpful in offering you additional information or individual counseling. Keep trying out different methods until you find one that suits you, but *do not have sex without using some form of birth control.* You owe that to yourself and to your partner.

■ SEXUALLY TRANSMITTED DISEASES (STDs)

Aside from birth control, the other important topic that belongs in a discussion of intimate relationships is sexually transmitted diseases (STDs). According to the World Health Organization, 250 million new cases of STDs are reported each year. In the United States, the annual incidence of new cases is 12 million, and two-thirds of these occur in women and men under the age of 25. If current trends continue in this country, at least one person in four will contract an STD at some point in his or her life.[24] If you are involved in a relationship that includes sex, information on this subject is literally a matter of life and death. Of course AIDS is the disease on everyone's mind today, but other STDs can also result in severe illness, sterility, and even death if they are not treated. Figure 10.5 presents some of the facts associated with STDs.

Acquired Immunodeficiency Disease Syndrome (AIDS)

AIDS involves a set of symptoms caused by the body's inability to fight infection. When your body's natural immune system is destroyed, you become susceptible to a host of diseases that are not troublesome to people with normally functioning immune systems. Although AIDS was first described as originating in Africa around 1981, many authorities mark 1977 as the beginning of the

Figure 10.5   *Some Facts Associated with STDs*

One out of four Americans has an STD. (*New York Times,* 1995.[25])

HIV infection is now the most common cause of death among people aged 25 to 44 years. (U.S. Centers For Disease Control and Prevention, 1996.[26])

There are more than 12 million new cases of STDs (non AIDS) each year in the United States. (U.S. Public Health Service, 1995.[27])

Eighty-six percent of diagnosed STDs occur in 15- to 19-year olds. (U.S. Public Health Service, 1995.[28])

Women are more severely affected by STDs than men because they are more susceptible to infection and less likely to experience symptoms which makes detection more difficult until serious problems develop. (U.S. Public Health Service, 1995.[29])

Sixty percent of college-age women who contract STDs have had sex under the influence of alcohol. (U.S. Public Health Service, 1995.[30])

More than one million Americans have tested positive for the AIDS virus. Approximately half will develop AIDS within 10 years. (*New York Times,* 1996, U.S. Department of Health & Human Services, 1994.[31, 32])

Chlamydia is the most common STD. In 75 percent of chlamydia infection cases, there may be no symptoms. Chlamydia can cause serious pelvic inflammatory disease (PID), urinary tract infections (UTIs), chronic pain, and sterility. (U.S. Public Health Service, 1995.[33])

By the year 2000, 30 to 40 million people world-wide will be infected with the HIV virus; 6000 new cases are added to the list of infected individuals *each day.* (*New York Times,* 1995.[34])

There is no cure for herpes. Symptoms may include blistery sores, pain, fever, headaches, burning during urination, and a general run-down feeling. (U.S. Public Health Service, 1995.[35])

The pattern of AIDS infection has changed; in this country and throughout the world, it is increasingly spread through heterosexual intercourse. (*New York Times,* 1995.[36])

Eighty percent of women who have gonorrhea show no symptoms. It can cause serious pelvic inflammatory disease (PID), heart problems, central nervous system disorders, and sterility. (U.S. Public Health Service, 1995.[37])

HIV epidemic in the United States. Cases have been reported in all 50 states, and the number of people affected continues to increase.

According to recent reports from the White House Office of National AIDS Policy and the Centers for Disease Control, one of every four people who become infected with the virus is under the age of 20, and HIV infection has now become *the most common cause of death* among people aged 25 through 44 years. More than 300 thousand people in the United States have died from AIDS, and more than one million people have tested positive for the AIDS virus.[38, 39, 40]

Aside from the increase in deaths among young people, the pattern of who is contracting AIDS has changed in recent years. In the 1980s, about half the individuals who became infected were gay men, more than a quarter were intravenous drug users, and fewer than 10 percent were heterosexuals. HIV

infections in the mid-1990s, show a very different pattern: Only a quarter of these infections occur in gay men, about half are among drug users who shared needles, and *about a quarter are heterosexually transmitted.* About 70 to 80 percent of the people who are contracting HIV infection through heterosexual intercourse are women; the majority contract the disease during crack, alcohol, or other drug binges when they are careless about safe sex practices.[41]

It is little consolation that the news from the international front is even more bleak. The World Health Organization predicts that by the year 2000, 30 to 40 million people will be infected with the HIV virus; eighty-five hundred new cases are added to the list of individuals infected each day.[42] Experts estimate that parts of Africa will lose a quarter of their adult population to the disease, and that 10 million Asians will die of AIDS before the year 2015.[43] The overwhelming majority of AIDS cases are reported in developing countries. On almost every continent, AIDS is a leading cause of death among young women, and most of them have been infected through heterosexual intercourse.

There is no medical treatment available at this time that will cure the disease nor is there any vaccine that can protect against it. Although recent research indicates that various drugs may be effective in slowing the progress of the disease, AIDS is almost always fatal. More than 300,000 people have died from AIDS in the United States, but many more are carriers of the virus.[44] Most of them feel well, they are not under medical care, and they may not even know that they are infected. They are, therefore, capable of spreading the disease to others with whom they share sex or needles.

Diagnosis of AIDS is made when a person contracts a disease that indicates that his or her body's natural defense system is not working. The two most common diseases that are used in the diagnosis of AIDS are Kaposi's sarcoma, a rare form of cancer that results in purplish blotches and bumps on the skin, and *Pneumocystis carinii* pneumonia, a lung infection characterized by a persistent cough and fever with difficulties in breathing. Since these diseases are not usually found in people whose natural immune systems are working properly, they are indicative of the damaged defense systems found in people with AIDS.

AIDS seems to be caused by the T-lymphotropic human immunodeficiency virus (HIV). We now have accurate tests available, such as the enzyme linked immunosorbent assay (ELISA) and the Western blot test, which can detect antibodies to the AIDS virus in the blood. These antibodies are almost always present when an individual has AIDS or one of the AIDS-related conditions. Early diagnosis and treatment can markedly extend the quality and duration of life in infected individuals.

A certain percentage of the people who have the HIV virus do not seem to develop any symptoms, but they are contagious and can transmit the disease to others. About half the people infected with HIV develop AIDS within 10 years.[45] Ten or more years may pass between the time an individual is infected with the virus and the time the symptoms first appear. A person may, therefore, be contagious to others without even knowing that he or she has the disease.

Although more than one million people have tested positive for AIDS in the United States, the disease occurs in higher percentages among certain groups of people. These high-risk groups include gay or bisexual men, illegal drug users who inject their drugs intravenously, individuals who require frequent blood donations, partners (male and female) of people who are infected with AIDS, and babies born to women who have AIDS. The disease is much more widespread among men than women, among blacks and Hispanics than other races, among people from ages 20 to 49 than other ages, and among city dwellers than rural residents.

Don't assume that how people label themselves (heterosexual or homosexual) tells you much about their actual sexual behavior. Studies of men from the general population, which is mostly heterosexual, show that more than 30 percent have had at least one sexual experience with another male since puberty. Three studies of homosexual men reported that between 62 and 79 percent had engaged in heterosexual intercourse. Four other studies found that 15 to 26 percent of homosexual men had been married. A recent study by the Kinsey Institute of lesbian women found that 74 percent had engaged in heterosexual behavior at least once since age 18.[46]

At the present time, the rate of HIV infection is increasing most steeply among heterosexual women (and their babies) whose male partners are infected with the AIDS virus.[47] In other words, heterosexual intercourse is increasingly replacing exposure to gay sex and shared needles among intravenous drug users as the major avenue for new HIV infections.

A study analyzing blood samples taken from clinics on 19 college and university campuses across the country found that 0.2 percent (1 in 500) were positive for the HIV virus.[48] If the results of this anonymous testing reflect the situation around the country, then approximately 25,000 of the nation's college students are infected with the virus.[49] (The study did not include schools from the New York or Florida areas where HIV infection is particularly high.)

Transmission of AIDS

Thirty-four to 43 percent of college students surveyed would hide sexual infidelity to maintain a relationship.

Many people hide experiences in their past or present lives from their partners. This is particularly true when they are beginning romantic relationships and wish to make a good impression. They are unlikely to mention intravenous drug use, bisexual encounters, or experiences with male or female prostitutes. A survey of 18- to 25-year-old students attending college in southern California concluded that more than 40 percent would understate the number of previous sexual partners in order to have intercourse, that 34 to 43 would not disclose an episode of sexual infidelity to maintain a sexual relationship, and that 20 percent of men and 4 percent of women would lie about having a negative HIV test in order to have sex.[50]

Twenty percent of men and 4 percent of women would lie about a positive HIV test in order to have sex.

Researchers have determined how the AIDS virus is transmitted, and their findings explain why certain groups are at much higher risk of contracting the disease. The virus is spread through contact with bodily fluids such as blood, semen, fluids from the vagina or penis, urine, and feces. If such infected fluids come in contact with another person's body, the AIDS virus may gain entrance through a cut or a place where the skin is very thin and porous. The skin is thin around the mucus linings of the sex organs, the anus, the mouth, and the eyes. Contact between these parts of the body and the infected fluids from another person's body is likely to result in transmission of the virus.

AIDS is spread through sexual contact, but certain sexual practices, such as anal sex, are more likely to result in transmission because the virus can cross the thin mucus linings that are often damaged during this type of sex. The virus in the semen then has the opportunity to enter the partner's blood system through the torn or damaged area. Oral sex is also risky because of the increased likelihood of contact between damaged mucus linings in the mouth and throat and the virus which is present in pre-ejaculatory fluid and vaginal secretions.

These high-risk behaviors are common among homosexual and bisexual men, and they explain why the incidence of AIDS is higher among these groups. Heterosexuals who participate in these types of sex, however, are also more likely to get AIDS if they have sex with a contagious partner. If you must engage in these high-risk sexual practices, use a condom to minimize the likelihood of contact between infected body fluids from your partner and your mucus membranes. Studies have shown that condoms, especially those treated with nonoxynol-9, are effective in decreasing the probability that you will contract the disease. Use synthetic (latex) condoms rather than natural (animal membrane) condoms.

Another common way that AIDS is spread is through the sharing of infected needles between illegal drug users. The virus, present in the blood and on the needle of the infected user, is directly injected and transmitted into the blood of the partner. The common practice of sharing needles among intravenous drug users explains why AIDS occurs more frequently among this group of people. If you must use illegal drugs, do not share needles with other people. The popularity of tatoos among young people also presents risks for the transmission of HIV if sterilized or disposable equipment and pigments are not used.

If you travel in other countries, be alert to medical facilities that do not use disposable needles. Sharing needles with other patients is a high-risk

VANESSA WAS IN A FATAL CAR ACCIDENT LAST NIGHT. ONLY SHE DOESN'T KNOW IT YET.

Every year, thousands of young people die in car accidents caused by drugs and alcohol. But now you can wreck your life without hitting the gas pedal. The number of reported AIDS cases among teenagers has increased by 96% in the last two years. If you get high and forget, even for a moment, how risky sex can be, you're putting your life on the line. Call 1-800-662-HELP for help and information. **AIDS. ANOTHER WAY DRUGS CAN KILL.**

National Institute on Drug Abuse, U.S. Department of Health & Human Services.

Photo by Ken Nahoum

Reprinted courtesy of the Advertising Council.

ACTIVITY

Understanding People Who Have AIDS

The Whitney Project began when Whitney, an 11-year-old girl with AIDS in Chicago, was befriended by a sixth-grade class in rural New Mexico. It has since connected American students with children suffering from HIV infection in Africa, Russia, and the United States. Exchanges of letters, visits, and phone calls have helped students learn more about HIV and AIDS, develop compassion for people who have life-threatening illnesses, and discover the positive impact of community action.

Contact the Whitney Project (P.O. Box 2511, Santa Fe, NM 87504) or a clinic, hospital, or hospice in your area that treats people who have been diagnosed with HIV infection. Tell them that you want to befriend a person with AIDS. Often people with this diagnosis feel isolated, rejected, or stigmatized. Visit or begin a correspondence with the person and offer your friendship and sympathy. Write a report about the experience of living with AIDS and share that report with your instructor or classmates.

---

practice because you cannot be sure that the other patient does not have AIDS or some other contagious disease. Medical facilities in this country use disposable needles so you need not fear infection if you donate blood or require injections for other medical reasons. If you come into contact with needles that have not been properly disposed of or blood vials that may be infected, handle them carefully. If you puncture your skin with the needle or broken glass, you may become infected with the AIDS virus.

A third way that AIDS is contracted is through infected blood products. This explains the higher incidence of AIDS among hemophiliacs, who require frequent donations of blood products, and among babies born to infected women, who share blood systems with their mothers. If you have AIDS and become pregnant, consult your doctor, as your baby will most likely be born with the disease. Early detection and treatment can improve the chances for a healthy baby.

Since 1985, tests in this country have been used to screen all blood products for the presence of the AIDS virus. The ELISA test is reasonably accurate for this purpose, and testing has reduced the number of people who contract AIDS because they require blood transfusions or the donation of blood products. If you are injured while traveling in a foreign country, be aware that careful screening of blood products is not practiced in many places.

AIDS cannot be spread through casual contact with people who are infected. Studies show that even family members who live in close contact with AIDS victims and share food, towels, cups, and other personal possessions do not become infected. It is also a myth that AIDS can be spread through contact with infected insects, cats, dogs, or toilet seats. Nor can you contract AIDS from donating blood in this country. Disposable needles are used, so it is not likely that you will come in contact with a needle that had been used for another donor. AIDS can only be spread through sex or contact between infected body fluids and an opening into your blood system. If you do not expose yourself to these things, you are not likely to be infected by the virus.

The only certain way to avoid AIDS is to abstain totally from sex and to avoid contact with infected body fluids. However, if you have decided to go ahead with a sexual relationship, review the precautions listed in Figure 10.6

Figure 10.6   *Precautions Against AIDS*

1. **Know your partner's medical and sex history.** Do not have unprotected sex with someone who has been infected with the AIDS virus. Unfortunately, it is difficult to know whether a person has AIDS; many people do not even know when they have the disease. If, in the last twelve years, your partner has had sex with anyone who was infected with the disease, your partner may be infected with the virus. When it comes to contracting AIDS, remember that each time you have sex with someone, you are having sex with all that person's partners over the past ten to twelve years.

   Although AIDS seems to spread more easily from men to women, reports from Africa and Asia indicate that female prostitutes are spreading the disease among their male clients, and the fastest-growing group of people who are diagnosed with AIDS in this country are the female partners of infected men. In many parts of the world, AIDS is spread primarily through sexual contact between men and women, and the World Health Organization says that heterosexual contact is expected to account for 70 percent of AIDS cases while homosexual contact and intravenous drug use will each account for only 10 percent of AIDS infections. You do not have to be gay or bisexual to get AIDS!

2. **Use a condom whenever you are having sex.** Unless you are absolutely certain that, in the past twelve years, your partner has not slept with anyone who might have been exposed to AIDS, use a condom. Unfortunately, the virus is present in the body fluids that might be touched even before intercourse actually takes place. The virus could enter through a cut on your hand or in your mouth unless a condom is worn throughout the entire sexual interaction. Using condoms, especially those treated with nonoxynol-9, lowers the probability of contracting AIDS and also protects you against other STDs.

3. **Limit the number of people with whom you have sex.** The more people with whom you sleep, the more likely it is that you will be exposed to the virus. If you have sex with partners who come from the high-risk groups, such as homosexual or bisexual men, intravenous drug users, or persons who require regular blood donations, use a condom and avoid high-risk sexual practices.

4. **Avoid high-risk sexual practices such as oral and anal sex.** Avoid high-risk sexual practices with both male and female partners. If you engage in these practices, use a condom throughout your sexual encounter.

5. **Avoid contact with body fluids of people who might be infected.** Never share needles with anyone. Handle needles or body fluids of infected people with care. Do not allow these items to touch parts of your body, such as places with open cuts or your eyes, where the virus might be able to enter your blood system. Do not share contact lenses or makeup with people who might be infected.

6. **Do not have unprotected sex with anyone who has ever used illegal intravenous drugs.** People in this high-risk group are very likely to be carriers of the AIDS virus.

so that you can lower your risk of contracting AIDS. As former Surgeon General C. Everett Koop said, "Who you are has nothing to do with whether you are in danger of being infected with the AIDS virus. What matters is what you do."[51] This message has been emphasized by the growing list of prominent celebrities, such as Magic Johnson, Arthur Ashe, and Greg Louganis who have died from HIV or announced that they are infected with the virus.

Other STDs

Herpes

Each year there are 200,000 new cases, and recurrent infections are much more common. It is estimated that 30 million Americans are infected with the herpes simplex virus.[52] Herpes is a virus of the same sort that causes colds, mumps, measles, chicken pox, or the flu. Type 1 herpes causes cold sores around the mouth, while Type 2 usually involves small, painful sores that develop on the sex organs. These sores may last from two to three weeks, and they may be accompanied by fever, swollen glands, and an overall itchy or run-down feeling. If you have active herpes virus on your skin, there is a good chance that you will spread it to your partner when you have sex.

After the sores heal, you will not be contagious to other people, but the virus is still in your system. Approximately one-third of the people who become infected with herpes will never experience another infection. For the other two-thirds, however, recurrent infections are likely sometime in the future. For some people, these repeated infections do not occur frequently, but for others, recurrent infections may appear every month or two. For some people, the recurrent infections are just as painful as the first one. We do not know why people have different reactions to the herpes virus, nor do we know what triggers the repeated infections.

Genital herpes is contracted by contact with active herpes viruses. Thousands of these viruses are present in the sores. A person may experience an itching or tingling feeling before a sore appears on a certain area of the skin. Contagious virus is present on that part of the skin from the time the tingling or itching occurs until the sore has healed and disappeared. You can spread herpes by touching one of your sores and then touching another part of your body or by touching another person's sore with your skin. Infection is particularly likely if you touch a cut that allows the virus direct access into your blood system or if you touch a part of your body where the skin is thin, such as your eye, mouth, or genital area.

If you avoid touching the sores and do not allow anyone else to touch the sores, you can stop the spread of herpes. It is not wise to have sex when active herpes virus is on your skin. This will be true from the time you experience the first tingling or itching until the time the sore has completely healed and disappeared. Occasionally, small numbers of herpes virus may also be present even though you have not experienced any symptoms. This may happen in the case of someone who does not even know that he or she has herpes. In order to prevent the spread of herpes, it is wise to always use a condom and nonoxynol-9 spermicide whenever you have sex.

Outbreaks of herpes should be treated by your physician. There is no cure at the present time, however, the oral antiviral medication, acyclovir, has been helpful in reducing symptoms.

Chlamydia

Genital chlamydia infections have become the most common bacterial STD, and they are the leading cause of preventable infertility and ectopic pregnancies.

There are 4 million new cases in the United States each year. These infections spread easily because infected individuals often do not seek medical attention since the symptoms are mild.[53]

The chlamydia parasite can infect the internal sex organs or the eyes. In many men and women, the infection results in itching and burning during urination, and it also results in pelvic inflammatory disease in women. In some cases, however, the infection is more problematic because the person experiences only mild symptoms or no symptoms at all after contracting the infection. The infected person does not realize that he or she requires treatment, nor does the person know that he or she is contagious to others. The disease can lead to blindness and to more serious urinary problems if it is not treated.

Diagnosis is made by a doctor who will prescribe antibiotics to cure the disease. Physicians are currently seeing many cases in which an individual contracts both chlamydia and gonorrhea at the same time, so the medical examination should cover both diseases. People who have suffered from several sexually transmitted diseases are more likely to become infected with the AIDS virus. You will not contract chlamydia, syphilis, or gonorrhea from toilet seats, swimming pools, or from casual contact with infected people. These diseases are only transmitted through contact with infected sexual organs.

Gonorrhea

There are 1 to 2 million new cases of gonorrhea in the United States each year. It is the most commonly reported communicable disease in this country.[54] Gonorrhea is caused by bacteria (gonococcus or GC), and it can result in a discharge (pus) from the urinary tract, a frequent urge to urinate, a burning sensation during urination, an inflammation of the vagina and internal sex organs, and rash, fever, and sores in the mouth. Gonorrhea is particularly dangerous when it does not cause any symptoms because the person does not

ACTIVITY

Communicating about STDs

This activity is designed to answer any questions that you may have about sexually transmitted diseases, to make you aware of where you can get answers to your questions, and to help you become more comfortable in talking about this important topic.

1. Take three index cards and write a question about STDs (or any question about sex, if you do not have one about STDs) on each of the three cards. If you really cannot think of three questions about sex, just write that you have no questions; you must write something on the cards. Do not put your name on the cards; this part of the exercise is *anonymous.*

2. Hand the cards to your instructor. He or she will have the questions typed or written on new cards and will distribute them to the class at the next session so that each person receives between one and three questions to research. Take the cards to the health services office at your college or call your physician or a family planning clinic and explain that you have a class assignment to find the answers to the questions on your cards. Ask the questions and any others that you may have. Then come back to class and report on your research.

know that he or she needs treatment, nor does the person realize that he or she can spread the disease to sex partners.

If gonorrhea is not treated, it will infect the internal sexual organs and can lead to sterility. It can also infect the liver and cause serious urinary problems so that the person is unable to urinate. Arthritis, infection of the heart valves, and widespread infection all through the body may also occur. If a pregnant woman has gonorrhea, her newborn infant will also contract it; this leads to blindness in the baby. The disease can be successfully treated by a course of antibiotics.

Syphilis

There are approximately 40,000 new cases of syphilis in the United States each year.[55] Syphilis is caused by a type of microorganism called a treponema pallidum. It may result in a chancre, or sore, on the skin of the sex organs or mouth. The sore is usually painless and appears two to six weeks after the infection. The sore disappears after a short time, but the organism is still active in the body. If the person is not treated, the disease may spread throughout the body.

All symptoms will disappear as the organism becomes inactive for anywhere from two to forty years. During this time, the treponeme spreads through the blood and lymph glands to all parts of the body. When the symptoms appear again, they are very serious, resulting in severe damage to brain, heart, liver, kidney, and other vital organs. The person may, for example, develop a serious mental disorder; a certain percentage of people even die from the disease when it has reached this advanced stage. Syphilis can be diagnosed and successfully treated by antibiotics.

Hepatitis B

The hepatitis B virus, which is now spread predominantly through sexual contact, results in 150,000 new cases each year. Many of these cases result in chronic liver disease, cancer, and death. No specific treatment exists for hepatitis B, but it is the only STD for which we have a vaccine. Researchers suspect that sexual transmission may also play a part in the spread of hepatitis C virus.[56]

Genital Warts

Herpes and hepatitis are not the only STDs caused by a virus. There are 3 million new cases of genital warts due to the human papilloma virus diagnosed each year. It has been estimated that up to one half of all sexually active young women in the United States are infected with this virus. Single or multiple painless growths may appear on the genital organs. They may enlarge and destroy tissue or cause complications during pregnancy. Several treatments are available including surgery, topical solutions, and cryotherapy.[57]

Pediculosis Pubis

Pediculosis pubis ("crabs," or pubic lice) is a condition in which lice are spread from one sexual partner to another. (Fleas can also be transmitted in the same way.) The lice generally remain in the hair surrounding the sex organs, although they may travel up to the hair on the chest, the eyelashes, and the eyebrows. The lice multiply rapidly and feed on the person's blood, causing tremendous itching. The condition can be successfully treated with a physician's prescription for a medicated shampoo.

Your Responsibilities

If you contract an STD, it is important that you get treatment for it. It is also important that you tell your sex partner about it so that he or she can get treatment; otherwise, your partner will infect you again and may also spread the disease to other sexual partners.

A number of courts have recognized a legal and moral obligation to inform a partner about a sexually transmitted disease. For example, a court awarded $14 million to the lover of a famous actor because the lover was not informed that the actor had AIDS. It is important that you learn to feel comfortable while talking about this subject.

ACTIVITY

A Safer Sex Mixer

This activity is designed to help you feel more comfortable talking about contraception and sexually transmitted diseases. It involves statements concerning safer sex. Move quickly around the room until you find someone who agrees with one of the statements on the following list and ask that person to sign his or her name on the line next to the statement. *No one may sign more than one statement.* The winner is the person who gets all statements signed first, or who has the most signed at the end of the allotted time.

Find Someone Who

1. Thinks schools should take a more active role in educating students about sex. _____

2. Knows someone who has changed their sexual behavior because of AIDS. _____

3. Can name 3 terrific alternatives to intercourse. _____

4. Believes ALL parts of the body are sexy. _____

5. Knows someone who has NOT changed their sexual behavior because of AIDS. _____

6. Can name 3 ways condoms improve sex. _____

7. Has talked with their parents about sex and AIDS. _____

8. Has encouraged someone to be more careful about sex. _____

9. Would insist a partner have a HIV antibody test before considering intercourse. _____

10. Has read a book about safer sex. _____

11. Thinks the dangers of AIDS and other sexually transmitted diseases have been exaggerated by the media. _____

12. Has no trouble saying "no," when they want to say "no." _____

13. Would be embarrassed to buy a condom. _____

14. Would not be embarrassed to buy a condom. _____

15. Believes AIDS will change most people's sexual behavior. _____

16. Believes that people who get a sexually transmitted disease really deserve it. _____

17. Believes that "NO" means no. _____

18. Believes it is useless to try to get people to practice safer sex. _____

19. Thinks it's OK for a woman to be prepared by buying and carrying condoms. _____

20. Can describe the steps to proper condom use. _____

21. Thinks that a woman is never responsible for her own rape. _____

22. Can name 3 ways to improve the effectiveness of a condom. _____

"A Safer Sex Mixer" is reprinted courtesy of Planned Parenthood of Greater Northern New Jersey from P. Brick et al., *Teaching Safer Sex,* 1989, Hackensack, NJ: Planned Parenthood of Greater Northern New Jersey.

ACTIVITY

Collecting Information about Sexually Transmitted Diseases

This activity is meant to familiarize you with the location and workings of a local family planning clinic; it is also meant to give you more practice in communicating about STDs.

Choose one of the following STDs for a research project. Visit a family planning clinic. (Planned Parenthood holds clinics on many college campuses, so you may not have to leave campus to complete this assignment.) Ask for a pamphlet about the disease. If the pamphlet does not present complete information or if the center has no pamphlet on the disease you have chosen, interview a counselor at the center to find information about the disease. Write down the name of the person you interview and the location of the center.

SEXUALLY TRANSMITTED DISEASES

- Acquired immunodeficiency disease syndrome (AIDS)
- Acute urethral syndrome, or cystitis
- Cervical intraepithelial neoplasia
- Chancroid
- Chlamydia
- Cytomegalovirus infections
- Enteric infections
- Genital warts
- Gonorrhea
- Granuloma inguinale
- Hepatitis B
- Herpes genitalis

■ Lymphogranuloma venereum
■ Molluscum contagiosum
■ Mucopurulent cervicitis
■ Nongonococcal urethritis
■ Pediculosis pubis
■ Pelvic inflammatory disease

■ Scabies
■ Syphilis
■ Vulvovaginitis
■ Trichomoniasis
■ Bacterial vaginosis
■ Candidiasis

Bring the pamphlet back to class and present a report to the class. If your instructor does not have enough class time to process this activity, he or she may prefer that you hand it in as a written assignment. In that case, attach the pamphlet to your report.

———

Reproduced, with permission, from R. A. Hatcher et al., *Contraceptive Technology,* 16th rev. ed. Atlanta, GA: Printed Matter, Inc., and New York: Irvington Publishers, 1994, pp. 86–103.

✍ REFLECTIONS FOR YOUR JOURNAL

1. Reflect upon the major factors that have influenced your values in intimate relationships. How have your religious beliefs, parents' values, friends' ideas, and your readings affected your values?

2. Do you feel confident of your ability to communicate and stand by your values? How has your ability been tested? If you do not feel comfortable in this area, what would give you greater confidence?

3. If you know someone who has decided to delay or abstain from sexual intercourse, how do you feel about that decision? Which strategies described in this chapter can help reinforce such a decision?

4. If you decided to engage in a sexual relationship but were not ready to begin a family, which contraceptive method would you choose? Explain your choice.

5. What responsibilities do you believe sexual partners have to communicate with each other about sexually transmitted diseases? How would you go about ensuring such communication?

Notes

1. R. P. Keeling, "Student Health in the 1990s," *The Chronicle of Higher Education, 38,* no. 7 (9 October 1991).

2. "Teenage Reproductive Health in the United States" New York: The Alan Guttmacher Institute, 1994.

3. G. Corey, *I Never Knew I Had a Choice,* 2nd ed. Montgomery, CA: Brooks/Cole Publishing Co., 1986.

4. J. Steinhauer, "Big Benefits in Marriage, Studies Say," *New York Times,* 10 April 1995, p. A9.

5. Ibid.

6. Ibid.

7. R. A. Hatcher, J. Trussell, F. Stewart, G. K. Stewart, D. Kowal, F. Guest, W. Cates, and M. Policar *Contraceptive Technology,* 16th rev. ed. New York: Irvington Publishers, 1994, p. 146.

8. Ibid, 142.

9. U.S. Public Health Service, *Get Real: Straight Talk About Women's Health,* Washington, DC: U.S. Public Health Service Office on Women's Health and Society for the Advancement of Women's Health Research, 1995.

10. M. L. Usdansky, "Teen Births: Formula For Disaster," *USA Today,* 22 February 1994, pp. 1a, 2a.

11. Ibid.

12. R. Pear, "Bigger Number of New Mothers Are Unmarried," *New York Times,* 4 December 1991, p. A20.

13. U.S. Public Health Service, op. cit.

14. M. L. Usdansky, op. cit.

15. M. T. Erickson, *Behavior Disorders of Children and Adolescents.* Englewood Cliffs, NJ: Prentice-Hall, 1987.

16. R. Pear, op. cit.

17. R. Hatcher, et al., op cit, p. 141–142.

18. U.S. Public Health Service, op. cit.

19. "Contraceptive Use: Facts in Brief. "New York: Alan Guttmacher Institute, 1996.

20. Ibid.

21. "Birth Control Update: Women's Health News," *Redbook,* September 1990, p. 36.

22. Hatcher et al., op. cit., p. 198.

23. Hatcher et al., op. cit., p. 170.

24. W. E. Leary, "Billions Suffering Needlessly, Study Says" *New York Times,* 2 May 1995, p. C5.

25. Ibid.

26. Centers For Disease Control, "Update: Mortality Attributable to HIV Infection Among Persons Aged 25–44 Years," *Morbidity and Mortality Weekly Report, 45,* no. 6, (February 1996), p. 1.

27. U.S. Public Health Service, op. cit.

28. Ibid.

29. Ibid.

30. Ibid.

31. T. Egan, "Donated Sperm Viewed As Rare Cause of AIDS," *New York Times,* 17 January 1996, p. A10.

32. Department of Health and Human Services, *HIV Infection and AIDS: Are You At Risk?* Washington, DC: U.S. Centers For Disease Control & Prevention, September 1994.

33. U.S. Public Health Service, op. cit.

34. W. E. Leary, op. cit.

35. U.S. Public Health Service, op. cit.

36. G. Kolata, "New Picture of Who Will Get AIDS," *New York Times,* 28 February 1995, p. C3.

37. U.S. Public Health Service, op. cit.

38. L. Alvarez, "Still Lives With AIDS," *New York Times,* 10 March 1996, p. 33.

39. Centers For Disease Control, op. cit.

40. T. Egan, op. cit.

41. G. Kolata, op. cit.

42. L. K. Altman, "India Suddenly Leads in H.I.V., AIDS Meeting Is Told," *New York Times,* 8 July 1996, p. A3.

43. "AIDS Epidemic, Late to Arrive, Now Explodes in Populous Asia," *New York Times,* 21 January 1996, p. A1, A8.

44. T. Egan, op. cit.

45. Department of Health and Human Services, op. cit.

46. Hatcher et al., op. cit., p. 8.

47. G. Kolata, op. cit.

48. H. D. Gayle, R. P. Keeling, M. Garcia-Tunon, B. W. Kilbourne, J. P. Narkunas, F. R. Ingram, M. F. Rogers, and J. W. Curran, "Prevalence of the Human Immunodeficiency Virus Among University Students," *New England Journal of Medicine, 323,* no. 22 (1990), pp. 1538–1541.

49. S. Okie, "Study Finds 1 in 500 College Students Infected with Virus That Causes AIDS," *The Journal News,* 29 May 1989, p. A3.

50. Hatcher et al., op. cit., p. 10.

51. C. E. Koop and Centers for Disease Control, "Understanding AIDS" (brochure), 1988.

52. Hatcher et. al., op. cit., p. 95.

53. Ibid, p. 90.

54. Ibid, p. 92.

55. Ibid, p. 101.

56. Ibid, p. 94.

57. Ibid, pp. 90–92.

Resources for More Information

AIDS Hotline
1-800-433-2437

American College of Obstetricians and
   Gynecologists
409 12th Street, SW
Washington, DC 20004-2188
202-638-5577

Centers for Disease Control and
   Prevention
National AIDS Hotline
P.O. Box 13827
Research Triangle Park
Research Triangle Park, NC 27709
1-800-342-AIDS

Centers for Disease Control and
   Prevention
National Center for Injury Prevention
   and Control
Division of Violence Prevention
Mail Stop K-60
4470 Buford Hwy., NE
Atlanta, GA 30341-3724
770-488-4362

Centers for Disease Control and
   Prevention
National STD Hotline
P.O. Box 13827
Research Triangle Park
Research Triangle Park, NC 27709
1-800-227-8922

Family Violence Prevention Fund
383 Rhode Island Street, Suite 304
San Francisco, CA 94103-5133
415-252-8900

National AIDS Information
   Clearinghouse
P.O. Box 6003
Rockville, MD 20850
1-800-458-5231

National Clothesline Project
P.O. Box 727
Brewster, MA 02631
508-385-7004

National Coalition Against Domestic
   Violence
P.O. Box 18749
Denver, CO 80218
303-839-1852

National Resource Center on Domestic
   Violence
1717 Lamont Street, NW, Apt. D
Washington, DC 20010
202-387-6729

9to5, National Association of Working
   Women
614 Superior Avenue, NW, Room, 852
Cleveland, OH 44113
1-800-522-0925

Planned Parenthood Federation of
   America
810 7th Avenue
New York, NY 10019
1-800-829-7732 (for general information,
   brochures)
1-800-230-7526 (for a clinic in your area)

Rape Crisis Hotline
P.O. Box 34125
Washington, DC 20043
1-800-656-4673

Rape Hotline
1-212-577-7777

Sida Hotline (Espanol)
1-800-233-7432

U.S. Public Health Service's Office on
   Women's Health
200 Independence Avenue, SW, Room
   730B
Washington, DC 20201
202-690-7650

CHAPTER

A HEALTHY LIFESTYLE

■ HEALTHY BODY, HEALTHY MIND

Why is a chapter on health included in a text on succeeding in college? Because you can't survive, let alone succeed, unless your body is functioning well. Your mind cannot function effectively without a body to nurture and protect it. If you abuse your body or do not get adequate rest, proper nutrition, or sufficient exercise, your body will eventually break down on you. If you deny yourself those essentials, you compromise your immune system and fall prey to whatever diseases are lurking about. The same holds true if you abuse your body with excessive doses of stress, caffeine, nicotine, alcohol, or other drugs. Your daily eating habits and level of physical activity now directly influence your risk for the nation's top killers: heart disease, cancer, and stroke. Alcohol, cocaine, and other drugs may kill you faster, but any of the abuses listed above will eventually lead to serious breakdown. You can't study if your physical plant has shut down!

■ GUIDELINES FOR GOOD NUTRITION

Follow generally accepted health guidelines.

Fad diets come and go, as do nutrition "experts." There are, however, certain guidelines for a healthy diet that are generally accepted by most physicians. If you follow as many of these guidelines as possible, you will be rewarded by a mind and body that feel better, function better, and resist disease better.

Reduce salt, sugar, and fat in your diet.

Reduce the amount of salt, fat, and sugar in your diet. The typical American diet is one of the worst in the world. Our infatuation with meat, fried foods, and highly processed foods results in serious health problems. Leading causes of death in this country, such as heart disease, cancer, stroke, and diabetes, are all associated with our poor eating patterns. Excessive salt intake is strongly linked with high blood pressure, and foods that are high in saturated fat also increase your risk of heart attacks. Reduce cholesterol (which clogs your arteries and endangers your heart) wherever possible by switching to skimmed or partially skimmed dairy products, cutting back on the amount of meat you eat, and using vegetable oils instead of butter.

Reduce alcohol consumption.

At 7 calories per gram, alcohol is almost as fattening as fat but supplies little or no nutrition. What is worse is that alcohol interferes with your judgment, so after a few drinks you are more likely to overeat. Alcohol is associated with other more serious consequences for your health such as illness and death from a host of cancers, heart disease, cirrhosis of the liver, gastritis, hepatitis, and various accidents due to impaired judgment and perception. Instead of alcohol, make a spritzer with your favorite juice and carbonated water.

Excessive consumption of sugar may be related to diabetes and mood swings such as those experienced during depression; the "empty" calories in sugar also discourage you from eating nutritious foods that your body needs. Increasing the percentage of calories in your diet that comes from complex carbohydrates will automatically help you reduce fat and sugar levels. Complex carbohydrates are found in foods that are high in starch and fiber (whole-grain bread, rice, pasta, cereals, etc.) as opposed to the carbohydrates present in high-sugar foods such as candy and soda. Complex carbohydrates enter the bloodstream more slowly, giving you longer lasting energy. On the other hand, sugar will give you a sudden boost in energy followed by a sharp drop. Complex carbohydrates also prevent hunger longer. Try a toasted English muffin with jam for a snack instead of a doughnut or a candy bar.

Reduce sugar.

Increase complex carbohydrates.

Look at the nutrition labels of the foods you eat. You can often reduce the amount of sugar, salt, fat, and calories by choosing different brands of the same product. For example, a cup of Extra Triple Brownie Overload ice cream will contribute 40 grams of fat to your diet; a cup of lowfat ice cream has just 6 grams of fat. Burger King's BK Broiler contains 29 grams of fat, whereas Mc-Donald's McGrilled Chicken has only 12. Gwaltney, Grillmaster, Mr. Turkey, and Weaver all make chicken and turkey frankfurters with 11 grams of fat. But Healthy Choice, Butterball, Hormel, and Oscar Meyer make pork, beef, and turkey franks with only 1 to 1½ grams of fat.[1]

Read labels.

Many baked goods contain palm oil, coconut oil, or coconut butter, which are high in saturated fats and raise cholesterol levels. Choose products made with sesame, soy, or peanut oils instead. These unsaturated fats help to lower your cholesterol level. Processing makes a difference, too. For example, canned vegetables often contain a lot of salt. Frozen vegetables usually have no added salt.

At other times, you may wish to substitute a lower calorie food or a healthier food for one you have been used to eating. For example, plain yogurt has fewer calories and less fat than sour cream, but it tastes almost as good on a baked potato. One tablespoon of whipped butter has 30 calories less than a tablespoon of regular butter. Using low-fat yogurt flavored with fruit juice instead of whole milk yogurt flavored with fruit and syrup can lead to savings in both fat and calorie levels. The fat in margarine is unsaturated, so it is less harmful to your cholesterol count than the fat in butter. Remove the skin from chicken to cut both calories and fat. Try tuna packed in water instead of tuna packed in oil to reduce fat and save 30 calories. A blueberry muffin has 100 fewer calories and less sugar than a glazed doughnut. A baked apple has less fat and saves you 205 calories over a slice of apple pie. Low-fat snacks include pretzels, popcorn (without the butter), and fruit. Substitute jams, jellies, and apple butter for high-fat spreads such as peanut butter, butter, and cream cheese. They will satisfy your sweet tooth without adding fat to your diet. Other sweet treats that are lower in fat include sorbet or nonfat frozen yogurt (instead of ice cream) and angel food cake (instead of cheesecake).

Substitute foods with lower calories and more nutrition.

■ WEIGHT LOSS

A recent Harris poll reports that 74 percent of Americans are overweight.[2] New research estimates that 300,000 deaths per year are attributable to overweight in the United States; this takes second place only to cigarette smoking which causes 400,000 deaths a year.[3] According to Yale University psychologist Kelly Brownell, nearly half of the adult women and a quarter of the adult men in the United States are dieting at any one time.[4]

You have probably heard of "middle age bulge" and "the freshman 10." The first phrase refers to the extra pounds many people gain as they enter middle age (about 10 pounds for each decade) because metabolism slows down and lifestyles become more sedentary. The "freshman 10" refers to the extra 10 pounds that many students gain during their first year of college because of a diet heavy in fat and junk foods.

Eating just one 250-calorie candy bar a day can add 26 pounds to your frame during one year. (Many of the most popular two-ounce candy bars contain 280 and even 300 calories. Multiply 250 calories by 365 days, and you get 91,250 calories. Divide that number by the 3,500 excess calories in your diet that make a pound of body fat, and you arrive at 26 pounds gained over the course of one year.) Being overweight is associated with heart disease, high blood pressure, stroke, various cancers, the most common type of diabetes, and other illnesses. If you establish good eating and exercise habits, you are less likely to accumulate the extra calories that turn into fat.

Regulate the number of calories you consume.

The number of calories you may consume each day without gaining weight depends on your body frame (the amount of muscle and bone in your body) and how active you are. The daily calorie levels in Figure 11.1 are recommended by the U.S. Department of Agriculture and can help you maintain your current weight level. If you wish to lose weight, you will need to consume fewer calories and be more physically active. If you wish to gain weight, you should increase the number of calories you consume.

If you are trying to lose weight, do it gradually. Experts recommend that you aim for a weight loss of one-half to one pound per week. More rapid weight loss can damage both your health and appearance; you are also more likely to gain the weight back quickly if you reduce too rapidly.

Lose weight slowly.

One pound is equivalent to 3,500 calories. If you reduce your daily calorie consumption by 500 calories a day, you will lose one pound a week (52 pounds in a year!). The pounds you lose slowly are the ones that are more likely to stay off. It is also true that losing weight too rapidly results in loss of muscle tissue (including heart muscle) as well as fat. Do not try to lose more than one to two pounds a week. Any weight loss program should incorporate extra water intake and, possibly, a multivitamin.

Combine diet with exercise.

Even better, combine a reduction in calories with an increase in exercise. Reduce your food intake by only 100 calories and burn only 100 extra calories a day through a small increase in activity level, and you will lose 1 pound every 2.5 weeks. That represents a loss of 4 pounds in just 10 weeks (almost 21 pounds in a year!) with virtually no deprivation or effort. Figure 11.2 shows the number of calories burned by men and women during various activities. A study at the Baylor College of Medicine showed that dieters who also exercised lost an average of 20 pounds in a year. Those who only dieted gained most of their weight back.[5] If you combine a change in diet with an exercise program, you will lose weight faster, build up muscle tone for a more attractive appearance, and live longer.

Figure 11.1 *Approximate Number of Calories per Day That Will Maintain Your Current Weight Level*

1,600 Calories per Day	2,200 Calories per Day	2,800 Calories per Day
Many sedentary women Some older adults	Teenage girls Active women Many sedentary men Most children	Teenage boys Many active men Some very active women

Derived from M. Burros, "Plain Talk About Eating Right," *New York Times Magazine*, Part 2, 6 October 1991, pp. 10–13.

Figure 11.2   *Number of Calories Burned during Various Activities*

Activity	Calories Burned per Hour	
	Man	Woman
Sitting quietly	100	80
Standing quietly	120	95
Light activity (cleaning house, office work, playing baseball, playing golf)	300	240
Moderate activity (walking 3.5 mph, gardening, cycling 5.5 mph, dancing, playing basketball)	460	370
Strenuous activity (jogging 9 mph, playing football, swimming)	730	580
Very strenuous activity (running 7 mph, racquetball, skiing)	920	740

Figures are for a healthy man weighing 175 pounds and for a healthy woman weighing 140 pounds. People who have more bone and muscle burn more calories per hour than people who weigh less. The number of calories may also vary depending on environmental conditions.[6]

Derived from W. McArdle, F. Katch, V. Katch, *Exercise Physiology*, 3rd ed., Philadelphia: Lea & Febiger, 1991. Reproduced with permission.

The minimum number of calories for a female diet is 1,200. Do not go below that level unless you have consulted with a physician. Studies have shown that going below 1,000 calories for a few weeks will slow down your metabolism by 10 to 30 percent so that you will burn calories more slowly. You'll be depriving yourself of food, but you won't be losing weight as fast, and much of the weight you lose will come from muscle, not from fat deposits. When you go back to your old eating habits, you will gain the weight back, and you may even gain more weight since your metabolism may remain in low gear. It is also difficult to obtain all the nutrients your body needs when you are on a very low-calorie diet. Instead of reducing your calories below 1,000, add exercise to burn those extra calories. You'll feel and look better.

Do not cut calories too much.

■ EATING DISORDERS

If you find yourself losing too much weight or weighing considerably less than the ideal weight for your height and frame, see a physician. You may have an illness that requires medical treatment. Aside from various parasites, illnesses, and hormonal imbalances that may cause unnatural weight loss, a disorder called anorexia nervosa results in dangerously high levels of weight loss. Anorexia is an eating disorder in which young women try to lose weight, but lose control over their eating. (Men account for only a very small percentage of individuals who are diagnosed with eating disorders.) They lose too much weight, upset the chemical balance in their bodies, and become dangerously undernourished. Up to 10 percent of anorexics die from the disorder or its complications. For singer Karen Carpenter, death from anorexia was the end result of a diet she began after a newspaper article called her "chubby." One in 10 college students suffers to a significant degree from anorexia, bulimia, or binge-eating disorder.[7]

Do not lose too much weight.

ACTIVITY

Warning Signs of an Eating Disorder

Check off the warning signs listed below that apply to you or a friend. Any of them may be indicators of an eating disorder that can seriously compromise your health. If you are concerned about yourself or a friend, contact your college counseling center. The National Association of Anorexia Nervosa and Associated Disorders (ANAD) (Highland Park, IL, 847-831-3483) offers free information, telephone counseling, and nationwide referrals to therapists, support groups, and physicians. The American Anorexia/Bulimia Association (New York City, 212-501-8351) can also provide information and referrals.

_____ Do you have an intense fear of gaining weight or becoming fat even though you are underweight?

_____ Do you weigh 85 percent or less than your expected weight level?

_____ Do you restrict your caloric intake to less than 500 calories a day or skip two or more meals a day?

_____ Have you missed three or more menstrual cycles?

_____ Do you eat a very large amount of food within a two-hour period while feeling out of control?

_____ Do you eat large amounts of food when you are not hungry?

_____ Do you use laxatives, vomiting, excessive exercise, diuretics or other purging behaviors to lose or control your weight?

_____ Is your evaluation of yourself based too much on your body shape or weight?

_____ Do you feel that food controls your life?

_____ Do you feel disgusted with yourself, depressed or very guilty after overeating?

_____ Do you stay at home or avoid social situations to maintain your eating or exercise schedule?

Adapted from J. E. Brody, "Help for Youths Beset by Eating Disorders," *New York Times*, 31 January 1996, p. C10 and *Desk Reference to the Diagnostic Criteria for DSM-IV*. Washington, DC: American Psychiatric Association, 1994.

Bulimia, an eating disorder that may be related to anorexia, also seems to be spreading among young women. Women who have this disorder go on eating binges, consuming huge quantities of high-calorie foods; they then attempt to control their weight gain by abusing laxatives or inducing vomiting. It is a dangerous disorder that may lead to serious medical problems. Bulimia can result in severe damage to the digestive system and teeth over a period of several years. It can also destroy the body's delicate electrolyte balance, leading to death in the short term.

Bulimia, like anorexia, seems to strike most heavily at women in their teens and twenties. It is at least partially caused by our culture's obsession with the "thin is beautiful" syndrome. Thin was not always beautiful, as can be seen in the pleasingly plump models of classic painters such as Rubens or da Vinci. Thin did not become popular in our country until the 1920s, and even in 1950s, female movie stars had voluptuous figures rather than the type of thin frame popularized by today's high-fashion models. In many European countries, in Africa, and in the Arabic world, a woman today must be "pleasingly plump" in order to be considered attractive.

Yet American women blindly embrace the "thinner is better" doctrine. Most dieters in this country are women, and most women are on perpetual diets. The preoccupation with thinness is beginning at earlier and earlier ages. One survey even found that one-half of a group of fourth graders were dieting! Many women are trying to lose more weight than is medically recommended. The truth is that women's bodies are biologically meant to have some fat on them. This fat is necessary in order to ensure regular menstrual cycles, normal pregnancy, and the ability to breast-feed. If you try to go below your weight range, you are likely to face a frustrating, never-ending battle that you cannot win. In addition, you may damage your health.

Figure 11.3 presents weights for adults suggested by an advisory committee to the Department of Health and Human Services and the Department of Agriculture. Due to newer and more extensive research on longevity, the ranges refer to people of all ages and no longer allow the 15-pound gain in middle age that was supported by earlier flawed research. The higher weights in the range apply to people with more bone and muscle in comparison to body fat; the lower weights represent ideal weights for those who tend to have less muscle and bone.

Beware of malnutrition.

Studies show that female adolescents are likely to be the most undernourished members of the American family, and many of them are actually suffering from malnutrition. Malnutrition seems impossible in a wealthy country where food is plentiful. It is due, however, to improper dieting and to the American love affair with easily available junk foods that contain few nutrients. If you do not get the vitamins, minerals, and protein that your body needs, you are endangering your health. You may also be endangering the health of your child. One-third of the women in this country between the ages of 15 and 20 experience at least one unwanted pregnancy.[8] This is the most undernourished group

Figure 11.3 *Suggested Weights for Adults*

Height without Shoes	Weight in Pounds without Clothes	Height without Shoes	Weight in Pounds without Clothes
5' 0"	97–128	5' 10"	132–174
5' 1"	101–132	5' 11"	136–179
5' 2"	104–137	6' 0"	140–184
5' 3"	107–141	6' 1"	144–189
5' 4"	111–146	6' 2"	148–195
5' 5"	114–150	6' 3"	152–200
5' 6"	118–155	6' 4"	156–205
5' 7"	121–160	6' 5"	160–211
5' 8"	125–164	6' 6"	164–216
5' 9"	129–169		

Draft Guidelines Submitted by an Advisory Committee to the Department of Health and Human Services and the Department of Agriculture, in J. E. Brody, "Personal Health," *New York Times,* 20 September 1995, p. C11.

Eat frequently.

in our country, and we know that malnutrition in the mother before and during pregnancy is likely to result in birth defects in her baby.

Regulate the number of meals you eat. Smaller, more frequent meals work better. Your body is less likely to store calories as fat if you eat more frequently and engage in some activity before going to bed. Eat at least three meals a day, and don't skip breakfast! Breakfast should make up approximately 25 percent of your daily calories. People who skip breakfast actually end up eating more calories during the day than if they had eaten a meal in the morning. Try to eat *Eat early in the day.* your largest meals early in the day so that you have a chance to burn the calories. Avoid large dinners and late-night snacking.

■ THE HEALTHY BALANCED DIET

Eat a balanced diet.

Although there has been some political controversy over the traditional food groups during the past few years, nutritionists are basically in agreement about what constitutes a balanced diet. The U.S. Department of Agriculture (USDA) has updated the "Four Basic Food Groups Wheel" that used to hang in many school classrooms. Instead of giving equal weight to the original four food groups, the new pyramid shows suggested daily servings from five basic food groups. Complaints from the meat and dairy industries delayed release of the new pyramid because of the smaller proportion of daily food intake given to these food groups.[9] The nation's top nutritionists do, however, endorse the USDA's "Food Guide Pyramid" which is presented in Figure 11.4 and promote it as the best way to control weight and live a healthier and longer life.

The pyramid is used in conjunction with the categories presented in Figure 11.1 on page 200. For instance, the pyramid recommends six to eleven servings from the bread, cereal, pasta, and rice group. A less physically active

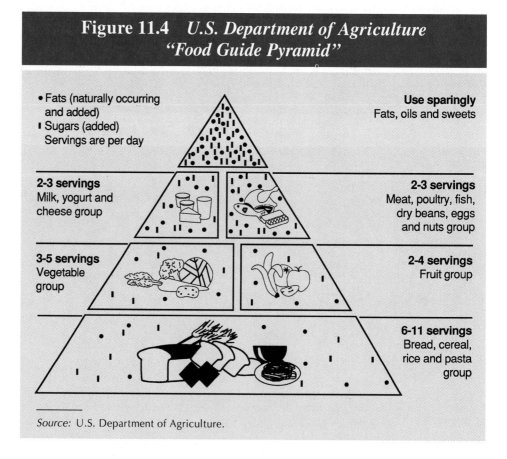

Figure 11.4 *U.S. Department of Agriculture "Food Guide Pyramid"*

- Fats (naturally occurring and added)
- Sugars (added)
Servings are per day

Use sparingly
Fats, oils and sweets

2-3 servings
Milk, yogurt and cheese group

2-3 servings
Meat, poultry, fish, dry beans, eggs and nuts group

3-5 servings
Vegetable group

2-4 servings
Fruit group

6-11 servings
Bread, cereal, rice and pasta group

Source: U.S. Department of Agriculture.

ACTIVITY

Eating Smart Quiz

The Eating Smart Quiz developed by the American Cancer Society will help you determine whether you are eating a healthy diet. Give yourself 0, 1, or 2 points for each item depending on which of the choices best represents your eating habits. Then total the number of points on your quiz.

YOUR POINTS

Baked Goods
Pies, cakes, cookies, sweet rolls, doughnuts
- I eat them 4 or more times a week. — 0
- I eat them 2–4 times a week. — 1
- I seldom eat baked goods, or eat only low-fat baked goods. — 2

☐

Poultry & Fish
- I rarely or never eat these foods. — 0
- I eat them 1–2 times a week. — 1
- I eat them 3 or more times a week. — 2

☐

High-Fat Meat
Luncheon meats, bacon, hot dogs, sausage, steak, regular & lean ground beef
- I eat these every day. — 0
- I eat these foods occasionally. — 1
- I rarely eat these foods. — 2
- I don't eat meat. — 2

☐

Low-Fat Meat
Extra lean hamburger, round steak, porkloin, roast, tenderloin, chuck roast
- I rarely eat lean meats. — 0
- I eat lean meats occasionally. — 1
- I eat mostly fat-trimmed lean red meats. — 2
- I don't eat meat. — 2

☐

Cured & Smoked Meat & Fish
Luncheon meats, hot dogs, bacon, ham & other smoked or pickled meats and fish
- I eat these foods 4 or more times a week. — 0
- I eat some 1–3 times a week. — 1
- I seldom eat these foods. — 2
- I don't eat meat or fish. — 2

☐

Legumes
Dried beans & peas (kidney, navy, lima, pinto, garbanzo, split-pea, lentil)
- I eat legumes less than once a week. — 0
- I eat these foods 1–2 times a week. — 1
- I eat them 3 or more times a week. — 2

☐

Snacks
Potato/corn chips, nuts, buttered popcorn, candy bars
- I eat these every day. — 0
- I eat some occasionally. — 1
- I seldom or never eat snacks. — 2

☐

Dairy Products

• I drink whole milk or 2% milk.	0	
• I drink nonfat or 1% milk.	1	☐

• I eat ice cream almost every day.	0	
• Instead of ice cream I eat ice milk, low-fat frozen yogurt, or sherbet.	1	☐
• I eat only fruit ices, and seldom eat frozen dairy desserts.	2	

• I eat mostly high-fat cheese (jack, cheddar, colby, Swiss, cream)	0	
• I eat both low- and high-fat cheeses.	1	☐
• I eat mostly low-fat cheeses (pot, 2% cottage, skim milk mozzarella).	2	
• I don't eat cheese.	2	

Oils & Fats

Butter, margarine, shortening, mayonnaise, sour cream, lard, oil, salad dressing

• I always add these to foods in cooking and/or at the table.	0	
• I occasionally add these to foods in cooking or at the table.	1	☐
• I rarely add these to foods in cooking and/or at the table.	2	

• I eat fried foods 3 or more times a week.	0	
• I eat fried foods 1–2 times a week.	1	☐
• I rarely or never eat fried foods.	2	

Whole Grains & Cereals

Whole grain breads, brown rice, pasta, whole grain cereals

• I seldom eat such foods.	0	
• I eat them 2–3 times a day.	1	☐
• I eat them 4 or more times a day.	2	

Vitamin C-Rich Fruits & Vegetables

Citrus fruits and juices, green pepper, strawberries, tomatoes

• I seldom eat them.	0	
• I eat them 3–5 times a week.	1	☐
• I eat them 1–2 times a day.	2	

Deep Green/Deep Yellow Fruits and Vegetables

Broccoli, cabbage, carrots, peaches

• I seldom eat them.	0	
• I eat them 3–5 times a week.	1	☐
• I eat them daily.	2	

Vegetables of the Cabbage Family

Broccoli, cabbage, brussel sprouts, cauliflower

• I seldom eat them.	0	
• I eat them 1–2 times a week.	1	☐
• I eat them 3–4 times a week.	2	

Alcohol

• I have more than 2 drinks a day.	0	
• I drink alcohol every week, but not daily.	1	☐
• I occasionally or never drink alcohol.	2	

YOUR POINTS

Personal Weight

- I'm more than 20 lbs. over my
  ideal weight.   0
- I'm 10–20 lbs. over my ideal
  weight.   1
- I'm within 10 lbs. of my ideal
  weight.   2

SCORE   **TOTAL POINTS**

0–12   A Warning

Your diet is probably too high in fat, and too low in fiber-rich foods.

13–17   Not Bad

You still have a way to go.

18+   You're Eating Smart

You have been careful to limit your fats, and to eat a varied diet.

The "Eating Smart Quiz" is reprinted from *Eating Smart,* courtesy of the American Cancer Society, 85-250m, 1987, Rev. 3/89, No. 2042. 800-ACS-2345.

person who should eat no more than 1,600 calories per day would need only six servings from that group. The very active teenager who needs 2,800 calories to maintain his weight would need eleven servings from that group. The moderately active person in the 2,200 calorie category should eat eight to nine servings from the grain food group.

If you cannot eat enough servings from the vegetable and fruit group, take a vitamin and mineral supplement. Try to obtain at least 60 percent of your calories from complex carbohydrates (starches, rather than sugars). Limit your fat intake to no more than 30 percent of your calories; no more than half of those fat calories should come from animal sources (eggs, meat, dairy products). Keep your consumption from the protein group to no more than 15 percent of your calories: dried beans, low-fat dairy products, and fish and chicken contain less fat than red meat, frankfurters, pork, or sausage. Lean meats, light meats (chicken breast instead of chicken legs), and meat without skin contain less fat and fewer calories.

Make sure that you get enough calcium. If your body doesn't take in enough calcium from the foods you eat, it will draw the calcium out of your bones. This can result in a crippling disease called osteoporosis (weak and brittle bones) that afflicts many women as they grow older. Teenagers need 1,200 milligrams of calcium a day; adults require 1,000 milligrams. It is better to get your calcium naturally from skim milk and dairy products, but if this is not possible, take a calcium supplement. (Other foods that are rich in calcium include tofu, calcium-fortified orange juice and cereals, buttermilk pancake mix, cornmeal, cheese pizza, broccoli, collard greens, baked and white beans, sardines or canned salmon that includes the bones.)   *Include enough calcium.*

The average American eats the equivalent of almost a whole stick of butter a day. That's almost 800 calories worth of fat, or 40 percent of the total day's   *Eat less fat.*

calories, rather than the maximum 30 percent or less recommended by the USDA and the American Heart Association. (Many top nutritionists recommend less than 20 percent fat.) If you are in the 1,600 calories per day category, the maximum recommended limit for your daily fat consumption is 54 grams; if you are in the 2,200 category, the maximum amount of fat you should consume is 74 grams; if you are in the most active category of 2,800 calories per day, you should try to consume less than 94 grams of fat each day.

To calculate the maximum amount of fat recommended for your activity level, take the maximum number of calories recommended for your activity level, multiply that number by 30 percent (0.30), and divide by 9 because each gram of fat has 9 calories. Even if you eat only the lowest fat foods, you will still use up half of your daily fat limit. So you should only add extra fat from desserts, salad dressings, or bread spreads with caution. For example, a pecan roll from AuBon Pain contains 800 calories and 45 grams of fat, almost a total day's recommended maximum ration of fat for a person in the 1600-calories per day category. A Mrs. Field's 420-calorie fudge brownie contains 25 grams of fat, and a Starbuck's cinnamon scone has 26 fat grams.[10] Remember that fat contains 9 calories per gram, while carbohydrates contain only 4. So you can eat twice as many carbohydrates and still consume fewer calories.

Use unsaturated fats.

When you eat fats, try to use unsaturated fats that come from vegetable products such as oil rather than saturated fats that come from meat or dairy products such as butter or cream. Use monosaturated oils such as olive, soy, peanut, or sesame instead of coconut or palm oils that are saturated and raise cholesterol. Include skimmed dairy products that will give you the calcium you need without adding too much fat. It is the saturated fat in the American diet that is mainly responsible for the heart attacks that kill such a large number of people in this country each year.

Drink eight 8 oz. glasses of water each day.

Water is vital to almost every function your body performs from regulating your body temperature and eliminating waste products to transporting nutrients and protecting internal organs. Milk and juice may form part of your "daily eight"; coffee, sodas, and alcohol are not good substitutes for water because they actually cause your body to lose water. Maintaining adequate hydration levels can prevent fatigue and overeating in addition to regulating vital body functions.

■ FAST FOOD

Cut down on fast food consumption.

Fast-food chains can present a problem to a healthy diet in terms of adding too much salt, too much sugar, too much fat, and too many calories. Catsup, pickles, sauces, and other condiments are usually very high in salt content. Buns and catsup are often loaded with sugar. Fried foods and meats contain a great deal of fat, and it is easy to consume more than one-third of the daily calories you should be having at any one meal. If you know that you will be eating a fast-food meal during the day, try to make your other meals that day lower in fat and salt.

Although it will be high in salt, calories, and saturated fats, a meal at McDonald's consisting of a Big Mac, fries, and shake is reasonably well balanced. It breaks down to 41 grams of fat, 40 grams of protein, and 143 grams of carbohydrates. That comes out to a distribution of 18 percent fat, 18 percent protein, and 62 percent carbohydrates, which is within the guidelines of the Public Health Service. A Whopper, fries, and shake at Burger King has a similar distribution, although it totals 1,200 calories instead of the 1,100 for the McDonald's meal. At 1,200 calories, this meal is higher than the 625 to 950 calories that the average female college student should have at lunch or dinner, and a bit high even for the 950 to 1,250 calories suggested for the average male.

Meals at many of the other fast-food restaurants vary in calories and fat content. With 48 grams of fat, an extra-crispy dinner (two pieces of chicken, mashed potatoes, gravy, cole slaw, and roll) at Kentucky Fried Chicken will set you back a total 902 calories. Add 145 calories to that total if you are drinking a 12-ounce soda. The Fish & More platter (two pieces of battered fish, "fryes," cole slaw, and two hush puppies) at Long John Silver's is higher in calories and fat content at 976 calories with 58 grams of fat.

At Pizza Hut you can indulge in a 10-inch Supreme Thin 'N Crispy pizza, with sausage, pepperoni, mushrooms, and so on, for 1,200 calories and 35 grams of fat. Or, you can share a 13-inch pie with a friend for only 800 calories. That pizza is reasonably well-balanced at 13 percent fat, 28 percent protein, and 59 percent carbohydrate. If you are willing to leave off the toppings except for cheese and tomato sauce, you can save 12 grams of fat, 600 milligrams of salt, and 120 calories on half of a 13-inch pie. Mexican fast food can be low in both calories and fat if you go easy on the sour cream, guacamole, and meat fillings.

Figure 11.5 can help you make better choices when you eat at fast-food restaurants. Choose the dishes that are lowest in fat, cholesterol, and salt. You may find some surprises here. Although chicken and fish are usually lower in fat and calories, they may not be when they are fried. If you are concerned about your weight, you may also want to consult the calories column. If you eat at fast-food restaurants frequently, you may wish to invest in Art Ulene's *The Nutribase Complete Fast-Food Restaurant Nutrition Counter*. The small paperback evaluates 3,000 menu entrees from over 65 fast-food restaurants. The *Nutrition Action Healthletter*, published by the Center for Science in the Public Interest, Washington, DC (1-800-237-4874) also includes comparisons of the nutritional components in various fast-food menus.

■ THE IMPORTANCE OF EXERCISE

Improvements in your exercise patterns can be as important as changes in your diet when it comes to leading a healthier lifestyle. Exercise can help you to lose weight and to maintain an ideal weight. It can energize you, and it can also curb your appetite. Exercise relieves stress; it can help you to relax and get a better night's sleep. Evidence also shows that it can help to control and counteract feelings of depression. Exercise strengthens your immune system (for example, people who walk frequently have fewer colds and other respiratory illnesses), lowers the risk of developing diabetes, osteoporosis, and some cancers. In fact, physical activity is as important as good nutrition and giving up smoking to maintaining and extending a healthy life.[11, 12]

While the evidence on the health benefits of exercise continues to grow, most people are inactive. American Sports Data which conducts an annual survey of people that inquires about regular participation in any of fifteen fitness activities found that 60 percent of respondents do nothing, and only approximately 20 percent participate in activity on a fairly regular basis.[13] Roper Starch Worldwide, a polling firm that has been conducting monthly surveys since the 1970s, reports that the largest growth in people who are doing nothing is among younger people, ages 18 to 29. There has been an 8 percent increase during the past 9 years in the number of people of this age category who do not walk, jog, swim, play golf or tennis, or dance.[14] The Centers for Disease Control and Prevention report that 73 percent of women age 18 and older do not get the recommended amount of exercise.[15]

Increase activity.

Exercise improves your blood circulation and helps your heart, lungs, and other vital organs to work more efficiently. A strong heart does not have to beat as often, and it pumps more blood with each stroke. Exercise also seems to counteract some of the unhealthy effects of high cholesterol levels in your diet. Studies show that people who exercise regularly live longer, and they are able

Figure 11.5 *Nutrition Comparisons for Fast Foods. Source: Company Analyses*

	Fat (Grams)	Cholesterol (MG)	Sodium (MG)	Percent (%) Calories from Fat	Total Calories
Hamburgers					
McDonald's McLean Deluxe	10	60	670	28	320
Wendy's Single (Plain)	15	65	500	40	340
McDonald's Big Mac	26	100	890	47	500
Burger King Whopper	36	90	865	53	614
Hardee's Big Deluxe Burger	30	70	760	54	500
Chicken					
Hardee's Grilled Chicken Sandwich	9	60	890	26	310
Wendy's Grilled Chicken Sandwich	13	60	815	34	340
Burger King BK Broiler Chicken Sandwich	18	53	764	43	379
McDonald's McChicken Sandwich	20	42	770	43	415
McDonald's Chicken McNuggetts (6 pc.)	15	56	580	50	270
Kentucky Fried Chicken Lite'n Crispy	12	60	354	55	198
Fish					
Hardee's Fisherman's Fillet	24	70	1030	43	500
McDonald's Filet-O-Fish	18	50	930	44	370
Burger King Ocean Catch Fish Filet	25	57	879	45	495
Wendy's Fish Filet Sandwich	25	79	994	49	460
Arby's Fish Filet	29	79	994	49	537
Other					
Arby's Regular Roast Beef	15	39	588	38	353
Hardee's Turkey Club	16	70	1280	37	390
Arby's Turkey Deluxe	20	39	1047	45	399
Taco Bell Taco Salad	61	80	910	61	905
Taco Bell Soft Taco	12	32	554	29	225
Taco Bell Nachos Supreme	27	18	471	66	367
Pizza Hut Personal Pan Pizza	29	53	1335	39	675
2 Slices Pizza Hut Thin'N Crispy (no extra toppings)	17	33	867	38	398

Portions reprinted with permission from The Hope Heart Institute, Kalamazoo, MI. "How Fast Foods Compare," *Hope Health Letter*, 11:9 (September 1991).

to work and play more efficiently for longer periods of time. The American Heart Association recognizes inactivity as the fourth major risk for heart disease along with overweight, hypertension, and cigarette smoking.[16] Finally, exercise tones your muscles and gives you a more attractive appearance regardless of your weight level.

Perform aerobic activity.
Increase your activity level. Aerobic activity, which stimulates the heart and lungs, is most beneficial in reducing the risk of heart disease. Examples of

ACTIVITY

Burning Calories through Exercise

To calculate the number of calories that will maintain your weight, multiply your weight by 15. If you want to lose weight, you will either have to eat less or burn more calories through exercise. It is better to lose weight by doing both: reduce calories and increase activity level. Remember that 3,500 calories a week equals 1 pound. The table below will give you an idea of how many calories are burned in various activities by a 150-pound person. If you weigh less than 150 pounds, you will burn fewer calories; if you weigh more than 150 pounds, you will burn more calories. For example, a person between the ages of 17 and 21 who weighs 125 pounds will use approximately 219 calories per hour while watching television. A person who weighs 180 pounds will use 249 calories.

Calories Burned per Minute by a 150-Pound Person

Activity	Number of Calories Consumed per Minute	Aerobic Benefits
Skiing (cross-country, uphill)	18.6	Very good
Running (at 7.5 miles per hour)	13.2	Very good
Squash	14.4	Very good
Basketball	9.4	Very good
Skiing (cross-country)	9.7	Very good
Swimming (at 2 miles per hour)	8.1	Very good
Tennis	7.4	Very good
Skiing (downhill)	7.1	Fair
Aerobic dancing	6.6	Very good
Bicycling (at 9.4 miles per hour)	6.35	Very good
Golf (no cart)	5.8	Poor
Walking (at 3 miles per hour)	3.8	Good

As we age, preventing damage to joints and bones during exercise becomes more of a concern. This is also an issue for people who have been injured playing sports, for people who have back problems, arthritis or other joint disorders, for people who are overweight, and for pregnant women. Low-impact aerobics programs were developed to deal with these concerns. The following table presents a list of high- and low-impact activities. You can get an effective aerobic workout with either form of exercise.

Consider low-impact aerobic activities.

High and Low-Impact Aerobic Exercise

High-Impact Aerobic Activities	Low-Impact Aerobic Activities
Skipping rope	Swimming
Jogging	Walking
Running	Bicycling
Basketball	Stairclimbing
Volleyball	Cross-country skiing
Racquetball	Low-impact aerobics class
Handball	
High-impact aerobics class	

More recently, water exercise programs have been developed that offer essentially a no-impact aerobic workout. Whereas jogging on land subjects your body's joints to a force of three times your body weight, and walking results in a force one-and-a-half times your weight, water's buoyancy reduces body weight to only 10 percent of what it is on land. Working out in the water is also ideal for people who become overheated and tire easily during land exercises.

If you know that a brownie is equal to 95 calories and you want to eat that brownie, you can now calculate that you will have to burn 95 calories by running for 7 minutes, swimming for 12 minutes, bicycling for 15 minutes, or walking for 25 minutes in order to keep your weight at the same level. Using the same calculations, you will realize that a can of beer will cost you 11 minutes of running, 19 minutes of swimming, 24 minutes of bicycling, or 39 minutes of walking. In addition to burning calories, *regular,* periodic exercise increases the metabolic rate, which helps the body burn fat faster. You can lose, gain, or maintain weight by adjusting your diet and your activity level.

---

aerobic activity include brisk walking, cycling, rope jumping, swimming, rowing, and jogging. These types of activity also burn calories and tone muscles for a more attractive appearance.

Consult your physician before you begin a strenuous exercise program.

If you are middle-aged or older, if you have not exercised on a regular basis for some time, or if you are at risk for heart disease, you should consult a physician before you undertake a strenuous exercise program. In addition to checking your overall physical condition, he or she may recommend a stress test before you begin an exercise program. This test can reveal abnormalities in the way your heart functions, and your physician might suggest that you avoid strenuous exercise if your heart is damaged.

In February 1995, the Centers for Disease Control and Prevention and the American College of Sports Medicine issued a new joint recommendation that adults should engage in moderate activity for at least 30 minutes a day, even if this exercise is accumulated in 10-minute spurts. But health experts agree that any amount of exercise is better than none in improving your mood, burning calories, keeping joints supple, and strengthening bones. Researchers also agree that more exercise is associated with more benefits like disease prevention and longer life. A long-term study of Harvard graduates concluded that those who regularly engage in vigorous exercise like jogging and fast walking increased their life expectancy significantly over those whose activities rarely caused them to break into a sweat. However, too much exercise, to the point of loss of menstruation in women, for example, may be harmful to health by contributing to osteoporosis, decreasing hormone levels, and accelerating aging of various body components.[17, 18]

Figure 11.6 shows how researchers quantify levels of physical activity. Experts have recommended a pyramid approach to fitness, much like the food-guide pyramid recommended by the Department of Agriculture: At the base would be routine, nonstructured physical activities such as walking the dog or climbing stairs. Farther up on the pyramid are more active pursuits such as dancing, swimming, tennis, or basketball. At the top of the pyramid would be three times a week of more vigorous activity such as brisk walking, using a stair-climbing or ski machine, singles tennis, or racquetball for the purpose of promoting fitness.[19]

Until recently, most fitness instructors emphasized aerobic exercise to strengthen the heart and cardiovascular system. More recent studies show that people who participate only in aerobic exercise actually lose muscle mass and strength over time. This loss can mean that individuals lose their ability to live independently as they get older. The Framingham Disability Study showed that 66 percent of women between the ages of 75 and 84 were unable to lift an

Figure 11.6   *Examples of Three Levels of Exercise*

Level of Exercise Activity	Amount of Time per Week	Number of Sessions per Week
Light Exercise		
Walking slowly (strolling)		
Swimming (slowly treading water)		
Golf (using a powered cart)		
Mowing lawn (using a riding mower)		
Home care (like carpet sweeping)		
Moderate Exercise		30 minutes/day
Walking briskly	3 to 4 miles per hour	
Swimming, using moderate effort		
Racket sports (like table tennis)		
Home care (like general cleaning)		
Mowing lawn (using power mower)		
Vigorous Exercise		
Walking briskly uphill or with a load, 4 to 5 miles per hour	45 minutes/day	5 times/per week
Swimming (fast treading or crawl) swimming laps	3 hours/week	
Cardiovascular exercise (stair-climbing or ski machine)	2–3 hours/week	
Racquet sports (singles tennis or racquetball)	3 days/week	
Moving furniture		
Mowing lawn (using hand mower)		

Thirty minutes of moderate activity per day confers significant health benefits and may have life-prolonging value. Significant increases of life expectancy are found in individuals who engage in vigorous activity at least 3 hours per week.

Adapted from J. E. Brody, "Trying to Reconcile Exercise Findings," *New York Times,* 23 April 1995, p. 22.

object weighing more than 10 pounds; this was also true for 28 percent of the men in that age group.[20] Strength training builds up muscle mass. The more muscle you have, the more calories you burn. So people who engage in strength training continue to burn more calories even when they are at rest.[21]

The guidelines of the American College of Sports Medicine, the leading organization of sports researchers, call for at least two strength workouts each week in addition to three sessions of aerobic exercise. In addition to burning more calories, the best reason for people to get stronger is to lower the risk of

Perform strength training or weight lifting activity.

ACTIVITY

Promoting Healthy Activities

USING THE HEALTH ACTIVITIES FORM

For at least two days, use the Health Activities Form to record the type and amount of food you eat and the amount of alcohol, caffeine, tobacco, and drugs you consume. You might wish to make one of those days a Saturday or Sunday. In addition, record each instance of exercise in which you engage. Record these data on a continuous basis. If you wait to record until the end of the day, you will forget many of the items that you have consumed. When you have completed two days of recording, you should be able to tell where you need to make changes in order to live a healthier lifestyle. You may wish, for example, to cut down on the amount of junk food you eat or to increase the number of fruits and vegetables you eat. Most of us are not aware of what and how much we really eat until we keep a daily record. Compare your eating habits with the balanced diet recommended by the U.S. Department of Agriculture on page 204.

Health Activities Form

Name _____   Day/Date _____

Time	Food Type & Amount	Exercise Type & Amount	Alcohol Type & Amount	Tobacco Amount	Drugs Type & Amount	Reasons, Circumstances, & Feelings at That Time

How do your exercise patterns compare with the recommendation of exercising vigorously three times a week? You may feel that you should increase the amount of exercise in your life. Take a particularly hard look at how you use cigarettes, alcohol, or other drugs. (Yes, alcohol is a drug, too.) We will talk about these in more detail in the chapter on substance abuse, but you may want to make some changes at this time. The less you use these drugs, the healthier you will be.

The last column asks you to record the circumstances and feelings you experience during consumption. An analysis of this column should give you insight into the reasons why you consume certain foods or drugs. You may then be able to find more healthy ways of dealing with tension, boredom, anger, or other emotions than having a drink or eating a pizza.

Health Activities Form

Name _____   Day/Date _____

Time	Food Type & Amount	Exercise Type & Amount	Alcohol Type & Amount	Tobacco Amount	Drugs Type & Amount	Reasons, Circumstances, & Feelings at That Time

Prevent osteoporosis. osteoporosis, a loss of bone mass that can lead to frequent fractures. The risk of osteoporosis increases as we age. One in three postmenopausal women suffers from the condition. Each year, approximately 240,000 women with osteoporosis fracture their hips; 19,000 of them die of complications within six months, and most others experience increasing difficulty in walking.[22] Experts believe that weight lifting increases bone mass to the point at which osteoporosis can be prevented. There is even evidence that strength training can increase bone mass in women who already have the condition.

The activity on pages 214–215 will help you to become more aware of your patterns of food, alcohol, nicotine, and other drug consumption. It will also bring your exercise habits into sharper focus.

■ STRESS AND STRESSORS

Stress consists of challenges from the environment: both physical challenges, such as hunger, cold, and viral infection; and psychological challenges, such as transferring to a new school, feeling pressured to accomplish too much in too little time, and facing a difficult exam. Stress occurs each time the environment presents you with problems that require solutions.

The categories from the following stressors exercise can serve as a rough guide to the levels of stress in your life. If you have experienced moderate or severe stress, you may wish to consult a counselor to find ways to lower your stress level. Each of us differs somewhat in what we find stressful and in how we respond to stress. Some people will find a change of school to be a refreshing challenge; others will dread the adjustments they have to face under the same circumstances. Some people thrive under pressure, others find it difficult

ACTIVITY

Measuring the Stress in Your Life

Complete the following checklist, and estimate how much stress you are experiencing. These events have been selected from several popular stress inventories.[23] You may be surprised to find that the list includes pleasant changes, such as a vacation, in addition to unpleasant changes, such as the death of a close family member. Both positive and negative changes require adjustment, and adjustment involves stress.

The following listed events are grouped into four categories from most stressful (Category A) to least stressful (Category D). Check the events that have occurred in your life within the past year. If an event has occurred twice, count it two times.

Life Stressors Checklist

Category A

_____ Death of a close family member

_____ Personal injury or illness

_____ Marriage

_____ Change in health of a family member

_____ Divorce of parents

_____ Pregnancy

_____ Placement on academic probation

Category B

_____ Financial problems (e.g., not having sufficient money to continue with school)

_____ Death of a close friend

_____ Taking out a major loan

_____ Dismissal from dormitory or other residence

_____ Beginning a new school experience at a higher level (e.g., going from high school into college)

_____ Change in living conditions

_____ Failing a course

Category C

_____ Fired at work

_____ Transferring to a new school at the same level (e.g., transferring from one college to another)

_____ Change in residence

_____ Change in church activities

_____ Joining a fraternity or sorority

_____ Change in social activities

_____ Change in work hours or conditions

_____ Failing an important exam

Category D

_____ Change in sleeping habits

_____ Change in eating habits

_____ Change in major program at college

_____ Dropping a course

_____ Christmas

_____ Minor violation of the law

_____ Vacation

Estimating Your Stress Level

Little Stress: Even if you have experienced all the events in Category D, you are probably feeling relatively little stress.

Mild Stress: If you have experienced all the items in Category C plus one item from any other category, you may be experiencing mild stress. If you have experienced most of the items from Category C and several items from other categories, you may also be feeling mild stress.

Moderate Stress: If you have experienced all items from Category C and Category D, you may be undergoing moderate stress. Three items from each of Categories A, B, and C might also indicate moderate stress.

Major Stress: If you have experienced four events from Categories A and B, you may be experiencing major stress.

Circle the category that best describes the level of stress you have experienced during this year.

Little Stress   Moderate Stress

Mild Stress   Major Stress

If you have any concern about the stress in your life, you should consult a professional at the counseling center.

to function when they are hard-pressed. If you have any concerns about the stress in your life, you should consult a professional at the college counseling center.

■ SOURCES OF STRESS

It may be worthwhile to evaluate which areas of your life are particularly stressful. Consider the academic, interpersonal, and vocational areas. For example, if you work, the list of job stressors might include pressure from your boss, commuting hassles, inconvenient work hours, or unreasonable demands. An examination of academic stress might result in a list that includes difficulty in passing a course required for your major, an instructor who consistently gives

ACTIVITY

Determining Your Sources of Stress

This activity concerning the sources of stress will give you the opportunity to take stock of the different types of stress in your life. By sharing this list with your class, you may discover common sources of stress or additional sources that did not originally occur to you. You may later wish to consider whether any of these areas is causing you enough stress to warrant some change. What types of stress do you experience from school, from your interpersonal relationships, or from your job?

Break into small discussion groups of four individuals. If you hold a paying job, you should be in a group with at least one other person who also does. For each of the three major areas in your life, list and share with your group members any specific item or event that results in stress for you. Some typical sources of stress are:

Academic: Failing an important course
Social: Quarreling with a friend
Job-related: Asking for a raise

You will probably discover that you have many sources of stress in common with your peers. Do any of them cause enough stress so that you should consider taking some type of action?

Academic Stressors	Social Stressors	Job Stressors

surprise quizzes, the inability to enroll in the courses you need at registration, or a course in which assignments are not clear. Interpersonal stressors might include quarrels with your roommate, disagreements with your spouse or girl-friend/boyfriend, disputes with your parents, hassles with your children, or disagreements with a friend.

Reactions to Stress

Stress also refers to the pattern of responses that you make when a stimulus challenges your ability to cope. This pattern of responses involves major

ACTIVITY

Determining Your Reactions to Stress

1. This activity will help you become aware of your responses to stress. Often people are not aware that they are under stress until they take an inventory of their responses to recent stressors. The following lists contain examples of psychological and physical reactions to stress. What reactions do you notice in yourself when you are under stress?

Psychological Reactions to Stress	Physiological Reactions to Stress*
Irritability	Drug or alcohol abuse
Inability to concentrate	Upset stomach
Shifts in mood	Sweaty palms
Impatience	Frequent urge to urinate or defecate
Racing mind	Loss of appetite
Always late or rushed	Urge to eat when you are not hungry
Forgetfulness	Insomnia
Depression	Tiredness
	Headache
	Stomach cramps

2. List the reactions you experience when you are stressed, and compare your observations with those of your classmates. You may discover additional reactions in yourself that you had overlooked before. When you become aware of your responses to stress, you can more easily tell when you are experiencing stress. Once you are aware of stress, you can take steps to cope with it.

Psychological Reactions to Stress

Physical Reactions to Stress

_____   _____

_____   _____

_____   _____

_____   _____

_____
*Physical symptoms may be caused by a medical problem. Consult your doctor before you assume that a physical symptom is caused by stress.

physical changes in your hormonal system, autonomic nervous system, and brain: increases in rate of breathing, heart rate, and blood pressure and in the discharge of steroids and adrenaline. All of these complicated physical changes are involved in preparing your body for "flight or fight"; your body becomes physically prepared to face the danger and fight or run from the danger.

You are probably more familiar, however, with the psychological reactions to stress such as anxiety, depression, anger, burnout, irritation, and difficulty in concentrating or making decisions. People respond to stress differently; the activity "Determining Your Reactions to Stress," will help you identify your typical reactions to stress.

■ STRESS AND ILLNESS

Stress has been implicated in many illnesses from colds to heart attacks, asthma, ulcers, and possibly even cancer. People who are under chronic stress seem to become ill more frequently than those who experience stress less frequently. Psychologists have identified people with certain personality traits who seem to be constantly stressed. Type A personalities put pressure on themselves continuously. They are hard-driving, aggressive, competitive, always-in-a-rush individuals who try to juggle two or three activities at the same time. Many studies have found a high correlation between these personality characteristics and the occurrence of heart disease, even when other correlates of heart disease, such as diet, smoking, and genetic history, are factored out.[24]

Heart disease, for example, is twice as frequent among Type A businessmen as among men in the general population. The Type A personality pattern is still relatively rare in nonindustrialized societies. It seems to be spreading, however, among individuals in high-pressure professions in our society. It is also becoming increasingly evident in college, high school, and even elementary school students in our country. The number of women who show this personality pattern is also increasing, as women juggle careers, child rearing, and household maintenance all at the same time.

You may wish to consider the extent to which your behavior fits the Type A pattern. Our society does seem to reward this type of behavior to a large extent. Are the costs in damaged health and frayed nerves worth the rewards? Is it possible to be successful without taking on the Type A personality?

Individual Responses to Stress

People vary in their responses to stress. They also vary in their interpretations of stress. Situations that are stressful for one person may be viewed by another person as challenging or as stimulating growth experiences. Some people thrive on excitement, challenge, and change; they find daily structure and routine boring; they seek out diversions such as roller coaster rides, horror movies, and bungee-jumping in order to increase their level of stimulation. They look for change and seize the opportunity for new jobs, new projects, new routines. Other people function best within familiar environments where the expectations are a known quantity. They prefer lower levels of stimulation and familiar structure; they find high-risk activities unsettling.

Eustress is good stress, a level of stress that feels comfortable and invigorating. Eustress leads to growth and development. Without change or challenge in our lives we become bored, and boredom is itself a stressful stimulus. It is useful for each of us to know the level of stimulation that works best for us when the time comes to make decisions about careers, relationships, and leisure activities.

■ BURNOUT

Burnout is caused when we try to keep going even though our levels of physical and emotional exhaustion are too high to maintain. The symptoms may include physical and mental fatigue, irritability, anxiety, feelings of hopelessness and helplessness, and general lack of motivation and enthusiasm.[25] We tend to feel burnout when we believe that we have put more into something than we receive in return, whether it is a course, a job, or our families.

Much of the blame for burnout rests with the workplace. Americans are working longer hours under more pressure than in past years. Technological improvements such as fax machines, laptop computers, e-mail, and cellular phones have made the instant response possible and therefore, necessary, in the competition of the marketplace. People can literally work any time, any place. Weekends, evenings, vacations, and the home are no longer sacred havens of refuge from a career. Many people feel that they can never satisfy the demands of their instructors, their bosses, or their families, and so they become frustrated. Many people feel that they receive less satisfaction from these endeavors and have less control over their lives. This situation is likely to result in burnout.

Women are particularly vulnerable to burnout because they are more likely to be juggling several roles, such as student, mother, wife, employee, and homemaker. Women with children and responsibility for household chores who also work outside the home work an average of 15 hours more per week than their partners. At the same time, due to distance from extended family members and less stability within families, many parents are forced to cope with child-rearing singlehandedly.

Check to see whether you are at high risk for burnout by considering the characteristics listed in Figure 11.7. If burnout may be looming on your horizon, consider the options for solutions described in Figure 11.8.

Figure 11.7   *Characteristics of Burnout*

Who Is at Highest Risk for Burnout?

- Fulltime students who also are employed fulltime
- Unmarried people
- Women who juggle a variety of roles such as student, employee, and homemaker
- People without children
- At-home parents who are isolated from peers
- Younger workers

Who Is Less Likely to Experience Burnout?

- People who maintain a balance between family and work and play
- People who believe there is more to life than just work or family duties
- People who have strong religious or spiritual beliefs
- People who can fall back on hobbies and or other interests

Adapted from "Burnout: The Epidemic of the '90's," *The Female Patient*, Supplement, S1 1995, pp. 31–32.

Figure 11.8 *Common Mechanisms for Coping with Stress*

- *Recognize that you have a problem when stress levels escalate.* Don't deny that something is wrong, and don't think of it as your fault. It is a problem related to your work or social situation.

- *Take responsibility for finding solutions to the problem of stress.* Seek out likely sources of support.

- *Use relaxation or meditation exercises.* If you do not have a routine that works for you, you may wish to order the audiocassette on page 384 that teaches progressive muscle relaxation, diaphragmatic breathing, autogenic training, and relaxation through imagery.

- *Get physical exercise.* Studies show that a brisk fifteen-minute walk can be more calming than a tranquilizer. A regular program of aerobic exercise can keep tension from building up.

- *Find emotional support from friends or relatives.* Talk to others; share your anxiety.

- *Write your feelings down or dictate them onto a cassette.* If you want to keep your situation confidential, destroy the letter or erase the cassette afterwards.

- *Breathe slowly and deeply.* Learn diaphragmatic breathing and practice taking slow, deep breaths periodically during the day so that you can use this technique effectively when you are stressed.

- *Take a warm bath or shower.* Use progressive muscle relaxation while you are soaking.

- *Try the blow-up technique.* Describe your situation to yourself in exaggerated terms. Blow it totally out of proportion to the point of absurdity. You will be able to smile and get a calmer perspective on your predicament.

- *Practice better time management.* Review the chapter on time management and practice with your daily planner.

- *Prioritize tasks.* Take care of the most important tasks first and let the others wait.

- *Seek professional help.* Talking to a supportive counselor can help you get a better perspective on your situation and give you ideas for change.

- *Redefine your goals or set more realistic standards.* Do not try to achieve the impossible.

- *Take control of your life.* Systematically reduce some of the sources of stress. Review the section on assertiveness training and learn to say "No" to unreasonable demands. Find a way out of a dead-end job or relationship.

- *Try to see your problem in a different light.* Highlight the positive aspects of your situation. Focus on the long-term benefits or reasons for your problem. Try to find a funny side to the situation in which you find yourself.

- *Distract yourself.* Some problems cannot be resolved now, so do not think about the situation. Go out with a friend, see a movie, immerse yourself in a book that has no socially redeeming value.

- *Plan your life so that you find satisfaction in more than one place.* You are more likely to find support and appreciation if you engage in a variety of activities.

■ RESISTANCE TO STRESS

Certain attitudes and traits can help you withstand stress. Psychologists have called this constellation of characteristics "hardiness." The items in the activity "Measuring Your Resistance to Stress" are similar to those used in a professional questionnaire that measures hardiness. The activity on page 224 can give you some idea of how well you might resist stress.

■ TECHNIQUES FOR COPING WITH STRESS

Once you are aware of the amount of stress you are experiencing, the sources of your stress, and your reactions to it, you can take steps to cope with your stress. It is useful to know how to reduce stress levels when you are feeling overwhelmed. We all use a variety of techniques to ease tension when the going gets tough. Do your coping mechanisms include any techniques from the list shown in Figure 11.8? The activity on page 225 will help you identify ways to cope with stress.

Relaxation Training

Learning to relax is a coping technique that many people have found helpful in dealing with stress. It is normal to feel nervous and tense when you are facing a challenge such as an important exam. Not only is this anxiety normal, it is also helpful! If you feel totally calm and collected during a test, you may not perform as well as you could. A small amount of anxiety is helpful in activating all your systems so that you are motivated to do your best.

On the other hand, too much anxiety is disruptive; it interferes with your concentration. If you are distracted by your racing mind, pumping heart, or sweaty palms, you will not be focusing on the test. Psychologists have developed very successful techniques for lowering anxiety. Two of the most successful ones are relaxation training and systematic desensitization.

Progressive deep muscle relaxation and autogenic training were developed by therapists in the 1930s to help patients relax. Since that time, both techniques have been used extensively by psychologists to help clients cope with various discomforts and anxieties. If you learn to recognize tension in your muscles and practice reducing it, your whole body will feel more relaxed. The key is to recognize and catch the tension before it builds up. Once you have learned how to relax your body, you will find that your mind relaxes as well. You can then condition yourself so that deep breathing and certain phrases will automatically trigger a more relaxed state when you wish to relax.

The exercise on pages 226–227 uses a muscle-scanning technique to help you relax. Many people have found it very helpful. If you are experiencing a great deal of anxiety, however, you may wish to learn progressive deep muscle relaxation, which is taught using the audiocassette described on page 384. This cassette will also teach you how to use other relaxation techniques such as self-hypnosis, relaxation through imagery, diaphragmatic breathing, and systematic desensitization.

One caution before you begin: Relaxation is a learned skill. The more you practice it, the more deeply you will be able to relax. Ten minutes of practice once or twice a day over a period of several weeks should enable you to reduce anxiety during situations that cause moderate tension. Continued practice, along with the desensitization exercises, should allow you to handle more difficult situations. These exercises are an abbreviated version of those that a therapist might use. If you find that they are not helping you to reduce anxiety, try the audiocassette described on page 384 or consult a therapist at the counseling center.

A C T I V I T Y

Measuring Your Resistance to Stress

Measure Your Resistance to Stress

Write in how much you agree or disagree with each statement. Use the following scale:

0 = *Strongly disagree*   2 = *Mildly agree*
1 = *Mildly disagree*   3 = *Strongly agree*

_____ A. Trying my best at work makes a difference.

_____ B. Trusting to fate is sometimes all I can do in a relationship.

_____ C. I often wake up eager to start on the day's projects.

_____ D. Thinking of myself as a free person leads to great frustration and difficulty.

_____ E. I would be willing to sacrifice financial security in my life if something really challenging came along.

_____ F. It bothers me when I have to deviate from the routine or schedule I've set for myself.

_____ G. An average citizen can have an impact on politics.

_____ H. Without the right breaks, it is hard to be successful in my field.

_____ I. I know why I am doing what I am doing at work (or at school).

_____ J. Getting close to people puts me at risk of being obligated to them.

_____ K. Encountering new situations is an important priority in my life.

_____ L. I really don't mind when I have nothing to do.

Calculate Your Score

These questions measure three dimensions of hardiness: control, commitment, and challenge. For half the questions, a high score indicates hardiness; for the other half, a low score indicates hardiness. Thus you must do a combination of addition and subtraction to get your score on each dimension. Fill in the following blanks to calculate your score.

Control score = _____ + _____ − _____ − _____ = _____
                  A   G   B   H

Commitment score = _____ + _____ − _____ − _____ = _____
                     C   I   D   J

Challenge score = _____ + _____ − _____ − _____ = _____
                   E   K   F   L

Control score + Commitment score + Challenge score
= Total hardiness score _____

Total Score Interpretation

10–18 = Hardy personality   0–9 = Moderate hardiness   Below 0 = Low hardiness

This exercise is reprinted with permission from S. O. Kobasa, "How Much Stress Can You Survive?" *American Health Magazine* © 1984, p. 66.

A C T I V I T Y

Decreasing Stress with Coping Techniques

1. List several of the methods you use to cope with stress. Include the techniques that you think are successful in addition to the ones that you would like to change.

_____

_____

_____

_____

_____

_____

2. Many individuals engage in maladaptive techniques (abusing drugs or alcohol, having a nervous breakdown, overeating, dropping out of school, procrastinating, and so on) in order to relieve stress. Such mechanisms may reduce stress temporarily; they do, however, have important disadvantages. What are they?

_____

_____

_____

_____

_____

_____

3. Break into small discussion groups, and share your coping techniques with group members. You may discover new techniques that work for you. Have each group present its coping mechanisms to the class so that you can construct a master list on the board. Discuss the advantages and disadvantages of the various techniques.

Successful Coping Techniques   Unsuccessful Coping Techniques

_____   _____

_____   _____

_____   _____

_____   _____

_____   _____

_____   _____

_____   _____

_____   _____

ACTIVITY

Decreasing Stress with Muscle Scanning

Find a quiet place where you will not be disturbed for ten minutes. A reclining chair that supports your head and legs is the best tool for practicing muscle relaxation; however, the exercises may also be done on a carpeted floor. You will find it helpful to have a friend record the relaxation instructions on an audio-cassette so that you can listen to the recording when you are first learning the exercises. A slow, monotone narration in someone else's voice is most effective at the beginning. As you get better at the exercises, you will discover that saying the instructions in your head or just saying the word *relax* to yourself will result in decreased tension.

Sit or lie down, and make yourself as comfortable as possible. Loosen any clothing that is restricting you (a belt, a collar, a hair clip, a pair of glasses), and close your eyes. Now tense up all the muscles in your body. Hunch your shoulders up to your ears; push the small of your back against the chair or the floor; squeeze the muscles in your buttocks; suck in your stomach muscles as though you were trying to avoid a punch; point your toes toward your head (tensing the muscles in your feet, calves, and thighs); make fists with your hands; bend your arms at the elbows so that your forearms are straining against your biceps muscles; take a deep breath and hold it (tightening the muscles in your chest); push your head against the chair or the floor (to tense your neck muscles); clench your jaws; wrinkle your nose as though you were smelling something bad; squeeze your eyes shut (but not so tightly that you become dizzy); squeeze your eyebrows together as though you were frowning or lift them so that you wrinkle your forehead as if you were surprised; hold all that tension for a moment, and then release it!

Let go of the tension, allow all of your muscles to relax, allow them to let go, allow the chair or the floor to take all the weight of your body, so that your muscles are free to relax.

Begin breathing deeply and regularly. Continue breathing slowly and deeply, allowing the air to flow in and out at a comfortable rate. Allow your body to begin relaxing. Allow the chair or the floor to take the weight of your arms and legs. Become aware of the point where your buttocks sink into the chair. Allow your shoulders to sink back against the floor or chair. Let the floor take all the weight of your body so that your muscles are free to relax, to let go, and to release their tension. Just continue breathing deeply and regularly.

Now let your mind focus on your feet. Become aware of the muscles in the toes of your right foot, the muscles in the arch of your foot, the muscles in your ankle. As you become aware of the muscles, allow them to loosen up and relax; allow them to release all tension. Now shift your attention to the muscles in your right leg, the muscles in your calf, the muscles behind your knee, the muscles in your thigh. Relax the tension; allow the muscles to loosen up; allow the chair or the floor to take all the weight of your leg.

Do the same thing now with your left foot. Focus on the muscles, become aware of how they are feeling, and just by scanning them, release any tension and allow them to relax. Then shift your attention to the muscles of your left leg. As you become aware of them, allow them to loosen up; allow them to let go; allow them to enjoy the pleasant sensations of relaxation.

Now allow those pleasant sensations of relaxation to spread upward from your legs into your stomach. Allow those warm, pleasant feelings to pool into your stomach muscles. As you become aware of the muscles in your stomach and in your buttocks, allow them to let go; allow them to loosen up; allow them to release a little more tension with each breath outward.

As you release the tension, allow the relaxed feelings to continue spreading upward, all along your spine, up into your shoulders and into the muscles across your back. You do not have to do anything at all. Just continue breathing deeply and regularly, allowing your attention to rest on the different groups of muscles. As you scan your body, as you become aware of each consecutive group of muscles, allow them to loosen up, allow them to let go, allow them to become a little more relaxed with each breath outward.

Now allow the relaxation to spread from the muscles in your shoulders down through your arms. Feel the pleasant sensations of relaxation spreading down through your right arm, to your elbow, to your forearm, and into the muscles of your right hand. Your fingers are loosening up, letting go, becoming more and more deeply relaxed with each breath outward. Now let the wave of relaxation spread back up through your right arm, all the way up to your shoulder and across your back into the left shoulder and down through your left arm. The muscles are loosening up, letting go, releasing their tension, becoming more deeply relaxed with each breath outward. Allow your hands to rest comfortably on the chair or in your lap. Notice how different the muscles feel when they are tense and when they are relaxed.

Now allow the pleasant wave of relaxation to travel back up through your left arm, to your shoulder, and into the muscles of your neck, the muscles in the back of your neck, the muscles at the side of your neck, the muscles in the front of your neck, all loosening up, letting go, becoming more and more deeply relaxed with each breath outward. Just continue breathing slowly and regularly, and bring the feelings of relaxation up into the muscles of your face.

Become aware of the muscles around your mouth, the muscles in your jaws, the muscles around your nose, the muscles around your eyes, the muscles in your forehead. Just becoming aware of the sensations in a particular group of muscles allows those muscles to release a little more tension. Each time you focus on a group of muscles, allow them to loosen up; allow them to let go; allow them to relax a little more.

Use the exhalation phase of your breathing to spread the warm, pleasant feelings of relaxation through all your muscles. Feel your body relaxing a little bit more with each breath outward as you continue scanning your muscle groups. If you find a muscle that does not feel relaxed, tense it for a moment, and then release the tension. Notice how different the muscles feel when they are tense and when they are relaxed. Allow your mind to focus one by one on the muscle groups in your body. As you become aware of your muscles, as you think about them, allow them to relax a little more. Continue to spread the pleasant sensations of relaxation from your face, down through your neck, across your shoulders, down through your arms and hands, and back up to your neck, and then down again through your chest into your stomach, your legs, and your feet. Your entire body is becoming more and more deeply relaxed with each breath outward.

You should feel relaxed and refreshed after doing the preceding relaxation exercises. You may experience some pins and needles or some feelings of heaviness or drowsiness. Some people experience feelings of lightness or floating. All of these sensations are normal. They are associated with deep feelings of relaxation.

Relaxation exercises have proven helpful with a variety of problems from insomnia to headaches to back pain. Many people have found these exercises useful in controlling excessive anxiety connected with exams, snakes, driving over a bridge, or giving a speech in front of a large audience.

In order for the exercises to work, you must practice them. Practicing ten minutes once or twice a day should bring you up to a useful level of expertise within two to three weeks. The more you practice, the more effective you will become in reducing your anxiety. Remember that you must catch your tension before it builds. Become adept at quickly checking your major muscle groups or trouble spots and beginning relaxation exercises before the tension increases. As you become more experienced at relaxing, taking just a few deep breaths or

A C T I V I T Y

Using Autogenic Phrases to Relax

You can also learn to relax by conditioning yourself with autogenic phrases that suggest feelings of warmth and relaxation. Say each of the following phrases to yourself twice, slowly and rhythmically. You may prefer to record the phrases on an audiocassette and say them to yourself as the tape plays.

> My breathing is deeper and deeper.
> My breathing is deeper and deeper.
>
> My entire body is warm and relaxed.
> My entire body is warm and relaxed.
>
> My mind is clear and tranquil.
> My mind is clear and tranquil.
>
> I feel calm and alert and relaxed.
> I feel calm and alert and relaxed.

saying a few of the autogenic phrases should be enough to relieve the tension. If you find that these exercises are not helping you to reduce your tension, try the more complete activities on the audiocassette described on page 384 or consult a professional at the counseling center.

Systematic Desensitization

Relaxation exercises can help you to feel more comfortable during exams or other problematic situations, if your anxiety level is not too high. If, however, anxiety really interferes with your performance, you may wish to consider a technique called systematic desensitization, through which you actually condition yourself to replace anxiety with relaxation during the situations that are troublesome for you.

Psychologists have demonstrated the effectiveness of systematic desensitization in thousands of studies. This method has proven successful with a wide range of fears from public speaking to snakes to exams. Ordinarily, the technique is conducted with the guidance of a psychologist. There is evidence, however, that individuals can develop effective programs for themselves.

The audiocassette described on page 384 teaches you how to set up a systematic desensitization program or you may seek out a professional at the counseling center who can help you to use this technique.

■ EFFECTS OF LONG-TERM STRESS: DEPRESSION AND SUICIDE

Aside from physical illness that may result from prolonged stress, another common reaction to stress involves depression. Depression symptoms vary, of

A C T I V I T Y

Recognizing Signs of Depression

1. How do you feel when you are depressed or "down" ? What changes do you notice in your behavior or thinking?

_____

_____

_____

_____

_____

_____

_____

2. Common signs of depression include the following. Check off the symptoms that you experience when you are down.

_____ Sleep problems (inability to fall asleep, waking up too early even when tired)

_____ Difficulties in concentration

_____ Overeating or loss of appetite leading to a decrease in eating

_____ Irritability, tearfulness

_____ Apathy, nothing seems to matter

_____ Loss of energy, constant fatigue

_____ Inability to enjoy previously enjoyable activities

_____ Feelings of worthlessness or guilt

_____ Feelings of pessimism

_____ Feelings of sadness

_____ The desire to take one's life

course, in terms of severity, duration, and the degree to which they interfere with our functioning. Most of us have experienced the symptoms of at least the milder forms of depression.

Usually, when we are "down" or "blue," these feelings go away in a few days. When the blue feelings linger for a long period, however, or when they begin to interfere with your daily functioning, it is time to seek help, from a friend, a family member, or a professional. Often, just talking about your feelings will help you to feel better. At other times, counseling or psychotherapy may be effective. Psychologists have now developed a number of techniques (especially cognitive therapy) that are particularly effective in dealing with depression.

Suicide and Depression

There is a strong link between depression and suicide. Statistics show that 80 percent of those who commit suicide are depressed,[26] and the suicide rate among young men 15 through 24 has tripled in the last 35 years. Among young women, the rate has doubled. Suicide is now one of top three leading causes of death among young people of ages 15 to 24, and the rates are even higher in older age groups.[27, 28] It seems that at least one-fourth of American college students are depressed at any given point in time and that suicide is 50 percent more frequent among college students than among other young people who are not enrolled in course work. Approximately ten thousand college students attempt suicide each year in the United States, and one thousand succeed.[29]

Since many students will not approach a professional when they are suicidal or seriously depressed, it is worthwhile for all of us to recognize the warning signs of a potential suicide. Check off warning signs of suicide that you may have noticed in a friend. If one of your peers is experiencing any of the symptoms listed in Figure 11.9, convince that friend to see a counselor.

Most colleges have a counseling center where professionals meet with students who are experiencing difficulties. Some schools also have clergy or peer counselors who can offer support or guidance. If your friend will not consider counseling, contact a residence assistant, a faculty member, or the counseling center about the situation.

Resources in case of a suicidal situation.

Other resources include the American Suicide Foundation at 1-800-531-4477, a 24-hour mental health emergency service or suicide hotline in your area, the emergency room at the local hospital, a member of the clergy (many colleges are affiliated with clergy from several faiths), or the police.

Figure 11.9   *Warning Signs of Suicide*

- Feelings of depression, hopelessness, or helplessness.
- Feelings of agitation, restlessness, sleeplessness.
- Giving away prized possessions.
- Recent loss of loved one through death or rejection.
- Recent loss of job; financial difficulties.
- Invention of a suicide plan and the means to carry it out.
- History of one or more suicide attempts or suicide threats. (The majority of suicides are carried out by people who have talked about or attempted suicide previously.)
- Absence of family or friends who are willing to help. Contact with family members has deteriorated or ceased. Family and friends are rejecting or nonsupportive.
- Failing health or presence of chronic illness.
- Deterioration in school performance.
- Abusing alcohol or other drugs. (Many studies show that the majority of suicides are committed when the person is intoxicated. Forty percent of the high school and college youths who commit suicide have a history of substance abuse.[30])
- Antisocial behavior. Research is beginning to document the fact that some youths resort to suicide when they have been detained or arrested by police officials for illegal behavior. Youths involved in violent behavior are also more likely to commit suicide.

ACTIVITY

Assessing Your Mental Health Each Day

Most of us have a certain idealized lifestyle and a clear set of values, but our actual life and the values we express in our daily actions may be something else. Using this checklist may help you to integrate what you *want* to do with your life with what you *are actually doing.* The key is raising your consciousness about how you spend each of the precious days allotted to you; there are 25 thousand if you live to age 70, and many of them have been spent already.

SELECT a time of day when you are at your best, happiest, and clearest: when you first waken if you are a morning person, or just before bed if you are a night person. Then assess your just completed day on each of the following six points.

1. FUN-PLEASURE: Was there any? It might have been big or little; thrilling to a magnificent symphony on the car radio as you admired the dawn or the sunset . . . laughing at a funny joke . . . thoroughly enjoying a good meal or a short story. You may not put a check in this column every day of your life, but if you go several days or a week with no fun, then give some thought to the reasons: Overstressed by work and responsibilities? Depressed? Or is something else wrong?

2. A HARD TASK: Did you spend any time at all today, even 10 or 15 minutes, doing something you would rather have not—because, although it was boring, unpleasant or difficult it was important or worthwhile to do? If you go too many days without doing so, you are in danger of accumulating a lot of tough things—dirty laundry, unpaid bills, unfiled income taxes—which can collectively cause you much stress and worry. But doing one or a little each day can give you a great sense of goodness and accomplishment.

3. HELP SOMEBODY: Did you, in the course of the day, do anything generous, altruistic, kind, or caring for another person? If you did, you deserve to feel good about it. If you didn't, be aware that during the last whole rotation of Planet Earth on its axis not one other person had a new reason to be glad that you exist.

4. PHYSICAL ACTIVITY: Did you do anything strenuous and demanding of your body today, in recognition of your animal origins and nature? If you ran, biked, swam, danced, walked vigorously, or did some equivalent, you reaffirmed that you are totally alive as a biological being and a warmblooded mammal, as well as a sensitive human being.

5. INTIMACY; CLOSENESS: Did you, in the course of the day, spend any time—from minutes to hours—in a close and warm way with someone you care about? It might have been a loved one—spouse, son, daughter—or lunch or a chat with a good friend. Sometimes because of a hectic schedule we have to have such conversations over the phone, calling someone close just to make contact, find out what's happening in that person's life, perhaps bring them up to date on our own. A few days without any such closeness may be no problem, but if they string together, take stock. Perhaps despite your good intentions you have worked your way into a lifestyle in which you have failed to create time and opportunity for this most basic, rewarding, and health-giving activity.

6. IN TOUCH WITH NATURE: Was there a time today when you admired a cloud or a mountain or a flower; enjoyed the breeze or chill on your cheek, noted a sign of the season, or in some other way became again aware that you are a part of the Kingdom of Nature?

Reprinted courtesy of Dr. Bert Pepper, former Commissioner of Mental Health, Rockland County from "A Checklist You Can Use To Assess Your Own Mental Health Each Day."

Figure 11.10 *Ways to Help a Depressed or Suicidal Friend*

- Listen to your friend with concern. Do not ignore your friend; do not put him or her down.
- Share your feelings about a time when you felt badly. Reassure your friend that things got better for you and that things can also get better for him or her.
- Ask your friend if he or she has suicidal thoughts.
- Let your friend know that many people think about suicide but that they do not act on those thoughts.
- Stay with your friend. Talk with him or her or do something together.
- Give your friend a suicide hot line number. Call that number and get advice if your friend will not do it on his or her own.
- If your friend is suicidal and refuses to get help, notify a responsible person (a counselor, the dormitory manager, an instructor, a minister, etc.).
- Make a date with your friend to see him or her the next day.

Literature about suicide is filled with testimonials from grateful individuals whose plans for suicide were interrupted. When people are depressed, their perspectives are warped; death seems to be the only solution to their problems. Once they have been helped to see other alternatives, they cannot imagine why they ever considered suicide. Consider the steps listed in Figure 11.10 that you could take to help a suicidal friend.

The activity on page 231 will help you to keep a sense of balance and perspective in your own life. If you make each day a balanced and fulfilling experience, you will find yourself resisting depressive episodes.

■ SIGNS OF MEDICAL EMERGENCIES

Despite your best efforts to maintain a healthy lifestyle, there will probably be times when you become sick. This section offers some remedies for the most common symptoms you are likely to encounter, but more important, it alerts you to symptoms that may be dangerous and require immediate medical attention.

> *These guidelines are offered only as general advice. You may need to see a doctor earlier or under different circumstances based on your own particular medical condition. If you are concerned about a symptom or have any questions, call your doctor or the health services nurse on campus.*

Colds and influenza ("flu") are the most common health complaints on college campuses. Unfortunately, we are all familiar with the symptoms: sneezing, sore throat, runny nose, "stuffy" head, coughing, headaches, fever, and aches and pains all through the body.

There is no cure for the virus that causes colds or flu; you just have to ride out the symptoms. You can, however, decrease the probability of contracting the virus by getting enough sleep, eating a balanced diet, washing your hands frequently with soap, and avoiding hand to nose or eye contact. (Wash your hands every one or two hours, especially before eating and do not touch your nose or eyes. That's how the viruses are spread.) If your body's immune system is working well because you are rested and well fed, your natural defenses will be more likely to fight off the virus. If you do get cold or flu symptoms, you can make yourself more comfortable by using decongestants to clear your nose and throat, sucking on hard candies, and taking aspirin or aspirin substitutes. (If you have a fever [any temperature higher than 98.6 degrees], use one of the aspirin substitutes to bring it down.)

■ *If your fever goes higher than 103° F or if a low fever persists more than three days, consult a doctor.*

■ *If you get a sore throat and swollen glands and experience headaches, chills, pain when you swallow, extreme fatigue, or a rash, see your doctor. You may have either mononucleosis or strep throat. Strep throat must be treated with antibiotics in order to avoid serious medical problems.*

What if you get stomach symptoms? If you are nauseous or vomiting, suck hard candies or ice chips for a few hours. Then try water, tea, or broth. You might try dry crackers and fruit juice the next day. If you experience diarrhea, try water, tea, or broth for a day, and then try dry crackers, toast, or plain rice. Avoid fruit juices and dairy products.

■ *If your symptoms do not improve within 48 hours or if your stomach hurts continuously, call a doctor. If you suspect that you have food poisoning (from mayonnaise salads left out too long on a warm day, canned foods or leftovers that were not reheated, meat or stuffing that was not cooked long enough), call a doctor quickly.*

■ *If a pain begins near your navel and then becomes worse in the lower right section of your abdomen, call a doctor immediately. You may have appendicitis, which can be fatal if it is not treated quickly.*

■ *If you regularly experience pain in the upper part of your stomach approximately one to three hours after eating, call a doctor. You may have an ulcer. Ulcers can be dangerous if they are not treated promptly.*

■ *If you have a headache or a neck ache and a fever, call your doctor immediately.*

Bring your vaccinations up to date. You should have been vaccinated against polio, mumps, measles, rubella, diphtheria, tetanus, and whooping cough as a child. Tetanus vaccinations should be updated every ten years throughout your adult life. Because of measles outbreaks, most schools now require that everyone 12 years and older have two doses of live measles vaccine on or after 12 months of age or have acceptable (laboratory) proof of immunization. These doses must be taken at least one month apart. If you contract measles as an adult, you can become seriously ill. If you contract rubella when you are pregnant, you may give birth to a seriously disabled baby.

■ *If you were not vaccinated during childhood, get your shots now.*

If you think that you may be pregnant, consult an obstetrician (a physician who specializes in pregnancy and birth) as soon as possible. Many diseases that might not even be noticed by an adult can result in serious damage to an unborn child. These diseases are particularly dangerous during the first three months of pregnancy. You should be tested and treated for them or you may give birth to a disabled infant. You should also learn how to change your diet and take care of yourself so that you will enjoy a healthy pregnancy and give birth to a healthy baby.

■ *See a doctor as soon as possible if you think that you are pregnant.*

The symptoms listed in Figure 11.11 are reasons to see a doctor as soon as possible. They may be signs of an illness that can be treated in order to prevent more serious illness or death. Depending on your own particular medical

Figure 11.11   *Signs of Serious Illness*

- If you have a sore that has not healed within two weeks.
- If you lose more than ten pounds of weight in ten weeks or less and you see no particular reason for the weight loss.
- If you have severe headaches that linger, and you do not know the reason for them.
- If you find a mole on your skin that bleeds or changes shape or color.
- If you cough or vomit up blood.
- If you vomit although you did not feel nauseous.
- If you are short of breath for no reason.
- If you faint or experience double vision for no reason.
- If you find that you are bleeding from your rectum or that your bowel movements are black and tarry.
- If you find it difficult to urinate or if you experience pain when you urinate.
- If your urine is cloudy, pink, or red.
- If you find a lump in your breast.
- If you experience bleeding from your vagina in between your menstrual periods.
- If you find a lump or a change in a testicle.
- If you feel pain or pressure in your chest and you do not know any reason for it.
- If you have a persistent cough.
- If you bruise or bleed easily.

ACTIVITY

Practicing a Healthier Lifestyle

Staying healthy means more than just surviving and staying alive. It means using the strategies we have discussed in this chapter that relate to nutrition, physical activity, controlling stress, and taking care of medical problems. But it also means practicing psychological health: affirming your being and enjoying life. This activity is meant to remind you of the pleasures of life as well as the responsibilities you have toward yourself. After all, if we don't take time to smell the roses, what's the point of being here?

Take some time for yourself each week to complete at least three of the activities that follow; they will prompt you to change old habits, discover new pleasures, and reexperience some of the simple joys of life. Do not think of this activity as selfishness or time wasted. Look at it as an investment in your health that will pay back double dividends. You will feel more energized and be better able to cope with your hectic schedule and many responsibilities!

- Try a sport that you have always wanted to try.
- Make a list of things you have never eaten and try one.
- Take a warm bath and practice deep muscle relaxation.
- Call a friend you have not spoken to in a long time and catch up with him or her.

- Pay someone a compliment.
- Smile at a stranger and say "Hello."
- Take a walk or a bike ride.
- Spend some time doing something silly or enjoyable with a child. If you do not have one of your own, borrow a child from a friend or relative for a few hours.
- If you smoke or drink alcohol or caffeine regularly, try giving it up for a day.
- Avoid the elevator for a day. Take the stairs!
- Volunteer an hour to help a friend, a neighbor, or someone who needs cheering up.
- Set the table with your fancy tablecloth, dinnerware, and glassware when you are not having company. Play some soothing music, and take twice as long over the meal as you usually would.
- Schedule half an hour for yourself to daydream, soak in a warm bath, or do something creative.
- Let someone get ahead of you in line at the supermarket or the cafeteria, or while you are driving.
- Plan on speaking up for yourself to someone with whom you are not usually assertive.
- If you watch television regularly, give it up for a day.
- Schedule ahead so that you can eat a meal at home with your whole family. Plan on some fun food that everyone enjoys.
- Think about some major life goals that you have set. Write a journal entry to yourself that describes your feelings about how things are going for you.
- Schedule time to spend an hour talking with someone who makes you feel good.
- If you regularly use salt at the table, skip it for a day.
- If you have not seen your doctor, dentist, gynecologist, or eye doctor in more than a year, schedule a checkup.
- Schedule some time to clean out your desk, a closet, the garage, or your purse.
- Make an appointment to visit the local gym; try out an exercise class or some equipment that you have never tried before.
- Pamper yourself. Make an appointment for a massage, a manicure, a haircut, or a day at a health spa.
- If you regularly eat fast food, skip it for two days. Indulge instead in a fancy vegetarian meal (Indian and Chinese restaurants are a good source for vegetarian dishes) or a deluxe salad bar.

---

condition, you may need to see a doctor earlier or under different circumstances. If you are concerned about a symptom or have a question, call your doctor or the health services nurse on campus.

REFLECTIONS FOR YOUR JOURNAL

1. Evaluate your diet. Is it well balanced? Do you follow the guidelines in this chapter for reducing your intake of fat, salt, sugar, fast foods, alcohol, and junk foods? Are you overweight? What changes can you make to approximate a healthier diet?

2. What benefits would a program of regular exercise give you? What type of exercise would fit most easily into your lifestyle? How can you make exercising more attractive?

3. If you believe that you experience too much stress, reflect upon the techniques you use to reduce the stress in your life. Discuss any stress-reducing techniques that you feel are maladaptive. How can you introduce healthier stress reduction techniques into your life?

4. Think about the last time you or a person who is close to you was depressed. How did you bring yourself (or your friend) out of the depression? How can you prevent future episodes of depression? If you cannot prevent depression, what can you do to make depressive episodes less severe?

5. If you know anyone who has contemplated suicide, write about that person's experience. How can you help a person who is close to you avoid suicide?

Notes

1. "Nutrition & Safe Foods IQ Test," "10 Foods You Should Never Eat," *Nutrition Action Newsletter.* Washington, DC: Center for Science in the Public Interest, 1995.
2. M. O'Neil, "The Morality of Fat," *New York Times Magazine,* 10 March 1996, p. 37.
3. "Even Moderate Weight Gain Can Become Deadly," *New York Times,* 14 September 1995, pp. A1, B11.
4. K. Brownell, "News of Medicine," *Reader's Digest,* 140, no. 838 (February 1992).
5. K. Baar, "Time for a Fitness Pyramid?" *New York Times,* 29 March 1995, pp. C1, C6.
6. U.S. Department of Health and Human Services, *Nutrition and Your Health: Dietary Guidelines for Americans,* 3rd ed. Washington, DC: U.S. Department of Agriculture, 1990, Doc. A 1.77:232/990.
7. J. E. Brody, "Help for Youths Beset by Eating Disorders," *New York Times,* 31 January 1996, p. C10.
8. M. T. Erickson, *Behavior Disorders of Children and Adolescents.* Englewood Cliffs, NJ: Prentice-Hall, 1987, p. 70.
9. "Meat and Dairy Industries Not Thrilled," *Hope Health Letter.* Seattle, WA: Hope Heart Institute.
10. M. Burros, "Favorite Pastries Weigh In," *New York Times,* 6 June 1996.
11. S. Gilbert, "Fitness Helps, Even for Smokers," *New York Times,* 17 July 1996, p. C7.
12. J. E. Brody, "More of the Elderly Seeking the Benefits of Exercise," *New York Times,* 4 October 1995, p. C11.
13. Ibid.
14. Ibid.
15. "Lack of Exercise Cited in U.S. Women," *New York Times,* 19 August 1995, p. 29.
16. J. E. Brody, "Trying to Reconcile Exercise Findings," *New York Times,* 23 April 1995, p. 22.
17. K. Baar, op. cit.
18. U.S. Public Health Service, Office on Women's Health, *Get Real: Straight Talk About Women's Health.* Washington, DC: U.S. Public Health Service and Society for the Advancement of Women's Health Research, 1995.
19. J. E. Brody, 23 April 1995, op. cit.
20. E. Kaufman, "The New Case for Woman Power," *New York Times Magazine,* Part 2, 28 April 1989, pp. 18–22.
21. K. Baar, op. cit.
22. E. Kaufman, op. cit.
23. T. H. Holmes and R. H. Rahe, "Social Readjustment Rating Scale," *Journal of Psychosomatic Research,* 11 (1967), pp. 213–218; I. G. Sarason, J. H. Johnson, and J. Siegel, "Assessing the Impact of Life Changes: Development of the Life Experience Survey." *Journal of Consulting and Clinical Psychology,* 46 (1978), pp. 932–946.
24. R. H. Rosenman et al., "Coronary Heart Disease in the Western Collaborative Group Study: Final Follow-Up Experience at $8^{1}/_{2}$ Years," *Journal of the American Medical Association,* 233 (1975), pp. 872–877; C. D. Jenkins, S. J. Zyzanski, and R. H. Rosenman, "Risk of New Myocardial Infarction in Middle Age Men with Manifest Coronary Disease," *Circulation,* 53 (1976), pp. 342–347.
25. "Burnout: The Epidemic of the '90's'," *The Female Patient,* Supplement, S1, 1995, pp. 31–32.
26. American Association of Suicidology.
27. Government Printing Office, U.S. Department of Commerce, Bureau of the Census, *Statistical Abstracts of the United States.* Washington, DC: 1995.
28. American Suicide Association, "Prevention Through Research and Education." New York, 1991.

29. J. C. Coleman, J. N. Butcher, and R. C. Carson, *Abnormal Psychology and Modern Life.* Glenview, IL: Scott, Foresman, 1980.
30. American Suicide Association, op. cit.

Resources for Further Information

The American Anorexia/Bulimia
    Association
293 Central Park West, Suite 1-R
New York, NY
212-501-8351

American Dietetic Association
216 W. Jackson Blvd.
Chicago, IL 60606
1-800-366-1655

Anorexia Nervosa and Related Eating
    Disordrs
P.O. Box 5102
Eugene, OR 97405
503-344-1144

Depression and Related Affective
    Disorders Association
Meyer-3-181
600 N. Wolfe Street
Baltimore, MD 21287-7381
410-955-4647
202-955-5800

National Association of Anorexia
    Nervosa and Associated Disorders
P.O. Box 7
Highland Park, IL 60035
847-831-3483

National Institute for Mental Health
Public Inquiries Section
5600 Fischers Lane, Rm. 7 C-02
Rockville, MD 20857
301-443-4513

National Mental Health Association
10201 Prince Street
Alexandria, VA 22314
1-800-969-6642

Osteoporosis and Related Bone
    Disorders
National Resource Center
1150 17 Street, NW, Suite 500
Washington, DC 20036
1-800-624-BONE

Overeaters Anonymous
P.O. Box 44020
Rio Rancho, NM 87174
505-891-2664

U.S. Department of Agriculture
Nutrition Policy and Promotion
1120 20 Street, NW
Suite 200, North Lobby
Washington, DC 20036
202-418-2312

U.S. Public Health Service's Office on
    Women's Health
200 Independence Avenue, SW, Rm. 730B
Washington, DC 20201
202-690-7650

CHAPTER 12

SUBSTANCE ABUSE

■ THE "INSTANT" CURE

You have undoubtedly heard that we live in a "drug happy" society. Whatever your complaint, physical or psychological, someone is likely to offer you a solution that involves drugs. Are you tense, tired, depressed, or upset? There's a pill that will help you. Do you have a cold, a headache, a skin rash? Your friendly pill pusher will find a cure. Would you like to have fun, lose weight, or deliver a better speech? Modern pharmacology can fix you up with an instant "cure." Some of these drugs are legal; others are illegal. Some have short-term effects; others cause permanent damage. Some are highly addictive; others may be used with less fear of developing a dependence. Experimenting with drugs can be dangerous. You will have to pay a price in the end, no matter which ones you try.

Drugs may cost some students their lives if they lead the students to engage in risky behaviors (such as unprotected sex with a partner infected with the AIDS virus, a dash through an intersection to beat a yellow light, or an exhilarating climb taken on a dare) that might not have become fatal temptations if their judgment or reflexes were fully intact. For other students, the cost of drug use is their college education. They may be forced to withdraw from college when drugs lead to behaviors that violate campus disciplinary codes or when drugs interfere with the ability to study and keep up grades. Drugs can become a particular problem during the freshman year when students may be experiencing freedom from their parents' supervision for the first time. If they misuse that freedom and abuse drugs, they will find themselves failing or expelled from college in a very short time.

After a decade of decline, several national surveys indicate that adolescent drug use has increased sharply. Significant increases have been reported in the use of marijuana, cigarettes, cocaine, and hallucinogens. This is the fourth straight year that the National Parents' Resource Institute for Drug Education (PRIDE) survey of 200,000 youths has reported a rise in teen drug use.[1, 2, 3]

■ ALCOHOL AND COLLEGE STUDENTS

When she was asked what the biggest problem on her campus was, former University of Wisconsin Chancellor Donna Shalala answered, "alcohol."[4] Her sentiment was shared by other college presidents responding to a Carnegie Foundation Survey who also classified alcohol abuse as the campus life issue of greatest concern to them.[5]

A very conservative estimate of the annual consumption of alcohol by American college students is more than 34 gallons per person per year. The

A lot of campus rapes start here.

Whenever there's drinking or drugs, things can get out of hand.
So it's no surprise that many campus rapes involve alcohol.

But you should know that under any circumstances, sex without
the other person's consent is considered rape. A felony, punishable
by prison. And drinking is no excuse.

That's why, when you party, it's good to know what your limits are.
You see, a little sobering thought now can save you from a big
problem later.

© 1990 Rape Treatment Center, Santa Monica Hospital.

Printed courtesy of Rape Treatment Center, Santa Monica Hospital Medical Center.

annual beer consumption of American college students is just under 4 billion cans.[6] Students in the United States spend more money on alcoholic beverages each year than they spend on textbooks.[7]

Administrators at approximately 200 colleges and universities estimate that on the average, alcohol is involved in 68 percent of the violent behavior and 52 percent of the physical injuries on their campuses. This includes tragedies such as the death of an alcohol-impaired Maryland student who drowned in a bathtub.[8]

Alcohol is responsible for a wide range of problems among college students. A national survey of almost 18,000 students on 140 campuses indicated that students who are frequent binge drinkers tend to have more problems than students who binge less frequently or not at all. For example, frequent binge drinkers, that is students who have had five or more drinks at one sitting on at least three occasions within the past two weeks, were 7 to 10 times more likely than nonbinge drinkers to not use protection when having sex, to engage in unplanned sexual activity, to get into trouble with campus police, to damage property, or to get hurt or injured.[9]

Figure 12.1 shows the number of problems reported by binge drinkers and non-binge drinkers. It is estimated that approximately 41 percent of

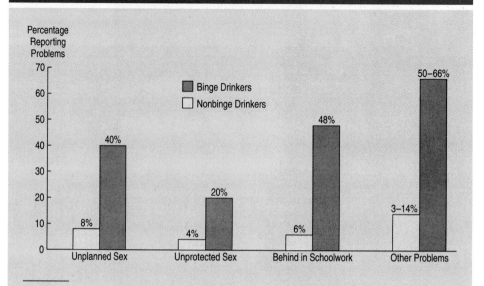

Figure 12.1   *Consequences of Binge Drinking in College*[10]

Based on data from H. Wechsler, A. Davenport, G. Dowdall, B. Moeykens, S. Castillo. "Health and Behavioral Consequences of Binge Drinking in College: A National Survey of Students at 140 Campuses," *Journal of the American Medical Association (JAMA),* 7 December 1994, pp. 1672–1677.

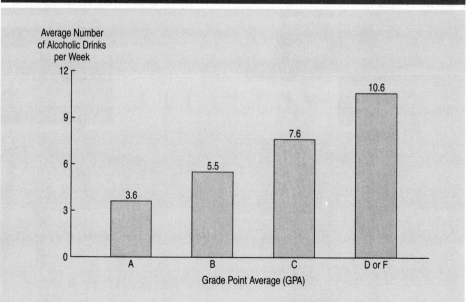

Figure 12.2   *The Relationship between the Number of Alcoholic Drinks Consumed per Week and Students' Grade Point Averages*

Based on data reported in "Campus Drinking: Who, Why, and How Much?" *US News and World Report,* 20 June 1994, p. 21.

students' academic problems and 28 percent of college dropouts are related to alcohol use.[11] Over 120,000 first-year students (7 percent of the freshman class) will become dropouts for reasons related to alcohol. Figure 12.2 may provide a partial explanation for these dropouts: There is a direct relationship between the amount of alcohol a student consumes and his or her grade point average. "A" students consume, on average, 3.6 drinks per week while D or F students average 10.6 drinks in a week.[12] It is also interesting that first year students consume, on the average, more alcoholic drinks than sophomores, who in turn drink more than juniors; the smallest average number of drinks consumed per week is reported by seniors.[13]

■ COPING WITH ALCOHOL

You may be surprised to see alcohol discussed in a chapter on drugs. Alcohol is classified as a drug because its main ingredient, ethanol, depresses the central nervous system just as sleeping pills do. At high enough doses, it can act as an anaesthetic, numbing your sensations. Like other drugs, alcohol produces a tolerance in the user so that larger and larger doses become necessary to achieve the desired effects. It acts as a toxin, or poisonous substance, to almost all organs: brain, heart, lungs, liver, bone marrow, intestines, ovaries, and testicles.

■ THE CONSEQUENCES OF ABUSING ALCOHOL

The most serious health consequence of alcohol is death. Close to 18,000 Americans are killed each year in alcohol-related auto fatalities.[14] Over twice as many Americans were killed in automobile crashes during the Vietnam War than were killed by the Viet Cong. And for every one of these fatalities, there were many more serious injuries. Alcohol is the leading factor in deaths among young people ages 16 through 21 because it leads to fatal accidents.

Although alcohol use increases the risk for motor vehicle accidents for all drivers, the risk for younger drivers begins to increase at very low blood alcohol levels (BACs). In addition, in young drivers who drive after drinking, the risk of an accident is greater at all levels than for older drivers.[15] This probably results from a combination of fewer years of experience in driving and in drinking along with the increased risk-taking among youths that is associated with lower feelings of vulnerability.

This is probably the reason that New York recently became the thirty-third state to enact a zero-tolerance law for drivers under the age of 21. This legislation authorizes the Department of Motor Vehicles to suspend the driver's license of a minor who is arrested while driving with a BAC level as low as two-hundredths of one percent—the equivalent, for most people, of one beer or one glass of wine.[16]

Despite the higher risks for young people who drink and drive, research at the University of Iowa and other studies of youthful driving patterns report that 40 percent of the students admitted to driving after drinking, and 40 percent knowingly rode with a driver who had had too much to drink.[17]

Despite the fact that the overall level of drinking among college students has declined slightly, abusive or binge drinking remains a problem. It is a much more frequent problem among members of the sororities and fraternities, but almost half of the nation's college students report patterns of binge drinking. A national survey indicates that 80 to 86 percent of sorority and fraternity residents are binge drinkers compared with 45 percent of men and women who are not affiliated with fraternities or sororities. Binge drinking puts students in a group that has higher risk for alcohol-related problems such as missing classes, getting hurt or injured, and having trouble with the police.[18]

A C T I V I T Y

Testing Your Alcohol IQ

Take the following quiz and see how you score in your knowledge about drinking. You can find the answers to the questions in this chapter. Answer the ones you do not know as you read the text. You may check your responses with the answer key on page 269.

_____ 1. Which has the most alcohol?
    a. 12 ounces of beer
    b. 5½ ounces of wine
    c. 1½ ounces of liquor
    d. they all have the same amount of alcohol

_____ 2. If you want to slow down the effect that alcohol is having on you
    a. eat something before you drink
    b. eat while you are drinking
    c. drink more slowly
    d. all of the above

_____ 3. When you have had too much to drink, how do you sober up?
    a. Stop drinking and eat something
    b. Drink a few cups of coffee
    c. Take a cold shower
    d. Wait 45 minutes before you have another drink

_____ 4. If you do not want to get drunk, you should
    a. drink beer
    b. drink wine
    c. switch from liquor to beer
    d. drink a nonalcoholic beverage

_____ 5. True or False? Alcohol is an aphrodisiac. (An aphrodisiac makes sex better.)

_____ 6. True or False? People can tell when they are too drunk to drive.

_____ 7. True or False? Alcohol is a depressant.

_____ 8. True or False? Alcohol is a stimulant.

_____ 9. True or False? Some people cannot metabolize alcohol. It makes them sick even if they drink only a small amount.

_____ 10. If a woman drinks while she is pregnant, her baby
    a. may be born smaller and will not grow as much or as fast
    b. may have certain deformities of the face or limbs
    c. may have minimal brain dysfunction
    d. may have all of the above

_____ 11. Most states define the level of intoxication for legal purposes at a blood alcohol concentration of
    a. .03   c. .10
    b. .06   d. .50
    What is the legal level of intoxication set by your state?

_____ 12. At what blood alcohol concentration level are you likely to lose consciousness?

   a. .03   c. .10
   b. .06   d. .50

_____ 13. How many drinks does it take for the average person to reach the level of intoxication as it is defined by the legal system?

   a. 1 to 2   c. 3 to 4
   b. 2 to 3   d. 4 to 5

_____ 14. If one of your parents has a drinking problem

   a. you are more likely to develop a drinking problem than the average person
   b. you are less likely to develop a drinking problem than the average person
   c. you have the same probability as the average person of developing a drinking problem
   d. your parents' drinking problem has no bearing on how likely it is that you will develop a problem

_____ 15. True or False? Alcohol is not addictive.

_____ 16. True or False? Alcohol is a leading factor in deaths of youths ages 16 through 21.

_____ 17. Which of these factors can speed up the effect alcohol has on you?

   a. your rate of drinking
   b. the concentration of alcohol in your beverage
   c. your emotions (e.g., fear, anger, stress)
   d. all of the above

_____ 18. True or False? Mixing alcohol with carbonated mixers such as soda is likely to speed up alcohol's effect on you.

_____ 19. True or False? A person's mood can influence the way alcohol affects him or her.

_____ 20. True or False? Mixing alcohol with depressant drugs can be fatal.

_____ 21. True or False? A person can die from an overdose of alcohol.

_____ 22. True or False? Switching to another kind of alcoholic drink will make you drunker than staying with the same kind of alcohol.

_____ 23. True or False? A blackout is the same as passing out.

_____ 24. Alcohol

   a. raises your body temperature
   b. lowers your body temperature
   c. gives you the feeling of warmth
   d. b and c

_____ 25. Using marijuana impairs your ability to drive and use machinery. Combining alcohol with marijuana

   a. leads to greater deterioration than using just one of them
   b. leads to less deterioration because they cancel each other out
   c. cancels the effect that each drug would have by itself
   d. has no effect on your ability to process information, control your eye movements, or perform tasks requiring manual dexterity

_____ 26. If you want to drink but you do not wish to become intoxicated, how far apart should you space your drinks?

   a. about 15 minutes   c. about 45 minutes
   b. about half an hour   d. about an hour

It is interesting that at the same time that the number of binge drinkers on college campuses is increasing, the number of teetotalers or nondrinkers is also increasing. In 1971 one in four students reported that they abstained from even drinking an occasional beer. Today, according to a national survey of more than 300,000 students conducted by the University of California at Los Angeles, almost half of the students say they do not drink. For those students who do drink regularly, the average consumption has dropped to 13 drinks a week, down from 14.3 in 1982.[19]

The list of problems associated with alcohol on campuses is long. Sixty percent of women who contract STDs, including HIV, have had sex under the influence of alcohol.[20] Drinking is involved in one-third of suicides, a leading cause of death among college students.[21] Sixty-nine percent of drowning deaths are related to alcohol, as are 17 to 53 percent of fatal falls.[22] There is also a very high correlation between drinking and rape on college campuses. This is especially true for victims and rapists in incidents of gang rape. One college president put it very succinctly when he said, "College men get smashed and break something; college women get smashed and get broken."[23]

In addition to its role in suicides, drownings, and rapes on campus, alcohol is also implicated in many accidents, including the death of a freshman who went to relieve himself during a fraternity hayride and was killed by an oncoming car, the fatal shooting of a student by a fellow student in his residence hall, the death of a first-year student who fell from a 2-inch-wide, 27-foot-high ledge she was trying to cross at a fraternity house, and nine out of the ten deaths that occur during fraternity hazings each year.[24] The four leading causes of death among young adults, vehicular crashes, homicides, suicides, and drownings, are all associated with alcohol use.[25]

Immediate death from alcohol-related events is actually a lower risk for college students than a later death caused by drinking. Between 240,000 and 360,000 of the students currently enrolled in American colleges will eventually die of alcohol-related causes. Cirrhosis of the liver will kill more of our current college students than the number who will ever get doctorates in business, communications, or management combined.[26] Various cancers are also associated with drinking, as well as other diseases such as gastritis, hepatitis, anemia, cerebellar degeneration, and heart disease. Although alcohol is a legal drug in this country, the statistics associated with its use are harrowing (Figure 12.3).

■ REASONS FOR DRINKING

The reasons that many people drink are well known: to release inhibitions and feel more relaxed, to escape from problems, or to comply with peer pressures. When drinking is used to escape from problems, alcohol can set a real trap, especially for young people who still have many of life's skills to learn. Drinking does not result in a solution to a problem, just a temporary escape from it. Once the alcohol wears off, the problem is still there or it will return in the future. Since the person has not learned to cope with the problem while drinking, the only way out is to start another round of drinking when the alcohol wears off or when the problem reappears.

This can lead to a vicious cycle of addiction from which you may not be able to escape. In the meantime, you do not learn any of the social or academic skills that would allow you to solve your problem. This is, perhaps, one of the most damaging aspects of any drug addiction. The "easy way" out leads only to addiction; it does not lead to learning the skills that can help you to cope effectively with life's challenges. In particular, it is likely to ruin your college career because you will not be able to meet the academic or social challenges presented on campus.

Figure 12.3 *Statistics of Alcohol Abuse*

■ Research by Harvard and Columbia Universities shows that 95 percent of all violent crimes committed on campuses nationwide are alcohol-related. (New York Times, 1996).

■ An analysis of 900 insurance claims against fraternities over a six-year period shows that one out of four resulted from a death, paralysis, or other serious injury. Alcohol had been a factor in more than 80 percent of the claims. According to national fraternity executives, fraternities spend a third of their budgets, approximately $30 million a year to pay liability costs. (Harris & Harris of Kentucky, Inc. in New York Times, 1996).

■ Fourteen to 16 million Americans meet the diagnostic criteria for alcohol abuse or dependence. They are physically addicted to alcohol or experience serious problems in living and health associated with its use.(American Psychiatric Association, 1994).

■ Between 30 and 40 percent of drivers aged 18- to 24-years who were involved in fatal automobile accidents had blood alcohol concentration levels (BACs) of .01 or more. (Centers For Disease Control and Prevention, 1995)

■ The four leading causes of death among young adults, vehicular crashes, homicides, suicides, and drownings, are all associated with alcohol use. (OASIS, State of New York, 1994)

■ Sixty percent of women who become infected with STDs, including HIV, have sex under the influence of alcohol. (U.S. Public Health Service, 1995).

■ About two out of every five Americans will be involved in an alcohol-related crash at some time in their lives (National Highway Traffic Safety Administration, 1991).

■ Approximately 2,886,000 people were arrested for alcohol-related offenses in 1993. (U.S. Department of Justice, 1995)

■ Alcohol abuse accounts for approximately 98,000 deaths each year. This includes deaths from cirrhosis and other medical problems, alcohol-related motor vehicle accidents, and alcohol-related homicides, suicides, and other accidents (National Council on Alcoholism).

■ Statistics indicate that about 355,000 people were injured in crashes where alcohol was present, an average of one person injured every 1.5 minutes. About 96,000 of these people suffered serious injuries. Close to 17.5 thousand people were killed in alcohol-related crashes. (National Highway Safety Administration, 1991; U.S. Department of Justice, 1995).

■ Costs to the American economy from alcohol abuse were close to $99 billion in 1990.(Robert Wood Johnson Foundation)

■ Four percent, or one-half million, of all college students drink every day. (Office of Substance Abuse and Prevention, 1993)

■ The short period between Thanksgiving and New Year's Eve is a particularly dangerous time. Mothers Against Drunk Driving predicted that the annual death toll in alcohol-related crashes during this narrow window would take 2000 lives. (MADD, 1995)

■ Suicide is the second leading cause of death among high school and college students. Forty percent of these youths had a history of substance abuse (American Suicide Foundation).

Figure 12.3   (Continued)

■ Between 80 and 86 percent of fraternity and sorority residents are binge-drinkers: They consumed 5 or more drinks on at least one occasion during the two weeks before the survey. Between 36 and 46 percent of college students who are not affiliated with Greek societies report patterns of binge drinking (*New York Times,* 1995).

■ Violent crime is heavily correlated with alcohol: 54 percent of those convicted of murder and attempted murder, 68 percent of those convicted of manslaughter, 52 percent of those convicted for rape, 48 percent of those convicted of robbery, 62 percent of those convicted of assault, and 44 percent of those convicted of burglary had been drinking in the time period immediately preceding the crime (U.S. Department of Health and Human Services, 1991). Drinking is estimated to be involved in 50 percent of spouse abuse cases and 38 percent of child abuse cases (National Council on Alcoholism).

■ Alcoholic males may experience shrunken testes, reduced testosterone levels, and even impotence. Alcohol kills brain cells and interferes with memory. People who drink regularly are at greater risk of developing cancer of the liver, mouth, esophagus, pancreas, intestine, prostate, and lung. (National Traffic Safety Student Workbook, 1994).

When alcohol is used because of pressure from your friends, it can also result in problems, though they are not as severe as the ones described in the preceding paragraph. The danger here is that the relationships with these people may be based solely on alcohol. You may not truly become close to these people, and you may not really get to know and like them. You also may not learn any social skills about how to make friends, give support, or share feelings. In some cases, the only basis for the friendship is drinking, and that will not result in a true friendship. Figure 12.4 suggests twenty-five ways to say "No" to peer pressure about drinking.

The use of alcohol to release inhibitions and to help you enjoy a social event is a more adaptive reason to drink. If it is used in moderation, alcohol can help you to relax and enjoy the company of others. It can enhance the taste of food, the sound of music, and the pleasure of a social event. Just be sure that you can recognize the difference between using alcohol to make a social event more pleasant and going to a social event just so you can abuse alcohol. If you are involved in the second scenario, you are probably using alcohol to escape from some type of problem. Whatever your reasons for using alcohol, given the unsettling statistics presented above, it is in your interests either to abstain from drinking or to learn to drink responsibly.

■ PROBLEM DRINKING

Drinking responsibly means making sure that alcohol does not create problems for you. If you begin partying during the week and missing classes or failing exams, then you may be sacrificing your college education and future career for a few hours worth of pleasure. If you find that you are beginning to experience hangovers, blackouts, or trembling hands, you may be giving up your health in exchange for false feelings of security and acceptance. If you are getting into trouble with the law or driving while intoxicated, you may

Figure 12.4 *Twenty-Five Ways to Say "No" to Booze*

1. I'd rather OD on pizza.
2. I don't need to loosen up—I just got it together.
3. Chocolate and alcohol don't mix.
4. I might forget where I parked my mind.
5. I'd rather hang loose than hangover.
6. If I were any more mellow, I'd melt.
7. I'm saving my brain cells for science.
8. If I'm going to blow my diet, I'd rather do it on junk food.
9. I think, therefore, I am not going to drink.
10. I use my money for better things.
11. I'm high on life.
12. My life is weird enough as it is.
13. I sing off key as it is.
14. My liver and I have this understanding.
15. I become so witty no one can stand me.
16. I don't need any more hair on my chest.
17. I drink no wine before it is time.
18. My weekends are made for something else.
19. For all I do, I don't need a brew.
20. I've got the time, you can keep the beer.
21. Liquor is quicker, but I'm in no hurry.
22. Life is a puzzle with the guzzle.
23. I've got all the gusto I can handle.
24. If I want the high life, I'd rather go sky-diving.
25. I'm performing neurosurgery in the morning.

Reprinted with permission of the Office of Highway Safety, State of Delaware, from a series of posters created by the Office of Highway Safety.

literally be giving up your life for only a few hours of escape from feelings of anxiety or boredom.

Force yourself to think about the choices you are making each time you decide to go out and drink for an evening. Make sure that the price you pay for that outing is worth the cost. Try to limit your partying to Friday and Saturday nights. A party is not much fun, after all, if you will be constantly worrying about the exam for which you should be studying. A problem drinker is someone who continues to drink even though the drinking causes problems for him or her. Be sure that you are not creating problems for yourself when you decide to go out and drink. Do not drink and drive.

As the activity on page 248 demonstrates, problem drinking can be very expensive. In Massachusetts, the Governor's Highway Safety Bureau calculates that costs for a first offender with a clean record who is arrested for driving while intoxicated come to $4,167. This includes $1,800 for the defense attorney, $1,050 increased insurance assessment for three years, $360 loss of safe driver credits for three years, $682 for the Alcohol Education Program (six

ACTIVITY

Evaluating the Consequences of a Drinking Problem

This activity will help you to become aware of the many different consequences that a drinking problem can cause. Break into small groups of four
to six students. Read the entire story, then read all of the items (consequences) before making any decisions.

During his senior year of college, John was involved in an automobile accident while returning home from a party. The accident was John's fault, and
it resulted in about $2,000 damage to his car and $7,000 damage to the other
car, and his girlfriend received injuries to her back. (Luckily, they were all
wearing seat belts at the time of the crash so that no one was killed or seriously injured.)

John was arrested for driving while impaired by alcohol; he was taken to
jail, booked, and released on bail after spending six hours in the "drunk tank."
When he appeared in court and pleaded "guilty," the judge determined that he
was really an upstanding citizen who had made a mistake so he did not send
John to jail. Because it was his first arrest for DWI, the judge fined John only
$400 plus $100 court costs and suspended his license for 60 days. John felt that
he had gotten off easy, but a number of things happened to him as a result of
his arrest and conviction.

Read all of the items first and then put an "X" next to the three consequences that would bother you most if they happened to you. When all group
members have ranked the items, try to reach a group consensus through discussion about which consequences would be most troublesome.

1. He discovered that he has a criminal record that will follow him for life.
2. He had to pay $950 for a lawyer to handle his case in court.
3. He had to pay an additional $350 per year for auto insurance premiums.
4. His parents found out about his arrest and conviction.
5. His girlfriend, whose back was injured in the accident, missed three
   weeks of school because of her injuries and had to drop out for the semester.
6. A promising job offer was withdrawn when the company's insurance/
   risk department determined that he was a poor driving risk due to his
   conviction.
7. He had to withdraw his name temporarily from the volunteer list at the
   youth agency where he had worked for three years because he was not
   available on Saturday mornings—he had to attend traffic school.
8. He did not get called back for "second interviews" at the placement office, since all major employers check the driving records of prospective
   employees.
9. The other driver, who was not at fault, lost his job because his car was destroyed and he missed too much work.
10. John's younger brother, Sam, used John's conviction as an excuse for com-
    ing home drunk: "If John can do it, why can't I?"
11. A report of his arrest and conviction was published in the local newspa-
    per; his friends, teachers, and minister found out about it.

This activity was adapted from exercises developed at Indiana University and the University of
Vermont.

months of intensive counseling sessions), $100 in court costs, $100 minimum fine, and smaller fees for car towing, car storage, and the magistrate's night-time bail fee. In addition, if you register 0.10 or over in blood alcohol concentration on the Breathalyzer test, your license will be revoked for 90 days. If you are convicted of a first offense, you will be fined up to $1,000, you may be sentenced up to two years in jail, and your license will be revoked for one year.

A brief survey of the costs involved in other states should convince you that drinking and driving is expensive in addition to being dangerous. The Ohio Department of Highway Safety warns that a conviction for driving under the influence of alcohol will cost $3,500 in cash fines, legal fees, and high-risk insurance premiums. Conviction of driving under the influence of alcohol in Colorado results in a jail term (five days to one year), a fine ($300 to $1,000), a public service obligation (48 to 96 hours), a $100 alcohol education fee, court costs, $60 to the Law Enforcement Assistance Fund, $25 to the Victim Compensation Fund, a 500 percent increase in car insurance for three to five years, and suspension of driving privileges. The Maine Alcohol & Drug Abuse Clearinghouse reports that a conviction for drunk driving will cost $3,260. What are the consequences for being arrested or convicted while driving under the influence in your state?

Use the strategies in Figures 12.5 and 12.6 to make sure you do not become a victim of driving under the influence.

Alcoholism in Families

Research shows that certain people are more likely to become problem drinkers than others. Studies of adopted children show that, on the average, children of alcoholics are four times more likely than other people to become alcoholic. This is true even if the children are adopted by nonalcoholics at a young age. Researchers have known for years that alcoholism runs in families, but a growing number of studies lends support to the theory that a tendency toward alcoholism may be inherited.

Data from the Alcohol Research Center at Washington University are typical of the strong family patterns found among alcoholics (see Figure 12.7).

Dr. Reich estimated that by the age of 40, more than one-half of the men and women who have one alcoholic parent will have developed a drinking disorder. For those who have two alcoholic parents, he estimated that 60 percent will become alcoholic. By comparison, national statistics show that only 3 percent of the women and 8 to 10 percent of the men in the general population will

Figure 12.5 *Strategies for Safer Drinking*

Control Your Drinking

You can control your use of alcohol if you:

- **Don't Start Drinking.** Once you start, your resistance will become weaker. Have a nonalcoholic drink instead.

- **Set a Limit.** Decide before you go out how many drinks you can have during the time you will be drinking. Pace yourself and stick to your limit.

- **Pace Yourself.** Do other things while you are drinking to slow down your rate of consumption.

Figure 12.6 *Strategies for Safe Driving*

Control Your Driving

If you don't control your drinking, you can control your driving.

- ■ Leave the Car at Home. When you know that you will be drinking, leave your car at home so that you will not be tempted to drive. Arrange for other transportation.

- ■ Leave the Car There. It's better to leave your car at the party, get a ride home, and pick your car up later.

- ■ Wait it Out. Wait until your system has had time to eliminate the alcohol. It will take about one hour per drink. No other method works.

Adapted from "Decide Before You Ride," National Highway Traffic Safety Administration, U.S. Department of Transportation, 1990.

---

become alcoholic. Children of alcoholic parents are at much greater risk for developing a drinking problem. Studies at the University of Kansas Medical Center showed that grandchildren of alcoholics are also at greater risk than the general population, even if their parents do not drink much.

Researchers think that the enzyme that breaks down a poisonous byproduct of alcohol, acetaldehyde, may explain why some people become more easily addicted to alcohol than others. If you do not have this enzyme, the buildup of acetaldehyde after drinking even small amounts of alcohol can give you a headache and make you feel nauseous, dizzy, and uncomfortably flushed. People who feel uncomfortable when they drink are less likely to drink much. People of Asian descent are particularly likely to be deficient in this enzyme, and, indeed, the rates of alcoholism among Asians are relatively lower than for other races. Women and Jews are also more likely than Gentile men to have this deficiency. The lower rates of alcoholism among women and Jews lends support to this theory.

A survey by the New York State Division of Alcoholism and Alcohol Abuse indicated that people who knew that they were at risk for alcoholism tried to cut down the amount they drank. Only 5 percent of the adult children of alcoholics realized that they were more likely to become alcoholic than the children of nonalcoholics, and they tried to limit their drinking. The adult children of alcoholics who did not realize that they were at greater risk drank

---

Figure 12.7 *Alcoholism Runs in Families*

- ■ 38 percent of the problem drinkers had alcoholic fathers
- ■ 21 percent of the problem drinkers had alcoholic mothers
- ■ 57 percent of the problem drinkers had alcoholic brothers
- ■ 15 percent of the problem drinkers had alcoholic sisters
- ■ 32 percent of the problem drinkers had alcoholic sons
- ■ 19 percent of the problem drinkers had alcoholic daughters

ACTIVITY

Warning Signs of a Drinking Problem

Place a check next to any of the statements that apply to you.

1. Getting into fights because of alcohol.

2. Doing things when you are drunk that you regret when you become sober.

3. Drinking when you have no particular reason to drink.

4. Experiencing hangovers that result in missed classes, missed appointments, or missed days at work.

5. Getting into accidents and hurting yourself or others while you are drinking.

6. Building up a tolerance. Finding that you need more and more alcohol to get the relief or good feelings that smaller quantities used to give you.

7. Experiencing blackouts. Finding that you can't remember what you did while you were drinking even though you were awake and conscious at the time.

8. Finding that you are beginning to lie about your drinking or about what you are or should be doing.

9. Becoming dependent on alcohol. Finding that you cannot function without it. Stockpiling and hiding alcohol so that you will never run out when you need it.

10. Getting into trouble with the police or the courts because of your drinking.

11. Suffering from withdrawal symptoms such as shaking hands, racing pulse, faster breathing, hallucinations, or anxiety when you have not had a drink in a while.

12. Receiving warnings from your doctor about damage to your liver, heart and arteries, stomach (ulcers, gastritis), and brain (loss of memory, confusion, and permanent damage to your coordination and your vision).

13. Trying to "go on the wagon."

14. Taking a few drinks before you go out with friends or go to a party where alcohol will be served.

15. Drinking when you are alone.

16. Worrying about your drinking.

17. Having your friends (or family) tell you that they are worried about your drinking.

18. Drinking because you are depressed, worried, or upset.

19. Going out in order to get smashed or wasted.

20. Trying to control your drinking by switching brands. Drinking only during certain times of the day, or sticking to only one type of drink.

If you find yourself checking off four or more of these items, talk to a counselor at your college counseling center. It is much easier to deal with a drinking problem in the early stages before it becomes serious. The counselor will be able to tell you whether or not you are developing a problem and will help you explore ways to get around your dependency. If you prefer to get help from a group rather than from an individual counselor, look up a chapter of Alcoholics Anonymous (AA), Bacchus, Al-Anon, Adult Children of Alcoholic Parents (ACOA), or your state alcohol authority. Toll-free telephone numbers for many organizations that can help you are listed on pages 271–272. Most are also listed in the local telephone directory.

---

three times as much and seven times as often as did those who were aware of their higher risk status. Figure 12.8 gives a prescription for sane drinking.

Your Body and Alcohol

The extent to which alcohol will affect you depends on many variables; the variables that make the most difference are your weight, how many drinks you have had, how fast you are drinking, and how much food is in your stomach. All of these variables affect the rate at which alcohol is absorbed into your bloodstream. The concentration of alcohol in your blood determines the extent to which alcohol impairs your ability to function. Figure 12.9 shows how individuals are affected by the number of drinks they consume as a function of their weight.

Figure 12.10 outlines the effects of alcohol on your body at different blood alcohol concentration levels. Psychology research on information processing shows that impairment occurs at all levels of blood-alcohol levels. Attention is narrowed so that subjects fail to see important peripheral events. They look at fewer sources of information and acquire less information about their circumstances. Tracking (steering), psychomotor skills (coordination), vision (eye movements), perception (narrowed field of vision), attention, and information processing are affected even at blood-alcohol levels as low as .02 and .01.[27] At a blood alcohol concentration of .06, most people are experiencing the warm, relaxing feelings associated with alcohol. Only a small amount of alcohol is necessary to experience these feelings. If you continue drinking, you will find that your coordination and judgment become markedly impaired by the time you reach the .10 blood alcohol concentration level.

Figure 12.8 *A Prescription for Sane Drinking*

- If you are male and your father was (or is) an alcoholic, don't drink at all. The risk that you will become alcoholic is very high.
- If you are male or female and have a father, mother, or grandparent who was alcoholic, try to control your drinking.
- Do not drink when you are alone.
- Do not drink when you are upset or depressed.
- Limit your drinking to two drinks (or less) per occasion.
- If you find that your drinking is beginning to get out of control (you suffer from blackouts, you have five or more drinks on one occasion, you drink in order to get drunk), see a counselor or therapist as soon as possible. You have a problem. Do something about it!

Figure 12.9   Blood Alcohol Level and Impairment as a Function of Individual's Weight and Number of Drinks Consumed

To find out your approximate BAL:

1. Determine your weight category (go to lower weight if between two listed).
2. Determine the number of drinks (12 oz. beer, 5 oz. wine, or 1¼ oz. 80-proof alcohol = 1 drink) you will (or have) consume(d).
3. Subtract one drink per hour of drinking time.

WEIGHT VERSUS ALCOHOL   **KNOW YOUR LIMITS**

APPROXIMATE BLOOD ALCOHOL PERCENTAGE

Drinks	Body Weight in Pounds								
	100	120	140	160	180	200	220	240	
1	.04	.03	.03	.02	.02	.02	.02	.02	Influenced Possibly
2	.08	.06	.05	.05	.04	.04	.03	.03	
3	.11	.09	.08	.07	.06	.06	.05	.05	
4	.15	.12	.11	.09	.08	.08	.07	.06	Ability Impaired
5	.19	.16	.13	.12	.11	.09	.09	.08	
6	.23	.19	.16	.14	.13	.11	.10	.09	
7	.26	.22	.19	.16	.15	.13	.12	.11	
8	.30	.25	.21	.19	.17	.15	.14	.13	Definitely Under the Influence
9	.34	.28	.24	.21	.19	.17	.15	.14	
10	.38	.31	.27	.23	.21	.19	.17	.16	

Reprinted from *The National Traffic Safety Institute Student Workbook*, Staten Island, NY: National Traffic Safety Institute, Rev. 1994.

Figure 12.10   Effects of Alcohol on Your Body

Effect	Blood-Alcohol Concentration	Number of Drinks
Warm, relaxed feelings	.06	2 drinks, each containing 1½ ounces of alcohol 2 glasses wine (11 ounces) 2 cans beer (24 ounces)
Legal intoxication	greater than .09	more than 3 mixed drinks 3 glasses wine (16½ ounces) 3 cans beer (36 ounces)
Unconsciousness	.50	17 mixed drinks 17 glasses wine (93½ ounces) 17 cans beer (264 ounces)
Death	greater than .55	more than 18 mixed drinks 26 glasses wine (98½ ounces) 24 cans beer (204 ounces)

Most states define the legal level of intoxication at the .10 concentration. This is the point at which coordination is sufficiently impaired to make driving dangerous. You are seven times more likely to have an accident when you have raised the alcohol concentration level in your blood to this .10 concentration level. Unconsciousness sets in somewhere between the .40 and .50 concentrations. Your body may become unconscious in order to keep you from drinking any more because drinking more is likely to result in death. These figures will vary according to the amount of food in your stomach, how much you weigh, and how fast you are drinking. It is wise to know your limitations. *It is even wiser not to drink and drive.*

Alcohol enters your blood directly through the walls of your stomach. It quickly reaches your brain, where it depresses the higher centers of your brain, resulting in a less-critical, less-inhibited attitude about your behavior. This is the reason that many people think alcohol is a stimulant. Actually, it is a depressant. You may be more talkative and outgoing because you are more relaxed and less concerned about what you are saying, not because the alcohol stimulates you to talk more.

In order to maintain this pleasant, relaxed state, you need only one drink per hour (one beer, one mixed drink, or one 5-ounce glass of wine). Your body can only metabolize one drink per hour. As long as the alcohol is active in your system, those relaxed feelings will remain with you. If you drink more than one drink per hour, you will begin raising your blood-alcohol concentration, hampering your judgment and coordination, and moving toward the levels associated with hangovers, blackouts, and unconsciousness.

The Physiology of Alcohol

If you drink more than one drink per hour, your body cannot dispose of the poisons associated with the alcohol until you slow down your drinking rate. Some of the unpleasant side effects of alcohol are due to the effects that these poisons are having on your system. Other side effects result from your body's attempt to avoid death from an alcohol overdose. The large number of people in crisis who are brought into hospital emergency rooms because of alcohol-related problems proves that the body's defenses will not always be successful.

It is not uncommon, for example, for a person to lose consciousness from drinking too much. This frequently happens at the same time that the brain's function in regulating breathing has been depressed by the alcohol. The person may stop breathing for long periods and then be jolted into a deep breath when the lack of oxygen reaches critical levels. If the person takes this deep breath at the same time that his or her stomach is trying to get rid of the irritating effects of the alcohol by throwing up, this person may choke and die of suffocation.

Aside from helping you to feel relaxed, alcohol also increases your heart rate, changes your ability to see (blurs your vision), impairs your coordination, slows your reaction time, and reduces your judgment. It is these effects of alcohol that get you into trouble when you drive. Without your usual sense of judgment, you may take that turn too quickly to hold the car on the road. Because of slower reaction time, you may not swerve out of the way of an oncoming auto in time. Due to blurred vision and impaired depth perception, you may not turn enough to avoid that pedestrian. With poorer coordination, you may not be able to handle the turn signal and the brake at the same time, and you may end up crashing into a wall. When you have been drinking, you are less likely to remember your seat belt or to think you need it. Of all fatally injured drivers, 14 percent of drunk drivers, 23 percent of drivers who had done some drinking, and 35 percent of sober drivers used seat belts.[28] After two to three drinks, with a blood alcohol concentration level of .10 (the legal level of intoxication in most states), you are seven times more likely to have an accident. *Don't drink*

MAKE A PLEDGE.
TAKE THE KEYS.
CALL A CAB.
TAKE A STAND.

Friends Don't Let Friends Drive Drunk.

Printed from materials developed by the National Highway Traffic Safety Administration.

and drive, and remember to buckle up. Studies show that safety belts reduce the risk of fatal injury by 45 percent and serious injury by 50 percent. In just one year, safety belts saved the lives of about 4,800 people riding in the front seat.[29]

If you are stopped for driving while intoxicated (DWI), you may be fined or jailed. You may lose your license. Your insurance rates will go up anywhere from three to five times. You may kill or injure yourself, your friends, or other innocent drivers or pedestrians. Aside from lifelong disability, you may leave yourself with a lifetime of guilt about the other lives you have destroyed. *If you drink, don't drive.* Call a cab, call a friend, sleep over where you are, or take turns, with your friends, being the "designated driver" who does not drink. If friends or family tell you that you are too intoxicated to drive, do not drive until your body has had the chance to rid itself of the alcohol. Remember that alcohol is a leading cause of death among young people ages 15 through 24.

If you abuse alcohol, you are likely to become addicted. Your body will build a tolerance for alcohol. This means that you will begin to need larger and larger quantities of alcohol to feel good after drinking. Your body will also become dependent on the drug. It will no longer be able to function normally without alcohol. When the alcohol level in your blood drops, your body will go into withdrawal, raising your blood pressure, your pulse, your temperature and your rate of breathing. You will begin to feel uncomfortable. Within the first 24 to 36 hours you will most likely experience seizures and convulsions. You may have hallucinations or memory loss, which can become permanent.

Aside from continued increases in your vital signs (blood pressure, temperature, pulse, and breathing), your brain will stop functioning properly and you will literally lose your mind. You will become confused and disoriented. If you do not receive medical treatment during this stage, you may die.

Some of the psychotic (ranting, raving, and hallucinating) symptoms are caused by a thiamine (Vitamin B-1) deficiency that is common among alcoholics. Problem drinkers generally suffer from malnutrition because alcohol is so high in calories. Since a beer contains 148 calories, a glass of wine, 114 calories, and the hard liquor in a standard drink, approximately 88 calories, heavy drinkers feel full from the non-nutritional calories in the alcohol and are less likely to eat properly. The damage to the intestine that is frequently caused by alcohol also compromises its ability to absorb many nutrients and vitamins. In addition, a person who abuses alcohol may lose the motivation to eat a balanced diet. Permanent damage to the liver, heart, brain, and stomach, along with the high incidence of accidents and suicides among alcoholics, is responsible for the steep death rates and shorter life expectancy of heavy drinkers.

■ COCAINE

Cocaine is known by a number of names on the street: coke, crack, blow, toot, C, nose candy, and so on. The U.S. Department of Health and Human Services reports that more than 12 percent of young adults, almost 3.5 million people, between the ages of 18 and 25 years have used cocaine. In estimating the total number of people across all age groups who have used cocaine in this country, the number is almost 22 million.[30] Although the number of people who report that they use cocaine has declined somewhat over the past few years, the daily reports of murders, robberies, assaults, and deaths associated with cocaine's use have forced Americans to realize that we have a crisis on our hands.

More than a million young adults between the ages of 18 and 25 years have used the drug within the past year. Students who try cocaine for the first time often get into serious trouble because of the damage the drug can cause to their bodies or to their ability to study. Cocaine provides a very effective avenue for short-circuiting a college career.

Your Body and Cocaine

Cocaine is a powerful stimulant that affects every vital system in your body. The most dramatic attention has been given to sudden, unexplained deaths in healthy individuals who have experimented with cocaine: sudden heart attacks, fatal arrhythmias, strokes, seizures, and suicides. These deaths have occurred in chronic users, but they have also been reported in young, healthy people when they used cocaine for the first time. The much publicized death of University of Maryland's all-American sports star, Len Bias, is an example of cocaine's dramatic fatal effects. Some people cannot metabolize the drug, and this can lead to an overdose from small quantities. The "Casey Jones" reaction immortalized in a song by the Grateful Dead can result in failure of the body's major systems, leading to convulsions and death within a few minutes.

These deaths occur because cocaine has dramatic stimulatory effects on electrical and chemical activity in the brain; this leads to increases in heart rate, blood pressure, and breathing. It is difficult to predict the precise effects cocaine may have on any given individual because these effects depend on the dose of cocaine, its purity, the individual's personal physical makeup, and the mode of administration.

There are three basic ways that cocaine is used: it can be "snorted," injected, or smoked. Snorting, or sniffing, cocaine into the nose is the most common method. Users often form a line of cocaine on a mirror and snort it through a straw or a rolled-up dollar bill.

Shooting up, or injecting, cocaine by needle is a riskier method because you can introduce impurities and infection directly into your bloodstream. These impurities damage the heart valve, allowing infection to occur. The result, endocarditis, is 100 percent fatal unless treated by intravenous antibiotics for four to six weeks in a hospital. Even if you survive, it can lead to chronic heart damage or strokes. In addition, shared needles have caused an epidemic spread of AIDS and hepatitis among intravenous drug users and their sex partners.

Figure 12.11   *Signs of a Medical Emergency Due to Cocaine*

- Gasping for breath
- Irregular breathing
- Accumulation of fluid in the lungs
- Failure to breathe
- Irregular heart rate
- Sudden, rapid fall in blood pressure
- Weak or irregular pulse
- Blue or gray skin color resulting from lack of oxygen

The third method of administration is smoking; the fastest way to get cocaine to the brain is by smoking it in a free-base form such as "crack," or "rock." Smoking produces addiction just as quickly as injection.

Cocaine can result in mild to life-threatening symptoms in the respiratory and cardiovascular systems. Any of the eight symptoms listed in Figure 12.11 are grounds for an immediate trip to the hospital emergency room.

Smoking and injecting cocaine pose the greatest dangers to the heart. Injection is associated with endocarditis, pulmonary edema, blood clots, hepatitis, and AIDS. All of these side effects represent serious medical conditions. Of the various methods of administering cocaine, free-basing is the one that most often results in heart attacks.[31]

Mood and Personality Changes

Since cocaine can have such dangerous consequences, the question remains as to why the drug has become so popular. Most users are attracted by the initial "rush": feelings of well-being, confidence, euphoria, competence, energy, power, and control. Many cocaine users feel that the drug helps them to perform better socially and on the job. Unfortunately, these "high" feelings are short-lived: they last from fifteen to thirty minutes.

The major problem is the "crash" that users experience as the drug effects wear off: depression, fatigue, paranoia, hallucinations. These negative feelings then prompt the many compulsive users to abuse the drug. The "low" is so bad, especially compared to the high they have just experienced, that users have to turn right around and use any means to get high again. This results in cocaine's vicious cycle of abuse.

Although everyone who uses the drug does not become an addict, few individuals can control a cocaine habit for long. The brief high is followed by a severe slump, and users feel that the only way out of that depression is another dose. Larger and larger doses are required to reach the high, and the time between doses becomes shorter and shorter. It is horrifying to read reports from successful individuals in every age group that describe how cocaine has taken over their lives. Chronic use leads to persistent mood and personality changes and paranoia.

Successful doctors, students, engineers, athletes, business executives, songwriters, and lawyers have all reported the same result: cocaine has destroyed their lives. It is a powerfully addictive drug, and they are not able to give it up. They have lost their families, their careers, their fortunes, their self-respect, and the values that formed the foundations of their lives.

If you have used cocaine and find that you need larger doses to get the high you once received from smaller doses, if you find that you cannot turn down cocaine when it is offered, if you are afraid that you will be too depressed or unmotivated to function at your present level when you stop using the drug, if you notice that you have changed your precocaine values (that is you no longer care about school, your career, your home, your family or that you may lie or steal to get cocaine), if you have lost your precocaine friends, if you usually use cocaine alone, if you tend to crash or get depressed when you stop using the drug, or if you notice other persistent or troublesome changes, you have a problem. Get help as soon as possible from a counselor. Cocaine has destroyed the lives of many individuals who thought they were strong enough to fight the addiction on their own. Do not let it destroy your life or college career.

The counseling center at your college has professionals who can help you unravel the problems that cocaine is causing in your life. You can also get advice by calling national hot lines at 1-800-COCAINE, 1-800-662-HELP, or your local community mental health center. Self-help groups such as Cocaine Anonymous (CA) and Narcotics Anonymous (NA) are listed in your telephone directory. These groups can provide you with long-term support from others who are struggling with similar problems. Coke Anon and Nar-Anon are self-help groups that can help the family members of an addict through the difficult times ahead.

■ CIGARETTES

Cigarette smoking is the single most important preventable cause of death in the United States.[32] It is estimated that 400,000 Americans die from smoking-related diseases each year.[33] Yet 46 million Americans continue to smoke, including 41 percent of young adults between the ages of 18 and 25 years, 36 percent of those between 26 and 34 years of age, and almost 30 percent of those who are 35 years or older[34, 35]

The age at which people begin smoking has been dropping in recent years.[36] Major studies by the University of Michigan's Survey Research Center and the Centers for Disease Control and Prevention suggest that smoking among teenagers is increasing sharply even as it declines among adults. Although it is illegal to sell cigarettes to young people under the age of 18, the Federal Drug Administration has estimated that the country's 3 million underage smokers spend $1.26 billion worth of the $46 billion in annual domestic cigarette sales collected by the American tobacco industry. Approximately 1 million teenagers become addicted to cigarettes each year.[37, 38]

Many carefully controlled studies in the United States show that the death rate is much higher among smokers at all ages than among nonsmokers. One in three smokers will die as a result of this habit. Experts estimate that each cigarette shortens a smoker's life by seven minutes.[39]

Smokers are at greater risk for lung cancer, heart attacks, and emphysema. Mortality rates are directly related to the number of cigarettes smoked: heavy smokers, people who have been smoking longer, and individuals who began smoking at an earlier age have higher death rates. People who smoke less than one pack per day have a death rate four times as high as nonsmokers. Those who smoke more than a pack a day have a death rate that is seven times as high.[40]

It seems that smokers also endanger the health of their family members, friends, and colleagues at work. Breathing secondhand smoke is almost as dangerous as smoking. A panel of scientists reports that secondhand smoke causes cancer, and another study concludes that the nonsmoking spouses of smokers suffer 33 percent more heart disease than the spouses of nonsmokers.[41]

The United States Labor Department recently settled the first compensation claim related to secondhand smoke in ruling that the death from lung cancer of a nurse who worked at a Veterans' Administration hospital was at least partly due to secondhand smoke; it awarded $21,500 per year to the husband of the nurse. Hundreds of claims have been filed by living victims of secondhand

Figure 12.12   *What's in Tobacco Smoke?*

- **Acetylene:** an asphyxiating gas used in welding
- **Ammonia:** a gas that irritates eyes and lungs; used to clean, bleach, deodorize; etches aluminum
- **Arsenic:** a crystalline solid used in rat poison; causes skin irritations, lung cancer, and lymphatic cancer
- **Benzene:** a gas that causes leukemia
- **Beta-Naphthalamine:** suspected of causing bladder cancer
- **Cadmium:** a metal that causes lung cancer and prostate cancer and damages the kidneys
- **Carbon Monoxide:** a gas that robs the body of oxygen
- **Cresol:** a caustic poison toxic to skin, the kidneys, the liver, and the pancreas; used as a disinfectant
- **Formaldehyde:** a suffocating carcinogen with a pungent odor; used as a disinfectant and preservative
- **Hydrazine:** a corrosive, fuming liquid hazardous to skin, blood, and the liver; used as rocket fuel
- **Hydrogen Cyanide:** the gas employed in execution chambers
- **Oxides of Nitrogen:** the same lung-searing smog that motor vehicles emit
- **Naphthylamine:** a cause of bladder cancer
- **Nickel:** a metal that causes cancer of the nose and lungs
- **Nicotine:** an addictive alkaloid toxic to the heart; used as insecticide
- **Nitrosamines:** a variety of carcinogenic compounds
- **Phenol:** hazardous for skin, the eyes, the liver, the kidneys, and the nervous system; used as a disinfectant
- **Polonium:** a radioactive metal
- **Propane:** the malodorous gas used as fuel
- **Toluene:** a solvent that depresses the central nervous system
- **Urethane:** a fungicide and pesticide
- **Vinyl Chloride:** a gas that causes liver cancer

Excerpted from "Health Consequences of Smoking: The Changing Cigarette." Report of the Surgeon General: 1981. Rockville, MD: U.S. Department of Health and Human Services, Public Health Service, Office on Smoking and Health, 1981. DHHS No. (PHS) 81-50156.

smoke.[42] Researchers at the University of Massachusetts and Brigham and Women's Hospital in Boston have estimated that smoking by pregnant women causes the death of 5,600 babies and 115,000 miscarriages in the United States each year.[43] Figure 12.12 presents a partial listing of the chemicals released by a burning cigarette and the hazards typically associated with them.

Aside from decreasing the smoker's life expectancy, cigarettes contain nicotine, which has a few other unfortunate side effects. By increasing heart rate and constricting blood vessels, nicotine causes smokers to lose their healthy skin color, to age and wrinkle faster, to have cold hands and feet, and to have bones that heal more slowly. Smoking also lowers men's sperm count, affects women's fertility, and lowers the birth weight of their babies, exposing the babies to a whole host of physical and psychological problems. Smoking even increases the risk for car accidents; it is not the nicotine that is responsible for this, but the momentary inattention to the road as you light a cigarette or tap

Check off any of the symptoms of nicotine addiction that apply to you.

_____ 1. Tobacco use is regular and compulsive.

_____ 2. Tobacco use alters your moods.

_____ 3. Tobacco use creates physical dependence which is characterized by withdrawal symptoms such as nervousness, insomnia, and drowsiness, irritability, headaches, and an intense craving for nicotine.

_____ 4. With continued use, tolerance to tobacco has developed resulting in diminished effects which cause you to increase the amount you smoke.

ACTIVITY

When Smokers Quit

The goal of this activity is to help you focus on the health benefits that you gain when you give up smoking.

Consult a counselor, look for a smoking clinic in your phone book, make a pact with a friend to quit, contact the American Cancer Society, the American Lung Association (1-800-LUNG-USA/586-4872), or Smoke Enders to begin quitting or to help a friend or relative make a commitment to quit. Then check off the benefits that apply to you and imagine your body becoming healthier with each milestone.

Yes

_____ 20 Minutes After Your Last Cigarette, your blood pressure drops to normal, your pulse rate drops to normal, the temperature in your hands and feet increases to normal.

_____ 8 Hours After Your Last Cigarette, the carbon dioxide level in your blood drops to normal, the oxygen level in your blood increases to normal.

_____ 24 Hours After Your Last Cigarette, your chance of having a heart attack decreases.

_____ 48 Hours After Your Last Cigarette, your nerve endings start regrowing, your ability to smell and taste is enhanced, walking becomes easier.

_____ 2 Weeks To 3 Months After Your Last Cigarette, your circulation improves, your lung function increases up to 30 percent.

_____ 1 To 9 Months After Your Last Cigarette, your coughing, sinus congestion, fatigue, and shortness of breath decrease.

_____ 1 Year After Your Last Cigarette, your risk of heart disease is half that of a smoker.

_____ 10 Years After Your Last Cigarette, your risk for heart disease is essentially the same as someone who has never smoked.

Excerpted from the American Cancer Society, Centers For Disease Control and Prevention, Reader's Digest, April 1996.

out your ashes. This is the reason that many companies offer lower car insurance rates to nonsmokers.

Nicotine, the active ingredient in cigarettes, seems to be a stimulant in terms of its biochemical action in the body, yet many smokers report that smoking helps them to relax. Part of this relaxing effect may come from relief of the withdrawal symptoms. As is the case with other drugs, the large number of people who are addicted to nicotine develop tolerance and experience uncomfortable withdrawal symptoms when the level of the drug in their bodies falls below the amount they need.

The tobacco industry's own research indicates that nicotine meets all four criteria that determine whether a drug is addictive.[44]

Cigarettes also have side effects that affect people's social lives. Smokers smell bad; the odor remains in their breath, clothes, and hair. Their teeth and fingers become stained and yellow. Smokers' skin ages and wrinkles prematurely, and the cigarette tars rot the gums. Smoking decreases respiratory reserve, or "wind," when exercising, so smokers age faster and die sooner. In a recent national survey of almost 50 thousand teenagers, both smokers and nonsmokers reported that they find smokers less attractive and were less interested in dating them.[45] Cigarettes are also expensive! They use money that could be spent on social activities.

The withdrawal symptoms and craving make it very difficult to stop smoking. Many ex-heroin users report that they found it easier to give up heroin than cigarettes. This craving may last as long as nine years in the case of some ex-smokers. Cigarettes are not likely to force you to withdraw from college, but they will shorten your life and impair your health.

There is, however, good news. Just 20 minutes after you have smoked your last cigarette, your body begins to make a series of healthy changes. If you are successful in giving up smoking for one year, you will substantially reduce your risk for heart attack. Ten years after quitting, your risk for heart disease is essentially the same as someone who has never smoked! Millions of people have given up smoking. Resources that can help you quit are listed in the activity, "When Smokers Quit." Check off the benefits that apply to you which are listed in the activity "When Smokers Quit."

■ OTHER DRUGS

Caffeine

Caffeine is a stimulant found in coffee, cocoa, chocolate, tea, cola, and other soft drinks. It belongs to a class of drugs known as xanthine stimulants. Caffeine has been implicated in research on depression, peptic ulcers, esophageal reflux (heartburn), ovarian cancer, insomnia, irritability, and cardiac irregularities. There are conflicting studies regarding the role of caffeine in heart disease. If it does increase the risk for heart disease, it would do so for people who drink the equivalent of five or more cups of coffee per day. If you are feeling anxious or depressed, try to avoid caffeine, because it may make your symptoms worse.

There is no question that people acquire tolerance for caffeine (requiring larger doses to achieve the same effects over time) and that withdrawal symptoms occur at the five-cup or more daily dosage level.[46] Headaches, trembling hands, irritability, fatigue, and heart palpitations are some of the symptoms that make it difficult for caffeine addicts to cut back on the amount they consume. At higher doses of five to ten cups a day, the user may suffer from a disorder called caffeinism, which includes unpleasant symptoms of mental disorder, such as confusion, disorientation, restless excitement, fatigue, and insomnia. Such symptoms can seriously interfere with your ability to study, and for this reason, you should not abuse caffeine pills or other substances containing caffeine if you cram for exams. (If you have read Chapter 6, you know that cramming is not an effective way to study for your exams, and if you have studied that chapter carefully and mastered the techniques in Chapter 3 on time management, you will never need to cram!)

Depressants

Depressants, which include narcotics (such as heroin), barbiturates, and tranquilizers, are a class of drugs that work on your brain to reduce pain, tension, and anxiety. Because they slow down your thinking and coordination, they can interfere with your ability to study. All of them lead to tolerance so that you need larger and larger quantities of the drug as time goes on, and all of them cause withdrawal symptoms when the level of the drug in the body drops so that you feel very uncomfortable. Withdrawal from any depressant is a dangerous business, and it should be supervised by a physician. Life-threatening seizures are common, and you may die without medical attention. All drugs in this class are fatal at high doses because they slow down vital functions such as breathing. They are particularly dangerous when combined with alcohol, which is also a depressant.

Heroin

Heroin, first cousin to morphine and opium, is a narcotic that comes from the poppy plant. Estimates from the National Household Survey on Drug Abuse indicate that up to 2.5 million Americans have used heroin. As cocaine use has declined somewhat, heroin consumption is rising. This renewed surge in heroin use seems to be related to a new, plentiful supply of relatively inexpensive, but potent heroin that has become available in the United States in the past few years. Evidence of this renewed surge is found in the sharp increase in emergency room admissions where heroin is a factor and in the greater number of prisoners who are addicted to heroin.[47, 48]

Heroin users usually inject the drug under their skin ("skin popping") or directly into their veins ("mainlining"). It is this practice of injecting heroin and sharing needles that led to the epidemic spread of AIDS among heroin users and their sex partners. The new powerful strains allow abusers to get high by sniffing the drug; some users mistakenly believe that heroin is not addictive when the drug is injected.

Users experience a rush that lasts about 5 to 15 minutes and then a high for 3 to 5 hours. The withdrawal symptoms are miserable, resulting in anxiety, hot and cold flashes, headaches, cramps, sweating, diarrhea, and sometimes, hallucinations. Because of this discomfort, addicts eventually spend most of their time and energy making sure that they can secure their next dose. This often leads to burglary, auto theft, and robbery to support the habit and leaves little time for study or social relationships. If withdrawal is carried out under a doctor's supervision, the doctor will prescribe medication that reduces the discomfort of the withdrawal symptoms.

Barbiturates and Tranquilizers

Sedatives or barbiturates include drugs such as Seconal, Rohypnol ("roofies"), Valium, and Nembutal ("downers"). The pills are prescribed by doctors in order to help patients relax and fall asleep. Unfortunately, they are habit-forming and can result in worse sleep problems so that the person gets into a vicious cycle of taking more and more pills until he or she is addicted. Sleep problems often become worse, causing exhaustion and irritability. This can certainly interfere with a college career, not to mention any other aspects of a sane life.

These pills often result in death when the person drinks alcohol in addition to taking the pill. (This situation occurred in the deaths of Marilyn Monroe and Judy Garland.) Taking the two drugs together magnifies the effect four times over that of taking either alcohol or barbiturates alone. Barbiturates have similar psychological effects to alcohol: released inhibitions, relaxation, and distorted judgment and coordination. It is, therefore, dangerous to drive if you have taken any of these pills, and your ability to study will also be impaired. Withdrawal symptoms are very unpleasant and can easily lead to seizures or death. Withdrawal should be supervised by a physician.

Rohypnol, a prescription drug which is not approved for use in the United States, has become the fastest-growing abused drug among young people in Florida, and its use has spread to at least a dozen other states. It has become as widely used as marijuana and LSD, threatening to become the "Quaaludes of the '90s." Officials in a number of counties have begun routine testing for the drug in cases where drivers appear drunk, but register low for alcohol, and in cases where women might have been raped but do not remember.[49]

When combined with alcohol or other drugs, the pills, known as "roofies" among American users, and sometimes as "roach" or "rope," can cause respiratory depression and death. Kurt Cobain, the rock singer, collapsed and slipped into a coma a month before his suicide after ingesting Rohypnol with champagne. Prosecutors have convicted rapists where the pill was slipped into a woman's drink prior to the rape. One man bragged that he had done this to a dozen women. Rohypnol has become the most "popular" drug after marijuana and cocaine among drivers in Dade County who are stopped because they are driving so dangerously. The drug is a controlled substance in this country, and its possession is punishable by fines and prison.[50]

Tranquilizers such as Librium and Valium are rarely abused by young people because they do not really produce a high. They are habit-forming, however, and have become addictive to many people who use them to decrease anxiety. Since their side effects include drowsiness and poor coordination, they should not be taken if you are going to drive. They are also likely to interfere with your ability to work effectively in college because of these side effects.

Amphetamines

Stimulants are a class of drugs that make users feel energetic, alert, and self-confident. We have already discussed cocaine, caffeine, and nicotine, which belong to this group. Amphetamines such as Benzedrine, Dexedrine, Methedrine ("speed," "ice," "crank,"), are other members of this group that are increasingly abused. In addition to their energizing effects, they decrease appetite; for this reason, they are sometimes abused by dieters, although this practice often leads to life-threatening seizures. Stimulants improve coordination, so they are popular with some athletes. They hold off the effects of sleeplessness, so they tend to be misused by students who are cramming for exams late at night. (It is not true, as some students believe, that amphetamines help you think better, and cramming, as you learned in Chapter 6, is not an effective way to study for exams.) Abuse of any of these drugs is dangerous because it may lead to fatal seizures.

Methamphetamine, a synthetic drug often marketed under the name "Ecstacy," is more stimulating to the brain than any other drug. It continues to work on brain receptors for 8 to 24 hours after it is taken, and its letdown or "crash" is much nastier than that produced by cocaine.[51, 52] Amphetamines produce tolerance so that users go on to higher levels, and at high levels these drugs can be quite dangerous. "Speed freaks" can carry on for several days at high-energy levels without eating or sleeping. They are likely, however, to literally "go crazy," becoming suspicious and violent when they lose touch with reality.

An example involves a man in New Mexico who was high on methamphetamine and alcohol; he beheaded his 14-year-old son and tossed the severed head from his van window onto a busy highway. Some parents in Newton, Iowa, have become so neglectful that their children have been taken away from them. People with no history of crime have been arrested for committing strings of burglaries. Nationwide, methamphetamine deaths have soared 145 percent over two years. The drug has been blamed for more than 400 deaths from overdose and suicide in California and 122 deaths in Phoenix in the past year. It was the number one cause of overdoses in San Diego where it has also been responsible for 26 homicides. In Des Moines, arrests for methamphetamine surpassed arrests for drunk driving, accounting for 65 percent of all arrests. More than 35 percent of the people going to Iowa prisons in 1995 reported using the drug, and 90 percent of the people committed to mental hospitals in Polk County, Iowa, have used methamphetamine.[53]

New forms of the drug are more potent and deadly because they may contain up to 90 percent of ephedrine, the active ingredient, as compared to only 20 percent ephedrine in the versions that were available years ago. It seems that use of the drug is spreading among college students and young professionals, and some experts fear a national epidemic similar to that caused by crack. Paranoia, violence, chronic psychosis, and brain damage are all common in amphetamine abusers. None of these symptoms is conducive to becoming a straight *A* student.

Concern is growing over a Chinese herb, ma huang or ephedra, which is being marketed under names such as *Herbal Ecstacy, Cloud 9,* and *Ultimate Xphoria.* The Commissioner of the Food and Drug Administration (FDA) plans to issue a warning about the potential dangers of the herb. The herb has been promoted by marketers as a natural, "safe, legal, and FDA-approved" alternative to methamphetamine. Although advertisements on the Internet have claimed that the drug is a "carefully formulated and thoroughly tested organic alternative to MDMA or Ecstacy," the FDA has never tested or approved any of the herbal compounds.[54]

The drug is being sold as pills in natural-food stores, pharmacies, boutiques, and novelty shops. It has been advertised as a "smart drug" because it is supposedly not addictive and gives a nice feeling. The FDA knows of 395 adverse reactions since 1993 and 15 deaths that may have been caused by ephedrine which is a component of the herb ephedra or from synthetic ephedrine which is used in some drugs. The physiological effects are the same whether the drug is natural or synthetic: too much can cause irregular heartbeat, heart attack, stroke, seizures, psychosis, or death. Eighty percent of the adverse reactions have occurred after people have taken the recommended dose. At least 20 states have enacted or are considering laws to restrict the sale of ephedra and ephedrine.[55]

Hallucinogens

Hallucinogens such as lysergic acid diethylamide (LSD), phencyclidine (PCP), dimethyltryptamine (DMT), and mescaline distort perceptions. Use of these drugs can lead to fantastic images and new awareness or it can lead to a "bad trip" involving terror and panic. Some people have suffered long-term mental illness and hospitalization because of the distorted images and perceptions they experienced during a trip that went bad. Users also sometimes experience frightening flashbacks in which they are suddenly on a "trip" even though they have not taken the drug for days, weeks, and even years. A hallucinatory flashback can happen long after a user has stopped taking the drug, and it can create problems in functioning on a day-to-day basis.

ACTIVITY

Recognizing Your Patterns of Drug Use

This activity is meant to encourage you to think about your patterns of drug use, to share your thoughts with your peers, and to evaluate your own use of drugs. Remember that the word *drugs* includes alcohol, tobacco, and caffeine, as well as other drugs that are illegal.

Break into small groups of four and discuss the following questions. After your discussion, regroup as a class and share your group's reflections with the whole class. Do not identify any group members' personal habits in the class discussion or in any remarks you make outside of class. Be especially careful not to identify anyone's use of an illegal drug.

1. If you drink or use drugs, when did you start using them?
2. Why did you first try alcohol or other drugs?
3. If you continue to use alcohol or other drugs, what encourages you to use them at this point in your life?
4. If you do not use alcohol or other drugs, why have you avoided them or stopped using them?
5. How much of the drug do you use (number of cigarettes, number of drinks, number of times you get high per week)?
6. Do you feel that the drug is causing problems for you (interfering with your work or social life, damaging your health)? If it is causing problems, what type of problems are they?
7. Do you drive after you have taken a drug (alcohol, cocaine, barbiturates, marijuana, or other hallucinogens)?
8. How do you feel about people who drive after they have taken a drug? What can you do about these feelings?
9. Do you experience any of the warning signs of a drinking or cocaine problem?
10. Do any members of your family have a drinking problem? (Check with your parents about this question. Often there is or was a family member who had a problem, but this person is not discussed. Tell your parents why you are asking about grandparents, cousins, uncles, etc.)
11. If you feel that you would like to decrease the amount of drug that you use, where can you go for help in cutting back?

These drugs do lead to tolerance, although they do not seem to be physically addictive. There are no particular withdrawal symptoms. PCP, or "angel dust," received a bad reputation in the 1970s because of its poisonous and frequent overdoses. Users often ended up hurting themselves or others because their perceptions were so distorted, and they became suspicious of others. Many users have become "vegetables" in mental hospitals or nursing homes because of extensive damage to their brains.

Marijuana ("pot," "dope," "grass") and hashish ("bhang," "dope," "weed") are classified as minor hallucinogens because their effects are not as dramatic as those of drugs such as LSD and PCP. One in three Americans has tried marijuana or hashish, which makes these the most common illegal drugs in the country. The most recent national PRIDE survey reports that more than 33 percent of high school seniors have used marijuana at least once in the past year.[56]

Marijuana, made by crushing the dried leaves of the cannabis plant, is usually smoked in cigarette form ("joints"), while the stronger hashish, made from the resin of the plant, is usually smoked in a pipe. Either form can also be eaten. The active ingredient in marijuana, delta 9, tetrahydrocannabinol (THC), increases heart rate and turns the whites of the eyes red. If you smoke marijuana while shooting cocaine, you may increase your heart rate to the point of serious overload.

THC also slows down reaction time and judgment of time and distance. For these reasons you should not drive for four to six hours after you have smoked marijuana. If you smoke marijuana and drink alcoholic beverages, your driving will be more impaired than if you used either drug alone. A study of the most seriously injured accident victims admitted to the Maryland Institute for Emergency Medicine in Baltimore found that one-third of the patients had used marijuana within two to four hours before being admitted for their injuries. Among patients thirty years old or younger, 40 percent were under the influence of marijuana at the time of the accident.[57]

The potency of the marijuana available now has increased more than 275 percent over the last decade; this makes it much more dangerous than the marijuana of the 1960s.[58] It is clear that marijuana leads to lung cancer and other respiratory illnesses. It has 50 percent more of the same carcinogenic substances that result in lung cancer from tobacco. Because of this higher level of toxicity and the fact that marijuana users try to hold the smoke in their lungs as long as possible, one marijuana cigarette may produce approximately the same lung damage as smoking four tobacco cigarettes.[59]

Low doses of marijuana lead to relaxed feelings, more vivid sensations, and a mild high. Higher doses result in a "spaced out" feeling. Some users experience a "bad trip," in which feelings of severe anxiety, depression, or separation from the self are magnified. Studies in animals show that marijuana also decreases the body's immune response to various infections and diseases. By interfering with hormonal systems, it lowers the sperm count in men and may cause infertility in women.[60]

Researchers have found that THC changes the way sensory information gets into and is processed by the hippocampus, the part of the brain that is crucial for memory, learning, and the integration of sensory experiences. It acts directly on the part of the brain many scientists believe forms the basis of our memory systems.[61] This is not good news for students who want to smoke a joint before going to class or studying for an exam. Remember that marijuana can stay in your system for a month after you smoke it; smoking over the weekend may interfere with your ability to process information and remember it for weeks to come.

Figure 12.13 presents an overview of the effects associated with many of the drugs that are abused today. Most of them can ruin your college career by interfering directly with your ability to concentrate, causing you to lose interest in your future and your studies, ruining your health so that you are unable to study, or bringing you into conflict with disciplinary rules and the legal system so that you are suspended from college.

■ HOW TO HELP SOMEONE WHO HAS A DRUG PROBLEM[62]

If you are worried about someone's drinking or his or her use of other drugs, do not be afraid to bring the subject up. Many recovered substance abusers did not realize they had a problem until a friend or relative brought it to their attention. If you care about the person, then you should show your concern. Wait for a time when the person is calm and not under the influence of the drug. Tell the person that you are concerned about his or her drug use.

Instead of *telling* the person that he or she has a drinking or drug problem, ask the person to be honest about his or her use of the substance. Describe the inappropriate aspects of the person's behavior during a recent high or period of

Figure 12.13   *A Listing of Facts on Drugs*

Drug	Street Names	Effects	Withdrawal Symptoms	Adverse/Overdose Reactions
Satiation				
Narcotics:				
Heroin	H, hombre, junk, smack, dope, horse, crap	Apathy, difficulty in concentration, slowed speech, decreased physical activity, drooling, itching, euphoria, nausea	Anxiety, vomiting, sneezing, diarrhea, lower back pain, watery eyes, runny nose, yawning, irritability, tremors, panic, chills and sweating, cramps	Depressed levels of consciousness, low blood pressure, rapid heart rate, shallow breathing, convulsions, coma, possible death
Morphine	Drugstore dope, cube, first line, mud			
Codeine				
Percodan	Perks			
Demerol				
Methadone	Meth			
Sedative Hypnotics:				
Nembutal	Yellow jackets, yellows	Impulsiveness, dramatic mood swings, bizarre thoughts, suicidal behavior, slurred speech, disorientation, slowed mental and physical functioning, limited attention span	Weakness, restlessness, nausea and vomiting, headache, nightmares, irritability, depression, acute anxiety, hallucinations, seizures, possible death	Confusion, decreased response to pain, shallow respiration, dilated pupils, weak and rapid pulse, coma, possible death
Seconal	Reds			
Tuinal	Tueys			
Phenobarbital				
Quaaludes	Ludes, 714's			
Valium	V's			
Librium				
Equanil				
Arousal				
Benzedrine	Speed	Increased confidence, mood elevation, sense of energy and alertness, decreased appetite, anxiety, irritability, insomnia, transient drowsiness, delayed orgasm	Apathy, general fatigue, prolonged sleep, depression, disorientation, suicidal thoughts, agitated motor activity, irritability, bizarre dreams	Elevated blood pressure, increase in body temperature, facepicking, suspiciousness, bizarre and repetitious behavior, vivid hallucinations, convulsions, possible death
Dexedrine	Speed			
Desoxyn	Speed, crystal methedrine			
Biphetamine				
Ritalin	Black beauties, speed			
Preludin				
Cocaine	Coke, blow, toot, snow, lady			
Methamphetamine	Ecstacy, Herbal			
Ma Huong/Ephedra	Ecstacy, Cloud 9,			
Ephedrin	Ultimate Xphoria			
Fantasy				
Hallucinogens:				
LSD	Electricity, acid, quasey, blotter acid, microdot, white lightning, purple barrels	Fascination with ordinary objects, heightened aesthetic responses to color, texture, contours, music, vision and depth distortion, hear colors, see music, slowing of time, gestures, magnified feelings of love, lust, hate, joy, anger, pain, terror, despair, etc., paranoia, panic, euphoria, bliss, impairment of short-term memory, projection of self into dreamlike images	Not reported	Nausea, chills, increased pulse, temperature, and blood pressure, trembling, slow deep breathing, loss of appetite, insomnia, longer, more intense "trips," bizarre, dangerous behavior possibly leading to injury or death

Figure 12.13　(Continued)

Drug	Street Names	Effects	Withdrawal Symptoms	Adverse/Overdose Reactions
Mescaline	Peyote buttons, (natural form)	Similar to LSD but more sensual and perceptual, fewer changes in thought, mood, and sense of self	Not reported	Resemble LSD, but more bodily sensations, vomiting
Psilocybin	Mushrooms, shrooms, rooms	Similar to LSD but more visual and less intense, more euphoria, fewer panic reactions	Not reported	Resemble LSD, but less severe
Cannabis Marijuana Hashish Hash Oil	Bhang, kif, ganja, dope, grass, pot, smoke, hemp, joint, weed, bone, Mary Jane, herb, tea	Euphoria, relaxed inhibitions, increased appetite, disoriented behavior	Hyperactivity, insomnia, decreased appetite, anxiety	Impaired memory and coordination problems. Severe reactions are rare, but include panic, paranoia, fatigue, bizarre and dangerous behavior
Phencyclidine	PCP, angel dust, hog, rocket fuel, superweed, peace pill, elephant tranquilizer, dust, bad pizza	Increased blood pressure and heart rate, sweating, nausea, numbness, floating sensation, slowed reflexes, altered body image, altered perception of time and space, impaired immediate and recent memory, decreased concentration, paranoid thoughts and delusions	Not reported	Highly variable and possibly dose-related, disorientation, loss of recent memory, lethargy/stupor, bizarre and violent behavior, rigidity and immobility, mutism, staring, hallucinations and delusions, coma

Reprinted with permission from *Psychology Today Magazine* Copyright © 1983 (PT Partners, L.P.).

intoxication. Tell the person that you like him or her, but that you do not like the *behavior* that he or she exhibits under the influence of the drug. Make sure that you *emphasize your concern and caring. Do not judge the person's behavior.*

Tell the person the facts about drug abuse. Describe the consequences that you fear continued drug abuse will have for the person's health, career, social life, and relationship with you. Help the person contact a treatment facility. The counseling center on campus might be a good place to start or try Narcotics Anonymous, Alcoholics Anonymous, Cocaine Anonymous, or your local community mental health center, which are all listed in your phone book. Additional resources with addresses and telephone numbers are listed below. You may wish to attend meetings of Al-Anon, Coke Anon, or Nar-Anon so that you can receive support while you help your friend or family member through the difficult times ahead.

Answers to Activity "Testing Your Alcohol IQ"

1. d	16. true
2. d	17. d
3. a	18. true
4. d	19. true
5. false	20. true
6. false	21. true
7. true	22. false; but it may make you sicker
8. false	23. false; a person is conscious during a blackout but does not remember what she or he has done.
9. true	
10. d	
11. c	24. d
12. d	25. a
13. c	26. d, for the average size person drinking ½ ounce of alcohol
14. a	
15. false	

✍ REFLECTIONS FOR YOUR JOURNAL

1. If you drink or use other drugs, when and why did you start using them? (Remember that the word "drugs" refers to alcohol, cigarettes, caffeine, as well as illegal drugs such as cocaine and marijuana.)
2. If you do not use drugs, why have you avoided them?
3. Do any members of your family have a drinking problem? Check with your parents about this. Quite often there is or was a family member who had a problem, but this person is not discussed. Share with your parents the information you have learned about the increased risk for family members whose relatives had a drinking problem. Explain why you are asking about grandparents, uncles, cousins, and so on.
4. If you use alcohol or other drugs, what encourages you to use them at this point in your life?
5. Do you feel that alcohol or another drug is causing problems for you (e.g., interferes with your work or social life, endangers your health)? If drugs are causing problems for you, describe these problems.
6. If you know someone who is having a problem with alcohol or other drugs, how can you help him or her cope with the problem?

Notes

1. R. D. Levine, "Drugs Are Back—Big Time," *Reader's Digest,* February 1996, pp. 71–76.
2. PRIDE, "Teen Drug Use Rises for Fourth Straight Year." Atlanta, GA: National Parents' Resource Institute for Drug Education, November 2, 1995.
3. M. Janofsky, "Survey Reports More Drug Use by Teenagers," *New York Times,* 13 December 1994, pp. A1, A26.
4. *Time,* April 23, 1990, in L. D. Eigen, *Alcohol Practices, Policies, and Potentials of American Colleges and Universities: A White Paper.* Rockville, MD: U.S. Department of Health and Human Services, Alcohol, Drug Abuse, and Mental Health Administration, 1991; DHHS Publication No. (ADM) 91-1842, p. 1.
5. Carnegie Foundation for the Advancement of Teaching, "Campus Life: In Search of Community." Princeton, NJ: Princeton University Press, 1990 in *Alcohol Practices, Policies, and Potentials,* op. cit., p. 1.
6. *Alcohol Practices, Policies, and Potentials,* op. cit., p. 6.

7. Ibid., p. 4.

8. U.S. Department of Health and Human Services, *Strategies for Preventing Alcohol and Other Drug Problems.* Rockville, MD: Alcohol, Drug Abuse, and Mental Health Administration 1991; DHHS Publication No. (ADM) 91-1843, p. 8.

9. U.S. Department of Justice, *Sourcebook of Criminal Justice Statistics 1994.* Washington, DC: Bureau of Justice Statistics, 1995, p. 301, Table 3.88. H. Wechler, A. Davenport, G. Dowdall, B. Moeykens, S. Castillo, "Health and Behavioral Consequences of Binge Drinking in College," *Journal of the American Medical Association,* 7 December 1994, pp. 1672–1677.

10. Ibid.

11. D. S. Anderson and A. F. Gadaleto, "The College Alcohol Survey," in *Alcohol Practices, Policies, and Potentials,* op. cit., p. 20.

12. "Campus Drinking: Who, Why, and How Much?" *U.S. News and World Report,* 20 June 1994, p. 21. C. A. Presley and P. W. Meilman, *Alcohol and Drugs on American College Campuses.* Carbondale, IL: Student Health Program Wellness Center of Southern Illinois University-Carbondale, 1991.

13. Ibid.

14. U.S. Department of Justice, op. cit., p. 302, Table 3.91

15. Centers for Disease Control and Prevention, *Vital and Health Statistics: Health Risk Behaviors Among Our Nation's Youth, 1992.* Washington, DC: U.S. Department of Health and Human Services, National Center for Health Statistics, 1995, p. 9. Centers for Disease Control and Prevention, "Update: Alcohol-Related Traffic Crashes and Fatalities Among American Youth and Young Adults," *Morbidity and Mortality Weekly Reports, 44,* no. 47 (1995), pp. 870–871.

16. J. Dao, "Pataki Signs Bill to Combat Drinking by Young Drivers," *New York Times,* 26 June 1996, p. A1.

17. B. Petroff and L. Broek, "The University of Iowa Alcohol and Other Drug Use Assessment: Spring Semester." Ames: University of Iowa Student Health Services, 1990 in *Alcohol Practices, Policies, and Potentials,* p. 11.

18. W. Celis, "Fewer on Campuses Drink, but Deadly Abuses Endure," *New York Times,* 31 December 1991, pp. A1, A14.

19. W. Celis, III, "Tradition on the Wane: College Drinking," *New York Times,* 5 February 1995, pp. A1, A20.

20. U.S. Public Health Service, *Get Real: Straight Talk about Women's Health.* Washington, DC: Office on Women's Health and Society for the Advancement of Women's Health Research, 1995.

21. American Suicide Foundation, "Prevention Through Research and Education."

22. U.S. Public Health Service, "Alcohol and Health: Sixth Special Report to Congress." Washington, DC, 1987 in *Alcohol Practices, Policies, and Potentials,* p. 11; R. Hingson and J. H. Howland, "Alcohol as a Risk Factor for Injury or Death Resulting from Accidental Falls: A Review of the Literature," *Journal of Studies of Alcohol, 48* (1987), pp. 212–219.

23. *Alcohol Practices, Policies, and Potentials,* op. cit., p. 29.

24. Ibid, p. 12.

25. Office of Alcoholism and Substance Abuse Services, "Alcohol: Some Thoughts for Parents." Albany, NY: State of New York Office of Alcoholism and Substance Abuse Services, 1994.

26. Ibid, p. 13.

27. H. Moscowitz & M. Burns, "Effects of Alcohol on Driving Performance," *Alcohol, Health, and Research,* 14, (1990), pp. 12–14.

28. National Center for Statistics and Analysis, "Drunk Driving Facts." Washington, DC: U.S. Department of Transportation, National Highway Traffic Safety Administration, 1991.

29. National Center for Statistics and Analysis, "1990 Traffic Fatality Facts." Washington, DC: U.S. Department of Transportation, National Highway Safety Administration, 1991, p. 6.

30. Substance Abuse and Mental Health Services Administration, *National Household Survey on Drug Abuse.* Washington, DC: U.S. Department of Health and Human Services, 1995, p. 31.

31. M. S. Gold, *800-COCAINE.* New York: Bantam Books, 1985.

32. Centers for Disease Control. "The Health Benefits of Smoking Cessation: A Report of the Surgeon General 1990." Rockville, MD: U.S. Department of Health and Human Services, Public Health Service, 1990, DHHS Publication No. (CDC) 90-8416.

33. J. F. Ross, "What You Don't Know About Risk," *Reader's Digest,* April, 1996, p. 90.

34. J. E. Brody, "Fighting the Nicotine Habit with Nicotine," *New York Times,* 14 April 1995, p. C10.

35. Substance Abuse and Mental Health Services Administration, op. cit., p. 91.

36. Centers for Disease Control, "Tobacco Use Among High School Students—United States, 1990," *Morbidity and Mortality Weekly Report, 40,* no. 36 (13 September 1991), pp. 617–619.

37. S. H. Verhovek, "Young, Carefree and in Love with Cigarettes," *New York Times,* 30 July 1995, p. A1.

38. T. S. Purdum, "Clinton Proposes Broad Plan To Curb Teen-Age Smoking," *New York Times,* 11 August 1995, pp. A1, A19.

39. J. F. Ross, op. cit., p. 88.

40. "Prevalence of Selected Chronic Respiratory Conditions," *Vital Health Statistics,* Series 10, no. 84. Washington, DC: U.S. Department of Health, Education and Welfare, 1970.

41. I. Springer, "Heart Report: Are You at Risk?" *Family Circle,* 18 February 1992, p. 70; W. Ecenbarger, "The Strange History of Tobacco," *Reader's Digest,* April 1992, p. 142.

42. "Husband Wins Claim in Secondhand Smoke Death," *New York Times,* 17 December 1995, p. 28.

43. "5600 Infant Deaths Tied to Mothers' Smoking," *New York Times,* 13 April 1995, p. A3.

44. Federal Drug Administration in T. S. Purdum, op. cit.

45. L. Kutner, "Why Children Smoke and Why They Won't Listen," *New York Times,* 6 February 1992, p. C12.

46. *Licit and Illicit Drugs.* Mt. Vernon, NY: Consumers Union, 1972.

47. Substance Abuse and Mental Health Services Administration, op. cit., p. 105.

48. M. Purdy, "New Inmates Reflect Surge in Use of Cheap But Potent Heroin," *New York Times,* 3 December 1995, p. 49.

49. M. Navarro, "In South, Drug Abusers Turning to a Smuggled Sedative," *New York Times,* 9 December 1995, p. 6.

50. Ibid.

51. D. Johnson, "Good People Go Bad in Iowa, and a Drug Is Blamed," *New York Times,* 22 February 1996, pp. A1, 19.

52. C. S. Wren. "Sharp Rise in Use of Methamphetamines Generates Concern," *New York Times,* 14 February 1996, p. A16.

53. D. Johnson, op. cit.

54. M. Burros & S. Jay, "Concern Grows Over Herb That Promises A Legal High," *New York Times,* 10 April 1996, pp. C1, C6.

55. Ibid.

56. Substance Abuse and Mental Health Services Administration, op. cit., p. 25; PRIDE, op. cit., p. 8.

57. National Institute on Drug Abuse, "Marijuana Update." Rockville, MD, 1989; NIDA Capsule 12.

58. Office for Substance Abuse and Prevention, *Turning Awareness into Action,* (Rockville, MD: National Clearinghouse for Drug and Alcohol Information, 1991), p. 56.

59. Ibid.

60. Office for Substance Abuse and Prevention, op. cit., p. 56.

61. National Institute on Drug Abuse, op. cit.

62. This section is adapted from material developed by the University of Massachusetts Health Service, Health Education Division, University of Massachusetts/Amherst.

Resources for Further Information

Alcoholics Anonymous
P.O. Box 459
Grand Central Station
New York, NY 10163
212-870-3400

American Cancer Society
1875 Connecticut Avenue, NW, Suite 730
Washington, DC 20009
1-800-ACS-2345

American Council on Alcoholism
2522 St. Paul Street
Baltimore, MD 21218
1-800-527-5344

American Council on Alcohol Problems
3426 Bridgeland Drive
Bridgeton, MO 63044
314-739-5944

American Council for Drug Education
204 Monroe Street, Suite 110
Rockville, MD 20850
1-800-488-DRUG

American Heart Association
7320 Greenville Avenue
Dallas, TX 75231
1-800-AHA-USA1

American Lung Association
475 H Street, NW
Washington, DC 20001
1-800-LUNG USA

Centers for Disease Control and
    Prevention
Office on Smoking and Health
1600 Clifton Road, NW
Atlanta, GA
404-488-5705

Cocaine Anonymous
3740 Overland Avenue, Suite G
Los Angeles, CA 90034
1-800-347-8998

Narcotics Anonymous
P.O. Box 9999
Van Nuys, CA 91409
818-773-9999
1-800-COCAINE

National Cancer Institute
Public Inquiries Section
9000 Rockville Pike
Bldg. 31, Rm. 10A-24
Bethesda, MD 20892
1-800-4-CANCER

National Clearinghouse for Alcohol
    Abuse and Drug Information
P.O. Box 2345
Rockville, MD 20847-2345
1-800-729-6686

National Council on Alcoholism and
    Drug Dependence
12 West 21 Street
New York, NY 10010
212-206-6770
1-800-622-2255

National Drug Information Treatment
    and Referral Line
11426-28 Rockville Pike, Ste. 410
Rockville, MD 20852
1-800-662-HELP

CHAPTER

VALUES CLARIFICATION

One of the most important developmental processes involves the acquisition of personal values. *Values* are standards or philosophies for living or behaving. Having values implies living in a way that you consider important, worthwhile, or meaningful. As individuals mature, they learn that there are many different types of value systems.

Growing up involves making choices about which values you will adopt. Setting goals is one way to put your values into action. For recent high school graduates, college may represent the first opportunity to experiment with values that are different from those held by their parents. For students returning to school after years in the world of work or homemaking, college offers the opportunity to reassess their values in the light of new knowledge and perspectives.

■ A PYRAMID OF NEEDS

Values are closely related to needs. Some writers believe that people adopt particular values in order to fulfill psychological or physical needs. The humanistic psychologist Abraham Maslow describes human needs and values in terms of a pyramid, as shown in Figure 13.1. At the bottom of the pyramid are basic physiological needs for food, air, water, and sex. Once these basic needs are satisfied, the individual may turn his or her attention to higher needs, thus progressing from one level to the next until he or she reaches the top level where the primary goal is self-actualization.

Other theorists hypothesize that these needs are not hierarchically arranged. You may wish to satisfy any or all of these needs at the same time. But there will be times when you must choose among different needs. A decision to help a friend may satisfy the need for affection and belongingness, but it may conflict with the need to have justice or goodness. A job that satisfies the need for knowledge or beauty will not necessarily meet the need for recognition or security. Making choices among different needs can often involve difficult value judgments.

Your Personal Needs

To the extent that you know yourself and your value system well, you should be able to make decisions in your life, education, and career with which you can live comfortably. Making decisions requires that you know what you want or what you value. The activity on pages 274–278 will help you identify your

Figure 13.1 *Maslow's Hierarchy of Needs*

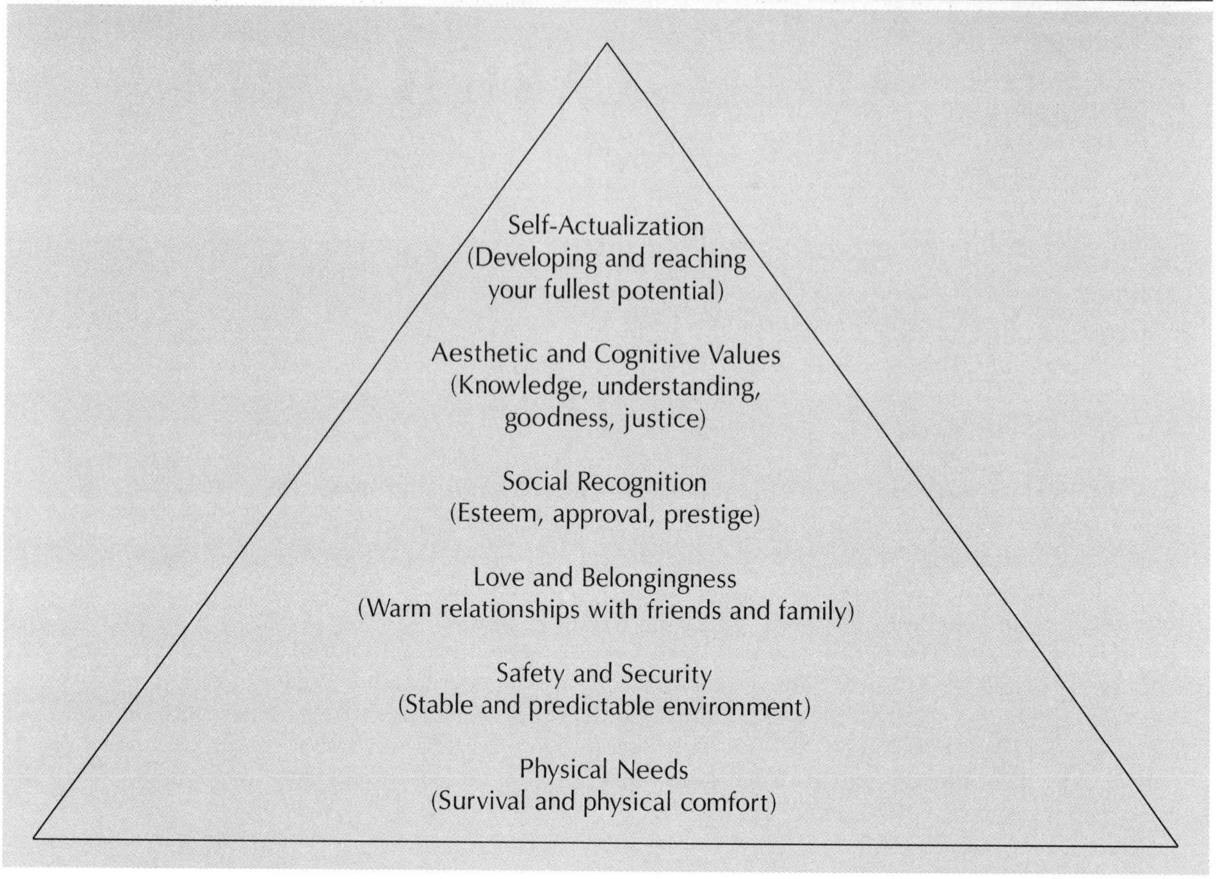

Self-Actualization
(Developing and reaching
your fullest potential)

Aesthetic and Cognitive Values
(Knowledge, understanding,
goodness, justice)

Social Recognition
(Esteem, approval, prestige)

Love and Belongingness
(Warm relationships with friends and family)

Safety and Security
(Stable and predictable environment)

Physical Needs
(Survival and physical comfort)

ACTIVITY

Identifying and Satisfying Personal Needs

1. The figure below lists twenty-eight needs commonly identified by adults. People attach different degrees of importance to each of these needs. Look over the items and think about how they relate to your life.

Choose the items that currently represent your five most important needs. Write your priority number next to each item, from most important (1) to fifth in importance (5). Then look through the remaining needs, choose a few that do not seem at all important to you, and mark them with a zero. There are three blank spaces in which you may add other needs that are not listed.

It may not be easy for you to identify and rank your needs. You are probably not accustomed to doing this. What's more, you may not feel completely comfortable with some of your choices. The purpose of this activity is not to judge whether your needs are good or bad or right or wrong, but rather to help you become more aware of what your needs are.

Needs Commonly Identified by Adults

_____ To feel that I am a good person	_____ To grow and develop
_____ To be economically secure	_____ To be respected
_____ To be with people I like	_____ To have power
_____ To feel needed	_____ To help others
_____ To have new experiences	_____ To be physically attractive
_____ To influence others	_____ To feel competent
_____ To be creative	_____ To feel like an adult
_____ To have time alone	_____ To be true to my beliefs
_____ To control my own life	_____ To be famous
_____ To take care of my body	_____ To achieve something important
_____ To enjoy life and have fun	_____ To have stability in my life
_____ To have wealth and luxuries	_____ To have aesthetically pleasing experiences
_____ To love and be loved	_____ To be intellectually stimulated
_____ To look up to others	_____ To feel a part of something larger than myself
_____ _____ (Write in another need you have)	
_____ _____ (Write in another need you have)	_____ _____ (Write in another need you have)

This activity is excerpted from *Catalyst's Campus Resource: A Guide to Exploring Career and Personal Life Options* copyright by *Catalyst* 1984. Reproduced by permission of Catalyst, 250 Park Avenue South, New York, NY 10003.

2. When class members have finished ranking their needs, your instructor will go around the room and ask each of you to read your most important need. If you do not feel comfortable responding to this question, just say "Pass," but do pay attention to your peers' responses. Your instructor will list the needs on the board as they are read and will put a check under a need each time a student reads it. You will thus be able to tally the most popular need.

Your instructor will then repeat this procedure for the needs ranked number 2 and number 3. Which needs appear frequently? How great is the variety of needs that are ranked as the top three priorities by your peers? Do the rankings of the women in the class differ from those of the men?

What are the three most common needs? Write them here:

1. _____

2. _____

3. _____

3. Your instructor will conduct a class discussion about the three most common needs. Consider the following questions:

■ What do you think makes people choose these needs?
Are they born with them?
Do they learn them?
How do they learn them?
Who teaches them to value those needs?

■ (If there are differences between the needs chosen most often by males and females . . .) Why do you think men (or women) chose this need more often?

■ For your first three needs, did you choose those that you are currently satisfying? If so, why? If not, why not?

4. The blank lists printed below will help you to identify the sources you might use to satisfy your needs. On the two final blank lists, write in any other sources of satisfaction that are relevant to you.

Needs I can satisfy best by having a career or job:

1. _____   5. _____
2. _____   6. _____
3. _____   7. _____
4. _____   8. _____

Needs I can satisfy best by having a spouse or partner:

1. _____   5. _____
2. _____   6. _____
3. _____   7. _____
4. _____   8. _____

Needs I can satisfy best by having a family or children:

1. _____   5. _____
2. _____   6. _____
3. _____   7. _____
4. _____   8. _____

Needs I can satisfy best by having leisure time:

1. _____   5. _____
2. _____   6. _____
3. _____   7. _____
4. _____   8. _____

Needs I can satisfy best by having close friends:

1. _____   5. _____
2. _____   6. _____
3. _____   7. _____
4. _____   8. _____

Needs I can satisfy best by volunteering my time to help others:

1. _____   5. _____

2. _____   6. _____

3. _____   7. _____

4. _____   8. _____

Needs I can satisfy best by belonging to an institutionalized religion:

1. _____   5. _____

2. _____   6. _____

3. _____   7. _____

4. _____   8. _____

Needs I can satisfy best by _____:

1. _____   5. _____

2. _____   6. _____

3. _____   7. _____

4. _____   8. _____

Needs I can satisfy best by _____:

1. _____   5. _____

2. _____   6. _____

3. _____   7. _____

4. _____   8. _____

Needs I can satisfy best by _____:

1. _____   5. _____

2. _____   6. _____

3. _____   7. _____

4. _____   8. _____

Needs I can satisfy best by _____:

1. _____   5. _____

2. _____   6. _____

3. _____   7. _____

4. _____   8. _____

5. After you have finished item 1 in this activity, consider the lists of needs and their sources of satisfaction. Match your needs with ways that you can satisfy them by writing the needs on the blank lines of each source of satisfaction list associated with them. Then determine which list has the most needs written on it.

Your instructor will ask for a show of hands to find out which source of satisfaction lists have the most needs assigned to them by class members. Write

in the three sources of satisfaction lists that satisfy the most needs for members of your class.

a. _____

b. _____

c. _____

6. Participate in a class discussion that addresses the following questions:

   ■ Did you find any needs that you could satisfy through more than one source?
   ■ (If applicable) Why do you think men or women want to satisfy their needs mostly through _____ (most frequently chosen item)?
   ■ Do any of your needs conflict with one another? Do you think that you will have to stifle one need in order to satisfy another? Which needs are in question?
   ■ Do you think it is possible to satisfy all of your needs? Why or why not?
   ■ Do you think the search for satisfaction of your own needs might conflict or interfere with the satisfaction of needs for people who are close to you?

personal needs and will give you the opportunity to think about what needs and values are most important to you. Such introspection can help you to define your value system. Chapter 15, "Careers," contains additional activities that will help you explore your needs and values, specifically those that relate to your career.

Sources of Satisfaction

You should realize that the importance you assign to various needs and the way you choose to satisfy them may change over time. Goals that seem very important now may become less pressing in a few years. You may be satisfying some needs through work now whereas you may choose to satisfy those same needs through another avenue in the future.

Perhaps the most important thing to realize is that few people ever completely satisfy all of their needs. By keeping an open mind about what are your possible sources of need satisfaction, you may be more pleased with the results of your search. In that way you can avoid being labeled as workaholic, hooked only on the kids, fun crazy, or workout freak.

■ COMMUNITY VALUES AND VOLUNTEERISM

Figure 13.2 lists a number of your needs that you can meet by volunteering some of your time to help other people.

Most people volunteer in order to help others and because they enjoy the work,[1] but the list in Figure 13.2 shows just how much the volunteers can benefit from the services they provide. A 10-year study of 1,300 Michigan men found that those who participated in organizations outside the home lived longer and healthier lives than those who did not. People who donate their time, money, or both say volunteering makes them feel great.[2] Other reasons to volunteer your time include adding experiences that enhance your resume,

Figure 13.2   *Personal Needs That Can Be Met through Volunteer Work*

To Feel That I Am a Good Person	To Be with People I Like
To Be Respected	To Have Power
To Help Others	To Feel Like an Adult
To Feel Competent	To Love and Be Loved
To Grow and Develop	To Be True to My Beliefs
To Have New Experiences	To Control My Own Life
To Influence Others	To Look Up to Others
To Be Creative	To Achieve Something Important
To Be Intellectually Stimulated	To Feel a Part of Something Larger
To Enjoy Life and Have Fun	Than Myself
To Have Aesthetically Pleasing	To Meet People with Similar
Experiences	Values and Interests

learning a new skill, or practicing skills that you would like to improve for future employment situations.

When you learn or practice a new skill as a volunteer, you can learn at your own pace, you can practice in a more supportive environment, and you can often be more creative than you could be if you were working under the pressures of a paid position. Volunteer work also offers the opportunity to work with people from different cultures, a skill that is becoming increasingly valued by today's employers.

Participation in volunteer work in this country continues at high levels. According to a recent national survey, more than half of all Americans over age 18 volunteer an average of four hours a week, up 23 percent from 1987[3] For example, New York Cares, a clearinghouse that connects New Yorkers interested in helping others with dozens of projects around the city, has a mailing list of 13,000 volunteers, and its model has been replicated in 26 cities across the country.[4]

A national umbrella organization, City Cares of America, helps to form new groups and spread successful ideas. In the smallest city involved, Greenville, South Carolina, membership is growing 10 percent each month. The calendar of Hands on Atlanta listed 187 projects including park cleanups, tutoring programs, and soup kitchens available every day of the month.

Some of these volunteers come from schools that have developed community service requirements for graduation, and others volunteer as a result of corporate incentive programs for employees. But the increased demand for volunteers from social agencies has more than made up for the increase in the number of people offering their services.

The need for volunteers has been spurred by cuts in social services made by the federal government through the 1980s, by the recession of the early 1990s that created more needy people, and by the public's growing awareness of problems highlighted in newspapers, on TV talk shows, and movies.

Types of volunteer opportunities have expanded tremendously. According to Annette Alve of the Volunteer Center of the United Way, some of the more popular volunteer positions involve working with people in homeless shelters or soup kitchens, tutoring children, putting out newsletters for social agencies (e.g., writing, computer programming, illustrating), working in classrooms with nursery school children, designing brochures for charitable organizations,

giving tours in museums, fielding phone calls for agencies such as the Better Business Bureau, staffing hot lines for suicide prevention or substance abuse programs, becoming a "big brother" or "big sister" to a young person who has gotten into trouble with the law, or working with historical materials at organizations such as the Westchester Archives.

San Diego Cares provides moving crews for people with AIDS who have to relocate frequently as their finances diminish. Volunteers at Hands On Miami read bedtime stories to children in shelters, New York City Cares collects winter coats every December—71,000 last year. Many of the groups collect a major part of their annual budgets on a single day of volunteerism when participants collect pledges from corporations and individuals in the community for the number of hours they work. About 7,500 people participated in the Hands on Atlanta Day raising more than $400,000.[5]

These new groups make volunteering easy, meaningful, and fun. Because they insist on direct involvement in the community, as opposed to stuffing envelopes or selling raffle tickets, they provide instant gratification to volunteers. Many programs, such as providing Thanksgiving dinners to homeless people, are scheduled in the evenings and weekends for the convenience of students and people who work. Increasingly, many of the more popular volunteer positions involve episodic work—time-limited commitments to see a certain project through rather than regularly-scheduled, ongoing commitment. For example, volunteers might organize a party at a residential treatment center for children, pick up a word-processing or printing job from an agency and complete it at home, or pitch in to clean up an area that has suffered an environmental accident. Some projects may involve only one or two hours.

The types of people volunteering have also changed. The little, old lady pushing a cart of library books through the corridors of a hospital is no longer an accurate picture of the typical volunteer. The majority of people who volunteer (60 percent) are employed either part-time or full-time outside their homes. Young professionals have been recruited by programs where they work and by organizations such as New York Cares, which has 13,000 members who are mostly between the ages of 25 and 35. The highest percentage of volunteers comes from the 25- through 44-year-old groups, but 43 percent of the people in the 18- through 24-year-old group volunteer, and more than 70 percent of college freshmen offered their services to nonprofit agencies during high school.[6]

Contact a member of the clergy or a local school to find out how you can offer your services. Fraternities and sororities on campus also sponsor many volunteer activities or you can find opportunities for volunteering in your telephone directory. Other resources for volunteer work are listed at the end of this chapter. People are increasingly feeling that they should be giving something back to the community, and they are increasingly getting hooked on the satisfaction they receive from sharing a few hours of their lives with others who are in need.

■ CAREER AND PERSONAL LIFE CHOICES

In addition to values that encourage community service, you will find that values are also important factors closer to home in your relationships with family and friends. The ten scenarios on pages 281–287 will help you consider how values affect your career and personal life choices. They will also help you see how priorities change according to circumstances and stages of a person's life. Finally, they will encourage you to find solutions to problems should you find yourself in similar situations.

ACTIVITY

Identifying Values, Goals, and Priorities: Relationships versus Careers

Break into small discussion groups of five students. Your instructor will assign three of the following scenarios to each discussion group. Read over the scenario, discuss all the issues, and answer the questions that follow the scenario. Decide how *you* might react in a similar situation.

These scenarios present very difficult conflict situations similar to those in which many people find themselves today. The resolution to these problems is based on individuals' personal value systems. *There are no right or wrong answers.* Decide how you might react in a similar situation. Reaching group consensus about what people in the scenario should do or whether they are right or wrong is not the goal of this exercise. Values, goals, and priorities are highlighted here because they are so rarely discussed and yet are so often at the root of many disputes in life.

SCENARIO 1

Andy, twenty-four, is a sales manager for a midwestern company that makes power tools. His wife, Paula, does not work outside the home and spends her time caring for their six-month-old son. Andy's job involves a lot of traveling; he supervises sales over a large area of the Midwest. He drives a great deal every day, calling directly on hardware stores, factories, schools, and the wholesalers who distribute his company's products. Andy often has to travel evenings and weekends to reach his clients who are spread out geographically; in addition, he spends at least two weeks out of every month away from home.

When he travels, he stays in close phone contact with his wife, but he sometimes feels as if his son is growing up without a father. Andy works on salary plus commission; he and Paula both realize that the harder and longer he works, the higher will be his earnings, but neither one is completely happy with the current situation.

Questions for Scenario 1

1. Andy and Paula have a traditional relationship. Because there is only one income for the family, the income produced by Andy's job is critical. How do you feel about this relationship? Does it seem satisfactory? Unsatisfactory? Why?

2. Would you suggest that Andy and Paula try to change their situation? If so, why? If not, why?

3. How might you change the situation to give Andy more time with his child (look for a new job, decide/try to live on less money, have Paula work part-time so that Andy could work less)?

4. How do you think Andy's job affects Paula's attitude toward him? Toward herself?

5. How do you think Andy's child will be affected by Andy's long periods away from home?

6. If you were in the couple's situation, would you find it acceptable temporarily? For how long? Would it be all right over a long period of time?

7. Could you imagine yourself in a situation similar to the one Andy and Paula have? (If you're a male, you would be in Andy's position; if you're a female, you would be in Paula's position). How might you react?

SCENARIO 2

Anne, now twenty-seven, is a stage actress who has played major roles in community theater and Off-Broadway productions in New York. She and her husband, Vincent, would like to have a child by the time Anne is in her thirties. Anne has had an offer to join a London repertory theater for one year. It is an opportunity to broaden her experience, work with a highly regarded director, and boost her chances for career advancement. When she returns to New York, she hopes to perform on Broadway and join a touring theater company. Eventually, she would like to go to Los Angeles and have an opportunity to work in films.

Vincent teaches history in a small private school in New York City. If Anne takes the London offer, he must decide whether to give up his position to go with her or remain in New York and see Anne only a few times during the year. He is aware that Anne will probably relocate several times because of her career, but the couple never seem to have time to thoroughly discuss their plans or how children and Vincent's career will fit into their future.

Questions for Scenario 2

1. In this relationship Anne has the "dominant" career. What do you think about this relationship? Is it workable? If it is, what makes it work? If not, why?

2. If Vincent relocates with Anne what could happen to his career? To their relationship?

3. What do you think will happen to Anne's career if she *doesn't* take the opportunity in London? What will happen to their relationship?

4. How would you suggest that Anne and Vincent work out their possible career conflict?

5. Would you want to be in Vincent's position? How would you feel if Anne asked you to relocate?

6. Would you want a career like Anne's? How would you feel about asking your spouse to relocate?

7. What kind of spouse would *you* have to have (if you were in Anne's position) to make a high-level acting career *and* a stable personal relationship possible?

SCENARIO 3

Joe, who is in his mid-twenties, just landed a job with a very important private law firm that employs over one hundred attorneys. Joe graduated with top honors from his law school and his firm has great expectations for him. Right now, Joe is what is called an "associate," and he spends much of his time assisting experienced attorneys with their cases. He has very little contact with clients and instead does a lot of research. But Joe knows that he has to prove himself before he's given more responsibility. He puts in very long days, often working through dinner and sometimes into the early morning hours at the office or in the local law library.

Over the next few years, Joe hopes to prove himself so that his responsibility for clients and cases will steadily increase, and the firm will offer him a partnership. Not many associates "make partner," and the competition is fierce. For the moment, he keeps working conscientiously anyway, hoping that it will pay off, but his profession is leaving him with little time for anything but work. In fact, he can't remember the last time he spent an evening "just relaxing." He's single but would like to have a family "someday"; he just doesn't know when he'll find the time.

Questions for Scenario 3

1. What do you think of Joe's job? What do you like about it? Dislike about it?

2. If you were in Joe's position, would you stay in the job at the law firm?

3. If Joe were a single parent with custody of his children, would you feel differently about the job? Why?

4. If Joe were a single woman with no children, would you feel differently about the job?
5. How do you feel about the fact that Joe's job gives him little contact with people?
6. How do you feel about a high-pressure, competitive job with the possibility of substantial rewards at the top?
7. How do you feel about the fact that these rewards are uncertain in the case of this job?

SCENARIO 4

Dorothy is a vice president at a large oil company. She is thirty-three and returned to work three months ago after having her first child (a daughter) and taking a two-month maternity leave. She had hoped to take a longer leave, but her office was in the midst of negotiating an important contract for which her services were needed. Her husband, Lee, requested a brief paternity leave from the hospital where he practices psychiatry, but it was denied because hospital policy does not give men parental leaves.

Both Dorothy and Lee worked hard to attain their current career levels and do not wish to leave their jobs. So they decided to hire a daytime caretaker for their daughter and alternate taking time off from work when the baby or the caretaker is sick. They had thought about maintaining this type of arrangement until their child is about two years old. At that time the couple expects to enroll her in the hospital's child care center.

Dorothy and Lee work long hours. Although their schedules are less hectic than they once were, each of their positions demands at least nine or ten hours of work per day. They are beginning to worry that neither of them has the time or energy to be the kind of parents they had hoped to be. They are also worried about the quality of their own relationship, which has suffered since the baby was born.

Questions for Scenario 4

1. Do you think it was wise for Dorothy and Lee to have a child at this point in their careers? Why or why not?
2. How do you feel about Dorothy and Lee leaving their baby with a hired caretaker all day, every day? Under the same circumstances, what would you do?
3. Imagine you are Dorothy's boss. How do you think you would respond if she asked you for additional time off to care for her child, even if it was without pay? How long would you guarantee to hold her full-time job open? How would you respond if she asked for a part-time position? What are some of the problems either of these arrangements (more leave, part-time work) might cause?
4. How do you feel about Lee wanting to take a leave to care for his baby? (*For women*) Would you want your spouse to take such a leave? Why or why not? (*For men*) Would you be willing to take such a leave? Why or why not?
5. If you were Dorothy, and you decided to quit your job to care for your child, what would be the most difficult part of leaving? What might be some of the advantages?
6. If you were Lee, and you decided to quit your job, what would be the most difficult part of leaving? What might be some of the advantages?
7. Picture yourself as a policy maker in an organization, institution, or company. Do you think it would be your responsibility to provide paternity leaves? If so, why? If not, why?

SCENARIO 5

Eleanor recently returned to college as a full-time student. She has spent the last fifteen years raising her three children (ages 8, 10, and 15) and taking responsibility for most of the household chores. She feels as though her personal identity has completely disappeared while caring for her family's needs. She feels the need for some intellectual stimulation and long-range goals. This is her first experience as a student in seventeen years. She hopes to get her degree and pursue a career in accounting. She feels that time is running out for her. If she does not go to school full time to get her degree, it will soon be too late for her to pursue a meaningful career.

Her husband, Keith, works full time as a manager for the telephone company. He supports her decision to return to school but is learning the "hard way" how much he took for granted Eleanor's contribution to managing the household.

Eleanor is also experiencing problems with the transition; sometimes she is too tired at night to be a patient mother or take full responsibility for household tasks. In fact, one night Eleanor yelled at Keith for buying the wrong kind of steak for dinner. On several occasions, she could not study adequately for important exams or complete research in time for class papers because of time she spent on housework and child care.

All family members are aware of the upheaval that the change in Eleanor's life caused in their routines, but they haven't really talked as a family about how to cope with these new arrangements.

Questions for Scenario 5

1. How do you feel about Eleanor's decision to return to school?
2. Do you feel that she should have returned to school sooner?
3. Do you feel she should have postponed her plans for school until the children were older?
4. Do you think she has an obligation to stay in the homemaker role permanently since that was the role she chose when she got married?
5. Would you take time from your husband's (or wife's) and children's needs to get a degree and make a meaningful life for yourself?
6. Would you take time from your husband's (or wife's) and children's needs to get a degree if it meant that you could improve their lives by earning (more) money in the long run?
7. What suggestions can you offer Eleanor, her husband, and her children that might ease tensions in their household?

SCENARIO 6

Vivian is a graduate student in history. She shares an off-campus apartment with Chris, who is an advanced undergraduate engineering student. They have been friends since they were in high school. This year Chris has to buy a personal computer to do her course work, or her grades will suffer. Chris lives on a fixed income from her family and has no extra money to contribute to the purchase. Vivian lives on a small teaching fellowship and has a loan from her parents. Both women share the apartment expenses equally.

Vivian is considering paying for the computer. She remembers that when they graduated from high school, Chris paid for Vivian to accompany her on a three-month trip to Europe. In order to buy the computer for Chris, Vivian would need to use her parents' loan, take an additional part-time job, and delay completion of her thesis. She must decide soon.

Questions for Scenario 6

1. If you were in Vivian's situation, what personal values might you consider in making this decision?
2. If you had to prioritize these values, which one(s) would be most important? Least important?
3. What external factors, or influences, might affect Vivian's decision? Which is the strongest factor? Which is the weakest?
4. If you were Chris, how would you feel if Vivian decided against buying the computer? What would you do?

5. Do you think it would be wise for Vivian to delay her educational/career goals? What might be the advantages? What might be the disadvantages?

6. If you were Vivian, what kinds of feelings might you have if you decided to buy the computer? How would you feel if you decided against it?

SCENARIO 7

Jose, twenty-six, is a computer technician for a large computer company. He and his wife, Luisa, who is twenty-six also, have been married for four years. They have both been working full time and are thinking about starting a family within a year. Jose's job pays well, but there is very little room for advancement in his department. He is also on call at night and on weekends, a schedule he doesn't want to maintain when he has children.

Recently, he took some aptitude tests at a local government employment agency and learned that he might do very well as a computer systems designer. If he decided to move into that field, he would need to return to school full time for three or four years. The company will not pay for his training or give him a leave of absence or a part-time position. Jose would have to quit *this* job to go back to school.

Luisa understands and supports Jose's ambitions but is very anxious to have children. She knows that if she becomes the sole wage earner and contributes to Jose's tuition, they will have to delay having children for at least five years. Although their finances will be better then, and their schedules will be less demanding, Luisa will be thirty-one years old, and she's worried about starting a family at that age.

Questions for Scenario 7

1. Do you think Jose should leave his present position and return to school? Why or why not?

2. If Jose returns to school now, how might it affect Luisa and Jose's relationship?

3. Which spouse do you think must make the most sacrifices if Jose returns to school? If he stays in his current job? Why?

4. If you were Luisa, how would you feel when Jose told you about his plans to leave his job? How would you respond?

5. How would you feel if you were the one asking Luisa to make this sacrifice? How could you deal with her feelings about the decision?

6. If Luisa were the one who wanted to return to school instead of Jose, do you think the same conflicts would exist? Why or why not?

7. Putting off childbearing for four or five years would make Luisa 30- or 31-years-old when she tries to start a family. How do you feel about the idea of starting a family at that age? Do you think these feelings would be different for Luisa than for Jose? Why or why not?

8. Do you see any alternatives for resolving this conflict?

SCENARIO 8

Jerome is 48 years old; he is a writer for a local newspaper in a small town. He lives alone and has never had a family of his own, but he loves his work and is very involved with his friends and the welfare of his town. His elderly mother also lives alone on a farm about twenty miles from town. She has recently suffered a fall and will need continuous care for six months, and possibly will never be able to care for herself completely. Jerome has no siblings or relatives nearby to bear this responsibility. He will not be eligible for retirement for several years.

He loves his mother and wants to be able to take care of her. He has thought about having her move in with him, but he realizes that he needs some space and time for his own friends and leisure activities. He has considered the possibility of hiring a live-in nurse for his mother, finding a nursing home in the community, or asking his sister (who lives in another state) to care for her part of the year.

Questions for Scenario 8

1. If you were Jerome, how would you feel about having the sole responsibility for your mother's well-being? Among the options Jerome is considering, which would work best for you? Why?

2. Do you think Jerome should be the one carrying the whole responsibility? (What about other relatives, her friends, her religious community, society itself?)

3. If you were Jerome's mother and the choice were yours, what would you decide to do? Why?

4. Jerome does not have a spouse or partner and has only his own career to consider. Do you think this increases or decreases his opportunities to find a solution to his mother's situation? In what ways?

5. Given this situation, whose needs do you think Jerome should consider first—his or his mother's? Why?

6. Do you know anyone personally who is in a similar situation (that is, someone solely responsible for an elderly parent)? If so, how are they resolving the problem? How do you feel about their method of handling the situation?

SCENARIO 9

Cynthia works for the personnel department of a small retail company. The personnel division is very small—just Cynthia and her boss. Since there are only two employees, Cynthia's job has many different responsibilities, from interviewing job applicants and recruiting new employees to overseeing employee benefits and the company's small cafeteria.

Cynthia is divorced and has one child, age 4, who is in a family day care home close to where they live. Cynthia's job has very regular hours (9–5) and that helps her to arrange for the care of her daughter. She never has to take work home and her weekends are free to spend with her child. Cynthia's boss is also very flexible, and if her daughter is sick, or Cynthia can't come in for some other reason, she and her boss can usually make some arrangement that's agreeable to both.

Cynthia's salary is moderate; she has friends who work in the personnel divisions of much larger companies and they make more money than she does. They also have a lot more responsibility and opportunities to move up within their companies. Cynthia knows that there won't be much room for advancement if she stays with her company, but she also appreciates the flexibility and "atmosphere" of her workplace. Still, sometimes she envies her friends with the high salaries and more stimulating work. But as long as her daughter is little, she feels she should make some tradeoffs as far as her career is concerned.

Questions for Scenario 9

1. What do you think of Cynthia's job? What do you like about it? Dislike about it?

2. As a single parent, Cynthia has total responsibility for her child and their economic survival. If you were in Cynthia's position, do you think you would stay in the job at the retail company? If so, why? If not, why?

3. If Cynthia were a man with custody of his child, would you feel differently about the job? Why?

4. Cynthia is trading possible career growth and higher salary for flexibility and regular hours. Do you think at some point she should try to get a more demanding, high-paying career? When? Would it make a difference if her child were older? If she got married again?

5. Today, would you rather have a 9-to-5 job that tended to be routine or would you rather have a more challenging career that paid well but left less time for fun, for your spouse/partner, or for your children? How do you think you'll feel 15 years from now?

6. If you had (have) a spouse/partner, which type of job would you like him/her to have? Why?

SCENARIO 10

Renee is in her 50s and has been working for years as a dental hygienist. She is married, has two grown children, and lives in the suburbs of a large city. She first began working as a dental hygienist because her husband became ill and could not work while their children were small. Renee's husband, Charles, was eventually able to work again, but her income was still essential to the family, so she continued working. She is very close to her family and enjoys working within walking distance of her home. However, the need for her services has dwindled in their community, her job has become part-time, and she expects to be laid off soon.

Renee is beginning to think about the possibility of changing jobs. She'd like to commute to the city where there are more opportunities. She is torn between the possible excitement of a new job and her fears of leaving her community and being exposed to the large city. She wants to begin looking for a new job now, while she is still employed, but Charles thinks she should wait until she's actually fired before looking for a new position. He usually supports her decisions, but he, too, is afraid of the dangers and risks of going to work in the city everyday.

Questions for Scenario 10

1. If you were Renee, what do you feel would be most important in making this decision about your job?

2. Do you think that Renee's desire to seek fulfillment through a new job is worth the risk of some physical and emotional distance from her family? If so, why? If not, why?

3. If you were 50 years old, what *feelings* might you have about leaving the security of your old job and neighborhood? What if Renee were 25 years old instead of 50?

4. Suppose one of Charles's fears is that once Renee gets used to the new job and the city she will become dissatisfied with him and leave him alone. How might this affect Renee's thinking about her future? Do you think Charles's fears are reasonable? Why?

5. If you were Charles, how would you feel about the whole situation?

6. If you were Renee would you talk about some of these concerns with your husband? Do you think she should discuss the issue with her grown children? Why? How much influence should her family members' opinions have on her final decision? Why?

7. Do you think you'd need support from people beyond the family, if you had to make a decision like Renee's? What sort of support group might Renee look for to discuss the issues as she thinks about this transition?

8. What do you think Renee's chances of finding a fulfilling position are, given her age? Should her age be a factor in her decision? Why?

This activity is excerpted from *Catalyst's Campus Resource: A Guide to Exploring Career and Personal Life Options*, copyright by Catalyst 1984. Reproduced by permission of Catalyst, 250 Park Avenue South, New York, NY 10003.

■ VALUES AND RELATING TO OTHERS

Values enter into your personal relationships in other ways, too. You might experience a conflict if you find that a friend has cheated on an exam in your class. Would you report him or her? Would you lecture your friend about honesty? What would you do if you found that a roommate was selling drugs? How would you react if your boyfriend or girlfriend made a habit of drinking at parties and then driving while intoxicated?

ACTIVITY

Identifying Interpersonal Values

1. For this activity, break into small discussion groups of five. Read the following scenario.

THE SCENARIO

Susan came from a small town in Pennsylvania where her widowed father was an evangelical Christian minister. He raised her very strictly, and it was only with great reluctance that he allowed Susan to go to the University of Pittsburgh. He feared that the big city would corrupt her morals. As Susan boarded the bus, he warned her, "If I ever find out that you've been fooling around with boys or using alcohol or drugs, I'll cut you off from all financial support and never let you enter my home again."

Susan had always obeyed her father and intended to do so while at college. She did stay away from drugs and alcohol, but in October she began dating Larry, a fellow student in her religion class. By December they were sleeping together. When she returned from Christmas vacation, Susan discovered that she was pregnant. Since neither her father nor the private church-affiliated schools she had attended ever mentioned birth control, she had not taken the proper precautions.

Larry did not want to get married. He said, "I'm sorry, but you should have been more careful." He then added, "Besides, how do I know that it's mine?" Rejected by Larry, Susan decided to turn to her father for help. Susan called her father and explained her situation. He said, "I warned you, and you know how I feel. From this day on, you are no longer my daughter," he added before hanging up on her.

Panic-stricken, Susan decided to have an abortion. Susan saw an article that an agency had placed in the *Pitt News* advertising help for unwanted pregnancies. The article said the cost for an abortion would be $400.00. Susan went to her best friend Allison for the money. "I don't approve of abortions," Allison said. "I can't lend you money to destroy a life." Susan then decided to call the agency. The agency head, after finding out that Susan did not have the money, referred her to the Department of Public Assistance. The social worker at the Department of Public Assistance told Susan that she was still the responsibility of her father. The clerk stated coldly, "If the Department of Public Assistance gave money to every irresponsible girl who got pregnant, there would be no money for people who really need it."

In desperation, Susan approached Dorothy. Dorothy was a popular, upper-class student in her dorm, who appeared to be very knowledgeable. "Sure, I've got a concoction that will make you miscarry—no charge," said Dorothy.

After taking the mixture, Susan did miscarry, but in the process, she hemorrhaged severely and died.

2. Discuss the scenario with your group members, and try to reach a consensus in which you rate each of the characters, according to how much he or she appeals to the group, from most appealing (1) to least appealing (6). Compare your group's ratings with the ratings of other groups in the class.

Susan _____   Larry _____   Social worker _____

Susan's father _____   Dorothy _____   Allison _____

3. Participate in a class discussion that addresses the following questions:

- What do you think your rankings reveal about your values?
- How do you feel about the following topics in relation to college students?
  Premarital sex
  Birth control
  Abortion
  Becoming parents before completing college
- Describe the obligations or responsibilities that you feel the characters in Susan's story owe to each other.
  Susan's father to Susan
  Susan to her father
  Larry to Susan
  Susan to Larry
  Allison to Susan
  Susan to Allison
  Dorothy to Susan
  The social worker to Susan
  Susan to her unborn child

This exercise is reprinted with permission of Professor Ina R. Hark, University of South Carolina, author of the "Modern Drawbridge Exercise."

Now that you are on your own in college, you may find that some of your values about what is right and wrong conflict with other values about loyalty, honesty, and security. The following activity will give you practice in confronting and thinking about some of the difficult questions that arise in the area of values and human relationships.

The activity, "Playing God" offers another opportunity to examine your values, specifically in a situation where the professional's responsibility to his client may conflict with certain universal values that form the basis of our society. It will also give you the opportunity to consider a situation that is becoming disturbingly common in contemporary personal relationships.

A report by the American Medical Association called domestic violence "a public health problem that has reached epidemic proportions." The association reported that "nearly one quarter of the women in the United States will be abused by a current or former partner some time during their lives."[7] Unfortunately, members of the college community are not exempt from dealing with these nasty realities. Over the years, I have had several students who found themselves in physically abusive and potentially lethal domestic situations.

Two to four million women are assaulted by boyfriends, husbands, or lovers each year, and the incidents cut across all racial, socioeconomic, educational, ethnic, and religious lines.[8] Three highly-publicized cases offer a sampling of the diversity of variables encountered: white, black, and hispanic individuals; extremely wealthy and middle class couples; highly educated and working class people; a married couple, a divorced couple, and a dating couple. What they all have in common is domestic violence.

The trial of O. J. Simpson on charges of murdering his wife, Nicole, riveted the nation for weeks. The arrest of Peter Martins, the ballet master in chief of the New York City Ballet on charges of assaulting his wife, the ballerina, Darci Kistler, rocked the artistic community. The recent case in New York City

ACTIVITY

Playing God: A Question of Values

Many students consider careers in law enforcement, in health services, or in the helping professions such as psychology, social work, the law, medicine, or police work. Situations like the ones described above are arising with increasing frequency. The goal of this activity is for you to consider some of the complex value decisions that confront individuals in our society's challenging professional and personal conflicts.

Break into small groups of 4 to 6 students and read the scenario. When you have finished reading, discuss the implications of Kitty's actions and her physician's response with the other members of your group.

PLAYING GOD

Why she called me first I never figured out. Maybe she had more brains than I gave her credit for. All she had said was,

My husband has passed away, Doctor. Can you come over?

That was it: flat monotone, no emotion, just matter-of-fact. Now I'm one of those old-fashioned doctors who still makes house calls on certain occasions, and this was definitely one of those occasions. I could feel it in the pit of my stomach. I grabbed my clothes, got dressed in the bathroom so as not to wake my wife, brushed the snow from the car, and headed over to their farm. A storm had passed through unannounced, leaving snow everywhere. It was the kind of night where, once you get out into it, you're glad you're there—everything blanketed in rolling white, not a rift in the cover—so cold and clear the stars hang down out of the sky just above the snow. On a night like that, you had trouble believing there could be any evil in the world.

From the bend in the road I could see the light from their kitchen far off, sparkling down the crystals of snow. I pulled the car in at the barest suggestion of a driveway, turned off the motor, and pushed through the drifts up to the porch. I let myself in. The house was quiet as a tomb. The kitchen clock gave off a quiet hum. On the face of the refrigerator were plastered the kids' school papers: spelling tests and arithmetic, maps colored in Crayola, and the minimal artwork of the early grades. There was a "Mom-Dad-and-Me" family portrait—"Mom" about a quarter the size of "Dad," who occupied center stage, and "Me" off to the side, a stick figure without arms—no mouth drawn in. I stepped through the kitchen and found Kitty sitting in the darkened living room in a straight-backed chair, staring off, trance-like, in shock maybe. What appeared to be small marbles lay scattered on the carpet. I picked one up. It was a pearl.

"Where's Earl?" I asked her.

"In the bedroom?" said Kitty. She always said everything as though it were a question. She motioned with her head.

"Where are the kids?"

"At my sister's?" she answered.

"You all right?" I asked.

She nodded.

I took a deep breath and headed into the bedroom, expecting the worst. I wasn't disappointed. Earl lay flat on the bed, a bullet hole above his right ear. The left half of his cranium and its contents were splattered next to him on the bedroom wall. I began to run a cold sweat. Even after all the years of small-town practice, being called in for mangled bodies and auto wrecks, botched amateur abortions, deceased elderly pensioners not found for days, and—worst of all—the abused children—that, worst of all—despite all of that hardening up, a scene like this still could weaken you at the knees. I swallowed against the sweat, looked away, looked back again, and had to look away. It was hard to stay clinical. Doctors have trouble with violent death. Disease we learn to accept. But not this.

I surveyed the scene. Earl's .30-.30 Winchester lay on the floor just inside the door. A half-empty bottle of Schenley's stood next to the bed, within easy reach. Earl lay on the bed fully dressed, shoes on, with that eternal gaze that can make your skin crawl.

The rest of the room was precise and neat. The top of the bureau was uncluttered: a brush, a comb, a mirror, all arranged just so, and an ash tray full of change. A wedding picture of Kitty and Earl stood off to the side. The bedside table held a small reading lamp, the shade a shocking white against the dark streaks of Earl's blood on the wall. There was a Bible and an old clothbound book, its title faded, and a pair of woman's reading glasses folded on top. There were no clothes lying about. The closet doors were closed. The window drapes hung just so. All this tidiness framing the mess of Earl's body.

I went back out to the living room to Kitty. She hadn't moved a muscle, except that her eyes had the look of a cornered mouse.

"What happened?" I asked her.

"He shot himself?" Kitty answered.

"Shot himself," I said.

She nodded.

"Kitty . . ." my voice trailed off. I sat down in a chair opposite her and looked at her for a long minute.

"Kitty, we go way back don't we?"

She nodded again.

Some thirty years ago I had brought her into this world, supported her through her mother's premature death, and twenty years later, delivered babies of her own. I had seen her boy through a bad case of spinal meningitis, and harped at her father's cigarette smoking, in the end burying him because of it.

But, through the most of it there had been Kitty. She held the record for most abused woman in Taylor County. There had been the time I had hospitalized her for a hairline fracture of the mandibular ramus, a both-bones fracture of the left forearm, and God knows how many internal injuries, for the better part of a week. We had Earl all wrapped up and ready to send down to the state prison. And then Kitty wouldn't sign the papers. The night I hospitalized her from that episode I stopped by her father's house just to check on things. Al was in a murderous rage. I could hardly blame him.

"I'm going to kill the son of a bitch. I'm going to kill the son of a bitch," was all he kept muttering. He'd look at me with his reddened, burning eyes, and I knew he meant it.

"Al," I said, "you do that and you'll wind up in prison yourself."

"I don't give a damn," he said.

"And Earl will get off."

"Earl will be dead," he answered.

"And your grandchildren will hate you for the rest of their lives," I said, "for killing their father."

At that, the hardness left him and he gave it up.

"I'm going to tell you something else, Al," I said. "In two weeks Kitty will be right back with him and there isn't a damn thing you can do about it."

Soon Kitty did go back with Earl. You had trouble saying whose sickness was worse. But there was no question about Kitty's suffering. Or her father's. It was the same scenario for some ten years, Kitty coming into the emergency room, badly beaten, meekly asking to see me, Al flying into a rage, and, in the early years, loading up his gun, resolving to put Earl away, later resigning himself to this terrible disease that both Earl and Kitty were torturing him with. Two other times Kitty had been so severely beaten that she required hospitalization. Each time we got the town police involved, had Earl arrested, had the complaint papers all filled out. All sealed, and delivered, except that Kitty would never sign the papers. And she always went back to him.

"You know, Doc," said the Chief of Police one day, "some day one of these two is going to wind up dead."

Kitty shifted in her chair and brought me back to the darkened living room. I turned to look at her. I was her doctor, her family's doctor. She'd level with me.

"What really happened?" I asked her.

"I heard the gun go off?" she said. "I went in. And he was dead."

"I didn't see a suicide note, Kitty," I said, pressing her. "Did he leave a note? People usually leave a note in these situations."

"No," she said. "There wasn't any note." Her voice fell. As tentative as she was, Kitty wouldn't budge. I thought later, looking back on it, that this was probably the first time in her life she had made up her mind and stuck to it.

"Kitty. . . ." I didn't know what else to say to her. She shifted nervously in the chair and I saw her wince. She held her left arm close to her body.

There she was, Al's little girl—everybody's little girl. I could remember Kitty skipping into my office at five full of happiness and life, for her preschool shots, and coming in again at twelve, the apple of her daddy's eye, for her camp physical. We were there, Al and I, on that crisp November day when Kitty bagged her first deer. And I sat at the head table, at her wedding reception—she and Earl the handsome couple—Kitty proudly wearing her mother's string of pearls that Al had surprised her with on that day. And after that all those hospital admissions . . . Kitty . . . most abused woman in the whole county.

But there was a lot more that went into this case. There had been Leon Tilley's murder two years before. He had been found dead in his hay field, two bullet holes at the base of his skull, relieved of a large amount of cash. For a year nothing happened. Tilley had been one popular old man, the kind of Norman Rockwell farmer everybody stops to talk to, wisdom written all over his face. The town was pretty unhappy with what they saw as police inaction. Then four teenagers and a drug dealer were apprehended and the papers were filled with yellow journalism for six months: stories of bad cops, barflies, drugs, and witnesses who lied. The kind of stuff that's not supposed to happen in the country. The whole county salivated. After all the publicity, the big-city lawyers, and backroom deals, the D.A. managed only one conviction. Now everybody was still screaming for the police chief's head and small-time entrepreneurs were getting rich selling T-shirts that read:

Come to Herkimer and get away with murder.

I looked at Kitty, and then into the bedroom, then back at Kitty again. I nodded to myself. Yes indeed, I thought, the Chief would dearly love to get his hands on this one. He needed this one.

One time back along, I had a bad baby on my hands, a newborn with hydrocephalus and a big cyst at the base of the neck—the crippled-for-life kind of baby you see once in a lifetime. I watched that baby struggle and watched and didn't do a damn thing to save it and apologized to the family afterwards, explaining it was a stillborn, lying to them. That was the one time I played God and it aggravated me, I can tell you. I went home that night and yelled at my wife, kicked the dog, and drank too much—brooded for weeks and never talked about it. It can eat at you. There had never been a second time until Kitty.

I grabbed one of the kitchen chairs and a dish towel and went back into the bedroom. In a few minutes I was on the phone and had the dispatcher get hold of the Chief. Shortly he was at the other end of the line, sleepy, gruff, trying to be important.

"Chief," I said, "I'm at Earl Staples' house. He's finally done himself in. He got drunk and shot himself with his deer rifle . . . yeah, I'm at the house now . . . well, it looks to me like he rested the gun on a chair next to the bed, and then lay himself down and shot himself in the temple. Clear suicide in my book. I'll be signing it out that way. . . . Yeah, she's here with me. I'll drive her over to her sister's. I'd sure appreciate it if you'd send one of your men over here to clean things up. . . . Thanks Chief."

I put the phone down and turned back to Kitty. She was staring at the floor. She hadn't moved. I sighed, slapped my thighs, and got up to go.

"Where's your coat, Kitty? I'll drive you over to Kate's, and in the morning," I said, nodding to her left arm, "you come over to the office so I can set that fracture for you one last time."

This article is reprinted with permission from M. A. LaCombe, "Playing God," *Annals of Internal Medicine,* 116 (15 January 1992), pp. 161–162.

QUESTIONS

1. Why did Kitty continue living with her husband? (Consider emotional, economic, and psychological variables.)
2. How do you feel about the murder?
3. Should physicians lie to protect murderers when there are extenuating circumstances?
4. Should Kitty be allowed to get away with murder?
5. How do you feel about the physician's actions in the earlier case involving the severely disabled baby?
6. How would you have behave if you were the physician in this case?

where a judge was removed from the bench after releasing a man who had attacked and threatened his girlfriend opened deep rifts between the mayor's office and the legal community. The man subsequently shot his girlfriend to death in the car dealership where she worked.

In this chapter you have identified some of your values and considered how they might affect your decisions in relationships, personal choices, and careers. Chapter 15, "Careers," will present additional exercises to help you determine which of your values might give you a sound basis for making career choices.

✍ REFLECTIONS FOR YOUR JOURNAL

1. Do any of your values conflict with the values of people who are important to you (e.g., your parents, children, spouse, girlfriend/boyfriend, or friends)? How do you cope with this conflict?

2. Reflect upon the five items you identified as your most important needs in the activity *Identifying and Satisfying Personal Needs*. Are you satisfying those needs at this time? What activities or relationships help you to satisfy those needs? If you are not satisfying those needs now, how do you plan to satisfy them in the future?

3. Think about the last time you helped someone. How did you feel about it? If you participate in volunteer work, what benefits do you receive from contributing to your community or helping others? If you do not participate in volunteer work, how can you make time to help others on an occasional or regular basis?

Notes

1. Fleishman-Hillard Research and the National Family Opinion Research, Inc. 1987, The J.C. Penney Company and Volunteer-The National Center.

2. M. Castleman, "There's Joy in Giving Yourself Away," *Reader's Digest,* November 1995, pp. 207–213.

3. Ibid.

4. K. Sack, "Making Volunteerism Easier for Busy Workers of Today," *New York Times,* 25 November 1995, pp. A1, 11.

5. Ibid.

6. "Campus Clips: Politics Passe for This Year's Freshmen," *On Campus,* 14, (1995), 2 and "1990/1991 Volunteer Center Media Kit." Arlington, VA: National Volunteer Center, abstracted from *Giving and Volunteering in the United States*. Washington, DC: Gallup Organization Studies, Independent Sector, 1828 L Street, NW, Washington, DC 20036, 1990.

7. C. Lawson, "Violence at Home: They Don't Want Anyone to Know," *New York Times,* 6 August 1992, pp. C1, C6.

8. L. Bullock, J. McFarlane, L. H. Bateman, and V. Miller, "The Prevalence and Characteristics of Battered Women in a Primary Care Setting," *Nurse Practitioner,* 14 (1989), pp. 53–56 in C. K. Cassel, Reflections on "Playing God," *Annals of Internal Medicine,* 116 (15 January 1992), pp. 163–164.

Resources for Volunteers

Campus Outreach Opportunity League (COOL)
386 McNeal Hall
University of Minnesota
St. Paul, MN 55108
(612-624-3018)

Provides assistance in setting up campus-based volunteer programs. Published resource book for students in community service.

College Student Volunteers
Campus Compact
Brown University
Box 1975
Providence, RI 02912
(410-836-1119)
An association of colleges/universities
   that have student volunteer programs.

National Society for Internships and
   Experiential Education
Second Floor
122 St. Mary's Street
Raleigh, NC 27605
(919-834-7536)
Provides information on service-learning
   opportunities.

Youth Service America
Suite 900
1319 F Street, NW
Washington, DC 20004
(202-783-8855)
Provides information and promotes
   development of youth service
   programs.

CHAPTER

14 MULTICULTURAL DIVERSITY

■ OUR MULTICULTURAL SOCIETY

The United States has been called the melting pot of the world. It is a country where people of varying races, religions, and ethnic backgrounds have come to work together and build a better society. A recent census report indicates that the percentage of our population that is foreign-born is at its highest level since World War II and accelerating rapidly.[1] Although our country is made up of people from various backgrounds, many of us come from communities and schools where we have experienced little in the way of diversity.

Your college experience may represent the first time that you will share a dormitory room with someone from a different race or work on a course project with someone from a different country. This may be the first time that you find yourself in classes with students who communicate by sign language or commute by wheelchair. Some students may be twenty years older than you are, with tastes in music, politics, clothes, and food that are radically different from your own. It is through your interactions with different types of students that some of the most important learning experiences at college take place. As you come into contact with different ideas, values, and customs, you will reflect upon, evaluate, and forge your own ideals. When you learn to communicate and work with individuals from varied backgrounds, you prepare yourself to function in the real world.

According to the U.S. Department of Labor, the workforce will be changing as women, minorities, and immigrants make up a disproportionate share of the 16 million new workers that will be added to the American economy by the year 2005. Since the growth rate of white males will be the smallest, managers will be trying to accommodate different gender, ethnic, and cultural work styles to meet the needs of the changing workforce.[2]

The increased diversity in the American workforce has been fueled by the declining birth rate of native-born Americans and a greater influx of immigrants, by federal legislation and equal opportunity laws, and by good business sense. The economy needs workers from new sectors as the post-baby boom generation contributes fewer employees to the work place. Corporations are also reaching out to minority workers so that they can tap the diverse American marketplace; exclusively white male management teams cannot come up with the most competitive and creative ways to reach this diversified market. For example, in the New York City region alone, there are separate bilingual, classified telephone business directories catering specifically to Korean, Dominican, Columbian, Portugese, Israeli, Cuban, Filipino, and Russian populations. The national Yellow Pages Publishers' Association in Michigan lists at least 27 Spanish directories and 11 Chinese guides across the country.[3]

If current trends in immigration and fertility continue, the minority and white populations in this country should be roughly equal by the middle of the twenty-first century.[4]

All predictions point to the fact that the workplace will consist of more women, more older workers, more people with disabilities, more African-Americans, more Asian-Americans, and more Hispanic-Americans and other ethnic minorities. If you wish to succeed in this type of work environment, you will have to learn to work effectively with people from a variety of backgrounds. Your college campus is a good place to undertake this kind of learning.

Although learning to work with people from diverse backgrounds can be exciting and fascinating, it is not always a smooth process. You may experience emotions such as anxiety, anger, embarrassment, or guilt as you begin to learn about and appreciate perspectives that differ from your own. It is worth persevering in the effort because you will broaden your experience and learn skills that you will need as you enter the more diverse world of the twenty-first century.

It is also worth persevering because learning to appreciate and tolerate other cultures can help maintain peace on the college campus. Many students have been suspended or disciplined because of racial incidents on campus. Some have even gone to jail. It may be helpful to review some of the material and activities on communication skills and conflict resolution in Chapter 9 if your campus has experienced multicultural tension. Good communication skills, knowledge, and understanding can go a long way to ease tensions and build a cooperative community.

A good place to begin a multicultural education is with a look at some of the problems minority groups have confronted in our society. This chapter will examine racial and ethnic issues, gender issues, and the issues facing people with disabilities and nontraditional students.

■ AFRICAN-AMERICANS

African-Americans constitute the largest disadvantaged minority in the United States. The 31 million African-Americans currently living in the United States make up 12 percent of the population.[5] This population has been growing at a faster rate than the white population, and African-American growth will continue to outstrip white growth. The Census Bureau estimates that this minority's population will grow more than 12 percent between the years 2000 and 2010 whereas white growth during that time will increase by less than 3 percent.[6]

African-Americans constitute a disadvantaged minority when we look at standard economic, educational, and political indicators such as average income, number of years of education completed, numbers represented in the professions, numbers holding political office, and number of families living below the poverty level. Many of these figures are directly related to discrimination experienced by this group. A brief look at the African-American experience in this country will explain some of the gaps between African-American and white standards of living.

History

The first African-Americans to enter the colonies arrived as slaves in 1619. Although African-Americans were freed from slavery after the Civil War, they have continued to face segregation and discrimination in education, employment, housing, and public services.

The Civil Rights Act of 1964 and the Voting Rights Act of 1965 guaranteed African-Americans access to public accommodations (such as restaurants and

ACTIVITY

Identifying Subtle Prejudice

Many subtle forms of discrimination continue on college campuses. Even these less blatant examples of discrimination can leave scars that prevent a person from reaching his or her fullest potential. Place a check next to the examples of prejudice against minority students that you have witnessed. Write in any additional examples that you may have seen on your campus. Your instructor will go around the room and ask you to volunteer examples. Compile a class list of the many forms that racial prejudice may take.

_____   Minority students are often chosen last as laboratory partners.

_____   Students frequently lean across a minority student to ask a white student what the professor said, implying that the minority student would not have understood the point.

_____   White students rarely ask to borrow the notes of minority students.

_____   Minority students are often left out of informal study groups organized by whites.

_____   Some professors and students frequently show surprise when minority students answer correctly in class or do well on exams.

_____   Many white professors and students avoid contact with minority students and are less likely to know them on a personal basis.

_____   Some professors or students interrupt minority students more frequently or do not call on them.

_____   Some professors or students avoid eye contact with minority students or do not acknowledge their comments.

_____   Some professors assume that minority students are not as competent as white students or cannot be in charge of a project.

_____   Minority students are often asked for an opinion on an issue relevant to the minority group as if they were spokespersons for all members of that group.

_____

_____

_____

_____

_____

hotels), voting booths, and jobs. Other federal laws followed that led to the active recruitment of African-Americans into businesses and colleges. These developments resulted in a growing African-American middle class. Despite continued discrimination, African-Americans made important gains in political representation, level of education, and economic status.

Politics

Examples of political gains include the election of an African-American governor in Virginia, an African-American mayor in New York City, and the overwhelming reelection of African-American mayors in Detroit and Los Angeles. African-Americans were appointed to the positions of ambassador to the United Nations, justice of the Supreme Court, and secretary of the Department of Housing and Urban Development. In 1988 and 1992, African-Americans were considered serious candidates for the Democratic presidential nomination. By 1985, African-Americans held 6,000 elective offices (sixty times as many as in 1954). There were 20 African-American members of the House of Representatives, 2 lieutenant governors, and 247 mayors. There were also 325 African-American judges.[7]

Economics

African-Americans have made tremendous strides in the area of economic status, but their standard of living still lags behind that of the white majority. After World War II, the federal government and most state governments passed fair employment statutes that made it illegal to ask questions about race on job applications. These laws made it more difficult for employers to discriminate on the basis of race. In the 1970s, the federal government went further in the battle against racial discrimination by requiring contractors to actually demonstrate that they were not discriminating: Contractors were forced to hire a reasonable number of minority workers. Together with improvements in the level of education, these affirmative action employment policies made it possible for many African-Americans to enter business and the professions; this combination resulted in a growing African-American middle class.

Between 1960 and 1980, the number of African-Americans entering the professions tripled, and the number of businesses owned by African-Americans rose sharply.[8] Unfortunately, the unemployment rate for African-Americans has been double the rate for whites as many farm and industrial jobs traditionally held by African-Americans have disappeared in an increasingly technological and service-oriented American economy.[9] Many people are also concerned that the debate over phasing out affirmative action programs may endanger the gains made by African-Americans.

Increased public assistance programs, the construction of subsidized housing, school lunch programs, Head Start programs, and Medicaid health insurance programs for the poor have raised the standard of living for many African-Americans living in poverty. African-American infant mortality was cut in half between 1960 and 1982. The life expectancy for African-Americans, during the same period, increased by five years to age 69, and the percentage of African-American families living below the poverty level fell from 55 percent in 1959 to 31 percent in 1994.[10, 11]

Despite these impressive economic gains, African-Americans are still more likely to suffer serious health problems, receive public assistance, be victims of crime, rent rather than own their residences, and be convicted of crime. As large increases occur in deaths among African-Americans from AIDS, alcohol, other drugs, and homicides, many researchers fear that the gap between African-Americans and whites will widen.

According to the Census Bureau, almost 33 percent of African-American households are made up of single mothers living with their children. The comparable figure for whites is 8 percent.[12] This tendency for African-American children to live in households without fathers is alarming because households headed by women tend to be poorer than households that are headed by men. A majority of African-American children living in female-headed households are being born and raised in poverty. Children raised in poverty are much more likely to suffer from a variety of childhood illnesses and disturbances, to drop out of school, to be unemployed, and to become involved in crime and drug abuse.

Education

In the eighteenth and nineteenth centuries, the legislatures of some states actually outlawed education for blacks. When African-American children *were* allowed to go to public school, they were forced to attend poorly funded schools where they received an inferior education. On 17 May 1954, the Supreme Court ruled that racial segregation in the schools violated the equal protection clause of the Fourteenth Amendment to the Constitution.

Since then, African-Americans have made impressive progress in raising their level of education. The percentage of African-Americans, ages 25 or over, who completed high school, increased from 13 percent to 59 percent between 1950 and 1984.[13] By 1994, almost 73 percent of African-Americans had completed high school or passed an equivalency test, while the percentage of whites with a high school education was 82 percent.[14] In addition, African-American college enrollment multiplied more than five times between 1960 and 1982.[15] By 1994, almost 38 percent of African-American high school graduates continued on to college, while the comparable figure for whites was 47 percent.[16]

African-Americans on Campus

Despite the impressive gains made by African-Americans, problems of discrimination continue to keep them in a subordinate position. Such problems are evident even in the nation's colleges and universities. The National Institute Against Prejudice and Violence, an independent research group based in Baltimore, reported incidents of racial harassment and violence at more than 300 colleges and universities between 1985 and 1990.[17] Although blatant examples of racism such as cross-burnings, students dressed in Ku Klux Klan costumes, and crude racial jokes broadcast on campus radio stations are becoming less frequent on college campuses these days, more subtle forms of discrimination seem to continue.

Research by Dr. Jaqueline Fleming, a psychology professor at Barnard University, indicates that African-Americans attending white colleges have a more difficult time than African-Americans who attend predominantly African-American schools. These students do not feel accepted on white campuses; they are frequently isolated and choose to socialize in racially-segregated dorms and fraternities; they are often resented.

Whites are often jealous of the extra help given to African-Americans through academic assistance and financial aid programs and also through preferential admissions policies. Racially-divisive incidents such as the Rodney King beating, the O.J. Simpson verdict, and racist remarks made by Louis

Farrakhan in connection with the Million Man March add to the flames of racial unrest on college campuses. The most recent annual report on hate crime statistics compiled by the U.S. Department of Justice lists 211 racially motivated bias crimes that were committed on the nation's campuses. (Almost 60 percent of the racially-motivated bias incidents reported across the country were anti-black, while 31 percent were directed against whites, and 6 percent against Asians.)[18]

African-Americans attending white schools report more dissatisfaction with their academic and social lives. They are less likely to make strong bonds

ACTIVITY

Social Barometer

Despite the impressive gains made by many minority groups, problems of discrimination continue to keep them in a subordinate position. This activity will help you explore some of the sensitive issues that arise in relationships between members of different groups. Your instructor will tape 8½ × 11-inch sheets of paper across a long wall of your classroom. Each sheet will have a large number (1, 2, 3, 4, or 5) written on it. The sheets will be placed so that they are high enough to show their numbers when class members stand under them.

Your instructor will read a statement. Listen to the statement carefully because you will be asked to "take a stand" on it. *There are no wrong or right answers.* Everyone's opinion is equally valuable.

After the statement is read, go and stand under the number that best describes the degree to which you agree or disagree with the statement: 1 = Agree Very Strongly; 2 = Agree; 3 = Neutral; 4 = Disagree; 5 = Disagree Very Strongly. There should be no discussion as you move toward the numbers.

After students have positioned themselves under the numbered sheets of paper, your instructor will ask why you chose to stand where you did. When you respond, try to use "I" statements that indicate why you feel the way you do. No one is to be harassed about his or her views.

Sample statements (you may wish to suggest additional ones):

1. I think interracial dating is wrong.
2. All whites are prejudiced.
3. Racial, ethnic, or religious jokes are harmful.
4. Members of minority groups have a "chip on their shoulders."
5. This campus does not have a problem with racism.
6. I think members of minority groups should not sit together at meals. They are separating themselves.
7. African-Americans are superior to whites in athletics.
8. Minority groups' history and achievements should be represented better in history books.
9. Members of minority groups have as many opportunities as whites in the business world.

This activity is used with permission of Professor Gail McGrail, Coordinator of Students Educating and Empowering for Diversity at the University of South Carolina, who has adapted it for her class.

with faculty members, they graduate in smaller proportions, and they are more likely to lower their vocational goals. On the other hand, predominantly white colleges offer African-American students access to more academic resources and to a broad social network that can lead to useful contacts for jobs and graduate training.

Integrated colleges can also help teach whites to live and work in a multicultural world. Since a diversified cultural experience is useful for both African-Americans and whites, it is worth looking at what we can do to increase the chances for African-American students to succeed on white campuses.

■ HISPANIC-AMERICANS

People who come from Spanish-speaking cultures are the second largest minority group in this country, making up more than 10 percent of the nation's population. There are more than 26 million Hispanic-Americans living in the United States, and the Census Bureau predicts the Hispanic population will increase by 30 percent between 2000 and 2010. In comparison, the white population is expected to grow by less than 3 percent during those years.[19]

Large numbers of Hispanic-Americans live in the southwestern portions of the United States. They make up approximately 38 percent of the population in New Mexico, 26 percent in California and Texas, 19 percent in Arizona, and more than 10 percent of the population in Florida, Colorado, and New York.[20] By the turn of the century, according to various projections, well under half the children in California will be "Anglos," or people of European origin; more than one-third will be Hispanic and, one in eight will be Asian.[21] In some cities, such as San Antonio, El Paso, and Miami, Hispanic-Americans constitute more than 50 percent of the population. These cities have become bilingual in a relatively short time. People who live in these cities will find it useful to learn Spanish to help them succeed in corporate positions, financial institutions, or business.[22]

Mexican-Americans

Although Hispanic-Americans share a common language and religion, they differ in most other respects. The people of Mexican descent living in the United States account for 60 percent of the resident Hispanic population in this country.[23] This group makes up the second largest disadvantaged minority in the United States. Many lived in the Southwest before their lands became part of the United States. Others are part of the immigrant stream that has entered the country since the beginning of the twentieth century. Because many workers in Mexico were unemployed, Mexican immigrants were willing to take jobs as migrant farm laborers or as road workers at low wages that most Americans rejected.

Mexico pays its workers about one-eighth what they can earn in the United States; therefore, immigration to this country, both legal and illegal, remains high. Unemployment has increased among many Hispanic workers during recessions as the "last-hired, first-fired" pattern of business lay-offs takes its toll. In addition, many employers have discriminated against Latino workers in the wake of anti-immigrant legislation such as California's Proposition 187 and rising unemployment among white workers. They often assume that Hispanic-Americans are immigrants or even illegal immigrants.[24] While many of those who immigrated before 1982 have been able to move up the economic ladder, more recent immigrants still earn less than the minimum wage at jobs in factories, warehouses, motels, and lawn services. Many live in segregated communities, and their children attend segregated schools.

Despite these hardships, Mexican-Americans have achieved some political gains. Arizona and New Mexico elected Mexican-American governors, and some Mexican-Americans have been elected to seats in Congress. Although Mexican-Americans have made economic and political progress in the past years, one-quarter still have incomes below the poverty level, one-half of their children drop out of high school, and only 6 percent earn bachelor's or higher educational degrees.[25]

Puerto Ricans

The second largest group of Hispanics in the country has emigrated from Puerto Rico. The United States acquired Puerto Rico from Spain after the Spanish-American War in 1898. Puerto Ricans have enjoyed American citizenship and unrestricted immigration into the United States since 1917. Many Puerto Ricans left their island seeking better economic conditions. Most who arrived were poor and uneducated, and they spoke little English. They could get only the lowest-paying jobs, and approximately half settled in New York City. Although the group continues to have a lower average income than Mexican- or Cuban-Americans, they have made substantial progress in the educational arena as 60 percent of their children graduate from high school, and almost 10 percent earn bachelor's degrees.[26]

Cubans

The third largest group of Hispanics entering the country came as refugees after Fidel Castro took over the government of Cuba in 1959 and confiscated the property of many Cubans. They have continued their emigration as economic conditions in Cuba have deteriorated over the years. Since most of the earlier immigrants were educated or professionally trained, they quickly became self-supporting. Although they started out in the lowest-paying jobs, their children did well in school, attended colleges in above-average numbers, established businesses, banks, and construction companies, and raised their median income close to the average income for the nation as a whole.

Other Hispanic-American Groups

Many Hispanic immigrants continue to enter the United States from other Central and South American countries seeking political freedom and better economic opportunities. The Dominican Republic, for example, where the average salary is $40 per month, sent more people to New York in the 1980s than any other country in the world.[27] Through hard work, some of these immigrants have achieved six-figure incomes within the past decade. For example, more than 120 major supermarkets in the New York area are owned by Dominicans, and they sell more than a billion dollars worth of groceries a year.[28]

Although many Hispanic-Americans have made considerable economic progress, the average family income of Hispanics as a group is still only 60 percent of the median income for white families. More than one out of four Hispanic families live below the poverty line (compared to only one out of nine white families), and the number of Hispanics who have completed four or more years of high school is approximately 29 percent lower than the number for whites.[29]

As mentioned above, discrimination against Hispanic-Americans continues in employment, housing, and education. In addition to ethnic prejudice,

ACTIVITY

Examining the Meaning of Discrimination

Look up and write down a dictionary definition of the words in the list below. Give an example of each term from your own experience, or make up some examples that illustrate each term. For each word, indicate how the term applies to racial, religious, or ethnic minorities, to women, to older people, or to people with physical disabilities. Share the examples with class members in small groups.

Discrimination:

_____

_____

_____

_____

_____

Stereotype:

_____

_____

_____

_____

_____

Racism:

_____

_____

_____

_____

_____

Sexism:

_____

_____

_____

_____

_____

Prejudice:

_____

_____

_____

_____

_____

Apartheid:

_____

_____

_____

_____

_____

This exercise is used with the permission of Professor Arnold Jones and Eileen Quaglino of Ramapo College, who developed it.

Hispanic-Americans may be exposed to racial bias. Most of the ethnically-based bias crimes (71 percent) listed in the Justice Department's most recent national survey of hate crimes were committed against Hispanic individuals. Unfortunately, these crimes occur even at institutions of higher learning: Twenty-two ethnically-biased crimes were reported specifically on university and college campuses in the Justice Department's latest annual report.[30] Many experts believe that this number underestimates the true situation since many bias crimes are not reported. What can colleges do to fight such prejudiced actions?

■ ASIAN-AMERICANS

The percentage of immigrants coming to the United States from Asia has risen dramatically so that Asian-Americans have now replaced Hispanics as the fastest growing minority in the United States. Experts predict that by 2010, Asian-Americans will make up more than 4 percent of the nation's population.[31]

It is difficult to speak of Asian-Americans as one group because they include people who differ in language, culture, and date of immigration. Asian-Americans have traditionally viewed themselves in ethnic (e.g., Japanese or Filipino) terms rather than as one racial group. Twenty-eight different Asian groups have been reported in census studies.

The Chinese were the first to come to the United States, arriving in large numbers during the middle of the nineteenth century. They worked in the gold mines, helped to lay the railroad tracks, and performed various domestic jobs. The Japanese were the second major Asian group to immigrate to the United States, providing a source of cheap labor for businesses on the West Coast at the turn of the century. Korean workers immigrated to Hawaii toward the end of the nineteenth century and filled the need for labor on the sugar cane and pineapple plantations. Filipinos also came to Hawaii to work on the plantations, but by the 1920s immigration from the Philippines to the American mainland had increased.

Racist propaganda and fears that Chinese laborers working for low wages would take jobs away from white workers resulted in the Chinese Exclusion Act of 1882 that prohibited Chinese from immigrating except under special circumstances. Similar fears resulted in acts that eliminated or severely restricted immigration from Japan, Korea, and the Philippines in 1907, 1924, and 1935. More general immigration laws passed in the 1920s were based on national quotas and favored immigrants from northwestern Europe at the expense of those from Asia. It was only in 1965 that the quotas were changed, opening the door to relatives of American residents and immigrants who possessed job skills needed in the United States.[32]

These changes in the immigration laws along with the many refugees created by the wars in Indochina have resulted in the most recent increase in Asian immigration. Although the Chinese and the Filipinos constitute the two largest groups of Asian-Americans in the country, the number of immigrants coming from India, Korea, Vietnam, Kampuchea (Cambodia), and Laos has been growing. California, Hawaii, and New York have the largest Asian-American communities.[33]

Much of the past discrimination against Asian-Americans has been enforced by the federal government. The Chinese were the first ethnic group, for example, to be singled out for exclusion from immigration, and Japanese-Americans were the first American citizens to be imprisoned in concentration camps solely because of their ethnic heritage.[34] This occurred during World War II when some Americans feared that Japanese-Americans might side with Japan against the United States.

Although it is no longer sanctioned by the government, evidence of continuing discrimination can be found in the occupational patterns and income levels of Asian-Americans. When adjusted for educational level, place of residence, number of family members working, and number of hours worked, the incomes of almost all Asian groups fall below the income of whites.

For example, Asian-Americans often earn less than whites who have an equivalent level of education; they tend to be overqualified for their jobs; they are more likely to be found in lower- to middle-level administrative jobs in government; and they are underrepresented in occupations such as upper-level management, communications, politics, and entertainment. When they hold professional and technical jobs, they tend to be paid less than whites who hold the same jobs.[35]

A recent study released by the National Asian Pacific-American Legal Consortium, an organization representing 40 groups, calculated a 35 percent increase in Anti-Asian hate crimes nationally over the previous year.[36] The large increase in Asian immigrants in recent years may have led to the upsurge in hate crimes. In San Francisco County, California, for example, Asians are now the largest minority, exceeding in numbers both blacks and people of Hispanic origin combined, and in northern California, the increase in anti-Asian hate crimes has been particularly steep, doubling over the previous year.[37]

Many incidents begin as simple name-calling and escalate into further violence. Incidents run the gamut from racist graffiti on buildings, to the firebombing of the home of a Chinese councilman in Sacramento, to the serious stabbing of an Asian man by a white youth who vowed, "I'm going to kill me a Chinaman."[38] The Justice Department reports that more than 5 percent of racially-motivated hate crimes nationwide are directed against Asians, and college campuses experienced 211 racially-motivated bias crimes in the most recent year documented.[39] How can we counter such racist attitudes?

Despite many years of discrimination, Asian-Americans have succeeded extremely well in this country and are often portrayed as a "model minority." In terms of the usual measures of socioeconomic achievement such as income, number of years of education completed, prestige of occupation, percentage of members in the workforce, and proportion of white collar workers, Asian-Americans generally meet or even exceed the levels reached by white Americans. Asians are the only racial group whose percentage of students enrolled in college exceeds their proportion of the national population: Asians make up only 3 percent of the country's population, but they represent 5.4 percent of the students enrolled in colleges and universities. Asian-Americans from India are

ACTIVITY

Sharing Your Experience of Discrimination

Your instructor will give each person in the class an index card. On that card, briefly describe one or two incidents of discrimination you have experienced personally or have witnessed. The discrimination may have been based on your race, religion, ethnic group, gender, age, or a physical characteristic (for example, a physical disability, your weight, use of eyeglasses, etc.). Include your reaction to the incident. (What did you do? How did you feel? How did the incident influence your behavior?) Do *not* put your name on the card.

When the class has finished writing, your instructor will collect the cards, shuffle them, and pass them back to class members so that everyone has a card written by someone else. (It is unlikely that you will receive your own card back, but if you do, you may ask your instructor to shuffle a few cards and distribute them again.) Each person will read out loud the card she or he has received, and class members may respond as each card is read.

This activity will demonstrate the many forms that discrimination takes, the effects it has on different people, and how widespread it is in our society.

---

the most educated ethnic group in the country. Japanese- and Chinese-Americans earn higher incomes than whites, and two-thirds of all Asian-Americans were born abroad. [40] This success seems to be based on their willingness to work hard and live frugally and the high values they place on education and family cohesiveness.[41]

In contrast to the success enjoyed overall by Asian-Americans, groups of Asian refugees who have arrived in recent years are less likely to bring the advanced education, technical skills, background in American language and culture, or ties to relatives in American communities that helped earlier Asian immigrants and their children move up so rapidly. For example, the average family income of recent Laotian refugees is much lower than the national average, and among some Hmong communities, the majority of families live below the federal poverty level.[42]

■ OTHER MINORITIES AND INTERNATIONAL STUDENTS

African-Americans, Hispanic-Americans, and Asian-Americans are by no means the only minorities that have experienced discrimination in this country. Many ethnic, racial, and religious minority groups that have immigrated in large numbers started out at the bottom of the economic ladder and experienced barriers to educational, vocational, and social advancement.

Like African-Americans, Hispanic-Americans and Asian-Americans, these other immigrant groups contributed thousands of gifted individuals who made important contributions to science, technology, literature, and the arts. They strengthened the American economy by providing needed skills and labor, and they added to the richness of the American fabric with contributions from their cultures. Immigrants who entered this country contributed their drive, ideals, and motivation to raise American morale. They often worked harder than other Americans in order to succeed economically and strengthen the American economy.

Yet discrimination against immigrant groups continues today. If you are an international student who has come to study in the United States, you may

ACTIVITY

Recognizing the Contributions of Minorities and Peacemakers

Choose an ethnic or minority group (e.g., Japanese, Italians, African-American, women) and research the contributions that two members of that group have made to American society. You may wish to look at contributions in areas such as the arts, theater, sports, entertainment, politics, science, or literature. Or, you may wish to consider the contributions of individuals who were considered peacemakers such as Martin Luther King, Cesar Chavez, Nelson Mandela, Golda Meir, Mother Teresa, Sojourner Truth, Eleanor Roosevelt, and Itzhak Rabin. Write a paragraph about each person you have chosen and share that information in an oral report to your class.

You may wish to list five or six persons who interest you most. In that way, your instructor can approve your choice of person or minority group, before you do your research, to avoid duplications or to assure that a good sampling of minority groups and types of contributions are covered.

Choice of Minority Group or Peacemaker

First Choice: _____

Second Choice: _____

Third Choice: _____

Choice for Area of Contribution (Literature, Politics, Science, etc.)

First Choice: _____

Second Choice: _____

Third Choice: _____

Choice of Famous Person

First Choice: _____

Second Choice: _____

Third Choice: _____

Fourth Choice: _____

Fifth Choice: _____

also run into prejudice. It seems that many new groups go through a period of stereotyping and discrimination after arriving, while their members struggle to achieve economic, academic, and social success. As members of the group succeed and become somewhat assimilated into American culture, discrimination seems to decrease. Most of us no longer remember the discrimination and prejudice that greeted early groups of Jews, Italians, Irish, Poles, and Germans who entered the country. These people had to work hard to overcome poverty as well as academic and social barriers to success.

These days, many politicians are proud to emphasize their ethnic heritage or minority status, but it was not that long ago, in 1960, when many people wondered whether a Catholic (John F. Kennedy) could succeed in being elected president of the United States. More recently, in 1984, a woman (Geraldine Ferraro) ran for the vice presidency for the first time. In 1992 and 1988, African-Americans (Governor L. Douglas Wilder and Jesse Jackson) were seriously considered for the presidential slot and even more recently, Colin Powell, the first African-American Commander of the Joint Chiefs of Staff of the Armed Forces, was proposed as a presidential candidate. Our prejudicial attitudes toward minorities are decreasing somewhat, but we still have a long road to travel before we erase the barriers that keep minority members from contributing to our society as fully and freely as they are able.

■ MINORITY GROUPS ON CAMPUS

Despite the impressive gains made by many minority groups, problems of discrimination continue to keep them in a subordinate position. Such problems are evident even in the nation's colleges and universities. The U.S. Department of Justice enumerates 343 bias-motivated crimes at the nation's universities and colleges in the most recent year of its *Hate Crime Statistics* report. This includes 211 crimes based on race, 55 crimes based on religion, 55 crimes based on sexual orientation, and 22 crimes based on ethnicity. Experts agree that these numbers underestimate the incidence of bias crimes since many are not reported. Approximately 59 percent of the racially-biased crimes reported nationwide were directed against blacks, 31 percent against whites, and 5 percent against Asians.[43]

Although the *1995 Audit* published by the Anti-Defamation League reports the first decrease (17%) in college campus incidents of anti-Semitism since 1987, the 118 incidents listed include examples such as the following: Two Jewish students at the University of Pennsylvania were taunted with anti-Semitic epithets and then threatened with a shotgun, a student received death threats accompanied by anti-Semitic comments at Central Connecticut State University, at the University of Wisconsin, Oshkosh, a student found "Kill the Jews" written on his floor, and the Columbia University *Daily Spectator* published an article describing Jews as "devils," "leeches," and "tricksters."[44]

On many college campuses, the growing number of incidents of discrimination against Jews, women, and gay people indicates that prejudicial attitudes are still strong. At the State University of New York, Binghamton, for example, members of the Jewish Student Union, the Women's Center, and the Gay Peoples' Union led a week-long series of protests over the administration's handling of incidents such as the vandalism of the Jewish Student Union, a report alleging the rape of a female student at a fraternity party, and a threatening homophobic letter posted outside the Gay People's Union.[45]

African-American, female, and homosexual students and faculty at Dartmouth University received threatening and obscene messages: "Go home feminist cunt" was written in toothpaste across one woman's door. A gay student at the University of Hartford was assaulted and suffered a broken cheekbone. Slogans such as "Drink Beers, Kill Queers" were painted on cars and buses.[46]

Extremely sexist letters were sent to women students at the State University of New York (Buffalo) law school. Female Jewish students have been targets of JAP ("Jewish American Princess") baiting at Syracuse University and several other campuses. At the University of Delaware, President Russel C. Jones was asked to resign after making the following remark: "I didn't learn to hate Blacks when I was young, because there weren't many around. I learned to hate Pollacks and some other kinds of people."[47] Polish jokes are still considered funny in some circles. Figure 14.1 relates an account of one courageous teacher's efforts to eliminate such discrimination.[48]

Promoting Minority Students' Success on White Campuses

Special cultural and social programs can help minority students to feel less isolated by reducing mistaken stereotypes and teaching other students more about minority culture. The more we learn about another culture and its individual representatives, the less likely we are to harbor fears, misconceptions, and anger toward that group.

Harvard University's Foundation for Intercultural and Racial Relations spends approximately $300,000 each year on creative programming to help students appreciate and understand multicultural perspectives. Caribbean festivals, appearances by noted members of minority groups such as the Reverend Desmond Tutu of South Africa, performer Debbie Allen, former United Nations Secretary General Javier Perez de Cuellar, and boxer Sugar Ray Robinson, help to destroy racial and ethnic stereotypes.[49] Once we get past cultural stereotypes, relationships with individuals can form the basis for more productive cooperation on campus and in the workplace.

Figure 14.1   *An Experiment in Discrimination*

Discrimination is a vicious practice that can seriously wound both the victims and the perpetrators. Jane Elliot, an elementary schoolteacher in Riceville, Iowa, carried out a courageous experiment with her third-grade classes for a number of years. She decided to teach her students firsthand what the experience of discrimination felt like.

On one day, all brown-eyed children in the class were the underdogs; they experienced discrimination in hundreds of blatant and subtle ways. They wore collars around their necks so that they could be identified from a distance; they were not allowed to play on the gym set if the blue-eyed children wished to use it. They were the last ones in line to go to recess. They were not allowed to use paper cups at the drinking fountain. They were not allowed to play with their blue-eyed friends.

If a brown-eyed child did not know the answer to a question, Ms. Elliott made disparaging comments about all brown-eyed children who never listened and, therefore, learned more slowly than blue-eyed children. If a brown-eyed child forgot an assignment, she generalized about the fact that all "brown-eyes" were forgetful. If a brown-eyed child did not complete an assignment, she commented on how lazy all "brown-eyes" were. On the following day, roles were reversed, and the blue-eyed children became the underdogs.

After the experiment, the children discussed the anger, resentment, rage, and despair they felt when they were the underdogs. They talked about how hurt they were when their friends would not play with them. They recounted how guilty and embarrassed they were when they belonged to the group on top.

One of Ms. Elliot's classes later met for a twenty-year reunion. Even after twenty years, the experience in discrimination had left important marks on the students and had guided many of their actions later in life. This experiment has since been replicated in many settings with adults as well as children. It is a powerful tool that can help us to learn firsthand about the painful emotional wounds that are left by discriminatory practices in our society.

■ A MULTICULTURAL ROLE MODEL

Research shows that students are more likely to succeed in college if they have mentors, or role models, from their own culture who are in positions of power at the institution. It may be difficult for minority students to find role models who work in higher education because the number of minority individuals employed in colleges and universities continues to grow very slowly. You are more likely to succeed in college if you can find a mentor with whom you identify. These mentors can lend a sympathetic ear, give you survival tips, and identify resources that help you to resolve problems. These people have come from where you are now and have succeeded in the system. They can identify differences in the expectations between your culture and the culture you are entering. They can give you advice on how to hold onto your cultural identity and still succeed in the majority system.

As a result of segregation and problems in urban public schools, minority students often enter college with poor academic preparation. Along with white students who have similar problems, they may need extra help with basic academic skills, tutoring in various subjects, and orientation to the expectations and structure of the college. Students from poor families may need information and help in obtaining financial aid. Many colleges have successfully instituted freshmen seminar programs that help all students in these areas. Others have experimented with mentor programs in which successful juniors or seniors are assigned to incoming students to "show them the ropes."

ACTIVITY

Finding a Mentor

Choose a minority group with which you identify. This may be women; African-Americans; Hispanic-Americans; a particular ethnic group, such as Italians or Irish; or a religious group, such as Jews. If you are an international student, you may wish to study your ethnic group. If you have a learning or physical disability, you may wish to focus on the issues affecting these populations. If you are a nontraditional student who is over 25 years of age, you may wish to do this project on the issues that affect older students.

The point of this activity is to realize that all groups experience some degree of culture shock and adjustment in entering a new environment. Find a person, from a group with which you identify, who can help you ease into that adjustment. This person may be a faculty member, an administrator, or a successful upper-level student. If you cannot find someone from your cultural group on campus, look off campus for a person who has succeeded in the system and who may be sensitive to the differences between your culture and the one you are entering. This person can be a professional, a community leader, or a successful businessperson. You may wish to do this activity with more than one interviewee. An upper-level student from your own generation may be able to give you different insights from those of a faculty member or a community leader. Both may be able to share support and helpful information.

Make an appointment to interview that person. The questions listed on the following pages are suggestions, but you may wish to delete some or add others that occur to you. Take the questions with you to the interview; record the answers you receive so that you can share them with your peers, in a class discussion, or with your instructor, through a written assignment.

Interview Questions

1. Is the relationship between faculty and students at this college different from what we might expect in our culture? How do students typically address faculty (Doctor, Professor, Mr. or Ms., by first name)? Are relationships more formal or less formal? Are faculty likely to discriminate against our cultural group?

_____

_____

_____

_____

_____

2. What type of contact do faculty and students have outside of class? Is there social contact? Are faculty available to help students with personal or academic problems that are unrelated to the course?

_____

_____

_____

_____

_____

3. How can I get to know faculty better and work with them more closely?

_____

_____

_____

_____

_____

4. How do relationships among students differ at this college from those among students in our culture? Are they more formal or less formal?

_____

_____

_____

_____

5. What types of social activities do students share? What types of academic activities do they share?

_____

_____

_____

_____

6. Is there anything I should know about differences in relationships between men and women? Are relationships in the majority culture different from those in our culture?

_____

_____

_____

_____

_____

7. What is the best way to meet other students and make friends?

_____

_____

_____

_____

8. What types of problems or frustrations have you encountered because you have come from a different background and tried to adjust to this culture? How have you coped with those problems?

_____

_____

_____

_____

9. What have you found to be the expectations for work at college? How do these expectations compare with those of our culture?

_____

_____

_____

_____

10. Are there differences in how the work must be presented (format, mechanics, appearance, etc.)? Must the work be submitted on time? How should I approach the work (through research, personal experience, summaries, or critiques)?

_____

_____

_____

_____

11. Are there particular behaviors, beliefs, or values among people in our culture that will lead to problems with the majority culture at this college (e.g., differences in dress, assertiveness, eye contact, formality of relations, punctuality)?

_____

_____

_____

12. Are there any clubs, organizations, or activities that you recommend I join in order to help me become more comfortable in this culture?

_____

_____

_____

_____

_____

13. Are there any other people or resources that might be helpful to me in adjusting to this culture?

_____

_____

_____

_____

_____

Individual Effort

The ideas previously described refer to ways that the college community can help minority students succeed in the college environment, but there are also important steps that each student must take to ensure his or her success. Any student needing help must take responsibility for identifying the necessary resources on campus: academic advisors, successful advanced students, key administrators, the financial aid office, the counseling center, or the academic support center, which may offer tutoring services, remedial courses, counseling, or support services such as readers or interpreters. Students should seek out the necessary resources early, and follow through to make sure they get the help they need.

Students should also be wary of assuming that admission to college automatically guarantees success. The dropout rate for minority students is high. Every individual must gain the skills and complete the work to achieve those As and Bs.

Professors will expect minority students to compete with other students even though the academic preparation of some students may be different. There can be no separate standards for minority students despite past discrimination or poor high school preparation. If a double standard were established, employers and graduate admissions officers might assume that minority college graduates are not competitive with majority graduates. Disadvantaged students can learn the skills they need to succeed in the world after college through their own individual efforts and through finding the necessary resources for help.

■ WOMEN

Many people are surprised when they hear a reference to women as a "minority." Women are not a minority in the statistical sense, but they have been treated like a disadvantaged minority group in many ways.

Sex Stereotypes

In our society, many people have very fixed ideas about masculinity and femininity. Men are expected to behave in masculine ways, while women are supposed to respond in feminine ways. These expectations are rigid enough so that many researchers refer to them as sex stereotypes: fixed traits or patterns of behavior that are ascribed to each of the sexes. Stereotypes are important because they influence our perceptions of ourselves, our perceptions of others, and how we actually behave.

If a girl believes that little girls are supposed to be relatively quiet and follow the rules, she may often try to meet her own and others' expectations for subdued behavior and submissiveness. If a little boy knows, on the other hand, that boys are supposed to roughhouse and engage in aggressive behavior, he may also live up to those expectations and unleash his exuberance in physical activities.

Girls and boys are treated differently from the moment they are born. What is the first question that proud, new parents are asked? Right! "Is it a boy or a girl?" From that moment on, female babies are dressed in different colors and clothes so that everyone will immediately recognize their sex and know

---

Figure 14.2   *Categories in Which Girls and Boys Are Raised Differently*

Girls		Boys
Wear pinks and pastels.	*Colors*	Wear blues and primaries.
Wear fragile, delicate clothes (dresses and skirts) that encourage subdued behavior.	*Clothes*	Wear sturdy clothes (pants) that allow freedom and encourage action.
Play with dolls and domestic equipment (dish sets, stoves, etc.).	*Toys*	Play with trucks, sports and action equipment, work equipment (tools, science kits).
Set the table and wash dishes.	*Chores*	Take out garbage and do outdoor, yard work.
Behave quietly, in a dependent, submissive manner; make marriage and family life goals.	*Expectations*	Behave in an independent, assertive manner; make school achievement and career life goals.
Behave "properly" and "safely."	*Restrictions*	Bend rules of etiquette; have later curfews; go out unescorted.

how to treat them. Girls receive different toys, and they are assigned different chores in the household.

Boys receive more roughhousing when they play with their parents. They are given more praise and more punishment. Their chores involve more outside work. Their clothes are sturdier and allow them more freedom. Fewer restrictions are placed on their behavior, and they are encouraged to explore independently. They also receive more parental pressure to achieve in school and careers. Figure 14.2 presents some of the categories in which girls and boys are raised differently.

Eventually, the different expectations and stereotypes have important consequences for the way men and women behave in social relationships, the types of education they choose, the careers they pursue, the amount of money they earn, and how they feel about themselves.

Many researchers believe that stereotypes restrict both sexes and make it difficult for men as well as women to achieve their full human potential. To the extent that you try to live up to certain idealized expectations for men or women in general, you may put pressure on yourself to achieve certain goals that do not truly reflect your needs. You may limit the way you express yourself in personal and professional relationships, and you may restrict the range of hobbies and interests you pursue.

Many research studies have shown surprising consistency about interests and characteristics that are judged masculine and feminine by college students, but such stereotypes tend to be oversimplifications. There is little

ACTIVITY

Recognizing Stereotypes and Identifying Ideal Characteristics

1. Look at the list of personality characteristics and interests on page 316. In the first column, mark the items that you believe are more characteristic of men in general, and in the second column, mark the items you believe apply more to women. Are the items for men and women different? Are there any characteristics that you feel both sexes share?

2. Now that you have noted some of the general characteristics that are often ascribed to women and men, go over these characteristics again and list those items that you would find desirable in the ideal woman and the ideal man in the last two columns of page 316. Are the two lists different?

3. Bring the exercise lists to class so that your instructor can tally the number of students who listed given traits or interests for men or women. Discuss the following questions with your classmates:

- Is there general agreement among class members about which traits are more characteristic of men or women?
- Do your perceptions agree with those of your classmates?
- Do you believe that the lists you have compiled reflect true differences between men and women? Do you know men or women whose personalities or interests do not fit the stereotypes?
- Which lists, the ones for men or the ones for women include traits that are more highly valued in our society?
- Are there differences between the traits seen as desirable for the ideal woman and those seen as desirable for the ideal man?

	More Characteristic of Men	More Characteristic of Women	More Characteristic of the Ideal Man	More Characteristic of the Ideal Woman
Aggressive	_____	_____	_____	_____
Independent	_____	_____	_____	_____
Emotional	_____	_____	_____	_____
Easily influenced	_____	_____	_____	_____
Active	_____	_____	_____	_____
Submissive	_____	_____	_____	_____
Competitive	_____	_____	_____	_____
Logical	_____	_____	_____	_____
Manipulative	_____	_____	_____	_____
Passive	_____	_____	_____	_____
Easily hurt	_____	_____	_____	_____
Weak	_____	_____	_____	_____
Adventurous	_____	_____	_____	_____
Tough	_____	_____	_____	_____
Self-confident	_____	_____	_____	_____
Gentle	_____	_____	_____	_____
Shows leadership	_____	_____	_____	_____
Sneaky/devious	_____	_____	_____	_____
Ambitious	_____	_____	_____	_____
Dependent	_____	_____	_____	_____
Talkative	_____	_____	_____	_____
Quiet	_____	_____	_____	_____
Sensitive to others	_____	_____	_____	_____
Sloppy	_____	_____	_____	_____
Decisive	_____	_____	_____	_____
Strong	_____	_____	_____	_____
Compassionate	_____	_____	_____	_____
Neat in personal habits	_____	_____	_____	_____
Interested in literature	_____	_____	_____	_____
Enjoys sports	_____	_____	_____	_____
Interested in math and science	_____	_____	_____	_____
Enjoys art	_____	_____	_____	_____
Other traits	_____	_____	_____	_____

ACTIVITY

Imagining Your Ideal Spouse or Partner

This exercise will help you become aware of your own values in the area of sex roles. Many of us are not conscious of the biases we carry and bring to our relationships.

1. In the following space, write a short paragraph describing your concept of the ideal spouse or partner. List the characteristics, values, and strengths *you* (not your friends, parents, or society) would look for in that person. The Merriam-Webster dictionary defines the word *ideal* as existing only in the mind, lacking practicality, or relating to perfection. So, let your imagination fly, think about the best of all possible situations, and be as honest as you can.

You might want to consider the following questions about the ideal spouse or partner:

- Would your partner work?
- What would he or she do?
- What attitudes or beliefs would your partner hold?
- What would his or her personality be like?
- Would your partner be older or younger than you?
- What kind of family would he or she come from?
- What physical or sexual characteristics would your partner have?
- Would you be your partner's first "real" love?
- What kinds of things would you enjoy doing together?
- What intellectual interests would your partner have?
- What beliefs and goals would be important to your partner?

2. Does your ideal partner reflect any of the stereotyped male or female characteristics you listed above? Why do you think the characteristics you chose might be attractive or important to you?

_____

_____

_____

_____

_____

_____

_____

_____

_____

_____

_____

3. If you are married, living with a partner, or dating someone special, you might want to consider how close that person comes to the stereotyped ideal for males or females. How close does your partner come to the ideal you described? Remember that few people ever find a perfect match. How close do you think you might be to your partner's ideal?

_____

_____

_____

_____

_____

_____

_____

_____

_____

_____

_____

_____

evidence to support generalized differences between the sexes. Where differences do exist, they may be the result of past experience and training.

As women enter the world of sports, for example, they are catching up in many of the areas where men have traditionally excelled. (The best female performance in the marathon run improved by more than 20 percent between 1970 and 1982; the best male performance improved by only 0.1 percent. In 1973, Billy Jean King beat Bobby Riggs, the men's champion tennis player, in a celebrated "match between the sexes," and more recently, Ginny Doyle passed the national record for men and women by making 66 straight freethrows in basketball.[50] Hall and Lee's study of girls who had spent a year or more in a coeducational physical fitness program found that they performed at similar levels to boys on most physical fitness items.) In any event, strength and size do not carry as much importance in our technological society where much of the work that was previously done with brute strength is now accomplished by the press of a button.

The traditional stereotypes are simply not accurate about the two sexes on the whole, and they are certainly likely to be wrong about any given individual. You certainly know some women who are stronger or more aggressive or more decisive than some of the men that you know. You also undoubtedly know men who are more sensitive, more easily influenced, and more compassionate than some of the women that you know. You have probably met some women who are better than men at special skills like map reading, picking out a figure hidden in a complex background, or catching a ball, while you probably also know some men who perform better than women on tests of manual dexterity, speed of perception, and verbal fluency.

Many professionals believe that the list of traits for the ideal man and the ideal woman is the same. There is one list of traits for what constitutes the ideal mature adult, and this list includes the best traits that are traditionally ascribed to both males and females. When this view is adopted, men need no longer fit the "strong, silent" stereotype. They become free to express their emotions as fully as women so that they can experience the satisfactions of intimate relations with their lovers, children, and friends. They need no longer live with the stress of pretending that they are never afraid and never depressed. When this happens, they need no longer feel pressured to always take charge, to always have the answers, to be the sole supporters of their families.

In order for men to be freed from the restrictions of sex stereotyping, however, women must also be released from false generalizations about what they can and cannot do. They must be allowed to show their strength and competence to achieve in their careers. They must receive help with household duties and child care so that they are not required to shoulder the sole responsibility for the domestic sphere at the same time that they are trying to advance professionally. They must be allowed to participate in decisions and take the initiative in important projects. Men and women will be free to pursue their full potential only when we are able to let go of some of the false stereotypes about what constitutes masculine and feminine behavior.

Recent research indicates that changes may be occurring in some of the traditional sex stereotypes. As the traditional stereotypes become looser, there does seem to be some movement towards androgyny: combining the best traits associated with each of the sexes into a single individual. Thus it may become acceptable for one person, male or female, to be warm, compassionate, and affectionate and also independent, assertive, and self-reliant.

Discrimination in the Classroom

Although some of the stereotypes may be changing, many of the discriminatory practices based on them still exist. A landmark study by Professors Serbin and O'Leary showed that discriminatory practices exist even at the nursery school level, where teachers treat boys and girls very differently. Boys received more attention from the teachers, they were praised more often, and teachers were twice as likely to have extended conversations with them. Teachers were also twice as likely to give boys detailed directions on how to do things for themselves.[51]

A three-year study by Professors Myra and David Sadker showed that the same trends continued through elementary school.[52] The Sadkers evaluated teaching in more than one hundred fourth-, sixth-, and eighth-grade classrooms. Their researchers found that teachers were giving boys more academic help, that they praised boys more than girls, and that they were more likely to accept boys' comments during class discussions.

Teachers responded differently, for example, when boys and girls called out answers. If girls called out answers, they were reprimanded with comments such as, "In this class we don't shout out answers, we raise our hands." When boys called out answers, teachers were much more likely to accept their answers. It is no wonder that boys are eight times more likely to call out in class than girls![53] They are rewarded for behaving in this way, while girls are punished for this behavior.

Although many people believe that sexism in the classroom died out in the 1970s, clearly it still exists. The Sadker's study showed that boys were encouraged to dominate the class. Although the teachers thought that girls were talking more, detailed counts of classroom interactions showed that boys were outtalking the girls by a ratio of three to one![54] The teachers were unconsciously giving boys a superior learning experience. This was true in all subject areas, at all grade levels, and in all communities. Sexual stereotypes can affect our perceptions and behaviors even though we are not aware of them.

A report by the American Association of University Women that examined more than 1,000 publications about girls and education, including hundreds of research studies, also concluded that teachers pay less attention to girls than boys; many science teachers and some math teachers tend to ignore girls in favor of boys, school textbooks still ignore or stereotype women, and some tests remain biased against girls, hurting their chances of scholarships and getting into college.[55] For example, despite the 43-point gap that favors men on the SATs, women get better grades in identical courses.[56]

Sex stereotypes also influence instruction at higher levels of the educational system. Sociologist Safilios-Rothschild found similar results in her study of sex desegregation at the Coast Guard Academy to those found in nursery, elementary, and high schools.[57] Teachers tended to give detailed instructions to male students on how to complete an assignment; when female students needed help, the instructors did the job or operated the equipment for them.

Despite this discrimination, women seem to be doing better in school. A fifteen-year follow-up of the high school class of 1972 conducted by the U.S. Department of Education Office of Research reported that women's mean high school rank exceeded that of men by at least 10 points, that among students who took more than four semesters in math, science, and foreign language, women outranked men in the top quintile of all three categories by at least 20 percent, that the percentage of women who earned bachelor's degrees in four years was 12 percent higher than men, that women's GPAs at the time they received their bachelor's degree were higher than men's, even when majors like engineering, science, math, and business were included, and that, on the average, women who went on to graduate school had higher GPAs than men. Despite all of these educational achievements, 13 years after graduating, women without children earned, on the average, 32 percent less than men.[58]

Roberta Hall and Bernice Sandler[59] have reported that many prominent colleges and universities are conducting research to measure the extent to

ACTIVITY

Recognizing Sexist Behavior in the Classroom

Hold a group discussion and compare notes with your classmates. To what extent have you noticed any of the following practices in your classes? Give examples from your experience. How might such practices make it difficult for female students to receive an education equal to that of male students?

You might consider some of these discussion questions about sexist behavior in the classroom:

- Are faculty more likely to call on male students?
- Do instructors tend to ask the same types of questions of both male and female students?
- Do female students receive the same encouragement as male students to think for themselves?
- Do female students receive as much praise, encouragement, and feedback as male students on their academic work?
- Are female students interrupted more frequently than male students?
- Do professors make eye contact with male students more when they are asking a question of the class? (This would encourage male students to participate more in class discussion.)
- Are some instructors more likely to remember the names of male rather than female students?
- Are instructors equally likely to choose female students as they are to choose male students for research assistants and to give them the same types of responsibilities?
- Do advisors discourage female students from enrolling in traditionally masculine or "hard" majors?
- Do some teachers use sexist humor to liven up their classes?
- Do some instructors make discriminatory or disparaging remarks about female students or their abilities in their courses?
- Are advisors more likely to contact male rather than female students for job openings or other professional opportunities?
- Do females receive more criticism of their work from faculty than males?
- Do advisors encourage female students to enroll in typically feminine majors?
- Are male faculty more likely to call on "good-looking" females more often?

which their female students are facing discrimination in the educational environment. Women are still reporting differences, such as those listed in the activity above, in the ways they are treated by their instructors.

As a result of such discriminatory practices, universities are finding that many female undergraduates feel less confident about their preparation for graduate school than do the male students in their classes. Female students continue to avoid many fields (e.g., math and science) that have been traditionally identified as masculine, and they lower their academic and career goals during their college years.

Women continue to be viewed as less capable by both men and women in our society. A series of studies have been done where two groups of people were asked to evaluate items such as articles, resumés, paintings, and so on. One group was led to believe that the work was associated with a woman, while the second group of evaluators believed that the identical work belonged to a man. Regardless of the items, when they were ascribed to a man, identical items were rated higher than when the evaluators thought they belonged to a woman.

Discrimination in the Workplace

Such prejudicial attitudes toward women and their work have followed women into the workplace. Fifty-eight percent of the women over the age of 16 are employed, and they constitute 45 percent of the work force.[60] Women have entered the labor force in record numbers, and the percentage of growth for women who are employed is projected to grow by twice the annual rate of the men's employment participation through the year 2005.[61] Yet despite passage of the Equal Pay Act of 1963 and Title VII of the Civil Rights Act of 1972, which prohibits sex discrimination in employment, women are still earning only 72 cents for every dollar earned by men![62]

This difference in salaries for males and females is not based on years of education, type of occupation, number of hours worked, years of experience, or any other relevant variables. Men earn more money than women, even when all of these factors are taken into account.

For example, among university professors, the gap between men's and women's salaries is about 30 percent. Even when both sexes reach the rank of full professor, women continue to earn 10 percent less than their male colleagues. [63] In managerial and professional positions, the median weekly earnings for women are 74 percent of their male counterparts', and in technical, sales and administrative occupations, they earn only 67 percent of male wages.[64] "Workforce 2000," a study commissioned by the U.S. Department of Labor, predicts that by the year 2000, the average female salary will still lag 74 percent behind the average male salary.[65]

People often assume that a man needs to earn more because he is supporting a family, but according to a recent Harris survey, more than half of the employed women, including single and married women, reported that they provided at least half of their household's income. Many women work because their families cannot live on their husband's salaries alone. Even among the married women surveyed, 48 percent said they contributed half or more of the family's income.[66] In addition, the number of households headed by women has been rising steeply, and the proportion of families with children headed by women living below the federal poverty level is almost 50 percent.[67]

The major explanation for the discrepancy between male and female earnings seems to lie in the fact that women and men have different occupations and that female-dominated occupations are paid less than male-dominated occupations. A man who dropped out of high school may well earn a salary similar to a woman college graduate because he is more likely to be a union worker or craftsman whereas she is more likely to be a nurse or a teacher. Women in the work force tend to be concentrated in five occupations: secretary, bookkeeper, elementary school teacher, waitress, and retail sales clerk.

Men's occupations are spread over a wider range of categories, and the occupations that they dominate are more highly paid than the occupations dominated by women. Women constitute 99 percent of dental assistants, but only 9 percent of dentists; 94 percent of registered nurses, but only 24 percent of physicians; 85 percent of data entry keyers, but only 33 percent of computer programmers; 85 percent of elementary school teachers, but only 41 percent of college and university teachers.[68]

Women are making progress. For example, a recent survey of freshmen indicated that more women than men planned to earn medical degrees, whereas in 1965, male premed students outnumbered women 4 to 1.[69] Women now represent 50 percent of accountants, 34 percent of journalists, 38 percent of psychologists, and 27 percent of lawyers.[70] Women will continue, however, to be second-class citizens with regard to power, property, and prestige unless they begin to enter the male-dominated occupations in larger numbers or unless female-dominated occupations are reevaluated so that they are compensated on a similar basis to male-dominated occupations. Until the traditional sex stereotypes are re-evaluated, both men and women will continue to suffer, as members of neither sex will be able to develop to their fullest human potential.

■ STUDENTS WITH DISABILITIES

Examine Figure 14.3 and see what the individuals listed in it have in common (the answer is given at the end of the chapter).

The Constitution of the United States guarantees equal opportunity for all Americans. For 49 million Americans with disabilities, this guarantee has proved elusive. Members of this minority group are undereducated, underemployed, unable to socialize as much as other Americans, and unable to develop their fullest potential.

A disability is a health-related condition that prevents a person from participating fully in work, school, or other normal activities. A Harris poll reports that 60 percent of Americans with disabilities feel that life has gotten much better for them over the past ten years; many, however, are still not happy with the quality of the lives they lead.[71] Life for people with disabilities is less satisfying and more restricting than for the general population; as a result, they often feel shut out of mainstream American society.

Americans with physical disabilities are unable, for example, to socialize as much as other Americans. Two-thirds of them report that their physical disability keeps them from getting out to socialize or to attend cultural and sports events as much as they would like. Almost 60 percent of those surveyed did not go to the movies even once in the past year (as compared to only 30 percent of the general American population who missed out on movies). Over 70 percent failed to attend any sports events (compared to 44 percent of the

Figure 14.3 *What Do These People Have in Common?*

Hans Christian Andersen[93]	Jose Feliciano	Itzak Perlman
Beethoven	Lou Ferrigno	Mackenzie Phillips
Alexander Graham Bell	Sigmund Freud	Jason Robards
Julius Ceasar	Annie Glenn	Nelson Rockefeller
Roy Campanella	Ernest Hemingway	Auguste Rodin[93]
Agatha Christie	Katharine Hepburn	Franklin D. Roosevelt
Leonardo Da Vinci[93]	Stephen Hopkins	Wilma Rudolph
Sandy Duncan	Bruce Jenner	Daniel Travanti
Thomas Edison	Helen Keller	Herve Villechaize
Albert Einstein[93]	Josh Logan	Woodrow Wilson
Dwight Eisenhower[93]	Mary Tyler Moore	Stevie Wonder
Nanette Fabray	George Patton[93]	William Butler Yeats[93]

This exercise is printed by permission of AHSSPSE, 1984 (American Handicapped Student Services in Post Secondary Education).

general American population).[72] Although access to public transportation has improved considerably, it is still either unavailable or inaccessible for many of our citizens who have disabilities.

The Americans with Disabilities Act which went into effect in 1992 helped to expand the independence of people with disabilities. It bans discrimination on the basis of physical or mental handicap in employment, public accommodations, transportation, or telecommunication services. This law has resulted in changes such as widening aisles in supermarkets to accommodate wheelchair users, installing Braille signs in elevators, widening doorways to restrooms and elevators in public buildings, lowering counter tops and installing ramps to insure accessibility for wheelchair users. As a result, three-quarters of people with disabilities think that access to public facilities, such as restaurants, theaters, stores, and museums has improved. [73]

Students with Learning Disabilities

A learning disability is a disorder that affects the way people process information. "Learning disabled adults receive inaccurate information through their senses and/or have trouble processing that information. Like interference on the radio or a fuzzy T.V. picture, incoming or outgoing information may become scrambled as it travels between the eye, ear, or skin and the brain."[74] A learning disorder is not a form of mental retardation (these individuals have average or above average intelligence), it is not an emotional disorder, and it is not caused by a problem with eyesight, hearing, or mobility.

Whereas more than 9 percent of first-year college students report having a disability, the largest growth has occurred among students reporting a learning disability: almost one-third of disabled students, or 3 percent of all college freshmen.[75] Figure 14.4 gives an example of the difficulty a person with a learning disability may face in reading because of letter reversals, letter substitutions, and misperceptions in spacing.

Figure 14.4 *Difficulties in Reading Caused by a Learning Disability*

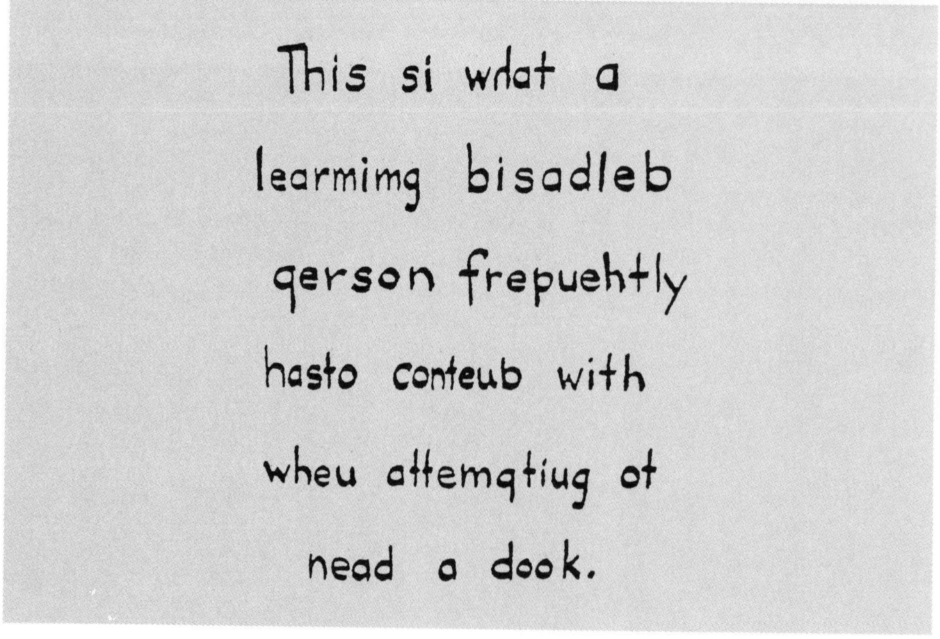

This si wdat a
learmimg bisadleb
qerson frepuehtly
hasto conteub with
wheu attemqtiug ot
nead a dook.

An adult with a learning disability typically has problems in one or more of these areas: Reading, comprehension, spelling, writing, math computation, and problem solving. She or he may also experience difficulty in time management, organizational skills, and social skills. Adults with learning disabilities are often doubly frustrated because, in addition to their problems in performance, they may have to prove that their invisible disability is just as problematic as more visible challenges like deafness, blindness, or paraplegia.

We usually assume that if a person understands individual words, he or she will understand the meaning of a passage made up of those words, but that is not the case for many individuals with a comprehension learning disability because of difficulties in processing or making connections between words. For example, a student with a learning disability processing the question "Who was the first president of the United States?" may go through the following steps: 'Who'—it must be a person; 'was'—he must be dead; 'the first'—oh, at the beginning; 'president'—the one in Washington.[76] While the disabled student is doing all this laborious processing, the rest of the class has long since answered the question and gone on to another topic. Figure 14.5 gives an example of a passage that people who do not have a learning disability might find difficult to process even though they know all of the individual words in it.[77]

One resource for individuals who suspect they may have a learning disability is the Parents Educational Resource Center in San Mateo, California, founded by millionaire discount stock broker Charles Schwab and his wife, Helen. Schwab, a graduate of Stanford University, suffers from severe dyslexia or reading disability. The Center has put together "Bridges to Reading," a package of pamphlets, audiotapes, and checklists that offers the latest information on reading disabilities in addition to practical strategies and tips. The Resource Collection for Learning Differences at the San Francisco Main Library which includes audiotapes, videotapes, printed materials, and an on-line database of information and references offers further resources in the area.[78]

Figure 14.5   *An Analogy for Learning Disability: Knowing Individual Words Does Not Insure That We Will Be Able to Easily Process a Passage Made Up of Those Words*

23 Known Words

are	draws	graph	often
between	variation	if	with
consists	one	isolated	table
continuously	points	known	values
corresponding	relation	making	variables
curve	set	only	

Paragraph Consisting of Those 23 Known Words

If the known relation between the variables consists of a table of corresponding values, the graph consists only of a set of isolated points. If the variables are known to vary continuously, one often draws a curve to show the variation.

Employment and Income

One of the most important areas where people with disabilities experience a disadvantage is in work. Sixty-eight percent of working-age Americans with disabilities are not working. This unemployment rate is higher than for any other minority group in the country, and among those disabled individuals who *are* employed, only one-third work full-time.[79]

Many Americans who have disabilities report that they have experienced job discrimination. Forty percent say that they are not able to work because employers will not believe that they can do a good job. Others feel that they do not have the necessary education, the marketable skills, or the access to transportation necessary to get a job.[80]

Workers with disabilities have demonstrated their productivity and ability to work in the past. During World War II, when the country's labor pool was drained of potential workers, many businesses realized that those who had traditionally been excluded from the work force made excellent workers. Large numbers of workers with disabilities (as well as women and minority group members) pitched in to maintain the production that helped us win the war.

Now America is facing competition in a global economy and the end of the postwar baby boom. Companies are finding that skilled workers who have disabilities make valuable employees. More than three-quarters of corporate managers give disabled employees a "pretty good" or "excellent" rating. Eighty-two percent rate the overall job performance of disabled employees as "about the same" as other employees; 6 percent of the managers say their performance is better, and only 2 percent report that it is worse.[81]

Federal legislation has joined with economic pressures to open employment opportunities for individuals with disabilities. As of 1994, the Americans with Disabilities Act passed by Congress applies to all businesses with 15 or more employees. It bans discrimination on the basis of physical or mental handicap in employment. Once these workers are hired, they are entitled to extra support and accommodation from employers as long as they are able to perform the essential job requirements.[82] Many companies are finding that making the reasonable accommodations that allow employees with disabilities to work makes good economic sense. Approximately half of the companies surveyed say their costs to accommodate people with disabilities have increased "a little" as a result of the Americans With Disabilities Act, while almost one-third reported no change at all.[83]

Some companies have cut the legs on drafting tables to make them accessible to workers in wheelchairs; other companies have installed inexpensive ramps for wheelchairs or dog walks for Seeing Eye dogs. Many companies are taking advantage of advances in computer technology that allow workers with physical disabilities to transfer work performed at home to the company's terminals. A national search for new technology to accommodate individuals with disabilities at home and at work has spurred development of devices like a telephone that allows deaf people to see messages typed in by callers on touch-tone phones, a computer keyboard with large, wide keys for people who have difficulty manipulating a standard keyboard, a software system which generates sound and speech to help a blind user manipulate a computer's rotary control or mouse, and a communication system that allows individuals with severe disabilities to communicate by using eye movements.[84] The ideas that appeal to the widest market are the keys to developing affordable technology for individuals who have disabilities. For example, the ramps cut into sidewalks are not used only by people in wheelchairs; they are also helpful to mothers with strollers, bicycle riders, and people making deliveries.

ACTIVITY

Recognizing Signs of a Learning Disability

Carol Frome, coordinator of the State University of New York-Plattsburg Learning Center, has developed a list of characteristics, that when they arise in combination, may indicate the need to refer students for extra help or diagnosis. If a number of these seem familiar, you may wish to consult with a staff member at your campus' Learning Center or Office of Specialized Services.

■ Poor, illegible or nearly illegible handwriting

■ Organizational problems, as evidenced by wrinkled papers, a messy backpack or messy appearance

■ Poor social skills and immaturity

■ Letter and number reversals

■ Unable to follow a *string* of instructions

■ Tangential thinking, making comments unrelated to the conversation

■ Able to explain something, but unable to put it on paper

■ Able to explain something one minute, but then "forgets" it the next

■ A fierce need to be right, intellectually stubborn, without evidence of reason

■ Time and again, people saying, "What's wrong with you? You aren't trying. What are you talking about? C'mon, you could do it a minute ago! Don't you have any common sense? Get to the point!"

These accommodations often save employers money as workers who have become physically disabled can be rehired in order to reduce the costs of training new workers. Such measures also reduce the high costs of disability payments. Workers with physical disabilities who are employed more than make up for the cost of their rehabilitation by paying income taxes and lowering the cost of support payments.

There is a close relationship between unemployment and income. One-quarter of the people with disabilities under the age of 65 must rely on government or insurance payments for some part of their income; as a result, they are poorer than other groups. Forty percent of adults with disabilities live in households with earnings of $15,000 or less, compared with 18 percent of adults without disabilities.[85]

Education

One of the important factors that affects employment and income is education. As a group, individuals with disabilities have made considerable progress in educational achievement. Three-quarters have completed high school, and 44 percent have completed some college (compared to only 47 percent of the nondisabled population).[86]

Progress is occurring in this area, once again, due to federal legislation. We are beginning to see more students with disabilities on campus. The Rehabilitation Act of 1973 first guaranteed to children with disabilities an appropriate education in the public schools. Section 504 of the law further stipulates

ACTIVITY

Simulating a Physical Disability

One way to appreciate some of the difficulties that students with physical disabilities experience on a daily basis is to simulate a physical disability for a few hours or for a day. If your campus has extra wheelchairs, try borrowing one and experience the challenge of getting around campus without the use of your legs for a class period. A way to simulate a motor disability is to tape your thumbs to your palms with masking tape and then trying to perform a task that requires fine motor skills like writing, tying shoelaces, or handling money. Or wear earplugs and see how well you can lip-read the contents of a lecture, a discussion, or a conversation. You might simulate blindness by having a friend act as your guide while you go around campus for a few hours blindfolded. Or wear a "blindfold" made of wax paper to simulate a visual impairment.

As you go through your simulation, try to focus on the feelings you are experiencing: frustration, anger, humiliation, embarrassment, anxiety, jealousy, exhaustion, irritation, or confusion. Come back to class and discuss the simulation and your feelings with your classmates. You may now be in a better position to identify with students who have physical disabilities and experience these stresses and humiliations on a daily basis.

---

that all colleges and universities that receive federal funding must be accessible to qualified students who have physical disabilities. Before this law was passed, most schools were not accessible to students with disabilities because of attitudes and policies that did not allow them to get past the admissions process or because of physical barriers that made it impossible for them to negotiate their way around the campus.

Many administrators believed, for example, that students with physical disabilities could not become teachers because they would not be able to handle their classes during a fire drill. Others closed off careers in engineering and science to blind or deaf students because they believed that their physical disability would be dangerous around specialized scientific equipment. Campuses were constructed so that students in wheelchairs could not get into classrooms or bathrooms. Textbooks were not available in braille or on taped cassettes. Interpreters who translated lectures into sign language were not available on campus. Recorders were not available to help students with learning disabilities write their exams.

The government's equal opportunity laws have literally opened the doors of higher education to students with disabilities. In 1978, less than 3 percent of the freshmen enrolled full time in college reported that they had a disability. More recently, the proportion of freshmen was greater than 9 percent, while the number of all graduate and first-year professional students reporting a disability represented 4 percent.[87]

Success for Students with Disabilities

As students with disabilities enter college in larger numbers, institutions and instructors must provide services that will give these students an equal opportunity to obtain a college education. Electric doors, ramps, elevators, and

ACTIVITY

Simulating a Learning Disability

You are probably familiar with the game of Simple Simon, in which you follow the leader's instructions as long as he or she says, "Simple Simon says . . ." If the leader does not say "Simple Simon says . . ." you should not do what he or she says or does.

This particular version of Simple Simon is a bit more challenging: we are going to reverse left and right because many people with learning disabilities have to concentrate carefully in order to avoid reversing left and right. They may often read the word *bad* as *dab* or transpose material from the right-hand side of the board to the left-hand side of their papers.

So now, if your leader says, "Raise your right foot," what are you going to do? I hope that you all said "Nothing," because you should remember not to do anything unless "Simple Simon says" you should do it. Now, what would you do if Simple Simon says, "Raise your right foot"? Right! Raise your *left* foot.

We are also going to reverse the directions for the words *over* and *under,* to show you how frustrating many students with a learning disability find it when they have to process teachers' instructions and class materials through information channels that do not come easily to them. If your leader says, "Simple Simon says put your left hand over your right elbow," what are you going to do? Think about this now. I hope that you will put your *right* hand *under* your *left* elbow. Now that you have practiced with the rules a bit, we are ready to begin our "simple" game. Some sample instructions might include the following:

- Put your right hand over your left ankle. Ah ha! Did some of you forget about "Simple Simon says"?
- Simple Simon says, "Hold your right elbow and touch your index finger to your right eye." Did we lose some of our students there?
- Simple Simon says, "Hop on your left foot."
- Simple Simon says, "Hold your right hand."
- Hold your left hand.
- Touch your head with your right hand.
- Simple Simon says, "Put your right hand over your chin."
- Simple Simon says, "Touch your head with your left hand."
- Put your left hand under your right ankle.
- Simple Simon says, "Hold your left ankle and touch your eye with your right hand."
- Simple Simon says, "Touch your right hip."
- Touch your left hip.

It seems that many of you are making mistakes or responding very slowly. I cannot understand why you are having difficulty with such an easy game! If you are having trouble following directions, come to the front of the room where the teacher can give you extra help (and where the other students can see just how much trouble you are having following "simple" instructions). (Students with learning disabilities are often singled out and ridiculed in this way.)

How do you feel after ten minutes of this game? Are you experiencing some confusion or frustration? Do you feel overwhelmed or embarrassed? How would you feel if this were not just a game, but some type of assignment where success was important to you? Might you become irritable? Would you lose your temper or give up because it was so difficult to learn what everyone else was doing with ease?

This activity is adapted from "Simulations Approximating Learning Disabilities" by D. Raschke and C. Dedrick, *TEACHING Exceptional Children,* Summer, 1986, pp. 266–271. Copyright 1986 by the Council for Exceptional Children. Reprinted with permission.

special parking areas may be needed so that students who use wheelchairs are able to get around the campus. Some allowances must be made for students with disabilities. Some of these students may occasionally arrive late to class because it is difficult to commute by wheelchair, negotiate icy walks with a cane, or wait for assistance with dressing or personal hygiene.

Visually impaired, or blind, students may require tape-recorded textbooks or classmates who take duplicate sets of notes with carbon paper. Deaf students may need to attend class with an interpreter, and students with hand-function impairments may require a recorder or a computer to write exams. Students with learning disabilities may need extra time to read or type assignments due to their specific learning disabilities.

The attitudes of the students on campus can also make a tremendous difference in the success of students who have disabilities. If you tend to avoid eye contact with these students because you feel awkward, they may begin to feel isolated. Try saying "hello," and start a conversation instead. Talk directly to the person with the disability, not to someone (e.g., an interpreter) who is accompanying him or her. If you are having a conversation with someone in a wheelchair, step back to prevent the wheelchair user from straining neck muscles to make eye contact with you. If you will be having an extended conversation, kneel down or find a chair for yourself so that you are at eye level with each other. When holding a conversation with a blind person, identify yourself and any new people who join in.

If you are with a person who has a disability and do not know whether or how to help in a particular situation, ask him or her. If you automatically cut up food or push a wheelchair for a person with a disability, the student may feel that you are taking away his or her independence. If you make decisions for a person with a disability about what that person may or may not want to do, he or she will feel excluded. Some students who have a disability, for example, may be just as interested in sports or dancing as you are. A double amputee "ran" the New York marathon (on his hands) and another amputee competed in Olympic-level pole vaulting events (on one leg). Approximately 60 wheelchair athletes participated in the last New York City Marathon, and the world record for pushing a wheelchair over a 26.2-mile marathon course is 1 hour 2 minutes, 45 minutes faster than the world's best for running a marathon. [88] If you are going jogging or bowling, ask your friend who has a disability to come along.

Students who have disabilities, on the other hand, must take responsibility for explaining their needs to their peers and instructors. I remember one student whose disability was not obvious. He took an exam along with the rest of the class because he did not want to ask for special favors. Unfortunately, it was only after he failed the exam that he told me about the visual impairment that had made it difficult for him to complete the exam during the time allotted by the class period. It would have been much more appropriate for him to tell me about his physical limitation before the exam, so that we could have made arrangements for a reader or for extra time. Instead, he had to ask me to give him a make-up exam after failing the first test.

If your college has a program or service for students who have disabilities, ask whether a speaker might come to your class to talk about the difficulties that these students experience on campus. The speaker will be able to answer questions about some of the ways you might help them cope with campus barriers. As more and more people with disabilities enter the mainstream on campuses and workplaces, all of us will benefit from learning to work comfortably and competently with them. In the process, you will also undoubtedly learn that you share more similarities than differences with your friends who have a disability.

■ NONTRADITIONAL STUDENTS

Nontraditional or older students who return to college face many of the same problems as traditional students. The chapters in this book that help you to improve your skills in studying for exams, taking notes, reading and marking textbooks, writing papers, doing research, and taking advantage of college resources are helpful to all students. But nontraditional students do face certain issues that apply particularly to them. Some of these issues are treated in this section, but you will find other sections of special interest to nontraditional students in the chapters listed in Figure 14.6.

An increasing number of students are coming to the campus after several years in the workplace or the home. In many evening and Saturday programs, nontraditional students make up more than 80 percent of the class. Adult students now represent more than 43 percent of all college students, a 77 percent increase since 1979. In addition to the 5.7 million older college students, more than 35.5 million adults are engaged in formal employer-sponsored learning, hundreds of thousands of adults are learning through televised instruction, in the military, and in courses through their professional associations, community centers, social and religious groups [89]

In response to the changing nature of the student body, many colleges are modifying the services they offer. For example, in the 1980s, Virginia Commonwealth University allocated 147 thousand dollars for child care services so that children of their students could be cared for while their parents were in class. By the 1990s, that budget had grown 61 percent. Like many colleges, Virginia Commonwealth discovered that when the average age of the student body is 26 years old, students are more concerned with job placement services, child care services, and university services that are open at times when working students can take advantage of them.[90]

Although the majority of these older students are women between the ages of 25 to 34, married and working full time,[91] nontraditional students form a very diverse group. Some are returning to college after retiring from a career; others are enrolling in a few courses like computer literacy, accounting, or management in order to gain advancement or promotion in their professions; still others, who needed a break from school after high school graduation, are returning because they are not satisfied with the limited opportunities available to them in the work world. Some of these students are coming when their children grow older, and they are freed from the burdens of child care. Others are enrolling as they go through divorce, knowing that they will have to support themselves for the first time through work outside the home. Some of these students are enrolling because they feel the need for intellectual stimulation or for a worthwhile goal around which to structure their lives, but most are pursuing degrees in order to advance their careers.

Figure 14.6   *Chapters of Special Interest for Nontraditional Students*

Time Management	How to manage time for a job, commuting, family responsibilities, and studies at the same time.
Benefits and Goals of a College Education	The particular benefits that college offers to older, returning students in terms of changing careers, upgrading vocational skills, or expanding personal and intellectual horizons. Tips regarding choice of major for nontraditional students who may feel that they have less time than younger students to explore the many options that a college education offers.
College Resources	How to get college credit for life experiences outside of the classroom, how to transfer credit for courses you took earlier at another institution.
Studying for Exams	How to reduce exam anxiety, strategies for multiple choice, True/False, and essay exams.
Textbooks and Study Techniques	How to cope with math anxiety, how to study for math and science courses.
Healthy Lifestyle	Strategies for weight control despite sedentary lifestyles and no-impact/low-impact aerobics, strength training, calcium supplements and osteoporosis. How to manage stress caused by the strain of being a parent, a spouse, an employee, and a student at the same time. Relaxation training and systematic desensitization, coping with symptoms of depression, recognizing symptoms of suicide in family members or friends.
Relationships	Learning assertive communication, how to deal with sexual harassment, and avoiding rape.
Examining Values	How to establish priorities regarding marriage, family, education, and career.
Substance Abuse	Recognizing and dealing with substance abuse in family members (alcohol, cigarettes, and other drugs).
Minorities	Recognizing and coping with discrimination and sexism at work and in classes, dealing with unequal relationships between the sexes at home.
Careers	How to coordinate your college education and your career goals, how to get valuable experience in your field before you graduate.
Audiocassette	Featuring relaxation training and systematic desensitization to deal with overall stress and particular anxieties like exam anxiety, math anxiety, and anxiety about returning to school. The audiocassette is described on page 384.

Nontraditional Students' Assets and Problems

Whatever the reasons for nontraditional students to enroll, many instructors welcome them into the classroom. These students usually bring with them a high level of motivation with which to succeed in college. (Instructors enjoy teaching students who are eager to learn.) Nontraditional students often have a specific purpose for enrolling in college, and they are willing to work hard to achieve their goals. They bring a wealth of life experiences that enrich class discussions, and they contribute the perspectives of later stages in life development that lend a more-balanced view to a variety of topics.

Unfortunately, most nontraditional students also bring a high level of anxiety to class. They worry about competing with younger students who may be faster or brighter or more up-to-date in academic subjects. They worry that some of their academic skills are rusty. They fear that they will not remember as much or as well as they used to. They are afraid that their computer skills are not as good as those of younger students. They worry that their energy levels are not high enough. They are concerned that family obligations or responsibilities at work will not allow them enough time to succeed in college. They are afraid that their grades will not be as good as the ones they received in years gone by. They fear they will be embarrassed because they are too old to be in school.

Some of these fears are justified. It *is* much harder to juggle course work at the same time that you are responsible for child care or for running a household. Demands at work *can* indeed compete with demands in class. Study skills that have not been used for many years *may* need to be polished. If you are concerned about how you will perform in college, read the section later in this chapter on "Anxiety Coping Techniques," work through the activity "Practicing Techniques to Decrease Anxiety and Stress," and review Chapter 3, "Time Management" and the second half of Chapter 11, "Stress and Stressors."

Another technique you should try is changing your attitudes and what you say to yourself. Research has shown that cognitive therapy is a powerful tool in combating depression and inspiring performance. When people tell themselves often enough that they can succeed, they begin to believe it, and they begin to act like successful individuals. Every time you look at yourself in the mirror, make a positive statement about yourself. For example, you might say, "I will finish my paper today, and I will earn an *A* on it," or "I can learn those new computer (or statistics) skills because I am an intelligent person, and I work hard."

Try making some systematic substitutions in your vocabulary to words and self-statements that give you power and control over your life:

Change	I will try	to	I will
Change	I think I can	to	I know I will
Change	I should	to	I choose to
Change	I intend	to	I promise to
Change	I hope to	to	I commit to
Change	I have to	to	I want to

Burnout

Nontraditional students are at higher risk for burnout because they are often juggling several roles in addition to that of "student"; they also tend to have less leisure time than traditional students. "Burnout is caused when we try to keep going even though our levels of physical and emotional exhaustion are too high to maintain." The symptoms may include physical and mental fatigue, irritability, anxiety, feelings of hopelessness and helplessness, and general lack of motivation and enthusiasm.[92] We tend to feel burnout when we believe that we have put more into something than we receive in return, whether it is a course, a job, or our families.

Much of the blame for burnout rests with the workplace. Americans are working longer hours under more pressure than in past years. Because of technological improvements such as fax machines, laptop computers, E-mail, and cellular phones, people can literally work any time, any place. Evenings, weekends, and vacations are no longer sacred havens of refuge from a career. The boundaries between the workplace and home have become blurred. Many people feel that they can never satisfy the demands of their instructors, their bosses, or their families, and so they become frustrated. At the same time, many people feel that they receive less satisfaction from these endeavors and have less control over their lives. This situation is likely to result in burnout.

Nontraditional students and women are particularly vulnerable to burnout because they are more likely to be juggling several roles such as student, parent, spouse, employee, or homemaker. Adults with children and responsibility for household chores who also work outside the home work an average of 15 hours more per week than their partners. At the same time, due to distance from extended family members and less stability within families, many parents are forced to cope with child-rearing singlehandedly. Check to see whether you are at high risk for burnout by considering the characteristics listed in Figure 11.7. If burnout is looming on your horizon, consider the options for solutions described in the activity "Practicing Techniques To Decrease Anxiety and Stress." Figure 11.10, "Common Mechanisms for Coping with Stress," in Chapter 11 and the activities "Decreasing Stress with Muscle Scanning" and "Using Autogenic Phrases to Relax" which also form part of the stress section of Chapter 11 may also be helpful.

Anxiety Coping Techniques

If you are a nontraditional student who is experiencing anxiety, recognize your anxiety for what it is. Anxiety is a signal from your body that says you are facing a new challenge; to do your best, you need the extra energy that anxiety provides. Channel that anxiety constructively to help you try a little harder and work a little longer. If you find that your anxiety becomes uncomfortably

ACTIVITY

Practicing Techniques to Decrease Anxiety and Stress

_____   Enroll in school part time; take fewer courses until you have adapted to the campus environment and reassured yourself about your ability to succeed in college.

_____   Review the chapters in this book to improve your notetaking skills, your writing skills, your reading and study skills, and your approach to exams. There is no evidence that returning students cannot learn and remember as well as younger students.

_____ Enroll in courses in which you can brush up on academic skills. Many colleges offer noncredit courses in how to study, how to write research papers, how to use the library, and so on.

_____ Use the academic services available on your campus to review skills in math or writing that form the basis for college course work. Many schools offer review courses, tutoring, or laboratories in basic skills.

_____ Review the chapter on exams and use the strategies described in it for better preparation before exams and reduction of anxiety during exams. Practice the relaxation and desensitization techniques with the audiocassette on stress reduction described on page 384.

_____ Make friends with other nontraditional students. You may meet them in your classes, in orientation programs, in a Women's Center, in peer support groups, or in courses designed specifically for nontraditional students. Find out which of these are available on your campus. Form a support group and meet to discuss issues like assertiveness, study skills, financial assistance, and other topics of mutual interest. You can receive support and learn a great deal from people who are experiencing similar challenges.

_____ Seek out a good advisor or faculty mentor who knows the system and is willing to help you find your way through it. There are many services and many tricks that can make your life on campus much easier. There is no reason to go through four years of college before you discover them.

_____ If you live with others, hold a planning session with the members of your household (e.g., spouse, children, partner, parents) early in the semester. Find out how these people feel about your return to school. Are they willing to support you so that you may succeed in college? This support can become crucial at "crunch" times during the semester when you have three exams or two papers due at the same time. Plan ahead for those times. Delegate responsibility. Decide what chores can wait for a less hectic time in your schedule.

_____ Evaluate your expectations realistically. Do you really have to be a straight A student? Must you really earn that degree in four years or less? Is it necessary to complete every optional reading assignment?

_____ Practice the relaxation exercises and coping techniques described in Chapter 11, and the exercises on the audiocassette tape described on page 384.

_____ Adapt the desensitization exercises described on the audiocassette tape to your particular fears.

_____ Seek help at the college's counseling center. A few sessions with a friendly, trained counselor can give you a clearer perspective on how to deal with your problem.

high, check off techniques in the activity on pages 334–335 that you might use to reduce it.

Above all, believe in yourself and allow yourself to enjoy the challenge and fulfillment your college career brings.

In general, nontraditional students tend to do as well as, if not better than, traditional-age students. One of the main reasons for this is their motivation: nontraditional students often work harder. They tend to be more focused about their reasons for attending college. Another factor is the skills they have perfected during the years they were managing a home or an office: time management, organization, assertiveness, and verbal and written communication. Although older students may make the same mistakes as traditional students, they usually ask what they are doing wrong, they are able to negotiate, and they improve quickly.

There is greater acceptance for nontraditional students on campus as people realize that our complex and rapidly changing society makes continuing education a necessity for many people. There is also greater acceptance as the census figures underscore the declining number of traditional-age students who can fill the seats in college classrooms.

Answers to Figure 14.3 "What Do These People Have in Common." All of these individuals have a learning or physical disability.

Hans Christian Andersen	Learning disability	Stephen Hopkins (a signer of the Declaration of Independence)	Cerebral palsy
Beethoven	Deafness		
Alexander Graham Bell	Hearing Impairment	Bruce Jenner	Learning disability
Julius Caesar	Epilepsy	Helen Keller	Blindness and deafness
Roy Campanella	Paraplegia	Josh Logan	Emotional disability
Agatha Christie	Learning disability	Mary Tyler Moore	Diabetes
Leonardo Da Vinci	Learning disability	George Patton	Learning disability
Sandy Duncan	Visual impairment	Itzak Perlman	Polio
Thomas Edison	Hearing impairment and learning disability	Mackenzie Phillips	Substance abuse (drugs)
		Jason Robards	Substance abuse (alcohol)
Albert Einstein	Learning disability	Nelson Rockefeller	Learning disability
Dwight Eisenhower	Learning disability	Auguste Rodin	Learning disability
Nanette Fabray	Hearing impairment	Franklin D. Roosevelt	Polio
Jose Feliciano	Blindness	Wilma Rudolph	Polio
Lou Ferrigno	Hearing/speech impairment	Daniel Travanti	Substance abuse (alcohol)
		Herve Villechaize	Short stature
Sigmund Freud	Cancer (facial prosthesis)	Woodrow Wilson	Learning disability
Annie Glenn	Stuttering	Stevie Wonder	Blindness
Ernest Hemingway	Learning disability	William Butler Yeats	Learning disability
Katharine Hepburn	Parkinson's Disease		

REFLECTIONS FOR YOUR JOURNAL

1. Think about an incident of discrimination or harassment that you experienced or witnessed. (The discrimination may have been based on race, ethnic group, religion, sex, physical disability, sexual orientation or age.) How did the experience affect you and the other people involved? Discuss your feelings, values, beliefs, and actions after the incident. What actions can you take to reduce the occurrence of such incidents?

2. Reflect upon sex discrimination in our society. How has it affected you or a woman who is important to you (e.g., your spouse, daughter, girlfriend, sister, mother)? Write about the effect of sex discrimination on self-esteem, education, career choices, relationships, and leisure activities. What are your feelings about sex discrimination?

3. Write about the experience of someone you know who has a physical or learning disability. How has that person coped with the challenges of daily

life, pursuing his or her education, participating in leisure activities, establishing a social life, or finding a job?

4. If you are a nontraditional student (more than 25 years of age), write about the sources of support that have encouraged you to attend and succeed in college (e.g., your family, a mentor, a friend, your own inner strength and motivation). What additional resources might you tap to help you succeed in college? How have you coped with the challenge of juggling the many roles in your life in addition to your role as a student? How do you feel about being an older student on campus?

5. If you are a traditional college student (less than 25 years of age), write about your experiences with nontraditional students. How have they enhanced your college education? Are there any disadvantages to having nontraditional students on campus? Can you think of circumstances in the future that might lead you to become an older student?

Notes

1. S. A. Holmes, "Surprising Rise in Immigrants Stirs Up Debate, *New York Times,* 30 August 1995, pp. A1, A5.

2. H. N. Fullerton, Jr., "The 2005 Labor Force," *Monthly Labor Review,* November 1995, pp. 29–44. Washington, DC: U.S. Department of Labor.

3. D. Carvajal, "Diversity Pays Off in a Babel of Yellow Pages for Specific Immigrant Groups," *New York Times,* 3 December 1995, pp. 1, 46.

4. S. A. Holmes, "Traditional Family Stabilized in the 90's, Study Suggests," *New York Times,* 7 March 1996.

5. Government Printing Office, U.S. Department of Commerce, Bureau of the Census, *Statistical Abstracts of the United States 1995.* Washington, DC, 1987, Table 19, p. 19.

6. Ibid, Table 19, p. 19.

7. W. M. Bagby, *Introduction to Social Science.* Chicago: Nelson-Hall, 1987, p. 35.

8. Ibid, p. 37.

9. Government Printing Office, op. cit., Table 49, p. 48.

10. Ibid, p. 38.

11. Government Printing Office, op. cit., Table 49, p. 48.

12. Ibid, Table 49, p. 48.

13. Bagby, op. cit., p. 36.

14. Government Printing Office, op. cit., Table 238, p. 157.

15. Bagby, op. cit. p. 36.

16. Government Printing Office, op. cit., Table 49, p. 48.

17. I. Wilkerson, "Racial Harassment Altering Blacks' Choices on College," *New York Times,* 9 May 1990, pp. A1, B10.

18. Department of Justice, *Uniform Crime Reports: Hate Crime Statistics Revised.* Washington, DC: US Department of Justice, FBI, 1995, Table 17, Table 1.

19. Government Printing Office, op. cit., Table 19, p. 19.

20. F. Barringer, "Census Shows Profound Change in Racial Makeup of Nation," *New York Times,* 11 March 1991, pp. A1, B8 .

21. R. Rheinhold, "Class Struggle," *New York Times Magazine,* 29 September 1991, p. 27.

22. J. Schmalz, "Hispanic Influx Spurs Step to Bolster English," *New York Times,* 26 October 1988, pp. A1, B8.

23. Government Printing Office, op. cit., Table 31, p. 31.

24. R. D. Hershey, Jr., "Bias Hits Hispanic Workers," *New York Times,* 27 April 1995, pp. D1, D3.

25. Government Printing Office, op. cit., Table 53, p. 51; Table 238, p. 157.

26. Ibid.

27. S. Rimer, "New York's Aspiring Dominican Immigrants," *New York Times,* 16 September 1991, pp. A1, B6.

28. A. R. Meyerson, "Thriving Where Others Won't Go," *New York Times,* 7 January 1992, pp. D1, D5.

29. Government Printing Office, op. cit., Table 53, p. 51; Table 238, p. 157.

30. Department of Justice, op. cit., Table 17, Table 1.

31. Government Printing Office, op. cit., Table 19, p. 19.

32. M. Wong, "Post-1965 Asian Immigrants: Where Do They Come From, Where Are They Now, and Where Are They Going?" *The Annals of the American Academy of Political and Social Science,* 487 (1986), pp. 150–168.

33. Government Printing Office, op. cit. , Table 31, p. 31; Table 8, p. 11.

34. W. M. Hurh and K. C. Kim, "The 'Success' Image of Asian Americans: Its Validity, and Its Practical and Theoretical Implications," *Ethnic and Racial Studies,* 12 (1989), pp. 512–538.

35. Ibid.

36. K. B. Noble, "Attacks Against Asian-Americans on the Rise, Especially in California," *New York Times,* 13 December 1995, p. B13.

37. Ibid.

38. Ibid.

39. U.S. Department of Justice, Federal Bureau of Investigation, *Hate Crime Statistics, 1993 Revised, Uniform Crime Reports,* Washington, DC: US Government Printing Office, 1995.

40. Government Printing Office, op. cit., Table 55, p. 52, N. Onishi, "New Sense of Race Arises Among Asian-Americans," *New York Times,* 30 May 1996, pp. A1, B6.

41. S. Awanohara, "Model Minority or Ethnic Grab-Bag? On an Uptick," *Far Eastern Economic Review,* 150 (1990).

42. Government Printing Office, op. cit., Table 55, p. 52.

43. U.S. Department of Justice, op. cit., Tables 17 and 1.

44. Anti-Defamation League, *Audit of Anti-Semitic Incidents, 1995,* New York: Anti-Defamation League, 1996.

45. H. J. Ehrlich, "Campus Ethnoviolence . . . and the Policy Options." Baltimore, MD: National Institute Against Prejudice and Violence, 1990, p. 66.

46. Ibid.

47. Ibid.

48. This experiment was powerfully recorded in a CBS documentary entitled "A Class Divided." The video is available from Public Broadcasting Services, Alexandria, VA, 800-424-7963.

49. E. T. Louis, "Black and Blue on Campus," *Essence,* August 1986, pp. 67, 68, 132.

50. G. Vecsey, "The Woman Who Outshot All the Men," *New York Times,* 6 February 1992.

51. L. A. Serbin et al., "A Comparison of Teacher Response to Preacademic and Problem Behavior of Boys and Girls," *Child Development* 44 (1973), pp. 769–804.

52. M. Sadker and D. Sadker, "Sexism in the Schoolroom of the '80s," *Psychology Today,* March 1985, pp. 54–55.

53. Ibid.

54. Ibid.

55. S. Chira, "Bias Against Girls Is Found in Schools with Lasting Damage," *New York Times,* 12 February 1992, pp. A1, A23.

56. "Sunday," *New York Times Magazine,* 10 September 1995, p. 22.

57. Sadker and Sadker, op. cit.

58. C. Adelman, "Women At Thirty-Something: Paradoxes of Attainment," U.S. Department of Education Office of Research, in "Women Produce More, Are Paid Less," *On Campus,* 11 (no. 2), 1991, p. 2.

59. R. Hall with B. Sandler, "The Classroom Climate: A Chilly One For Women?" *Project on the Status of and Education of Women.* Washington, D.C.: Association of American Colleges, 1982.

60. C. Costello and A.J. Stone (Eds.), *The American Woman: 1994–1995.* New York: W. W. Norton, Section 3: Employment.

61. H. N. Fullerton, "The 2005 Labor Force: Growing, But Slowly," *Monthly Labor Review: The Workforce in 2005,* 1995, pp. 29–44.

62. Government Printing Office, op. cit., Table 739, p. 477.

63. W. Honan, "Male Professors Keep 30% Lead in Pay Over Women, Study Says," *New York Times,* 11 April 1996, p. B9.

64. Government Printing Office, op. cit., Table 677, p. 433.

65. Hudson Institute, "Workforce 2000," Bureau of Labor Statistics, in "Jobs for Women in the Nineties," *Ms,* July, 1988, p. 77.

66. T. Lewin, "Women Are Becoming Equal Providers," *New York Times,* 11 May 1995, p. A27.

67. C. Costello and A. J. Stone, op. cit., p. 327.

68. Ibid, Table 3-10.

69. "Sunday," *New York Times Magazine,* 19 September 1995, p. 22

70. "Report Explaining Increasing Numbers of Women in Psychology," *APA Monitor,* 26, (December 1995), p. 15.

71. Louis Harris & Associates, *Closing The Gap: The National Organization on Disability/Harris Survey of Americans With Disabilities.* Washington, DC: National Organization on Disability, 1994, p. 28.

72. Ibid, p. 26.

73. Ibid, p. 28.

74. D. Brown, *Steps to Independence for People with Learning Disabilities.*

75. C. Henderson, "College Freshmen With Disabilities: Facts You Can Use." Washington, DC: HEATH Research Center of the American Council on Education, 1995.

76. R. D. Lavoie in D. Hevesi, "Learning Disabled for a Day," *New York Times,* 4 August 1991, Section 4 A, Education Life.

77. M. M. Michaelson, *Basic College Math,* 1945, in D. Havesi, Ibid.

78. R. L. Colvin, "Stockbroker Sheds Light on Dyslexia's Difficulties," *The Sunday Record,* 5 May 1996, p. L-13.

79. Louis Harris & Associates, op. cit., p. 9.

80. Ibid, p. 13.

81. Louis Harris & Associates, *The National Organization on Disability/Harris Survey on Employment of People with Disabilities.* Washington, DC: National Organization on Disability, 1995, p. 23.

82. M. Freudenheim, "New Law to Bring Wider Job Rights for Mentally Ill," *New York Times,* 23 September 1991, pp. A1, D4.

83. Louis Harris & Associates, 1995, op. cit., p. 7.

84. "A Rush to Solve Problems That Confront the Disabled," *New York Times,* 1 March 1992, p. A24.

85. Louis Harris & Associates, 1994, op. cit., p. 10.

86. Ibid, p. 22.

87. C. Henderson, Post-Secondary Students with Disabilities: Where Are They Enrolled?" *American Council on Education Research Briefs,* 6, 1995, p. 1.

88. J. Longman, "Proceeding with Caution: Wheelchair Athlete Face Risks When Training on Roads," *New York Times,* 7 November 1995, pp. B9, B12.

89. L. Smith and T. Walter, *The Adult Learner's Guide to College Success.* Belmont, CA: Wadsworth, 1995 and *USA Today,* 2 March 1991, in "Back to School," *The Serious Investor,* August 1991 (New York: Shearson Lehman Brothers).

90. J. P. Hicks, "Catering to a New Crowd," *New York Times,* 4 August 1991, Education Life, Section 4A, p. 19.

91. C. Sims, "Late Bloomers Come to Campus," *New York Times,* 4 August 1991, Education Life, Section 4A, pp. 16–17.

92. "Burnout: The Epidemic of the '90s," *The Female Patient,* Supplement, S1, 1995, pp. 31–32.

93. J. Sarno with K. Rosenchein and L. Maglione, *The Differently-Abled Student in Higher Education,* Mahwah, NJ: Ramapo College, 1985, pp. 6, 20.

CHAPTER

15

CAREERS

An American Indian legend tells this story of an orphaned eagle.*

> A young warrior found a lone eagle egg. Meaning to be helpful, he placed it in the nest of a prairie chicken. The little eagle hatched with his stepbrothers and stepsisters, the prairie chicks.
>
> Growing up friends, they pecked and clucked around the ground together, scratching for worms, insects, and seeds. Eaglethood was one pleasant day after another, with no challenges.
>
> When the eaglet flew, he imitated his prairie chicken family. With a lot of flap and little flight, the changeling eaglet never rose more than a few feet off the ground.
>
> As the years passed, the eagle grew up, matured and grew old. Scratching the ground one day, the changeling eagle happened to glance up and there in the clouds was the most splendid bird he'd ever seen. He couldn't look away from the magnificent bird as it played tag with the sun. And yet the bird's gorgeous, strong golden wings scarcely seemed to move as it commanded the sky.
>
> "This is the most noble bird I have ever seen," clucked the changeling eagle to the senior prairie chicken. "I wonder what it is."
>
> "Why, that's an eagle, the chief of birds," said the senior prairie chicken. "But he's far above you. Keep scratching."
>
> And so our eagle kept scratching the ground. He died never realizing he was not a prairie chicken.
>
> If you want to be a prairie chicken, that's fine. If you'd rather be an eagle, that's good, too. What's most important is that you know what you want and how to get it. If you drift through life not ever finding out who you are, you are certain to miss the thrill of soaring."

■ CAREER GOALS AND PLANNING

According to the U.S. Department of Labor, total employment in the United States is expected to increase by 17.7 million jobs in the next decade. In addition to a bewildering number of jobs, today's college graduates are faced with tremendous changes in the job market. New jobs are constantly being created while old ones are phased out. The jobs that are most in demand one year are replaced by new listings the next year. "In general, occupations that require a bachelor's degree or other post-secondary education or training are projected to have faster than average rates of employment growth" during the next 10 years.[1]

The latest edition of *The Dictionary of Occupational Titles* describes more than 20,000 occupations, from abalone diver to zoo veterinarian. The Assistant

---

*From J. L. Kennedy, Career Book, 1988 in "Soaring Above the Crowd," *The Writing on the Wall*, Vol. 1, no. 1, Madison, WI: Cross-College Advising Service, University of Wisconsin-Madison, October 1994, p. 1.

Secretary for Employment and Training reports that a "revolutionary change" has taken place in the American workplace since the previous revision of the *Dictionary:* "The skills most in demand are not what they were fourteen years ago; educational requirements have steadfastly increased. Too many of America's young people are entering the world of work inadequately prepared."[2] Experts used to predict that the average person would have four jobs in a lifetime. Now, because of rapid changes in our economy, the average person is likely to have four careers with several job changes in each one of these careers.[3, 4] Education, flexibility, and the abilities to think critically and communicate clearly offer the keys to success in this challenging market.

Labor expert Lynn Martin indicates that "There is growing recognition of the need for lifetime learning, when rapid technological change is making the jobs of current workers more complex than they were even a few years ago."[5] According to a study by the Hudson Research Institute, more than half the new jobs created by the year 2000 will require some college education, and the gulf between the incomes of the college educated and the high school educated is widening.[6] Wages have been frozen for the average worker with a high school diploma or a little college. In factories, high-paid assembly jobs keep disappearing, and it has become harder to find a job paying even $8 an hour, the equivalent of $16,000 a year. What little increase has occurred recently in the average hourly wage is an illusion; inflation has outpaced it so that employees' dollars are worth less in buying power.[7] Studies show, for example, that the standard of living of high school graduates fell in the 1980s, while the college graduates' standard of living rose by nearly 8 percent.[8]

While many employers have frozen wages, they are demanding higher levels of skills and experience. A study by the National Center on Educational Quality of the Work Force reports that more than half of the 3000 employers surveyed have increased the skill requirements in their workplaces; only 5 percent said requirements have decreased.[9]

A college education is required to prepare for this increasingly technical and rapidly changing economy, but choosing among all of the options available and then preparing for that choice can present quite a challenge! Studies by the Carnegie Foundation and the American Council on Education indicate that today's freshmen are more concerned about job prospects and financial security than freshmen in previous years. Although a college education is not meant to prepare you for a particular job, many institutions of higher education are responding to student concerns by committing increasing resources to guiding students in career options.

Career planning should begin during your first year of college and continue through each succeeding year. The Four-Year Career Guide presented at the end of this chapter guides you through a check-off list of steps you should take throughout each of your four years at college. Doing this will help you achieve your career goals.

■ CAREER GUIDANCE AND PLACEMENT OFFICES

Most colleges have career guidance or placement offices that are stocked with a wealth of information about current trends in employment: what fields are growing and have the largest number of openings, what salary ranges are like, what types of education are needed for various careers, what parts of the country (or world) are opening up new career opportunities, and so on.

These offices also offer vocational testing that can help you discover careers in which you might be interested and also help you evaluate the skills necessary to succeed in those careers. In addition to paper-and-pencil tests, an increasingly popular form of vocational testing is a computer-based interactive guidance system. The computer asks you questions about your interests, values, and abilities, analyzes your answers, and makes recommendations about career paths you might explore. Sigi is one example of a systematic, comprehensive program that takes you through three hours' worth of exploration and then offers individualized career recommendations.

Services at career offices often include individual and group counseling sessions with career advisors, workshops with alumni who are employed in various fields, and job fairs where you can meet and question representatives from a number of corporations. All of these activities are aimed at helping you to explore and decide on career options.

In addition to helping you with long-range career planning, these offices frequently offer placement services for part-time and summer jobs where you can earn money, try out a career that interests you, and gain valuable work experience while you are still enrolled in college. Internships may also be available through cooperative education programs or through practicum courses associated with various majors. Some of these fieldwork placements offer a salary in addition to the opportunity to explore career options before you graduate. The hands-on work experience you gain through a practicum course, a summer job, or part-time work can be very valuable in helping you to land that first job after college.

Besides offering information and services related to jobs, career planning offices are often the place to go for information about graduate school and professional training programs. Some of the careers that interest you may require advanced educational degrees. The career planning office or graduate school advisory office is where you will go to find directories that describe the types of graduate programs there are, where these programs are located, what the admissions requirements are, how much they cost, and how long they take to complete. If you are thinking about going to graduate school or pursuing professional training after college, you should set up an appointment for postgraduate counseling in your sophomore or junior year. Many of the programs require that you complete particular course sequences and take certain admissions exams while you are still enrolled in college.

It is useful for you to begin thinking about career possibilities early so that you can coordinate your vocational interests with your academic program and explore as many options as possible while you are still attending college. It doesn't make sense to program yourself for a certain type of career all through your college years, only to discover after you graduate that that type of work does not suit you.

■ WORK VALUES

The activity concerning work values on pages 343–344 will help you to think about the job-related satisfactions that are most important to you. Salary should not be the major consideration in choosing a career. People who enjoy their work tend to put in the time and effort that help them succeed in their careers. Hard work is necessary for any career and so is a commitment of time, usually several years, to learn the skills needed in that area. Job dissatisfaction will limit your commitment. It can also spread to the other areas of your life and have negative effects on your relationships and leisure time. Since your values will change over time, you might want to complete this activity again in a year or two.

■ INTERNSHIPS AND SUMMER JOBS

It will be helpful if you begin exploration of career options through internships and summer jobs while you are still enrolled in college. Such experiences give you concrete bases for making decisions about whether a particular career

ACTIVITY

Identifying Your Work Values

1. The following list describes a variety of satisfactions that people obtain from their jobs. Look over the definitions of these satisfactions, and using the following scale, rate how important each satisfaction is for you.

1 = Not important at all   *3 = Reasonably important*
2 = Not very important   *4 = Very important in my choice of career*

_____ *Help Society:* Do something to contribute to the betterment of the world I live in.

_____ *Help Others:* Be involved in helping other people in a direct way, either individually or in small groups.

_____ *Public Contact:* Have a lot of day-to-day contact with people.

_____ *Work with Others:* Have close working relationships with a group; work as a team toward common goals.

_____ *Affiliation:* Be recognized as a member of a particular organization.

_____ *Friendships:* Develop close personal relationships with people as a result of my work activities.

_____ *Competition:* Engage in activities which pit my abilities against others where there are clear win-and-lose outcomes.

_____ *Work Under Pressure:* Work in situations where time pressure is prevalent and/or the quality of my work is judged critically by supervisors, customers or others.

_____ *Power and Authority:* Control the work activities or (partially) the destinies of other people.

_____ *Influence People:* Be in a position to change attitudes or opinions of other people.

_____ *Work Alone:* Do projects by myself, without any significant amount of contact with others.

_____ *Knowledge:* Engage myself in the pursuit of knowledge, truth and understanding.

_____ *Intellectual Status:* Be regarded as a person of high intellectual prowess or as one who is an acknowledged "expert" in a given field.

_____ *Artistic Creativity:* Engage in creative work in any of several art forms.

_____ *Creativity (general):* Create new ideas, programs, organizational structures or anything else not following a format previously developed by others.

_____ *Aesthetics:* Be involved in studying or appreciating the beauty of things, ideas, etc.

_____ *Supervision:* Have a job in which I am directly responsible for the work done by others.

_____ *Change and Variety:* Have work responsibilities which frequently change in their content and setting.

_____ *Precision Work:* Work in situations where there is very little tolerance for error.

_____ *Stability:* Have a work routine and job duties that are largely predictable and not likely to change over a long period of time.

_____ *Security:* Be assured of keeping my job and a reasonable financial reward.

_____ *Fast Pace:* Work in circumstances where there is a high pace of activity, work must be done rapidly.

_____ *Recognition:* Be recognized for the quality of my work in some visible or public way.

_____ *Excitement:* Experience a high degree of (or frequent) excitement in the course of my work.

_____ *Adventure:* Have work duties which involve frequent risk-taking.

_____ *Profit, Gain:* Have a strong likelihood of accumulating large amounts of money or other material gain.

_____ *Independence:* Be able to determine the nature of my work without significant direction from others; not have to do what others tell me to.

_____ *Moral Fulfillment:* Feel that my work is contributing significantly to a set of moral standards which I feel are very important.

_____ *Location:* Find a place to live (town, geographical area) which is conducive to my life-style and affords me the opportunity to do the things I enjoy most.

_____ *Community:* Live in a town or city where I can get involved in community affairs.

_____ *Physical Challenge:* Have a job that makes physical demands which I would find rewarding.

_____ *Time Freedom:* Have work responsibilities which I can work at according to my own time schedule; no specific working hours required.

2. Now choose five of these work values that are most important to you and write them on the following blanks. If you can think of any other values or satisfactions you would like from your work that were not included in the previous list, add them to the five values you have listed.

Example
1. Help Others
2. Security
3. Power and Authority

4. Creativity
5. Adventure

Work Values

1. _____

2. _____

3. _____

4. _____

5. _____

When you are considering a career or a job, ask yourself whether it will give you the satisfactions you have rated as most important for yourself. When you are interviewing people who hold various types of jobs, ask them what they like about their jobs so that you can judge whether those jobs would satisfy you.

This exercise is reprinted by permission from H. E. Figler, (1979). *PATH: A Career Workbook for Liberal Arts Students.* Cranston, RI: The Carroll Press, pp. 77–79.

ACTIVITY

Assessing Your Abilities

1. In addition to considering work values and satisfactions, another factor that is likely to influence your success in a particular career is ability. Do you have the skills that are needed to do the job? The following list will help you to evaluate your abilities and identify skills that are needed in various types of jobs. Think about how well you typically perform on different tasks. What types of grades have you received on assignments that require these skills? Have you had much success on tasks where you must use these abilities? Evaluate yourself on each of the abilities categories according to the following scale:

1 = No ability here at all   3 = Some ability
2 = Enough ability to get by with help from others   4 = Strong ability in this area

Self-Rating   VERBAL-PERSUASIVE

_____   *Writing:* Express myself well in written forms of communication.

_____   *Talking:* Relate easily with people in ordinary conversational settings.

_____   *Speaking:* Able to deliver a talk or address to an audience.

_____   *Persuading:* Able to convince others to believe something that I hold to be true.

_____   *Selling:* Able to convince others to buy a product that I am selling.

_____   *Dramatic:* Able to portray ideas or stories in a dramatic format.

_____   *Negotiation:* Able to bargain or discuss with a view toward reaching agreement.

SOCIAL

_____   *Social ease:* Relate easily in situations which are primarily social in nature; i.e., parties, receptions.

_____   *Deal with public:* Relate on a continual basis with people who come to an establishment for information, service or help, including a broad cross section of people.

_____   *Good appearance:* Dress presentably and appropriately for a variety of interpersonal situations or group occasions.

_____   *Deal with negative feedback:* Able to cope with criticism.

NUMERICAL

_____   *Computational speed:* Able to manipulate numerical data rapidly without the aid of a mechanical device, demonstrating considerable accuracy in the process.

_____   *Work with numerical data:* Comfortable with large amounts of quantitative data, compiling, interpreting, presenting such data.

_____   *Solve quantitative problems:* Able to reason quantitatively so that problems having numerical solutions can be solved without the aid of a computer or other mechanical equipment.

_____   *Computer use:* Able to use electronic computers to solve quantitative problems; knowledge of programming, computer capabilities, etc.

INVESTIGATE

_____ *Scientific curiosity:* Ability to learn scientific phenomena and investigate events which may lead to such learning.

_____ *Research:* Gather information in a systematic way for a particular field of knowledge in order to establish certain facts or principles.

_____ *Technical work:* Work easily with practical, mechanical or industrial aspects of a particular science, profession or craft.

MANUAL-PHYSICAL

_____ *Mechanical reasoning:* Able to understand the ways that machinery or tools operate and the relationships between mechanical operations.

_____ *Manual dexterity:* Skill in using one's hands or body.

_____ *Spatial perception:* Able to judge the relationships of objects in space, to judge sizes and shapes, manipulate them mentally and visualize the effects of putting them together or of turning them over or around.[10]

_____ *Physical stamina:* Physical resistance to fatigue, hardship and illness.

_____ *Outdoor work:* Familiar with the outdoors, ability to work outdoors without encountering obstacles or knowledge deficiencies.

CREATIVE

_____ *Artistic:* Keenly sensitive to aesthetic values, able to create works of art.

_____ *Imaginative with things:* Able to create new ideas and forms with various physical objects.

_____ *Imaginative with ideas:* Able to create new ideas and programs through conceiving existing elements of behavior in new ways; able to merge abstract ideas in new ways.

WORKING WITH OTHERS

_____ *Supervising:* Able to oversee, manage or direct work of others.

_____ *Teaching:* Able to help others learn how to do or understand something; able to provide knowledge or insight.

_____ *Coaching:* Able to instruct or train an individual to improve his or her performance in a specific subject area.

_____ *Counseling:* Able to engage in a direct helping relationship with another individual in situations where the person's concern is not solvable through direct information giving or advice.

MANAGERIAL

_____ *Organization and planning:* Able to develop a program project to set of ideas through systematic preparation and arrangement of tasks, coordinating the people and resources necessary to put a plan into effect.

_____ *Orderliness:* Able to arrange items in a systematic, regular fashion so that such items or information can be readily used or retrieved with a minimum of difficulty.

_____ *Handle details:* Able to work with a great variety and/or volume of information without losing track of any items in the total situation; comfortable with small informational tasks that are part of the larger project responsibility.

_____   *Make decisions:* Comfortable in making judgments or reaching conclusions about matters which require specific action; able to accept the responsibility for the consequences of such actions.

2. Look back over the abilities you have rated, and in the following space write down the areas in which you are strongest:

Abilities

_____

_____

_____

_____

_____

When you are researching careers, see which ones require abilities that you have rated 3 or 4 in yourself. When you interview job holders, ask them what skills helped them to succeed in their careers. You will eventually have to consider your strengths and weaknesses when you make a decision about career paths. Reevaluate your abilities from time to time. You may find yourself improving in certain skills as you progress through your college years.

_____

This exercise is reprinted with permission from H. E. Figler (1979). *PATH: A Career Workbook for Liberal Arts Students.* Cranston, RI: The Carroll Press, pp. 94–97.

ACTIVITY

Researching a Career through an Interview

Your first year in college is not too soon to begin some of the research that will help you find a satisfying career. One of the best ways to find out whether a particular career is right for you is to interview people who are working in the field. Choose a field that interests you, and make an appointment to interview someone who works in that area. You might interview someone you know or ask your parents, a faculty member, or a career advisor for suggestions.

The questions on the following pages can guide you in obtaining information that will help you to make decisions about future career paths. Take the questions with you and write down the answers so that you can share the information with your classmates, through an oral presentation, or with your instructor, through a written assignment.

INTERVIEW QUESTIONS

1. What is the nature of the work?

_____

_____

_____

2. What are the major duties of workers in this occupation? (Be aware, however, that although you should be able to determine a general job description, duties are likely to vary somewhat by employer and size of the employing program.)

_____

_____

_____

3. What are the entry-level positions in the field?

_____

_____

_____

4. What is the next rung to which I can aspire?

_____

_____

_____

5. How long should I anticipate it will take to reach that level?

_____

6. What training and other qualifications do I need for entry into this field?

_____

_____

_____

7. Is on-the-job training or a formal training program available?

_____

8. What are the characteristics or traits one should have in order to enter this field?

_____

_____

_____

9. What will I need to do in order to advance?

_____

_____

_____

10. Do you feel it is more beneficial to go to graduate school first or to obtain work experience before entering graduate school?

_____

11. What graduate level program do you feel is best in order to enhance one's ability to advance in this field?

_____

12. What are the criteria on which performance in this field is evaluated?

_____

_____

_____

13. What are the advantages of working for a small rather than large firm or vice versa?

_____

_____

_____

14. What are the entry-level salaries in this field? What can established professionals earn?

_____

_____

_____

15. What are the working conditions like? Are there likely to be long hours, physical demands, etc.?

_____

_____

_____

16. Will I be required to travel or relocate?

_____

17. What do you perceive to be the major rewards in this field? Major frustrations?

_____

_____

_____

18. What are the most frequently recurring problems? What undergraduate experiences do employers in this field find valuable? How can I gain these experiences?

_____

_____

_____

19. Is the field different from what it was in the past? What changes do you anticipate for the future?

_____

_____

_____

20. What is the employment outlook for this field?

_____

_____

_____

21. If you had it to do over again, what would you do differently?

_____

_____

_____

22. Can you give me any tips or suggestions?

_____

_____

_____

23. What professional associations could I join now as a student?

_____

_____

_____

24. Where can I obtain further information about this field?

_____

_____

_____

_____

Excerpted with permission from Tepper, R. (1988). _Career Manual._ Mahwah, NJ: Ramapo College, p. 20.

is right for you. They also provide work experience that you may list on a re-sumé and a source of recommendations (from supervisors) who can commend your sterling abilities to future employers. Many colleges offer courses in your major that include an internship or fieldwork as part of the course work. If your college offers that type of course, take advantage of the experience. Find out whether your college has a cooperative education program. These programs, in which you work for a semester or more at a job related to your major, offer an additional way to gain valuable hands-on experience during your college career.

■ THE FOUR-YEAR CAREER PLANNING GUIDE

The following Four-Year Career Planning Guide offers a year-by-year program of activities that will bring you closer to reaching your career objectives. Make plans now to participate in activities that will keep you moving toward success on your career path. Check off the date you complete each activity, and be sure to look over the entire guide before registering for the semester; this will keep you moving toward your career goals.

ACTIVITY

Following through on the Four-Year Career Planning Guide

The Freshman Year

Date
Completed

1. Begin to consider possible career choices through exploratory activities.

_____   Complete "Identifying Your Work Values" in this chapter (see pages 343–344).

_____   Complete the "Assessing Your Abilities" in this chapter (see pages 345–347).

_____   Complete the "Researching a Career through an Interview" in this chapter (see pages 347–350).

_____   Make an appointment at the career planning office to work with Sigi or another computerized career guidance system that will help you explore your values and interests and give you information about careers that interest you.

2. Visit the career planning office.

_____   Visit the career planning office at your college. Take a look at the library and materials they have available for you. Find out what types of services they offer that will help you explore career and graduate training options.

3. Participate in extracurricular activities.

_____   Attend meetings of several clubs or organizations, and join at least one. Student organizations offer the opportunity to develop career-related skills, make friends, and serve the college community. You can join a club related to your major, participate on an athletic team, or work on the college newspaper, student government, or radio station.

4. Attend workshops given by the career planning office.

_____   Most career planning offices offer workshops during the year on job search methods, résumé writing, interviewing skills, particular career fields, and preparation for graduate school. Attend several of these.

5. Get to know the faculty at your college.

Faculty, administrators, and counselors can advise you about careers. Faculty who really know you and your work can write better letters supporting your applications for jobs or graduate programs. Begin building those relationships now.

_____   Set up appointments with faculty during their office hours to discuss your work and interests.

_____   Ask your professors about opportunities to work with them on research projects.

6. Begin to develop communications skills.

Most employers consistently list writing and speaking skills as most desirable in new employees.

_____   To improve your speaking skills, take a public speaking course or another course that requires oral presentations.

_____   Register for courses that require several writing assignments so that you can improve your writing skills.

_____   Work on the college newspaper, yearbook, or literary magazine to improve your writing skills.

_____   Work at the college radio station, the student government, or a theater production to improve your speaking skills.

7. Choose your part-time and summer jobs carefully.

If you need to work while you are attending college, try to find a job on campus that is related to your career goals.

An on-campus job will cut down on the amount of time you spend commuting. Being a student should be your first priority, since your education is a lifelong investment. Spend as much time as you can on your course work and extracurricular activities. Work only as many hours as is required to meet necessary expenses.

_____   A job related to your major or career will give you valuable experience that you can list on your résumé or graduate school applications. Use your jobs as opportunities to evaluate your career interests and develop important work skills.

The Sophomore Year

1. Continue career exploration at the career planning office.

_____   Look over materials in the career planning office library. *The Encyclopedia of Careers* and *The Occupational Outlook Handbook* can give you basic information on many careers and fields. Other books and pamphlets on particular fields offer information on how to prepare for specific careers and how to find employment in them.

_____ Make an appointment for vocational testing. Individual testing and meetings with a career counselor can help you zero in on careers that will suit you.

2. Conduct informational interviews.

_____ Schedule informational interviews with professionals who are working in fields that interest you. Counselors in the career planning office may be able to give you names of people to interview and suggestions for questions to ask.

3. Meet with career advisors or faculty in your major.

_____ Make appointments to discuss your choice of courses to maximize your career options. Ask about second majors or minors that might enhance your vocational opportunities.

4. Participate in a cooperative education program, if your college has one.

_____ Cooperative education counselors may be able to place you in a job where you will earn money, college credits, and work experience related to your career. Make an appointment with a counselor as soon as you are eligible for the program.

5. Enroll in internships.

_____ Some of the courses associated with your major may offer a practicum component where you can acquire hands-on experience in your field. Faculty may know of agencies that will give you supervision and job experience in exchange for volunteer work during the semester or over the summer. The career planning office may have books that list corporations offering internships. Explore these options early in the year. Many summer internships have applications deadlines in January.

The Junior Year

1. Choose your courses carefully.

Many colleges encourage you to explore a variety of areas and to broaden your general knowledge during your first two years of college. General education courses and electives expose you to many different fields and help to make you a more well-rounded individual. By your junior year, however, most colleges expect that you will have chosen a major. The junior and senior years are traditionally the years in which students delve deeper into their majors and strengthen skills and commitment to their area of specialization.

_____ Be certain that you are enrolling in the courses that you will need in order to graduate with a degree in your major. Check the college catalog or other handouts from your department that list required courses.

_____ Meet with an academic advisor in your major to discuss your courses. Many colleges give you a choice in selecting courses that fulfill requirements in your major. Some of these courses may prepare you better than others for a particular graduate program or career.

_____ In addition to taking the courses required by your major program, enroll in electives that will complement or broaden your knowledge in the major. A student specializing in business management may find, for example, that courses like Industrial/Organizational Psychology from the psychology program, Business Ethics from the philosophy program, or Advanced Microcomputer Applications from the computer science program add important career skills to the program in his or her major. A psychology major may find that courses like Sociology of Deviance, Child Welfare, and Cultural Anthropology round out his interests in the major's program. Ask your advisor which courses from other programs at the college best complement your interests and career goals.

_____ Be sure that you are taking courses that will help you develop strong speaking and writing skills.

2. Work as a research assistant.

_____   Find out which faculty members are doing research in areas that interest you. Make appointments to talk to them during their office hours, and ask whether you can work as a research assistant. Graduate admissions officers and employers appreciate the initiative and commitment that such experience shows. They also know that you will have gained valuable hands-on experience and individualized supervision from such work.

3. Join a professional organization.

_____   Many professional programs encourage college students to join by offering reduced student membership rates. State or county organizations like the New Jersey State Psychological Association or the Westchester County Psychological Association may be more accessible to you than national associations like the American Psychological Association.

_____   As a member, you will receive journals or newsletters that will keep you up to date on the newest developments in your field. Read those publications regularly. Ask your academic advisor which organizations might be of the most interest to you.

_____   Attend the conferences of some of the professional organizations in your field. In addition to learning about new trends, some organizations also offer the opportunity to meet with employers at these conferences.

4. Continue your career research.

_____   Be certain that you will be qualified to work in your field. Check the requirements for entry-level skills. Consult career advisors and books in the career planning office library.

_____   Schedule interviews with professionals who are working in your field.

5. Continue to gain work experience related to your field.

_____   Choose your part-time and summer work experiences wisely. Continue to search out cooperative education and internship experiences related to your career interests.

_____   Think about skills you have acquired through job experience, extracurricular activities, or course work that might be of interest to an employer. Organizational ability, leadership skills, and the ability to cooperate or work effectively with different types of people are valuable. Computer skills, fluency in a foreign language, statistical analysis, accounting skills, and research abilities may make you more marketable to many employers. You should be able to talk about such skills during a job interview. You may wish to include some of them on your résumé.

6. Take steps to prepare for graduate school.

_____   Make an appointment to talk with an academic advisor in your field about graduate school. What advantages would graduate or professional training give you? What are your chances of gaining admission to a graduate or professional program?

_____   Check the literature in the graduate advisement office of your college or department to find out about admissions requirements and scholarships.

_____   Many colleges organize a graduate school fair where you can meet admissions officers from a number of schools and programs. Use this opportunity to ask specific questions in addition to picking up general literature about various programs.

_____   Most graduate programs require admissions examinations. Check with the graduate advisement office to see when and where these are scheduled. Take advantage of practice books and practice tests in order to do your best. If you are dissatisfied with your scores, you may be able to take the tests a second time, but both sets of scores (the lower and the higher scores) will be forwarded to the graduate school admissions committees.

_____   Plan to visit graduate schools that interest you while classes are in session. Call ahead and ask whether you can sit in on classes. Talk to students and faculty at the school when you go for an interview or visit. Make a list of questions ahead of time that will help you decide whether you wish to apply for admission to this school.

The Senior Year

1. Check your courses against the graduation requirements.

_____   Make an appointment with your academic advisor to be sure that you have completed all the requirements for graduation. April of your senior year is no time to discover that you are missing a required course or credit!

2. Step up your job campaign.

_____   If you have not yet prepared a résumé, meet with a career advisor who can give you pointers on how to write one. The career planning office will also have literature available on content, layout, printing, and so on. This is one of your most important tools in getting a job. Give it the time and attention it deserves.

_____   Use on-line resources to raise your visibility by strategically placing your vita in resume databases. *The Electronic Job Search Revolution* by Joyce Kennedy will give you additional ideas on using electronic technology in your job search.

_____   Attend a workshop on interview skills. Ask a career advisor about the types of questions that are frequently posed by employers during interviews. Read *Sweaty Palms: The Neglected Art of Being Interviewed* by H. Anthony Medley.

_____   If your college participates in on-campus recruiting programs, make appointments for interviews with companies that interest you. A career advisor may be able to suggest additional appropriate employers for you to contact. Make a list of people you have met who are working in your field. Tell them that you are looking for a job. Give them a copy of your résumé, if that is appropriate.

_____   Always do some research on a company before you go for an interview. Prepare some comments or questions before the interview that will show the employer that you know something about his or her company. This demonstrates both your initiative and sincere interest in the company. On-line resources can help you research a potential employer. Many career planning offices maintain corporate files that include literature and annual reports that can give you information about your prospective employer. Most offices also have directories of employers in specific industries. Do not neglect books like *The 100 Best Companies to Work for in America, The National Job Bank,* and *U.S. Employment Opportunities.*

_____   Attend the job fair, if your college sponsors one. This is a good opportunity to speak to employers about your interests, to ask questions, and to set up interviews. Bring copies of your résumé to the fair, and dress as you would for a job interview.

_____   Make appointments with former employers and faculty members who know your work, to discuss a letter of reference. Give them a copy of your transcript, and highlight the course(s) that you have taken with them. Attach a list of extracurricular activities or other accomplishments that should be mentioned in the letter of recommendation. Ask them to send a copy of the letter to the career planning office so that a copy can be kept in your file for future job applications.

3. Complete the applications process for graduate school if you are planning to continue your education.

_____   Make certain that you have taken the necessary admissions tests, and have the scores mailed to the schools where you are applying.

_____   Send away early in the semester for applications forms from the schools in which you are interested. These forms require considerable time and attention; almost all schools require that you ask faculty to send letters of recommendation, and many ask you to write essays that require some careful thought on your part. Getting your forms in early gives you an advantage at many schools.

_____   If the school suggests that you come in for an interview, take advantage of the opportunity to visit, ask questions, and make a favorable impression. If you have not done so earlier, make an appointment to sit in on classes and talk with students enrolled in the program.

_____

Adapted with permission from Tepper, R. (1988). *Career Manual.* Mahwah, NJ: Ramapo College, pp. 6–15.

✍ REFLECTIONS FOR YOUR JOURNAL

1. Interview someone who enjoys his or her work. (If you work, you may wish to "interview" yourself.) What satisfactions does this person receive from working? You may wish to look over the activity *Identifying Your Work Values* for a review of the satisfactions that a job can offer. How did this person come to do this kind of work?

2. Interview someone who does not enjoy his or her work. (If you wish, you may "interview" yourself.) What aspects of working make this person unhappy? How does she or he cope with this dissatisfaction?

3. If you have chosen a career path, evaluate how your choice will mesh with your values and with other goals in your life (e.g., plans for a family, social relationships, service to your community, leisure activity, and so on). Review the scenarios described on pages 248-254 of chapter 13. Is it likely that any of the conflicts between career choices and other life goals described in that chapter might affect you? How would you resolve such a conflict?

4. Evaluate your prospects for a satisfying career. Why do you think you might (or might not) be happy with your career choice?

Notes

1. G. T. Sivestri, "Occupational Employment to 2005," *Monthly Labor Review: The Workforce in 2005,* November 1995, pp. 60–84.

2. R. Jones, in *Dictionary of Occupational Titles,* 4th ed. Washington, DC: U.S. Department of Labor Employment and Training Administration, 1991, p. v.

3. M. J. Yate, quoted in C. McIntosh, "Giving Good Answers to Tough Questions," *McCall's,* May 1991, pp. 38, 40.

4. "Where The Jobs Are," *Moneysaver, Gannett Suburban Newspaper* (from the *L.A. Times*), 1 April 1995, p. 1.

5. L. Martin, in *Dictionary of Occupational Titles,* op. cit., p. iii.

6. The Hudson Institute, "Workforce 2000" in J. Bailey, "Jobs for Women in the Nineties," *Ms,* July 1988, pp. 74–79. L. Uchitelle, "Surplus of College Graduates Dims Job Outlook for Others," *New York Times,* 18 June 1990.

7. P. T. Kilborn, "In New Work World, Employers Call All the Shots," *New York Times,* 3 July 1995, pp. 1, 7.

8. The Hudson Institute, op. cit.

9. P. Applebome, "Employers Wary of School System," *New York Times,* 20 February 1995, pp. A1, 13.

10. D. E. Super and J. O. Crites, *Appraising Vocational Fitness,* rev. ed. New York: Harper Brothers, 1962, p. 287.

THE COMPUTER
A Student's Best Friend

In speaking of the days when he graduated from college, Daniel Schorr, Senior Public Analyst for National Public Radio noted that

> In those days, pot was something you cooked in and coke was something you drank and grass was something you mowed . . . hardware was a hammer and software wasn't in the dictionary.[1]

Times have changed, so welcome to the age of the computer! Some people hate computers, and other people love them. Nearly everyone finds them useful, and many people cannot live without them. Now that one-third of households in the United States and 50 percent of American teenagers have a personal computer, it is becoming difficult to avoid higher technology. Experts estimate that 30 million people are using the Internet, and this population is increasing at 10 percent per month.[2, 3] Regardless of your feelings about computers, there will be few places to hide from these machines when you go out into the work world. For this reason many colleges now insist that each student own or have access to a computer. If you are new to the world of computing, prepare yourself for some wonderful discoveries and a few frustrations.

◼ COMPUTER TECHNOLOGY ON CAMPUS

Some first-year college students have never used a computer, while others have been involved with word processing or computer games for years. Other groups of students may most accurately be described "hackers" or techno-wizards; they feel at home on the Web and may even be quite familiar with the intricacies of computer programming. If you are new to computers, this chapter will help you learn some of the basics and suggest other resources on campus that can ease you into the world of computing. If you have already had some experience with computers, this part of the text may widen your horizons and help you upgrade your skills. If you are quite proficient in computer technology, this chapter may serve as a guide towards identifying and making the best use of computer resources on your campus.

If you are new to computers, if you are not familiar with the computer system at your college, or if you need help with certain computer applications such as electronic mail, you may wish to enroll in an orientation or workshop given by the computing center. A word of caution is in order here: The support center for academic computing which teaches the application of computers to coursework or research is not usually the same as the department which offers computer science courses for credit. Ask one of your instructors or an upper class student where to find these non-credit computer workshops.

When you find the computing center, you might inquire whether there are online tutorials or manuals available that will help you to learn a particular word-processing program, windows applications, or some other skill that you need. Computer labs in the libraries, residence halls, or departments of the college usually have lab assistants who are there to help when you get stuck. Fellow students who know more than you about a particular computer application may also be helpful. The best teachers are people who do not talk down to you, people who are patient, and people who allow you to perform the keystrokes rather than doing them for you. It is often helpful to take notes on the keystrokes as you perform a new operation so that you can remember how to do it the next time.

According to the American Council on Education, the number of computers distributed in colleges and universities across the country in just one recent year was 9.3 million.[4] Computer networks on an increasing number of campuses allow students to pay tuition, update financial aid information, order tickets to athletic events, register for courses, or request grade reports. Routine college tasks are handled through custom-tailored voice response systems, touch-screen systems, or networked campus computer databases. Students may access this information by telephone, through student information kiosks scattered around campus, or from personal computers in their dormitory rooms. For example, the University of Toledo installed a campus computer system that provides students with easy, rapid access to information about extracurricular activities, bills, grades, and so on, eliminates the need to wait in long lines, and saves the university $185,000 a year.[5]

"Computing is not about computers anymore. It is about living."

Nicholas Negroponte, Being Digital, *(New York: Alfred Knopf, 1995.)*[6]

■ THE INTERNET

The *Internet*, also known as the *Net*, is a worldwide network of more than 50,000 individual computer networks and over 30 million computer users that now includes almost every large corporation, university, government, organization, and many small businesses.[7] The computer facilities owned by colleges, businesses, or other organizations are connected by high-speed telephone and satellite data links and a public, freely available communications software standard.

The rapid growth of the Internet was spurred when the American government turned over operation of the high-speed data links to commercial communications networks. At the same time, we were experiencing phenomenal growth in the number of personal computers, local area networks (private networks of computers within businesses, colleges, and other organizations), bulletin board systems, and consumer-oriented online services. It is estimated that the Internet is growing at a rate of 15 to 20 percent per month, and half the Internet sites are outside the United States. [8, 9] The Internet is best known for three main features: electronic mail, for rapid communication among individuals or groups; Usenet groups, thousands of online discussion groups that cover an incredible variety of personal, technical, and business subjects; and the World Wide Web.

The World Wide Web

The World Wide Web, or the *Web* as it is more commonly known, is a method of combining the display of graphics, text, video and audio clips into a standardized system that lends itself easily to research, entertainment, interaction, and access to an impressive world of personal and business information. A recent survey indicates that more than 14.5 million Americans have used the Web, and almost two million of them have bought something on line.[10] The Web essentially provides a coding system where elements of a text such as titles of articles,

subheads, images, and key words may be highlighted by special bracketed codes known as *HyperText Markup Language* or *HTML* and turned into *hotlinks*. These hotlinks become easily and instantly accessible if you have a Web browser running on your personal computer. You may use your *Web browser* to find and display items such as articles about a topic you are researching, pictures from museums exhibitions, or audio clips of popular music that interest you.

MOSAIC was the first browser developed to access Web documents and graphics. The group that developed MOSAIC then went on to form the Netscape Communications Corporation which is now one of the largest providers of browsers on the Net. Browsers like MOSAIC, *Netscape Navigator,* and *Netcom's NetCruiser* have been joined by browsers provided by major online computer services such as America Online, Compuserve, Prodigy, and MCI. You will need a browser in order to take advantage of the Web's awesome research capabilities.

Experts estimate that the number of subscribers who use the Web is doubling every day and that 100 new individual websites are being added each day.[11] *A website* is a collection of files about a particular subject located on a computer that is connected to the Internet. A website may be created by an individual, a group, a company, or another organization and may consist of a page or many pages. It usually includes pictures, text, graphics, and video or audio clips. You may download any of these materials, store them, and use them freely on your own computer. Each website has a *Uniform Resource Locator* or *URL* that indicates its address or location on the Web. This URL must be typed into your browser exactly as it appears, including the correct use of upper and lower case letters, slashes, and other punctuation. For example, http://lycos.cs.cmu.edu/ is the URL for Lycos, a search engine discussed in the paragraph below which describes searches on the Web.

Websites include a wealth of information such as tips on finding a new job, advice and resources for your hobbies and interests, new travel and vacation destinations, articles or books housed in libraries around the world, paintings in museums, government archives, and connections to people on the Internet who have interests in common with yours. Many of the authors of websites, who are often experts in their fields, invite direct e-mail contact with people who connect to their sites.

Hotlinks or links are the Web's most famous and useful research feature. These are words or groups of words that are highlighted by Hypertext on the Web pages. When you click on a hotlink with your computer mouse, you are immediately linked to another website or location containing information related to the original link. If you are reading an article on the Civil War, and come across a reference to the battle at Gettysburg that is hotlinked in the paragraph you are reading, you may click on the word "Gettysburg;" you will immediately jump to more detailed information about the battle at Gettysburg that has been linked by the website's creator. This jump may lead you to another portion of the same website or to another website located halfway across the world.

These "jumps" to hotlinked sites do not require typing in the location code for the new site. You are automatically taken to the cross-linked reference when you click on it with your mouse. You may, however, wish to save the URL of the new site on the *hotlist* file or *bookmark* of your computer's browser so that you may access it easily in the future without looking up or keying in the location number.

Since the Web is growing very rapidly, it is hard to keep track of new sites that are added every day and what type of information they contain. For this reason, several programmers have developed software that "travels" all over the Net, collecting new site locations, taking samples of text from Web pages, and building up lists of keywords. These *search engines* or *web worms* can help you find the sites you need. Such engines as Lycos and WWWW (World Wide Web Worm) are especially helpful in finding new websites.

Lycos, which is operated by Carnegie Mellon, performs weekly scans of the Web's two million plus sites, indexes them, abstracts them, and allows you to locate a website by typing a subject key word. It will return a list of up to 999 "hits" or sites related to your subject including the Web page titles, summaries of content, and URLs so that you can easily jump to a site that interests you. A recent search under the word "investment" turned up 1,132 "hits," and another using "Beatles" uncovered 266 sources, each offering a summary of the information on the site.[12]

Oliver McBryan's "World Wide Web Worm" (WWWW) scans a Web database of more than 300,000 websites and lists sites by their location, key word, or file type. So you could, for example, find all the home pages about colleges or universities or the Web pages for particular countries.

■ ELECTRONIC MAIL OR E-MAIL

Much of the Net's growth is due to the acceptance of the Internet as the standard for electronic mail which is rapidly replacing the FAX machine and the postal service as the preferred means for sending and receiving business and personal communications. Electronic mail, or e-mail, as it is more commonly known, allows you to send messages through the computer to other students and faculty on your campus or to other individuals or organizations anywhere in the world. These messages arrive at their destination immediately. (Enthusiasts of e-mail sneeringly refer to traditional mail service as "snail mail" because it is so slow.)

If your recipient is using the computer when the message arrives, you may "talk" back and forth, using the keyboard, the way you would during a telephone conversation. If your party's computer is not turned on at the time you send the message, the communication will wait for the person to turn on the computer and check his or her "mailbox." The person may then answer your message at any time, and the response will travel back to your computer immediately and wait for you to check your mailbox. As long as the recipient of your message has access to an e-mail address, the maximum charge for sending your message anywhere in the world should be the cost of a local telephone call, and your message arrives immediately!

On many campuses, students are automatically given e-mail addresses. Many faculty communicate with students through e-mail, and at an increasing number of colleges, syllabi and other course materials are distributed through e-mail, assignments are turned in over e-mail rather than in printed form, and students receive feedback on their work through e-mail. E-mail makes it easier to contact faculty members since neither of you has to "catch" the other or waste time playing "telephone tag." You may each communicate when it is convenient, and the messages will wait until the recipient has an opportunity to respond. Inquire at the computing center whether your campus has an electronic mail system that is available to students and whether there is a charge for this service.

E-mail makes it very easy to respond quickly to a message. People often dash off a hasty reply or comment about a situation. Once you press the "send" command, you cannot retract your message. For this reason, it is wise to pause and think about your message especially if it involves an upsetting or emotional event. Because it is also very easy to "forward" messages to a third person or a whole group of people when using e-mail, you should realize that your communication may be seen by someone in addition to your intended recipient. In light of these issues, you may wish to consider more carefully what you say and how you say it when you are using electronic communication. Each campus is likely to have guidelines and address certain ethical issues that arise in the use of electronic mail. Be sure that you understand these guidelines and

act responsibly. If you have any questions or concerns in this area, check with a staff member at the computing center or one of your instructors.

■ COMPUTERS AND LEARNING

The "virtual university" is replacing the classroom for many students. Students may attend thousands of on-line degree and non-degree courses offered by hundreds of institutions of higher education. For example, a college in Arizona teaches English, via the Internet, to students in Russia; in North Dakota, 11 institutions have joined together to offer courses through video conferences, Compuserve's Education Forum lists more than 70 educational institutions such as Purdue and Columbia that offer on-line courses.[13]

In addition, many college classes today use computers as an integral part of the learning process. In some courses, computers help students work their way through practice exercises in accounting, engineering, or statistics. In other courses, computers simulate laboratory experiments in psychology, biology, or physics. Courses such as "Berlitz Live! Japanese" use CD-ROM's with 256 colors, sound boards, headphones, and microphones that allow students to hear the sounds of a foreign language they are learning, see the lip movements involved in producing the correct sounds, and receive feedback on their own attempts to mimic native speakers.[14] Social work students use computers to practice the interviewing skills they will need with clients. Premed students try their hand at solving challenging diagnostic cases, nurses learn to insert IV lines into simulated human bodies that feel no pain, and surgical residents practice difficult and costly procedures on virtual, three-dimensional organs that can be removed and then replaced.[15] One of the most widespread uses for computers in the classroom is in the area of writing.

■ COMPUTERS AND THE WRITING PROCESS

Many writing instructors are now holding their classes in computer laboratories rather than in conventional classrooms. Students report that computers make writing more fun. Those who used to dread writing find that word processing takes the drudgery out of composition.[16] They no longer have to retype whole pages in order to correct a typographical error or to make changes in organizational structure.

Because corrections and changes are so easy to make, they feel free to try out new ideas. Students can keep making changes until their texts are perfect. They can add sentences, delete words, move paragraphs around, and check spelling. Because computers save so much time, students are willing to experiment with new techniques. They can try free-writing, brainstorming, or heuristic aids to composition.[17] They can compare several drafts to see which organizational structure works best.

Students who have experienced difficulty sitting still and concentrating on a piece of paper find that the lighted screen captures their attention. Students who have lost their train of thought during the laborious process of writing out ideas by hand report that the keyboard makes communication a snap. Students who were not willing to edit because it was too difficult to read their handwriting are eager to read over their printed pages. Students who were not willing to reorganize their papers because retyping was so boring and time-consuming find the computer's "cut-and-paste" options to be fun and efficient. Reluctant writers become enthusiastic writers. They write more; they are more willing to revise their work; and they take greater pride in their writing.[18]

Computers offer special advantages for students who have physical disabilities. Students with visual impairments find that special software with

large-print letters makes reading easier. Many students who cannot write because of motor disabilities are able to use the keyboard. For students with motor impairments, the voice-activated computers provide a way to express their thoughts in writing.

Some reasons students give for using computers include the following:

- Computers make writing fun.
- Corrections and changes are easy to make.
- Fewer errors appear in the finished work.
- The final product looks neat and professional.
- Writer's cramp is eliminated.
- New techniques can be explored.
- Minor errors do not create the need to retype whole pages.
- Several drafts can be prepared and the best one chosen.
- Papers can be prepared over several work sessions; the computer can keep track of notes and outlines.

One word of caution before you go on to the magic keyboard. Although you are about to discover the many advantages of working with a computer, you are also about to discover some of the limitations. The computer can make writing easier and more enjoyable. It can also produce a more professional-looking product that has fewer spelling and grammatical errors, but it cannot write for you. *You* must produce the ideas, *you* must develop them, and *you* must organize them. This still takes time and work.

If you have not worked with a computer before, you will have to learn the system and practice with it. It is likely to take you a quite a few hours of study and practice before you are feeling comfortable with the word processor. The more you use it, the more competent you will become.

Following are some typical frustrations overcome by beginning students:

- It takes time to learn the command keys. If you hit the wrong key, you may erase a word or a sentence unintentionally. On the other hand, the computer makes it very easy to correct such errors.
- If you have never typed before, you will have to learn. With a little practice, you will find that keying on a computer keyboard is much faster and easier than using a typewriter.
- You may lose your work if you are not careful about storing it in the appropriate places.
- You will have to learn to control the appearance of your work on paper. It will take time to learn how to produce double-spaced printing, to position the printer in the right place, to have page numbers typed automatically, and to produce a title page.

All of these problems can be avoided or overcome through practice sessions on the computer. Most students report that the pains of this learning process are well worth the final rewards.

■ BASIC WORD-PROCESSING SKILLS

The word processor is a set of instructions, or a program, that tells your computer what to do. It allows you to create, edit, and print a document. Some of the most popular word-processing programs are WordPerfect, WordStar, Word, AppleWorks, and MacWrite. There are too many of these programs on the market to go through the specific steps of using each one. The programs do share many common features, however, and a review of the basic features will help you use the computer to improve your writing.

If your word-processing program comes with a tutorial, work your way through it. The step-by-step directions will give you the basic procedures necessary to begin writing. If you do not have a tutorial, read the manual that comes with the word-processing program and practice the basic procedures. It is best to do this when you have a friend or a tutor close by who is familiar with the program you are using.

The first thing you must learn is how to start up your word-processing program. Most college computer laboratories provide students with access to microcomputers that use diskettes to store information. Your computer will probably use 3½-inch hard shell diskettes. Ask the laboratory assistant about the type of diskette your computer uses; you will probably have to buy one so that you have a place to store your work.

Format a blank diskette only once.

Before you use a new diskette, you must first format, or initialize it. This process sets up the storage space on the diskette so that your computer and word-processing program can work with it. Initializing a diskette is a very quick, easy process. Read about it in your manual, or ask the laboratory tutor to show you the procedure. Do not use a diskette that has not been properly formatted; you will lose your work! Be careful to format a diskette only once. Formatting a diskette wipes out all the information you have stored on it. If you have stored a draft of your paper on the diskette, you probably do not wish to lose it by formatting the diskette again!

Load the word-processing program.

Some microcomputers require that you place a diskette containing the word-processing program in one drive of the computer and that you place another personal, or data, diskette, on which you store your work, into a second drive. Be sure that you place the diskettes in the correct drives. Find out if the diskettes should be placed in the disk drives before or after you turn on the computer. If your computer has only one drive, you will have to load the word-processing program first, remove that diskette, and then place your personal, or data, diskette into the slot. In many computer laboratories, a word-processing system is already loaded onto the hard drive of the computer before you arrive. If you have previously worked on your diskette in a different computer, be sure that the work stored on your diskette is in a word-processing system that is compatible with the system used by the hard drive.

Insert your personal or data diskette.

If your computer uses an internal hard drive, you may not need to insert a program diskette. Select the word-processing option when it appears on the screen, and then insert your data diskette so that you will be able to save your work.

Storing Your Work

Before you type any work onto a computer, learn how to store your work. Most word-processing programs call this "saving." While you are working on the computer, your work will be held in a temporary memory system. This memory is temporary in the sense that your work can be lost if you exit from the word-processing program or turn off the computer.

Store your work frequently.

My most frustrating computer lesson occurred one morning, when, after I had been working on the computer for three hours, the electric power to my home was momentarily interrupted. I had not saved my work during this time, so that momentary blip in electric power cost me three hours of work! I had to reconstruct my work as best I could and key it in from the beginning. I have never made that mistake again. I now save my work every few minutes.

Once you store your work on a hard disk or on a diskette, a permanent record is made. You can retrieve that piece of work at any time in the future. It is wise to get into the habit of saving your work every fifteen minutes or so. Saving your work is a quick and easy process. Consult your manual or laboratory tutor for the proper procedure. You will have to tell the computer the name of the piece on which you are working; you must also tell the computer where to store your work.

Name your file.

Each time you begin a new document, the computer will ask you what you wish to name it. Naming a document sets up a text file for it in the computer so that you can store it and return to work on it at another time. Choose a name that will help you remember which work you stored in that particular file. A laboratory report on DNA might be called DNALAB. Check your manual to find out the maximum number of letters you may use in the file's name and whether your computer allows spaces or numbers in the name.

Check manual for appropriate file names.

When you write several drafts of a document, you might wish to store each of them under a separate name: DNALAB1, DNALAB2, and so on. This will allow you to compare drafts and to incorporate material from earlier drafts. It will also serve as evidence that the work is yours, should a question of plagiarism ever arise, and it will give you a backup in the event that your most recent draft is accidentally erased.

Store later drafts under different names.

In addition to telling the computer the name of your document, you must also tell it where you want the work stored. If your machine has a hard drive, you may want to store your document there. In that case, you might specify "C:DNALAB" to indicate that your laboratory report should be stored on Drive C. If you share the computer with other students or if your computer does not have a hard drive, you will want to store the document on your personal diskette. If you placed that diskette in Drive A, then you will key in "A:DNALAB" after giving the command to store your work.

Store your work on the appropriate drive.

It is always a good idea to back up your work. Make two copies so that if one is lost or damaged, you still have the second disk. You may store one copy on the computer's hard disk and one copy on a data disk, or you may choose to make a duplicate copy of your data disk and keep the two disks in different locations.

Back up your work.

Remember to save your work every fifteen minutes or so. Saving your work frequently and regularly may save you hours of frustration. Also remember to save your work before you print it. Your work can get lost between the computer and the printer, but as long as you have saved the work, you can quickly retrieve it and reissue the print command. Always store your work before you walk away from the computer and before you exit from the word-processing program.

Save before printing.

Store before exiting.

Handling Disks

Label your disk so that you know what work it contains and under what name you have stored a particular document. Write on the label before you put it on the diskette. If you wish to write on it later, use a felt-tip pen. A labeled disk gives you some insurance against accidentally reformatting a disk that contains documents you wish to save.

Label disks.

Handle your disks carefully. Keep them in their protective covers or plastic baggies when they are not in the computer. Avoid bending or exposing them to high temperatures. Damaged disks result in lost work that you cannot retrieve. When you wish to work on a document or print it out again in the future, you need only give the computer the file name after entering the retrieve command. If you do not remember the file name or if you enter it incorrectly, issue a display or directory command, and the computer will list the names of all files contained on that disk.

Handle disks carefully.

Retrieve your work.

ACTIVITY

Practicing the Basics of Word Processing

It is time to sit down and begin work with your computer! Ideally, you will be able to schedule a class session at the computer laboratory when an instructor or a laboratory assistant will be available to assist you. If this is not possible, choose a time when you have at least an hour to work with the computer. It might be helpful to work with a friend; two heads are often better than one in finding solutions to problems that arise.

Bring this book and two blank diskettes with you when you begin work with your computer. This activity will take you through the steps to begin using your word-processing program. Write down the answers to the questions in your text so that they are available for reference should you forget any procedures during future writing sessions.

If your instructor or the computer laboratory tutor is available, he or she can help you with the answers to these questions. The answers can also be found in the tutorial or the manual that accompanies your word-processing program.

1. Turn on the computer. If the monitor (screen) does not light up, find its switch and turn on that, too.

2. If you are using a new data disk that has not been formatted, insert the disk in the appropriate drive and format it before you begin to work. What steps are involved in formatting a disk?

   _____

   _____

   _____

   _____

   _____

3. Insert the program disk into the appropriate drive, and load the word-processing program, if necessary. Which is the proper drive for the program disk?

   _____

4. Insert your data disk into the appropriate drive, if you have not already done so. (If your computer has only one drive, you will have to remove the program disk before you insert your data disk.) Which is the proper drive for your data disk?

   _____

5. Which option must you select from the menu to begin writing or editing? Select that option now, and press enter (↵),if necessary.

   _____

6. If you are creating a new file, must you name it before you begin writing or may you name it when you are ready to save? Let LESSON.TXT be the name of your file.

   _____

7. List any restrictions that govern your choice of file names (e.g., What is the maximum number of letters in a name? Are spaces or numbers permitted? Must the file have a name "tag" or extension like the one in FILE.TXT?).

_____

_____

_____

_____

_____

_____

8. What command must you issue to create or open a new file? Issue that command and name your file LESSON.TXT if you have not yet done so.

_____

9. What command must you issue if you wish to work on a file that already exists?

_____

10. Type in the following text. (Do not worry about any typographical errors you make at this point.)

I pledge allegiance to the flag of the United States of America and to the republic for which it stands, one nation, under God, indivisible, with liberty and justice for all.

My country 'tis of thee
Sweet land of liberty
To thee I sing.
Land where my fathers died
Land of the pilgrims' pride
From ev'ry mountainside
Let freedom ring.

11. a. In each of the following situations, write, on the answer line, which key(s) you would press to move the cursor (the blinking, lighted bar).

_____ move(s) the cursor one character to the left without erasing text

_____ move(s) the cursor one character to the right without erasing text

_____ move(s) the cursor one word to the left

_____ move(s) the cursor one word to the right

_____ move(s) the cursor to the right-hand margin

_____ move(s) the cursor to the left-hand margin

_____ move(s) the cursor to the bottom of the screen

_____ move(s) the cursor to the top of the screen

_____ move(s) the cursor to the end of the text

_____ move(s) the cursor to the beginning of the text

_____ move(s) the cursor to indent a paragraph

(On many computers you cannot use the space bar to move the cursor to a new position in your text without erasing text as you move. It can be frustrating to break this habit if you are accustomed to a typewriter where the space bar is used to move from one point to another.)

b. Position the cursor at the beginning of the Pledge of Allegiance, and try out each of the cursor movements listed above.

12. a. Must you press a particular key to insert text? Or does your word-processing program automatically move existing text to the right to make room for additional material as you key it? Many word-processing programs have a toggle switch (a key on the keyboard) that controls this function. (That key is often labeled *Ins.*) Once you have pressed the key that activates insert mode, you will remain in that mode until you press the key again.

How do you activate the "insert" mode?

_____

_____

b. Insert the following text after the word *flag* in the first line of the Pledge of Allegiance material that you typed: *which is red, white, and blue.*

13. a. Must you press a particular key to type over text that you wish to delete? Or, does your processor automatically erase existing text as you type on top of it? In many word-processing programs, pressing the insert (Ins) key will activate type-over mode so that existing text is erased as you type over it.

How do you activate the "type-over" mode?

_____

_____

b. In place of "and to the republic for which it stands," type the following text: *and to the nation it represents.*

14. a. Does your word-processing program automatically reform your paragraph to eliminate blank spaces and line up your margins as you insert or delete material? If it does not do this automatically, which key must you press to reform your paragraph so that the blank spaces are eliminated?

_____

b. Before you press that key, be sure to place a hard carriage return, by pressing the enter key, or the end-of-paragraph symbol that your program uses at the end of the paragraph. (Press the enter key after "and justice for all.") If you do not perform this operation, the Pledge of Allegiance will be merged into one paragraph with "My Country 'Tis of Thee."

c. Press the correct key and reform your paragraph.

15. Which key(s) would you press to delete

_____ a single character?

_____ a single word?

_____ a whole line?

_____ a whole section of text?

a. Delete the *g* in *flag.*

b. Delete the word *pledge.*

c. Delete the second line of "My Country 'Tis of Thee."

d. Delete the last three lines of "My Country 'Tis of Thee."

e. Recover sentences or paragraphs you have previously erased. (Many programs allow you to change your mind about material you have deleted.)

16. a. How do you save your file?

_____

_____

_____

    b. Save your text on your personal disk.

17. a. How do you back up your file (make a second copy in a different location)?

_____

_____

    b. If your computer has a hard drive that you can use, save your text onto the hard drive.

    c. If the hard drive is not available to you, copy the contents of your diskette onto a second diskette. Write down the steps involved.

_____

_____

18. a. After you have saved your file and wish to end your computer session, how do you exit from the program?

_____

_____

    b. Exit from the program now.

19. Call up the program again.

    a. How do you retrieve your text (LESSON.TXT)?

_____

_____

    b. Retrieve your text and add the following to the end of your text: *Congratulations to me!* Put your name at the top of the page.

    c. Save your text.

20. Check that the printer is turned on and connected to your computer and that it has an adequate supply of paper.

    a. How do you tell the computer to print your text?

_____

_____

    b. Print your text.

    c. Collect your printout.

    d. Exit from the program.

    e. Collect your data disk.

    f. Turn off the computer if this is appropriate.

Congratulations! You have made it through the first session on your word-processing program. Best wishes for a long and productive relationship with computers.

Keying in Work

Find the function keys.

Keying work on a computer keyboard is much easier and faster than typing on a typewriter because it is so easy to correct errors. Since you will not be worrying about accuracy, you will find yourself keying much more quickly.

The computer keyboard has more keys than a regular typewriter. You will find a whole set of function keys (usually labeled F1, F2, F3, etc.) that allow you to give the computer various commands such as "move a paragraph" or "underline a sentence." You will find yourself pressing many of these function keys in conjunction with the Ctrl key, the Alt key, or the shift key (⇧) to issue a variety of commands.

Find the keys that move the cursor.

You will also find a number of keys that allow you to move the cursor. The cursor (the blinking bar on your screen) tells you where on the screen your next keystroke will take effect. Some keys move the cursor one letter at a time; other keys move it to the end of the next word, to the end of a line, to the end of the page, or to the end of the paper. You will find yourself moving the cursor in order to add words, delete sentences, or rearrange the order of paragraphs.

Note the wrap-around feature.

Note the hard carriage return.

As you are keying, you will notice that the computer automatically takes you to the next line when you come to the edge of the right-hand margin setting. You do not have to keep track of margin settings in order to move to the next line. If you wish to move to the next line before you come to the edge of the margin, just press the enter key (↵), and the computer will move the cursor to the next line.

Note insert, delete, and escape keys.

Memorize help key.

You will also notice keys that allow you to insert (Ins) and delete (Del) characters, backspace (←) to delete characters, escape (Esc) from various options, and move to various tab settings (➡). Practice using these keys with your tutorial or manual until you feel comfortable with them. Many word-processing programs come with templates that you can mount on the keyboard to help you remember which keys control which functions. Most of these programs also use a help key with which you can call up a display of the key functions. This display will tell you which keys control which functions. As long as you memorize which key calls up the help menu, you will not need to memorize all of the key functions. As you work with the word-processing program, you will find yourself automatically remembering the keys that you use most often.

Printing Work

You must learn how to send your work from the computer to the printer in order to hand your instructor a "hard copy" of your paper. Each word-processing program uses a slightly different method for accomplishing this. Ordinarily, you select the print option from the menu, tell the computer which text you wish to print, and press the enter or return key.

Save before printing.

Check printer and paper.

Again, be sure that you have saved your work before you issue the print command. Work is often lost on the way to the printer and is sometimes lost when several computer terminals in a laboratory are connected to the same printer. Before you issue the print command, check that the printer is turned on, that it is connected to the computer, and that it has enough paper. You are less likely to lose your work. If you have saved your work and it is lost on the way to the printer, you can easily retrieve it and issue the print command again.

■ WORD PROCESSING ALL STAGES OF WRITING

Instructors generally identify four processes that are necessary to produce a finished piece of writing:

1. Prewriting, or planning
2. Writing, or drafting
3. Rewriting, or revising
4. Editing, or proofreading

Stage One: Prewriting

Prewriting is the planning process in which you define a topic, explore what you know about it, find out what you need to know, generate ideas, do research, read, take notes, and produce an outline. Professional writers usually spend more time on this planning stage than they do on the writing phase.

Sitting down and planning a paper is often the most difficult part of writing. The computer can be very helpful at this stage. You may wish to review Chapter 8 to refresh your memory on how the computer can help you organize your paper with an assignment page and how it can make it easier for you to generate ideas for your paper with the brainstorming, free-writing, and posing questions techniques.

Heuristic Questions

Aside from its utility in generating ideas, the computer can also be helpful during the prewriting phase in gathering information and organizing it. Some writers use a "shell," or template, as a frame on which to construct a paper.

The Journalist's Shell

One example of this kind of strategy involves the six heuristic questions traditionally asked by journalists:

■ What?   ■ Who?   ■ When?
■ Why?   ■ Where?   ■ How?

ACTIVITY

Gathering Information through a Journalist's Shell

If you were going to do a paper on watermelons, for example, you might start out with the word *what* on your screen. You would then insert, under that heuristic word, several paragraphs on what watermelons are like. Define watermelons and describe them. Discuss different types of watermelons; how do they look, taste, feel, and smell?

When you have finished writing all that comes to mind under the *what* of watermelons, go to the word *why* and insert as many paragraphs as you can on why people grow watermelons, why they eat watermelons, and why they enjoy watermelons.

Continue inserting paragraphs under each of the heuristic words and answer the questions prompted by that particular key word. You will find that the ideas for your first draft practically write and organize themselves.

The Classical Shell

A more sophisticated form of the shell technique uses a framework proposed by classical Greek writers. Like the journalist's questions, this framework can help you discover or remember important information about your topic. Aristotle proposed twenty-eight items, but the five that follow should give you a good idea about how to proceed:

- Definition
- Comparison and contrast
- Connections
- Testimony
- Circumstance

If you were writing a paper on sin, you might begin with

- A definition of sin—
  How is sin defined?
  Is there more than one definition?
  Does sin really exist?
  What are the different kinds of sin?
  Are there various components to sin?

- A comparison and contrast of sin—
  What does sin resemble?
  How does sinful behavior differ from other behaviors?
  What is sin most like? Why?
  How do sins differ from each other?
  How do various sins resemble each other?

- Connections of sin—
  What are sin's origins?
  What are the consequences of sin?
  Does sin serve any purpose?
  Is sin related to any other traits?

- Testimony—
  What do the experts say about sin?
  What is your own experience with sin?
  How do most people feel about sin?

- Circumstance—
  How do we gather information about sin?
  Is there such a thing as sin?
  What circumstances make sin possible or impossible?

ACTIVITY

Gathering Information through a Classical Shell

1. Key in the framework and questions previously described but substitute an X for the word *sin*. Save that text under the file name SHELL. Doing this will preserve your blank shell so that you can call it up for a future paper.

2. Now go back and systematically answer the questions in relation to a topic on which you have to write a paper. This activity will give you some idea about what you know and what you still have to research for your paper. It will also help you to organize your information.

When you are ready to store your work, save your text under a name that will remind you of the file's content. If you were writing a paper on sin, you might name the file SHELLSIN. When you have completed your research and filled in as much information as you can under each question, you may erase the questions and begin organizing your paragraphs into a draft of your paper.

Using an Outline Program

Some word-processing systems include an outline program. When you activate this program, the computer will display an outline structure beginning with the Roman numeral I. After you have keyed in your heading and pressed the appropriate key, the heading will automatically be indented and you will be presented with an *A* for a subheading. When you give the appropriate command, the outline will then indent further and print a *1* so that you may enter the next level of subheadings. This type of outline program allows you to insert, delete, and move headings and sections so that you can change the organization of your outline quickly and easily. The computer keeps track of your categories so that you do not have to remember whether the next subheading should be a *b* or *c;* the word-processing program will automatically print the correct prompt for you.

Such outlines are a lot of fun, and they can help you to organize the topics for your paper. If your word-processing program does not contain an outline program, you may purchase a separate program. PC-Outline is one example of an outline program designed for personal computers. You may use the outline headings as a shell while you type in appropriate sentences or paragraphs under each heading. When you are ready to write your first draft, it is easy to erase the titles of the outline's categories. You will then be left with a neatly organized set of paragraphs.

If you have access to an outline program, check the manual or documentation for it and try it out. Many of these programs come with on-screen directions and help options available at a keystroke. These may be so simple and helpful that you do not need the manual.

Stage Two: Writing or Drafting

Once you have defined your topic, generated some ideas, and thought about the overall organization of your paper, you are ready to write your first draft. Word-processing programs have a number of options that can be very helpful at this point.

Working with Several Files Simultaneously

Many word-processing programs allow you to work with several files at the same time. You may have your notes or an outline in one file and your draft in another. If your processor has a split screen option, you will be able to see the outline on half of the screen and to incorporate parts of it into the draft you are writing on the other half of the screen. You can also use the split screen to view two drafts of your paper at the same time. In this way, you can choose the best features of each and integrate them into one paper.

Instead of using a split screen, some word-processing programs allow you to work with two or more files simultaneously by placing material from several files in "windows." You are able to view material from various files by opening and closing windows that are located in different segments of the screen.

If your word-processing program offers options that move material back and forth among files and that merge files, learn to use them. They will save you much time in scrolling back and forth through lengthy documents to find the sections you want. They will also eliminate the need to copy lengthy sections of text from one file into another.

Stage Three: Rewriting or Revising

Professional writers rarely present their first drafts to the public. In fact, the difference between a poor writer and a competent writer usually lies in the revision stage. Many writers require three and even four drafts before their work is refined enough for publication. The word-processing program takes the drudgery out of revisions. Making corrections and changes is quicker, easier, and more fun.

The Block Move

Once you learn to move the cursor efficiently, you will find that it is very easy to make changes in your work. One or two keystrokes will take you to a place in your document where you can insert or delete material. You may add or subtract letters, words, sentences, paragraphs, or even whole pages with a single keystroke.

If you have written material in one part of your paper that you would like to move or copy to another place, you can do this easily by marking the boundaries of the material that is to be moved and then indicating the new location with the cursor. This operation is often called block moving or cut and paste. It allows small or large sections of text to be erased, moved, or duplicated without the need to retype the material. Learning this procedure will make your editing much easier.

Paragraph "Busting"

Paragraph "busting" can be a useful technique for checking on cohesiveness, organization, and transitions in your paper. One option is to use the search-and-replace command described below to search out each instance of a period and to replace it with a hard return. Each sentence of a paragraph will then be displayed on a separate line. You will be able to examine sentences more easily to be sure that they are related and that they flow logically into each other.

Another option involves the display of the first and last sentences of each paragraph. When you see these two sentences without the distraction of intermediate material, you can readily judge whether you have consistently followed through with the thought you introduced. You can also check whether you have provided a smooth transition between the last sentence of one paragraph and the first sentence of the one that follows.

You may use a similar strategy to check the cohesiveness of the paper by isolating the thesis statement and comparing it with the conclusions in your final paragraph.

Stage Four: Editing or Proofreading

The word-processing program is a very handy aid when you reach the last phase of writing: proofreading. A number of options make this task more accurate and less boring.

The Search-and-Replace Command

One useful procedure is the search-and-replace command that is available on many word-processing programs. This feature allows you to specify a group of letters, a word, or a punctuation mark for which your computer will mount a search. When it comes to the designated symbol, it will pause and automatically replace that word or punctuation mark with another one that you have specified. If you do not want automatic replacement, the computer will pause and allow you to decide whether you wish to make a change in that location. It will then go on to find the next instance of the designated word so that you may examine that piece of text. It will continue to search and pause until it ferrets out each instance of the designated characters in the entire document.

If you know, for example, that you tend to confuse *their* with *there,* you may instruct the computer to stop each time it finds the word *their.* You can then examine each instance and decide whether you wish to replace it with *there.* On the other hand, if you find that you have consistently misspelled Sigmund Freud's name in a twenty-page psychology paper, you may instruct the computer to search for each instance of *Frued* and automatically replace it with the correct spelling of *Freud.*

If you know that you tend to get caught up in run-on sentences, you may instruct the computer to pause at each period. Isolating each sentence in this way will make it easier to judge whether or not you are dealing with a run-on sentence.

A final example of the usefulness of search-and-replace commands involves the elimination of sexist language from a paper. If your instructor criticizes your prose on this basis, instruct the computer to replace each instance of the word *he* with *he or she.* You might also have the computer search for all instances of the word *man* so that you can replace *chairman* with *department chair,* *postman* with *mail carrier,* and *policeman* with *police officer.*

The Spell Checker

The "spell checker," available as part of many word-processing systems, is one of the most-popular editing options. You may instruct the computer to search through your text and to pause each time it comes to a word it does not recognize. You then have the option of activating a display of words that resemble the one you tried to spell. One of them is likely to be the correct version of the word you misspelled.

Some spell checkers work as you are typing; the computer will automatically beep when you type in a word it does not recognize. You may then correct the word or activate a list of words that resemble the one you were trying to spell. In addition to helping you with spelling, this type of checking will alert you to many typographical errors. It cannot, unfortunately, serve as a substitute for careful proofreading. The computer will not beep if you mistakenly keyed in *heroin* for *heroine,* because *heroin* is a properly spelled word that also appears in its dictionary.

■ SPREADSHEETS

Spreadsheets such as Lotus 1-2-3 and EXCEL have opened up exciting possibilities for students in areas as varied as engineering, mathematics, manufacturing, management, economics, and statistics. These programs allow students to build and play with models in their fields much the way a word-processing program allows writers to play with the component parts of the writing process.

A student in manufacturing might build a model of an assembly line and try out different ways of breaking down the task to see which would be most efficient. A spreadsheet can give a mathematician access to Monte Carlo programming, the analysis of complex statistical probabilities through the use of multiple random events. Models for complex economic phenomena can be readily constructed and examined by students in economics and political science.

I was converted to spreadsheets when I had to perform the statistical analysis on data from a large research project. After some preliminary preparation, I found that a single keystroke was able to complete in one second calculations that had taken me six hours on a hand calculator. I had to perform more than ten of these analyses, so I was very impressed! Since most of the work took place in creating the spreadsheet, I just typed in the ten different sets of data and each calculation was done in a second. The total saving in time was sixty hours!

Spreadsheets can also be helpful outside of the classroom. You can create a spreadsheet to keep track of your personal investments, noting dividend and interest payments, sales, purchases, profits, losses, and maturity dates. As each payment comes in, you just log it in the appropriate slot. As April 15th rolls around, the press of a single button can tally your reckonings for the Internal Revenue Service.

A spreadsheet can also help you keep track of the courses you must complete to graduate from your college. Create a spreadsheet that lists the categories of courses you must complete for your degree. As you complete each course, key it in under the appropriate category: basic skills requirements, general education requirements, requirements in your major, requirements in your minor, or requirements for certification in a specialty area. Whenever it is time to register for the upcoming semester's courses, you will know exactly what you have to take.

■ WIDENING YOUR COMPUTER HORIZONS TO OTHER FIELDS

Mathematics students rejoice in programs such as TK Solver or MathCAD that allow them to watch as the computer actually goes through the steps of solving complex mathematical formulas on the screen. These students can now understand and play with various aspects of complex mathematics formulations in a way that was previously impossible.

Music majors may enjoy working with a program that helps them compose, orchestrate, transcribe, and play their original compositions. The computer also helps poetry students with their creative process. Students may specify a given structure, and the computer will help them write poetry by keeping track of meter and phrase length, by suggesting words and rhymes.

Students who request counseling (personal or vocational) can find answers to their needs from a computerized "counselor" such as Sigi or the Discover program. Chess, backgammon, bridge, and Go enthusiasts can refine their skills by practicing against computerized "opponents."

Indeed, there seem to be almost no limitations to the variety of ways that computers are helping students in the learning process. It is well worth the investment of your time to become familiar with this fascinating technology.

✍ REFLECTIONS FOR YOUR JOURNAL

1. If you regularly use a computer for coursework, describe how the computer has helped you to improve your writing or enhanced the quality of other work you complete for your courses.

2. If you do not regularly use a computer, describe your feelings about computers. What frustrations have you experienced or what reservations do you have about learning to use computers? How can you overcome these negative experiences or feelings?

3. Why is it worthwhile for you to become comfortable with computers?

Notes

1. D. L. Schorr, Brandeis University commencement address, May 21, 1995, in "Graduation: Words from the Famous to Those Who May Be," *New York Times,* 29 May 1995, p. 9.
2. G. Fabrikant, "The Young and Restless Audience: Computers and Videos Cutting Into Children's Time For Watching TV and Ads," *New York Times,* 8 April 1996, p. D1.
3. N. Negroponte, *Being Digital.* New York: Alfred A. Knopf, 1995, pp. 5, 6.
4. "Techfacts," *On Campus, Vol. 15,* no. 2 (October 1995), p. 11.
5. R. A. Nicholson, "Reengineering the Way Education Does Business," speech given at 9th Annual National Conference on Student Retention, New York, July 28, 1995, ©1995 USA GROUP, Inc, pp. 13–16.
6. N. Negroponte, op. cit, p. 6.
7. E. Gagnon (ed.), *What's on the Web, 1995/1996?* Fairfax, VA: Internet Media Corporation, 1995, p. 3.
8. Ibid, pp. 4–5.
9. A. Pollack, "A Cyberspace Front in the Multicultural War," *New York Times,* 7 December 1995, pp. D1, D4.
10. P. H. Lewis, "In a Recount, Cyber Census Still Confounds," *New York Times,* 17 April 1996, pp. D1, D5.
11. E. Gagnon, op. cit., p. 7.
12. Ibid, p. 34.
13. R. A. Nicholson, op. cit., pp. 17–18.
14. L. R. Shannon, "The Latest Language Skills Via CD ROM's," *New York Times,* 30 May 1995, p. C6.
15. L. Flynn, "Virtual Reality and Virtual Spaces Find a Niche in Real Medicine," *New York Times,* 5 June 1995, p. D3.
16. J. Strickland, "The Reluctant Writer and Word Processing," *Conference for Secondary School English Department Chairpersons (CSSEDC) Quarterly* (1988), pp. 4–5.
17. W. W. Wresch, "Computers and Composition Instruction: An Update," *College English* 45 (1988), 8:794–799.
18. W. V. Costanzo, *The Electronic Text: Learning to Write, Read, and Reason with Computers.* Englewood Cliffs, N.J.: Englewood Cliffs Publications, N.J. Educational Technology, 1989.

Bibliography and References

ADELMAN, C. "Women At Thirty-Something: Paradoxes of Attainment." U.S. Department of Education Office of Research, in "Women Produce More, Are Paid Less." *On Campus,* 11 (no. 2), 1991, p. 2.

"AIDS Epidemic, Late to Arrive, Now Explodes in Populous Asia," *New York Times,* 21 January 1996, pp. A1, A8.

ALTMAN, L. K. "India Suddenly Leads in H.I.V., AIDS Meeting Is Told," *New York Times,* 8 July 1996, p. A3.

ALVAREZ, L. "Still Lives With AIDS," *New York Times,* 10 March 1996, p. 33.

American Council on Education. "American Freshmen: National Norms for 1987." Washington, DC: American Council on Education, 1988.

American Suicide Association, "Prevention Through Research and Education." New York, 1991.

ANDERSON, D. S. and GADALETO, A. F. "The College Alcohol Survey." In *Alcohol Practices, Policies, and Potentials of American Colleges and Universities: A White Paper.* Rockville, MD: U.S. Department of Health and Human Services, Alcohol, Drug Abuse, and Mental Health Administration, 1991; DHHS Publication No. (ADM) 91-1842, p. 20.

Anti-Defamation League. *Audit of Anti-Semitic Incidents, 1995.* New York: Anti-Defamation League, 1996.

APPELBOME, P. "After Rising Faster Than Inflation for Years, Tuition Begins to Drop at Many Colleges," *New York Times,* 24 January 1996, p. B7.

APPLEBOME, P. "Employers Wary of School System," *New York Times,* 20 February 1995, pp. A1, 13.

"A Rush to Solve Problems That Confront the Disabled," *New York Times,* 1 March 1992, p. A24.

AWANOHARA, S. "Model Minority or Ethnic Grab-Bag? On an Uptick," *Far Eastern Economic Review,* 150 (1990).

BAAR, K. "Time for a Fitness Pyramid?" *New York Times,* 29 March 1995, pp. C1, C6.

BAGBY, W. M. *Introduction to Social Science.* Chicago: Nelson-Hall, 1987, pp. 25–27, 31–38.

BANE, V., GRANT, M., ALEXANDER, B., KELLY, K., BROWN, S. A., WEGHER, B., and FELDON-MITCHELL, L. "Silent No More," *People,* 17 December 1990, pp. 94–104.

BARRINGER, F. "Census Shows Profound Change in Racial Makeup of Nation," *New York Times,* 11 March 1991, pp. A1, B8 .

BERNSTEIN, N. "Behind Some Fraternity Walls, Brothers in Crime," *New York Times,* 6 May 1996, pp. A1, B8.

"Birth Control Update: Women's Health News," *Redbook,* September 1990, p. 36.

BRICK, P. and COOPERMAN, C. "Choice and Consequences: Making Decisions About Birth Control." *Positive Images: A New Approach to Contraceptive Education.* Bergen County, NJ: Planned Parenthood.

BRODY, J. E. "Fighting the Nicotine Habit with Nicotine," *New York Times,* 14 April 1995, p. C10.

BRODY, J. E. "Help for Youths Beset by Eating Disorders," *New York Times,* 31 January 1996, p. C10.

BRODY, J. E. "More of the Elderly Seeking the Benefits of Exercise," *New York Times,* 4 October 1995, p. C11.

BRODY, J. E. "Trying to Reconcile Exercise Findings," *New York Times,* 23 April 1995, p. 22.

BROWN, D. *Steps to Independence for People with Learning Disabilities.* Louisville, KY: Youth-Adult Committee of Jefferson County, 1980.

BROWNELL, K. "News of Medicine," *Reader's Digest,* 140, no. 838 (February 1992).

"Burnout: The Epidemic of the '90s," *The Female Patient,* Supplement, S1, 1995, pp. 31–32.

BURROS, M. and JAY, S. "Concern Grows Over Herb That Promises A Legal High," *New York Times,* 10 April 1996, pp. C1, C6.

"Campus Clips: Politics Passe For This Year's Freshmen." *On Campus,* 14, (1995), p. 2.

Carnegie Foundation for the Advancement of Teaching. "Campus Life: In Search of Community." In *Alcohol Practices, Policies, and Potentials.* Princeton, NJ: Princeton University Press, 1990, p. 1.

CARVAJAL, D. "Diversity Pays Off in a Babel of Yellow Pages for Specific Immigrant Groups," *New York Times,* 3 December 1995, pp. 1, 46.

Catalyst. *Catalyst's Campus Resource: A Guide to Exploring Career and Personal Life Options.* New York: Author, 1984.

CELIS, W. "Fewer on Campuses Drink, but Deadly Abuses Endure," *New York Times,* 31 December 1991, pp. A1, A14.

Centers for Disease Control. "The Health Benefits of Smoking Cessation: A Report of the Surgeon General 1990." Rockville, MD: U.S. Department of Health and Human Services, Public Health Service, 1990, DHHS Publication No. (CDC) 90-8416.

Centers for Disease Control. "Tobacco Use Among High School Students—United States, 1990." *Morbidity and Mortality Weekly Report,* 40, no. 36 (13 September 1991), pp. 617–619.

Centers For Disease Control. "Update: Mortality Attributable to HIV Infection Among Persons Aged 25–44 Years." *Morbidity and Mortality Weekly Report,* 45, no. 6, (February 1996), p. 1.

Centers for Disease Control and Prevention. "Update: Alcohol-Related Traffic Crashes and Fatalities Among American Youth and Young Adults." *Morbidity and Mortality Weekly Reports,* 44, no. 47, 1995, pp. 870–871.

Centers for Disease Control and Prevention. *Vital and Health Statistics: Health Risk Behaviors Among Our Nation's Youth, 1992.* Washington, DC: U.S. Department of Health and Human Services, National Center for Health Statistics, 1995, p. 9.

CHIRA, S. "Bias Against Girls Is Found in Schools with Lasting Damage," *New York Times,* 12 February 1992, pp. A1, A23.

CHENEY, L. "Students of Success," *Newsweek,* 1 September 1986, p. 7.

"Chain Must Pay Male Sex-Harassment Victim," *New York Times,* 24 November 1995.

COLVIN, R. L. "Stockbroker Sheds Light on Dyslexia's Difficulties," *Sunday Record,* 5 May 1996, p. L-13.

Consumers Union. *Licit and Illicit Drugs.* Mount Vernon, NY: Author, 1972.

"Contraceptive Use: Facts in Brief." New York: Alan Guttmacher Institute, 1996.

COREY, G. *I Never Knew I Had a Choice.* 2d ed. Monterey, CA: Brooks/Cole Publishing Co., 1986.

COSTANZA, W. V. "The Electronic Text: Learning to Write, Read, and Reason with Computers." Englewood Cliffs, NJ: Englewood Cliffs Publications, New Jersey Educational Technology, 1989.

COSTELLO, C. and STONE, A. J., (Eds.). *The American Woman: 1994–1995.* New York: W. W. Norton, Section 3: Employment.

DAO, J. "Pataki Signs Bill to Combat Drinking by Young Drivers," *New York Times,* 26 June 1996, p. A1.

DEVINE, T. G. *Teaching Study Skills: A Guide for Teachers.* Boston: Allyn & Bacon, 1987.

DUNPHY, L., MILLER, T. E., WOODRUFF, T., and NELSON, J. E. In *Increasing Retention: Academic and Affairs Administrators in Partnership. New Directions for Higher Education,* no. 60. Edited by M. M. Stodt and W. M. Klepper, San Francisco: Jossey-Bass, 1987.

EGAN, T. "Donated Sperm Viewed As Rare Cause of AIDS," *New York Times,* 17 January 1996, p. A10.

EHRLICH, H. J. "Campus Ethnoviolence . . . and the Policy Options." Baltimore, MD: National Institute Against Prejudice and Violence, 1990, p. 66.

EL-KAWAS, E., (Ed.). "Campus Trends, 1984: A Survey of the American Coucil on Education." *Higher Education Report,* no. 65, 1985, p. 9.

ERICKSON, M. T. *Behavior Disorders of Children and Adolescents.* Englewood Cliffs, NJ: Prentice-Hall, 1991, p. 70.

EVANS, G. "Black Students Who Attend White Colleges Face Contradictions in Their Campus Life." *Chronicle of Higher Education,* 30 April 1986.

"Even Moderate Weight Gain Can Become Deadly," *New York Times,* 14 September 1995, pp. A1, B11.

FABRIKANT, G. "The Young and Restless Audience: Computers and Videos Cutting into Children's Time For Watching TV and Ads," *New York Times,* 8 April 1996, p. D1.

"Families Reel from Borrowing Explosion," *On Campus,* March 1996, Vol. 15, no. 6, p. 3, Washington DC: American Federation of Teachers.

FIDLER, P. P. "Evidence of Effectiveness of the Freshman Seminar." In *Enhancing the Success of the First Year Students: The Freshman Experience.* Edited by J. N. Gardner and M. L. Upcraft. San Francisco: Jossey-Bass, 1989, Ch. 15.

"5600 Infant Deaths Tied to Mothers' Smoking," *New York Times,* 13 April 1995, p. A3.

FIGLER, H. E. *Path: A Career Workbook for the Liberal Arts Student.* Cranston, RI: The Carroll Press, 1979.

FLYNN, L. "Virtual Reality and Virtual Spaces Find a Niche in Real Medicine," *New York Times,* 5 June 1995, p. D3.

FREUDENHEIM, M. "New Law to Bring Wider Job Rights for Mentally Ill," *New York Times,* 23 September 1991, pp. A1, D4.

FULLERTON, H. N. "The 2005 Labor Force: Growing, But Slowly," *Monthly Labor Review: The Workforce in 2005,* November 1995, pp. 29–44.

GAGNON, E., (Ed.). *What's on the Web, 1995/1996?* Fairfax, VA: Internet Media Corporation, 1995.

GARDNER, J. (1991). Paper presented at Fifth National Conference on Student Retention, New York, NY. E. El-Kawas, (Ed.). (1985). *Campus Trends, 1984: A Survey of the American Council on Education, Higher Education Report,* 65. Washington, DC: American Council on Education, p. 9.

GARDNER, M. "19 Tips Guaranteed To Give You What You Want," *Working Mother,* February 1996, p. 19.

GAYLE, H. D., KEELING, R. P., GARCIA-TUNON, M., KILBOURNE, B. W., NARKUNAS, J. P., INGRAM, F. R., ROGERS, M. F., and CURRAN, J. W. "Prevalence of the Human Immunodeficiency Virus among University Students," *New England Journal of Medicine,* 323:22 (1990), pp. 1538–1541.

Get Real: Straight Talk About Women's Health. Washington, DC: U.S. Public Health Services Office on Women's Health and Society for Advancement of Women's Research, 1995.

GILBERT, S. "Fitness Helps, Even for Smokers," *New York Times,* 17 July 1996, p. C7.

GOLD, M. S. *800-COCAINE.* New York: Bantam Books, 1985.

GOLDBERG, C. "Company to Pay Record Amount in L.I. Sexual Harassment Case," *New York Times,* 3 August 1995, pp. A1, D8.

GOLEMAN, D. "Sexual Harassment: It's About Power, Not Sex," *New York Times,* 22 October 1991.

GORDON, V. N. and GRITES, T. J. "The Freshman Seminar Course: Helping Students Succeed." *Journal of College Student Personnel,* July 1984, pp. 315–320.

GROSS, J. "Schools Are Newest Arena for Sex-Harassment Cases," *New York Times,* 11 March 1992.

HALL, R., with SANDLER, B. "The Classroom Climate: A Chilly One for Women?" *Project on the Status and Education of Women.* Washington, DC: Association of American Colleges, 1982.

HARTH, M., personal communication (1987).

HATCHER, R. A., GUEST, F., STEWART, F., STEWART, G. K., TRUSSELL, J., BOWEN, S. C., and CATES, W. *Contraceptive Technology.* 16th ed. Atlanta: Printed Matter, Inc.; New York: Irvington Publishers, 1994.

HATCHER, R. A., TRUSSELL, J., STEWART, F., STEWART, G. K., KOWAL, D., GUEST, F., CATES, W., and POLICAR, M. *Contraceptive Technology.* 16th rev. ed. New York: Irvington Publishers, 1994.

HAYES, D. W. "Violence: Another Burden for Some Historically Black Colleges and Universities," *Black Issues in Higher Education,* 24 February 1994, pp. 22–25.

HENDERSON, C. "College Freshmen with Disabilities: Facts You Can Use." Washington, DC: HEATH Research Center of the American Council on Education, 1995.

HENDERSON, C. "Post-Secondary Students with Disabilities: Where Are They Enrolled?" *American Council on Education Research Briefs,* 6, 1995, p. 1.

HERSHENSON, R. "Pain Is Common Thread in Exhibition on Rape," *New York Times,* 25 November 1995, Sec. 13, p. 1.

HERSHEY, JR., R. D. "Bias Hits Hispanic Workers," *New York Times,* 27 April 1995, pp. D1, D3.

HINSENKAMP, P. *How To Use Undergraduate Libraries for Academic Success.* Mahwah, NJ: Ramapo College, 1991.

HITCHCOCK, S. T., and BENNER, R. In "Life after Liberal Arts" by W. Raspberry. *Bergen Country Record,* 19 June 1986.

HOLMES, S. A. "Surprising Rise in Immigrants Stirs Up Debate," *New York Times,* 30 August 1995, pp. A1, A5.

HOLMES, S. A. "Traditional Family Stabilized in the 90's, Study Suggests," *New York Times,* 7 March 1996.

HOLMES, T. H., and RAHE, R. H. "Social Readjustment Rating Scale," *Journal of Psychosomatic Research,* 11, 1967, pp. 213–218.

HONAN, W. "Male Professors Keep 30% Lead in Pay Over Women, Study Says," *New York Times,* 11 April 1996, p. B9.

HONAN, W. H. "State Universities Reshaped in the Era of Budget Cutting," *New York Times,* 22 February 1995, pp. A1, B7.

Hudson Institute. "Workforce 2000." Bureau of Labor Statistics, in "Jobs for Women in the Nineties," *Ms,* July, 1988, p. 77.

HUGHES, T. "Word Processing: Changes in the Classroom, Changes in the Writer," *Conference for Secondary School English Department Chairpersons (CSSEDC) Quarterly* 10:31 (1988), pp. 2–3.

HURH, W. M. and KIM, K. C. "The 'Success' Image of Asian Americans: Its Validity, and Its Practical and Theoretical Implications." *Ethnic and Racial Studies,* 12 (1989), pp. 512–538.

"Husband Wins Claim in Secondhand Smoke Death," *New York Times*, 17 December 1995, p. 28.

JANOFSKY, M. "Survey Reports More Drug Use By Teenagers," *New York Times*, 13 December 1994, pp. A1, A26.

JENKINS, C. D., ZYZANSKI, S. J., and ROSENMAN, R. H. "Risk of New Myocardial Infarction in Middle Age Men with Manifest Coronary Disease," *Circulation*, 53 (1976), pp. 342–347.

JOHNSON, D. "Good People Go Bad in Iowa, and a Drug Is Blamed," *New York Times*, 22 February 1996, pp. A1, 19.

JOHNSON, J. H. and SIEGEL, J. "Assessing the Impact of Life Changes: Development of the Life Experience Survey." *Journal of Consulting and Clinical Psychology*, 46 (1978), pp. 932–946.

JONES, R. in *Dictionary of Occupational Titles*. 4th ed. Washington, DC: U.S. Department of Labor Employment and Training Administration, 1991, pp. iii, v.

KAUFMAN, E. "The New Case for Woman Power," *New York Times Magazine*, Part 2, 28 April 1989, pp. 18–22.

KEELING, R. P. "Student Health in the 1990s," *The Chronicle of Higher Education*, 38:7 (9 October 1991).

KILBORN, P. T. "In New Work World, Employers Call All the Shots," *New York Times*, 3 July 1995, pp. 1, 7.

KOBASA, S. O. "How Much Stress Can You Survive?" *American Health*, 66, September 1984.

KOLATA, G. "New Picture of Who Will Get AIDS," *New York Times*, 28 February 1995, p. C3.

KOONTZ, K. "Major Matters, or Does It?" *Connections*, Winter Preview, 1989, American Express Card, pp. 3–4, 16.

KOOP, C. E. and Centers for Disease Control. "Understanding AIDS" (brochure), 1988.

KUTNER, L. "Why Children Smoke and Why They Won't Listen," *New York Times*, 6 February 1992, p. C12.

"Lack of Exercise Cited in U. S. Women," *New York Times*, 19 August 1995, p. 29.

LACROIX, A. Z., MEAD, L. A., LIANG, K. Y., THOMAS, C. B., and PEARSON, T. A. "Coffee Consumption and the Incidence of Coronary Heart Disease," *New England Journal of Medicine* 315 (1986), pp. 977–982.

LAVOIE, R. D., in HEVESI, D. "Learning Disabled for a Day," *New York Times*, 4 August 1991, Section 4 A, Education Life.

LEARY, W. E. "Billions Suffering Needlessly, Study Says," *New York Times*. 2 May 1995, p. C5.

LEDERMAN, D. "Colleges Report 7500 Violent Crimes. . . ." *The Chronicle of Higher Education*, 20 January 1993, pp. A32–A41.

LEVINE, R. D. "Drugs Are Back—Big Time," *Reader's Digest*, February 1996, pp. 71–76.

LEWIN, T. "Chevron Settles Sexual Harassment Charges," *New York Times*, 22 February 1995.

LEWIN, T. "Sexual Harassment Charged at Cornell," *New York Times*, 27 January 1995, p. B5.

LEWIN, T. "Women Are Becoming Equal Partners," *New York Times*, 5 November 1995, p. A27.

LEWIN, T. "Women Are Becoming Equal Providers," *New York Times*, 11 May 1995, p. A27.

LEWIS, P. H. "In a Recount, Cyber Census Still Confounds," *New York Times*, 17 April 1996, pp. D1, D5.

Licit and Illicit Drugs. Mt. Vernon, NY: Consumers Union, 1972.

LINE, L. "Ticks and Moths, Not Just Oaks, Linked to Acorns," *New York Times*, 16 April 1996, pp. C1, C6.

LOMBARDI, K. S. "New Policy Is Aimed at Preventing Date Rape on Campuses," *New York Times*, 25 October 1992, Sec. 13, pp. 1, 4, 5.

LONGMAN, J. "Proceeding with Caution: Wheelchair Athletes Face Risks When Training on Roads," *New York Times*, 7 November 1995, pp. B9, B12.

LOUIS, E. T. "Black and Blue on Campus," *Essence*, August 1986, pp. 67, 68, 132.

Louis Harris & Associates. *Closing The Gap: The National Organization on Disability/Harris Survey of Americans With Disabilities*. Washington, DC: National Organization on Disability, 1994, p. 28.

Louis Harris & Associates. *The National Organization on Disability/Harris Survey on Employment of People With Disabilities*. Washington, DC: National Organization on Disability, 1995, p. 23.

LURIA, A. R. *Mind of a Mnemonist*. Translated by L. Solotaroff. New York: Basic Books, 1968.

MCWHORTER, K. *College Reading and Study Skills*. Boston: Little Brown, 1982.

MCWHORTER, K. *Study and Thinking Skills in College*. Glenview, IL: Scott, Foresman, 1988.

"Man Wins Harassment Suit Against Man," *New York Times*, 13 August 1995.

MARTIN, JOHN YATE in C. MCINTOSH, "Giving Good Answers to Tough Interview Questions," *McCall's*, May 1991, p. 38.

MATHEWS, A. "The Campus Crime Wave," *The New York Times Magazine*, 7 March 1993, pp. 38–47.

"Meat and Dairy Industries Not Thrilled." *Hope Health Letter*. Seattle, WA: Hope Heart Institute.

MEYERSON, R. "Thriving Where Others Won't Go," *New York Times*, 7 January 1992, pp. D1, D5.

National Center for Statistics and Analysis. "1990 Traffic Fatality Facts." Washington, DC: U.S. Department of Transportation, National Highway Safety Administration, 1991, p. 6.

National Center for Statistics and Analysis. "Drunk Driving Facts." Washington, DC: U.S. Department of Transportation, National Highway Traffic Safety Administration, 1991.

"National Dropout Rates." The American College Testing Program. Compiled from ACT Institutional Data File. Iowa City, IA: Noel-Levitz Center for Student Retention, 1995.

National Institute on Drug Abuse. "Marijuana Update." Rockville, MD, 1989, NIDA Capsule 12.

National Institute on Drug Abuse. *National Household Survey on Drug Abuse: Population Estimates 1994*. Washington, DC: U.S. Department of Health and Human Services, 1994.

National Institute on Drug Abuse. *National Trends in Drug Use and Related Factors Among American High School Students and Young Adults, 1975–1986*. Washington, DC: U.S. Department of Health and Human Services, 1987. DHHS Publication No. (ADM) 87-1535.

NAVARRO, M. "In South, Drug Abusers Turning to a Smuggled Sedative," *New York Times*, 9 December 1995, p. 6.

NEGROPONTE, N. *Being Digital*. New York: Alfred A. Knopf, 1995.

NICHOLSON, R. A. "Reengineering the Way Education Does Business." Speech given at the Ninth Annual National Conference on Student Retention, New York, July 28, 1995, © 1995 USA GROUP, Inc., pp. 13–16.

NOBLE, K. B. "Attacks Against Asian-Americans on the Rise, Especially in California," *New York Times*, 13 December 1995, p. B13.

"Nutrition & Safe Foods IQ Test, 10 Foods You Should Never Eat." *Nutrition Action Newsletter*. Washington, DC: Center for Science in the Public Interest, 1995.

Office for Substance Abuse and Prevention. *Turning Awareness into Action*. Rockville, MD: National Clearinghouse for Drug and Alcohol Information, 1991, p. 56.

OKIE, S. "Study Finds 1 in 500 College Students Infected with Virus That Causes AIDS," *The Journal News*, 29 May 1989, p. A3.

O'NEIL, M. "The Morality of Fat," *New York Times Magazine,* 10 March 1996, p. 37.

PETROFF, B. and BROEK, L. "The University of Iowa Alcohol and Other Drug Use Assessment: Spring Semester." In *Alcohol Practices, Policies, and Potentials,* p. 11. Ames: University of Iowa Student Health Services, 1990.

POLLACK, A. "A Cyberspace Front in the Multicultural War," *New York Times,* 7 December 1995, pp. D1, D4.

POSTMAN, R. D., KECKLER, B., and SCHNECKER, P. *College Reading and Study Skills.* New York: Macmillan, 1985.

"Prevalence of Selected Chronic Respiratory Conditions." *Vital Health Statistics,* Series 10, no. 84. Washington, DC: U.S. Department of Health, Education and Welfare, 1970.

PRIDE. "Teen Drug Use Rises for Fourth Straight Year." Atlanta, GA: National Parents' Resource Institute for Drug Education, November 2, 1995.

PRITCHARD, C. *Avoiding Rape On and Off Campus.* Wenonah, NJ: State College Publishing Co., 1985.

PURDUM, T. S. "Clinton Proposes Broad Plan to Curb Teen-Age Smoking," *New York Times,* 11 August 1995, pp. A1, A19.

PURDY, M. "New Inmates Reflect Surge in Use of Cheap but Potent Heroin," *New York Times,* 3 December 1995, p. 49.

RASCHKE, D., and DEDRICK, C. "Simulations Approximating Learning Disabilities," *TEACHING Exceptional Children,* Summer 1986, pp. 266–271.

RAWLINGS, H. R., III. "Sexual Harassment." Ithaca, NY: Cornell University Office of Public Services, 1995.

"Report Explaining Increasing Numbers of Women in Psychology," *APA Monitor,* 26 (December 1995), p. 15.

RICHARDSON, L. *The Dynamics of Sex and Gender: A Sociological Perspective.* New York: Harper & Row, 1988.

RHEINHOLD, R. "Class Struggle," *New York Times Magazine,* 29 September 1991, p. 27.

RIMER, S. "New York's Aspiring Dominican Immigrants," *New York Times,* 16 September 1991, pp. A1, B6.

ROARK, M. L. "Helping High School Students Assess Campus Safety," *The School Counselor,* 39, March 1992, pp. 251–256.

RODEN, M. "What Men Need to Know About Date Rape." Santa Monica, CA: Rape Treatment Center, Santa Monica Hospital Medical Center, 1990.

ROSENMAN, R. H., BRAND, R. J., JENKINS, C. D., FRIEDMAN, M., STRAUS, R., and WURM, M. "Coronary Heart Disease in the Western Collaborative Group Study: Final Follow-up Experience at 8½ Years," *Journal of the American Medical Association,* 233 (1975), pp. 872–877.

ROSS, J. F. "What You Don't Know About Risk," *Reader's Digest,* April, 1996, p. 90.

SACK, K. "Making Volunteerism Easier for Busy Workers of Today," *New York Times,* 25 November 1995, pp. A1, 11.

SADKER, M., and SADKER, D. "Sexism in the '80s," *Psychology Today,* March 1985, pp. 54–55.

SAFILIOS-ROTHSCHILD. Reported in M. Sadker and D. Sadker, "Sexism in the '80s," *Psychology Today,* March 1985, pp. 54–55.

SARASON, I. G., JOHNSON, J. H., and SIEGEL, J. "Assessing the Impact of Life Changes: Development of the Life Experience Survey," *Journal of Consulting and Clinical Psychology,* 46 (1978), pp. 932–946.

SCHATZKIN, A. et al. "Alcohol Consumption and Breast Cancer in the Epidemiologic Follow-up Study of the First National Health and Nutrition Examination Survey," *New England Journal of Medicine,* 316 (1987), pp. 1169–1173.

SCHLAADT, R. G., and SHANNON, P. T. *Drugs of Choice.* Englewood Cliffs, NJ: Prentice-Hall, 1982.

SCHMALZ, J. "Hispanic Influx Spurs Step to Bolster English," *New York Times,* 26 October 1988, pp. A1, B8.

SCHMITT, E. "Ex-Head of Navy's Sex Bias Fight Goes on Trial in Harassment Case," *New York Times,* 12 October 1995, pp. A1, B6.

SCHMITT, E. "New Navy Scandal: An Admiral Guilty of Sexual Harassment," *New York Times,* 9 December 1995, pp. A1, A11.

SEBOLD, A. "Speaking of the Unspeakable," *New York Times Magazine,* 26 February 1989, Sec. 6, p. 16.

SERBIN, L. A., O'LEARY, K. D., KENT, R. N., and TONICK, I. J. "A Comparison of Teacher Response to the Pre-academic and Problem Behavior of Boys and Girls," *Child Development,* 44 (1973), pp. 796–804.

SHAFII, M. et al. "Psychological Autopsy of Completed Suicide in Children and Adolescents," *American Journal of Psychiatry,* 142 (1985), p. 1061.

SHANNON, L. R. "The Latest Language Skills via CD ROM's," *New York Times,* 30 May 1995, p. C6.

SIEGEL, D. S. "What Is Behind the Growth of Violence on Campuses?" *USA Today,* May 1994, pp. 32–34.

SIMPSON, J. C. "Campus Barrier? Black College Students Are Viewed as Victims of a Subtle Racism," *Wall Street Journal,* 3 April 1987.

SIMS, C. "Late Bloomers Come to Campus," *New York Times,* 4 August 1991, Education Life, Sec. 4A, pp. 16–17.

SIVESTRI, G. T. "Occupational Employment to 2005," *Monthly Labor Review: The Workforce in 2005,* November 1995, pp. 60–84.

SMITH, H. M., and KENNEDY, M. L. *Word Processing for College Writers.* Englewood Cliffs, NJ: Prentice-Hall, 1989.

SMITH, L., and WALTER, T. *The Adult Learner's Guide to College Success.* Belmont, CA: Wadsworth, 1995 and *USA Today,* 2 March 1991, in "Back to School," *The Serious Investor,* August 1991, New York: Shearson Lehman Brothers.

"Special Report: Medical Complications of Cocaine Abuse," *New England Journal of Medicine,* 315 (1986), pp. 1495–1500.

SPRINGER, I. "Heart Report: Are You at Risk?" *Family Circle,* 18 February 1992, p. 70; W. Ecenbarger, "The Strange History of Tobacco," *Reader's Digest,* April 1992, p. 142.

STARKE, M. C. "A Longitudinal Study of the Freshman Seminar Program." Paper presented at Eleventh National Conference on the Freshman Year Experience, Columbia, SC: February 1994.

STARKE, M. C. "Retention and Bonding: The Effectiveness of the Freshman Seminar at Ramapo College." Paper presented at the Ninth National Conference on Student Retention, New York, NY, April 1995.

STARKE, M. C. "Retention and Bonding: The Success of the Freshman Seminar Program at Ramapo College." Paper presented at Fourth National Conference on Student Retention, Washington, DC, July 1990.

STARKE, M. C., and BEAR, G. "Grading in Higher Education: A Survey of American Systems and Practices," *Journal of Research and Development in Education,* 21:4 (1988), pp. 62–68.

STEIN, N., MARSHALL, N. L., and TRAPP, L. R. *Secrets in Public: Sexual Harassment.* Center for Research on Women at Wellesley College and NOW Legal Defense Education Fund.

STEINHAUER, J. "Big Benefits in Marriage, Studies Say," *New York Times,* 10 April 1995, p. A9.

STRICKLAND, J. "The Reluctant Writer and Word Processing," *Conference for Secondary School English Department Chairpersons (CSSEDC) Quarterly* (1988), pp. 4–5.

Substance Abuse and Mental Health Services Administration. *National Household Survey on Drug Abuse.* Washington, DC: U.S. Department of Health and Human Services, 1995, p. 31.

Substance Abuse and Mental Health Services Administration, op. cit., p. 91.

SUPER, D. E., and CRITES, J. O. *Appraising Vocational Fitness.* Rev. ed. New York: Harper Brothers, 1962.

"Techfacts." *On Campus,* Vol. 15, no. 2, October 1995, p. 11.

"Teenage Reproductive Health in the United States." New York: Alan Guttmacher Institute, 1994.

TEPPER, R. *Career Manual.* Mahwah, NJ: Ramapo College, 1988.

Time, April 23, 1990. In L. D. Eigen, *Alcohol Practices, Policies, and Potentials of American Colleges and Universities: A White Paper.* Rockville, MD: U.S. Department of Health and Human Services, Alcohol, Drug Abuse, and Mental Health Administration, 1991; DHHS Publication No. (ADM) 91-1842, p. 1.

UCHITELLE, L. "Surplus of College Graduates Dims Job Outlook for Others," *New York Times,* 18 June 1990.

U.S. Department of Commerce, Bureau of the Census. *Statistical Abstracts of the United States, 1995.* Washington, DC: Author, 1995.

U.S. Department of Commerce, Bureau of the Census. *Statistical Abstracts of the United States.* Washington, DC: Government Printing Office, 1995, Table 8, p. 11; Table 19, p. 19; Table 31, p. 31, p. 38; Table 49, p. 48; Table 53, p. 51; Table 55, p. 52; Table 228, p. 151; Table 238, p. 157; Table 281, p. 181; Table 677, p. 433; Table 739, p. 477.

U.S. Department of Commerce, op. cit, Table 228, p. 151; Table 281, p. 181.

U.S. Department of Commerce, op. cit., Table 271, p. 162.

U.S. Department of Commerce, op. cit., Table 294, p. 187.

U.S. Department of Commerce, op. cit., Table 742, p. 479.

U.S. Department of Health and Human Services. *The Fourth Special Report to the U.S. Congress on Alcohol and Health.* Washington, DC: Alcohol, Drug Use, and Mental Health Administration, 1981.

U.S. Department of Health and Human Services. *Nutrition and Your Health: Dietary Guidelines for Americans,* 3rd ed. Washington, DC: U.S. Department of Agriculture, 1990, Doc. A 1.77:232/990.

U.S. Department of Health and Human Services. *Strategies for Preventing Alcohol and Other Drug Problems.* Rockville, MD: Alcohol, Drug Abuse, and Mental Health Administration 1991; DHHS Publication No. (ADM) 91-1843, p. 8.

U.S. Department of Justice. *Sourcebook of Criminal Justice Statistics 1994.* Washington, DC: Bureau of Justice Statistics, 1995, p. 301, Table 3.88.

U.S. Department of Justice. *Uniform Crime Reports: Hate Crime Statistics Revised.* Washington, DC: U.S. Department of Justice, FBI, 1995, Tables 17, 1.

U.S. Department of Justice, Federal Bureau of Investigation. *Hate Crime Statistics, 1993 Revised, Uniform Crime Reports.* Washington, DC: U.S. Government Printing Office, 1995.

U.S. Public Health Service. "Alcohol and Health: Sixth Special Report to Congress." (Washington, DC, 1987) in *Alcohol Practices, Policies, and Potentials,* p. 11; R. Hingson and J. H. Howland, "Alcohol as a Risk Factor for Injury or Death Resulting from Accidental Falls: A Review of the Literature," *Journal of Studies of Alcohol,* 48 (1987), pp. 212–219.

USDANSKY, M. L. "Teen Births: Formula For Disaster," *USA Today,* 22 February 1994, pp. 1a, 2a.

VAN GELDER, L. "Patterns of Addiction: Dependencies of Independent Women," *Ms,* February 1987, p. 38.

VECSEY, G. "The Woman Who Outshot All the Men," *New York Times,* 6 February 1992.

VERHOVEK, S. H. "Young, Carefree and in Love with Cigarettes," *New York Times,* 30 July 1995, p. A1.

WECHLER, H., DAVENPORT, A., DOWDALL, G., MOEYKENS, B., and CASTILLO, S. "Health and Behavioral Consequences of Binge Drinking in College," *Journal of the American Medical Association,* 7 (December 1994), pp. 1672–1677.

WEINSTEIN, M. M. "Why They Deserve It," *New York Times Magazine,* 19 November 1995, p. 103.

"What Value Education? Counting the Whys," *New York Times,* 3 October 1987, p. 29.

"Where The Jobs Are," *Moneysaver, Gannett Suburban Newspaper,* (from the *L.A. Times*) 1 April 1995, p. 1.

WILKERSON, I. "Racial Harassment Altering Blacks' Choices on College," *New York Times,* 9 May 1990, pp. A1, B10.

WILLETT, W. C. et al. "Moderate Alcohol Consumption and the Risk of Breast Cancer," *New England Journal of Medicine,* 316 (1987), pp. 1174–1180.

WILLIAMS, G. D., STINTSON, F. S., PARKER, D. A., HARTFORD, T. C., and NOBLE, J. N. "Demographic Trends, Alcohol Abuse and Alcoholism 1985–1995," *Alcohol World: Health and Research,* 11 (1987), pp. 80–84.

WONG, M. "Post-1965 Asian Immigrants: Where Do They Come From, Where Are They Now, and Where Are They Going?" *The Annals of the American Academy of Political and Social Science,* 487 (1986), pp. 150–168.

WREN, C. S. "Sharp Rise in Use of Methamphetamines Generates Concern," *New York Times,* 14 February 1996, p. A16.

WRESCH, W. W. "Computers and Composition Instruction: An Update," *College English,* 45:8 (1988), pp. 794–799.

Index

STRESS MANAGEMENT AUDIOCASSETTE

Is anxiety or stress keeping you from performing your very best?

Have you tried to relax, but find you just can't block out the sounds around you?

Now you can get an audiocassette that will reduce your anxiety and stress and help you be successful!

This 60-minute audiocassette will direct you through four proven relaxation techniques

- Deep Muscle Relaxation
- Autogenic Training
- Imagery
- Systematic Desensitization

This audiocassette will take you step-by-step through the various muscle groups so that you learn how to relax your body. You will then learn how to use imagery, breathing, and autogenic phrases to calm your mind so that you can focus on a task and perform at your best.

Finally, you will learn to use systematic desensitization to condition yourself so that you become comfortable in situations that previously made you anxious. This tape focuses on overcoming your anxiety in exam situations and it will teach you how to construct a program that can help you overcome other fears that interfere with your success.

YES! Please send me the audiocassette!

Quantity _____ @ $10.95 each = $ _____

Shipping and Handling   + $2.00

HELP! I needed this cassette yesterday!

Please send me the tape overnight

$10.00 for 1–4 audiocassettes   + $ _____

$15.00 for 5 or more audiocassettes   + $ _____

Total $ _____

Name _____

Street Address _____

City _____ State _____ Zip Code _____

Telephone Number _____

Signature _____

Send this order form and your check or   Mary C. Starke, Ph.D.
money order payable to Mary C. Starke to: 516 North State Road
                                                Briarcliff, NY 10510

Thank you for your order!

Eyewitness
FORENSIC
SCIENCE

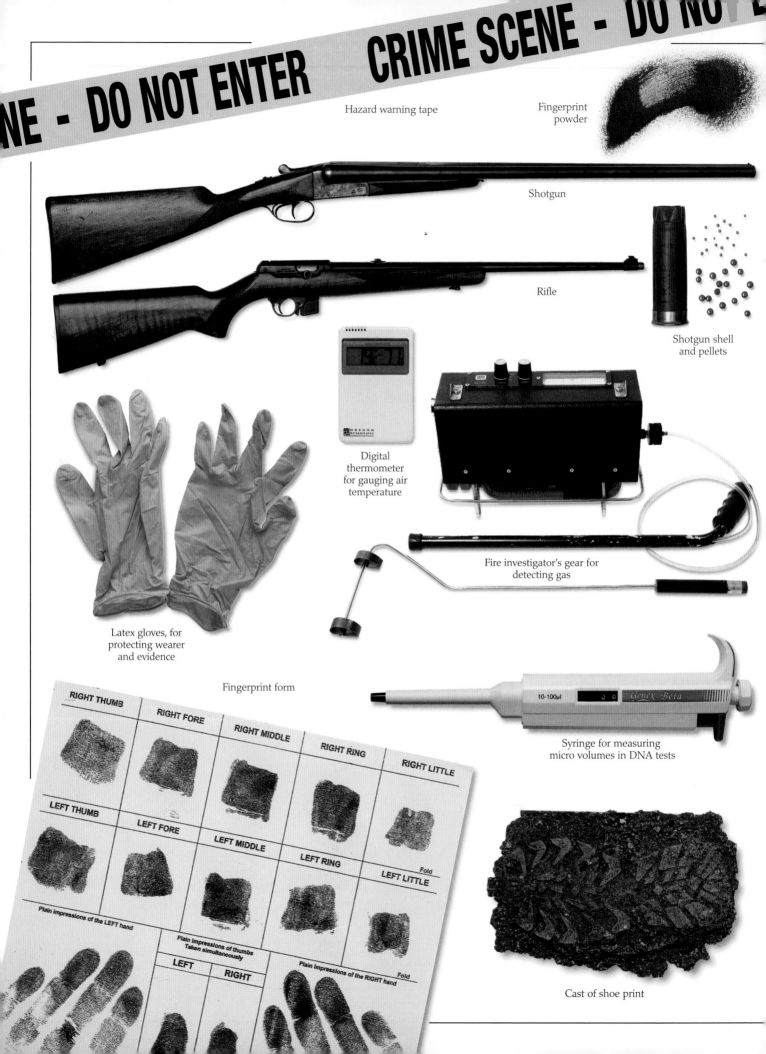

CRIME SCENE - DO NOT E

NE - DO NOT ENTER

Hazard warning tape

Fingerprint powder

Shotgun

Rifle

Shotgun shell and pellets

Digital thermometer for gauging air temperature

Fire investigator's gear for detecting gas

Latex gloves, for protecting wearer and evidence

Fingerprint form

10-100µl   Genex Beta

Syringe for measuring micro volumes in DNA tests

RIGHT THUMB	RIGHT FORE	RIGHT MIDDLE	RIGHT RING	RIGHT LITTLE
LEFT THUMB	LEFT FORE	LEFT MIDDLE	LEFT RING	LEFT LITTLE

Fold

Plain impressions of the LEFT hand

Plain impressions of thumbs
Taken simultaneously

LEFT	RIGHT

Plain impressions of the RIGHT hand

Fold

Cast of shoe print

Linen tester
for magnifying
fingerprints

Eyewitness
FORENSIC
SCIENCE

Beretta 92FS
pistol

Written by
CHRIS COOPER

Forensic investigator's toolkit

DK Publishing

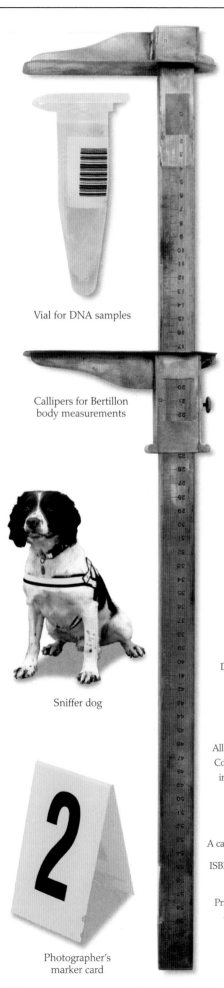

Vial for DNA samples

Callipers for Bertillon
body measurements

Sniffer dog

Photographer's
marker card

Pipette

Scalpel

Tweezers

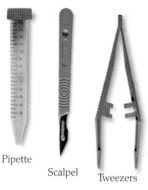

**LONDON, NEW YORK, MUNICH,
MELBOURNE, AND DELHI**

Consultant Dr. Clive Steele

Project editor Mary Lindsay
Art editor Neville Graham
Photographer Andy Crawford
Managing editor Camilla Hallinan
Managing art editor Owen Peyton Jones
Art director Martin Wilson
Publishing manager Sunita Gahir
Category publisher Andrea Pinnington
Picture researcher Sarah Hopper
DK picture library Rose Horridge, Emma Shepherd
Senior production editor Vivianne Ridgeway
Senior production controller Man Fai Lau

DK DELHI
Art director Shefali Upadhyay
Designer Govind Mittal
DTP designer Harish Aggarwal

This Eyewitness ® Book has been conceived by
Dorling Kindersley Limited and Editions Gallimard.

First published in the United States in 2008 by
DK Publishing, 375 Hudson Street, New York, New York 10014

A catalog record for this book is available from the Library of Congress.

ISBN 978-0-7566-3383-7 (HC), 978-0-7566-3363-9 (Library Binding)

Color reproduction by Colourscan, Singapore.
Printed & bound in Hong Kong by Toppan Printing Company Ltd.

Discover more at
www.dk.com

Fingerprint
powder brush

Camera for
photographic record

Magnetic wand

Sterile swab
and container
for sample

Contents

In pursuit of the criminal

FORENSIC SCIENCE IS THE USE OF SCIENTIFIC methods and knowledge to investigate crime—the word "forensic" comes from the Latin *forum* and means presenting and interpreting scientific information in court. Forensic scientists study evidence at the scene of a crime and perhaps at the homes and workplaces of suspects. They study the bodies of victims. Many sciences, from chemistry to engineering to entomology (the study of insects), are used in an investigation. If there is any doubt about what has happened, forensic science provides evidence that may link a suspect to a crime or prove him or her innocent. Experts investigate not only murder, assault, and bank robbery, but also smuggling animals or people, or committing fraud on the Internet—crimes of all types.

FORENSICS AT THE CRIME SCENE
Forensic investigators must collect evidence as soon as possible after the crime, while it is still fresh—even if the area is unsafe and they have to work under armed guard. These investigators are examining the victim of a terrorist killing in Northern Ireland in 2000. To protect the scene from contamination they wear cleansuits, which prevent traces from their clothes or skin from fouling the evidence.

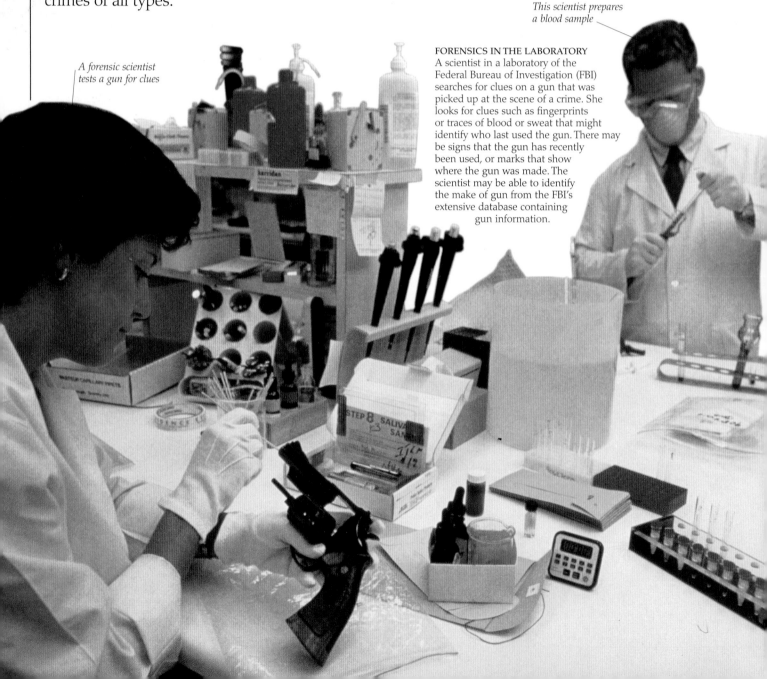

A forensic scientist tests a gun for clues

This scientist prepares a blood sample

FORENSICS IN THE LABORATORY
A scientist in a laboratory of the Federal Bureau of Investigation (FBI) searches for clues on a gun that was picked up at the scene of a crime. She looks for clues such as fingerprints or traces of blood or sweat that might identify who last used the gun. There may be signs that the gun has recently been used, or marks that show where the gun was made. The scientist may be able to identify the make of gun from the FBI's extensive database containing gun information.

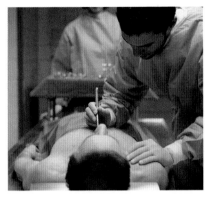

AT AN AUTOPSY

A forensic pathologist is making an incision in the chest of a dead man. His main job is to find out the cause of death and inform the police if there are signs of a crime. After checking any external markings for clues as to the cause of death, he cuts the body open to examine the internal organs. He will remove some of them in order to inspect them closely and also to examine underlying organs and other structures, but they will all be replaced in the body before it is buried or cremated.

FORENSICS IN COURT

At a criminal trial, it is the job of forensic scientists to provide evidence, regardless of whether it favors the prosecution or the defense. The results of the experts' painstaking work often end up in court. Here photographs made at the scene of the crime are presented in the sensational trial of the professional football player O. J. Simpson, who was accused of double murder. The defense and prosecution lawyers pitted their own forensic experts against each other. The jury doubted some of the prosecution's evidence, and the trial ended with O. J. Simpson's acquittal in October 1995.

Forensic expert presents evidence

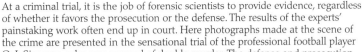

Aerial photo of location of crime scene

Close-up view of evidence at the crime scene

FBI officer talks to the press

FORENSICS BEFORE THE PUBLIC

An FBI officer talks at a press conference following the arrest of a suspected bank robber in New Jersey. The police rely on the forensic team behind the scene—information that goes to the press and the public must be absolutely accurate. The forensic experts' reconstruction of a crime and of the description of the suspects will play a large part in the investigation and prosecution that follow.

FORENSICS AS ENTERTAINMENT

Greg Sanders (played by Eric Szmanda) is a junior member of the forensic team in the hit TV show *CSI: Crime Scene Investigation*. Sanders uses his enthusiasm for science to track down criminals. Despite criticisms of the ways in which the show often sensationalizes forensic work, it is credited with creating unprecedented public interest in forensic science, and has spawned *CSI: Miami* and *CSI: NY*, as well as many other competitor programs worldwide.

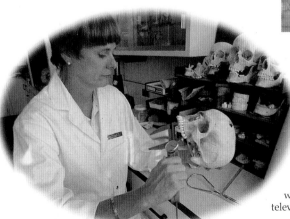

KATHY REICHS—SCIENTIST AND NOVELIST

Forensic experts often complain that books, films, and television shows are full of inaccuracies about the scientific nature of their work. Kathy Reichs, however, brings authenticity to her best-selling thrillers, which are all written with a forensic science angle. She is a highly respected college professor who also works as a forensic scientist for US and Canadian police, specializing in the evidence that can be provided by bones. Her novels feature a forensic scientist called Temperance Brennan, whose fictional work is very similar to the writer's. A television series, *Bones*, is based on the same character.

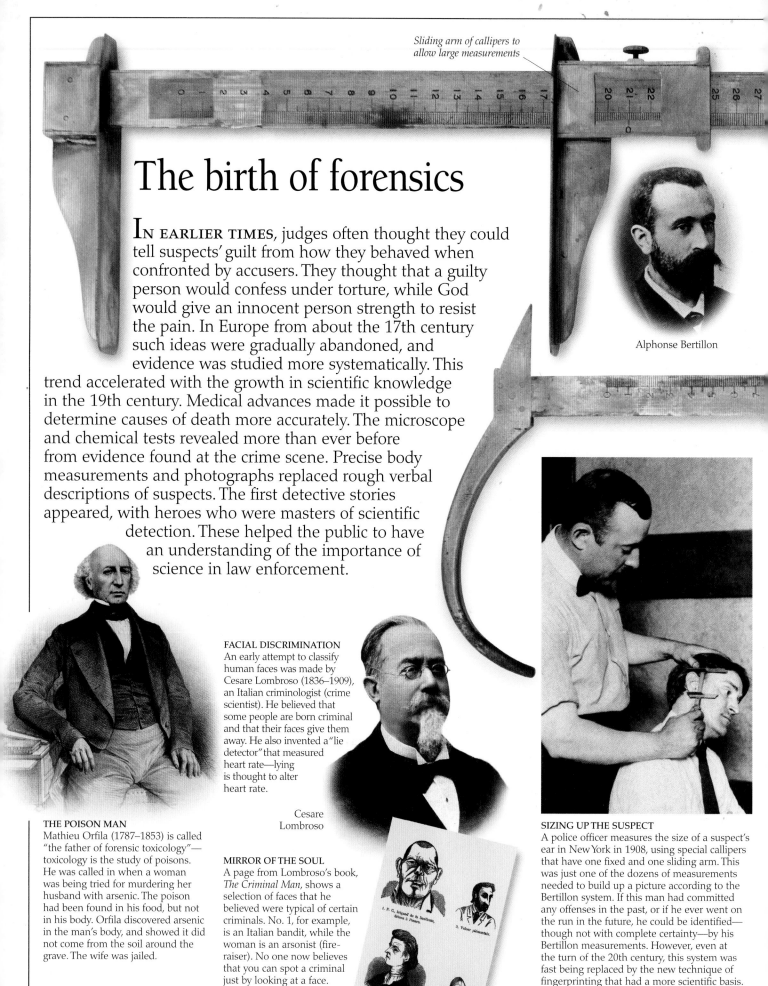

Sliding arm of callipers to allow large measurements

The birth of forensics

IN EARLIER TIMES, judges often thought they could tell suspects' guilt from how they behaved when confronted by accusers. They thought that a guilty person would confess under torture, while God would give an innocent person strength to resist the pain. In Europe from about the 17th century such ideas were gradually abandoned, and evidence was studied more systematically. This trend accelerated with the growth in scientific knowledge in the 19th century. Medical advances made it possible to determine causes of death more accurately. The microscope and chemical tests revealed more than ever before from evidence found at the crime scene. Precise body measurements and photographs replaced rough verbal descriptions of suspects. The first detective stories appeared, with heroes who were masters of scientific detection. These helped the public to have an understanding of the importance of science in law enforcement.

Alphonse Bertillon

FACIAL DISCRIMINATION
An early attempt to classify human faces was made by Cesare Lombroso (1836–1909), an Italian criminologist (crime scientist). He believed that some people are born criminal and that their faces give them away. He also invented a "lie detector" that measured heart rate—lying is thought to alter heart rate.

Cesare Lombroso

THE POISON MAN
Mathieu Orfila (1787–1853) is called "the father of forensic toxicology"—toxicology is the study of poisons. He was called in when a woman was being tried for murdering her husband with arsenic. The poison had been found in his food, but not in his body. Orfila discovered arsenic in the man's body, and showed it did not come from the soil around the grave. The wife was jailed.

MIRROR OF THE SOUL
A page from Lombroso's book, *The Criminal Man*, shows a selection of faces that he believed were typical of certain criminals. No. 1, for example, is an Italian bandit, while the woman is an arsonist (fire-raiser). No one now believes that you can spot a criminal just by looking at a face.

SIZING UP THE SUSPECT
A police officer measures the size of a suspect's ear in New York in 1908, using special callipers that have one fixed and one sliding arm. This was just one of the dozens of measurements needed to build up a picture according to the Bertillon system. If this man had committed any offenses in the past, or if he ever went on the run in the future, he could be identified—though not with complete certainty—by his Bertillon measurements. However, even at the turn of the 20th century, this system was fast being replaced by the new technique of fingerprinting that had a more scientific basis.

"MEASURING" THE PERSON

The earliest scientific system for identifying people by their physical appearance was called Bertillonage, after its French inventor Alphonse Bertillon (1853–1914). This system used measurements of the body, such as the lengths of arms and legs, the diameter of the head, and other statistics, as well as body markings such as scars or tattoos, and photographs of the suspect. Although the system was slow and cumbersome, and could not always tell people apart, it was used by many police forces for years. It suffered a blow in 1903 when an American called Will West was sent to prison, before it was discovered that another prisoner there had almost the same Bertillon measurements—and was named William West.

EARLY MUGSHOTS

Bertillon measurements were supplemented with photographs, which came to be called "mugshots." Usually a photograph would be taken from the side ("in profile") and from the front. If the person committed a crime at some future time, his mugshot would be widely distributed, so that he could be recognized by policemen on the beat or by the public. The profiles shown here are from just one of the many pages of Bertillon's original book of mugshots.

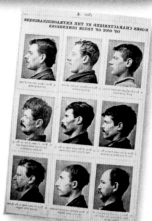

Window displaying recorded measurement

Rule measuring centimeters

Small sliding arm

POLICING BECOMES SCIENTIFIC

The pioneering forensic laboratory shown here was established in 1932 by the boss of the FBI, J. Edgar Hoover. Police forces began to realize that scientific principles were needed in their work. This laboratory was equipped for up-to-date tests using chemistry, physics, and engineering. Evidence began to be properly stored and protected until it could be examined. As scientific methods became more and more sensitive, so the precautions taken in collecting the evidence became greater. Today every major country has at least one advanced forensic science laboratory.

FICTIONAL FORENSICS

Sherlock Holmes, the fictional detective created by Sir Arthur Conan Doyle, is pictured studying a piece of evidence through a powerful magnifying glass. Close at hand are a microscope and various pieces of chemical apparatus. The most famous detective in fiction made his first appearance in print in 1887. He is described as paying attention to tiny pieces of evidence that others overlooked. The character of Holmes was wildly popular—this still is from the popular 1942 film, *The Voice of Terror*.

Basil Rathbone as Holmes

LETTER FROM THE RIPPER?

This is one of hundreds of letters—probably all hoaxes—claiming to be from the serial killer "Jack the Ripper," who terrorized London's East End in 1888. The primitive forensic methods of the time could discover little from this letter. Modern DNA testing suggests that it was from a woman. The letter is almost certainly a hoax.

Securing the scene

In the past, policemen would walk around the scene of a crime and handle evidence with their bare hands. This didn't matter much, since the simple forensic techniques available could not detect the effects of their actions on the evidence. Today, with the enormous advances in forensic science, the situation is very different. With a serious crime, the forensic specialists turn the scene into an area resembling a laboratory. Only authorized personnel are allowed past the police warning tape. The investigators record evidence on the spot, with photographs, sketches, notes, and measurements, and then take away essential evidence—including bodies, if there are any. At the same time, police officers locate witnesses and take statements. Speed is vital: witnesses must be questioned while memories are still fresh, and physical evidence must be preserved before it is altered by time or weather conditions. This precious window of opportunity is known as the "golden hour."

BY INVITATION ONLY
One of the first things the police do when they arrive at the scene of a crime is to make sure no one is in danger. Their next priority is to get help to anyone who has been injured. Then they cordon off the area. Curious onlookers, journalists, and cameramen often crowd around the scene of a crime. It is imperative to keep them away until the evidence has been collected. This is to ensure that they do not accidentally contaminate the scene and mislead investigators. Only authorized police officers are allowed to cross the line.

One member of the team takes notes

The forensic photographer makes a record of the scene

Tape used to cordon off a crime scene while evidence is collected

BEFORE THE TRAIL GOES COLD

If a body found at an incident shows signs of life, the person must be rushed to the hospital. If not, it must be certified dead by a qualified medical examiner before it is moved. This body was found in the aftermath of Hurricane Katrina in New Orleans in 2005. A forensic investigation was needed because the police couldn't assume that every body found was a victim of the hurricane and not of a crime committed some time before the hurricane struck.

FIRST ANSWER

Many crime investigations depend on a few facts among many thousands of items of information provided by people living near the scene of a crime. The whole area may be flooded with police officers asking the same carefully devised questions from a checklist. In addition, the police may be equipped with visual cues, such as photographs or drawings of victims or suspects. Such an enormous effort in terms of manpower and time can only be put into the most serious of crimes.

PLANE CRASH SCENE

Crash investigators study the scattered wreckage of an airliner that caught fire on landing at Yogyakarta, Indonesia. The cause of a disaster like this is usually discovered only after a long and painstaking investigation carried out by experts at the scene. Many questions must be asked: was it an accident or a crime? Was the airline negligent, or was the aircrew careless? Did someone sabotage the plane?

FINGERTIP SEARCH

A line of police officers wearing "cleansuits" advances on hands and knees, searching every square inch of a road. The body of a murdered woman was found nearby, and there could be signs of the killer's arrival or departure. Similarly thorough searches for clues may need to be made in the surrounding countryside, in streets, or through people's household waste. In many crimes, the searchers don't know what they're looking for. Although the vast majority of the objects found are not relevant to the investigation they still have to be cataloged and treated as potential evidence until events prove they have no part to play.

Search on hands and knees ensures no evidence is missed

SEARCH PATTERNS

There are many equally good patterns in which an area can be searched. Sticking to one pattern ensures the best cover of ground in the shortest possible time. The pattern of search should leave no area out, and preferably should cover each point twice, but shouldn't waste effort by searching the same area more than that. It should be directed by a single person to avoid any confusion.

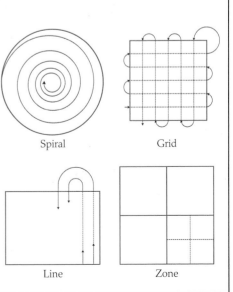

Spiral   Grid

Line   Zone

Recording the scene

WHEN FORENSIC INVESTIGATORS arrive at a crime scene, they make a permanent record of anything that is relevant to the crime. They write descriptions of what they see, draw diagrams, and take photographs. Not only does all this scrupulous care and attention to fine detail avoid having to rely on highly unreliable human memory, it also provides evidence that is likely to be accepted in a court. The investigators also behave according to a principle stated by the French forensics pioneer Edmond Locard:"Every contact leaves a trace."This means that everyone who visits a crime scene leaves microscopic traces of material—hairs, sweat, flakes of skin, fibers from their clothes, or soil from their shoes. He or she also carries away traces from the scene—dust, pollen, grease from a gun, fibers from a carpet or upholstery, or traces of drugs or explosives. The principle applies equally to the police and forensics experts at the scene—and so they take every precaution to make sure they do not contaminate the site by always wearing protective clothing and footwear.

Vital clue—dried blood on a brick

Hood to keep hair in place

Face mask in case of noxious substances

All-in-one protective cleansuit

FORENSIC FASHION
The "cleansuits" worn by forensic officers prevent particles, fibers, sweat, and dirt from passing from the investigators onto items of evidence. The work of the scientists would be made much harder if the evidence they were analyzing consisted of, for example, hair from one of the investigators, or soil that they had walked into the area. The cleansuits also help to prevent contamination if there is poison or infectious germs at the scene. Special "overshoes" with "POLICE" embossed in mirror writing on the soles ensure that the team's footprints are not confused with those belonging to the suspects.

CAPTURING THE SCENE
A forensic photographer, who wears a cleansuit just like all the other officers, records a suspicious object—a knife—at the crime scene. He photographs the crime scene from every angle, so that investigators do not have to rely on their memories or the sketches as they reconstruct the events that happened there. Often the photographer includes a scale in the photograph so that people viewing the picture at a later date have a clear idea of the size of the object.

PORTRAIT OF THE CRIME
An investigator's drawing of the crime scene shows where a body has been found, possibly the victim of a murder. The sketch also marks the positions of objects and the distances between them, and notes any peculiarities that a photograph does not bring out. The officer may use a handheld computer to aid in rapidly producing a high-quality diagram. The sketch is signed as a true record of the scene.

Position of body

12

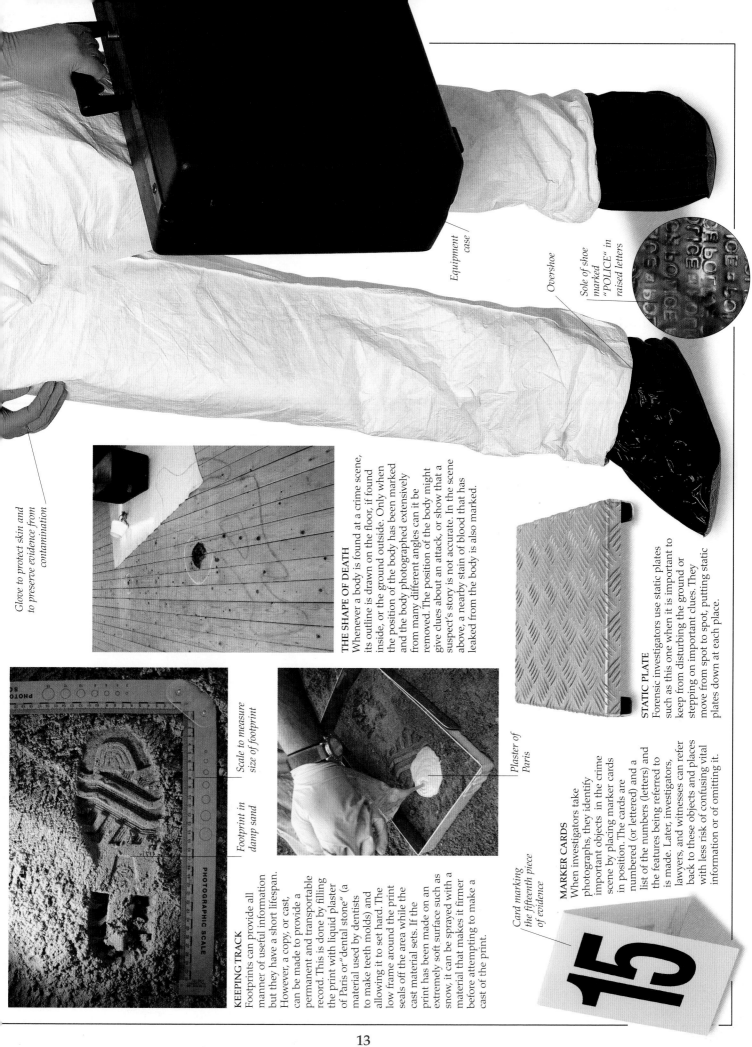

Equipment case

Overshoe

Sole of shoe marked "POLICE" in raised letters

Glove to protect skin and to preserve evidence from contamination

THE SHAPE OF DEATH

Whenever a body is found at a crime scene, its outline is drawn on the floor, if found inside, or the ground outside. Only when the position of the body has been marked and the body photographed extensively from many different angles can it be removed. The position of the body might give clues about an attack, or show that a suspect's story is not accurate. In the scene above, a nearby stain of blood that has leaked from the body is also marked.

STATIC PLATE

Forensic investigators use static plates such as this one when it is important to keep from disturbing the ground or stepping on important clues. They move from spot to spot, putting static plates down at each place.

KEEPING TRACK

Footprints can provide all manner of useful information but they have a short lifespan. However, a copy, or cast, can be made to provide a permanent and transportable record. This is done by filling the print with liquid plaster of Paris or "dental stone" (a material used by dentists to make teeth molds) and allowing it to set hard. The low frame around the print seals off the area while the cast material sets. If the print has been made on an extremely soft surface such as snow, it can be sprayed with a material that makes it firmer before attempting to make a cast of the print.

Scale to measure size of footprint

Footprint in damp sand

Plaster of Paris

MARKER CARDS

When investigators take photographs, they identify important objects in the crime scene by placing marker cards in position. The cards are numbered (or lettered) and a list of the numbers (letters) and the features being referred to is made. Later, investigators, lawyers, and witnesses can refer back to these objects and places with less risk of confusing vital information or of omitting it.

Card marking the fifteenth piece of evidence

15

13

Handling the evidence

AN INCIDENT SCENE IS A HIVE OF ACTIVITY as forensic investigators record and collect all the evidence that could possibly be relevant. Having taken great care—by wearing cleansuits, gloves, and overshoes—not to contaminate anything, the investigators must take equal care that no one and nothing else can damage the evidence during the course of its life, which is often long. Anything removed from the site goes into a container that is sealed and labeled. Seals on bags and bottles are "tamper evident," showing obvious signs if they've been opened. Containers carry "progress-of-custody" labels—each person who handles the evidence signs the label so a court has confidence in its contents.

1. Fingerprint forms— *prints are inked onto these*

2. Labels *to attach to items of evidence*

3. Lifting tape *to "capture" fingerprints on objects*

4. Fingerprint brushes *for applying powder to fingerprints*

5. Vials *of pure water to dissolve dried stains*

6. Roller *for pressing lifting tape onto fingerprints*

7. Digital thermometer *measures air temperature at scene*

TOOLKIT

There is no time to lose at the scene of a crime or other incident—all the investigator's tools must be ready and on hand. Evidence that needs to be preserved is put into bags, bottles, or envelopes. Blood and other fluids are gathered on swabs resembling household cotton swabs. Adhesive tape and scissors are handy. Many items in the toolkit are disposable—gloves, scalpels, and other things cannot be used again in case they contaminate the evidence. Containers are sealed, and labels track their movements.

PHOTOGRAPHIC RECORD

Crime-scene investigators normally use film cameras like this one. Digital images are sometimes challenged in court on the grounds that it is easy to alter them, but ways of guarding against this are being developed. As soon as full protection against tampering is possible, the use of digital photography in forensics is set to increase.

MEASURING SCALES

Forensic investigators carry various scales (rulers). Scientists measure objects at the scene and place scales next to objects being photographed to show their size. These right-angled scales can be placed inside a corner—of a room, for example—or outside corners—of furniture, for example—to provide quick and easy readings.

14

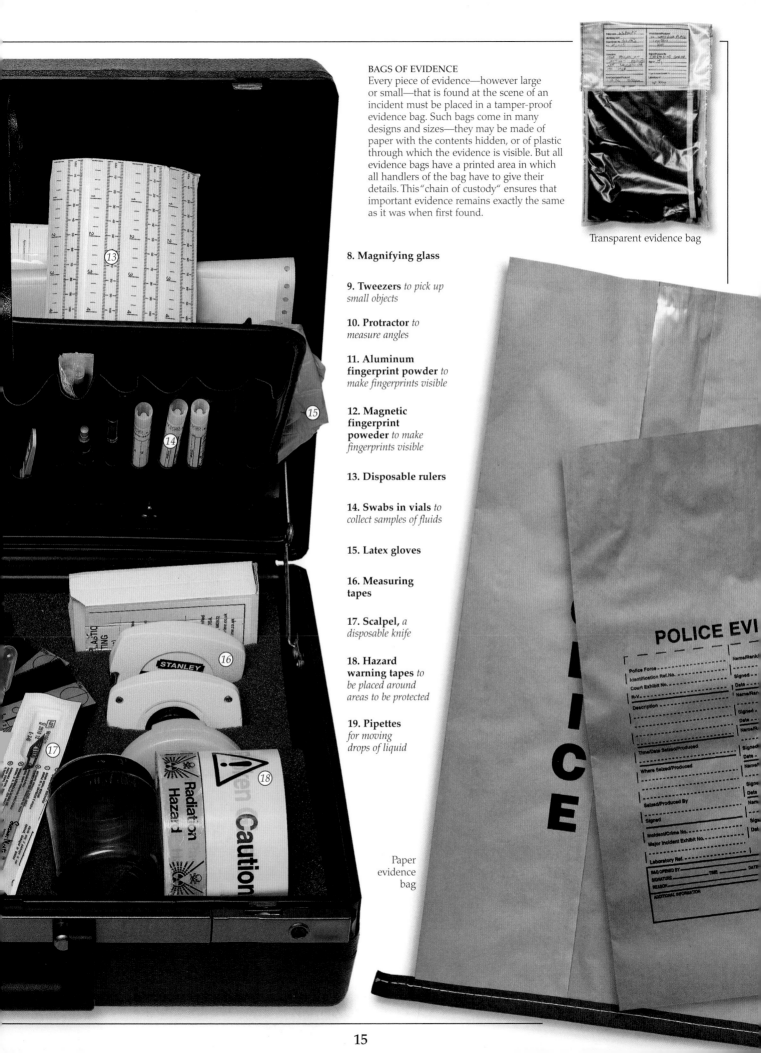

BAGS OF EVIDENCE

Every piece of evidence—however large or small—that is found at the scene of an incident must be placed in a tamper-proof evidence bag. Such bags come in many designs and sizes—they may be made of paper with the contents hidden, or of plastic through which the evidence is visible. But all evidence bags have a printed area in which all handlers of the bag have to give their details. This "chain of custody" ensures that important evidence remains exactly the same as it was when first found.

Transparent evidence bag

8. Magnifying glass

9. Tweezers *to pick up small objects*

10. Protractor *to measure angles*

11. Aluminum fingerprint powder *to make fingerprints visible*

12. Magnetic fingerprint poweder *to make fingerprints visible*

13. Disposable rulers

14. Swabs in vials *to collect samples of fluids*

15. Latex gloves

16. Measuring tapes

17. Scalpel, *a disposable knife*

18. Hazard warning tapes *to be placed around areas to be protected*

19. Pipettes *for moving drops of liquid*

Paper evidence bag

POLICE EVI

Police Force	Name/Rankin
Identification Ref.No.	Signed
Court Exhibit No.	Date
R-V-	Name/Ran
Description	Signed
	Date
	Name/R
Time/Date Seized/Produced	Signed
	Date
Where Seized/Produced	Name
	Signe
	Date
Seized/Produced By	Nam
Signed	Sigu
Incident/Crime No.	Dat
Major Incident Exhibit No.	
Laboratory Ref.	
BAG OPENED BY	TIME	DATE
SIGNATURE		
REASON		
ADDITIONAL INFORMATION		

Taking fingerprints

THE FIRST POLICE FORCE to collect and store fingerprints systematically to identify criminals was in Argentina, in the 1890s. Today, every country keeps a store of criminals' fingerprints. Forensic investigators try to find all the fingerprints at a crime scene. A print that is visible to the naked eye is called a patent print; one that appears invisible but can be made visible is a latent print. The investigators make permanent copies of the prints and photograph them. Prints are taken from everyone known to have been at the scene—including, for example, family members—so that they can be compared with those of suspects or people whose prints are held on file as a result of some earlier misconduct.

DUSTING FOR PRINTS
A police officer brushes fingerprint dust onto a car door. A smooth, metal surface readily takes fingerprints. Since cars come in many colors, investigators need a range of colors of fingerprint powder, so that they can choose contrasting ones to show up the prints. There are an enormous number of places in a car where prints might be found—the interior, the exterior body, the engine compartment, the trunk, and even perhaps underneath the car.

THE WIDER VIEW
The magnifying glass is one of the oldest and simplest aids for the detective, but still one of the most valuable. It is indispensable for getting a better view of fingerprints, significant marks and scratches, and small writing and printing.

BRUSHES
The fingerprint specialist uses brushes to cover areas where prints are visible or suspected with a fine powder. Sweeping away the excess leaves the pattern of the print revealed in the dust. A broad brush cleans larger areas; a narrower brush can be pushed into recesses. The type of brush also depends on the type of powder chosen.

FINGERPRINT POWDER
A small heap of fingerprint powder left after an investigator has taken a brushful to spread on a fingerprint. The consistency and color of the powder is chosen depending on the type of surface being checked. Dark fingerprint powder usually consists of fine particles of carbon, rather like soot. Light powders may be chalk, titanium dioxide, or other materials.

LIFTING TAPE
This clear adhesive tape can be pressed onto a surface carrying a fingerprint so that the print is transferred onto it. The print can then be removed for analysis and comparison with known prints on file.

ROLLER
A fingerprint roller is used to smooth lifting tape onto a fingerprint. The pressure from forcing the roller over the tape removes air bubbles and allows optimum contact between tape and print to make an accurate impression.

PROCEDURE FOR TAKING FINGERPRINTS

Fingerprint specialists have to know where to look for prints, how to dust an invisible or damaged print so that it produces a clear and accurate image, and how to preserve it so that it can be used as evidence, possibly years later. Brushing the surface with carbon powder is still the most widely used method.

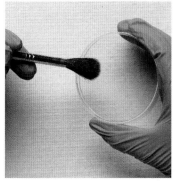

1 BRUSHING THE SURFACE
The fingerprints on this dish are barely visible. To show them up, fingerprint powder is brushed lightly over the surface with a brush. The investigator is careful to wear gloves.

2 REVEALING THE PRINT
A large print is now clearly visible on the surface of the object. However, to make it into a piece of evidence that can be used it needs to be made much clearer and more permanent.

3 USING THE ROLLER
The investigator lays lifting tape over the surface and runs the roller over it, pressing down firmly so that some of the grease making up the fingerprint is transferred to the film.

4 COPYING THE PRINT
The forensic scientist peels back the lifting tape away from the surface of the dish, being careful to do it in one smooth motion. The tape now carries its copy of the fingerprint.

5 FATE OF THE FINGERPRINT
The print on the lifting film is placed in a protective sleeve with a label recording when and where it was obtained. It may be examined visually (as here), photographed, or scanned electronically. Its details end up in a computer database, while the physical fingerprint is safely stored.

WAVING A WAND

A magnetic wand used with metal dust is an alternative to a brush used with nonmetallic powders. The fine dust of metal filings forms a bushy clump at one end of the wand. The fingerprint officer uses the wand to brush the dust onto the area being studied, and some of the metal sticks to the grease of the print pattern and produces a recordable print.

Magnetic tip attracts filings

MAGNETIC POWDER
Magnetic powder contains iron so that it is attracted by magnets. It comes in many colors but cannot be used on iron, steel, and many other kinds of metal.

Large magnetic wand

Smaller pen-size magnetic wand

1 GATHERING DUST
An investigator inserts the wand into the magnetic fingerprint dust and lifts a mass of dust on the tip of the magnetic wand. The dust forms a natural "brush" that has little chance of damaging a fingerprint.

2 MAKING CONTACT WITH THE PRINT
Gentle brushing of the magnetic dust over the surface shows up a large part of a hand. Normally only fingerprints are kept on file, but hand markings are also unique to each person and can be a useful addition to the evidence. One of the advantages of magnetic dust is that the excess is easily removed with the wand, more easily than ordinary dust is removed with an ordinary brush. This allows a cleaner print to be prepared in a shorter space of time.

Analyzing fingerprints

LINEN TESTER
This gadget is an alternative to a magnifying glass and is often used in forensics. It comes in different sizes and magnifications, and folds up compactly.

FOR HUNDREDS OF YEARS people occasionally commented on the fact that people's fingerprints—the patterns of looped and branching ridges on the fingertips—differ from person to person. It was not until the mid-19th century that they were first used by British officials in India in place of signatures on contracts. Then the British scientist Francis Galton published his studies of fingerprints, showing two crucial facts: that everyone's prints are different, and that everyone's prints stay the same through the whole of their lives. In 1891, Argentina started to make use of fingerprints; British and American police forces soon followed. Now every country has records of fingerprints and has police trained in collecting and analyzing them. Storage and analysis of fingerprints are computerized these days, and fingerprint information can be flashed between police forces around the world in a matter of seconds. Palmprints and footprints are also unique, and sometimes these are used to identify people, too.

SIR WILLIAM HERSCHEL
In the mid-19th century Herschel (1833–1918), a British official in India, started demanding that the local people put their palmprints on legal documents as a way of showing their agreement. Later he refined this to just requiring the marks of two fingerprints. At first he simply wanted to encourage the people to respect the authority of the document, but he soon came to realize that fingerprints were also unique individual identifiers.

QUICK PRINTING
Fingerprint specialists often use ready-inked pieces of film to speed up the process of taking fingerprints. When the protective layer has been peeled off, the witness or suspect presses each of his or her fingertips onto the ink. In turn, each fingerprint is transferred onto a specially printed fingerprint form. This ensures a consistency of recording that makes comparing prints easier.

Each finger of each hand has an individual and distinctive appearance

Pre-inked paper has made print taking quicker and less messy

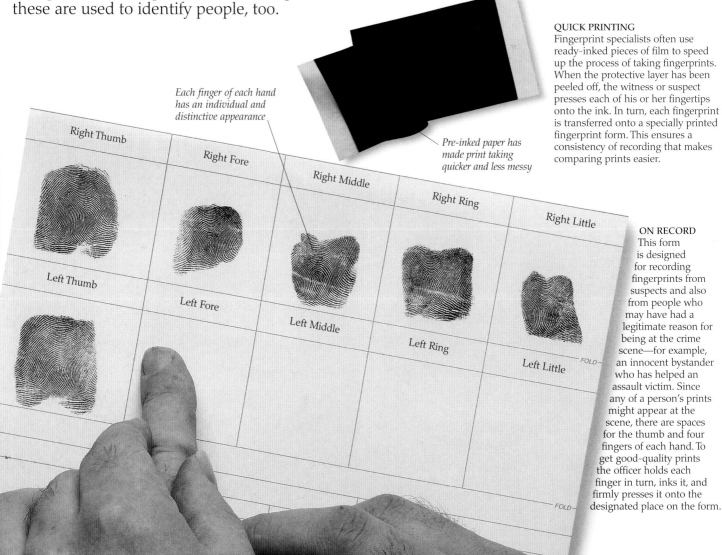

Right Thumb

Right Fore

Right Middle

Right Ring

Right Little

Left Thumb

Left Fore

Left Middle

Left Ring

Left Little

FOLD

FOLD

ON RECORD
This form is designed for recording fingerprints from suspects and also from people who may have had a legitimate reason for being at the crime scene—for example, an innocent bystander who has helped an assault victim. Since any of a person's prints might appear at the scene, there are spaces for the thumb and four fingers of each hand. To get good-quality prints the officer holds each finger in turn, inks it, and firmly presses it onto the designated place on the form.

PATTERNS OF PRINTS

The three pictures below show the most common fingerprint patterns. The details within each pattern are what the experts look at to determine similarity. In whorls, the ridges near the center of the pattern form closed curves. Loops are the most common type of print; each ridge enters and leaves on the right or left side of the finger. In an arch, each ridge enters and leaves on opposite sides.

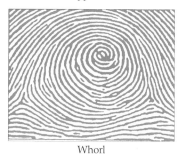

Whorl

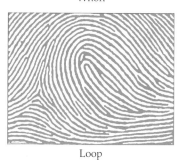

Loop

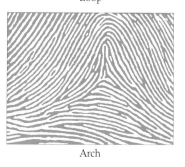

Arch

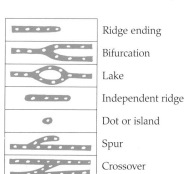

Ridge ending

Bifurcation

Lake

Independent ridge

Dot or island

Spur

Crossover

GALTON DETAILS

When they are comparing prints, fingerprint officers look at tiny features (listed above) that appear on the ridges. These are called Galton's details, after Sir Francis Galton (1822–1911), the fingerprint pioneer. The expert looks at where the details occur, and if there are many identical details he or she declares the two prints to come from the same person.

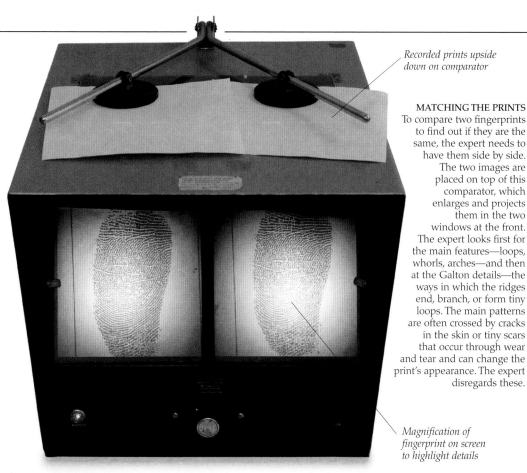

Recorded prints upside down on comparator

MATCHING THE PRINTS

To compare two fingerprints to find out if they are the same, the expert needs to have them side by side. The two images are placed on top of this comparator, which enlarges and projects them in the two windows at the front. The expert looks first for the main features—loops, whorls, arches—and then at the Galton details—the ways in which the ridges end, branch, or form tiny loops. The main patterns are often crossed by cracks in the skin or tiny scars that occur through wear and tear and can change the print's appearance. The expert disregards these.

Magnification of fingerprint on screen to highlight details

Can suspended in glue vapor

VISUALIZING FINGERPRINTS

A hard-to-see fingerprint can be made more visible by "super-glue fuming." The object—a can, in this case—is put in a cabinet with a small amount of a super-gluelike substance. When heated, the glue gives off fumes that react with the grease in the print. This forms a hard opaque deposit that is easy to see.

SHINING A LIGHT ON CRIME

Finding a fingerprint is one thing but getting a clear enough copy to be able to analyze it in detail is quite another matter. One way to help improve the quality of a print is to use laser light rather than ordinary light. Laser can often show up faint details more clearly. Here, it is shone on the can treated in the super-glue fuming process at left. The fingerprints have already been made clearer by the super-glue treatment that has now coated the can in a hard deposit. The laser light shows up the prints even more clearly. The prints will be photographed, and the can will also be kept as a permanent record until the crime is cleared up.

Fingerprint shown up by glue fuming

COMPUTERIZED MATCHING

A fingerprint expert in Taiwan compares the fingerprint image held in his left hand with two images on a computer screen. The handheld image is from the scene of a recent crime; the computer versions are from records of known criminals, which are held on a database. The original analysis of the electronic prints after they were first taken was largely carried out by computer. Computers can store and quickly process a lot of data, but human experts are involved at every stage, and only the human eye is capable of confirming the final match.

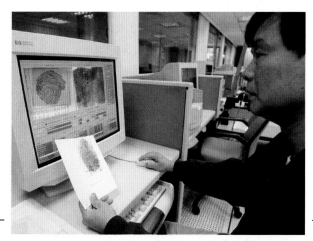

Written in blood

IN PAST TIMES, blood was not a very useful clue in a crime. If a farmer's clothes had a suspicious stain on them, for example, he could claim it was an animal's blood. A carpenter might say the stain was paint. But in the late 19th century, chemical tests were invented that could show whether a stain was blood or not. A very useful one that is still used as a quick, scene-of-the-crime test is the Kastle-Meyer test, but it cannot tell human from animal blood. Around 1900, Paul Uhlenhuth invented a chemical test that had to be performed in a laboratory; this showed whether blood was human. Since then, more sophisticated ways of analyzing blood have been invented. They may even show how the person died—if, for example, by poison or suffocation.

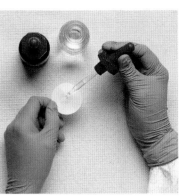

KARL LANDSTEINER
Around 1902, Dr. Karl Landsteiner (1868–1943) showed that there are several different types, or groups, of blood. This explained why blood transfusions were so often unsuccessful in those days: a patient can only receive blood of certain groups. In police work, if two bloodstains are of different groups, it follows that they must come from different people.

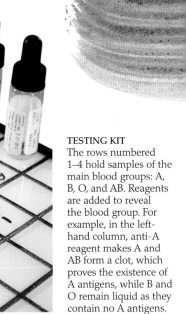

Blood sample   *Reagent (chemical used for testing)*

JOHN GLAISTER
John Glaister (1892–1971) classified bloodstains into six types, according to their shape, which depended on how they were produced. Much the same classification is still in use today. Glaister and his father were professors of forensic medicine, showing that the subject had been accepted as an important area of science by the latter part of the 19th century.

TESTING KIT
The rows numbered 1–4 hold samples of the main blood groups: A, B, O, and AB. Reagents are added to reveal the blood group. For example, in the left-hand column, anti-A reagent makes A and AB form a clot, which proves the existence of A antigens, while B and O remain liquid as they contain no A antigens.

KASTLE-MEYER TEST
The quick blood tests that investigators can do at the scene of the crime are called "presumptive" tests. The most common is the Kastle-Meyer test. If the test rules out a fluid or a stain as being blood, no further tests are needed. However, if it indicates that the stain or mark could be blood, more sensitive and specific tests must be carried out in a laboratory for confirmation. That detailed investigation will also reveal whether the blood is human or animal, what its group is, whether it shows signs of disease, and much more.

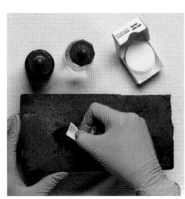

1 REMOVING A TRACE
A stain that has been found on a brick near the site of a crime is suspected to be dried human blood. The investigator rubs it with the corner of a disk of paper that has been folded into four in order to collect a sample consisting of just a few grains.

2 CHECKING THE SAMPLE
The disk of paper is unfolded, and the sample is clearly seen as a dot at its centre. The investigator wears gloves not only to protect the sample from contamination but also to protect the investigator from contamination from disease-bearing fluids.

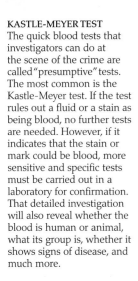

3 ADDING REAGENT
The investigator adds a few drops of a chemical reagent called phenolphthalein from a dropper onto the sample. The test is so sensitive that only a small quantity of the chemical is needed.

PATTERNS OF BLOODSTAINS

The shape that bloodstains make at the scene of an incident can give valuable information about their cause—whether they came spurting from an artery or whether they were the result of slower bleeding from smaller blood vessels, whether the victim was moving at the time, or whether the injury was caused by a blow, a knife wound, or in some other way. In the 1930s, Sir John Glaister classified bloodstains into six main types: drops; splashes; pools; spurts; smears; and trails. However, many factors can influence the shapes, and an expert has to be very cautious in his or her interpretation.

Blood is smeared over a large area

Point from which blood trails radiate

BLOOD SMEAR

The blood smear (left) is the result of a quantity of blood being spread over a surface, either by the injured person trying to get away from the scene, or by the person falling as he or she dies. A blood smear may also be caused by the victim being moved from or within the crime scene, either at the time of the injury or soon afterward. There is plenty of blood here from which investigators can take one or more samples for testing.

IMPACT SPLATTER

When a bloodstain found on the floor or ground splatters out from a central area, as in the picture above, it is a sign that the blood has fallen from a height. It is possible to estimate how far the blood has fallen, which can give the investigators certain information about the height of the victim, or about his or her location at the time of the attack.

SHOE PRINT

If there has been a very violent incident, with much blood shed, it is unlikely that anyone will leave the scene unmarked. Here, an excellent blood print of the sole pattern of a shoe has been left near the scene of the crime. In addition to giving clues to the size and make of shoe, the print shows some defects that may link it uniquely to its wearer.

TEARDROP SHAPE

Blood stains are often teardrop-shaped. Sometimes this is a result of a spherical drop flying through the air and spreading as it strikes a surface. This can give valuable clues about the movement of the victim as he or she was wounded. In other stains, such as this one, the teardrop shape is due to gravity forcing the blood downward.

CIRCULAR DROP

When a drop of blood is circular in shape, it indicates that it struck the surface at right angles—usually by falling vertically onto a floor. However, there is still a possibility that the victim was moving, even if very slowly.

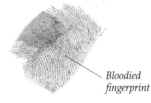

Bloodied fingerprint

FINGERPRINT

A fingerprint in blood is two pieces of evidence in one. But it is possible for the fingerprint to have come from the criminal and the blood to have come from the victim—or even vice versa. To discover the truth, scrupulous testing and analysis are essential.

More blood on intact side of shoe

Sole's wear and tear causes less blood here

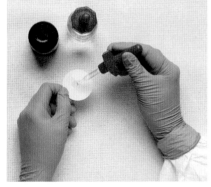

4 A SECOND CHEMICAL

The investigator then adds a few drops of hydrogen peroxide, a clear liquid that is often used as a household bleach or disinfectant. The combination of this chemical and phenolphthalein in the presence of even a minute quantity of blood causes an effect that is visible to the naked eye.

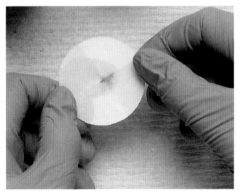

5 BLOOD REVEALED

The paper turns a bright pink in the area where the stain has mixed with the chemicals. This means the stain is likely to be blood. After confirmation, the sample will most likely be taken to a laboratory for more detailed tests.

DNA analysis

A REVOLUTION IN FORENSICS has been brought about by DNA typing, or "genetic fingerprinting." DNA (deoxyribonucleic acid) is the substance at the heart of every human cell. It carries genetic (inherited) instructions about how our bodies are built. It controls the way a baby is going to grow up—its sex and height, hair color, and susceptibility to certain diseases. DNA molecules are spiraling chains of atoms, packed into the center of every cell. Only identical twins, triplets, and so on have the same DNA. A single hair, a drop of blood, or a smear of saliva at the scene of a crime can reveal who the criminal was—provided the DNA is stored on a database and a match is made. A criminal can wear gloves to keep from leaving fingerprints, but it is hard not to leave any DNA.

SAMPLE TO PROFILE
These vials (small bottles) contain samples of DNA that have been prepared to go through a multistep DNA typing process. Samples may be taken from the scene of a crime—for example, from a blood stain—and from suspects, usually taken from cells scraped from inside the cheek. The test can show whether the crime-scene samples come from one individual or more than one, and whether the suspect is the same person as the person at the scene.

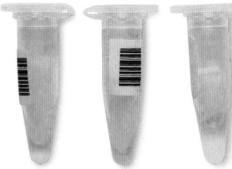
Scraper for collecting buccal (cheek) cells

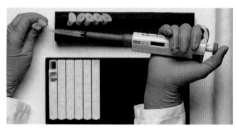
Vials containing samples of buccal cells

1 TRANSFERRING THE DNA
A scientist picks up some of the contents of the first vial and drops it into the first compartment of a multipart container. (Six containers are visible here.) She uses a pipette, or dropper, that has a digital scale showing the precise amount that she drops in. She repeats the process for the first compartment in each of the six containers.

PIONEERS OF DNA
Pictured right are the two scientists who first worked out the structure of the enormously complicated DNA molecule. All living matter contains DNA—it is the chemical blueprint of life. Francis Crick (1916–2004) (far right) and James Watson (b. 1928) discovered that DNA is in the form of a double strand. Each strand is a helix (similar to a spiral staircase) and consists of about 100 million chemical units (bases). Each base is a small group of atoms. A small fraction of the bases are "instructions" for the organism. The rest has no known function—but it's what is used in "genetic fingerprinting."

2 PREPARING TO PURIFY
The first compartment of each container now holds a different DNA sample. The investigator peels the foil off the six containers, ready for the purification process. The other compartments hold chemicals. In the process about to begin, reactions will take place in each compartment in turn.

SIR ALEC JEFFREYS
Alec Jeffreys invented DNA typing, or genetic fingerprinting in 1984. It was first used to investigate two murders committed in 1983 and 1986. A young man had confessed to both murders and had been charged, but he appeared to have the wrong type of blood. Jeffreys was able to show that the two murders had been committed by the same person, but that it was not the man who had confessed. Eventually, the DNA evidence showed that another man was the killer. In the first police use of DNA testing, Jeffreys had proved the innocence of one man and the guilt of another.

3 EXTRACTING AND PURIFYING
The scientist adds further chemicals (in the blue containers). The machine will automatically mix each DNA sample with the chemicals in the next compartment, then mix the results of this reaction with the next batch of chemicals, and so on. These processes extract and purify the DNA.

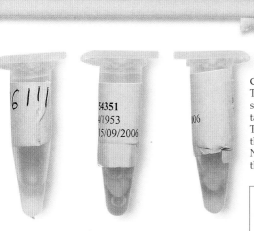

COMPARING PROFILES

The DNA profile for each sample is a pattern in which selected fragments of the DNA, called STRs (short tandem repeats), are spread out according to their sizes. There is more than one way of showing a DNA profile: the graphs below have been produced by electrophoresis. No two people have exactly the same peaks, or spikes, in the same positions in such a graph.

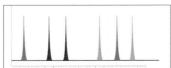

CRIME SAMPLE
A DNA sample from the scene can be compared with samples taken from various suspects.

VICTIM SAMPLE
The victim's DNA may be at the crime scene, and must not be confused with the offender's.

FIRST SUSPECT
This shows some peaks like those of the crime sample, but others, too. It can be ruled out.

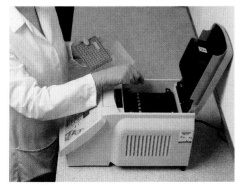

SECOND SUSPECT
This DNA pattern matches the crime sample. This suspect was at the crime scene.

ENDANGERED SPECIES

The parrots, macaws, hummingbirds, and other species in this print are just some of the rich array of birds of Central and South America. Their survival is threatened by illegal trading to countries where the demand for exotic pets flourishes. Traveling long distances in atrocious conditions leads to many casualties. Often the only way the authorities have of identifying smuggled birds and other animals is to analyze the DNA from their remains. DNA analysis can also confirm where the animal originally come from. If it belongs to a protected species, prison or a heavy fine can follow.

4 AMPLIFYING THE DNA

The next step in this complex process is to "amplify" the DNA—increase its amount by making copies of the molecules, and copies of the copies, repeatedly. This machine runs the samples through a multistep process called PCR (polymerase chain reaction), which doubles the number of molecules at each step. After doing this many times there may be hundreds of thousands of times as much DNA as there was to start with. Amplifying the DNA ensures that there is enough material for the scientists to work with.

5 CREATING THE PROFILE

Finally, the multiplied DNA samples are placed in an electrophoresis machine. Inside, a strong electric field of hundreds of volts drags the fragments of DNA along a thin tube called a capillary, separating them out according to the size of the fragments. The positions of the fragments are detected electronically and used to generate visible patterns or sequences of numbers. These form the DNA profiles of the person or people from whom the original DNA samples came.

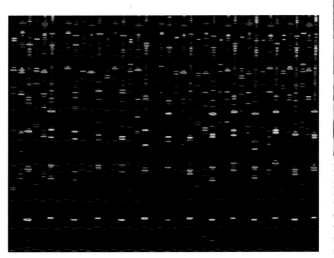

DNA PROFILES

The DNA profiles of several people are compared above. Through a series of complex chemical processes, even minute traces of a person's DNA can be displayed in this graphic way. This helps the forensic expert to make comparisons with other samples. DNA databases, which are maintained in most countries around the world, hold DNA records of offenders, whatever their crime or conviction. When a crime is committed, DNA from the scene of the crime is collected and compared with profiles that exist on the database. As the databases increase in size and sophistication, more matches are being made, even concerning crimes committed many years ago.

RELATIVELY GUILTY
In 2003, two drunk men on a highway overpass in the UK threw bricks into the traffic. One smashed through a truck windshield, causing the driver to have a heart attack. Some of the criminal's blood was on the brick, but the DNA was not on the national DNA database. The search was widened to look for similar DNA. A man who was on the database because he had a criminal conviction had very similar DNA. The man's brother proved to be guilty.

Trace evidence

FOLLOWING DR. EDMOND LOCARD'S exchange principle that "every contact leaves a trace" (see p. 12), forensic scientists study some very tiny traces indeed. They look for details that are too small to see with the naked eye. Often they use comparison microscopes, which are set up to look at two things at once. They also use scanning electron microscopes. Instead of beams of light, these scan objects with beams of tiny particles called electrons. Electrons are small particles that are found inside atoms. Studied at this level of detail, hairs that are apparently identical when viewed with the naked eye reveal very different surface textures. Flakes of paint from a car are seen to consist of multiple layers, with differences in thickness and color. If the flake looks identical under the electron microscope to a sample from a suspect car, it almost certainly came from that car.

VACUUM EVIDENCE
Forensic investigators use a specially designed type of vacuum cleaner to collect fibers, dust, and other trace evidence from furniture, carpets, curtains, clothing, and car interiors. The very small nozzle makes it possible to pick up fibers from otherwise inaccessible areas.

PAINT EFFECTS
A forensic scientist examines a sample of paint under an optical microscope and compares it with the vast range of samples in the foreground. This traditional method of examining paint can be used to compare color and type, for example, whether it is glossy or matte, oil- or water-based. With a scanning electron microscope, however, an investigator can see much more.

COMPARISON MICROSCOPE
When samples are compared, it is best done side by side so that differences and similarities show up clearly. There are various types of comparison microscope that present the two samples in the same field of view. In this design, there are two identical microscopes, each with binocular eyepieces (eyepieces for both eyes). The samples can be viewed separately by each person looking through the eyepieces one at a time. Alternatively, the images can be transmitted through cables to a TV screen, where they can be viewed more easily side by side.

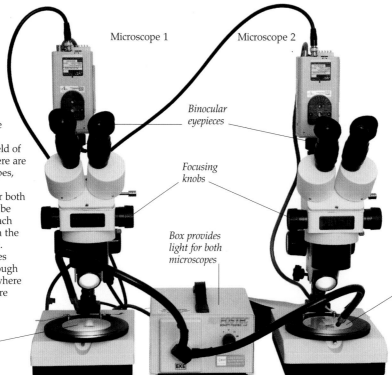

Microscope 1   Microscope 2

Binocular eyepieces

Focusing knobs

Box provides light for both microscopes

Sample 1

Sample 2

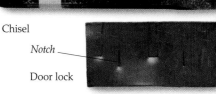

Chisel

Notch

Door lock

TOOL MARKS
The metal plate above, part of a door lock, was damaged when an edged tool was used in a burglary. Detailed examination shows that the notches are the same width and thickness as the tip of a chisel owned by a suspect. By itself this doesn't prove the chisel's owner was responsible for the crime, but it can convince the police that they should investigate him closely.

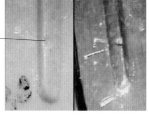

Tool mark shows nick in chisel

Suspect's tool mark   Crime scene tool mark

TOOLS COMPARED
The far left picture shows a mark made by a chisel found in the possession of a suspect. This is compared with a mark found at the scene of the crime (near left). The investigator looks at the general shape made by the tool, such as the rounded bottom end, as well as individual distinguishing marks, in this case the nicks halfway along its length. Although similar in shape, the nicks are not in the same position. So the expert would conclude that the suspect chisel was not the one used in the crime.

THE SCANNING ELECTRON MICROSCOPE (SEM)

Forensic scientists use scanning electron microscopes (SEMs) to study trace evidence. Unlike microscopes that use light to provide a magnified image, SEMs rely on a stream of electrons. These tiny particles are electrically charged and when separated from their atoms, they form an electric current. In the SEM, the electron beam produces a highly magnified and very detailed image. Anything viewed under an SEM must be coated with metal so that the electric charge from the beam is conducted away. (If not, the charge builds up and interferes with the beam.) Here, a hair is stuck to a small metal disk, about $2/5$ in (1 cm) in diameter, which is coated with a layer of gold in order to be viewed under the SEM.

1. Metal stub (small disk) for receiving sample hair

Adhesive film

Hair visible through gold

2. Adhesive film holds hair in place

3. Gold-plated stub

1 DISK ENTERING MACHINE
The sample, attached to the small metal stub, is placed carefully in the chamber of the sputtering (plating) machine. The airtight lid is closed before switching on the machine.

2 GOLD PLATING TAKING PLACE
Air is pumped out of the chamber. A high voltage is applied. This creates a gold halo around the sample (seen as a purple glow). Gold deposits stick to the surface of the sample.

3 TRANSFERRING TO SEM
The stub is taken from the coating machine and placed on a movable tray in the SEM. This is pushed into the electron gun chamber, and a beam of electrons is fired at it.

4 FORMING A PICTURE
The beam of electrons is focused onto the sample by powerful electromagnets. The result appears on the computer monitor—a highly magnified, 3-D picture of the hair.

Electron gun

Sample chamber

TV monitor views sample by infrared light

Controls for magnification and position of sample

SEM image of hair

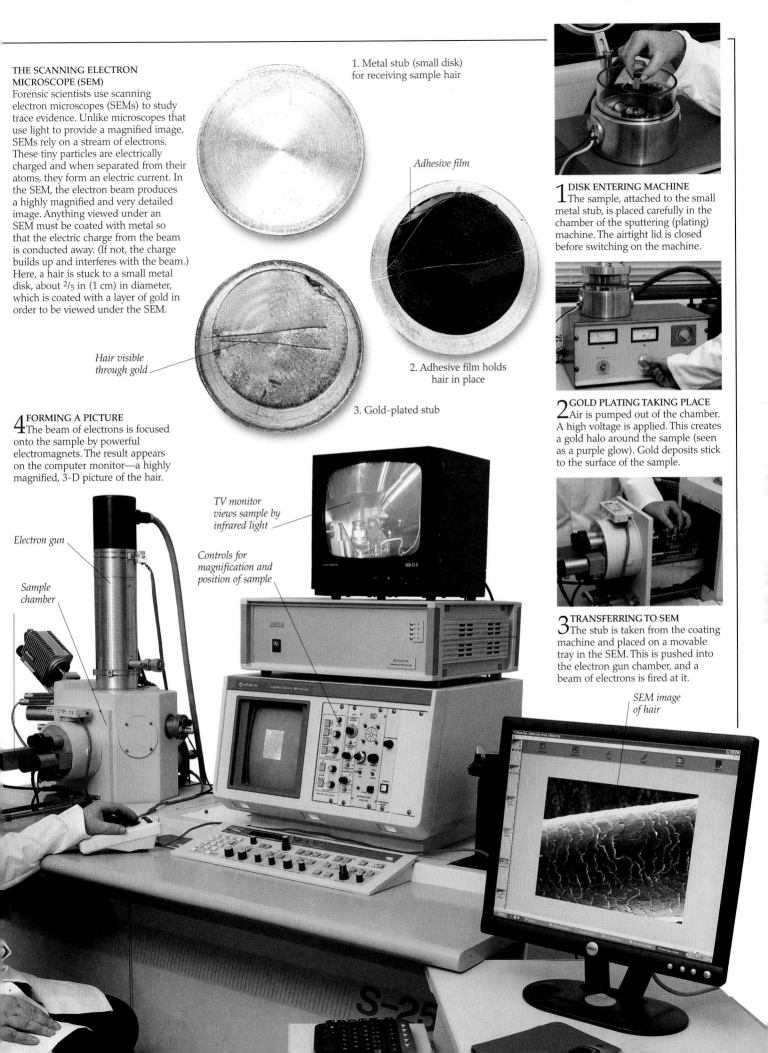

Natural clues

FORENSICS EXPERTS KNOW that the air is always rich with almost invisible dust. Powerful microscopes reveal flakes of human and animal skin and tiny animals called dust mites in household dust. Outdoor dust in addition includes grains of sand, soil, and pollen. Dust may also contain human and animal hairs, and fibers from our clothes. According to Edmond Locard, the famous French forensics scientist, whenever two things or people touch, material from one is transferred to the other and vice versa. So at any crime scene—including on the victim and the guilty person—there are many "invisible" clues. Once removed to the laboratory, such clues can be looked at more closely and compared with known samples on databases. For example, it may be possible to identify the type and manufacturer of a carpet on the basis of a few fibers picked up at the scene, which might even solve the crime.

SLIDE SHOW
Specimens are mounted on slides—small glass plates—for viewing under the microscope. The scientist can tell if hair (top) is animal or human and whether fabric is synthetic (middle) or natural (bottom).

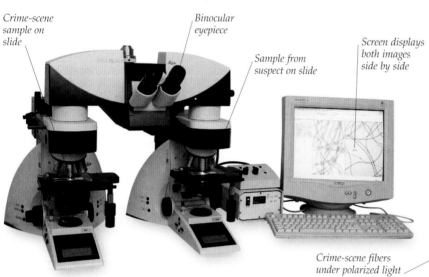

Crime-scene sample on slide

Binocular eyepiece

Sample from suspect on slide

Screen displays both images side by side

Crime-scene fibers under polarized light

COMPARING FIBERS
This advanced comparison microscope combines two microscopes. Two samples can be compared by observing through the binocular eyepiece, or on the computer screen. The central image (right) is a blown-up version of the screen. Two synthetic fiber samples are being compared: one is from the crime scene, the other from a suspect. The materials may be identified precisely by looking at the samples using polarized light. If the samples are found to be different, they provide no evidence that the suspect was at the crime scene. If they turn out to be the same, they provide some evidence, but not proof, that he or she was there.

LOOKING AT HAIRS
The color, type, and length of any hair found at the scene are all important clues but an SEM (scanning electron microscope) can show much more. The forensics expert looks for individual aspects of the hair that are not visible to the naked eye. The hair in the upper image is clearly damaged. This could be due to excessive use of hair-care products, which would immediately exclude some people. In the lower image, the blue specks are particles of dried shampoo, which may or may not be significant.

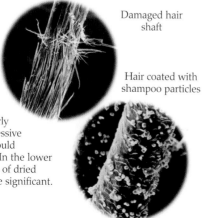

Damaged hair shaft

Hair coated with shampoo particles

LOOKING AT POLLEN
Under SEM, pollen spores are seen to have beautiful and intricate structures. In principle, the species of plant is clearly identifiable, but there are many thousands of plant species with which to compare the image so it is not always easy to find the right one. Each type of pollen is produced at definite times of year, so the presence of pollen in the clothing of a victim or suspect can give important clues about when and where they have been.

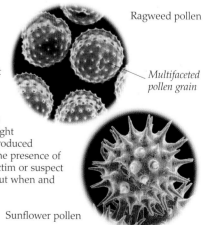

Ragweed pollen

Multifaceted pollen grain

Sunflower pollen

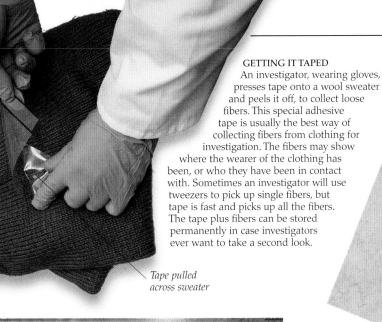

GETTING IT TAPED

An investigator, wearing gloves, presses tape onto a wool sweater and peels it off, to collect loose fibers. This special adhesive tape is usually the best way of collecting fibers from clothing for investigation. The fibers may show where the wearer of the clothing has been, or who they have been in contact with. Sometimes an investigator will use tweezers to pick up single fibers, but tape is fast and picks up all the fibers. The tape plus fibers can be stored permanently in case investigators ever want to take a second look.

Tape pulled across sweater

Wool and unidentified fibers seen sticking to tape

EDMOND LOCARD
Locard (1877–1966) was a leading French forensic scientist. During his lifetime his famous exchange principle—"every contact leaves a trace"—became more and more important, as scientific advances made it possible to detect even tinier traces at the scene of an incident. Among his many achievements was a huge textbook called *Treatise on Criminalistics.* (Criminalistics just means forensic science.)

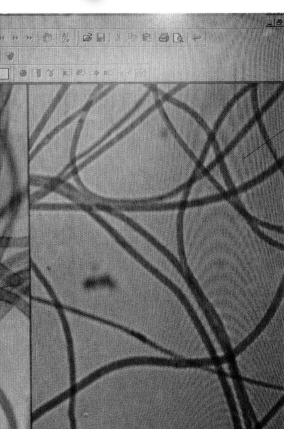

Fibers from suspect under polarized light

Spectrometer's FTIR machine

Microscope's binocular eyepiece

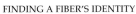

A sample fiber under visible and infrared light

FINDING A FIBER'S IDENTITY

Comparison of different fibers or other materials is just one method of identifying their origin. Sometimes scientists have only one sample so comparison is not possible, but they still have to try and find out where the fiber has come from. The machine above is a spectrometer, which uses both visible light and invisible infrared light. (Infrared light has wavelengths longer than ordinary light.) A fiber is being examined (inset). Ordinary visible light is shining on the fiber, but an infrared beam is also focused on it. The FTIR (Fourier transform infrared spectroscopy) machine analyzes the reflected infrared light by a highly sophisticated technique. The machine's output is a graph, which can be compared to information stored in a huge database of common and not so common materials.

SEEDS OF SUSPICION

Grass seeds solved the murder of Louise Almodovar in 1942. She was strangled on November 1 in Central Park, New York City. Her husband Anibal was held on suspicion. Witnesses testified that he had been dancing at a club that night, but it was only a few hundred yards from the murder spot. Grass seeds of a rare type were found in his pockets and pant cuffs. A botanist showed that in New York City they grew only in Central Park—at the spot where Louise had been killed. Anibal hurriedly produced a story about having walked in the park in September. The botanist pointed out that the grass produces its seeds in mid-October at the earliest. At this point, Almodovar broke down and confessed.

A good impression

FOOTPRINTS, DENTS, AND SCRAPES are a treasure trove for forensic specialists. If there are footprints and tire tracks at a crime scene, the investigators make a record of them. This is done by taking photographs and possibly by making a cast—a solid copy in hard material. The patterns of shoe prints are cataloged and kept on a computerized database. An officer provides a description of a footprint, in terms of its size and the design of diamonds, curves, squares, and other lines that make up the pattern of the sole. With these details, full information about the brand, the date it went on the market, and a picture of the whole shoe can all be quickly found. The same thing can be done with prints of tires—then a list of all vehicles that use that make of tire can be called up. The marks that an intruder leaves when forcing windows or doors during a break-in are individual—often specific to a particular tool—and harder to track down.

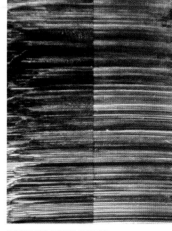

BOLT-CUTTER MATCH
Microscope photographs reveal the tool responsible for a break-in. Every cutting tool leaves its own "fingerprint" (pattern of marks). The left-hand picture above shows marks left on a chain-link that had been cut in a burglary. The right-hand picture shows marks made in a laboratory by a bolt-cutter found by the police. The pictures line up exactly, showing that the same blade made both cuts.

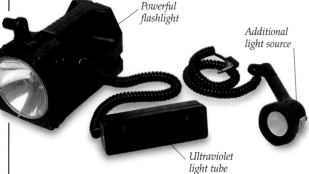

Powerful flashlight

Additional light source

Ultraviolet light tube

LIFTING FOOTPRINTS
A footprint can be a faint mark consisting of dust. This investigator has a powerful flashlight with an additional lamp attached for extra power. Shining the light at an angle rather than directly often shows up faint footprints. Other kinds of light can show up different substances more strongly. Ultraviolet light, for example, makes some substances glow. The forensic scientist can make a permanent record of a dusty footprint that he can take away to examine more closely in a laboratory. He lays a sheet of foil-backed plastic film over the print, and touches a high-voltage probe to the film. Dust is attracted from the print to the film, forming an impression that can be fixed with a spray.

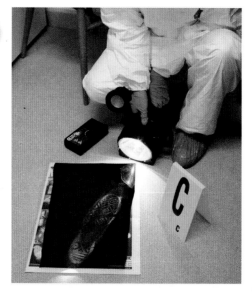

BURGLAR'S TOOLS
A crowbar and a chisel are two of a burglar's favorite tools. Fingerprints and unique marks on the blades of the instruments can give away their user's identity. Even the tiny fragments left after their use can provide clues; for example, they may have come from another crime scene if the criminal hasn't cleaned his tools well enough.

Chisel

Crowbar

TIRE TRACKS
A track left by a vehicle tire, such as this one in soft ground could be a valuable clue, so a permanent record needs to be made. A photograph will do, but even better is a latex (rubber) cast made in the same way as a footprint cast (see p. 29). The image can be compared with a computerized database of tire treads to narrow down the type of vehicle and the date and place of its manufacture. In addition, there will be unique wear marks that may help identify the vehicle that made the track.

Database tracks are compared with those from the scene

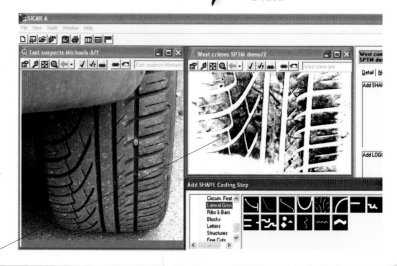

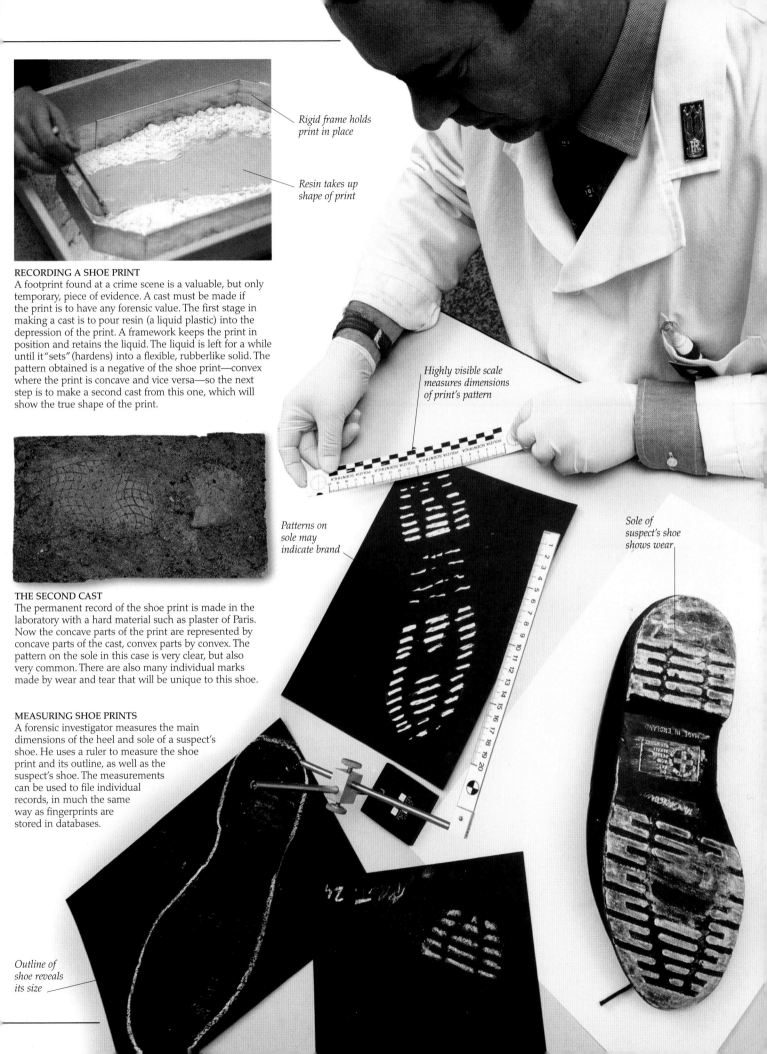

Rigid frame holds print in place

Resin takes up shape of print

RECORDING A SHOE PRINT
A footprint found at a crime scene is a valuable, but only temporary, piece of evidence. A cast must be made if the print is to have any forensic value. The first stage in making a cast is to pour resin (a liquid plastic) into the depression of the print. A framework keeps the print in position and retains the liquid. The liquid is left for a while until it "sets" (hardens) into a flexible, rubberlike solid. The pattern obtained is a negative of the shoe print—convex where the print is concave and vice versa—so the next step is to make a second cast from this one, which will show the true shape of the print.

Highly visible scale measures dimensions of print's pattern

Patterns on sole may indicate brand

Sole of suspect's shoe shows wear

THE SECOND CAST
The permanent record of the shoe print is made in the laboratory with a hard material such as plaster of Paris. Now the concave parts of the print are represented by concave parts of the cast, convex parts by convex. The pattern on the sole in this case is very clear, but also very common. There are also many individual marks made by wear and tear that will be unique to this shoe.

MEASURING SHOE PRINTS
A forensic investigator measures the main dimensions of the heel and sole of a suspect's shoe. He uses a ruler to measure the shoe print and its outline, as well as the suspect's shoe. The measurements can be used to file individual records, in much the same way as fingerprints are stored in databases.

Outline of shoe reveals its size

Guns and bullets

POLICE OFFICERS KNOW THE DEVASTATING HARM that firearms can cause. One of the first things to be done at any scene of crime where they have been used is to make safe any guns and ammunition that are present. The forensic investigation can then begin. The investigators record the positions of the weapons. They measure the damage caused by bullets to objects and human victims. They search for the bullets themselves—marks on them are like "fingerprints" of the weapons from which they were fired. The investigators carefully work out the positions from which the bullets were fired and the trajectories (paths) that they followed. They also search for tiny particles called firearm discharge residue (FDR) or gunshot residue (GSR), which are blasted out by a gunshot.

OPERATION TRIDENT
In 1998, London, England's Metropolitan Police set up a program, called "Operation Trident," which invited people to hand in guns and other weapons without fear of prosecution. The head of the initiative is shown with a cache of seized guns. Some had been used in violent crimes.

Twin triggers

Trigger guard

Stock

Rear sight

Foresight

Stock

Magazine clip

Trigger

Trigger guard

Safety catch

Rear sight

Hammer

Barrel

Slide

Foresight

Trigger guard

Grip

Trigger

13-round magazine within

Magazine release catch

RIFLE
A rifle is a long-barreled firearm that has spiral grooves called rifling running along the inside of its barrel. These make the bullet spin as it travels along the barrel, leaving characteristic marks on the bullet. The spin makes the bullet fly in a straighter path when it emerges. A rifle often has a magazine clip containing several cartridges (the bullet containers). The user steadies the rifle's stock against the shoulder when firing. This, the long barrel, the rifling, and (sometimes) a telescopic sight all make the rifle a very accurate firearm.

PISTOL
The Beretta 92FS is the pistol (handgun) that was adopted as the US military's official sidearm in 1985. Pistols like this are often called "automatics," but they are usually "semiautomatic," which means that a single pull of the trigger fires the bullet, ejects the used cartridge, and readies the next cartridge for firing. When the gun fires, the top part (slide) is driven back. A spring then forces it forward again to load the next cartridge into the chamber. A fully automatic weapon can fire repeated shots while the trigger is pressed once and held. Although intended for police and military use, such weapons have found their way into the hands of criminals.

DEATH IN DALLAS

The 1963 assassination of President Kennedy showed the lethal capabilities of powerful guns in criminal hands. The president was riding in an open-topped car through Dallas, Texas. Ex-marine Lee Harvey Oswald fired three shots from a sixth-story warehouse window. One shot killed the president. To this day, conspiracy theories abound about who shot the president and why, but they are hard to prove so long after the event.

The motorcade just before the shooting

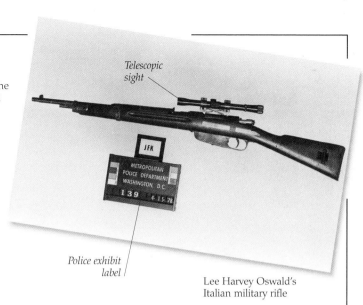

Telescopic sight

Police exhibit label

Lee Harvey Oswald's Italian military rifle

Twin barrels for quick firing

SHOTGUN

A shotgun is a long-barreled firearm that fires many small pellets (called shot) enclosed in a shell, rather than a single bullet. Unlike a rifle, the inside of its barrel is smooth. Its aim is less accurate than a rifle's, but this is made up for by the wide dispersal of the shot, which makes it easy to hit a target at close range. Criminals often like to carry shotguns during robberies to terrify people. A sawed-off shotgun has a shortened barrel, which reduces its accuracy. This weapon is favored by criminals because it is easy to hide in a bag.

Barrel

Plastic case

Metal head

Pellets

POWER OF THE GUN

Irrespective of shape or size, all guns produce an explosion that sends a bullet (or shot in shotguns) racing out of the barrel. In a rifle, the bullet is encased within a cartridge, together with gunpowder. A shotgun also holds cartridges, or shells, enclosing pieces of lead shot rather than a single bullet. With a pull of the trigger, the firing pin strikes and ignites the end of the cartridge, causing the gunpowder inside to explode. This forces the bullet or shot out of the gun with great speed.

RIFLE CARTRIDGE

A rifle cartridge is longer and slimmer than a pistol cartridge. The case is filled with gunpowder and the pointed bullet is on top. It is made of lead, usually covered with a metal jacket to prevent buildup of lead in the rifle barrel.

REPLICA BULLET

Although not designed to harm, these bullets can be made deadly by removing the plastic pellet inside and replacing it with a ball bearing. Replica guns are common in crime as they are easy to buy.

SHOTGUN SHELL

A normal shotgun shell contains many pellets, called shot, instead of a single bullet. These do not follow an accurate path, but spread out after leaving the barrel. The shotgun is good at hitting a close target, even when used by an inexperienced shooter. Shot can be of different sizes, described by a number—the larger the number, the smaller the shot.

MANIPULATED BULLET

A modified bullet—also known as a "dum-dum" bullet—is altered to do more damage when it hits a target. The bullet shown here has had the top of its metal jacket cut off, so that the jacket will spread when the bullet hits its target. If that target happens to be a human being, a larger, more damaging wound will be created, either at the point of impact or inside the body.

PISTOL CARTRIDGE

A cartridge used in a pistol differs from a rifle cartridge. It is shorter and broader in relation to its length. The empty cartridge left behind after firing is immediately ejected from the gun by the force of the explosive power. This same force brings the next cartridge into the firing chamber. The cycle continues until all the ammunition is used up.

Modified bullet

Standard bullet

Replica bullet

Rifle cartridge

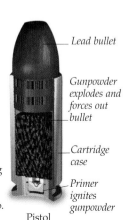

Lead bullet

Gunpowder explodes and forces out bullet

Cartridge case

Primer ignites gunpowder

Pistol cartridge

Firearms in the laboratory

THE STUDY OF GUN USE is called "ballistics." Internal ballistics is the study of the processes involved as the bullet is fired and travels down the barrel. Terminal ballistics is concerned with what happens when the bullet strikes the target. Chemistry is crucial, and analysis of firearm discharge residue (FDR) looks for key metals, including barium, antimony, and lead. The scanning electron microscope can form images of such particles, and can be used to analyze them chemically.

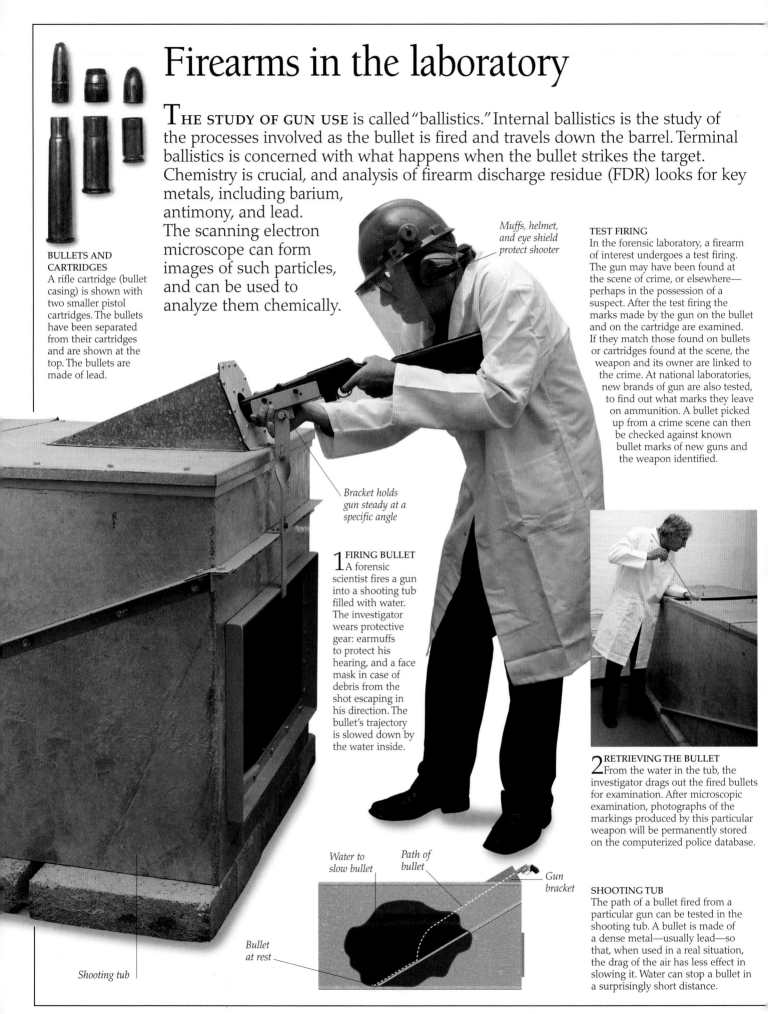

BULLETS AND CARTRIDGES
A rifle cartridge (bullet casing) is shown with two smaller pistol cartridges. The bullets have been separated from their cartridges and are shown at the top. The bullets are made of lead.

Muffs, helmet, and eye shield protect shooter

Bracket holds gun steady at a specific angle

1 FIRING BULLET
A forensic scientist fires a gun into a shooting tub filled with water. The investigator wears protective gear: earmuffs to protect his hearing, and a face mask in case of debris from the shot escaping in his direction. The bullet's trajectory is slowed down by the water inside.

Shooting tub

Water to slow bullet *Path of bullet* *Gun bracket*

Bullet at rest

TEST FIRING
In the forensic laboratory, a firearm of interest undergoes a test firing. The gun may have been found at the scene of crime, or elsewhere—perhaps in the possession of a suspect. After the test firing the marks made by the gun on the bullet and on the cartridge are examined. If they match those found on bullets or cartridges found at the scene, the weapon and its owner are linked to the crime. At national laboratories, new brands of gun are also tested, to find out what marks they leave on ammunition. A bullet picked up from a crime scene can then be checked against known bullet marks of new guns and the weapon identified.

2 RETRIEVING THE BULLET
From the water in the tub, the investigator drags out the fired bullets for examination. After microscopic examination, photographs of the markings produced by this particular weapon will be permanently stored on the computerized police database.

SHOOTING TUB
The path of a bullet fired from a particular gun can be tested in the shooting tub. A bullet is made of a dense metal—usually lead—so that, when used in a real situation, the drag of the air has less effect in slowing it. Water can stop a bullet in a surprisingly short distance.

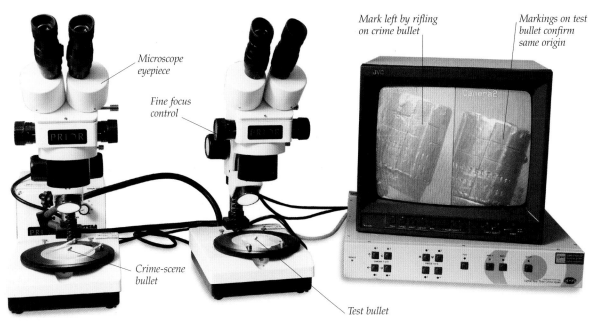

Microscope eyepiece

Fine focus control

Crime-scene bullet

Test bullet

Mark left by rifling on crime bullet

Markings on test bullet confirm same origin

IMPACT DAMAGE

A bullet is grossly distorted (above right) when it hits anything solid—even comparatively soft wood. A test bullet fired into a water tub (above left) is much less seriously damaged. Even so, the two can be compared for striations (grooves) and rifling on the sides of the bullet behind the deformed head. Even a deformed bullet indicates which types of gun could have fired it, and the distance from which it was fired.

SIGNATURE OF A GUN

A bullet from a crime scene is placed under a comparison microscope together with a bullet fired in the laboratory from a suspect weapon, in order to compare them at high magnification. The forensic investigator will be looking for several features in the comparison. Marks are left on the rear end of the cartridge when it is forced into the chamber on loading. Marks are also left by the hammer or firing-pin when it is fired. The rifling from the barrel leaves characteristic grooves running the length of the bullet. The best that such examination can achieve is to show a link between a gun and a crime. More evidence—for example, the discovery of a matching type of gunshot residue or a DNA link—is necessary to say conclusively that a particular person fired a particular shot.

RETRIEVING A CARTRIDGE

A forensics officer places a used cartridge into an evidence bag at the scene of crime, after marking and photographing its position. Cartridges are automatically ejected from most types of firearm, and a criminal rarely has time to grab them before fleeing, so they are a frequent source of information.

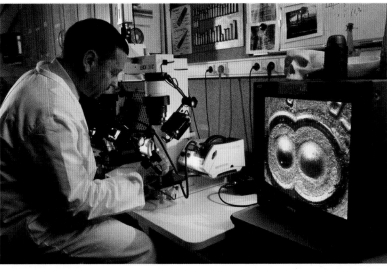

COMPARING CARTRIDGE CASES

Two cartridges, one from the crime scene and one from a test firing in the laboratory, are being studied under a comparison microscope. Visible here are the rims of the cartridges, and the central percussion caps, which were struck by the weapon's firing pin. Both these areas at the rear of the cartridge, being in contact with parts of the weapon, will carry markings that are unique to that weapon. Under high magnification, similarities and differences between these markings are visible and can help the investigator decide whether there is a connection between the two cartridge cases.

CONDEMNED BY BALLISTICS

The trial of Nicola Sacco and Bartolomeo Vanzetti was a sensation. In 1920, two payroll guards were shot and $16,000 was stolen in Braintree, Massachusetts. Sacco and Vanzetti were tried for the crime. They were political activists and many allies protested their innocence. The evidence against them was weak, but a firearms expert showed that the markings on a test bullet fired from Sacco's revolver matched those of one of the fatal bullets. The men were executed in August 1927.

Vanzetti

Sacco

DEADLY PATH

A policeman is using a rod to reconstruct the path followed by a bullet that struck this car. Laser beams or strings are sometimes used instead. If a bullet hole is deep enough, the police may slide a probe into it to show the direction of entry. Tracing trajectories in this way is especially important if more than one person was using a gun at the scene.

Probable position of gun

Rod links bullet hole with gun's position

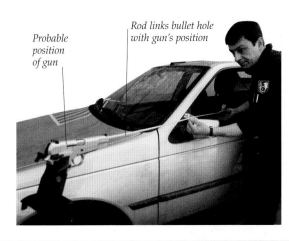

At the scene of the crime

A CRIME INVESTIGATION doesn't always begin with a crime scene or a body: it may be sparked by a missing-person's report. The police have to choose whether to launch a search right away, at the risk of finding that the person has simply gone away without telling anyone. The alternative is to wait until it is certain that something is wrong, when the trail may have gone cold and many clues may have been lost. If a person is found dead at a scene, whether following a search or not, the first question is who are they; the second is whether the death is due to foul play. Even a death arising in the course of a crime is not necessarily a murder. All the clues have to be collected that might help a court decide whether the death was due to accident, negligence, recklessness—or murder.

SNIFFING IT OUT
Sniffer dogs are shown here searching the scene after an unsuccessful bomb attack at Glasgow Airport in Scotland. Dogs are also used to find drugs, and missing people—dead or alive. Some dogs are specially trained to scent a dead body, even if buried—springer spaniels (left) are one breed that make good "cadaver dogs," as they are called.

EYE IN THE SKY
A police helicopter crew liaises with police and volunteer searchers on the ground before continuing its flight in quest of a missing person. Using a helicopter is a costly method of search but it can cover a wide area and access areas that would prove difficult for land vehicles. That is why it is the equipment of choice in incidents involving the sea, lakes, mountains, moors, deserts, and other inhospitable terrain. It can also carry infrared heat detectors and other sophisticated devices capable of detecting a living or dead human body from the air.

Cockpit provides 180° vision

WHO'S WHO

In the aftermath of a shooting outside a railroad station, the search to identify the victim begins. A clean-suited officer carries a stack of yellow position cards ready to be placed by evidence, which will be photographed and put into bags for safekeeping. Documents and other personal effects found on or near the body are included in this catalog since they will provide vital information to help identify the body. Friends or relatives may come forward with information, which may add to the picture. In this case, the victim who was shot was simply an innocent bystander who had intervened when criminals attacked two security guards.

THE BODY FARM

Dr. William Bass looks at a body at the Body Farm—a research center in the US that studies how bodies decompose. Bodies are buried in different types of soil, or left out in the open or in the trunks of cars. Studying the way in which the bodies decompose can help pinpoint time of death. Many people donate their bodies to the Body Farm.

A TRIPLE KILLER

In December 1993, "Big Mike" Rubenstein reported finding three of his relatives—a man, woman, and child—dead in their mountain cabin. He had visited twice in November and found the cabin empty, he said. Body Farm scientists used their knowledge of how bodies decay to determine that the victims had died in mid-November—so their corpses must already have been there when Rubenstein said the cabin was empty. He was eventually convicted of the three murders.

GOING DEEP

A diver searches a shallow stream in a hunt for a missing woman. Some of her possessions were found in the water, near where the diver was looking. Divers usually work in extremely poor visibility. However, they are now increasingly aided by sonar equipment, using high-frequency sound waves to generate an image of objects on the bottom. When this indicates objects of potential interest, divers go underwater to investigate them.

RADAR DOWN TO EARTH

A searcher steers a GPR (ground-penetrating radar) unit. GPR can be used when a body or other evidence is suspected to be buried in a well-defined area. The unit sends out radar (high-frequency radio) waves. These are reflected more strongly by some objects beneath the ground than by others. The image has to be interpreted by an expert and rarely shows definitely that a body is buried. However, what it can do is give a good indication that something unusual is present and with this knowledge experts can decide if it is worth conducting a more thorough search.

Police officer gives instructions to volunteers

Underground details relayed to monitor

A bug's life

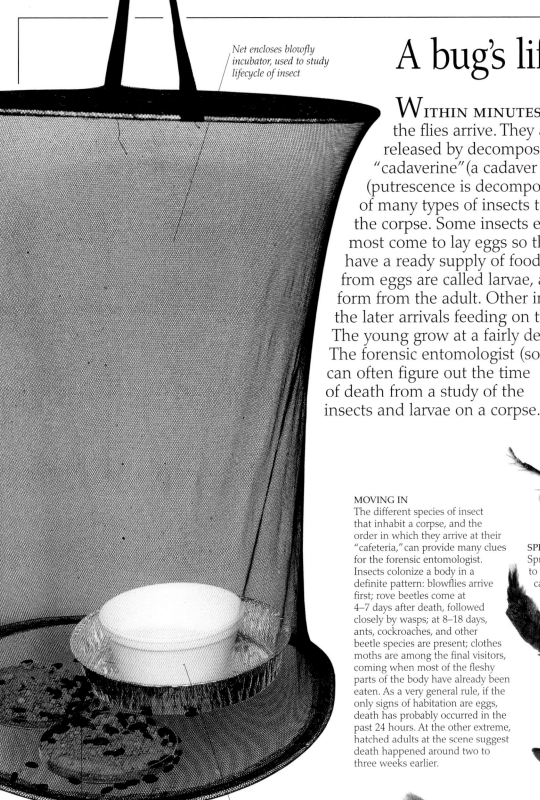

Net encloses blowfly incubator, used to study lifecycle of insect

WITHIN MINUTES OF A PERSON DYING, the flies arrive. They are guided by substances released by decomposing bodies—such as "cadaverine" (a cadaver is a corpse) or "putrescine" (putrescence is decomposition). The flies are the first of many types of insects to come and set up house on the corpse. Some insects eat the flesh themselves, bu most come to lay eggs so that their developing young have a ready supply of food. The young that emerge from eggs are called larvae, and are very different in form from the adult. Other insect species come in wave the later arrivals feeding on the larvae of the earlier one The young grow at a fairly definite rate for each species. The forensic entomologist (someone who studies insects can often figure out the time of death from a study of the insects and larvae on a corpse.

MITE
Mites arrive on dead body soor after flies. They often eat eggs an maggots of other insects, misleading forensic scientists.

MOVING IN
The different species of insect that inhabit a corpse, and the order in which they arrive at their "cafeteria," can provide many clues for the forensic entomologist. Insects colonize a body in a definite pattern: blowflies arrive first; rove beetles come at 4–7 days after death, followed closely by wasps; at 8–18 days, ants, cockroaches, and other beetle species are present; clothes moths are among the final visitors, coming when most of the fleshy parts of the body have already been eaten. As a very general rule, if the only signs of habitation are eggs, death has probably occurred in the past 24 hours. At the other extreme, hatched adults at the scene suggest death happened around two to three weeks earlier.

SPRINGTAIL BEETLE
Springtails are among the later insects to arrive at a corpse—they can indicate the person died some time ago.

WASP
Wasps do not usually fe on corpses, but on the insects that have arriv earlier. They may al· lay their eggs in t maggots on th body.

Water for consistent humidity

Blowfly pupae

MAGGOT FARM
This net houses a family of blowfly pupae growing on rotting meat in a forensic science laboratory. The scientists study their rate of growth, the stages they go through, the effects of light and temperature, and the effects on insect development of drugs or alcohol in the meat—this imitates the effects of these substances in dead bodies. All this information is valuable to forensic scientists trying to figure out the time and place of a suspicious death. Investigators carry out a similar process of growing eggs, maggots, or pupae from the scene. Since larvae of different species and different ages can look similar, they have to be grown to maturity to identify what insects are present, and their stage of development.

CLOTHES MOTH
In the final stages of decomposition, the larvae of clothes moths may feed on the corpse's hair.

ANTS
Although not partial to human flesh, ants are often found on and around a dead body. They are interested in feasting on the larvae and maggots of some of the other insects that are feeding from the corpse.

4 ADULT
Two to three weeks after the blowfly's eggs were first laid, the fully formed adult flies emerge from the pupae. They have all the characteristics of flies, including six legs, a single pair of wings, and eyes that are huge relative to the size of their bodies. The adults do not feed on flesh—only the maggots do this, in order to prepare for adulthood. The time taken for the adult to emerge is strongly dependent on temperature—the warmer the surroundings, the faster the development.

24 hours

1 EGGS
Each adult female blowfly that arrives at the corpse will lay about 250 eggs in the ears, nose, other openings, wounds, or folds in clothing—wherever it is warm and moist. The eggs are incredibly small, each one measuring about $1/12$ in (2 mm) in length. Through the translucent outer layers of the eggs, a faint mass—which is, in fact, the future larva—becomes visible. It takes only about 24 hours for the eggs to develop into the next stage of the cycle.

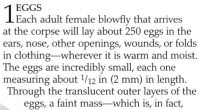

24 hours

LIFE CYCLE OF THE BLOWFLY
Blowflies are a family of insects that includes many species. Some of these are the familiar metallic-looking bluebottles. All blowflies lay their eggs on the flesh of decomposing bodies, and also on open wounds. The first blowflies to arrive at a fresh corpse typically show up within minutes. For this reason, the eggs, larvae, pupae, and adult forms of the fly found on a corpse are one of the best guides to the time since death. A forensic investigator will collect all the insect life he or she can see on or near the corpse and will grow them to maturity in the laboratory to identify them.

PUPA
The pupa [is t]he stage of [dev]elopment during which [the] blowfly turns from a [sha]peless maggot into the adult [fly.] The maggot first develops a hard [casi]ng, or puparium. The transformation [from] larva to adult takes place hidden [insi]de this apparently lifeless casing. The [pup]a cannot move or feed, and lives off [food] stored in its body. It spends as long [as a] week in this state. Then the newly [deve]loped fly forces its way out.

7 days

7–14 days (three larval stages occur)

2 MAGGOTS
Blowfly eggs develop into maggots. A maggot is an insect larva that is blind and legless, but able to move by wriggling, and able to feed. Blowfly maggots in a corpse molt, or lose their skins, twice, to go through three stages, each bigger than the previous one. If the maggots cluster into masses, they generate heat and attract other insects that feed on them. The last maggot stage ends one to two weeks after the eggs were laid.

MAGGOTS GIVE THE GAME AWAY
The charred remains of a man were found in a burned-out car 18 days after he'd been reported missing. The corpse was studied by the forensic entomologists at the Body Farm of the University of Tennessee. There were live maggots on his body, and from their size and weight, they were judged to be 2 days old. Did that mean the man had been dead for only 2 days? In his brain, there were also dead maggots. These had developed for about 14 to 16 days before they had been cooked in the fire. The investigators concluded that the man had been killed soon after his disappearance. Two weeks after his murder, the criminal had tried to disguise the cause of death by burning the car with the body in it. Insects returned to colonize the cooled body.

A burned-out car can initially disguise the cause of death

Cause of death

A POSTMORTEM (after-death) examination, or autopsy, begins with an external assessment of the state of the body. This is conducted by a scientist called a forensic pathologist, who looks for signs of injury. With stab or bullet wounds, it is necessary to study the angle of impact and the depth of penetration. Next, the pathologist cuts open the body to check the internal organs for further clues as to why the person died. The organs are removed and pieces of tissue are cut from them to be sent for laboratory analysis. This may reveal that death was caused by, say, a lack of oxygen due to carbon monoxide poisoning or suffocation. Finally, the organs are replaced and the body is sewn up so that it can be buried or cremated.

AUTOPSY ROOM
A body that has to be examined is brought from the mortuary (see p. 39) to an autopsy room— an operating room for the dead. Here a pathologist pieces together the facts behind a suspicious death. The body is placed on a specially designed stainless-steel table. After the body has been cleaned, the pathologist gets to work. Hygiene in the autopsy room is of utmost importance, both to protect the pathologist's health and to ensure that the evidence is not contaminated. Any organs removed are weighed, since an abnormal organ weight may indicate the cause of death.

Refrigerated cabinet for storing body parts

Raised lip prevents liquids from spilling on to floor

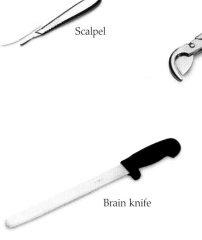

Scalpel

Bone cutters

Hand saw

Brain knife

Cranium chisel

TOOLS OF THE TRADE
As with any specialized job, a pathologist depends on having the right tools on hand. His or her job ranges from making large cuts through flesh and bones, which requires a saw and bone cutters, to small cuts and removing tiny pieces of tissue, which requires a scalpel. Removing and sampling the brain requires yet more specialized tools, including the brain knife and cranium chisel.

AUTOPSY PROCEDURE
If the initial examination of the body indicates suspicious circumstances, the pathologist will open up the body. He or she uses special surgical saws to cut through bone, and surgical tools to cut out and into each organ. The procedure follows a set sequence. First to be pulled out are the esophagus and stomach. (The esophagus is the tube that leads from the mouth to the stomach.) Then out come the heart and lungs, followed by the brain. Finally, the liver and kidneys are removed.

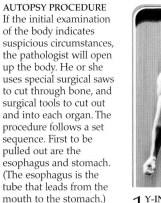

1 Y-INCISION
The first cut (or "incision") is Y-shaped— across the chest and down the body.

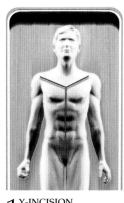

2 OPENING THE CHEST
The pathologist peels back the flesh of the chest to reveal the rib cage and the soft organs.

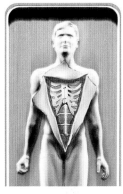

3 ACCESS TO ORGANS
The front ribs are removed using a saw. The internal organs can now be removed.

EXAMINING THE BRAIN
If the brain needs to be examined, the top of the skull is removed and the brain is first studied in position. Then its connection to the spinal cord is cut and the brain is removed and weighed. The organ can be kept in formalin, a preserving fluid, until it is returned to the skull for burial.

Scales for weighing organs

Chalk board for recording weights of organs

Autopsy table slopes toward drain at far end

Water to clean body and wash away fluids released by autopsy

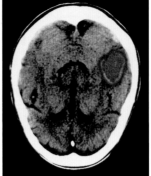

DEATH IN THE BRAIN

A major cause of death in violent crimes is a hemorrhage (bleeding) inside the skull, resulting from a blow to the head. If there are no outward signs of injury, the cause of death may not be apparent, so pathologists must open the skull to look for evidence. Brain scans can reveal hemorrhages without opening the skull, but they are usually only performed on living people. This scan shows bleeding (red area) in a 66-year-old woman. It did not prove fatal.

CUT TO THE BONE

Stab wounds can be so severe that they penetrate the soft tissues and go deep enough to damage the victim's bones, leaving clear marks. Just as burglary tools can be identified by the marks they leave at the crime scene (see pp. 24 and 28), pathologists can sometimes link a particular weapon to the stabbing, because imperfections in the blade match the marks it left on the bones.

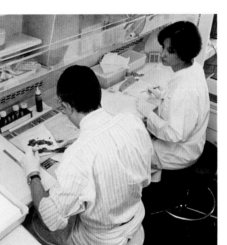

Groove made by knife blade

Fragment of thigh bone

TISSUE ANALYSIS

After an autopsy, scientists in a laboratory analyze tissue samples removed from the various organs to see what information they can yield. Blood is tested for its group, and to see what diseases the person might have had. Testing hair can reveal whether and when the person had taken drugs. However, the most important tissue test is DNA typing (see pp. 22–23), which can be performed on a wide range of body tissues and fluids.

AUTOPSY RECORD

As part of the general external examination of a body before it is cut open, the pathologist will usually draw a diagram showing all notable features—birthmarks, moles, tattoos, and so on, as well as any wounds, bruises, or other markings that may possibly be linked to the person's death. Increasingly, photography is also being used to record body marks, but photos still need to be interpreted and annotated by the pathologist. Often a pathologist will tape an audio commentary during the examination. The goal of all this is to ensure that a complete record is made of all the information at the time of the examination, so that later anaylsis does not have to rely on half-remembered facts.

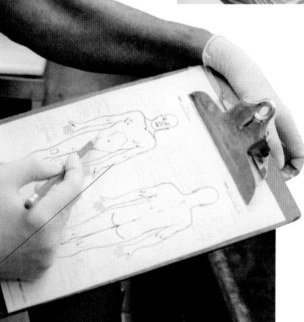

Notable features marked on standard autopsy diagram

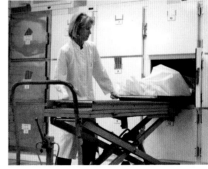

THE MORTUARY

Dead bodies are kept in a storage room called a mortuary, or morgue. Each body is kept in a body bag in a separate large drawer. If an autopsy is needed, or if the person has not yet been identified, the body is kept chilled so that it does not decompose and its condition remains much the same as at the time of death. After an autopsy, a body is returned to its drawer in the mortuary until burial or cremation.

Toxic world

WARNING—POISON!
Emblazoned on pirate flags long ago to instill fear in their enemies, the skull and crossbones symbol is still used today to warn of deadly danger. Seen on a chemical bottle, or on the door of a cabinet or room, the skull and crossbones means that there is poison—a toxic substance—inside. The implications of this traditional and universal symbol are understood by the public around the world.

IF DRUG USE OR POISONING is suspected in a crime, samples from an autopsy or crime scene may be sent to toxicologists, who test them for toxins. A toxin is any substance that is harmful, or poisonous, to the human body. The drugs we take for our health are medicines. Drugs taken for pleasure range from the mild stimulant caffeine (found in coffee, tea, and cola drinks), through alcohol and nicotine (the active ingredient in tobacco), to more powerful and harmful illegal drugs such as cannabis, cocaine, and heroin. Any drug can be toxic, even fatal, if taken in excess or used for the wrong purposes. In addition to looking for toxins in bodies, forensic scientists also investigate toxic hazards produced by our way of life. Industrial wastes are often toxic, and new and poorly tested materials can pose health risks.

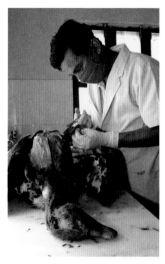

ENVIRONMENTAL CRIME?
Not all crime victims are human. A scientist studies the corpse of an Indian white-backed vulture that was allegedly killed by an environmental toxin. The cause might have been natural, or it might have been criminal activity—farmers deliberately setting out poison to protect their animals from predators, or a factory negligently releasing a harmful waste product. In fact, this vulture and many others seem to have been killed by feeding on the carcasses of cows that had been given diclofenac, a veterinary drug.

ANTHRAX ATTACK
On September 11, 2001, hijacked airliners destroyed the twin skyscrapers of the World Trade Center in New York City and damaged the Pentagon military headquarters in Washington, D.C. Nearly 3,000 people were killed. One week later, another terrorist attack against the United States began. Five letters containing spores of the deadly disease anthrax were sent to news companies and two US senators. Five people died and 17 others were infected. Millions of dollars were spent trying to locate the source, decontaminate dozens of office buildings, and screen mail to prevent future anthrax attacks. The spores must have been prepared in a laboratory—and the type involved was first prepared at a US research laboratory in the 1980s—but the source was never identified and no arrests were made.

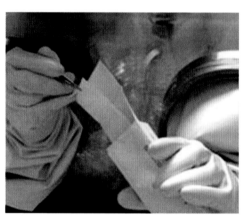

A forensic scientist checks a suspect package

One of the letters
containing anthrax

A CLASSIC MURDERER
When the remains of the missing Cora Crippen, wife of Englishman Dr. Hawley Harvey Crippen, were found buried in his basement he was already on board a ship bound for Canada with his lover. The ship's captain reported by radio that he'd recognized the fugitives, even though both were well disguised. A Scotland Yard officer boarded a faster ship and was waiting for them when they arrived in Canada. Crippen was found guilty of poisoning his wife and was hanged in November 1910.

TRENTON, NJ

PM

18 SEP
2001

USA
34

EDITOR
NEW YORK POST
1211 AVE. OF THE AMERICAS
NEW YORK NY 10036

TESTING FOR TOXINS

An important part of the forensic scientist's job is to identify toxins in samples taken from a crime scene or a victim's body. Even a tiny amount of some toxins can be deadly. One of the most sensitive instruments for analyzing small quantities of a substance is the mass spectrometer. It breaks up a sample into tiny molecules (groups of atoms). Molecules of different substances have different masses. By separating the molecules according to their mass, the spectrometer tells the scientist which substances the sample contains.

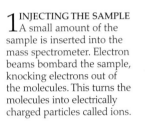

POISONS

Historically, poisons were a firm favorite with murderers, since it was often possible to make it look as if the victim had died naturally. With today's sophisticated toxicology, few criminals could hope to get away with murder using any of the three poisons below. But accidental poisonings occur and forensic scientists may be called in to investigate.

STRYCHNINE
The toxic leaves of strychnine cause a very unpleasant, slow death. Violent convulsions lasting some time eventually cause exhaustion and lung paralysis, which leads to suffocation.

MUSHROOM
The death cap mushroom is just one of many deadly types of fungi. Famously used to poison the Roman emperor Claudius, it causes an agonizing death with cramps, vomiting, diarrhea, delirium, and liver failure

ANTIMONY
This metal was once ground up and used in powdered form as a poison. It has a distinctive metal taste that is hard to disguise, so it would be given in small doses over a long period. Antimony ultimately causes death by heart failure.

1 INJECTING THE SAMPLE
A small amount of the sample is inserted into the mass spectrometer. Electron beams bombard the sample, knocking electrons out of the molecules. This turns the molecules into electrically charged particles called ions.

2 PINBALL SCIENCE
The mass spectrometer then plays "pinball" with the ions. A strong electric field fires the ions in a beam up the machine (from the bottom left-hand corner), and a magnetic field bends the beam around the curved track. Ions of different substances have different masses, so they follow different paths and separate out by the time they reach the detector (bottom right). The result is a graph showing if any toxins are present.

ILLEGAL DRUGS
Some drugs, such as marijuana, heroin, amphetamines, and cocaine, are so detrimental to health that their use is prohibited by law. In some countries alcohol is also illegal. If taken in large enough quantities, or in a "cocktail" with other drugs, these drugs can produce life-threatening symptons. If there are no signs of injury in a dead person, a toxicologist may test for evidence of drugs in the blood.

CANNABIS
Also known as marijuana, this is the most commonly used illegal drug. Strong concentrations of the drug have been known to cause abnormal behavior, so victims and suspects in apparently motiveless crimes are often tested for cannabis.

KILLED BY RICIN
Walking in London one day in 1978, Georgi Markov felt a jab in the back of his leg. He turned to see a man behind picking up a fallen umbrella and apologizing to him. The man jumped into a taxi and Markov thought no more of it. Three days later, Markov was dead. The umbrella was a weapon that had injected him with a tiny metal pellet containing the deadly poison ricin. Markov was a political dissident who protested about conditions in his home country of Bulgaria, and he was almost certainly assassinated by a Bulgarian agent.

Drilled hole to hold ricin

Actual size of pellet ●

HEROIN
Extracted from the opium poppy plant, heroin is a highly addictive drug and is commonly abused. Accidental overdose often causes death in addicts. Toxicologists can determine from a blood test whether heroin was responsible for the death.

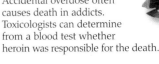

The bones of the matter

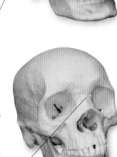

BARE BONES
The remains of a human being, reduced to mere bones after burial, are laid out on a forensic scientist's table. The investigator will almost certainly be able to tell the sex of the person, and also the height and age when he or she died. The ethnic group and state of health, and possibly even the cause of death, may also be revealed.

ONE STRAND OF INVESTIGATION is called forensic anthropology (the study of humankind for evidence). It is a branch of physical anthropology, which looks at how the human body varies among different peoples around the globe. Forensic anthropologists deal mainly with the skeleton—the part of a body that lasts longest when it's buried. People's skeletons change throughout their lives, which is why the size of the body in relation to the size of the head is greater in an adult than in a child. Skeletons also differ according to sex. The pelvis (consisting of the hip bones and a couple of smaller bones) is wider in a woman to allow for childbirth. In addition, skeletons vary around the world according to their ethnic origin. For example, there are significant differences between the skull shapes of Europeans, Africans, and East Asians. Forensic anthropologists sift through all this information to construct an accurate picture of the person whose bones they are investigating.

ETHNIC COMPARISON
The part of the skeleton that yields most information is the skull. To find a person's likely ethnic origin an anthropologist examines the depth (front to back) and breadth (side to side) of the skull. Other clues come from the cheekbones, eye sockets, and angle of the face, as well as the nose bridge and nasal opening. Teeth, too, are useful indicators of ethnic identity. The result is never conclusive, since there are wide variations within each ethnic population.

EUROPEAN SKULL
Skulls of Europeans are not as deep as those of Africans, nor as broad as those of East Asians. The face is relatively flat, since neither the cheekbones nor the jaw project.

Less deep than African skull

AFRICAN SKULL
Skulls of people from sub-Saharan Africa, or whose ancestors are from there, are deeper than those of Europeans. The cheekbones are lower, while the eye-sockets are wider, with more space between them.

Wide space between eyes

EAST ASIAN SKULL
Skulls of people from East Asia are long, and broad in relation to their depth, with rounded eye sockets. The incisors (the front cutting" teeth) are shovel-shaped.

Broad forehead

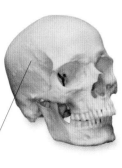

MASS GRAVES
United Nations forensic scientists dig at a communal grave in the Kosovo region of Serbia. In the late 1990s, civil war raged between the Serbian government and Kosovo, whose people are mostly of Albanian descent. Accusations of the mass murder of civilians were given credibility when communal graves were discovered. The investigators try to reunite the bodies' scattered bones to find out who the victims were (or at least which ethnic group they came from) and how they died.

ARTHRITIC KNEE
This X-ray of a knee joint shows little space between the bones, which is a sign of osteoarthritis. In this disease, the cartilage (elastic connecting tissue) in knees, hips, and other joints wears away, so bones rub together and get damaged. After death, this person might be identifiable from medical records describing their condition.

Reconstruction of head in clay

Photo of missing man

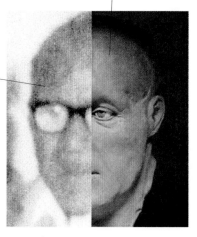

FROM THE ASHES
On November 18, 1987, a fire swept through King's Cross subway station in London, England. The identities of 30 people who died were pieced together over the days that followed. But one of the dead remained unidentified. Forensic sculptors reconstructed what they thought he had looked like from his fire-damaged skull (right). The victim was a short man who had undergone brain surgery. It was 15 years before the family of a homeless man, Alexander Fallon, 72 years old at the time of the fire, connected him with the event and matched his photo to the restoration.

WAKING THE DEAD

Sometimes the only way to identify a dead person whose skull or decomposed head has been found is to try to reconstruct his or her appearance and publicize it. The traditional way to do this is by drawing it or modeling it in clay. The clay reconstruction shown here is from a skull found in 1989 in Wales. The finished model was so lifelike that when it was published, the victim was immediately identified by her social worker.

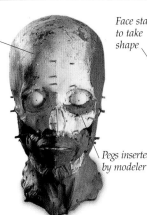

Cast of well-preserved skull

Pegs inserted by modeler

1 DEPTH PEGS
The sculptor inserts pegs over a cast of the skull. These show the typical depth of facial flesh and muscle on a person of the same sex and age.

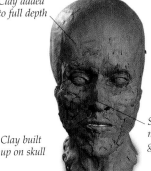

Face starts to take shape

Clay built up on skull

2 ADDING MUSCLES
The sculptor builds up clay around the temples and jaw, representing the muscles and underlying flesh in those areas.

Clay added to full depth

Shape of nose is guessed at

3 ADDING SKIN AND NOSE
When the pegs are completely covered, the sculptor smoothes clay (representing the skin) over the whole skull.

Hair added

Facial features assumed

4 HAIR AND COMPLEXION
The sculptor's biggest guesses must be made in the final stages, when he adds the hair, colors the skin, and hints at an expression.

COMPUTER MODELING

Facial reconstruction is increasingly being done by computer, using data from CT (computer tomography) scans of living people. CT is a special type of X-ray scanning that detects soft tissue as well as bone—conventional X-rays reveal only bone. A CT scan of a head shows not only the skull shape, but also the depth of the overlying flesh. To "flesh out" the skull of an unknown person, the computer wraps a CT scan around a digital model of the skull, then stretches and squashes it to fit. Once facial details such as skin, eye color, and hair have been added, the reconstruction is ready to send out to police forces and the media.

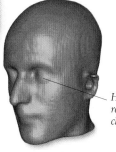

The facial tissue fits neatly over the skull shape

4 ADDED EXTRAS
After the CT skull is warped and merged with the model, the computer adds the CT scan's flesh and muscle tissues (blue).

Head resembles a clay model

5 SOLID RESULT
The computer generates a 3-D, 360° view, but it's not yet lifelike. Details of eyes and hair are added—sometimes from other evidence, sometimes by guesswork.

1 SCANNING A SKULL
A skull of an unidentified person rotates in front of a scanner in the University of Sheffield, England. A laser beam scans it, sending numerical information about its shape and size to a computer's memory. Now comes the challenge of reconstructing

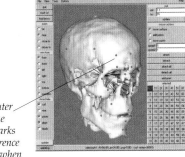

Computer uses the landmarks as reference points when attaching the CT scan

2 PREPARING A MODEL
The scanned skull is displayed on the computer screen as a digital model. The computer marks approximately the points where a CT scan will be fitted to the skull. These "landmark" points need to be positioned precisely. This fine-tuning is done by a human operator.

3 BEST FIT
A CT scan of a suitable skull is chosen from the computer's database, according to the forensic anthropologist's judgment of the sex, age, and race of the unkown person. The CT scan (red) is then superimposed on the model (blue) to show where they match and where the CT scan must be "warped" (distorted) to fit.

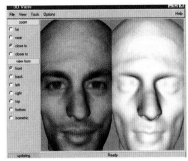

6 BACK FROM THE DEAD
To add authentic skin detail, a photo of a living face is wrapped around the model. Lastly, to make the face look realistic the computer adds highlights and shadows.

Spitting image

WHEN A CRIME HAS BEEN COMMITTED, getting a good picture of a suspect or a victim is vital. A likeness can be circulated to police officers and published in the press and on TV, recruiting millions of members of the public in a bid to find a criminal or identify someone whose remains have been found. The first source police go to is often any CCTV cameras in the area of an incident. CCTV (closed-circuit television) is non-broadcast TV, such as security cameras in stores and public places. If no pictures are available, or none is of sufficiently good quality, a picture of the person's face will be made from witness descriptions. People tend to be poor at describing faces in words, but they are usually good at judging whether a picture, on screen or paper, is a close resemblance to a face they have seen. The police method of producing a likeness from a witness consists of building up a picture of the face from different components, while the witness says whether it's getting more or less like the person they saw. Originally this was done by drawing a picture freehand under the witness's direction. Then ready-made drawings of facial features were used, and later on photographs. Today's computers can build up images with an even higher degree of accuracy from witness descriptions.

FACES IN A BOX
A photographic identification kit was a great advance in getting descriptions of suspects from eyewitnesses. Facial features were broken down into a fixed number of types and then put on to photographic cards. The technique was invented by a photographer, Jacques Penry, who called his system "Photo-Fit." It was capable of creating 15 billion different faces. This box contains dozens of different choices for each facial feature, such as hair, eyebrows, eyes, nose, and mouth. Witnesses who find it difficult to describe a briefly glimpsed face may find it much easier to select from a limited range of visual examples.

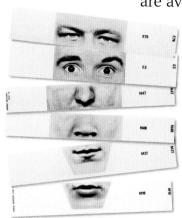

PHOTO FEATURES
Commonly called an "identikit," the photo identification system is made up of photos of facial features on strips of card (above). Witnesses trying to recall a face are shown cards for, for instance, the nose. They then pick the one that bears the closest resemblance to the nose they remember. This is assembled with other facial-feature cards to make a composite face (below left).

Facial jigsaw completed

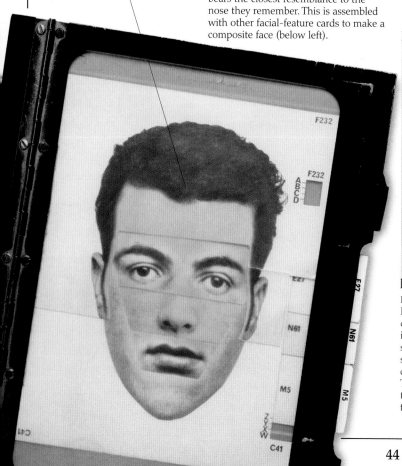

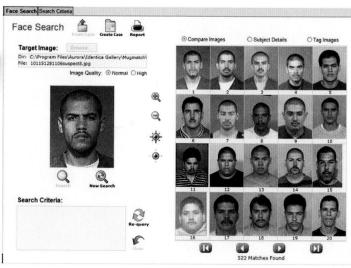

FINDING POTENTIAL MATCHES
In those cases where a good image of a suspect has been provided, the computer revolutionizes the task of searching through records to see whether information on the suspect has already been gathered. Here, the image of a suspect appears on the left-hand side of the computer display. On the right side of the screen there are 20 images retrieved by the computer from its database, which it has selected as good matches to the suspect's photograph. The computer can retrieve these matches within a few seconds from a database that may contain millions of faces. It is now up to a human expert to compare the selected images and decide if any of them really do depict the suspect.

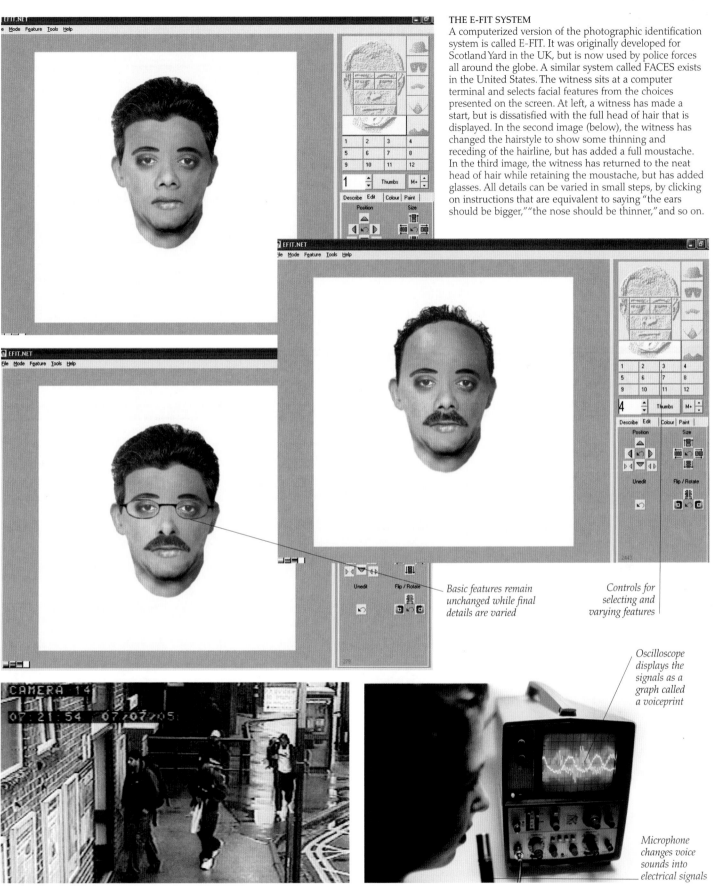

THE E-FIT SYSTEM

A computerized version of the photographic identification system is called E-FIT. It was originally developed for Scotland Yard in the UK, but is now used by police forces all around the globe. A similar system called FACES exists in the United States. The witness sits at a computer terminal and selects facial features from the choices presented on the screen. At left, a witness has made a start, but is dissatisfied with the full head of hair that is displayed. In the second image (below), the witness has changed the hairstyle to show some thinning and receding of the hairline, but has added a full moustache. In the third image, the witness has returned to the neat head of hair while retaining the moustache, but has added glasses. All details can be varied in small steps, by clicking on instructions that are equivalent to saying "the ears should be bigger," "the nose should be thinner," and so on.

Basic features remain unchanged while final details are varied

Controls for selecting and varying features

Oscilloscope displays the signals as a graph called a voiceprint

Microphone changes voice sounds into electrical signals

CCTV CATCHES TERRORISTS

This CCTV picture shows four inconspicuous-looking men entering a railroad station to travel 30 miles (50 km) to London, England. It could not show the bombs they were carrying in their backpacks, which would soon kill them and 52 others in central London. But this and other pictures afterward provided vital clues to their movements and the terrorist network they belonged to.

SOUND EVIDENCE

Every person has a unique voice. Forensic phoneticians are speech experts who can deduce a person's age, sex, and race by listening to voice recordings. They may also use voice spectrography. This measures variations in the sound as a person speaks, and produces a graphic representation called a "voiceprint." Like fingerprints, voiceprints can be compared to identify individuals.

Behavior of the offender

PROFILERS STUDY CRIMES to get a picture of the criminal's personality or way of life. Geographical profiling studies the locations and timings of a series of crimes. Burglars, for example, rarely commit robberies close to their own homes, and travel connections influence the pattern of their robberies. If a burglar lives close to a highway intersection, the most convenient places for him to target are residential districts close to the next intersections along the highway. If he has a legitimate daytime job, he has to commit his burglaries in the evenings and on weekends. Psychological profiling works back from the way the crime is carried out to deduce the criminal's personality and history. Someone who commits violent repeated assaults is more than likely to have displayed a violent personality in the past and to have a police record. Investigators also try to "get inside the mind" of a suspect during interrogation. The "lie detector," or polygraph, is based on the idea that someone who is lying will give themselves away by, for example, increased sweating and raised heart rate. However, in reality, few courts accept polygraph results.

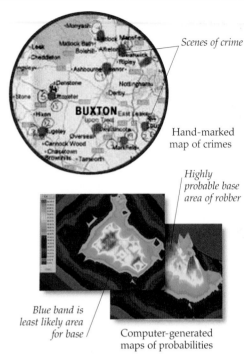

Scenes of crime

Hand-marked map of crimes

Highly probable base area of robber

Blue band is least likely area for base

Computer-generated maps of probabilities

GETTING WARMER
Red dots mark a series of bank robberies in central England (top). A profiler with expertise at geographical profiling was brought in. He came up with a computer map (center) that showed the probable location of the offender's base—his home or where he stored loot. Red areas are the most likely, blue the least. A 3-D version (bottom) shows the red areas as "peaks." The profiler reduced the search area to a tenth of the area covered by the crimes, and the criminal was soon caught.

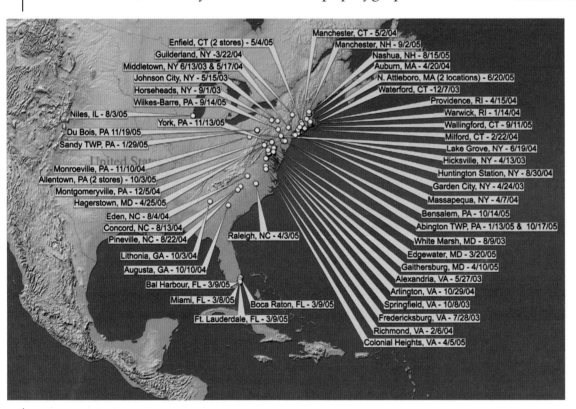

Manchester, CT - 5/2/04
Manchester, NH - 9/2/05
Nashua, NH - 8/15/05
Auburn, MA - 4/20/04
N. Attleboro, MA (2 locations) - 6/20/05
Waterford, CT -12/7/03
Providence, RI - 4/15/04
Warwick, RI - 1/14/04
Wallingford, CT - 9/11/05
Milford, CT - 2/22/04
Lake Grove, NY - 6/19/04
Hicksville, NY - 4/13/03
Huntington Station, NY - 8/30/04
Garden City, NY - 4/24/03
Massapequa, NY - 4/7/04
Bensalem, PA - 10/14/05
Abington TWP, PA - 1/13/05 & 10/17/05
White Marsh, MD - 8/9/03
Edgewater, MD - 3/20/05
Gaithersburg, MD - 4/10/05
Alexandria, VA - 5/27/03
Arlington, VA - 10/29/04
Springfield, VA - 10/8/03
Fredericksburg, VA - 7/28/03
Richmond, VA - 2/6/04
Colonial Heights, VA - 4/5/05

Enfield, CT (2 stores) - 5/4/05
Guilderland, NY -3/22/04
Middletown, NY 6/13/03 & 5/17/04
Johnson City, NY - 5/15/03
Horseheads, NY - 9/1/03
Wilkes-Barre, PA - 9/14/05
Niles, IL - 8/3/05
York, PA - 11/13/05
Du Bois, PA 11/19/05
Sandy TWP, PA - 1/29/05
Monroeville, PA - 11/10/04
Allentown, PA (2 stores) - 10/3/05
Montgomeryville, PA - 12/5/04
Hagerstown, MD - 4/25/05
Eden, NC - 8/4/04
Concord, NC - 8/13/04
Pineville, NC - 8/22/04
Raleigh, NC - 4/3/05
Lithonia, GA - 10/3/04
Augusta, GA - 10/10/04
Bal Harbour, FL - 3/9/05
Miami, FL - 3/8/05
Boca Raton, FL - 3/9/05
Ft. Lauderdale, FL - 3/9/05

JEWELRY ROBERIES
An FBI map shows the locations and dates of a string of related jewel robberies along the East Coast of the United States that began in April 2003 and continued for some years. In total, over 50 thefts occurred, amounting to over $5 million-worth of stolen jewelry. Creating a map like this is the first step in searching for behavior patterns that might reveal the perpetrators' base, their means of transportation, and perhaps where they will strike next. Even with a smaller number of incidents, this type of map can be helpful.

CRACKER
A psychological profiler featured in the hit TV series *Cracker* (a slang name for a profiler). The central character, "Fitz" Fitzgerald, was played in the British series by Robbie Coltrane (above), and by Robert Pastorelli in the US remake. Fitz has brilliant insight into the minds of criminals, but also severe personal problems of his own. In reality, the use of profilers is limited: police may listen to a profiler's views, but they keep an open mind. Police rarely work on "hunches," using a trained forensic psychologist to help plan a methodical approach to catching the criminal.

A PROFILING SUCCESS

In 1956, Dr. James A. Brussel, a psychiatrist, drew up a profile of the "Mad Bomber" who had been terrorizing New York City for years. He said the bomber was a neat and tidy, heavily built male, 40–50 years old, with a serious illness. He perhaps lived with an older female relative. And he might be wearing a double-breasted suit. The police eventually arrested George Metesky (above) at the house where he lived with his two older sisters. He fit the profile—even wearing a double-breasted suit to go to the police station.

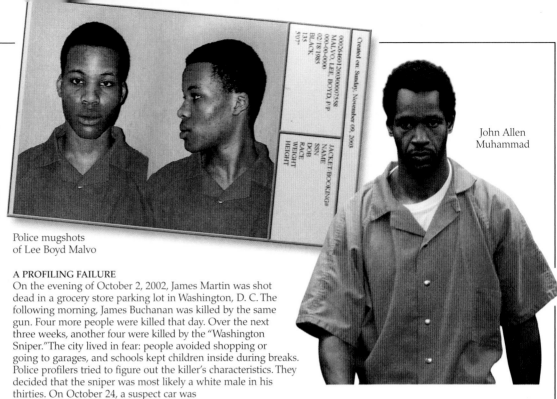

Police mugshots of Lee Boyd Malvo

John Allen Muhammad

A PROFILING FAILURE

On the evening of October 2, 2002, James Martin was shot dead in a grocery store parking lot in Washington, D. C. The following morning, James Buchanan was killed by the same gun. Four more people were killed that day. Over the next three weeks, another four were killed by the "Washington Sniper." The city lived in fear: people avoided shopping or going to garages, and schools kept children inside during breaks. Police profilers tried to figure out the killer's characteristics. They decided that the sniper was most likely a white male in his thirties. On October 24, a suspect car was seen at a highway rest stop. Inside were the killers—two black men, neither in his thirties. The instigator was John Allen Muhammad, aged 41. The younger man was Lee Boyd Malvo.

DETECTING LIES?

A man is interviewed as he sits hooked up to a polygraph, or "lie-detector," in a police station. Sensors record his pulse rate, blood pressure, breathing rate, and amount of sweating. Measurements are made when he answers "neutral" questions—about, for example, what he had for lunch. These are compared with measurements made when he is asked about the offense. High pulse rate, sweating, or raised blood pressure are taken to indicate nervousness and perhaps guilt.

Tubes record breathing

Fingertip sensor measures sweating

Cuff on arm measures blood pressure and pulse

PORTRAIT OF A KILLER

Jack Ruby was a nightclub owner in Dallas, Texas, in the 1960s. He was also the man who killed President Kennedy's assassin, Lee Harvey Oswald. There was no doubt that Ruby fired the gun, but investigators wanted to know his motive and whether he was part of a gang. His polygraph test (above) was examined for signs of untruthfulness in his story. He died before conviction.

Readings from "loaded" questions are compared with output from neutral questions to detect contrast

Fire starters

W<small>HEN A FIRE HAS THREATENED LIFE</small> or actually killed, forensic investigators move in to answer two main questions: how did it start, and how did it develop to become so damaging? Deliberately starting a fire is called arson. Some people do it for malicious pleasure, others because they have a grudge against the victims, and others to claim insurance on the property. But the great majority of fires start accidentally. The forensic investigators try to find out how the fire progressed once it started, because this can tell them whether dangerous materials played a part. A material that easily catches fire is said to be flammable, and materials sold for construction and furnishings must be nonflammable or have very low flammability. A fire might spread rapidly if a building has been badly designed, so forensic scientists have to keep up to date with the latest developments in architecture and building design, since sometimes these can create new fire hazards.

AFTERMATH OF FIRE
This room has been devastated by fire. Heat and smoke have destroyed the windows and all the furniture. The interior will need complete rebuilding if the house is to be used again. If anyone has died, forensic scientists will investigate to decide how the fire started, whether anyone did it deliberately, or whether someone was reckless or negligent. The electric heater in the center of the room will interest investigators.

SNIFFING FOR CLUES
After a fire, a forensic investigator uses "sniffing" equipment to search for traces of accelerant—a fluid used to make a fire burn more fiercely. If he finds it, it will suggest that the fire was deliberately started. The most commonly used accelerants are gas, paraffin, and turpentine. The apparatus seen here draws in air close to the area being examined, through the long tube.
  A miniature automatic chemical lab in the device analyzes the gases in the sample. If the device finds traces of an accelerant, detailed examination of that area begins, and samples are taken away to a forensic laboratory for thorough analysis.

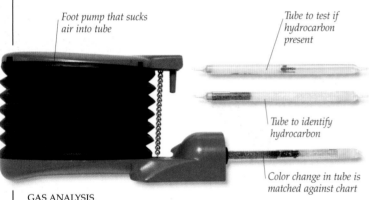

Foot pump that sucks air into tube

Tube to test if hydrocarbon present

Tube to identify hydrocarbon

Color change in tube is matched against chart

GAS ANALYSIS
This is one type of device used for analyzing gas samples at the scene of a fire. Called a Dräger tube after the German company that first started making instruments of this type, it consists of a foot-operated bellows that sucks air through a transparent tube containing chemicals. Different accelerants cause different color changes at various points along the tube.

THE THREAT OF FLASHOVER
Firefighters are trained to recognize signs that warn of imminent trouble. This fire, started artificially in a training area, has reached a dangerous point, called "rollover," in which snakes of flame begin to separate from the main fire. At any moment there is likely to be a "flashover," in which everything flammable in the surrounding area, having become intensely hot, bursts into flame, even without being in contact with the main fire. Forensic fire investigators must do part of their training in simulators like this in order to understand how fires work.

SPONTANEOUS COMBUSTION
Stories are often told of "spontaneous human combustion"—people bursting into flame with no apparent cause, as shown in this print from Charles Dickens' novel *Bleak House*. The real explanation, experts believe, is that an unconscious person gets caught in a fire that starts in a normal way.

A BURNED-OUT BUILDING
Many buildings near the Buncefield oil depot were destroyed in the blaze (right), including this house. The total destruction of its interior shows how ferocious, all-consuming, and fast-spreading a fire can be. Although the forensic investigators know the cause of this fire, it is still their responsibility to look for signs that might indicate how and why it spread so far from the main site and why the consequences were so disastrous.

EUROPE'S BIGGEST PEACETIME FIRE
A vast column of smoke is seen here rising from a burning oil depot at Buncefield, in southeast England. Described as the biggest fire in Europe since the World War II (1939–1945), it began when automatic equipment overfilled an oil tank with gasoline. The excess flowed into an open reservoir, and a large cloud of gas fumes built up over the unmanned site early on December 11, 2005. The inevitable explosion engulfed more than 20 large storage tanks. No one was killed, but nearby housing was severely damaged, 2,000 people were evacuated, and the oil depot was devastated. Soon, forensic scientists established the sequence of events and ruled out terrorism.

Smoke plume rose nearly 2 miles (3 km) high

Some fires were extinguished, but others were allowed to burn themselves out

Fire testing

Dᴉscovering the cause of a fire, why it spread, and why there were casualties can be difficult—which is not surprising, since burning itself is a complex chemical reaction. When a material burns, it combines with oxygen from the air. Heat is released and new substances are formed. These substances include smoke and ash. Invisible gases are also produced, such as potentially lethal carbon monoxide, hydrogen cyanide, and sulfur dioxide. Fires are often fatal. People are killed by the heat, by poisonous gases, and by choking smoke. Dense smoke is also dangerous because it reduces visibility, so that people cannot find their way to escape from the fire. Forensic experts do a huge amount of laboratory work to investigate how materials burn, which materials are dangerous because they combust readily or give off toxic gases, and how buildings can be improved to lessen the risk of fire. Armed with this knowledge, the scientists can advise companies that build and furnish hotels, offices, factories, and shopping centers. Such research also means that forensic scientists are better equipped to understand what actually happened when they investigate in the aftermath of a fire.

HOW DID IT START?
Samples of charred debris collected from a fire scene may yield valuable evidence. They are usually examined for traces of accelerant, which would suggest that the fire was a criminal act of arson. The collecting jars are always glass and the lids are made of a specially chosen plastic, neither of which contain chemicals that might contaminate the sample.

Piece of charred carpet from fire scene

HOW MUCH HEAT?
The cone calorimeter is a machine that tests the amount of heat energy materials give out when they burn, and the rate at which it is produced. (The word calorimeter means "heat measurer," and the cone referred to is a cone-shaped heater.) This is important, because the more heat the material gives out, and the quicker it does so, the more intense the fire is and the faster it spreads. The calorimeter subjects a sample to extreme heat until it ignites. A computer then calculates how much energy is released by combustion, and how rapidly.

1 PREPARING THE SAMPLE
Here, the material being tested in the cone calorimeter is a type of plastic. A square sample of the plastic is placed on aluminum foil to be mounted in the machine. The foil will reflect heat from the cone onto the sample.

HOW MUCH SMOKE?
Smoke is a killer, so it is vital to know the smoke-producing properties of materials used in furnishings and construction. This is what the smoke density chamber tests. A sample, such as a piece of carpet, is mounted on a stand (inset). Then a strong electric current is passed through the heating unit, which glows intensely hot. The machine records the time it takes for smoke to be given off by the heated sample and to build up to a maximum. It also measures the amount of smoke produced by detecting how strongly it absorbs light.

Sample mount   *Controls*

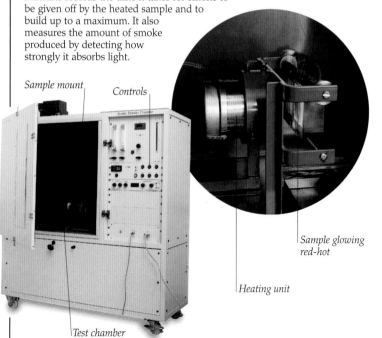

Sample glowing red-hot

Heating unit

Test chamber

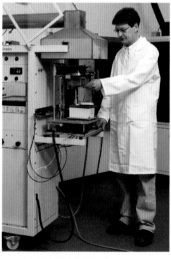

2 POSITIONING THE SAMPLE
The operator mounts the sample in the machine, on the platform near his left hand. Above the sample is the electrically heated cone. A shutter then opens to expose the sample to the cone's intense heat.

3 IGNITING THE SAMPLE
As the plastic's temperature rises, it starts to give off hot gases. When the gases are concentrated enough, they are ignited by sparks made by the thin white probe on the left. Sensors detect the energy released.

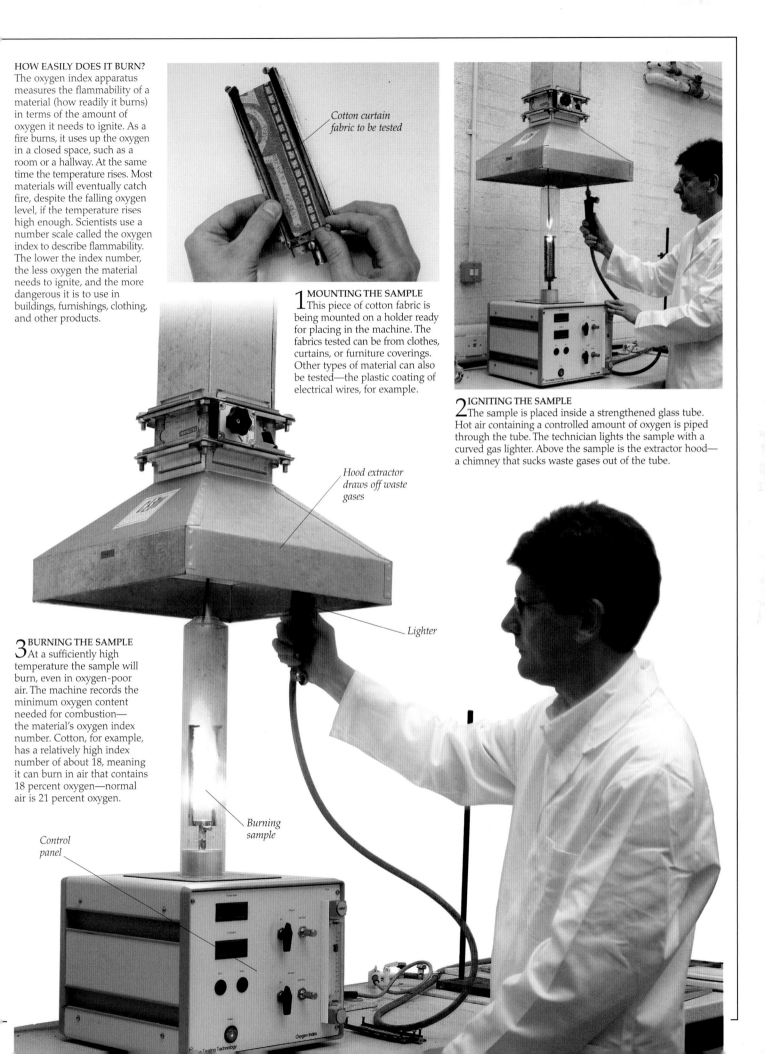

HOW EASILY DOES IT BURN?

The oxygen index apparatus measures the flammability of a material (how readily it burns) in terms of the amount of oxygen it needs to ignite. As a fire burns, it uses up the oxygen in a closed space, such as a room or a hallway. At the same time the temperature rises. Most materials will eventually catch fire, despite the falling oxygen level, if the temperature rises high enough. Scientists use a number scale called the oxygen index to describe flammability. The lower the index number, the less oxygen the material needs to ignite, and the more dangerous it is to use in buildings, furnishings, clothing, and other products.

Cotton curtain fabric to be tested

1 MOUNTING THE SAMPLE
This piece of cotton fabric is being mounted on a holder ready for placing in the machine. The fabrics tested can be from clothes, curtains, or furniture coverings. Other types of material can also be tested—the plastic coating of electrical wires, for example.

2 IGNITING THE SAMPLE
The sample is placed inside a strengthened glass tube. Hot air containing a controlled amount of oxygen is piped through the tube. The technician lights the sample with a curved gas lighter. Above the sample is the extractor hood—a chimney that sucks waste gases out of the tube.

Hood extractor draws off waste gases

Lighter

3 BURNING THE SAMPLE
At a sufficiently high temperature the sample will burn, even in oxygen-poor air. The machine records the minimum oxygen content needed for combustion—the material's oxygen index number. Cotton, for example, has a relatively high index number of about 18, meaning it can burn in air that contains 18 percent oxygen—normal air is 21 percent oxygen.

Burning sample

Control panel

Crash investigation

A MAJOR INCIDENT IS ALMOST ALWAYS followed by a thorough investigation. A train, plane, ship, or several cars may be involved, and a large number of people hurt or killed. Such disasters are usually the result of many rare events coming together by chance, or they may be an act of terrorism. Whether the cause is accident, carelessness, or sabotage, it is important to find out if anyone is to blame. Perhaps the correct safety and security procedures weren't followed, or maybe there was a design fault or equipment failure in the vehicle. These questions will be decided in court. The job of the forensic experts is to piece together the whole chain of events leading up to the disaster. They're helped by event recorders—"black boxes"—which are installed in airliners, trains, and ships. These hold instrument and voice recordings of everything that goes on in the vehicle's control center.

Radar showed plane broke up in midair

Retrieved fuselage confirms bomb damage

EMERGENCY STOP
The lengths of skid marks, together with a knowledge of the vehicle type and how heavily it was loaded, indicate the speed at which the vehicle was traveling. Weather conditions must also be considered. If skid marks start on the wrong side of the road, they may indicate reckless driving. If they start too close to some stationary obstacle, they indicate the driver was sleepy or not alert.

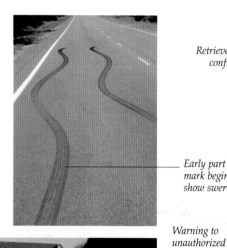

Early part of skid mark beginning to show swerve

Warning to unauthorized personnel

Signals in/out

Power supply meter

CRASH DUMMY
This "driver" has been saved from serious damage by the car's seat belt and inflated air bag. Car safety features are tested using crash dummies like this. The results are used not only in building safer cars but also in learning what the results of crashes are, so that forensic investigators can work backward from the aftermath of an accident to what actually happened. Such tests show, for example, that doubling the speed of cars in a collision results in a fourfold increase in damage.

Reflective stripes to aid recovery

Crash-resistant case

LAST WORDS
This is one of the two flight recorders from a crashed plane. Although called "black boxes," they are always bright red, and tough, to make them easily visible in wreckage. The one shown here is a Cockpit Voice Recorder (CVR), which records conversations among the crew. Current CVRs store the last two hours of conversation. The Flight Data Recorder (FDR) stores data from the plane's instruments.

PAN AM FLIGHT 103

The shattered body of a Boeing 747 airliner, Pan Am Flight 103, was painstakingly reassembled from hundreds of thousands of parts recovered over a vast area in and around the small town of Lockerbie, in Scotland. On December 21, 1988, the plane exploded on its way from London to New York. All 259 passengers and crew were killed, as well as 11 Lockerbie residents. Forensic scientists discovered that a bomb placed in the hold had torn the plane apart.

Air accident investigator

OFF THE RAILS

On June 3, 1998, a German Intercity Express train was involved in a catastrophic crash near Eschede. There were 101 dead, and 88 seriously injured. Forensics revealed that a wheel rim had broken due to metal fatigue—a problem foreseen by other train operators, who had altered the design. As the train traveled over a set of points, the displaced wheel hit a trackside lever, changing the points and derailing the rear cars. The train cars hit the pillars of a bridge, which fell onto the train. In complex cases like this, blame and responsibility can be difficult to establish. Although two officials and an engineer from the train company were taken to court, the charges were later dropped.

The big bang

INSIDE A BOMB, a chemical reaction generates very hot, high-pressure gas that suddenly blasts outward, potentially devastating anything nearby. Gunpowder and similar materials need oxygen from the atmosphere to make the reaction work. This limits their power, so they are called low explosives. High explosives, such as dynamite, already contain the oxygen they need, and are used for a stronger, more rapid blast. A typical bomb contains an easily detonated explosive, called the primary explosive. This in turn triggers a more powerful but harder-to-detonate material, called the secondary explosive. A bomb can be made more deadly by putting it in a tough casing, such as an iron pipe, or by packing shrapnel (nails or other pieces of metal) around the explosive.

BUS BOMBING
This double-decker London bus was wrecked by a bomb exploding at the rear of the top deck. The picture shows the devastation that can be inflicted by a quantity of explosive small enough to be contained in a backpack. The bombing was the last of four that took place in London on July 7, 2005. Forensics work established that the bus bomber was among the 16 dead, and that the explosive consisted of homemade materials.

Fragment of suitcase lining

SNIFFER DOG
Here, a dog trained to detect explosives alerts its handler to a suspicious garbage can in Jerusalem, Israel. "Sniffer" dogs like this are taught to sit or bark when they encounter something that smells of explosive. Dogs are more efficient than any sniffer machines developed so far. They are used to search for explosives when an attack is feared, and for traces of explosive after an attack.

CMS   10   20

SUITCASE BOMB
These fragments of a suspect suitcase from the wreckage of Pan Am 103—the airliner that exploded over Lockerbie, Scotland, in 1988—were meticulously gathered and numbered along with thousands of pieces from the plane (see p. 53). After extensive study, investigators decided that the bomb was hidden in a cassette recorder inside this suitcase, which was stowed in the plane's hold. They created controlled explosions in replicas of the hold, filled with luggage, to figure out exactly how strong the explosion was. Fragments of the electronics of the recorder and labels on shreds of clothing led to two men who were eventually charged with the crime.

THWARTED MISSION
A bomb placed in a vehicle is hard to detect, and the vehicle can park in a town center without attracting undue attention. These large canisters of gas were removed from a truck that was intended to cause death and destruction in a city in Colombia, South America. The gas is normally used in industry or homes to provide heat and light. The canisters are very strong, to keep the liquefied gas under high pressure. So the bomb included an extra explosive that was capable of cracking the canisters.

Back of bus peeled apart

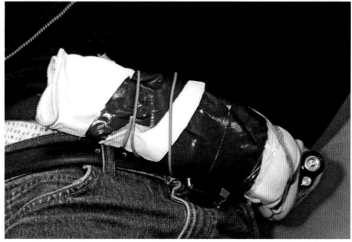

BOMB BELT

Although a dummy, this bomb is like a device worn around a suicide bomber's waist. This "bomb" is being used in a training exercise for security guards. A real bomb would be triggered by a switch held in the wearer's hand. A guard attempting to make the bomb safe has the problem of immobilizing the bomber instantly, without giving him or her a chance to trigger the device. A suicide bombing is one of the most difficult kinds of attack to deal with, because there may be nothing suspicious about the bomber except perhaps a bulky jacket. Since the bomber is prepared to die carrying out the attack, intercepting him or her with force may have little effect.

IMPROVISED BOMB

The hastily constructed bomb below was planted in a mosque in Hyderabad, Pakistan, but it was made safe before exploding. A liquid explosive is stored in the two aluminum flasks. The assembly is wrapped in plastic held together with adhesive tape. Wires to detonate the bomb lead into the cylinders from the circuit board, but are here partly disconnected. A radio signal, most likely from a cell phone, would have set off the electronic switch that triggered the bomb. When a sophisticated trigger mechanism like this is recovered, it often gives more information than any other part of the bomb about the makers.

Flask containing liquid explosive

Part of detonating device

TRAP FOR THE UNWARY

This metal box houses a lethal homemade bomb. The explosive, called Semtex, is in the plastic bag on the left. Wires lead to a radio receiver on the right, to which a signal is sent to detonate the bomb. If anyone but an expert had tried to open the box, they would have set off the mousetrap in the center—which also would have triggered the bomb.

Radio receiver

Semtex

Mousetrap acts as a booby-trap

COUNTDOWN TO DESTRUCTION

A bomb packed in a plastic box has a deadly extra attached to it—a plastic soft-drink bottle containing gasoline. On the side of the box is an ordinary kitchen timer, which controls the time of detonation. The explosive inside the box scatters the gas and ignites it, making this a potentially devastating incendiary (fire-starting) device.

Deadly soft-drink container

Circuit board triggers bomb when cell phone signal is received

Computer forensics

Today it is possible to strike up friendships, do business deals, and buy goods around the globe via the online computer and the cell phone. Crime is expanding fast in this digital world. Vast sums are stolen by criminals accessing someone else's bank account. People can be swindled by spam emails offering fake business propositions. Young people in chat rooms can be drawn into danger by older people posing as teenagers. Terrorists can share their knowledge of bomb making. But dealings in cyberspace are often not as anonymous as the criminals think. Police can find the rough location of a computer user who is visiting a suspect internet site. The position of a cell phone can be roughly localized when it makes a call. Everyone leaves information about themselves in many places, whenever they shop or travel, and the forensic investigator can take advantage of this electronic trail when trying to track down criminals.

THE PENTAGON HACKER
The internet makes it possible to commit "burglary" around the world no matter where the burglar lives. Computer users all over the globe are attempting to hack into (gain unauthorized access to) the computers of the Pentagon—the headquarters of the US armed forces (above). In 2005, the US military claimed that the biggest hacker attack in history had been carried out by Gary McKinnon (right), a computer administrator in Scotland. They said that he had snooped on 97 Pentagon computers. He claimed that he hadn't been interested in military secrets—he only wanted to find out what the US government knew about UFOs.

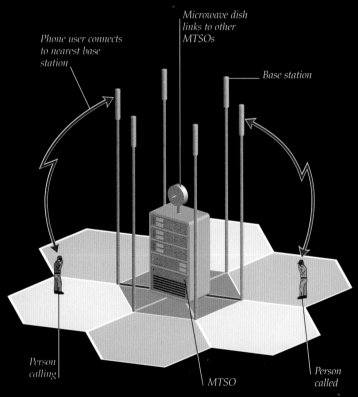

Phone user connects to nearest base station

Microwave dish links to other MTSOs

Base station

Person calling

MTSO

Person called

CELL PHONE NETWORK
Cell phones (cell phones) are so called because the phone company divides the area served into a grid of "cells"—areas roughly hexagonal in shape. Each base station (relay mast) is located at the point where three cells meet. Two people holding a phone conversation are each connected to their nearest base station. Base stations communicate through an MTSO (Mobile Telephone Switching Office) to other base stations. The phone company's log shows which base stations were involved in the call, and therefore which cells the callers were in, but not their precise locations.

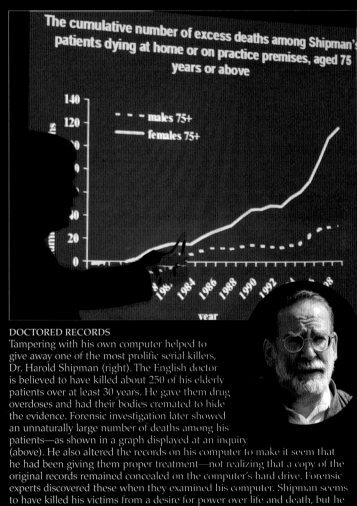

The cumulative number of excess deaths among Shipman's patients dying at home or on practice premises, aged 75 years or above

- - - males 75+
— females 75+

DOCTORED RECORDS
Tampering with his own computer helped to give away one of the most prolific serial killers, Dr. Harold Shipman (right). The English doctor is believed to have killed about 250 of his elderly patients over at least 30 years. He gave them drug overdoses and had their bodies cremated to hide the evidence. Forensic investigation later showed an unnaturally large number of deaths among his patients—as shown in a graph displayed at an inquiry (above). He also altered the records on his computer to make it seem that he had been giving them proper treatment—not realizing that a copy of the original records remained concealed on the computer's hard drive. Forensic experts discovered these when they examined his computer. Shipman seems to have killed his victims from a desire for power over life and death, but he altered one victim's will to inherit her money, exposing his part in her death.

COMPUTER DETECTIVE

A police expert is seen here removing the hard drive from a suspect's computer. Investigators have to follow a standard procedure when raiding computers to ensure they do not inadvertently destroy evidence. Any printing must be completed because the criminals might be printing incriminating files before deleting them on the computer. A computer should not be switched on because then it might be accessed remotely and tampered with. The police will sketch or photograph the computers' positions and connections before removing them, and look for written notes containing passwords.

A VIRUS STRIKES

An unexpected picture on a screen—such as this skull and crossbones—tells the shocked user that a virus has infected the computer. A virus is a malicious program that is spread from computer to computer. At best it causes inconvenience—the skull and message may be all this virus inflicts on the computer. At worst the virus can destroy information or make the computer unusable until major work has been done on it. Thousands of viruses are in circulation via the Internet or shared computer disks, and others are spreading through cell phones. Vast sums are spent on preventing viruses and "curing" infected computers.

SMART CARD

A smart card, such as the one exploded here, is a credit or debit card that can "remember" information about its user. The "brain" of the card is the microprocessor, or microchip—a tiny complex computer circuit. This "memory chip" encrypts data (translates into a secret code) for utmost securiy. The microchip is glued into a recess in the card. On top of the microchip is the larger printed circuit, which links the microchip to the outside world by connecting to terminals in a cash machine or a card reader in a shop. The microchip can carry information about the cardholder's identity, amount of money in the account, amount he or she is allowed to borrow, and so on. If the card falls into the hands of criminals, they will not be able to access the information unless they also get the user's PIN (personal identification number).

Printed circuit connects with outside world

Front of plastic card

Microprocessor or "brain" of card

Glue

Plastic support

Recess

Card holder's account number

Paper trail

FORENSIC SCIENTISTS OFTEN NEED to make a close examination of a paper document. It might be a blackmail letter or a threatening message, or a forged document such as a faked check. Sometimes a forensics expert compares samples of handwriting to see if the same person wrote them. In the past, when typewriters were widely used, it was possible to identify the machine used by imperfections in the letters typed. Today photocopiers and printers can often be identified by tiny imperfections in the copies. Many now print almost invisible information on their printouts that police can detect. Another kind of document that police often have to examine is paper currency. These days currency designs incorporate many safety features that are hard to fake—but sometimes a forgery is so good that it takes an expert forensic analyst to recognize it.

PRINTING AND PRIVACY

Many computer printers now print a microscopic code on the pages they output. Governments have requested this information to help the police identify when and where a document was printed. It is especially useful for tracking documents that criminals might create when planning business fraud or terrorism. Office printers can inform managers over the internet whether the printer needs to be repaired or is out of ink or paper. By the same means, it might be possible to say who was using a particular printer.

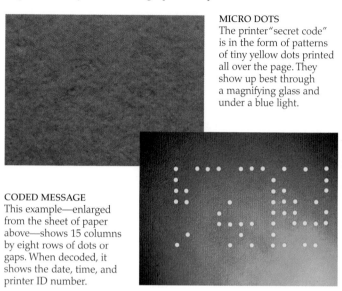

MICRO DOTS
The printer "secret code" is in the form of patterns of tiny yellow dots printed all over the page. They show up best through a magnifying glass and under a blue light.

CODED MESSAGE
This example—enlarged from the sheet of paper above—shows 15 columns by eight rows of dots or gaps. When decoded, it shows the date, time, and printer ID number.

BANKNOTE ANTIFORGERY FEATURES

Some criminals use high-quality color photocopiers to turn out fake currency. The copies can fool people who are too busy or careless to check that the money is real. But many features of genuine banknotes cannot be reproduced. They are printed on strong, high-quality paper, with their own characteristic "feel." If a cashier draws on the money with a counterfeit-detecting pen, the ink will turn gold if the paper is the right kind, but black if it is not. The designs on a genuine banknote are extremely intricate—a photocopier may blur them. The designs on the front and back are precisely aligned—hard to do on a photocopier.

SEE-THROUGH REGISTER
When this note is held up to the light, the incomplete "£" symbols on the front and back combine, showing the printing coincides accurately on both sides.

ULTRAVIOLET FEATURE
A UV banknote-testing lamp shone onto the British 20-pound note makes a large "20" appear in a red and green pattern. Similar patterns appear elsewhere on the note.

WATERMARK
In this banknote, a "ghostly" watermark—featuring Queen Elizabeth II and the number £20—becomes visible when held up against the light.

HOLOGRAPHIC STRIP
A series of foil patches forms a line. When you turn the note to catch the light at different angles, a face or the symbols "£" and "20" appears.

QUALITY
Banknotes have a special "feel," because of the heavy, high-quality paper used. Forgers use cheaper papers that are easily detectable.

MICROLETTERING
A magnifying glass reveals tiny lettering beneath the Queen: the value of the note in letters ("TWENTY") and numerals ("20").

RAISED PRINT
A finger run across the note can feel raised print in some areas, such as in the words "Bank of England" and on the figure "20" bottom right.

ELECTROSTATIC DETECTIVE

Forensic investigators can sometimes find traces of writing on a sheet of paper—even though they are invisible to the naked eye. When someone writes on the top sheet of a pad, a copy of the writing is left in the form of very slight impressions (dents) in the sheets beneath. The impression is greatest on the next sheet down, but if the writer presses hard, marks may be left on several sheets. The ESDA (Electrostatic Detection Apparatus) is a high-tech way of making the impressions on a lower sheet visible.

1 APPLYING THE FILM
The investigator lays the sheet of paper being investigated on a porous metal plate forming the top of the ESDA device. There are small holes in the plate. A pump sucks air through the holes, pulling the film and paper hard against the plate, in order to make a good contact between them.

2 CHARGING THE FILM
The operator waves a "wand," which is an electrode connected to a power supply at a very high voltage. This produces an electric charge all over the film (like static in hair). The charge is stronger where an impression in the paper creates a slight gap between film and paper.

3 SCATTERING THE TONER
The operator scatters powder, like the toner in photocopiers over the charged film, and then blows away the excess. Some powder remains, clinging to the film where the charge is strongest and revealing the writing (see right).

Fragile scrolls fell to pieces when found

THE DEAD SEA SCROLLS
Between 1947 and 1960, a treasure trove of Jewish religious writings was discovered in caves around the Dead Sea in the Middle East. Some were versions of parts of the Bible. But were they genuine, and how could the experts find out their exact age? Carbon dating was the technique used. This measures the radioactive carbon in the scrolls. It showed that the scrolls were written at various dates from the 2nd century BCE to the 1st century CE. Forgery was therefore ruled out.

THE FÜHRER FORGERIES
In 1981, a German journalist (far left) told his boss about some diaries supposedly written by Hitler. Handwriting experts and a historian declared them authentic. The journalist's magazine and a British newspaper paid millions of dollars to publish extracts. But forensics experts found the paper, inks, and bindings were modern and not available in Hitler's day. The forger and his accomplice, the journalist, were jailed.

Toner in grooves reveals writing

Every picture tells a story

GENUINENESS MAKES ALL THE DIFFERENCE to the value of an artwork. Even an inferior picture by a famous artist will fetch a higher price than an excellent one with an artist's signature that happens to be a fake. Forensic scientists study suspect paintings under light of various wavelengths. A forger might make a picture look convincing to the naked eye but X-rays and infrared light do not deceive. A forger has to be extremely talented and dedicated to produce an "old" picture without resorting to any modern materials.

Among the most notorious forgers of recent years are the Dutchman Han Van Meegeren and Londoner Tom Keating, who both managed to escape detection for a long time. With the development of sophisticated forensic science techniques, it has become easier to spot fakes. Paintings are not the only forms of art that are copied—photographs, ceramics, statues, and other artifacts have hoodwinked the experts.

MASTER FORGER
Tom Keating claimed to have painted 2,000 forged paintings during his lifetime. He felt that paintings in his own name did not get the recognition they deserved. He produced paintings in very varied styles, from the 16th century to the 20th. Only bad health saved him from being tried and perhaps jailed. He claimed that he always gave clues that experts should recognize—for example, by using modern paints, or putting historical errors into scenes. Remarkably, his paintings—including the forgeries—have increased in value ever since he was exposed.

VAN MEEGEREN PAINTING
Investigators decided that this picture, painted in the style of the 17th-century painter Vermeer, was one of many fakes painted by the forger Han Van Meegeren. Unusually, he was desperate to prove he was guilty of forgery—to prove that he was not guilty of treason. After World War II (1939–1945) he was accused of selling masterpieces to the Nazi invaders of his country. He had to paint a fake picture for the court to prove he had the skill to forge the old pictures. Although found innocent of treason, he was convicted of forgery but died before starting his sentence.

LOOKING FOR THE INVISIBLE
A technician aims a powerful spotlight (with a tungsten element) at an oil painting. The lamp illuminates the picture with both visible light (forming the bright patch on the painting) and infrared light, which is invisible radiation with wavelengths longer than those of visible light. The camera is loaded with special thermal imaging film that is sensitive to the infrared light reflected from the picture. In the photograph, details not visible in ordinary light, such as corrections and alterations, will show up. Infrared can also help determine whether the paint used is characteristic of a particular artist, and the picture is therefore genuine. X-rays, which penetrate beneath the surface of the painting, can see whether cracking occurs through all the layers—if it doesn't, the painting is probably a fake.

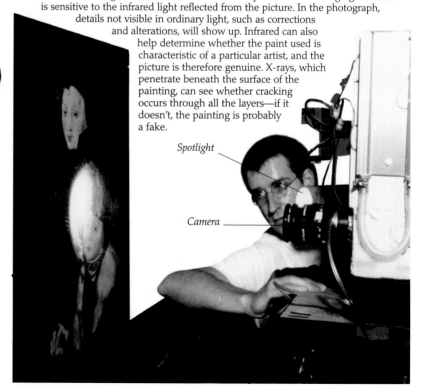

Spotlight

Camera

COTTINGLEY FAIRIES
Ten-year-old Frances Griffiths gazes dreamily at a troupe of fairies dancing in the garden. This photograph, taken by her 16-year-old cousin Elsie Wright in 1917, became world famous when published three years later. Many longed to believe these were real fairies—including Sir Arthur Conan Doyle, creator of the great detective Sherlock Holmes (see p. 9). Journalists questioned the girls to find out if the pictures were faked. Using a camera lent by an expert on the paranormal, the girls produced three more pictures of fairies. The images were said to have been retouched (altered) to make them clearer when printed in newspapers and magazines. This accounted for the flat, unconvincing look of the fairies. Many years later, Elsie and Frances admitted that the "fairies" were paper cutouts of pictures copied from a book.

STORED ENERGY
This African figurine is made of terra-cotta (baked clay). It could be several hundred years old, and may be very valuable. Measuring thermoluminescence (TL) can determine its age, and confirm its value. Clay continually stores energy from natural radioactivity—radiation from substances such as uranium that occur naturally in the ground. When a potter bakes the clay, this energy is released and the buildup of energy starts again. If a forensic scientist later heats a sample of the figure's clay, the stored energy is given out as light. The amount of TL shows how many years have passed since the potter made the figure.

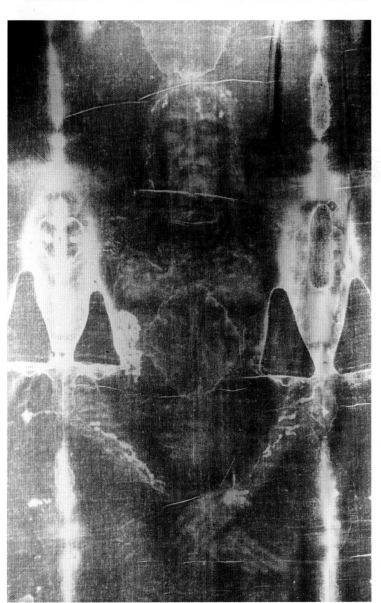

Shroud sample wrapped in foil

Sealed container in which sample was sent for testing

Wax seal of the Archbishop of Turin

THE TURIN SHROUD
For centuries, this linen cloth (left) was venerated as the shroud in which Jesus was wrapped when taken down from the Cross. The cloth's image of a man's body was said to have been made either miraculously or by some natural process. Fragments from the edge of the cloth have been sent to independent laboratories for analysis. Three radiocarbon dating tests place the cloth somewhere between 1260 and 1390 CE. However, the uncertainties in precisely dating a tiny piece of cloth taken from such a much-handled object are enormous.

Future forensics

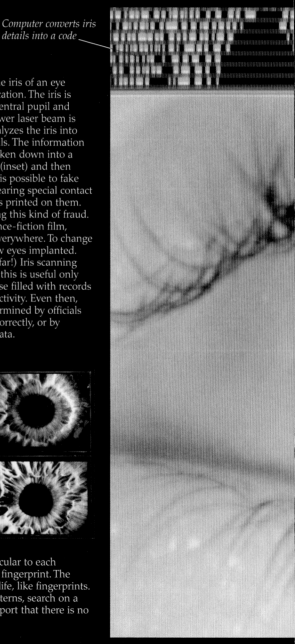

Injector, with RFID in place

Radio ID device

SCIENCE WILL OFFER AN IMPRESSIVE ARRAY of new techniques to police and forensic investigators in the near future. These can increase surveillance over our daily lives, helping the police to detect and solve crime. It will be possible to follow suspects by tracking their travel, their shopping, and their phone calls. From information hidden in digital photos, computer printouts, and computer drives police will be able to figure out a person's movements. Suspects will carry ID that can't be forged—in "biometric" details, such as facial features and eye patterns. Today, in most countries, such information is held only for those who have had a brush with the law. In the future, it may be gathered for everyone from birth. But is this desirable? There is a delicate balance between keeping tabs on criminals to combat crime and the state controlling the freedom of the individual.

UNDER THE SKIN
A radio frequency identification device (RFID) is a tiny implant that is inserted under a person's skin using the injector in order to keep track of his or her movements. Some criminals who are on probation and restricted to their homes at certain times already wear bulky radio-tagging devices. One day perhaps they will have these tiny implants, instead, so that the authorities can monitor where they are at all times.

Computer converts iris details into a code

IRIS SCANNING
This computer screen image is of the iris of an eye being scanned for personal identification. The iris is the colored area around the black central pupil and is unique in each person. A low-power laser beam is shone into the eye. The scanner analyzes the iris into eight circular areas to pick out details. The information about markings in each circle is broken down into a sequence of light and dark patches (inset) and then stored as numbers in a database. It is possible to fake the iris pattern—for example, by wearing special contact lenses with an image of iris patterns printed on them. However, there are ways of detecting this kind of fraud. (In the imaginary future of the science-fiction film, *Minority Report*, eye-scanners are everywhere. To change identity, a character has to have new eyes implanted. Few criminals today would go that far!) Iris scanning will identify someone correctly, but this is useful only when this identity links to a database filled with records showing past or possible criminal activity. Even then, the records' accuracy could be undermined by officials accidentally processing the data incorrectly, or by criminals deliberately altering the data.

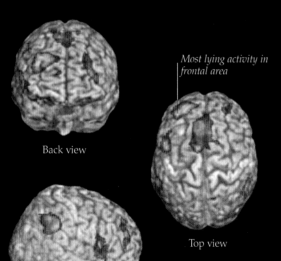

Most lying activity in frontal area

Back view

Top view

Right side

THE LYING BRAIN
Functional magnetic resonance imaging (fMRI) is used in medicine to observe how the brain works. The yellow and red areas above show brain cell activity during speech. The person being scanned was asked sometimes to lie and sometimes to tell the truth, while the activity of the brain was observed. Maybe one day police will be able to use a compact brain scanner that can show if a suspect is lying while being interrogated.

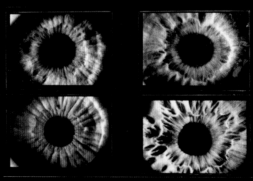

IRIS TYPES
Each iris is full of detail that is particular to each individual and more graphic than a fingerprint. The patterns are consistent throughout life, like fingerprints. A computer can analyze the iris patterns, search on a database, and make a match—or report that there is no match—within 3 seconds.

Standard set of points measured

Face shape scanned into computer

MAPPING THE FACE

A face can be scanned and its features summarized in a set of biometric measurements. A mesh of lines is projected in infrared light onto a face and a computer analyzes the way they're curved by underlying facial features. The distance between the centers of the eyes, the ends of the mouth, the length of the nose, and so on are measured rapidly. Facial recognition can be used as security passes as well as for locating criminals. However, as a person ages, facial features change and making a match becomes more difficult.

TRACKING THE TRAFFIC

Clusters of CCTV cameras high above a London street survey and make a record of the vehicles going past. The cameras are linked to computers that can "read" the license numbers. The cameras are at the entrance and exit points of the London congestion-charge zone. Hundreds of thousands of drivers pay a toll to enter the city each day from Monday to Friday. If a car's license goes onto the computer and the owner has not paid the charge, he or she will get a fine in the mail. Such charging may spread to the nation's highways and help to reduce the volume of traffic, while at the same time giving police a way of tracking vehicle movements around the country—modern criminals are highly mobile.

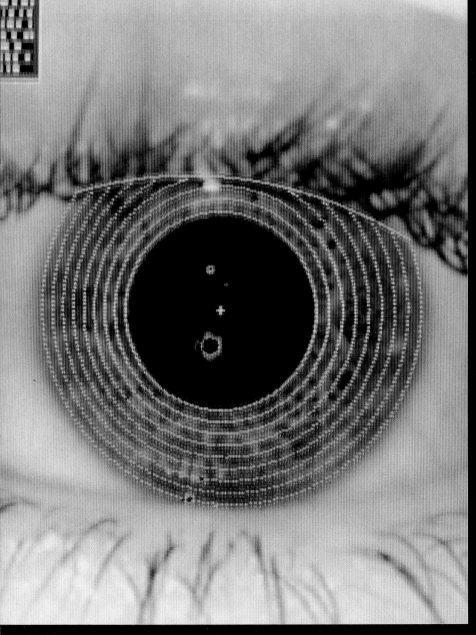

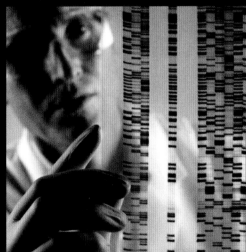

PERSONAL PROFILE

This scientist is examining DNA profiles. Soon it may be possible to get a DNA profile of a suspect as quickly as a breathalyzer test can detect alcohol in the blood. DNA databases are being built up in many countries, and often there are proposals to extend testing to the whole population. There is a danger that the public will think DNA testing is infallible and that it threatens only the guilty. Criminals know they can confuse DNA evidence by placing other people's DNA at the scene of crime. For example, scattering other people's cigarette butts to point the blame elsewhere. That's why forensic science can never stand still!

Hall of Fame

THE MAJOR PIONEERS AND CONTRIBUTORS to forensic science have come from many walks of life. Most are scientists, or police officers and detectives. Thanks to their work, there are now crime laboratories and databases all over the world, and forensics plays a key part in the criminal justice system, often providing evidence to convict the guilty and acquit the innocent.

ABAGNALE , FRANK 1948–
As a teenager, Abagnale taught himself the art of fraud and forgery and started writing checks. He ran away from home at the age of 16, and headed for New York. In a five-year crime spree he conned banks out of more than $2.5 million while posing as an airline pilot, doctor, lawyer, and teacher. By the time of his capture in 1969 Abagnale was wanted in 21 countries. However,

Frank Abagnale's incredible criminal career became the subject of a film in 2002

he served less than five years in prison when the FBI released him on the condition that he help them in their fight against fraud. He later founded his own security consultancy firm and became a legitimate millionaire.

BALTHAZARD, VICTOR 1872–1950
Balthazard was a professor of forensic medicine at the Sorbonne University in Paris, France. He made a comprehensive forensic study of hair, conducted research into bloodstain patterns, and used photographic enlargements of bullets and cartridge cases to determine weapon type. He was one of the first to attempt to match a bullet to a weapon.

BELL, JOSEPH 1837–1911
Dr. Bell was a professor at the medical school of the University of Edinburgh, Scotland, where one of his pupils was Arthur Conan Doyle. Bell had a habit of deducing a patient's occupation and history from studying his or her physical details. Conan Doyle used this trait for his fictional detective Sherlock Holmes. Bell's emphasis on close observation also made him a pioneer in his own field, forensic pathology.

BERTILLON, ALPHONSE 1853–1914
French detective and creator of anthropometry, the science of measuring the body. See pp. 8–9.

CRICK, FRANCIS 1916–2004
British codiscoverer, with James Watson, of the structure of DNA. See p. 22.

CRIPPEN, DR. HAWLEY HARVEY 1862–1910
American murderer captured by the use of new wireless communication. See p. 40.

DNA DATABASE 1995
The world's first DNA database was begun in Britain, and it is still the largest of any country. It holds DNA samples of around 3.5 million convicted criminals and suspects. Continuing technical advances in DNA collection and searching enable police to make new prosecutions for previously unsolved crimes, and to free those wrongly imprisoned.

FBI, 1908–
The Federal Bureau of Investigation, founded in 1908 as the Bureau of Investigation, under US President Theodore Roosevelt. See Hoover, J. Edgar.

GALTON, SIR FRANCIS 1822–1911
A cousin of Charles Darwin, Francis Galton was the author of *Fingerprints*. The book showed that fingerprints are individual and permanent,

and it established a first classification system, referred to as Galton's Details. This Victorian polymath also worked in statistics, psychology, geography, exploration, and meteorology.

GLAISTER, SIR JOHN 1856–1932
Scottish professor of forensic medicine and expert witness. See p. 20.

GODDARD, CALVIN 1891–1955
A pioneer in ballistics, Goddard headed the Bureau of Forensic Ballistics, the US's first independent crime laboratory. The Bureau took on fingerprinting, trace evidence, and blood analysis as well as ballistics. He encouraged the use of the newly invented comparison microscope to identify bullet markings, and was an expert witness at criminal trials.

GROSS, HANS 1847–1915
Gross was an examining magistrate and professor of criminal law at the University of Graz, Austria. His book *Criminal Investigation* explored the ways that physical evidence can be used to solve crimes He established the Institute of Criminology in Graz .

HAUPTMANN, BRUNO 1889–1936
This one-time criminal entered the US illegally from his native Germany in 1923. He lived quietly until 1935, when he was accused of the kidnapping and murder of the baby son of famous aviator Charles Lindbergh. "The trial of the century" convicted Hauptmann, partly because of similarities between his signature and a ransom note. But doubts about Hauptmann's guilt remained and, in 2005, three forensic document experts reexamined the handwriting evidence. All independently concluded that Hauptmann was indeed the author of the ransom note.

HERSCHEL, WILLIAM 1833–1918
British colonial magistrate and the first to use fingerprints for identification. See p. 18.

HOOVER, J. EDGAR
Founder and controversial director of the FBI in its present form, Hoover held this post for 48 years. The FBI investigates crimes and gathers intelligence about potential criminal activity. Hoover established forensics at the organization by setting up a fingerprint file, a crime laboratory, and the FBI National Academy for training elite officers. The headquarters in Washington, D. C., are named after him.

IAFIS 1999
The Integrated Automatic Fingerprint Identification System is the US's national fingerprint and criminal history system, and is maintained by the FBI. Submission, storage, and search are integrated in this one electronic

Hauptmann's signature

Composite signature made from ransom note

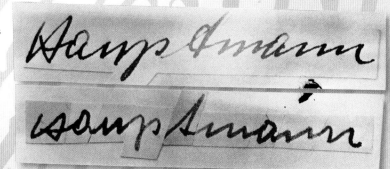

J. Edgar Hoover, founder of the FBI

known as "inheritance powder." Marsh was also a skilled inventor.

ORFILA, MATHIEU 1787–1853
Orfila was born in Spain but lived most of his life in Paris, France, where he was a professor of chemistry. He is the author of the influential *Treatise of General Toxicology*, published when he was just 26. The book detailed new techniques for detecting arsenic—a poison frequently used in murder cases—in the body. This, and other works, earned Orfila the title "the father of toxicology."

OSBORN, ALBERT SHERMAN 1858–1946
The author of *Questioned Documents* (1910), Osborn devoted his time to analyzing forged documents for more than 50 years. He was an expert witness in many important cases. In 1942 he founded the American Society of Questioned Document Examiners. He also designed a comparison microscope.

PARKER, ELLIS 1871–1940
Often described as America's real-life Sherlock

Wild West gunslinger Jesse James and "Boston strangler" Albert de Salvo have been examined by Starrs. His 2005 book *A Voice for the Dead* detailed his forensic researches. He is a professor of law and forensic science, and writes and edits the journal *Scientific Sleuthing Review*.

SURETe NATIONALE 1812–
The French National Police was founded by a former criminal, Eugène François Vidocq, in 1812, under Emperor Napoleon I. The Sûreté Nationale was the criminal investigative bureau of the Paris police, and most of its members—many of them former criminals—worked undercover. The science of secrecy was a huge success and the Paris crime rate was cut by 40 percent in eight years. Today, the Sûreté Nationale is known as the Police Nationale.

UHLENHUTH, PAUL 1870–1957
This German bacteriologist devised a test for distinguishing blood from other liquids, and one for distinguishing human blood from other animals' blood. See p. 20.

VUCETICH, JUAN 1858–1925
Argentine police officer and anthropologist Juan Vucetich made the first prosection based on fingerprint evidence, in a murder case. He developed a method of fingerprint classification that would be used by police forces all over the world. In 1904 Vucetich became the director of the Center for Dactyloscopy (fingerprint identification) in Buenos Aires.

WATSON, JAMES 1928–
British Nobel Prize winner and codiscoverer, with Francis Crick, of DNA's structure. See p. 22.

system, so that fingerprint checks, which used to take months, can be made in just hours. The IAFIS's database contains the fingerprints and criminal records of more than 47 million people.

KEATING, TOM 1917–1984
Successful British art forger. See p. 60.

KGB 1917–1991
The KGB was the Soviet Union's secret police. Its goal was to gather foreign intelligence and to pursue the state's enemies, often to the death. The organization used a mix of forensic science, new technology, and old-fashioned coercion to achieve its goals. When the Soviet Union was disbanded, so was the KGB.

JEFFRIES, SIR ALEC 1950–
British discoverer of DNA fingerprinting. See p. 22.

LACASSAGNE, ALEXANDRE 1844–1921
Sometimes referred to as the founder of forensic science, Lacassagne was a professor of forensic medicine at the University of Lyon, France, where one of his students was the future forensics start Edmond Locard. Lacassagne participated in criminal investigations and was an expert witness at criminal trials. He was the first to study bloodstain pattern analysis and bullet markings.

LANDSTEINER, KARL 1868–1943
Austrian discoverer of ABO blood groups and Nobel Prize winner. See p. 20.

LOCARD, DR. EDMOND 1877–1966
French forensic scientist most famous for his exchange principle. See p. 27.

MARKOV, GEORGI 1929–1978
Bulgarian dissident murdered with a poisoned umbrella. See p. 41.

MARSH, JAMES 1794–1896
British chemist who in 1836 devised a test for detecting arsenic, called the "Marsh test." Before the test, colorless, odorless arsenic was untraceable. The poison was used so widely to bump off family members that it became

Ellis Parker (right) discusses a case with his son, Ellis Parker Junior

Holmes, Ellis Parker was a Chief of Detectives in New Jersey for 45 years. He helped to solve more than three hundred violent crimes using a forensic mixture of close observation, deduction, and psychology. He became known for spotting details that other missed, and for asking questions that seemed pointless but which often led to an important discovery.

SCOTLAND YARD, 1829–
The headquarters for London's Metropolitan Police, founded in 1829 by Sir Robert Peel with the help of Eugène François Vidocq. The Met was an early adopter of forensic science and set up the Fingerprint Branch in 1901, using the Henry System of Classification.

STARRS, JAMES E.
American forensic anthropologist James E. Starrs has directed more than 20 exhumations of controversial murderers to try and discover new evidence. The remains of

Forensic scientist James E. Starrs examines DNA sequences

Timeline of forensic firsts

Forensic science has long been a weapon in the fight against crime, but today it is used more frequently, and more precisely, than ever before. Early breakthroughs included subjects as diverse as medicine, optics, and handwriting analysis. This timeline tracks the most significant of those advances.

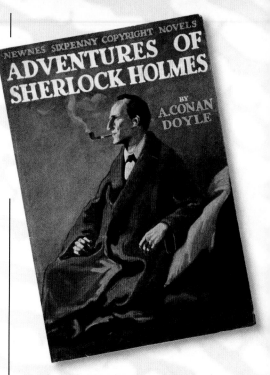

Published in 1892, this collection contained 12 of Holmes's adventures

1247
In China the first book on forensic science appears, called *The Washing Away of Wrongs*. Author Sung Tzuh, a lawyer, includes instructions on how to distinguish between suicide, murder, and natural deaths.

1609
The first study of handwriting analysis, by François Demelle, is published in France.

1642
The University of Leipzig in Germany begins a course on forensic medicine.

1670
The first powerful precision microscope is invented by Dutch scientist Anton van Leeuwenhoek. The device will become a vital tool for forensic scientists.

1776
During the Revolutionary War, the corpse of General Warren is identified by his false tooth, which was made from a walrus tusk.

1794
In Lancashire, Britain, murderer John Toms is convicted on the basis of a torn scrap of paper found on his victim matching a piece in Toms' pocket.

1804
German physicist Johann Wilhelm Ritter discovers ultraviolet radiation, which will be used to reveal trace evidence invisible in normal light.

Early precision microscope

1812
The world's first detective force, the Sûreté Nationale, is established in Paris, France. It becomes a model for Britain's Scotland Yard and the US's FBI.

1813
The influential book *Treatise of Toxicology* by Spanish doctor Mathieu Orfila is published.

1823
Czech physiologist Johann Evangelista Purkinje publishes a description of fingerprint types.

1828
Scottish physicist William Nicol invents the polarizing light microscope, which will become used for detecting trace evidence.

1835
British police officer Henry Goddard studies bullet markings, and demonstrates that a bullet can be matched to the gun that fired it.

1836
British chemist James Marsh devises a test for detecting minute quantities of arsenic in the body. The test is soon being used successfully in murder trials.

1841
The first detective story, *The Murders in the Rue Morgue* by American author Edgar Allen Poe, is published. From now on, developments in forensic science will be reflected in the adventures of fictional detectives.

1843
The first mugshots of suspects are taken by Brussels police in Belgium.

1850
In the US, murderer John Webster becomes the first to be convicted by medical evidence when doctors are able to determine the age, sex, and time of death of his victim.

1856
In India, administrative officer Sir William Herschel begins to use thumbprints on documents to identify illiterates.

1859
The US becomes the first country to allow photographs to be used as evidence in courts of law.

1861
In Germany, professor of pathological anatomy Rudolph Virchow makes a study of the value of hair as physical evidence.

1878
The Criminal Investigation Department (CID) is Britain's first plain-clothes detective force. The CID is controlled by Scotland Yard.

1880s
Italian criminologist Cesare Lombroso measures changes in blood volume to discover if any physiological changes are associated with lying.

1882
Anthropometry, a system of bodily measurements, starts to be used as a means of identifying criminals in Paris, France. It will become used by police forces all over the world.

1883
American humorist Mark Twain's book *Life on the Mississippi* features the identification of a murderer by fingerprints.

1887
Arthur Conan Doyle's *A Study in Scarlet,* the first story featuring Sherlock Holmes, is published in the UK. Holmes goes on to appear in four novels and 56 short stories and become the world's most popular fictional detective.

1891
Argentinian police officer Juan Vucetich makes the first criminal identification using fingerprints. As a result, a murderer is convicted. The following year, the Argentinian police force becomes the world's first to use fingerprinting as a means of criminal identification.

1892
Fingerprints, by British scientist Francis Galton, is first published. The book establishes a classification system, and shows that fingerprints are not inherited, and that even the prints of identical twins are different.

1893
The book *System der Kriminalistik* by German forensic scientist Hans Gross covers microscopy, serology, fingerprints, and ballistics. It appears in English in 1907 as *Criminal Investigation*.

1894
In France, Captain Alfred Dreyfus is wrongly convicted of treason by an incorrect handwriting identification by expert Alphonse Bertillon. The scandal rocks French politics.

1895
German physicist Wilhelm Conrad Röntgen discovers X-rays, which will earn him a Nobel Prize in Physics. X-rays will become a key tool for forensic anthropologists and odontologists.

1896
In Britain, Sir Edward Richard Henry publishes *Classification and Uses of Fingerprints*, which establishes a fingerprint classification system that will come to be used across Europe and North America.

1898
German chemist Paul Jeserich gets a killer convicted by firing a bullet from a suspect's gun and matching it with one from the crime scene.

1901
Austrian pathologist Karl Landsteiner demonstrates three blood types, leading to the ABO system of blood typing.

1901
German scientist Paul Uhlenhuth devises the precipitin test, which distinguishes human blood from the blood of other animals.

1902
Burglar Harry Jackson is the first person in the UK to be convicted by fingerprint evidence.

1904
In Germany, the precipitin test is first used in a criminal court, to convict brutal murderer Ludwig Tessnow.

1910
Questioned Documents by American document examiner and handwriting expert Albert Osborn is published. The book is still consulted by experts today.

1910
The world's first forensic laboratory is opened in France by Edmond Locard.

1911
Murderer Thomas Jennings is hanged after being convicted by fingerprint evidence in Chicago.

1913
Victor Balthazard, professor of forensic medicine at the University of Sorbonne, Paris, publishes an article detailing how bullet markings make every bullet unique.

1916
In the US, Albert Schneider uses a vacuum apparatus to collect trace evidence.

1920
French forensic expert Edmond Locard formulates his exchange principle, usually summarised as "every contact leaves a trace".

1920
An international catalog of firearms is begun by Charles E. Thwaite in the US. Five years later, the collection is complete and any bullet can be matched to the gun that fired it.

1920
Physicist John Fisher invents a device called a helixometer, for recording the interiors of gun barrels.

1920
American Luke May is the first to study how striation marks on tools can be compared and used as evidence.

1920
The Mysterious Affair at Styles is published in the US. Agatha Christie's first novel introduces the Belgian detective Hercule Poirot. He will feature in 33 novels and 54 short stories, and in many films.

1921
The first lie detector test, or polygraph, is invented by John Larson in the US. The machine measures blood pressure and rate of breathing.

1923
A US court rules that polygraph tests are not admissible as evidence.

1923
The US's first independent crime laboratory, The Bureau of Forensic Ballistics, opens for business.

1924
In the US, two killers are convicted when experts showed that one of them owned the typewriter used to write a ransom note.

1924
Los Angeles Chief of Police August Vollmer opens the US's first police crime laboratory.

1925
The first comparison microscope, important for matching bullet and other markings, is invented in the US by Philip Gravelle and Calvin Goddard.

1926
In the US, Italian-born laborers Nicola Sacco and Bartolomeo Vanzetti are convicted for robbery and murder, largely by ballistics evidence from the new comparison microscope.

1929
In Chicago, one of the hitmen responsible for gunning down seven mobsters in the St. Valentine's Day Massacre is identified when guns at his home are matched to cartridge cases from the crime scene.

The presence of maggots can help determine time of death

1930s
Mexico introduces the first test to identify gunshot residue on skin, the dermal nitrate test.

1930
In the US, the National Fingerprint File is started by the FBI.

1930
The *American Journal of Police Science* is founded and published by staff of the Bureau of Forensic Ballistics.

1932
The FBI opens its own crime lab, the Technical Crime Laboratory.

1936
In a murder trial, Scottish doctor Alexander Mearns uses the life cycle of maggots to estimate the time of the victim's death.

1936
Handwriting evidence helps convict German-born murderer Bruno Hauptmann in the US.

1941
The voice spectograph is invented by researchers at Bell Laboratories in the US. The device is intended to identify suspects from speech characteristics.

1945
The "Drunkometer," forerunner of the modern Breathalyzer, is developed by Dr. R.N. Harger of Indiana University.

1948
The American Academy of Forensic Sciences (AAFS) is founded, to bring together forensic scientists working in different disciplines.

A record of a suspect's fingerprints

1950
Tape lift method of collecting trace evidence is developed by Swiss criminalist Max Frei-Sulzer.

1953
Cambridge scientists James Crick and Francis Watson announce that they have discovered the double-helix structure of DNA.

1954
The breathalyzer, which estimates alcohol content in the blood from a sample of breath, is invented by Robert Borkenstein in the US. The device will be adopted by police departments around the world.

1959
A color test for gunshot residue is developed. Named the Harrison and Gilroy test after its inventors, the test is simpler and clearer than previous ones.

1965
In Britain, a team at Cambridge University develops the first scanning electron microscope (SEM). SEMs produce high-resolution 3-D images for analyzing samples in incredible detail.

1967
In the US, the FBI opens the National Crime Information Center to coordinate information about criminals and stolen goods.

Fibers in a needle's eye, as seen by a scanning electron microscope

1971
French photographer Jacques Penry creates the Photo-FIT ID System, capable of creating 15 billion different faces.

1975
The FBI introduces the Automated Fingerprint Identification System (AFIS).

1977
In Japan, trace evidence examiner Masato Soba discovers super-glue fuming—a method of revealing latent (hidden) fingerprints.

1978
The electrostatic detection apparatus (ESDA) is invented by British scientists Bob Freeman and Doug Foster. The device reveals impressions of handwriting in paper.

1983
The so-called Hitler Diaries, bought by the German news magazine *Stern*, are shown to be a fake by forensic document examiners.

1984
British geneticist Sir Alec Jefffreys discovers DNA fingerprinting, which uses variations in the genetic code to identify an individual.

1986
Polymerase Chain Reaction (PCR), a method of duplicating parts of the DNA molecule, is developed by American chemist Kary Mullis. PCR enables identifications to be made from a minute sample of DNA.

1988
In Britain, DNA fingerprinting is used to solve a crime for the first time. It exonerates a murder suspect, and then it nails the real culprit, Colin Pitchfork.

1989
In the US, Gary Dotson becomes the first person to have a conviction overturned by DNA evidence. He had served eight years in prison.

1991
University College Hospital, London, develops a laser scanning technique that enables a computer simulation of a human face based on the skull's shape.

1992
The FBI launches Drugfire, a firearms identification database that stores details of markings for search and comparison to find out if crimes were committed using the same weapons.

1993
75 years after their assassination, the remains of the last Russian czar, Nicholas II, and his family are positively identified by comparing samples of DNA from bone tissue with close relatives.

1994
The UK Home Office publishes a report called *CCTV: Looking Out For You*, which paves the way for a huge increase in the use of Closed Circuit Television cameras in

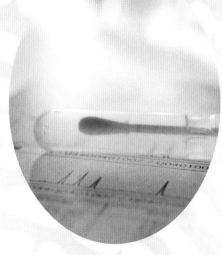

DNA sample on a swab

public places. The UK now has one CCTV camera for every 14 people.

1995
The world's first DNA database, containing the DNA records of convicted criminals, is set up in Britain. Other countries will soon follow suit.

1998
In the US, professor Don Foster helps police find serial bomber Ted Kaczynski through the new forensic science of literary analysis—studying documents the killer had written to discover who and where he was.

1999
The National Integrated Ballistics Network replaces the FBI's Drugfire database. It is a computer network containing digital images of ballistics evidence.

1999
The AFIS is integrated to create the Integrated Automated Fingerprint Identification System, making searching for matches much faster.

2000
The first episode of *CSI: Crime Scene Investigation* is broadcast on TV in the US. The program shows crimes being solved entirely by a team of forensic investigators. *CSI* will be a huge hit worldwide, and many other dramas about forensic science will follow. Experts complain that the "CSI Effect" gives the public unrealistically high expectations of what forensic science can achieve.

2001
Toxicologists examine a lock of hair that belonged to the French emperor Napoleon I, who died in 1821. It reveals that he suffered from long-term arsenic poisoning, which may have killed him.

2006
Automated Numberplate Recognition (ANPR) systems can now scan license plates at around one per second on vehicles traveling up to 100 mph (160 kmh). Using specialized CCTV cameras, ANPR reads the registration number and checks it on a database of stored license plates to identify the vehicle's owner.

Find out more

FORENSIC SCIENCE IS BECOMING increasingly popular, especially among young people. It has long been represented in books and TV, but now it is getting interactive, too—in museum exhibitions and on special websites. For budding forensic scientists, or anyone with an interest in forensics, there are plenty of opportunities to explore this fascinating subject.

USEFUL WEBSITES

- This site showcases forensic science resources for children and young adults
http:// www.all-about-forensic-science.com/science-for-kids

- Try some forensic science experiments and activities designed for children
http://www.hometrainingtools.com/articles/forensic-science-projects

- *Science News'* online magazine for 9–14-year-olds details the various fields of forensic science, and the inventions that made them possible
http://www.sciencenewsforkids.org/articles/20041215/Feature1.asp.

- Solve a make-believe crime and discover how you can practice forensic science at home
http://pbskids.org/dragonflytv/show/forensics.html

- London's Natural History Museum challenges the user to solve age-old crimes and mysteries using modern forensic science
http://www.nhm.ac.uk/nature-online/science-of-natural-history/forensic-sleuth

- *The CSI Experience: Web Adventure* has various games and activities based on the popular TV program
http://forensics.rice.edu/html/onlineactivities.html

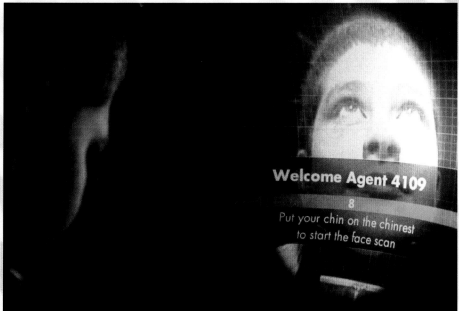

Welcome Agent 4109

8

Put your chin on the chinrest to start the face scan

Part of an interactive exhibition called "Please Identify Yourself!"

FORENSICS ON SHOW
This is an exhibit from an exploration of biometrics at London's Science Museum. The exhibition explores the ways that new technology, such as computer face recognition, is increasingly used for identification.

Police officer and K9, from Nebraska State Patrol, with local schoolchildren

THE SHERLOCK HOLMES MUSEUM
SOUVENIRS BOOKS ANTIQUES AND CURIOS

POLICE AT SCHOOL
In many parts of the world, police officers make educational visits to local schools. They may inform children about the role of the police in their community, and offer advice on keeping safe and asking for help when needed.

A museum guard dressed as a Victorian "bobby"

MUSEUM OF DETECTION
In London's Baker Street, the Sherlock Holmes Museum pays tribute to that fictional master of "deductive reasoning"—using observation and logic to deduce specific information about a person's habits and lifestyle. The famous study is kept exactly as it is described in the stories.

Glossary

ACCELERANT
A highly flammable substance that can be used to start a fire, such as gasoline.

ANTHROPOMETRY
A series of body measurements that was used by police forces for criminal identification before fingerprinting.

A bullet hole in reinforced glass leaves a clear record for the ballistics investigator

ARCH
The rarest of fingerprint patterns. Only around five percent of fingerprint patterns are arches.

ARSON
The crime of starting a fire deliberately in order to cause damage to property.

AUTOPSY
A medical examination of a corpse in order to discover the cause of death. Also known as a postmorterm.

BALLISTICS
In forensic science ballistics means the study of guns, bullets, and trajectories. In general use, the word may be used to describe the science of the flight of projectiles.

BLACK BOX
An event recorder, installed in planes, ships, and trains, that holds instrument and voice recordings, to be played in the event of a crash.

BLOOD GROUP
Everyone belongs to one of four main blood groups: A, B, AB, or O. A test determines which group a sample belong to.

CALIBER
Used as a measure of the inside diameter of a gun's barrel. Measurements may be inches, hundredths of inches, or millimeters.

CARTRIDGE CASE
A cylinder containing the explosive charge and the bullet or pellets for a gun.

CAUSE OF DEATH
The action that resulted in death (such as a blow to the head), as distinct from a medical condition (such as brain hemorrhage).

CHAIN OF CUSTODY
The trail followed from crime scene to court by a piece of evidence held by the police and forensic scientists. Written records must show who passed the evidence to whom and when.

CHROMATOGRAPHY
A series of laboratory tests designed to separate out the components of a mixture. In forensic science, chromatographic tests are used to discover the presence of drugs or poisons.

CLEANSUIT
Outfit worn by forensic investigators at at crime scene, designed to prevent contamination.

COMPARATOR
A device that enlarges and projects images of two different fingerprints for easy comparison.

COMPARISON MICROSCOPE
A double microscope for examining two similar items, often bullets, side by side.

COMPUTER TOMOGRAPHY (CT)
A method of X-raying the body in sections and creating three-dimensional images of its parts.

DATABASE
An organized collection of information—such as DNA, fingerprints, or firearms—usually computerized for quick and easy searching.

DUSTING
Brushing for latent fingerprints with a powder to make them visible.

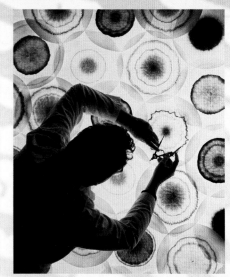

Scientist examining paper chromatograms

E-FIT SYSTEM
Computerized version of the photographic identification system that uses photographs of facial features to create a likeness of a suspect. A similar system called FACES exists in the United States.

ELECTROPHORESIS
Analytical method using an electric charge to grade substances by size and, in the case of DNA samples, generate DND profiles.

ELECTROSTATIC DETECTION APPARATUS (ESDA)
A device that reveals handwriting impressions on paper with static electricity and toner.

ENTOMOLOGY
The study of insects. A forensic entomologist studies the life cycles of insects found on corpses as an aid to estimating time of death.

EVIDENCE MARKER
At a crime scene, used for marking the location of key evidence and identifying any special features.

DNA—THE LADDER OF LIFE

Inside the nuclei of the cells that make up the different parts of our bodies is a spiral molecule called deoxyribonucleic acid, or DNA. It is a microscopic map of a person's unique features and characteristics, and a set of instructions for their development. The shape of DNA is often called the double helix, and it is composed of two strands that twist around each other. These are linked by rungs, which are composed of four different chemicals, shown here in different colors. It is the order of these chemical rungs that is different in every person—except for identical twins, triplets, and so forth, who are the only people on the planet to share the same DNA.

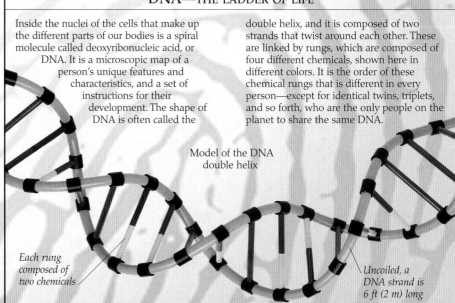

Model of the DNA double helix

Each rung composed of two chemicals

Uncoiled, a DNA strand is 6 ft (2 m) long

FIBER EVIDENCE
Evidence provided by human and animal hairs, or by synthetic fibers.

FINGERTIP SEARCH
A crime scene search carried out by several officers kneeling shoulder-to-shoulder.

FORENSIC ANTHROPOLOGY
The study of skeletons for identification. A forensic anthropologist typically tries to identify the victims of wars or major accidents when many are killed.

GUNSHOT RESIDUE (GSR)
Miscroscopic powder from explosive that is sprayed onto the hand of a person firing a gun. It is invisible, but can be detected with a hand swab up to six hours after firing.

HOMICIDE
The act of killing an individual. Can be manslaughter or murder.

LARVA
A stage in the development of an insect just before it undergoes metamorphosis. If larvae are found on a corpse, knowledge of their life cycle can help to indicate time of death.

LASER BEAM
An intense beam of monochromatic light. In forensic science, laser beams may be used at a crime scene to trace a bullet's trajectory.

LATENT FINGERPRINT
One that is not visible and requires special techniques to make it clear.

LIE DETECTOR
See Polygraph.

LINEN TESTER
An alternative magnifying glass often used by forensic investigators.

LOCARD'S EXCHANGE PRINCIPLE
The principle behind trace evidence collection and analysis—"every contact leaves a trace"—formulated by Edmond Locard.

LOOP
The most common fingerprint pattern, making up between 60 and 70 percent of fingerprints.

LUMINOL
A chemical spray used by forensic investigators to show up traces of blood. It can reveal years-old bloodstains.

MAGNETIC WAND
Used in conjunction with magnetic powder to dust for fingerprints on glossy surfaces.

MASS SPECTROMETRY
A technique used to measure very small amounts of substances, such as drugs, or to identify the presence of accelerants.

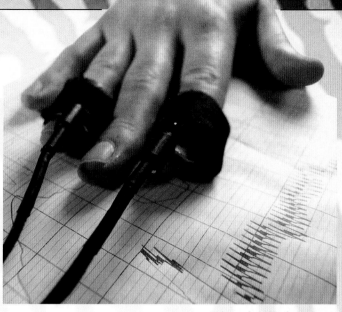
Polygraph or lie-detector test

MORTUARY
Also called a morgue, this is the place where dead bodies are kept before a funeral.

ODONTOLOGY
Forensic dentistry. This usually involves making identifications from bite marks, or matching a body's teeth to dental records.

PARAMEDIC
A person trained to give emergency medical treatment, often at a crime scene.

PATHOLOGY
The study of diseases from body tissue. A forensic pathologist examines suspicious deaths, and seeks to discover the cause of death by carrying out an autopsy.

PATTERN EVIDENCE
Evidence that is significant for its shape or pattern—in particular, bloodstains, which are classified in six different patterns.

POLYGRAPH
An instrument designed to discover whether a person is lying by recording changes in their blood pressure and pulse rate.

POLYMERASE CHAIN REACTION (PCR)
A method of duplicating fragments of DNA, until there is enough for DNA profiling or other analysis.

POSTMORTEM INTERVAL
The estimated time since death. *Post mortem* means "after death." See also Autopsy.

PRECIPITIN TEST
A test to distinguish human from animal blood.

PRESUMPTIVE TEST
A test, most commonly the Kastle-Meyer test, to show quickly whether a liquid is blood and therefore requires more detailed analysis.

PROVENANCE
A record of an object's history, including its origin and all of its owners. Important art and antiquities, provenance can be faked by forgers.

RIFLING
The raised, spiraling pattern in a gun barrel, which can cause distinctive marks on bullets.

RIGOR MORTIS
The stiffness of a corpse that occurs some hours after death. It can help investigators determine time of death.

SCANNING ELECTRON MICROSCOPE (SEM)
A powerful microscope that uses a beam of electrons instead of light to magnify an image.

SEARCH PATTERN
An organized method of searching a crime scene. There are many different search patterns.

SEROLOGY
The study of blood and other body fluids, usually for purposes of identification

SNIFFER DOG
A dog that has been trained to use its sensitive sense of smell to detect explosives, illegal drugs, missing people, or corpses.

SUSPECT
Someone who may be involved in a crime but who has not been formally charged.

TAPE LIFT
A method for recovering trace evidence—such as gunshot residue, fibers, or fingerprints—from a surface using adhesive tape.

TOOLMARK
Mark on a surface from which investigators may be able to identify the type of tool that made it, or even the individual tool.

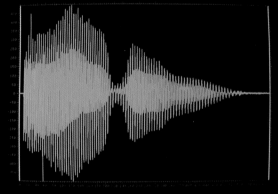
Voiceprint of a two-syllable word

TOXICOLOGY
The study of drugs and poisons.

TRACE EVIDENCE
Small objects or small amounts of substances that can be used as evidence—typically hair, fibers, or soil, transferred unknowingly by contact.

VOICEPRINT
Graphic representation of the sound of an individual's speech patterns, which may be used for identification.

X-RAY
A type of radiation used to scan and create an image of bones.

Index

Acknowledgments

Dorling Kindersley would like to thank
Peter Winfield for illustrations 11br, 32bc;
Stewart J. Wild for proofreading; Hilary Bird for the
index; David Ekholm-JAlbum, Sunita Gahir, Susan
St. Louis, Carey Scott, Lisa Stock, & Bulent Yusuf
for the clip art; Jim Green & Carey Scott for the
wall chart.

The publisher would like to thank the following
for their kind permission to reproduce their
photographs:

(key: a=above b=below/bottom c=center f=far
l=left r=right t=top)

Alamy Images: Si Barber 29tl; John Boykin 47br;
Scott Camazine 36crb; Jon Challicom 54bl; Chris
Gomersall 40tr; GOwst 69br; Mikael Karlsson 57tl,
69bl; Ellen McKnight 27b; Ian Miles-Flashpoint
Pictures 13cl, 13tl; Pablo Paul 12c, 28c; Pictorial
Press Ltd 56tl; Stocksearch 62ftl; Gari Wyn
Williams 13ca; Doug Wilson 52cl; **Ardea:** Pascal

Goetgheluck 37cl; Steve Hopkin 36tr, 37bc, 37cr,
37t; **CEPHOS Corporation:** 62bl; **Corbis:** 8cr, 31tr,
47cr; Lewis Allen 6tr; Morton Beebe 37br;
Annebicque Bernard 23br; Bettmann 20tr, 27tl,
31tl, 33bl, 47bl, 64-65br, 65t; Régis Bossu/Sygma
53br; Andrew Brookes 68r; Chesapeake City
Sheriffs Department/Reuters 47tc; Richard Chung/
Reuters 19br; John Mc Coy 7tr; P. Deliss/Godong
61l; Kieran Doherty/Reuters 56cla; epa 49r; **FDNY/
Assignment ID:** 30039450A 48tr; Federal Bureau
of Investigation/epa 46l; Laurence Fordyce/Eye
Ubiquitous 40tl; Hulton-Deutsch Collection 8cra,
40br; Nadeem Khawer/epa 55br; Micro Discovery
68l; Christopher J. Morris 7bc; Richard T. Nowitz
65br; Sebastian Pfuetze/zefa 7tl; Matt Rainey/Star
Ledger 7cl; Reuters 40bl, 40c, 41, 52-53t, 54c, 54cr,
54tr, 56cr, 63tr; Ron Sachs/CNP 47cr; Lucas Schifres
57tr; Scotland Yard/Reuters 45bl; Sion Touhig 54-
55tc; West Semitic Research/Dead Sea Scrolls
Foundation 59tr; Tim Wright 52bl; **Courtesy of
The Bank of England:** 58b; **The Design Works,
Sheffield:** 38cl, 38cr, 38tc, 38tl, 38tr; **DK Images:**

Courtesy of HM Customs and Excise 4fcl, 34ca;
Courtesy of the Metropolitan Police Museum,
London 4cl, 8-9ca, 8-9t, 9tr; **Dr Thomas
Heseltine/Aurora CS Ltd:** 63tl; Dr Thomas
Heseltine 44br; **The Electronic Frontier
Foundation:** 58tr; **Environmental Criminology
Research Inc.:** 46cra, 46tr; **Faro UK:** Neil Barnett
43cl; **Firearmsid.com:** 31br; **www.firetactics.com:**
48b; **Foster & Freeman Ltd.:** 28br; **Granada
Television Limited:** 46br; **The Kobal Collection:**
CBS-TV 7cr; Dreamworks 64-65l; Universal 9bl;
Lexis Public Relations: 69t; **London Fire
Brigade:** 48cr; **Mary Evans Picture Library:** 48br;
Chris Coupland 66t; **Missouri State Police Crime
Laboratory:** 28tr; **PA Photos:** 10-11b, 11ca, 11cl,
11cr, 34tr, 34-35b, 35tl, 39br, 41bl, 42c, 42tl, 42tr,
56br, 60l; Gareth Copley 35c; Ian Nicholson/PA
Archive 30tl; **Photoshot:** UPPA 20cl; **Reuters:** John
Sommers II 35tc; **Rex Features:** 55tc, 55cl;
Science Photo Library: A. Barrington Brown 22cl;
Dr Tony Brain 26bl; Dr Jeremy Burgess 70l; CNRI
42cr; Charles D.Winters 45br; Michael Donne 49t;
Mauro Fermariello 24tl, 29r; E. Gueho 26crb; James
King-Holmes 61bc, 62-63b; Mark Maio/King-
Holmes 62br; Peter Menzel 6-7bl; Hank Morgan
71b; Louise Murray 35br; Susumu Nishinaga 26br;
David Parker 22bl; Pasieka 66-67 (Background), 68-

69 (Backdrop), 68-69 (Background), 70-71
(Background); Philippe Psaila 33br, 33cl, 33cr;
David R.Frazier 16tr; David Scharf 26clb; Science
Source 67b; Volker Steger 60b; Tek Image 20c, 63br,
71t; Geoff Tompkinson 70tr; Volker Steger, Peter
Arnold Inc. 24tr; **www.skullsunlimited.com:**
42bl, 42cl, 42clb; **TopFoto.co.uk:** 9c, 60t, 65c;
Fortean 61t; **VisionMetric Ltd:** 45cl, 45cr, 45t; **The
Wellcome Institute Library, London:** 8bc, 8c,
8fcl; **Susan Moberly:** 23bc; **Jerry Young:** 43t

Wall Chart: PA Photos: John Giles / PA Archive
ca (fingertip search); **The Wellcome Institute
Library, London:** Susan Moberly clb (DNA
profiles)

Jacket: Front: **PA Photos:** Chris Young (b).
Punchstock: Digital Vision/John Lamb (tcr).
Science Photo Library: TEK Image (tl); National
Library of Medicine (tr); Philippe Psaila (tcl). Back:
Corbis: Ashley Cooper (b); Image 1 (cr). **Science
Photo Library:** Michael Donne, University of
Manchester (tr); Volker Sleger, Peter Arnold Inc.
(cl).

All other images © Dorling Kindersley
For further information see: **www.dkimages.com**